WARRIOR

DK

WARRIOR

A VISUAL HISTORY OF THE FIGHTING MAN

R.G.GRANT

LONDON, NEW YORK, MELBOURNE, MUNICH, AND DELHI

SENIOR ART EDITOR Sharon Spencer
ART EDITOR Victoria Clark
DESIGNERS Phil Gamble, Philip Fitzgerald, Kenny Osinnowo, Peter Laws
DTP John Goldsmid

SENIOR EDITOR Alison Sturgeon
PROJECT EDITORS Ferdie McDonald, Chris Stone, Andrew Szudek

MANAGING ART EDITOR Karen Self
MANAGING EDITOR Debra Wolter
ART DIRECTOR Bryn Walls
PUBLISHER Jonathan Metcalf

CONSULTANT Dr. Arnold Harvey

PICTURE RESEARCHERS Jenny Baskaya, Sarah Hopper, Romaine Werblow

PHOTOGRAPHY Gary Ombler, Roger Dixon

CARTOGRAPHY Advanced Illustration Ltd

PRODUCTION CONTROLLER Tony Phipps

First American Edition, 2007
This paperback edition published in 2010
Published in the United States by
DK Publishing
375 Hudson Street
New York, New York 10014

10 11 12 13 14 10 9 8 7 6 5 4 3 2 1
WD154—August 2010

Published in Great Britain by Dorling Kindersley Limited.

A catalog record for this book is available from the Library of Congress.

ISBN 978-0-7566-6541-8

DK books are available at special discounts when purchased in bulk for sales promotions, premiums, fund-raising, or educational use. For details, contact: DK Publishing Special Markets, 375 Hudson Street, New York, New York 10014 or SpecialSales@dk.com.

Color reproduction by GRB Editrice S.r.l., Italy
Printed and bound in Singapore by Star Standard

Discover more at
www.dk.com

CONTENTS

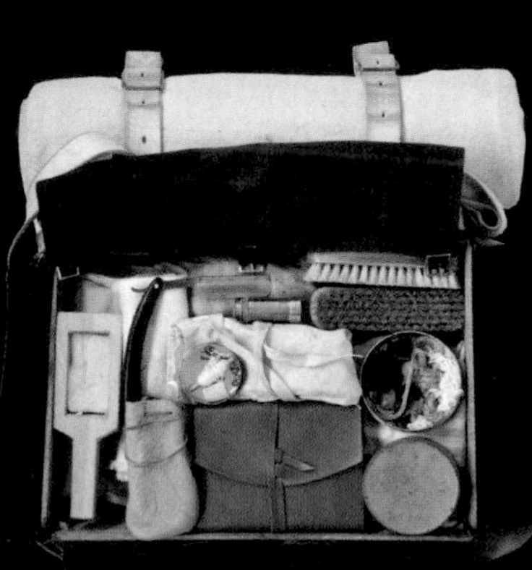

68
LI
2

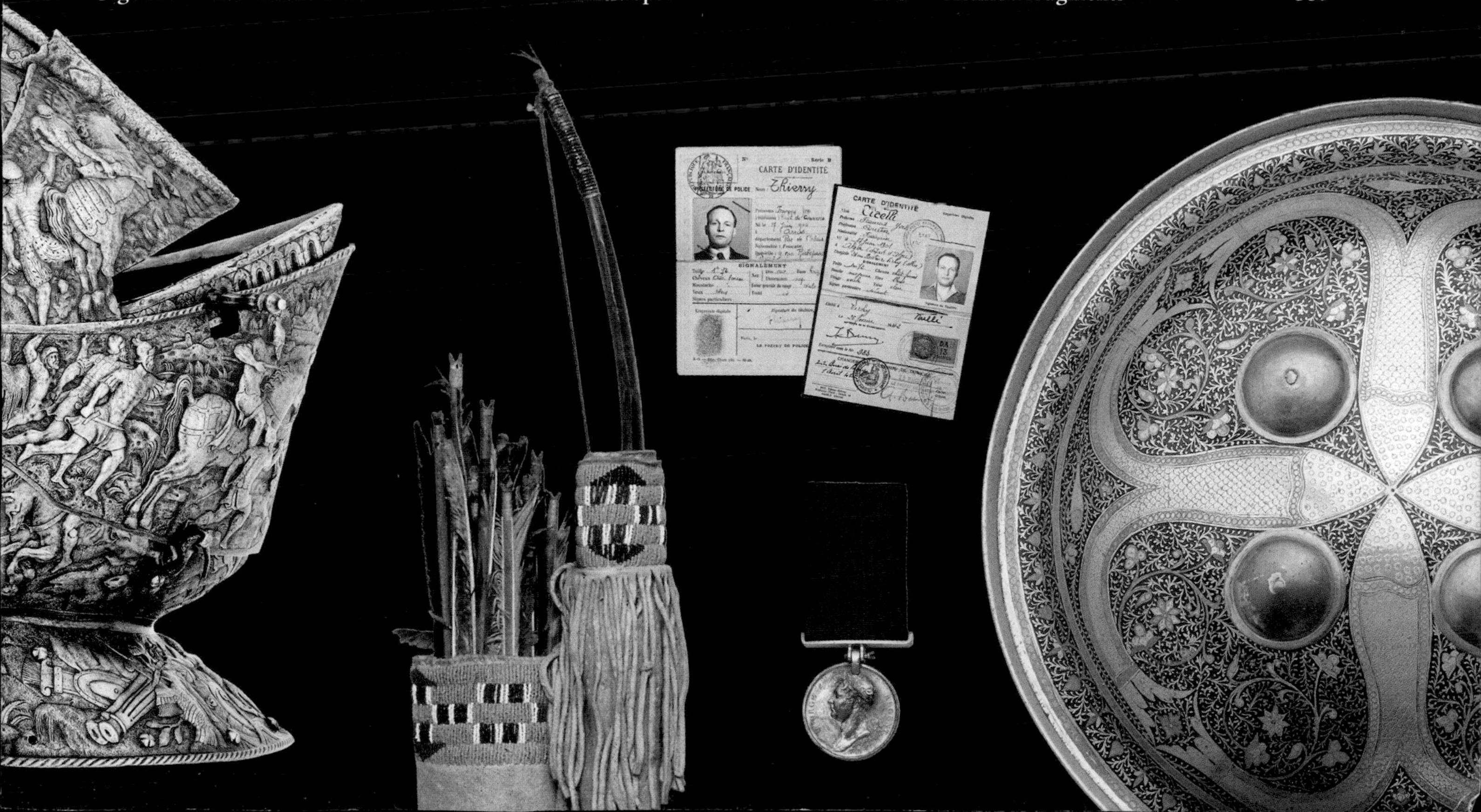

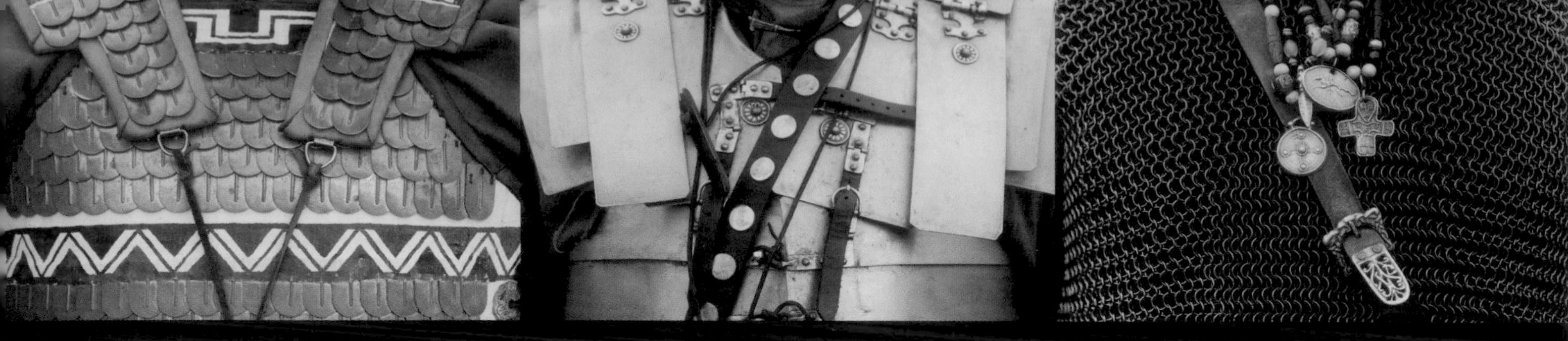

FOREWORD

My intention in writing this book has been to focus not upon wars, campaigns, and battles in themselves, but squarely upon the lives of the men who, through the length of human history, have fought them. Why did they become fighting men? How were they recruited and trained? How were they armed and fed and paid? What did they carry in their packs? How did they survive when on campaign? And how did they cope with that climactic experience of combat?

In the sweep of history covered by this book, certain principles of military life recur. The need for physical endurance and courage is a given, for it is hard to imagine any military training or campaigning that would not require these qualities. But the experience of comradeship-in-arms is equally omnipresent. A Mongol horseman, one of Wellington's or Napoleon's foot soldiers, a Japanese samurai, and a Viet Cong peasant guerrilla would have very little in common at most levels, but all will have bonded to some degree in a band of brothers, forged in the white heat of the traumatizing, exhilarating experience of combat. Yet this said, there can be no pretence of discovering a single character of the warrior or fighting man. On the contrary, fighting men have been as diverse as the cultures and societies that have produced them. The Plains Indian warrior and the US cavalryman, to take one instance, fought one another across a gulf of mutual incomprehension created by the sheer distance between a citizen of a 19th-century industrializing state and a member of a nomadic hunter-gatherer society.

This book features 30 key individual soldiers and warriors, including sailors and airmen, with over 70 others covered in lesser detail. Each of these fighting men is presented in the particularity of his own place and time. These warriors include not only the fighting elites of great empires, but also the inexperienced conscripts and volunteers that have formed the bulk of fighting men throughout history. For each of the key soldiers there is a full account of their organization and equipment, with insights into their motivation and an assessment of their achievements.

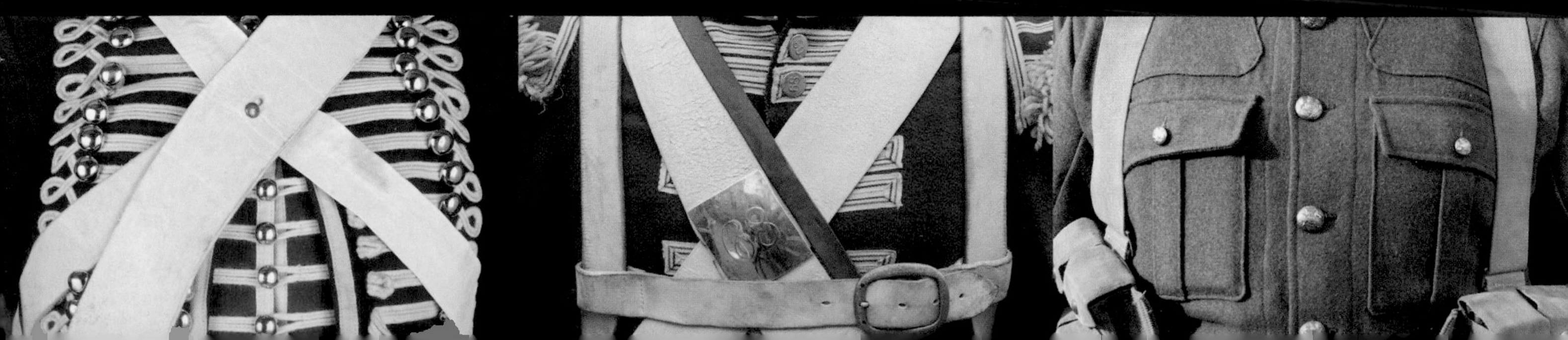

One of the main functions of an illustrated book such as this is to enable people to see the past as well as read about it. The original photography that makes up an essential part of this book presents, wherever possible, genuine weapons, armor, and artifacts that survive from the warfare of even the most ancient times. But the material historical record is perversely selective—wood and iron artifacts almost never survive long, for example, while both bronze and copper are relatively durable. Where necessary we have had recourse to replicas of military equipment, always scrupulously based upon precise historical information. Most of the gear of the Ancient Roman soldiers shown here, for example, has been recreated as a result of study of Trajan's Column and other contemporary representations of men at war. In a similar spirit, we have also depended in many cases upon those inspired amateurs, the historical re-enactors, to give a visual impression of the warfare of earlier times. These are people whose dedicated efforts have often made an original contribution to historical knowledge, as they actually attempt to do in practice what soldiers of the past are alleged to have done by the chroniclers and historians.

As an author I have tried to do justice to all the diverse warriors featured in this book, but inevitably I have my personal favorites. The flash elites of the military world, whether medieval knights and samurai or SAS troopers, will never warm my heart like the grumbling, hard-bitten soldier in the ranks, eternally put-upon, rarely rewarded, plagued by marching and drill, motivated by a dour sense of duty rather than a lust for glory. That is the sort of man on whose unpretentious shoulders, at critical moments of history, the fate of civilizations is liable to rest.

I have never been a fighting man, but my father, my grandfather, and many others of my older relatives were called upon to fight for their country. They were, on the whole, unwilling participants in war, but they did their duty, like other fighting men through history, under the most extreme circumstances. It is to them that this book is dedicated.

R. G. GRANT

INTRODUCTION

The societies of the past had no difficulty in embracing war as a positive activity. The medieval troubadour Bertran de Born declared: "I have no such joy as ... when I see both great and small fall in the ditches and on the grass: Lords, mortgage your domains, castles, cities, but never give up war!" In the contemporary world, this would at least superficially appear an unfashionable sentiment. The sheer destructiveness of modern weaponry and the vast death toll in the major conflicts of the 20th century has made war seem intolerable. And yet warfare continues to flourish, and the warrior tradition lives on. Indeed, warriors seem to have been with us since the very earliest of pre-state societies, in which, along with hunting, war was the definitive male activity. Whatever the specific pretext for combat, it constituted a necessary rite of passage for youths entering manhood, and had its essential place in the ritual life of the band or tribe. Warriors adopted costumes and equipment decorated with symbols of religious significance; combat was preceded by ceremony and sacrifice. Men of fighting age often lived apart in tightly knit groups to encourage bonding, while at the same time styles of fighting were ritualized to encourage demonstrations of individual prowess. These two superficially contradictory elements were to prove ubiquitous in the history of warfare: the bonding of fighting men in a brotherhood and the pursuit of individual glory.

BANDS OF BROTHERS

Bonding and individualism combined in one of the earliest permanent military organizations, the warband. This was a body of warriors bound by allegiance to a leader who was an acknowledged fighter of outstanding skill and courage. Its motivation was only partly material (the pursuit of plunder or land) because warfare also offered the individual his chance to improve his standing in the group. The Roman writer Tacitus, describing the German warbands of the 1st century CE, wrote that among these warriors "it is a disgrace to the chief to be surpassed in valour by his companions, to the companions not to come up to the valor of their chiefs." The warbands had to seek out conflict, says Tacitus, because "renown is easier won among perils." This attitude to warfare has been called the "warrior ethic." The warrior delights in combat

because it offers him a chance to display his courage, to achieve glory for himself, and to uphold his place among his fellows. A man's honor is valued above life itself. The warrior ethic was found among the Plains Indians of North America, the companions of Macedonian conqueror Alexander the Great, and the Vikings of early medieval Scandinavia. It was also encouraged among Luftwaffe fighter pilots in World War II. In some form it is likely to exist among any body of men who are going to perform outstandingly on the battlefield.

SOLDIERS AND WARRIORS

Of course, many fighting men down the ages have entirely lacked enthusiasm for war. When the first hierarchical state systems evolved, around 5,000 years ago, sharp distinctions opened up between the rulers and the ruled, the wealthy and the poor. Making war to extend or defend their empires, rulers pressed men from the lower orders of society into service. Hastily trained and poorly equipped, these troops had a relationship to warfare that was remote from the warrior tradition. An Ancient Egyptian papyrus that has survived from the time of the pharaonic New Kingdom gives this vivid description of the experience of the average soldier: "His march is uphill through mountains. He drinks water every third day; it is smelly and tastes of salt … The enemy comes, surrounds him with missiles, and life recedes from him. He is told: 'Quick, forward, valiant soldier! Win for yourself a good name!' He does not know what he is about. His body is weak, his legs fail him … If he comes out alive, he is worn out from marching." This was an experience with which many an unwilling foot soldier could identify down the ages.

The warrior ethic still existed in these hierarchical societies, but it became the preserve of the ruling class. Thus, at the same period as the papyrus quoted above, Egyptian pharaohs had themselves depicted in chariots, smiting their enemies with a club, or shooting them with arrows. Fighting was still a prestigious activity, but only when associated with status and power. This was, for example, the attitude of high-status mounted knights in the European Middle Ages, who felt contempt for foot soldiers recruited from the lower ranks of society. The distinction between a warrior and a mere soldier, in

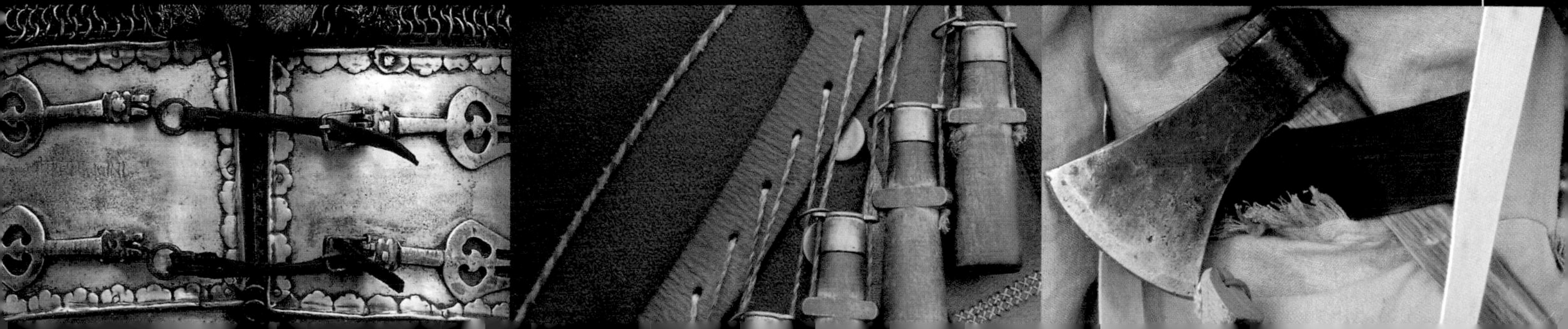

European history, often corresponded to the assumed superiority of the man mounted to the man on foot. But even in the hierarchical Aztec, Inca, or Maya societies of pre-Columbian America, which had no horses, the elite aristocratic warriors remained sharply distinguished from a mass of lowly stone-throwers.

PRACTICAL FIGHTERS

Unfortunately for the aristocratic warrior, who regarded war as an arena for personal feats of valor, warfare was always fundamentally a practical activity, in which the question of winning or losing could determine the future of whole societies. History repeatedly shows examples of men from the lower orders, properly organized and equipped, outfighting the warrior elites through a less individualistic, more down-to-earth approach to war. The legions of the Roman Empire established the paradigm for a professional force of career-soldiers recruited from the lower ranks of society and trained up to a high level of military effectiveness. These were men instilled with a strong sense of duty and devotion to the honor of their legion, as well as being subject to rigorous discipline. They had no ambition to achieve individual glory, only the more modest goal of promotion within a hierarchy of rank. When Europe's modern standing armies developed in the 17th and 18th centuries, discipline and drill were again at the heart of their effort to transform men often viewed by their officers as the scum of society into brave and reliable fighting men. The warrior principles of honor and glory were not forgotten, since the regimental system made the soldiers part of an enduring organization with whose banners and reputation they could identify. But individual initiative and fighting flair were strictly repressed. These uniformed armies made fixed hierarchies of rank and unhesitating obedience to orders the essence of military life.

CITIZEN-SOLDIERS

The concept of the citizen-soldier we owe to the Ancient Greeks. In Athens in the 5th century BCE, donning armor as an unpaid hoplite heavy infantryman was both a duty and a privilege of status as a free citizen. This was an idea that much appealed to modern Europeans when

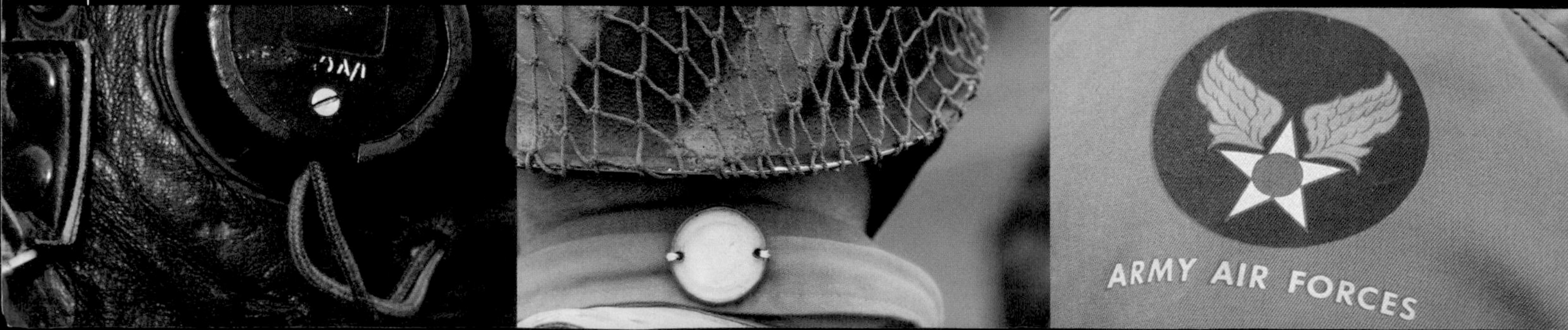

they rediscovered it during the Renaissance (15th and 16th centuries), but it took the French Revolution of 1789 to turn a whole people into the equal citizens needed to populate such a force.

The revolutionary regime's *levée en masse* of 1793 proposed conscription not as an arbitrary exercise of a ruler's power over its subjects but as an appeal to the duty of the citizens of a country to fight for their nation. The change in the status of the soldier that this implied was reflected, if imperfectly, in a change in how soldiers were treated, even in the armies that fought against revolutionary France. The regulations of the British Rifle Brigade, raised in 1800, state that an officer or NCO "shall give his orders in the language of moderation and of regard to the feelings of the men under his command" and that "duty should be done from cheerfulness and inclination, and not from mere command and the necessity of obeying." The men who fought in the American Civil War 60 years later initially elected their officers, and in many cases obeyed them only when they saw fit.

The mobilization of its citizens gave a modern state the potential to field armies numbered in millions. Western societies made a conscious effort to maintain or revive the warrior spirit in this age of mass warfare. Schoolchildren were taught of the glory of dying in battle for the homeland. The warriors of the past were praised as heroes to be imitated. At the outbreak of the American Civil War (1861–1865), and later of World War I (1914–1918), many otherwise peaceable young men rushed forward to enlist, keen to test themselves in combat. But the supremely destructive battlefields of the 19th and 20th centuries on the whole failed to fulfill the assumed promise of heroic adventure. Patriotic propagandists seeking for warriors to glorify found them among the ace fighter pilots of the two world wars or elite soldiers such as the German stormtroopers. But the reality of modern conflict was more honestly represented in the erection of Tombs of the Unknown Soldier, and in mass military cemeteries that celebrated the anonymous courage and sacrifice of the common man. The soldier who fought at Gettysburg, the Somme, or on the D-day beaches of France, was typically a most unwarriorlike individual, his natural habitat an office, factory, or farm. Yet these civilians in uniform proved time and again impressive fighting men when forced into the cauldron of battle.

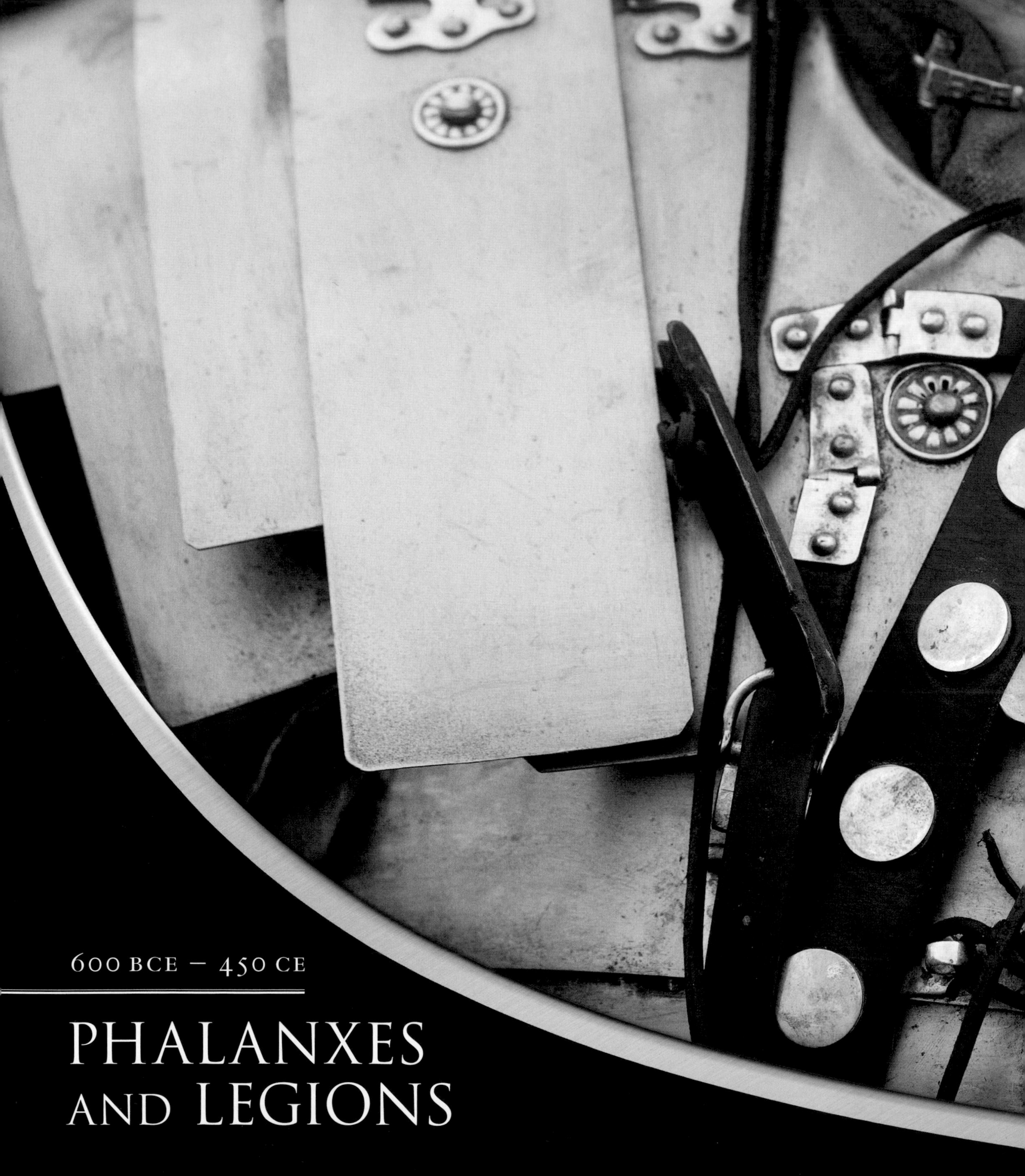

600 BCE – 450 CE

PHALANXES AND LEGIONS

Most of the basic weapons used up to the gunpowder age already existed before the appearance of the first hierarchical "civilized" states around 5,000 years ago. Bows and arrows, spears, clubs, and edged weapons grew in effectiveness during the period covered in this chapter, notably through the use of new materials—evolving from stone to copper, bronze, and finally iron. But the essentials of slashing, stabbing, and launching missiles at an enemy remained unchanged. Apart from a few specialized machines for siege warfare, the only major technical innovation was the introduction of horses around 1700 BCE, first to pull chariots and then to mount cavalry.

HIERARCHY AND COMMAND

There were only quite limited variations in the military technology available to different societies, so the key area for the evolution of warfare was in the organization and motivation of fighting men. The Ancient World was characterized by a dazzling diversity of fighting methods. Tribal societies in which each adult male was a warrior would find themselves confronted by armies of trained, professional soldiers who had a career structure and a fixed term of service. Men fighting exclusively as mounted archers battled with armies committed to close-quarters infantry combat.

The first hierarchically organized armies known to historians appeared in the city-states of Sumeria, Mesopotamia, in around 3000 BCE. From then until around 1000 BCE, similar military

Greek warfare
Hoplites, depicted naked, although they would have worn armor, battle with spears. The 7–9 ft (2–3 m) spear was the hoplite's primary weapon. When forming a phalanx they would point these forward while locking their shields together.

Roman discipline
With their gleaming helmets and armor, the well-drilled Roman legionaries of the late 1st century CE were a force that was more than a match for the various enemies that threatened the borders of their empire.

forces would appear wherever complex societies evolved—from the Nile valley to the Indus valley and China. These armies introduced for the first time the distinction between fighting men and civilians—and between different kinds of fighting man. Forces developed command structures and variously armed troops were assigned different roles on the battlefield. By the time the armies of the Egyptian New Kingdom (1552–1069 BCE) or of the Assyrian Empire (c.1000–600 BCE) were marching around the eastern Mediterranean, a familiar distinction had emerged between noble or royal warriors on the one hand—typically fighting in chariots or on horseback and bragging of their heroic deeds—and a reluctant mass of foot soldiers stoically enduring military service.

As powerful states developed empires, their armies also became variegated by the inclusion of forces from diverse ethnic groups. These graded seamlessly from mercenary bands earning a living by marketing their military skills to forces supplied by states that had been conquered by and owed tribute to the imperial power. According to the Greek historian Herodotus, the army of the Persian Empire in the 5th century BCE included soldiers of 35 different nationalities, each ethnic contingent employing its own typical weaponry and tactics. The Carthaginian army with which Hannibal invaded Italy across the Alps in 218 BCE was also an accummulation of armed bands, from North African cavalry to Iberian stone-slingers.

CITIZEN-SOLDIERS

The rise of the Greek city-states from the 6th century BCE brought an alternative to the dichotomy between the heroic aristocratic warrior and the faceless foot soldier, with the concept of the highly motivated citizen-soldier.

The Greeks were culturally familiar with the notion of the individualistic high-status warrior because of their legend of the Trojan Wars, which was fixed by the 8th century BCE and centered on single combat between the heroes of the two sides. But the city-states developed a system of collective heroism, in which war service was one of the duties and privileges of citizenship. Citizens fought as heavy infantrymen, or hoplites, in a tight-knit formation with their equals, glorifying the bravery of face-to-face close-range combat. The hoplite army was to prove an extremely influential military model, although it was only when twinned with the Macedonian cavalry of Alexander the Great that the infantry phalanx became a world-beating force in the 4th century BCE.

The effectiveness of Greece's armored foot soldiers was surpassed by the famous legions of the Roman Republic and Empire. Starting like the Greeks with an infantry force of part-time citizen-soldiers, the Romans developed a full-time professional army, while retaining the principle of citizenship as a qualification for service. With its discipline, training, and uniform equipment, the Roman legion encouraged the soldier to see himself as a man with a job to do. Glory and renown were collective, the property of the legion with which the soldier was expected to identify. The extension of Roman citizenship beyond the boundaries of Italy helped maintain the professional citizen-army, but Rome could never do without the auxiliaries drawn from non-citizen ethnic groups. By the time of the later Empire, it was dependent to a degree upon foreign troops fighting under their own leaders.

WARBANDS

The various "barbarian" peoples, who at times fought against the Romans and at other times fought for them in the service of the Western Empire, harked back to older principles of warriorhood. The Celtic peoples of France and Britain valued individual bravery and personal display above discipline and cohesion. The Germanic tribes, such as the Goths and Vandals, formed warbands of emotionally bonded fighters giving allegiance to a leader who was known for his exceptional skill or valor. In the end these simpler military structures proved more durable than the highly organized, well-disciplined Roman army. Warband leaders were the men who inherited the mantle of the Roman Empire in western Europe.

By 450 CE, cavalry were once more a major force on the battlefield. The Goths and Vandals had demonstrated the effectiveness of armored horsemen armed with lances, while the invading Huns, nomadic warriors from the Asian steppe, had shown Europe the power of fast-moving mounted archers. In Asia, the cataphracts (heavy cavalrymen) of Sassanid Persia (226–637 CE) were widely imitated by their enemies. The dominant warrior of the next era in the history of warfare would be a man on horseback.

600 BCE – 300 BCE

GREEK HOPLITE

GO NEAR, STRIKE WITH A LONG SPEAR OR A SWORD AT CLOSE RANGE, AND KILL A MAN. SET FOOT AGAINST FOOT, PRESS SHIELD AGAINST SHIELD, FLING CREST AGAINST CREST, HELMET AGAINST HELMET, AND CHEST AGAINST CHEST.

TYRTAEUS, A SPARTAN POET

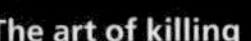

THE CITY-STATES OF ANCIENT GREECE invented a distinctive kind of armored infantry force: the hoplites. These spear-armed citizen-soldiers proved their worth in the 5th century BCE, first in the repulse of Persian invaders and then in the Peloponnesian Wars that pitted Athens against Sparta. Widely recognized as the finest foot soldiers of their time, Greek hoplites later served in the all-conquering army of Alexander the Great and as mercenaries in the service of other powers, including the Egyptians and Persians.

The Ancient Greek world embraced not only mainland Greece, but extended along the coast of modern Turkey and across the Mediterranean to Sicily, southern Italy, and even the south of France. Though the many city-states and their colonies showed great cultural unity, politically they were more often than not divided. They could unite to counter the threat of a common enemy, as they had done against the Trojans in the legendary era of prehistory described in Homer's epic poem, the *Iliad*. This they did again, although not without disagreements and near-disasters, when they thwarted the invasion attempts of the Persian kings Darius and Xerxes in the early years of the 5th century BCE. But in the second half of the century rivalry between Athens and Sparta provoked the so-called Peloponnesian War (431–404 BCE). The alliances formed by the two main powers during this period involved almost all the Greek city-states and as a result their citizens had to be in a state of permanent readiness for war. The warriors who did the bulk of the fighting in the long bloody struggle that developed were the hoplites.

WEAPONS AND TACTICS

Service as a hoplite was both a duty and a privilege of adult males enjoying full citizen status. The two most prominent city-state armies, those of Athens and of Sparta, were broadly similar in their equipment and tactics. The hoplite wore thick, heavy bronze armor consisting of a cuirass, greaves to protect his legs, and a helmet; he carried a large shield, a spear, and a short iron sword. He fought in a tight formation known as a phalanx, typically eight ranks deep, using the long spear as his primary weapon

The Trojan War
This relief shows Achilles dragging the body of Hector around the walls of Troy.

ATHENIAN HOPLITES

Athens and Sparta differed sharply, however, in their organization and training. In Athens hoplites were barely trained part-timers, expected to abandon their civilian occupation and present themselves for service whenever the state required. They had to buy their own equipment. A full panoply of armor was very expensive and almost certainly beyond the means of many Athenians, who will have presented themselves with only part of the standard gear. The wealthiest citizens, on the other hand, were decked out in the finest armor to proclaim their status. Those too poor to own any armor at all often ended up becoming oarsmen in the Athenian fleet. One man who served Athens in this way was the philosopher Socrates.

Although the traditional practice of foot-racing, wrestling, and other competitive sports provided the Athenians with a kind of physical conditioning, they seem to have had little or no formal military training or drill. But they were free men fighting for their city and their honor, and thus exhibited at times a high level of morale and commitment.

The art of killing
Depictions of Ancient Greek hoplites survive on countless ceramic dishes and drinking vessels. This painting on a bowl from c.500 BCE *(above)* gives a vivid impression of a group of warriors armed with spears, lying in ambush. Later Greek hoplites in the age of Alexander the Great used even longer spears and the *kopis*, a fearsome, curved knife that originated in Persia *(right)*.

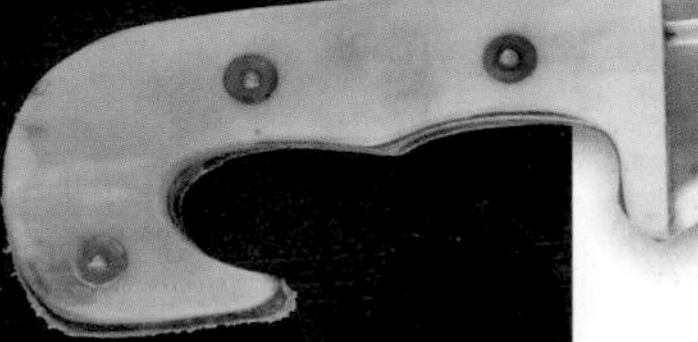

THE KOPIS, A LONG SLASHING KNIFE

Phalanx meets phalanx Ancient Greek warfare was highly symmetrical. When two phalanxes clashed, each presented exactly the same wall of shields topped by a bristling row of spears. On the left, a musician with a double flute plays a Spartan-style war song to keep up the spirit of the advancing hoplites.

By contrast, Sparta was a totally militarized state. The Spartan citizens, who were probably many fewer in number than the Athenians, relied on a large population of non-citizen laborers—the helots. These were essentially serfs that belonged to the state and, as such, posed a much greater threat to the security of the Spartan regime than did the slaves owned by individual Athenians. That all Sparta's male citizens were raised to be soldiers was partly through fear of a helot revolt.

SPARTAN UPBRINGING

Young Spartans were subjected to a rigorous system of military training and bonding. Male children were toughened up by exposure to the elements—they went barefoot and lightly clad through the winters—and punishments for failing tests of initiative and daring. At the age of 20, they were assigned to a barracks where they ate and slept, kept apart from women, for the following ten years. It was a system designed to create a disciplined fighting force, and it seems to have succeeded. The Spartans marched to battle in step to music, a skill that was quite beyond the Athenians. They had a coherent chain of command and could carry out relatively complex battlefield maneuvers without losing formation.

GREEK VERSUS GREEK

Campaigns fought by city-state citizen armies were of necessity short, usually restricted to the summer season. There was no proper supply system to maintain an army in the field, although large numbers of slaves—or, in the case of the Spartans, helots—accompanied an army on its march to meet the enemy, and foraging and preparing food would have been an important part of their duties. A military campaign often came to an end simply because most of the soldiers on both sides were farmers who had to go home to their fields to harvest their crops.

When city-state armies met, they first made sacrifices to the gods and then drew up in phalanxes facing one another, choosing the most level piece of ground available—phalanx tactics did not work well on rough terrain. The most experienced fighters were placed in the front three rows of the phalanx and in the back row, where it was their job to deter weaker spirits from attempting to run away. A crowd of skirmishing troops, many of them probably the personal slaves of the hoplites, operated around the phalanxes, harassing the enemy with a deluge of stones, javelins, and arrows.

The advance of an armored phalanx to contact—each man

Cooking on campaign
The Greeks made portable earthenware cooking stoves that were fueled by charcoal. These may well have been used by Greek armies on the march.

GREEK NAVAL WARFARE

Trireme
It took 170 men to crew the oars of a trireme and synchronizing the strokes was not easy, as volunteers aboard the reconstructed trireme *Olympias* discover.

The Greeks were famed for their skill at naval warfare, using the light, fast warships known as triremes. Each trireme was run by a captain, or "trierach." In Athens trierarchs were appointed from among those who owned "land and a house" in the city. It was the captain's responsibility to recruit and pay a crew, the majority of whom were oarsmen. Since a fleet of 100 ships might be assembled for a campaign, it was hard to find sufficient recruits. Most triremes went to sea with a mix of paid citizens, foreign mercenaries, and slaves at the oars. A trireme also typically carried ten armored marines and four archers.

A trireme was extremely cramped. There was room only for three days' supply of food and water. Crews usually went ashore to eat at midday and at nightfall to sleep. Much time was spent foraging for food and drink, unless the war fleet was supported by supply vessels.

The trireme had a heavy bronze ram at its prow. In battle, ships maneuvered around one another, attempting to ram an enemy in the flank. Meanwhile the marines and archers rained missiles upon the enemy—the marines threw their javelins from a seated position, to avoid unbalancing the ship. A trireme with a skilled helmsman and a disciplined crew could ram an enemy vessel or ride over its oars and then reverse, leaving it crippled in the water. Alternatively, the marines would board the rammed vessel, seizing it after hand-to-hand fighting with spears and axes.

> **"THE SPARTANS MARCHED SLOWLY AND TO THE MUSIC OF MANY PIPERS IN THEIR RANKS ... SO THAT THE MEN COULD CLOSE ON THE ENEMY STEADILY AND EVENLY AND NOT FALL OUT OF FORMATION."**
>
> **THUCYDIDES,** DESCRIBING SPARTANS AT THE FIRST BATTLE OF MANTINEA, 418 BCE, PELOPONNESIAN WAR

with his shield hooked over his left forearm and a spear held in his right hand—was an intimidating sight. The Spartans initiated the custom of singing a "paean," or war song, as they marched forward, a habit eventually adopted by most Greek forces. Singing helped men to cope with the desperate feeling of vulnerability as the shock of collision with the enemy approached. The Greek historian Thucydides recorded how an advancing phalanx tended to drift to the right, since "fear makes every man want to do his best to find protection for his unarmed side in the shield of the man next to him on the right, thinking that the more closely the shields are locked together, the safer he will be." There was always a risk of losing the tight phalanx formation. Greek writer Xenophon described an occasion when "part of the phalanx surged forward in front of the rest and the part that was left behind began to advance at the double" to catch up.

At a certain distance from the enemy, the hoplites would break into a run, charging forward while emitting a high pitched war cry. Then the two phalanxes clashed shield to shield, the hoplites in the front ranks thrusting with their spears through the gaps in the enemy shield wall. At some point in this struggle one part of a phalanx would collapse under the pressure of the attack. As the formation broke up and men attempted to flee the field, the defeated side could expect to suffer heavy casualties. It seems that losses on the winning side were typically around five percent—including a relatively high percentage of the hoplites in the front lines, the men actively engaged in the fighting. On the losing side, casualties would probably mount to around 15 percent of the soldiers in the field, many being butchered as they fled.

FIGHTING THE PERSIANS

The fighting qualities of the Greek hoplite were put thoroughly to the test when large Persian armies invaded Greece, first in 490 BCE and then again a decade later. On the first occasion a predominantly Athenian force clashed with a far larger Persian army, including cavalry, at Marathon. Despite their inferior numbers, the hoplites charged the Persian lines.

Greek warrior
This stylized figurine shows a hoplite with a crested helmet and a round shield. Hoplites dressed and fought in much the same way across all the small city-states of the Greek world.

Respite from war
During the Olympic Games, a pan-Hellenic festival held every four years, hostilities between warring cities were normally suspended. One of the best-preserved sites at Olympia is the *palestra* or gym where the athletes trained.

Ocher dye used to create red stripes on crest

Colors all created with natural dyes

Horsehair crest and tail

Articulated cheek piece can be raised to ventilate the face

Chalcidian helmet
Once thought to have originated in the Greek city of Chalcis, this ornate style of helmet was made in the Greek colonies of southern Italy in the 5th century BCE.

The Persians were unaccustomed to the Greeks' aggressive use of infantry, depending more upon archers, cavalry, and chariots. Despite their surprise at the tactics of the hoplites, they succeeded in routing the Greek center, but stronger Greek forces on each wing drove into the Persian flanks, forcing them to flee to their boats. The second invasion in 480 BCE was the occasion of the celebrated fight to the death by 300 Spartan hoplites holding the narrow pass at Thermopylae. Soon after this delaying action the Persian fleet was decisively defeated at Salamis, and the following year combined Greek forces won victories over the Persians on land at the battles of Plataea and Mycale.

AUXILIARY TROOPS

Although the defeat of the Persians was a tribute to the courage and fighting skills of the armored citizen-soldier, the account of the battles by Greek historian Herodotus makes it clear that many light troops fought on the Greek side. He states, for example, that "35,000 lightly armed helots" supported the 5,000 Spartan hoplites at Platea and that the Athenian forces at the same battle included 800 archers. In the course of the Peloponnesian Wars these skirmishers seem to have grown in importance. An example of the use of light troops—and of the pitiless brutality of Greek warfare—is given by Thucydides, who relates that in 459 BCE the Athenians managed to trap a large number of fleeing Corinthians and "surrounding the enclosure with light-armed troops, stoned to death all who were inside." The most famous skirmishers were Thracian peltasts. Wearing a flimsy tunic and carrying a light wicker shield, these fleet-footed soldiers harassed the enemy phalanx by throwing javelins into their midst. Slow-moving hoplites, overburdened with heavy shields and armor, were vulnerable to this form of attack. Fighting in the service of Athens, peltasts famously annihilated a Spartan hoplite brigade outside Corinth in 390 BCE.

> "WE ... ARE TO FIGHT MEDES AND PERSIANS, NATIONS LONG STEEPED IN LUXURY, WHILE WE HAVE LONG BEEN HARDENED BY WARLIKE TOILS AND DANGERS ... IT WILL BE A FIGHT OF FREE MEN AGAINST SLAVES."
>
> **ALEXANDER THE GREAT**, ADDRESSING HIS ARMY BEFORE THE BATTLE OF ISSUS, 333 BCE

Battle of Issus
Long Macedonian-style "sarissa" spears are a prominent feature in this depiction of Alexander the Great's defeat of the Persian king Darius in 333 BCE.

Styles of fighting
Ancient Greek images of warfare often depict men fighting with a sword and a small oval "Boeotian" shield *(far left)*. It is not clear whether this shield and style of fighting belong to an earlier heroic age or were still in use when war was dominated by hoplites in phalanxes. The shield was clearly held differently from the larger round shield carried by hoplites *(left)*.

The increasing effectiveness of light troops led to changes in hoplite equipment and tactics. In the early 4th century the Athenian general Iphicrates stripped his hoplites of their metal greaves and cuirass, and replaced their large bronze-covered shield with a smaller shield faced with leather. More lightly equipped, the Iphicratid hoplite was better able to face the challenge presented by the peltasts and other skirmishers. At the same time, he was given a longer spear to outreach more heavily armored hoplite opponents.

In general, Greek warfare underwent a gradual professionalization. Campaigns became too sustained and ambitious in scale to be conducted as a part-time activity by citizen-soldiers. Regular troops and mercenaries could provide specialist skills on the battlefield and conduct long, drawn-out sieges of fortified towns. Under the leadership of a military genius, Epaminondas, the Thebans became the dominant military force in Greece around 380 BCE with an army sharply different from the Athenian or Spartan forces that had fought Persia. At the heart of the Theban army was a body of full-time soldiers paid by the state, the Sacred Band. This elite force took the principle of comradely bonding to its limit, being composed apparently of homosexual couples. Theban tactics included an innovative use of the phalanx and a major role for cavalry, who were supported by lightly clad runners trained to keep up with the horses on foot. For battle the cream of the Theban hoplites, including the Sacred Band, were typically massed in a phalanx up to 48 ranks deep on the left wing, this shock force destroying the enemy while cavalry and light troops protected the centre and right.

MACEDONIANS AND ROMANS

From 337 BCE, the Greek city-states came under the dominance of Macedonian rulers, first Philip II and then his son, Alexander the Great. Hoplites became a crucial but secondary element in Macedonian-led armies, which had cavalry as their elite arm. On his astonishing campaigns of conquest from 334 to 323 BCE, Alexander used a phalanx 16 or 32 ranks deep, armed with the long "sarissa" spear, measuring 20–23 ft (6-7 m). The hoplites were no longer self-consciously brave and noble citizen-soldiers, but relatively lower-class professionals drilled into a steady performance on the battlefield. Many Greeks also fought against Alexander, for their renowned qualities as armored foot soldiers had made them sought-after mercenaries, whose services were bought by Persian emperors, as well as many other rulers in the eastern Mediterranean.

The hoplite style of warfare with phalanx and spear continued to show its worth until the armies of the Hellenistic world came into conflict with the rising power of Rome in the 2nd century BCE. At the decisive battle of Pydna in 168 BCE, the Romans deliberately retired over rough ground, which caused the pursuing Macedonians to lose their tight formation. The Roman infantry, armed with swords and javelins, were then able to slash a path into their phalanx. Once the fighting was at close quarters the long, unwieldy sarissa became a useless encumbrance. Hoplites threw away their spears and fought with daggers, but were cut to pieces by the Roman swords. A new era of infantry warfare was born.

HOPLITE BATTLE TACTICS

The tactics illustrated here are those of the 5th century BCE, when the tightly packed phalanxes of two opposing Greek city-states would line up to do battle in exactly the same formation. The men at the front advanced with their shields locked together and their spears ready to engage with the enemy. When the front ranks clashed, the men behind pressed forward with their shields on those ahead of them, contributing to the *othismos*, or "shoving match," with the rival phalanx. The details of Greek hoplite tactics are, however, the subject of dispute. Some historians have argued that as hoplites ran to attack they would have been forced to spread out, although they could have locked shields if standing on the defensive.

Advancing in a tight phalanx
Here the phalanx advances to meet an opposing phalanx in very tight formation, shoulder-to-shoulder and with shields up against the back of the man in front. Only the front three or four ranks could have reached the enemy with their spears. Later, when spears grew much longer, they were probably held underarm.

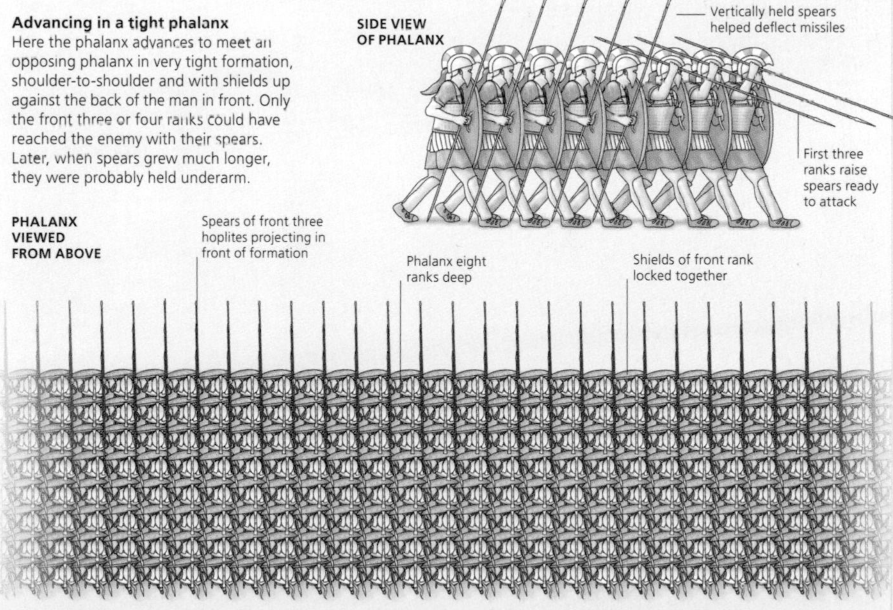

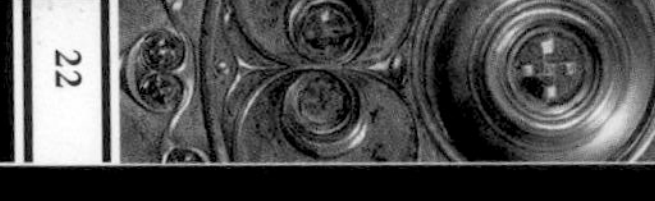

GREEK ARMS

Early armor was bronze but was later exchanged for cheaper, lighter, linen armor which afforded quicker movement as battle tactics changed. Appearance would have mattered as well as strength, as some standoffs could result in simply visually intimidating the enemy into conceding defeat without going to battle. The primary and secondary weapon of the hoplite was the *doru* or spear. If the front half of the spear broke off in the crush of the battlefield the hoplite could still utilize the heavier butt of the spear, which was also equipped with a point.

Horsehair crest in natural whites or browns

Corinthian helmet
Increased maneuvering during battle called for better communication, reflected in the design of this 400 BCE replica, allowing better hearing and visibility than earlier versions.

Larger eye holes for increased peripheral vision

Ear hole for responding to commands

Chiton
This was worn under the armor and would have been brightly dyed. Favored military colors were red and blue.

Braiding prevented fraying on stitching

Yoke

Dyed linen

Bronze scales

Decorative strip level with hoplite's navel

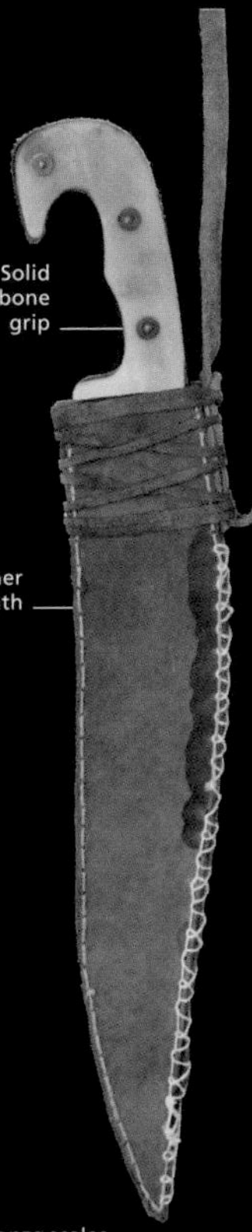

Kopis ("chopper")
A scythe weapon developed from agriculture, the *kopis* was used in a hacking motion.

Solid bone grip

Leather sheath

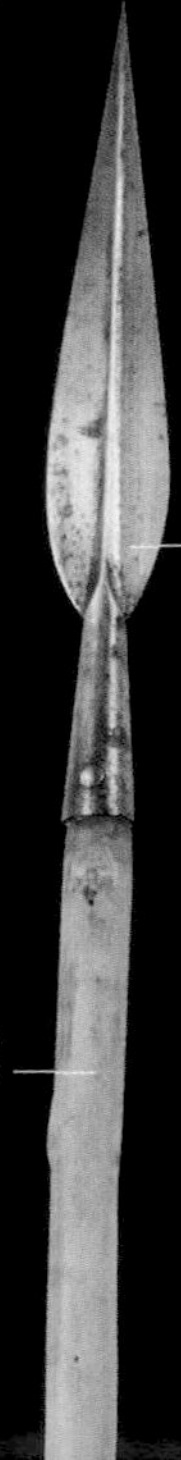

Doru (spear)
A stabbing rather than throwing spear, the point or *aichme* was the primary stabbing weapon. The butt end was called the *sarouter* or "lizard sticker," as it was used to skewer fallen enemies. The hand-turned ash shaft was about 7–9 ft (2–3 m) long.

Iron *aichme* with central ridge for strength

SPEAR POINT

Ash shaft

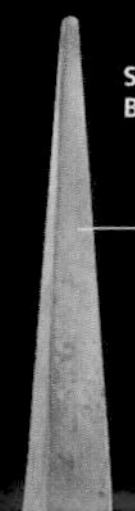

SPEAR BUTT

Square-sectioned bronze *sarouter* at rear end of spear

Doing up leather fastenings

Interior grip of shield

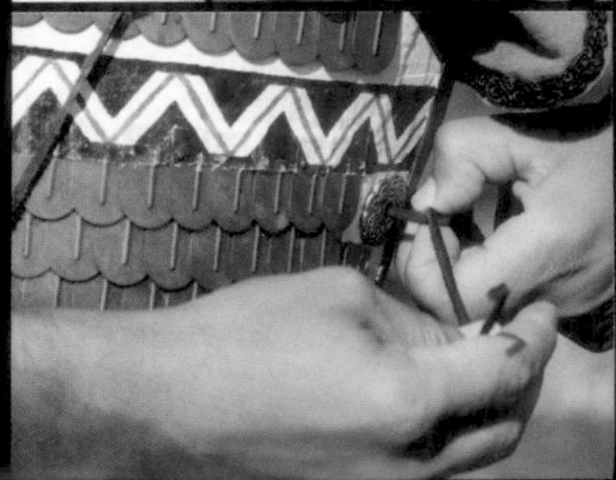

Linothorax fastened on lefthand side

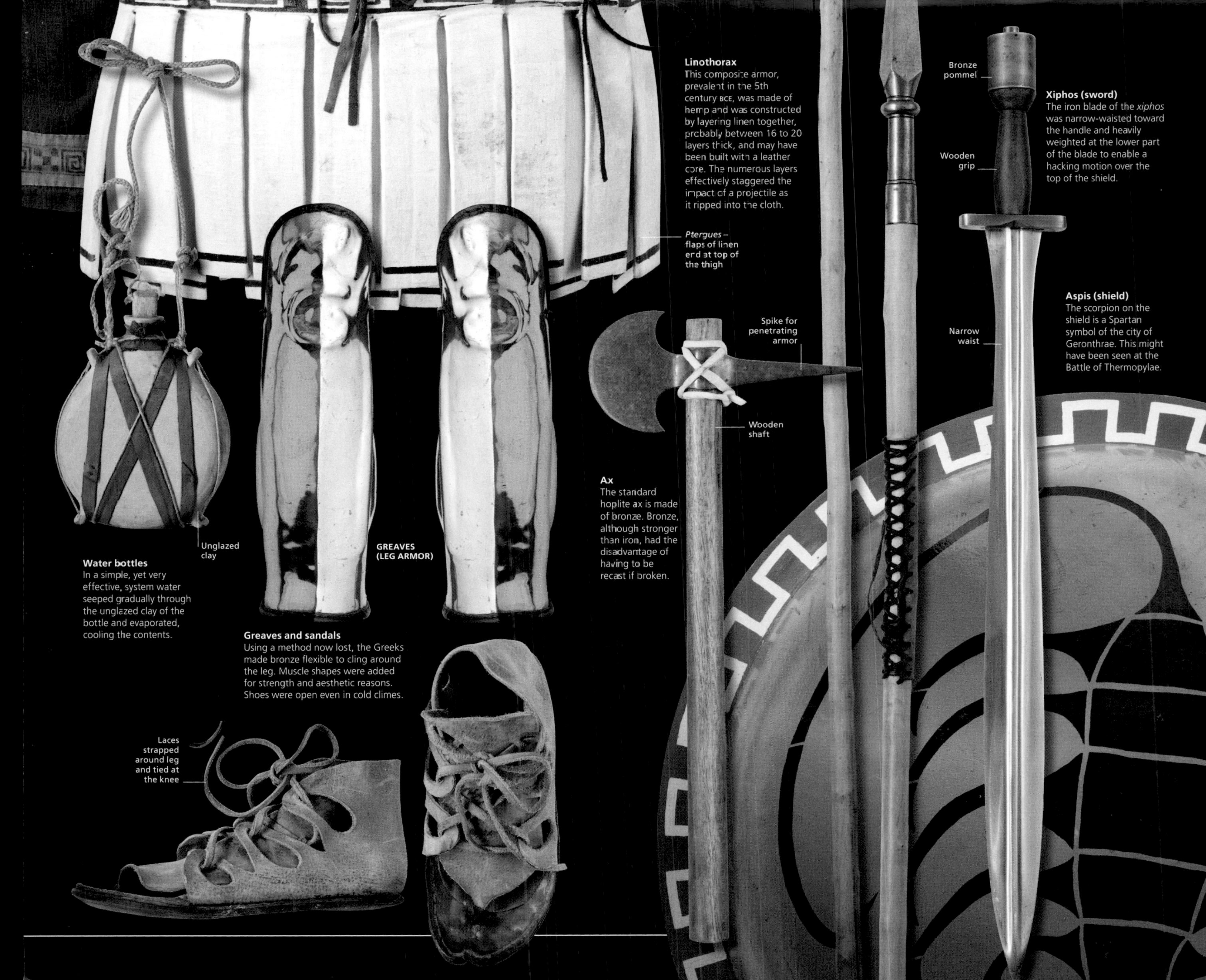

Linothorax
This composite armor, prevalent in the 5th century BCE, was made of hemp and was constructed by layering linen together, probably between 16 to 20 layers thick, and may have been built with a leather core. The numerous layers effectively staggered the impact of a projectile as it ripped into the cloth.

Xiphos (sword)
The iron blade of the *xiphos* was narrow-waisted toward the handle and heavily weighted at the lower part of the blade to enable a hacking motion over the top of the shield.

Aspis (shield)
The scorpion on the shield is a Spartan symbol of the city of Geronthrae. This might have been seen at the Battle of Thermopylae.

Ax
The standard hoplite ax is made of bronze. Bronze, although stronger than iron, had the disadvantage of having to be recast if broken.

Water bottles
In a simple, yet very effective, system water seeped gradually through the unglazed clay of the bottle and evaporated, cooling the contents.

Greaves and sandals
Using a method now lost, the Greeks made bronze flexible to cling around the leg. Muscle shapes were added for strength and aesthetic reasons. Shoes were open even in cold climes.

Roman military engineering
Roman soldiers cross the Danube on a newly constructed pontoon bridge during the Emperor Trajan's first campaign against the Dacians (101–102 CE). Danuvius, the stern god of the river, looks on in this scene from the frieze on Trajan's Column in Rome.

300 BCE – 450 CE

ROMAN LEGIONARY

"IN EVERY BATTLE VICTORY IS GRANTED NOT BY MERE NUMBERS AND INNATE COURAGE BUT BY SKILL AND TRAINING ... WE PREVAILED BY SKILFUL SELECTION OF RECRUITS, BY TEACHING THE PRINCIPLES OF WAR, BY PUNISHMENT FOR INDOLENCE."

AT ITS PEAK THE ROMAN ARMY was probably the most effective fighting force in the Ancient World. It conquered and maintained an empire that, by the 1st century CE, stretched from Britain to North Africa and from Spain to Egypt. At the heart of this formidable organization were the legionaries— tough professional infantry equipped with sword, shield, and javelin. Equally dominant in pitched battles and in siege warfare, they were used to cow or destroy the enemies of Rome in campaigns of ruthless efficiency.

The Roman army was originally a militia of part-time soldiers, with every propertied citizen owing periods of military service to the state. Around 300 BCE the legions began to assume the form and organization that would make them such an invincible force. The soldiers, although still not professionals, were extremely successful in combat, most notably in defeating the Carthaginians in the Punic Wars. But as victorious campaigns extended Roman rule over an ever wider area, part-time service became inadequate to Rome's military needs. Ordinary citizens could not be expected to engage in prolonged campaigns far from home or man permanent garrisons in distant provinces. By the time Julius Caesar was engaged upon his famous conquest of the Gauls (58–51 BCE), the Roman army had evolved into a permanent force of professional soldiers.

LEGIONARIES AND AUXILIARIES

The professionalization of the army was not without its drawbacks. Regular soldiers tended to develop an allegiance to the commander who led them rather than to the state, and Rome was for a time torn apart by civil wars between rival generals. But after Augustus established himself as Rome's first emperor (from 31 BCE to 14 CE), the regular army became the rock on which the Roman Empire stood. This army included auxiliary cohorts that would be recruited from various "barbarian" peoples who did not have the privilege of Roman citizenship. It also included cavalry, usually auxiliaries, who formed an important element of the army on the battlefield. But there is no question that the heart and soul of the army was the Roman citizen foot soldier.

Legionary emblem
This tile is embossed with a leaping boar, emblem of the 20th Legion, based in Chester.

The legionary, upon whom the burden of maintaining the Roman Empire at its apogee rested, was an infantryman trained to fight in close formation with short sword and javelin. Although conscription was not unknown at times of military crisis, he was generally a volunteer and in principle had to fulfil certain criteria. Firstly, he had to be a citizen. This did not mean he had to be born in the city of Rome, but in the early days of the Empire it did mean that he was probably at least from Italy. By 212 CE, however, citizenship had been extended to all free men across the Empire. Slaves were rigorously excluded from the ranks of the legions and any who had enlisted by falsely claiming to be free men could expect severe punishment if their deception was discovered. Men convicted of serious crimes or facing prosecution were also barred. Every potential recruit was subjected to a physical examination and some were rejected as too short of stature or as unfit for service on medical grounds.

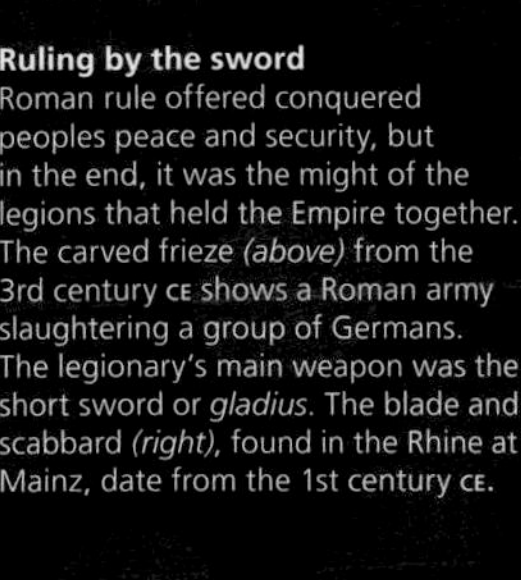

Ruling by the sword
Roman rule offered conquered peoples peace and security, but in the end, it was the might of the legions that held the Empire together. The carved frieze *(above)* from the 3rd century CE shows a Roman army slaughtering a group of Germans. The legionary's main weapon was the short sword or *gladius*. The blade and scabbard *(right)*, found in the Rhine at Mainz, date from the 1st century CE.

GLADIUS AND SCABBARD

> "IT WOULD NOT BE WRONG TO CALL THEIR DRILLS BLOODLESS BATTLES AND THEIR BATTLES BLOODY DRILLS."
>
> **FLAVIUS JOSEPHUS**, JEWISH HISTORIAN, DESCRIBING ROMAN TRAINING METHODS

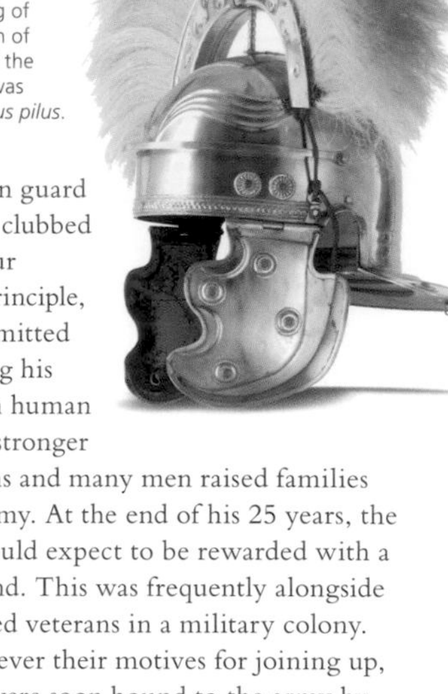

Centurion's helmet
In the early centuries of the Empire a legion usually had a total of 59 centurions. The highest-ranking of these was centurion of the First Century of the First Cohort, who was known as the *primus pilus*.

The existence of selection criteria should not be taken to imply, though, that legionaries were a hand-picked elite. Whereas the earlier militia legions had been recruited from citizens meeting a certain property qualification, volunteers for the professional army came predominantly from the lower ranks of society—from the sons of farmers and artisans down to plain vagrants. Roman recruiting parties may have preferred to select tall, robust citizens accustomed to physical labor, but much of the time they presumably had to accept whatever vaguely acceptable candidates presented themselves.

LIFE IN THE LEGIONS

The attractions of life in the legions were such as would appeal to men who otherwise faced lives blighted by insecurity and poor prospects. Employment as a legionary offered modest pay—probably no more than the income of an ordinary laborer—but a high level of job security, regular meals, and some chance of advancement in life. Usually recruited in his early 20s, the legionary was required to make a daunting commitment. He signed up for 20 years active service plus five years as a "veteran" with lighter duties. During that quarter-century he was likely to be stationed at remote locations on the frontiers of the Empire, subject to rigorous discipline and draconian punishments—the penalty for falling asleep on guard duty was to be clubbed to death by your comrades. In principle, he was not permitted to marry during his service, though human nature proved stronger than regulations and many men raised families while in the army. At the end of his 25 years, the legionary could expect to be rewarded with a grant of land. This was frequently alongside other retired veterans in a military colony.

Whatever their motives for joining up, soldiers were soon bound to the army by ties of group loyalty that were deliberately fostered at every level. Arriving at his designated unit with his lead identity tablet

Image *(imago)* of the emperor carried on a pole by a junior officer with the title *imaginifer*

Signum, the standard of an individual century, carried by a junior officer known as the *signifer*

Large curved trumpet used for communicating simple orders, played by a *cornucen* around his neck, the legionary was integrated into a tight-knit hierarchical organization. At the lowest level, he belonged to a *contubernium*, a group of eight men who shared rooms in barracks and messed together. Ten of these *contubernia* formed a century, commanded by a centurion; six centuries made a cohort and ten cohorts a legion. Each legion had its carefully preserved traditions and its symbols, creating a sense of identity for its soldiers, who would regard other legions than their own with rivalry or contempt.

The officers who regulated the legionary's daily life were the centurion and his various subordinates, known as *principales*. The centurion was a key figure in the Roman military system, a repository of experience and a resolute source of leadership at the level where it counted most. At least some, and possibly most, centurions had worked their way up through the ranks, although a legionary who aspired to this status could expect first to endure at least 15 years of military service. He would also need to be literate, for the running of any part of the Roman army generated large quantities of documents for official records. Above the centurion level, officers were members of the ruling classes appointed through the influence of powerful patrons.

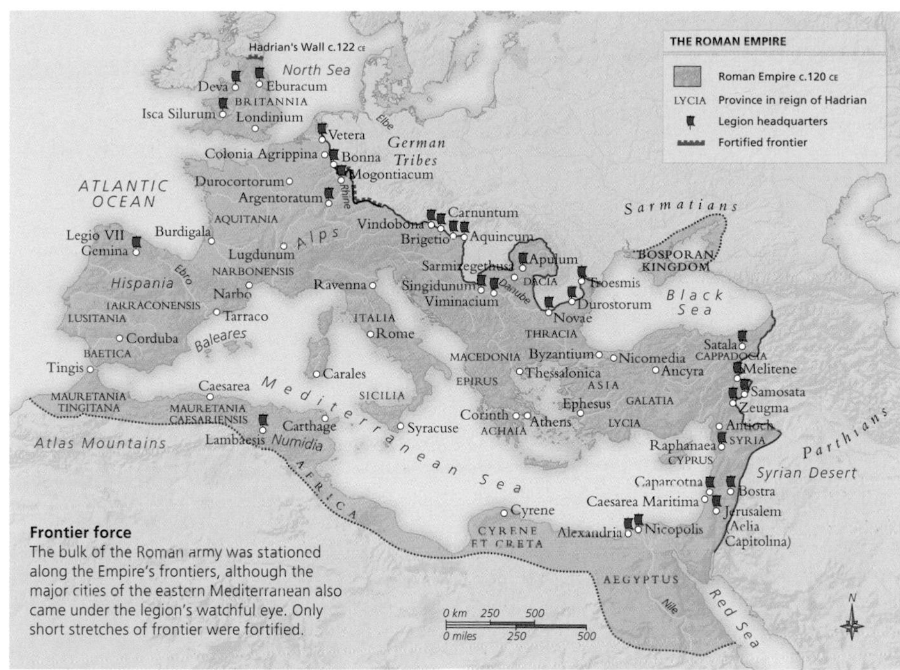

Frontier force
The bulk of the Roman army was stationed along the Empire's frontiers, although the major cities of the eastern Mediterranean also came under the legion's watchful eye. Only short stretches of frontier were fortified.

Square flag (*vexillum*) bearing the legion's symbol, which marked the position of the commander on the battlefield

TRAINING AND WORKING

Most legionaries were posted to some remote area near the frontiers of the Empire, or to one of the cities of the eastern Mediterranean, such as Jerusalem, that were considered sufficiently unreliable to require a strong military presence. Since warfare tended to be sporadic, they were likely to spend the majority of their time in the army on peacetime garrison duties in a barracks. Keeping militarily up to scratch under these circumstances was inevitably a challenge. The training of a legionary, which continued throughout his service, focused on three goals: physical fitness and endurance; the skilled use of weaponry; and disciplined action as part of a unit. Men were taken out on forced marches of 20–30 miles (30–50 km) with heavy packs and full equipment. They engaged in mock combat, from one-on-one fighting to elaborate exercises involving entire units. Naturally, they were taught to march in step and they carried out formation drills in preparation for close-order combat.

Apart from the routine of training, drill, guard duties, and fatigues, the legionaries fulfilled an essential everyday function in patrolling and policing areas prone to lawlessness, rebellion, or incursions by armed groups from across the border. They were also responsible for large-scale building work, carrying out both civilian and military projects, including the construction of roads, fortresses, and aqueducts. Hadrian's Wall in northern England is a notable example of a legionary-built structure, each section of the wall being completed by a different century. Legions also had an important role as manufacturers, their workshops supplying many of the army's material needs, from pottery to weaponry.

Roman battle order
Roman legionaries advanced on their enemies with swords drawn and shields raised. Flags and other standards were important symbols of Roman power and served as rallying points for the cohorts and centuries within the legion.

Although legionaries spent only a fraction of their time on active service, warfare was in the end what they were for. Probably most men welcomed campaigning as a chance to escape the dull routine of garrison duties and to put into practice the military skills endlessly rehearsed in training. Campaigns mostly involved the aggressive movement of forces into hostile territory in response to a revolt within the empire or attacks from outside it. The aim was punitive—to inflict such spectacular suffering and destruction on those responsible that the incidents would not recur.

Wooden fort
The fort at Lunt near Coventry in England is a reconstruction of one built there in the 1st century CE. The design of the gate tower is based on examples on Trajan's Column.

The legionary was expected to march at a speed of around 4 mph (6 kph) under normal circumstances, and faster if a crisis required it. But the practical speed of movement of Roman forces was set by their supply wagons, pack animals, and siege train. The logistical arrangements of Roman legions were generally excellent and both soldiers and animals could expect to be reasonably fed while on campaign, although a certain amount of foraging along the route was normal. Sometimes on punitive expeditions the main function of the legionaries was to devastate the area around the march, destroying crops and animals and laying waste to villages and towns. This was a task Roman soldiers performed with thoroughness and conscience-free brutality.

> "I GIVE THANKS ... THAT WHILE ALL ARE WORKING HARD THE WHOLE DAY CUTTING STONES, I AS A PRINCIPALIS GO ABOUT DOING NOTHING."
>
> **ROMAN SOLDIER** STATIONED IN EGYPT IN A LETTER TO HIS FAMILY, 109 CE

CONSTRUCTION DUTIES

At the end of every day the legionaries would construct a marching camp, a temporary defensive position surrounded by a rampart and ditch. The back-breaking work of digging ditches and building ramparts to establish the camp was done by contingents drawn from all the centuries involved in the campaign – perhaps ten men from each. Marching near the head of the column, these men would aim to have the site ready by the time their colleagues, near the rear of the column, arrived looking for rest.

Faced with natural obstacles, legions on the march would sometimes demonstrate impressive engineering skills. During his first campaign against the Dacians in 101 CE, Emperor Trajan's army crossed the Danube on a rapidly constructed bridge of boats. But returning for a second

Arch of Trajan, Thamugadi, Algeria
While legionaries built magnificent paved roads across the empire, emperors erected memorials to their military triumphs. This arch in a once prosperous North African city commemorates Trajan's victories over the Parthians in 114–117 CE.

decisive campaign five years later they built a monumental stone-and-wood arched bridge, accessed by an approach road cut into the cliffs lining the river. It has been suggested that the legionaries should be regarded more as combat engineers than as straightforward infantry.

The need to use tools as much as weapons was also much in evidence during siege operations, which formed such an important part of the warfare of the age. Taking a fortified position that was stoutly defended was a challenge to any attacking force, but the Roman legions achieved the feat time and again through a combination of engineering skills and indomitable fighting spirit.

SIEGE TACTICS AND WEAPONS

Sieges were normally long, drawn-out affairs, because an assault on a fortress or fortified town was a desperate business to attempt, even once the walls were breached. Fighting your way into a stronghold was a last resort, and defenders who made it necessary by refusing to surrender could expect no mercy. Victorious legionaries, who had seen colleagues killed or wounded by missiles as they advanced on the fortifications and in the confused close-quarters fighting that followed, indulged in an orgy of slaughter, rape, and pillage. This was the legionary's reward for the hardships and dangers of the siege and his revenge on those who had caused him so much trouble. It was also deliberate Roman policy, designed to deter others from attempting to defy Roman power.

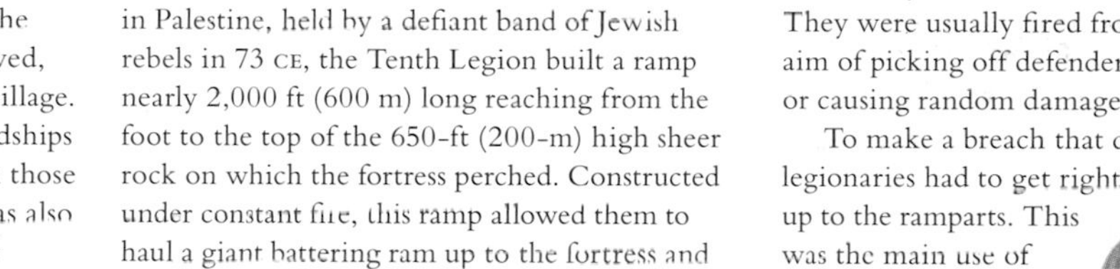

The stronghold of Masada
The taking of the cliff-top fortress in 73 CE showed great engineering skill and ruthless determination. When the Romans finally broke into the fortress after two years' siege, the few remaining defenders had committed suicide.

The scale of the siege works undertaken was often highly impressive. Besieging the Gallic army of Vercingetorix at Alesia in central Gaul in 52 BCE, Caesar's legionaries constructed a circular ditch-and-rampart wall around the Gauls' hill fort stretching 11 miles (18 km) and incorporating 23 forts and over 100 wooden towers. Having completed this massive work, they then built an even longer fortified wall facing outward, to defend themselves against a Gallic army arriving to relieve Vercingetorix.

At the siege of the mountain fortress of Masada in Palestine, held by a defiant band of Jewish rebels in 73 CE, the Tenth Legion built a ramp nearly 2,000 ft (600 m) long reaching from the foot to the top of the 650-ft (200-m) high sheer rock on which the fortress perched. Constructed under constant fire, this ramp allowed them to haul a giant battering ram up to the fortress and hammer a breach in its walls.

The Romans had siege artillery with which to bombard the enemy. These were mostly forms of *ballista*, a torsion machine superficially resembling a large crossbow. In the late empire period *ballistae* were supplemented by the *onager*, a one-armed catapult. None of these siege engines, however, packed sufficient punch to breach city walls or other solid fortifications. They were usually fired from towers with the aim of picking off defenders on the ramparts or causing random damage inside the walls.

To make a breach that could be stormed, legionaries had to get right up to the ramparts. This was the main use of the famous *testudo*.

ROMAN AUXILIARIES AND CAVALRY

The auxiliaries were troops recruited from "barbarian" peoples, usually living within the borders of the Roman Empire but not enjoying the privilege of Roman citizenship. They provided extra manpower and special skills that the Roman army very much needed. In particular, they constituted the majority of the army's skirmishing light infantry and of its cavalry.

Like the legionaries, auxiliaries were expected to serve for 25 years. On completing the full term of service, their reward was the grant of Roman citizenship to them and their descendants. An auxiliary cohort was composed of recruits from a single area or ethnic group, but it was usually stationed away from its home area. Auxiliaries were paid less than legionaries and seem often to have been thrown into the most dangerous fighting as relatively dispensable troops. On the other hand, they were subject to less strict discipline, did less work—they were not involved in engineering or building—and carried less weight on the march.

AUXILIARY SHIELD

Many of the auxiliaries were trained to fight in a similar manner to the legionary, but some regions supplied specialized troops—the Balearics produced stone-slingers, for instance, and Syria was a source of bowmen. Most important were the expert horsemen from areas such as Batavia, Pannonia, and Thrace. They were the cream of the Roman cavalry, armed with spears, javelins, and the *spatha*—a longer sword than the infantry gladius. Although they did not have stirrups, their horned saddles served to hold them firmly on their mounts in combat.

CAVALRY HELMET

Roman cavalry did not usually act as shock troops charging infantry, but instead defended the army's flanks, carried out encirclements, and hunted down defeated enemy soldiers in the pursuit after a victory. In the later period of the Empire, cavalry probably became more numerous and played an increasingly important role in battle.

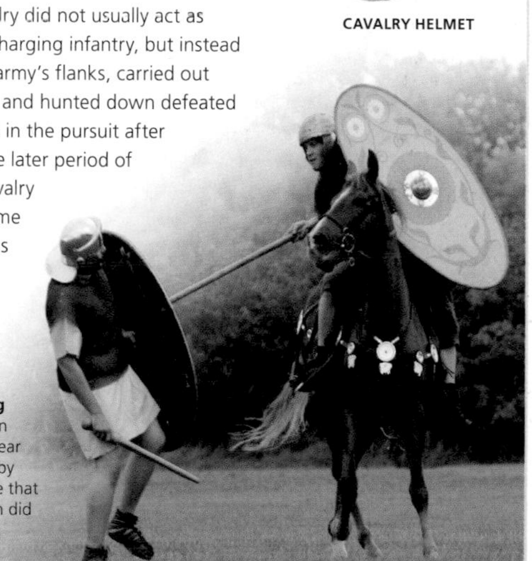

Cavalry training
Cavalry training in the use of the spear is demonstrated by re-enactors. Note that Roman horsemen did not have stirrups.

The tortoise
Using the tortoise formation to attack the walls or gate of a city required considerable practice to coordinate the movements of all the soldiers involved *(right)*. If they executed the maneuver successfully, they were immune to the arrows and other missiles directed against them by the defenders *(far right)*.

> "LEST THE SOLDIERS ... SHOULD BE SEPARATED FROM THEIR COMRADES, EVERY COHORT HAD ITS SHIELDS PAINTED IN A MANNER PECULIAR TO ITSELF. THE NAME OF EACH SOLDIER WAS ALSO WRITTEN ON HIS SHIELD, TOGETHER WITH THE NUMBER OF THE COHORT AND CENTURY TO WHICH HE BELONGED."
>
> **VEGETIUS**, *A MILITARY DIGEST*, 4TH CENTURY CE

In this aptly named formation—*testudo* is Latin for tortoise—a body of soldiers would advance with shields covering them from above as well as from all sides. When they reached the walls, they would either attack them with metal bars and picks or attempt to tunnel under them.

INTO BATTLE

Full-scale field battles were infrequent, but they were the ultimate test of a legionary's morale and fighting skills. Confronted with a "barbarian" army, the Romans had no crucial technological advantage on the battlefield. They did deploy field artillery in the form of small ballistae known as "scorpions," but although these were accurate and effective missile weapons they were not decisive. The Romans rarely made use of field fortifications, and then only to defend their flanks. It was the discipline, stamina, and strength of the legionary that so often brought victory. He was, it is true, better armored than his opponents, but sword, spear, and shield were common to both sides. The savagery of close-quarters combat demanded emotional commitment to counter his inevitable fear. Here his bonding with comrades fighting alongside and identification with the honor of the cohort and legion would have their full effect.

But the Roman legionaries were not invincible. In 53 BCE they were defeated by Parthian archers at Carrhae. In 9 CE three Roman legions were surrounded and massacred in the Teutoburg Forest by German tribes led by Arminius. The Ninth Legion was partially destroyed by Queen Boudicca of the Iceni in 60 CE, before the 14th and 20th Legions defeated her and reasserted Roman power in Britain. But their record of success against enemies from outside and within the Empire in the first two centuries of the Christian era was impressive.

From the 3rd century CE the legions often became tools in the power struggles of ambitious leaders. Economic problems led to the adoption of cheaper armor and political disruption made armies much harder to raise and supply. Most of the soldiers of the late Empire were conscripts and the distinction between the citizen-legionaries and "barbarian" auxiliaries was largely lost. But the eventual fall of the Roman Empire in the west in the 5th century CE was not the result of defeats suffered by the legions, and much of the tradition of the Roman army was preserved by the Empire in the east.

Roman artillery
A team of legionaries mans a ballista. Two of them prepare to winch back the bowstring into the firing position. This kind of ballista could fire stone projectiles or heavy darts.

ROMAN BATTLEFIELD TACTICS

Roman battle tactics obviously changed radically over time and depended on whether they were fighting fellow Romans or "barbarians." The Romans would also have to adapt their battle formations to the terrain and in order to counter forces employing large numbers of cavalry or chariots. The deployment of troops shown below is one that might have been adopted by a legion—along with its cavalry and assorted auxiliary troops—to confront a "barbarian" enemy fighting largely on foot, such as the Britons in the 1st century CE. Roman infantry drew up on the battlefield in close order, with the most reliable troops in the front lines. The first century of each cohort, the one with the best troops, was placed in front of the others with the veterans at the rear.

When the moment came for battle to be joined—usually after a prolonged exchange of arrows, slingshots, and artillery—the cohorts advanced in silence at a slow and steady pace to meet the warriors charging toward them. It was at this point that the discipline of the legionary was put most severely to the test, for there had to be no wavering as the enemy came ever closer. Then the order was given to charge. The previously silent legionaries would raise a spine-chilling shout and hurl their javelins into the mass of the enemy, then surge forward to make contact, shoving with their shields and stabbing with their short swords.

A legion in order of battle
Here the cohorts of a legion are lined up side by side, but they could also have been deployed with five cohorts in front and five behind. Gaps between the cohorts and between the individual centuries were essential to battlefield maneuvering, but they could be speedily closed in the event of an enemy charge.

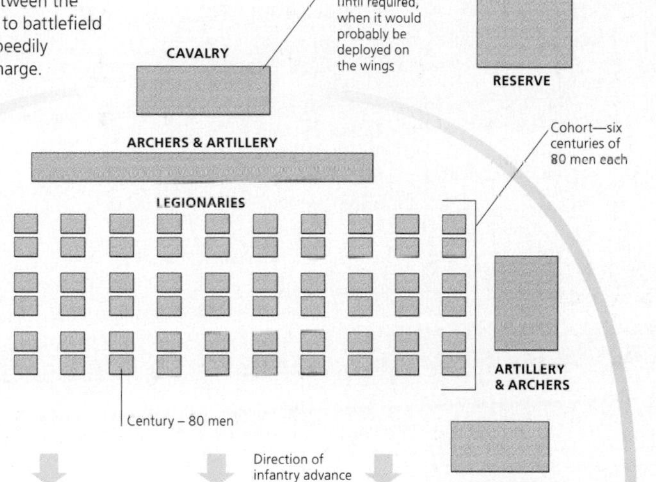

Order of battle
Depending on how the enemy lined up, the Romans might greet them with arrows and artillery bolts or harass them with skirmishers and slingers. The latter would withdraw as the main infantry force of legionaries advanced.

Century in marching order
The legionaries approached the battlefield marching in disciplined ranks and files, probably led by their centurion and *signifer*—the junior officer who carried the century's standard.

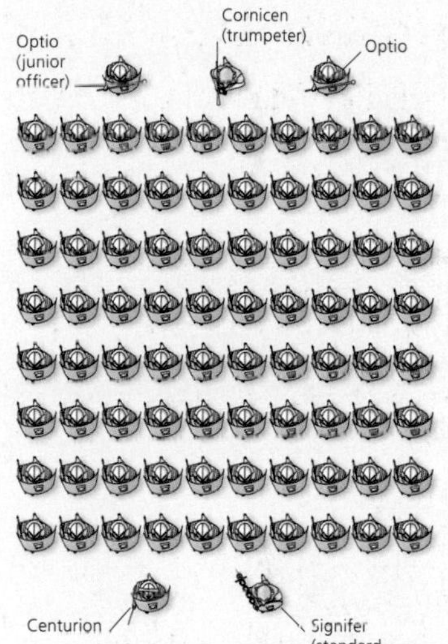

Century in attack formation
The century has deployed in four ranks to attack, first launching a volley of javelins, then assuming closer order to smash into the enemy front line with a wall of shields.

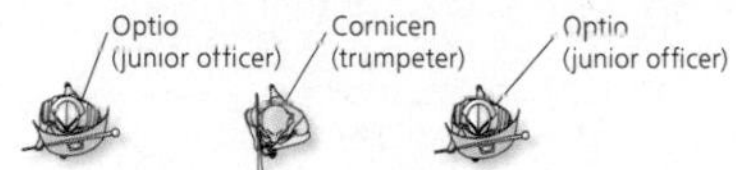

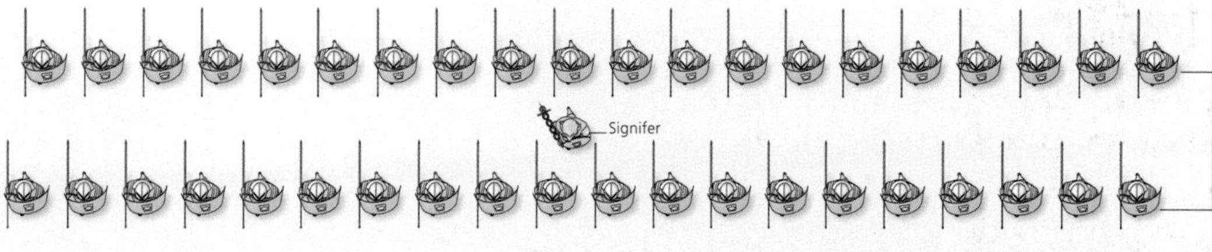

ROMAN ARMOR

The Roman legionary's armor was a compromise between protection and mobility. Head, shoulders, and torso were well protected by the iron helmet and cuirass, but arms and legs were uncovered. It is thought, however, that soldiers sometimes wore greaves to protect their legs and even flexible arm guards of overlapping plates. Although there was considerable uniformity in the appearance of the legions across the empire, especially in the 1st century CE, legions must often have been fitted out in a variety of different styles of armor and helmets.

THE YOUNG SOLDIER MUST BE GIVEN FREQUENT PRACTICE IN CARRYING LOADS OF UP TO 60 POUNDS WHILE MARCHING AT NORMAL SPEEDS.

VEGETIUS, *A MILITARY DIGEST*, 4TH CENTURY CE

Fitting for attaching crest

Helmet
A widely used model of the late 1st century CE, the design of the helmet was based originally on Gallic styles. It gave good protection to the legionary's cheeks and to the back of his neck. Helmets were fitted with the means of attaching a crest, but it seems that the ordinary legionary did not wear one in battle, so they were perhaps a feature of ceremonial parades.

Projecting ridge giving added protection from downward sword blows

Cheek guard

Large sloping neck guard for extra protection

Brass fittings

Iron plates, articulated by means of internal leather straps

Brass fastenings tied with leather thongs

Securing the cheek guards

Lucky medallion hanging around neck

Armor made with seven or eight overlapping plates

Plates with intricate designs in inlay or relief

Cuirass
Body armor made of overlapping iron plates was common, but by no means universal in the 1st century CE. It is the kind worn by the legionaries depicted on Trajan's Column in Rome. It may have weighed as much as 20lb (9 kg) and for the armor to sit comfortably there was probably some kind of padded lining worn underneath.

Fastening the cuirass

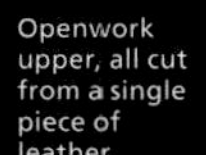

Leather purse attached to belt

Belt and apron
When a legionary was not wearing his armor, it was his ornate belt *(balteus)* and apron of studded straps which hung from it that marked him out as a soldier. And when a legionary was given a dishonorable discharge, he was formally stripped of his belt.

Tunic
Soldiers' woollen tunics were shorter than those worn by civilians, but were otherwise essentially the same. They were probably off-white or dyed red. The color may have had some significance in terms of rank.

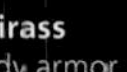

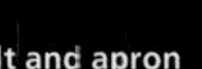

Openwork upper, all cut from a single piece of leather

Pattern of nails supporting heel and ball of foot

Army sandals
Soldiers' durable, iron-nailed sandals were known as *caligae* (boots). In the 1st century CE, they were made to more or less the same pattern all across the empire.

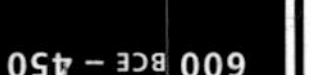

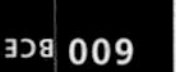

ROMAN WEAPONS AND EQUIPMENT

A legionary on the march not only had to bear the weight of his armor, shield, and weapons, which could be as much as 44 lb (20 kg), but also had to carry a bulky pack of equipment—ranging from entrenching tools to cooking pots and pans. This could add 33 lb (15 kg) or more to his total load. Heavier items of gear, such as quern stones to grind corn, were carried by mules or ox-carts. Ideally a number of soldiers would be spared the burden of their full gear so that they would be ready to fight in case of ambush. The standard weapons of an infantryman in the Imperial period were two *pila* (javelins), used either to halt a charge or to soften up the enemy before the Roman forces attacked, and a short sword for fighting at close quarters once battle was joined. Many legionaries also carried a short dagger.

A soldier's pay
This hoard of gold coins from the period of the Roman invasion of Britain in 43 CE, was found buried in Kent in southeastern England. It was perhaps the savings of one of the invading army—presumably an officer because it represents about four years' pay for an ordinary legionary. Soldiers carried their money in purses like bracelets that could only be opened when taken off the wrist.

Marching pack
A soldier's gear obviously varied according to the climate and nature of the campaign, but would normally include essential tools for setting up temporary camps and fortifications, as well as a pack holding three days' rations along with his personal effects. Additional items could easily be strapped onto the T-shaped carrying pole.

Short sword
The short, pointed sword *(gladius)* was an effective stabbing weapon for fighting at close quarters from behind shields in well-disciplined ranks. This example, about 28 in (70 cm) in length, dates from the late 1st century CE and is of the kind shown worn by the legionaries on Trajan's Column. The precise details of the handle, pommel, and blade are based on examples that were excavated at Pompeii. The blades of later Roman swords were significantly longer.

> THEY CARRY … A SAW, A BASKET, A PICK, AND AN AX, AS WELL AS A LEATHER STRAP, A SICKLE, A CHAIN, AND ENOUGH RATIONS … FOR THREE DAYS. IN FACT, THE INFANTRYMAN CARRIES SO MUCH EQUIPMENT THAT HE IS NOT VERY DIFFERENT FROM A MULE.
>
> **FLAVIUS JOSEPHUS,** THE JEWISH WAR, 1ST CENTURY CE

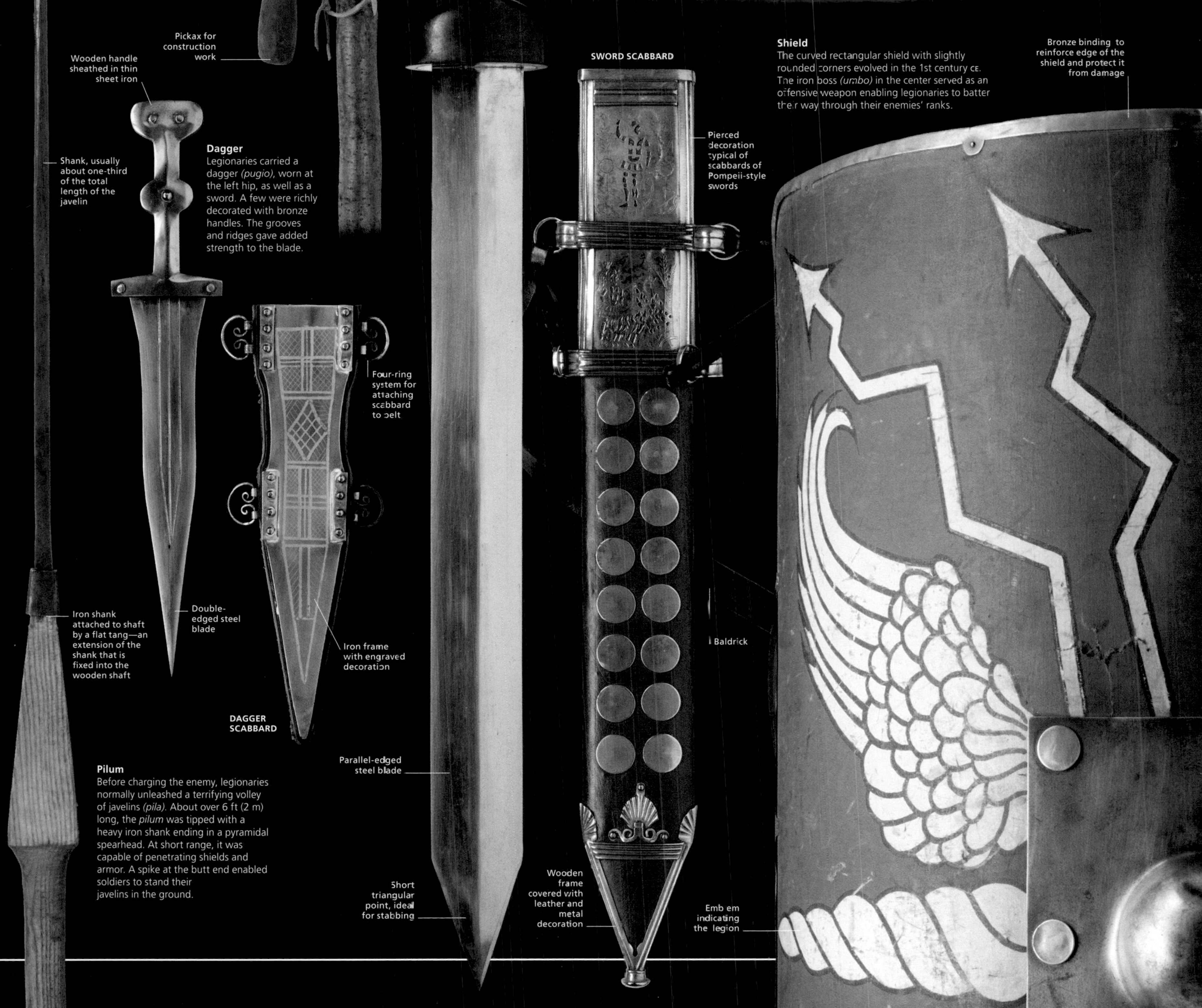

Pickax for construction work
Wooden handle sheathed in thin sheet iron
Shank, usually about one-third of the total length of the javelin
Dagger
Legionaries carried a dagger (pugio), worn at the left hip, as well as a sword. A few were richly decorated with bronze handles. The grooves and ridges gave added strength to the blade.
Four-ring system for attaching scabbard to belt
Iron shank attached to shaft by a flat tang—an extension of the shank that is fixed into the wooden shaft
Double-edged steel blade
Iron frame with engraved decoration
DAGGER SCABBARD
Pilum
Before charging the enemy, legionaries normally unleashed a terrifying volley of javelins (pila). About over 6 ft (2 m) long, the pilum was tipped with a heavy iron shank ending in a pyramidal spearhead. At short range, it was capable of penetrating shields and armor. A spike at the butt end enabled soldiers to stand their javelins in the ground.
Parallel-edged steel blade
Short triangular point, ideal for stabbing
SWORD SCABBARD
Pierced decoration typical of scabbards of Pompeii-style swords
Baldrick
Wooden frame covered with leather and metal decoration
Emblem indicating the legion
Shield
The curved rectangular shield with slightly rounded corners evolved in the 1st century CE. The iron boss (umbo) in the center served as an offensive weapon enabling legionaries to batter their way through their enemies' ranks.
Bronze binding to reinforce edge of the shield and protect it from damage

ROMAN FORT

The Romans were the greatest experts in fortification in the Ancient World. When on campaign, a legion would construct a fortified camp, surrounded by a rampart and ditch, at every stop. While fighting might often be left to less well-trained auxiliaries, building work was always the job of legionaries. They would have built the fort shown here at Arbeia in northern England, although it subsequently housed auxiliary troops.

Permanent forts and fortresses, like this one that has been reconstructed at Arbeia, were built of stone rather than the wood used for temporary camps. They acted as barracks, supply depots, and administrative headquarters to maintain Rome's military presence in potentially hostile territory. In addition to their military tasks, educated soldiers might be assigned to clerical duties, keeping the written records required by Roman bureaucracy. Outposts of Roman civilization, they made no concessions to local climate or cultures, displaying similar features throughout the empire. Living conditions were cramped and basic, but with their heated bathhouses and latrines cleaned by running water, the forts had a standard of hygiene far superior to any of the quarters provided for the armies that fought almost 2,000 years later in the Crimean War.

Settlements of local civilians grew up around forts and fortresses to service the Roman troops and many modern-day towns and cities trace their origins back to a Roman military base.

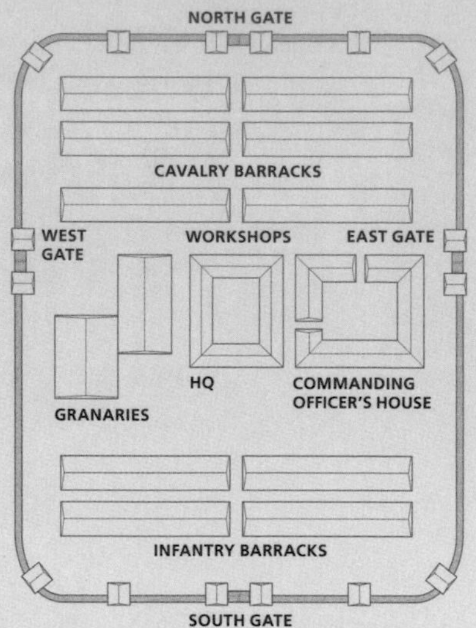

Layout of a Roman fort
Arbeia was a small fort housing about 600 men. Legionary fortresses, housing 5,000, were much larger, but had a similar layout with barracks for cavalry and infantry, workshops, granaries, and a headquarters building.

> "WHAT OTHERS WOULD HAVE SPREAD OVER SEVERAL DAYS TOOK YOU ONLY ONE TO FINISH: YOU HAVE BUILT A WALL ... IN NOT MUCH MORE TIME THAN IS REQUIRED FOR A TURF RAMPART."
>
> **EMPEROR HADRIAN** TO TROOPS AT LAMBAESIS IN MODERN ALGERIA

Garrisoning the fort
Barrack life would have been familiar to any soldier in a modern regular army. There was morning parade, drill, guard and patrol duties, training exercises, gear to maintain, and latrines to clean.

Building a fort
Legionaries on the Dacian campaign (101–102 CE) build a stone fort. They are working in full armor in case of a surprise enemy raid.

Gatehouse battlements
The plaque states that the fort was built by Legio VI Victrix under Sextus Calpurnius Agricola, governor of Britain c.163–166 CE.

Doorway
The solid walls and doors of the fort would have kept out the tribal fighters who might carry out raids in Roman-occupied Britain.

Gatehouse
The gatehouse of the fort of Arbeia, on the Tyne River estuary in northern England, has been recontructed to give an impression of its original appearance. Built in the 2nd century CE, the fort became a major supply depot for the troops manning Hadrian's Wall. Although the twin towers are imposing, they are smaller than those at some other Roman forts, which had gatehouses up to four stories high.

THE BARRACKS

The barrack blocks at Arbeia were built of plastered stonework outside with wattle-and-daub dividing walls inside. The auxiliary troops that were stationed there would have been divided, like legionaries, into eight-man *contubernia*, or "tent groups". Each infantry block housed five *contubernia* and each *contubernium* was allotted a cramped two-roomed suite, which also had to accommodate much of their equipment. The centurion and the lower ranking officers lived in a slightly larger suite at the end of the barracks. Cavalrymen were billeted in similar sized barracks. With 30 men and their horses housed in each block, conditions were even less enviable than those of the infantry.

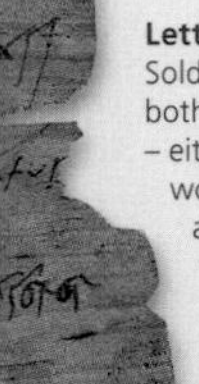

Letter and stylus
Soldiers wrote letters – both official and personal – either in ink on thin wooden panels or using a stylus to write on wax. The letters were about the size of a large postcard.

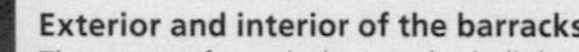

Exterior and interior of the barracks
There were few windows to let in light or fresh air, but the roof tiles were pierced intermittently with ventilators. The internal walls at Arbeia were made of wattle-and-daub *(left)*, a form of inexpensive plasterwork.

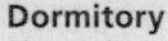

Dormitory
The ordinary soldiers of a Roman *contubernium* would have spent most of their time in the larger of their two rooms. It was here that they slept – either under woollen blankets on beds like these or simply on mattresses on the floor.

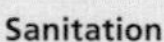

Sanitation
Many forts had a bathhouse outside the fort for the troops, while the commanding officer's family had their own baths in the house. This communal latrine near Hadrian's Wall makes up for lack of privacy with high-quality plumbing.

Courtyard of the house
The house was arranged around an open courtyard, which may have contained fountains. Courtyard walls are likely to have been decorated with garden scenes. The principal rooms led off a colonnaded walkway.

Single room
The smaller room of the suite allotted to a *contubernium* was either a living area or the space where the soldiers stored their military equipment.

Board game
Soldiers are known to have whiled away off-duty hours with a variety of board games played with dice and counters.

COMMANDING OFFICER'S HOUSE

In dramatic contrast to the privations of barrack-room life, the commanding officer of the fort was provided with a comfortable house. Since the Romans took their domestic architectural styles wherever they went, the building would have mimicked a typical Mediterranean town house, complete with dining rooms, bedrooms, a kitchen, stables, and its own hypocaust (under-floor heating system). No concessions were made to the local climate, and these airy houses built around an open central courtyard may not have been so appealing during mid-winter in the northern reaches of the empire.

Commanding officer's bedroom
Unlike the sleeping quarters in the barracks, the bedrooms in the house were spacious and kept warm by the hypocaust. Both the furniture and decoration reflect contemporary taste in Rome. The beds were richly carved and sometimes painted.

Food and drink
The officers and men seem to have enjoyed a reasonably varied diet based on bread and locally produced meat, vegetables, and fruit. Luxuries shipped in *amphorae* from Spain and Italy included wine, olive oil, and *garum* (a fermented fish sauce that the Romans used to add flavour to food).

ENEMIES OF ROME

The forces against which the Romans fought ranged from the armies of rival states or empires—including the Carthaginians in the west and the Parthians and Sassanid Persians in the east—to tribal warbands and nomadic cavalry. Although there was never any great technological gulf distinguishing these different forces from one another or from the Romans, they were extremely varied in their battle tactics, their level of organization and discipline, and their view of warfare. The contrast between Celtic or Germanic tribal fighters following their chiefs into battle and the complex polyglot army of Carthage translated into a very different battlefield performance—the Carthaginian army coming close to achieving the conquest of Rome.

THE CARTHAGINIANS

The army with which the inspired Carthaginian general Hannibal invaded Italy in 218 BCE was a multicultural force of mercenaries, chiefly recruited from Carthage's North African allies or tributaries and from Spain. No attempt was made to blend these troops into a uniform force. Instead each ethnic group stuck together and fought in its own style. Libyans made redoubtable foot soldiers, while the semi-nomadic Numidians were superb light horsemen, riding bareback armed with javelins and spears. Spanish hill tribesmen fought mounted or on foot, usually armed with short swords. Balearic Islanders specialized in the use of slingshots, firing a hail of stones or lead pellets. Hannibal's war elephants, a small African breed, were mostly supplied by the Numidians—the beasts served to disrupt enemy cavalry and provided a platform for archers or javelin-throwers.

What held this disparate army together was the shared experience of combat and, above all, allegiance to their commander. The mercenaries would fight forever as long as pay or plunder were available to reward them. At Cannae in 216 BCE Hannibal's army inflicted a thorough and bloody defeat on the Romans, and it sustained its campaign in Italy for 15 years. When the war eventually shifted to North Africa, local conscripts were drafted in to make up a large part of the Carthaginian ranks. This diluted army was definitively defeated by the Romans at Zama in 202 BCE.

ORNATE CARTHAGINIAN BREASTPLATE

Exotic army
A 16th-century artist's impression of Hannibal's Carthaginian forces attempts to convey their exotic variety of personnel. One of the uses of a war elephant may have been as a mobile command post.

THE GERMANS

Germanic tribes and federations—Teutones, Alamanni, Goths, Franks, Vandals, and many others—were among the most determined and persistent enemies of the Roman Empire from the 2nd century BCE to the 5th century CE. Like the Celts, the Germans were used to more or less permanent tribal warfare, often practiced by warbands of young men led by an experienced fighter of noted prowess. Their battlefield tactics seem to have differed from the Celts in so far as they involved a more compact formation and a larger measure of coordination. According to Julius Caesar, writing in the 1st century BCE, they fought in a tight infantry phalanx, armed with iron-tipped spears.

> "THEY THINK IT TAME AND STUPID ... TO ACQUIRE BY THE SWEAT OF TOIL WHAT THEY MIGHT WIN BY THEIR BLOOD."
> **TACITUS** DESCRIBING THE CHARACTER OF THE GERMANIC PEOPLES, 1ST CENTURY CE

The Germans were also adept at avoiding pitched battles, using ambushes and harassing hit-and-run tactics. It was in this way that they weakened and eventually destroyed the Roman legions led by Varus at the Teutoburger Wald in 9 CE. Over time cavalry became an important part of Germanic forces. Horsemen on short sturdy mounts rode forward armed with shield and javelin, accompanied by swiftly running foot soldiers similarly armed. Among the Ostrogoths and the Vandals there evolved an armored horse-riding aristocracy that pointed forward to the medieval knight.

Many German tribes found employment as Roman auxiliaries and, by the 4th century CE, had a dominant position in the forces of the later Western Empire. The Goths who sacked the city of Rome in 410 CE had been part of the Roman army, and it was Gothic and other German chiefs who ruled the successor states when the Western Empire finally disintegrated.

Germans defeated
Made in around 250 CE, this relief on the Ludovisi sarcophagus shows clean-shaven Romans triumphing over hirsute bearded Germanic warriors.

THE CELTS

The Celts of western Europe—Gauls, Iberians, Britons—had a distinctive style of warfare that contrasted strikingly with that of the Romans. Bands of young men, following a leader of acknowledged strength and courage, would regularly embark on raids on neighbouring peoples. Tribal battles were probably heavily formalized, with individual warriors first stepping forward to proclaim their prowess and challenge enemies to single combat. An attack involved a wild charge accompanied by a cacophony of noise. Although some Roman historians describe the Celts as fighting naked, they mostly wore a tunic and trousers. Elite warriors would have worn a helmet and even chainmail or leather armor, although shields were their main defense. Mostly fighting on foot, they wielded long slashing swords and short spears. Some Celtic peoples employed war chariots to disrupt the enemy formation.

The Romans first encountered the Celts when the latter invaded Italy in the 4th century BCE, and subsequently fought them on many occasions, most notably in the campaign against the Gauls under Vercingetorix in 52 BCE and the suppression of the Iceni revolt led by Boudicca in Britain in 60–61 CE. The Romans were impressed by the Celts' physical strength—they are described as tall, with rippling muscles—and by their wild courage in battle.

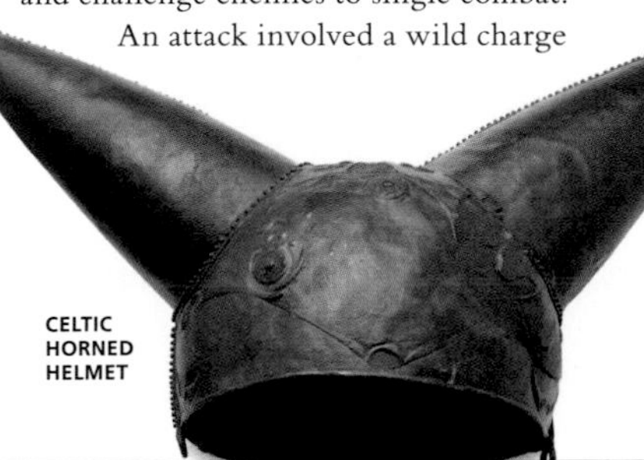

CELTIC HORNED HELMET

> "WEIRD, DISCORDANT HORNS WERE SOUNDED ... THEY BEAT THEIR SWORDS RHYTHMICALLY AGAINST THEIR SHIELDS."
> **DIODORUS SICULUS** DESCRIBING CELTS IN BATTLE, 1ST CENTURY BCE

Ceremonial shield
Made of bronze with studs of colored glass, this shield once belonged to an elite Celtic warrior in Britain. Dating from the 2nd century BCE, it was probably intended for ceremonial use rather than for combat.

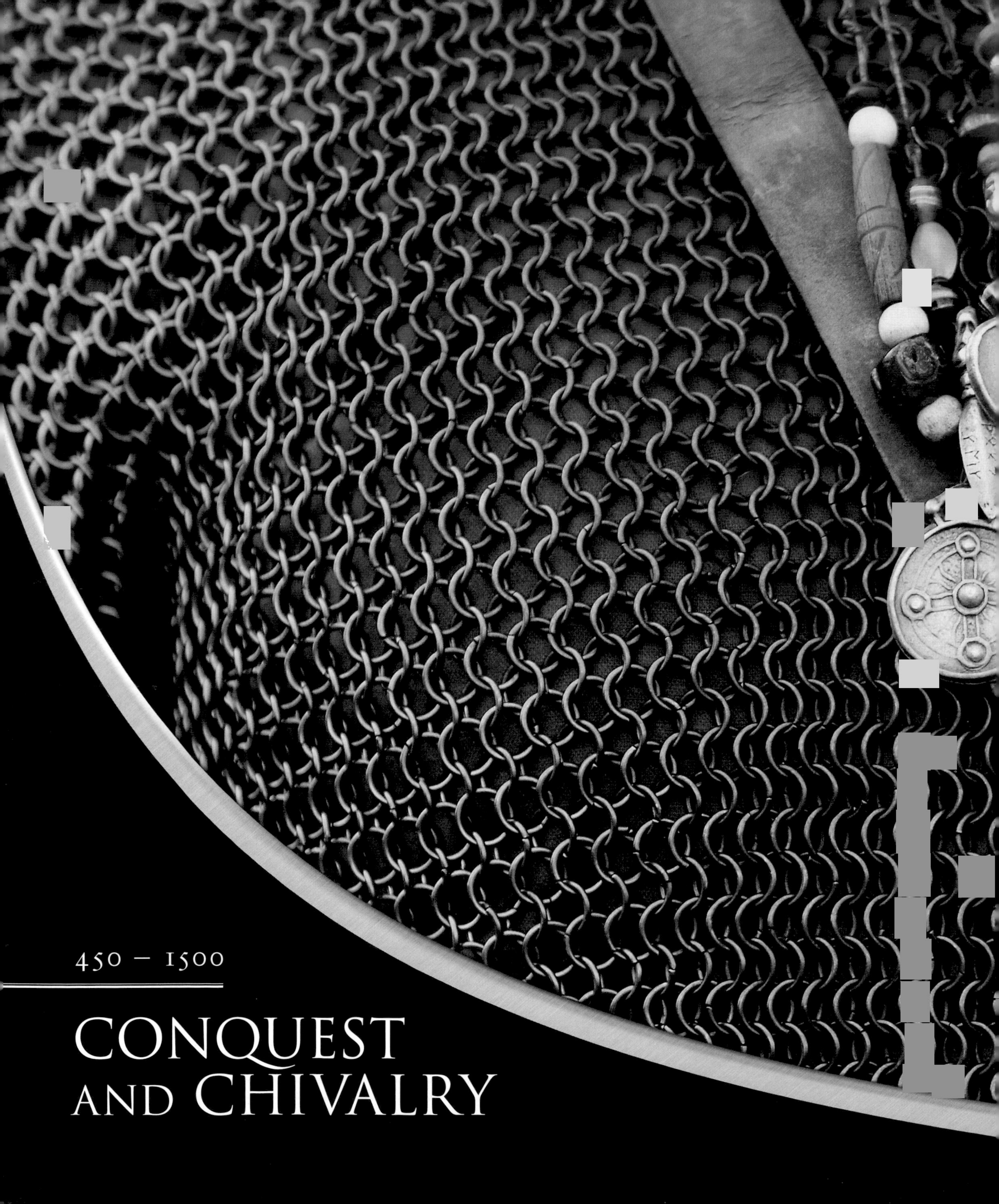

450 – 1500

CONQUEST AND CHIVALRY

In the warfare of the Middle Ages, cavalry were in the ascendant across most of Eurasia. A high-status warrior was by definition a horseman. In the Byzantine Empire, armored cavalry known as cataphracts were the core of the armed forces by the 6th century. The Arab armies that, inspired by the new creed of Islam, swept east as far as Afghanistan and west through North Africa and into Spain in the 7th and 8th centuries, achieved their conquests on horseback. The armored knight of medieval western Europe, charging with lance, is of course one of the most iconic fighting men in military history.

TURKS AND MONGOLS

The most consistently successful of medieval mounted warriors emerged from the tough nomadic peoples of Central Asia. Fighting with the composite bow as their primary weapon, they repeatedly defeated the slower-moving armies of settled civilizations. Both the Turkish Seljuks, who crushed the Byzantine army at Manzikert in 1071, and the Jurchen who conquered the northern part of the Chinese Song Empire in the following century, were Asian horsemen. The most famous of these steppe warriors, however, are the Mongols, whose astonishing conquests began under Genghis Khan in the early 13th century. By the time Genghis's grandson Kublai Khan died

Battle of Hastings
The Norman army that defeated the Anglo-Saxons at Hastings on 14 October, 1066 was a balanced force of cavalry and foot soldiers. The heavy cavalry did not yet have the social status of the medieval knight; they were professional fighting men who could afford to own a warhorse.

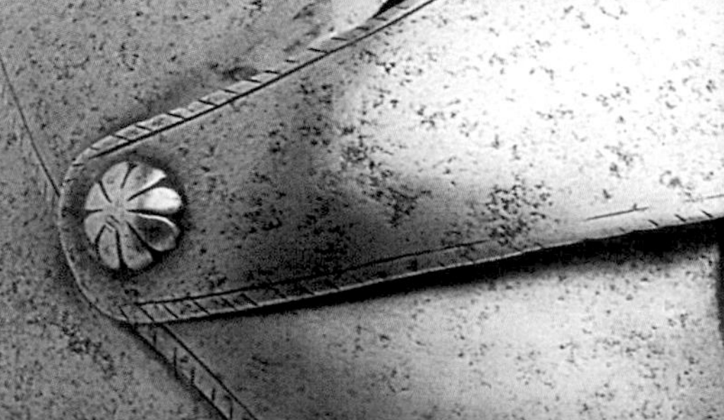

in 1294, the Mongols ruled all of China and Central Asia, and parts of the Middle East and eastern Europe. Western Europe escaped conquest purely because of distance—but when Mongol horsemen fought Christian knights at Liegnitz in 1241, the knights were crushed.

CHRISTIAN EUROPE

In the early medieval period, Western Europe was a relatively backward region dominated by Germanic peoples whose military system was based on the tribal warband. The region was exposed to aggressive raids and settlement by Muslims, Magyars, and Vikings. The Franks, by the 9th century claiming to be the successors to the Roman Empire in the west, struggled to defend their Christian domain, depending more upon cultural absorption than military might. The feared Vikings intermarried with Frankish subjects and adopted the French language; as Normans, indistinguishable from other Christian warriors, they conquered Anglo-Saxon England, Sicily, and southern Italy in the 11th century.

CHIVALROUS KNIGHTS

It was in that century that the armored knight emerged as an elite warrior in medieval Europe. The special status of knighthood was conferred by public ceremony, celebrated in literature, and buttressed by the code of chivalry. Committed to close-quarters combat with lance and sword as the only honorable form of warfare, knights benefited from progress in metalworking that over time produced highly effective edged weapons and plate armor. In the 1090s European knights embarked upon the first of the Crusades, an aggressive onslaught upon Muslim rule in the eastern Mediterranean. Some knights belonged to military orders such as the Hospitallers and Templars, modeled upon orders of monks. The wearing of the cross, however, did not stop crusaders from sacking Christian Constantinople in 1204. By the end of the 13th century the crusaders had been driven out of Palestine, but crusades continued around the margins of Christian Europe—against the Muslims in Spain and "pagan" peoples to the east.

INFANTRY AND GUNS

Since there was also near constant warfare between Christian states within Europe, the continent became a testing ground for fighting techniques and military technologies. Although the knight was regarded as the only true warrior, the search for success on the battlefield led to the development of more effective ways of using infantry. Lower-class foot soldiers, armed with pikes or halberds, and archers armed with the crossbow or longbow, were the most effective. Gunpowder weapons were probably first used on a European battlefield at Crécy in 1346, and cannon were improved through refinements in gunpowder manufacture and metal casting. By the second half of the 15th century, the combination of gunpowder weapons and better infantry brought an end to the dominance of armored cavalry on European battlefields.

Samurai victorious
One of very few peoples to defeat the Mongols in the 13th century, the Japanese repelled an attempted invasion by Kublai Khan in 1281. Here, Samurai defend a stone wall built along the coast to prevent the invading army from landing.

SEPARATE DEVELOPMENTS

In some parts of the world military developments followed their own path, with little influence from Eurasia. In Japan, the samurai resembled a medieval knight in being a warrior whose conduct was theoretically governed by a chivalric code, *bushido*. But the samurai had no equivalent of the mass cavalry charge with lances, nor did they despise the use of missile weapons, for the bow was initially their arm of choice.

In Central and South Americas a separate tradition of warfare had been established over millennia. In the absence of horses, battles were fought on foot, almost exclusively with weapons of wood and stone. Sophisticated empires had been built upon these limited military bases, but they were ill-equipped to survive the invasion by Europeans with horses, swords, armor, and gunpowder weapons in the 16th century.

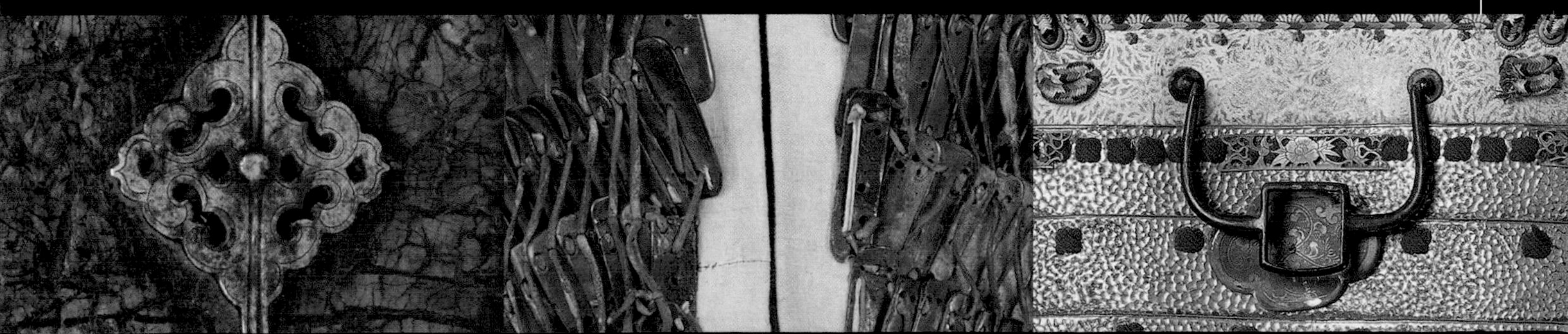

800 – 1100

VIKING

THE PAGANS FROM THE NORTHERN REGIONS CAME WITH A NAVAL FORCE TO BRITAIN LIKE STINGING HORNETS AND SPREAD ON ALL SIDES LIKE FEARFUL WOLVES, ROBBED, TORE AND SLAUGHTERED

VIKING WARRIORS FROM SCANDINAVIA first appeared in documented history in the late 8th century as seafaring raiders terrorizing the population of coasts and islands around Western Europe. Over time, raids expanded into campaigns of conquest and permanent settlement. Vikings voyaged as far as North America and, via Russian rivers, to the Black Sea. Although the excellence of their long ships and the boldness of their maritime enterprise was the key to their success, they were also formidable fighters on land.

Why the agricultural and fishing communities of Scandinavia should have suddenly generated a plague of raiders to prey upon the kingdoms of Anglo-Saxon England and the Frankish Empire is not known for certain. The most likely explanation is that in overpopulated coastal communities only the eldest son inherited his father's possessions, so younger siblings, with no means of making a living locally, sought fame and fortune overseas. The first raiding forces would have consisted of perhaps a couple of ships from two neighboring villages setting off in search of trade goods—silver and slaves seem to have been particularly desirable commodities. As few as 40 armed men could easily have overwhelmed an English coastal village or isolated monastery. The Anglo-Saxon invasion of England in the 5th century CE had begun in very much the same way, with small raiding parties developing into much larger invasion forces.

Swedish Viking pendant
Silver looted on Viking raids was often melted down and turned into personal jewellery.

The first recorded Viking landing in England probably took place in 787, but, although blood was shed, it did not develop into a raid. The shock of the first known raid is graphically described in the writings of monks and scholars. In 793 the monastery of Lindisfarne, a famed center of Christian learning on an island off the Northumbrian coast, was sacked by Vikings in a raid of sensational suddenness and violence. The scholar Alcuin wrote, in a letter to Northumbria's King Ethelred, "never before has such terror appeared as we have now suffered from a pagan race." A later chronicler, Simeon of Durham, described how the raiders killed some monks, carried others off "in fetters," and looted the monastery of its considerable treasures. Departing for Norway with a hoard of gold and silver plate, and with prisoners for sale as slaves, the Vikings presumably viewed the raid as a great success.

EXPANDING HORIZONS

Raiding was sporadic and small-scale until the 830s—hit-and-run attacks more akin to piracy than warfare. But then Danish Vikings began to mount more substantial operations against southern England, the Low Countries, and the coast of France. Antwerp, for example, was laid waste in 836 and Nantes in 843. In 845 a warrior called Ragnar led a fleet of ships up the Seine River and sacked Paris. Voyages became ever more ambitious, with at least one fleet rounding Spain and ravaging the western Mediterranean, while another reached the Black Sea via the rivers of Russia and Ukraine and appeared outside the walls of Constantinople.

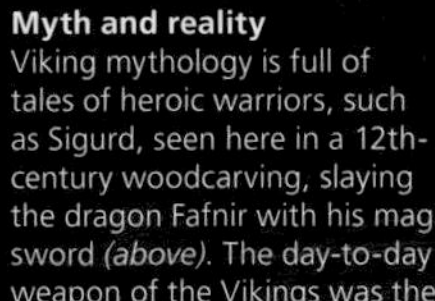

Myth and reality
Viking mythology is full of tales of heroic warriors, such as Sigurd, seen here in a 12th-century woodcarving, slaying the dragon Fafnir with his magic sword *(above)*. The day-to-day weapon of the Vikings was the sax *(right)*,a knife that doubled as a short sword if trouble arose.

SAX AND SCABBARD

The key to the Vikings' success was their ability to concentrate forces at an unexpected point with a rapidity of movement far superior to that of the defenders. When they sailed their longships across the North Sea or along the coastline, they could land wherever they chose, grounding their vessels on a stretch of beach. Although the Franks and Anglo-Saxons built watchtowers to look out for Viking raiding parties, they rarely had time to mount a significant armed response. On occasions when Vikings needed to make a rapid escape, they benefitted from the design of their ships, which had a prow at each end and thus could be relaunched without being turned around. When Vikings penetrated inland up rivers, their progress was slower, with much use of oars and possibly the need to move the ships for short distances on land around shallows or other obstacles. This gave the defenders a better chance to organize an army to meet them. With around 50 men in each ship, however, and probably between 100 and 200 ships involved in a major attack such as that on Paris in 845, the Vikings had a good chance of matching any force that could be mustered to halt their progress.

Badge of loyalty
Leaders of Viking warbands would sometimes reward an especially loyal follower with a heavy silver armlet. If the warrior subsequently fell on hard times, he could snap off pieces of silver when required.

Decorative inscriptions from the runic alphabet also known as "Futhark"

GANGING UP

The basic fighting force in Viking raiding warfare was the warband, a gang of adventurers attracted to the service of a warrior of proven courage and ability. Young men without prospects and keen for action would compete for admission into a successful warband. Proving yourself fierce, ruthless, and fearless in action would win you acceptance within the group and also, eventually, promotion to the warband leader's inner circle. The leader, for his part, had to provide action and plunder if he was to hold the loyalty of his followers and stave off competition from other warbands. Annual raiding expeditions kept up the supply of loot off which the men lived and satisfied their craving for excitement—for there can be no doubt that the Vikings thrived on the thrill of combat and enjoyed the thorough-going rape and massacre in which they indulged when given a chance. In the absence of outsiders to attack, Viking warriors would fight one another. Challenges to single combat were apparently common, either to settle issues of status or simply so that the winning fighter could claim the loser's property.

From out of nowhere
The first reported Viking raid on Britain was the sacking of the monastery at Lindisfarne in 793. The attack came completely without warning.

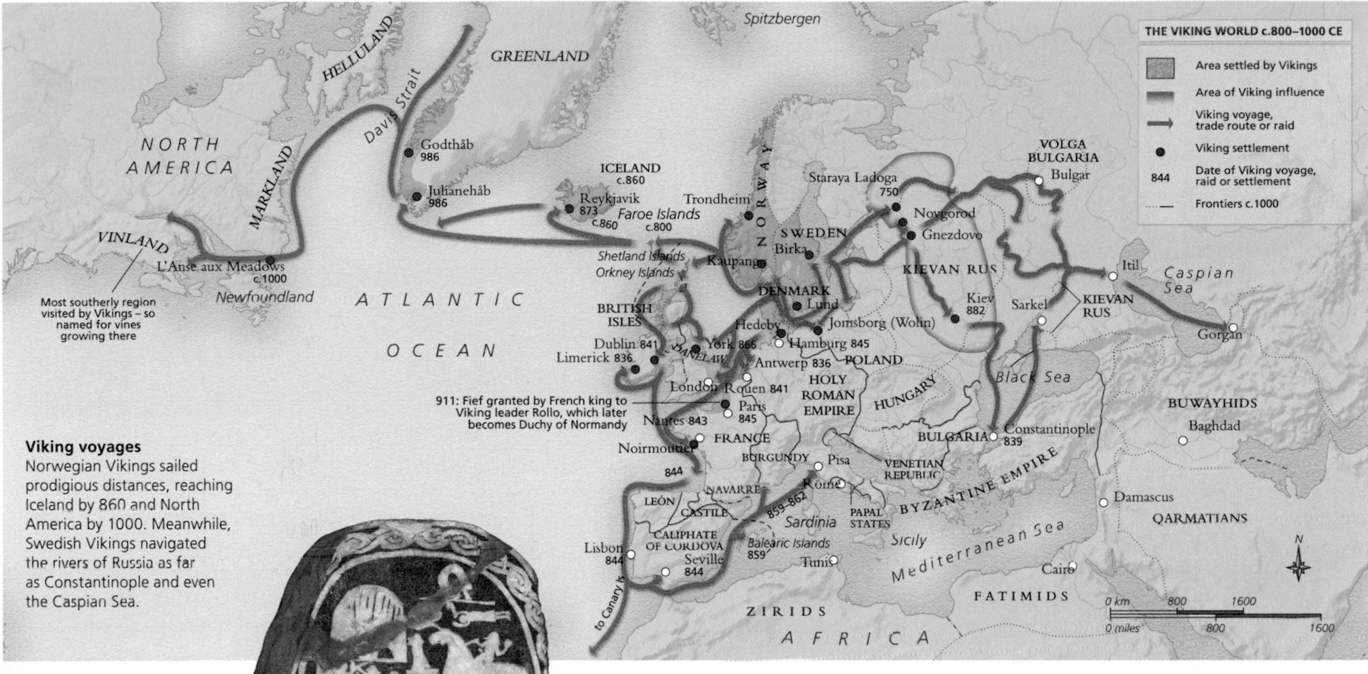

Viking voyages
Norwegian Vikings sailed prodigious distances, reaching Iceland by 860 and North America by 1000. Meanwhile, Swedish Vikings navigated the rivers of Russia as far as Constantinople and even the Caspian Sea.

Specific military training was probably more or less nonexistent among the Scandinavian peoples. The basic skills of sailing and of warfare were simply part of everyday life. Hunting and sports made all males familiar with the use of weaponry to some degree, as did the insecurity of Viking existence—a Nordic text of the 9th century advises: "Never part with your weapons when out in the fields, for you never know when you will need your spear." Skilled in metalworking, Scandinavian craftsmen supplied formidable slashing swords and iron axes—both long-shafted two-handed axes and shorter "bearded axes" wielded with one hand. Spears, knives, and bows were less costly and more common. For his defence a Viking warrior would hope to have a metal-bossed round shield and, if he could afford it, a knee-length chainmail coat, and metal helmet. The average Viking could probably aspire to no more than a padded leather or fur garment.

FROM RAIDS TO CONQUEST

Moving onto land Viking raiders did not seek out pitched battle. Their aim was to avoid serious fighting through their hit-and-run tactics. But over time raiding mutated into settlement and conquest, and when Vikings came to stay they inevitably had to stand and fight. From the 840s warbands started wintering at fortified camps at sites such as the Ile de Noirmoutier on the west coast of France, Dublin in Ireland, and the Isle of Thanet on the coast of southeast England. Some of these camps became permanent bases. In 865 a Danish force described in the Anglo-Saxon Chronicles as "a great heathen host" established itself in East Anglia, initiating a series of land campaigns that, over the following decade, brought the Danes victory over the kingdoms of Northumbria, East Anglia, and Mercia. Although hard-pressed by the invaders, the Anglo-Saxon kingdom of Wessex survived. In France, a Viking army besieged Paris for almost a year from 885 to 886, until bought off by the king of the Franks and Holy Roman Emperor Charles the Fat. The Norsemen were by then an unshakeable presence, a fact recognized by the Franks in granting them control of Normandy in 911. In the east, other groups of Vikings established kingdoms centered on Novgorod and Kiev.

The land armies formed by the Vikings still had a substantial core of warriors functioning as warbands, but larger forces would also include a considerable number of ordinary farmers or craftsmen drummed into the ranks for a fighting season. Some of these levies were probably armed only with spears. The Vikings had always had horses—even raiding parties had often carried a few in their boats.

Gotland picture stone
The top of this 8th-century carved stone from the Swedish island of Gotland depicts warriors entering Valhalla—the eight-legged horse is Odin's steed Sleipnir. The lower part of the picture shows a Viking longship.

Ship's prow
Longships had high curving stem and stern posts, often carved in the shape of dragons. These clearly helped strike terror into the victims of Viking raids.

> "THE NUMBER OF SHIPS INCREASES, THE ENDLESS FLOOD OF VIKINGS BEGINS TO GROW ... THEY OVERRUN ALL THAT LIES BEFORE THEM AND NONE CAN WITHSTAND THEM."
>
> **ERMENTARIUS**, FRANKISH MONK

Fighting methods and weaponry
The main weapons of the Vikings were spears and axes, wielded with great force. Swords, usually the weapons of leaders, were forged by skilled smiths. They play an important part in Norse mythology. The woodcarving *(far right)* shows an episode in the story of Sigurd: the testing of the sword Gram by banging it against an anvil.

More often, however, they would simply round up the horses in the area they were attacking and appropriate them for their own purposes. Although they did not fight mounted, the Vikings used the animals to increase their speed of maneuver—the transition from raiding to conquest did not alter the Vikings' taste for mobility and surprise. In their campaigns in England against King Alfred of Wessex in 877–78, they used both ships and horses to move men swiftly into occupation of Anglo-Saxon territory, forcing Alfred to take refuge in impenetrable marshes without a battle fought.

BATTLE FORMATION

When the Vikings were obliged to fight a pitched battle, they formed up on foot, probably with a line of men shoulder-to-shoulder creating a shield wall, their spears bristling outward through the small openings between shield and shield. The elite warriors with their armor and heavier weaponry would stand close to their leader, whose banner would be raised behind the front line. A battle always began with an exchange of missile fire, the Viking bowmen forming an essential if rarely mentioned part of the army. Skirmishers would throw spears or small axes and there would probably be slingshots also used. At some point one or other side would mount a charge. At the battle of Edington in May 878, the Danish army of Guthrum apparently failed to break through the Anglo-Saxon shield wall and was worn down until forced to abandon the field. But if the attackers broke through, the battle would fragment into a series of fierce contests between individuals or small groups of warriors.

VIKING SETTLEMENTS

As the amount of territory controlled by the Vikings in England, Ireland, and northern France increased, many warriors were rewarded with grants of land, and raids and expeditions of conquest became less frequent. Viking men began to intermarry with women from the local population and in regions such as Normandy, central and northern England, and the area around Dublin there were extended periods of peaceful coexistence. Far off Viking colonists in Iceland faced a different problem: there was no native population and consequently a severe shortage of women. These had to be shipped in from elsewhere and a recent genetic study has shown that the female ancestors of today's Icelanders were, almost without exception, Irish.

Dice cup
Archaeological finds show that the Vikings had exactly the interests you would expect in a warrior race – drinking and gambling.

The foundation of colonies and towns did not mean that the Vikings renounced their warlike culture. Their armies still struck terror into the neighboring kingdoms of the Anglo-Saxons and Franks. Face to face, the Viking warrior was a formidable opponent. Vikings were generally healthy and of large stature, partly a tribute to the quality of the diet they enjoyed in their Scandinavian homeland. In combat they wielded their large swords and axes with ferocious energy that put physical strength and endurance at a premium.

GOING BERSERK

The nature of Viking culture also mentally strengthened the warrior's commitment to the battle. The cult of Odin, the one-eyed god of war, stressed the importance of a warrior dying heroically in battle rather than shamefully in his bed. Odin's most enthusiastic devotees were the "berserkers." Although contested by some historians, the existence of these wild warriors is well attested in Norse literary sources.

Admittedly many of these were not committed to writing until 300 years after the events they describe. Beserkers appear to have fought naked but for bear or wolf skins, working themselves into a trancelike fury before combat. Once in their inspired state, they were allegedly immune to pain and uncontrollable in their aggression. One text describes them as "mad as dogs or wolves" and "strong as bears or wild bulls." They had the strange habit of chewing the edge of their shields before battle and

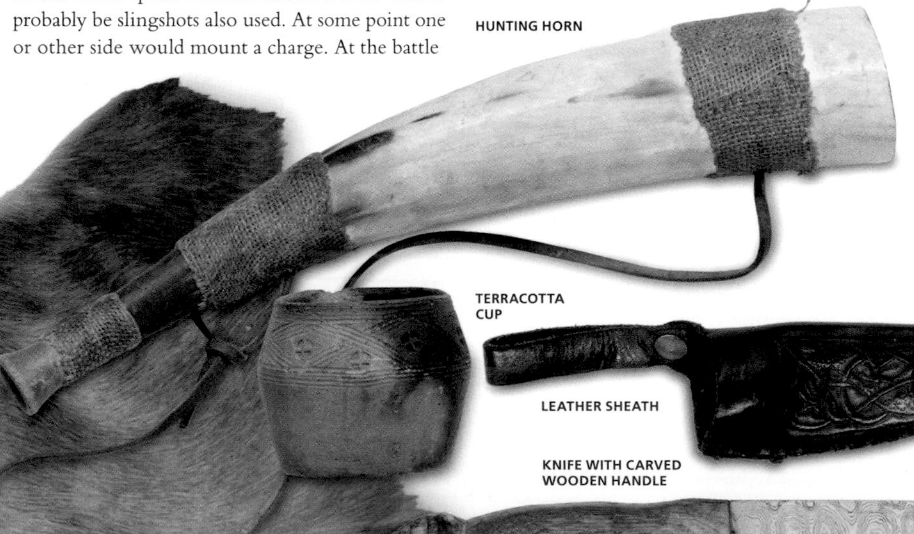

Hunting, eating, and drinking
These replicas of archaeological finds show that Viking craftsmen applied decoration to everyday objects as well as to weapons and jewelry. The interlacing pattern on the leather sheath is a common motif.

emitting roars and growls. We are told that they "killed people with a single blow" and were hurt "neither by fire nor iron." The berserkers' behavior may have been caused by ingesting drugs or large quantities of alcohol and must certainly have made them difficult to employ effectively on the battlefield. But although their cult was banned in places, some war leaders are said to have used them as personal bodyguard or as shock troops in battle.

Perhaps the most objective testimony to the quality of "non-beserker" Viking warriors was their employment in Constantinople as mercenaries of the Byzantine Empire. They distinguished themselves so effectively in warfare as far afield as Syria that, from the late 10th century, they were formed into the emperor's elite Varangian Guard. Naturally the Byzantines liked to patronize these foreign mercenaries, describing them as "ax-bearing barbarians." Their drunkenness was as much an object of astonishment to their sophisticated hosts as their fierceness in combat. But it was for their strength and loyalty that they were prized and often liberally rewarded.

Thor's hammer
Small silver pendants in the shape of Thor's hammer were widely used by the Vikings as religious amulets. Thor, the Norse god of thunder, was the son of Odin, the god of war.

LATER VIKING CONQUESTS

Relatively quiescent through much of the 10th century, Viking power underwent a resurgence from the 980s. Anglo-Saxon Britain suffered the aggressive raids of the fearsome Olaf Trygvasson, followed in the second decade of the 11th century by the conquest that made Norwegian King Cnut ruler of England. For a time Cnut ruled Denmark also, creating a shortlived North Sea empire. But this turned out to be a late flowering of Viking influence. In 1066 the Norwegian King Harald Hardrada, a formidable warrior who, during a period of exile, had served in Constantinople in the Varangian Guard, invaded Britain to uphold his claim to the royal succession, but was defeated at Stamford Bridge by Anglo-Saxon King Harold. Ironically, Harold was then defeated at the battle of Hastings by the Normans, descendants of the Vikings who had by then become French in language and culture.

> "YOU WORKED WELL IN THE SHIELD-WAR, WARRIOR-KING; BROWN WAS THE FLESH OF BODIES SERVED TO THE BLOOD-BIRD: IN THE SLAUGHTER, YOU WON, SIRE, WITH YOUR SWORD ENOUGH OF A NAME ..."
>
> *KNYTLINGA SAGA*, DESCRIBING KING CNUT WARRING IN ENGLAND, PROBABLY WRITTEN AROUND 1250

Warriors' resting place
The burial ground at Lindholm Høje in northern Denmark contains over 700 graves dating from about 700–1100 CE. The bodies were cremated, but grave goods show that men's graves were marked by stones arranged in the shape of ships.

VIKING ARMOR

Viking warriors' attire varied from the very basic to the more comprehensively equipped. The poorer Viking would have had to make do with a protective garment of padded leather, although reindeer hide was reputedly even more effective than chainmail. Chainmail was very labor-intensive to make, particularly if individually riveted. It was also extremely heavy, but very difficult to penetrate. Helmets took immense skill to make, and these were fashioned in various styles, one of which was the spectacled helm. However, the popular image of the horned or winged Viking helmet is a fiction.

Gjermundbu helm
The cheek flaps of this typical helmet, also called a spectacled helm, were sometimes tied against the head, perhaps giving rise to the idea of winged or horned Viking helmets.

Four steel plates riveted together by metal strips

Chainmail for neck protection

Hinged, fur-lined cheek flaps

Holes for leather ties to fasten flaps under the chin, or against the helm

Undertunic of unbleached linen

Undertunic and padded top
Undertunics were sometimes worn alone by poorer Vikings. The padded top had two layers of leather stuffed with horsehair. It was buckled at the back to prevent arrows from piercing between fastenings.

Stitches in sections to prevent the stuffing from shifting

Conical helm secured with strap

Sax worn across the waist

Sword worn at the left side

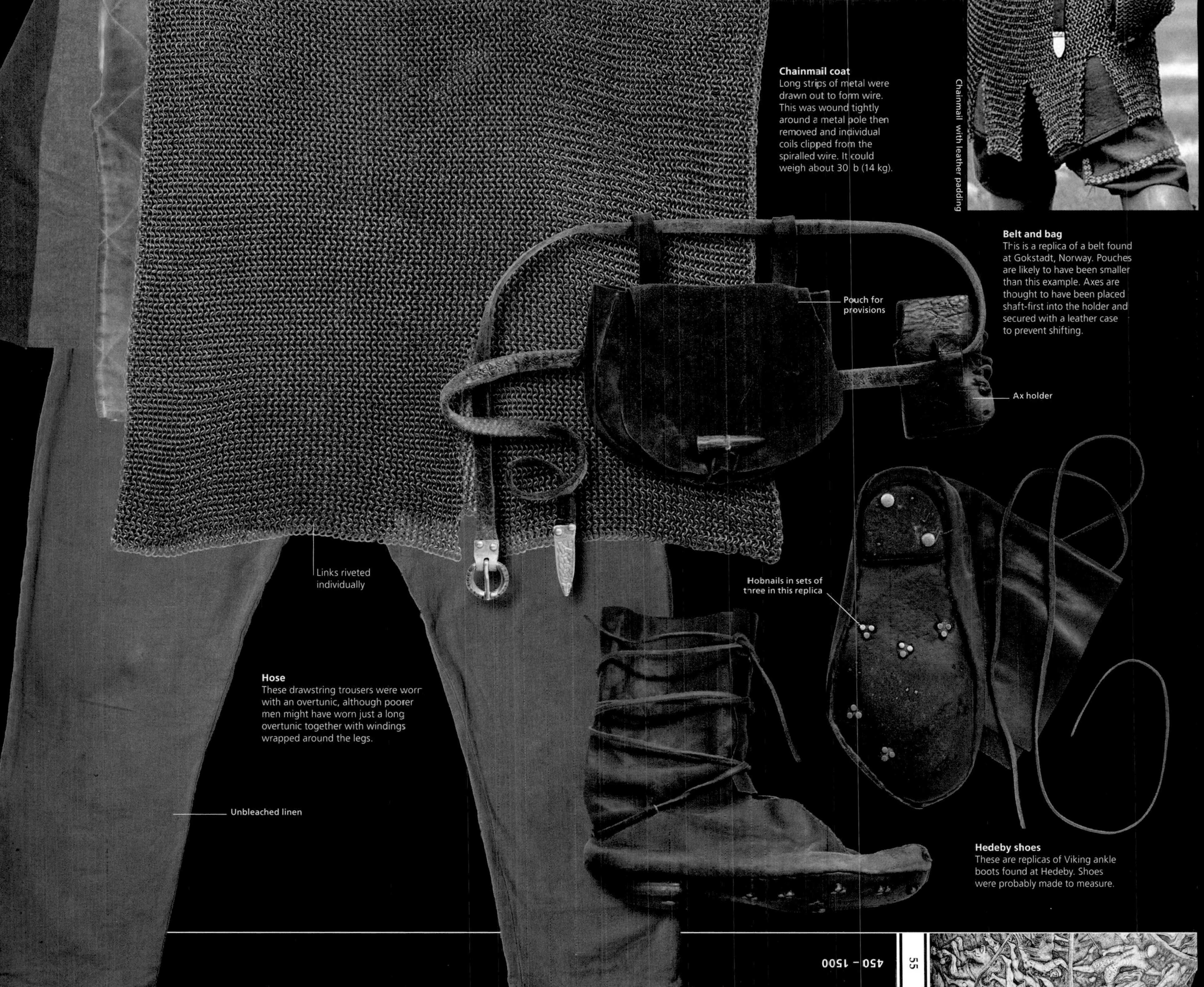

Chainmail coat
Long strips of metal were drawn out to form wire. This was wound tightly around a metal pole then removed and individual coils clipped from the spiralled wire. It could weigh about 30 lb (14 kg).

Chainmail with leather padding

Belt and bag
This is a replica of a belt found at Gokstadt, Norway. Pouches are likely to have been smaller than this example. Axes are thought to have been placed shaft-first into the holder and secured with a leather case to prevent shifting.

Pouch for provisions

Ax holder

Links riveted individually

Hobnails in sets of three in this replica

Hose
These drawstring trousers were worn with an overtunic, although poorer men might have worn just a long overtunic together with windings wrapped around the legs.

Unbleached linen

Hedeby shoes
These are replicas of Viking ankle boots found at Hedeby. Shoes were probably made to measure.

VIKING WEAPONS

Vikings used a variety of weapons according to the quantity of metal they could afford. Spears were the most common as the heads required little steel and shafts could easily be replaced if they splintered on the battlefield. A basic ax was something even the poorer farmer would possess for his domestic use, while swords were items of great value, owned by only the very successful Viking raider and passed down through generations. As signs of status and wealth, weapons were often decorated.

Spears
Spears were thrust rather than hurled. Vikings used smaller javelins for throwing, carrying three at a time, as well as an ax for defense once the javelins were released.

Arrows
Arrowheads varied enormously in shape and size. Shafts were about 28–32 in (70 to 80 cm) long and arrows were fired from a bow made of ash, elm, or yew, with a range of around 650 ft (200 m).

Swords
Viking blades were pattern welded, forged by twisting strips of metal together, beating and heating them, repeating the procedure several times for added strength. Sheaths hung on the left side so the right-handed warrior could easily withdraw his sword across his body.

Axes
These ranged from smaller battle-axes also used domestically, to the two-handed broad ax, which had to be used for quick hit-and-run attacks as the Viking could not carry a shield at the same time.

Sax
Primarily a tool, but also used as a weapon, it was worn across the front of the waist. The larger version was called a langsax or "long knife."

Round Shields
These were made from linden wood planks riveted together and edged with rawhide, then decorated with hand-painted designs.

VIKING LONGSHIP

The Viking longship was a swift, sturdy, and versatile military transport. Propelled either by a sail or by oars, it could cross the open seas but also, because of its shallow draught, penetrate inland along rivers or be pulled up onto a beach. The longship featured here, known as *Havhingsten fra Glendalough* (the *Sea Stallion from Glendalough*), is a reconstruction of a vessel excavated from Roskilde Fjord, Denmark, in the 1960s.

The original of the *Sea Stallion*, referred to as *Skuldelev 2*, was deliberately sunk, along with four other ships, in the late 11th century. This was done to block the entrance of the fjord, thus protecting Roskilde, at that time the Danish capital, against attack from the sea. Study of the oak from which the vessel was made revealed that it had been built around 1042 in Dublin, Ireland, then a major Viking settlement.

The longship has a prow at both ends and is steered by means of a side rudder. It is clinker-built—that is, with a hull made of overlapping planks. As far as possible, the reconstruction used tools, techniques, and materials of the Viking period; the timber from 300 oak trees was required to build it. A longship of this size would have been commissioned by a man of wealth and power and its construction would have taken an entire winter.

At least 60 men would have been needed to row the longship. Their muscle power could have delivered a sustained speed of 5-6 knots, but with its sail raised and a favourable wind the ship could have made 15–20 knots.

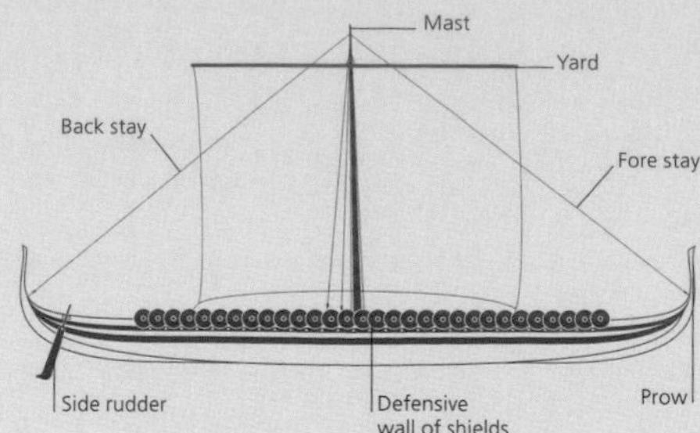

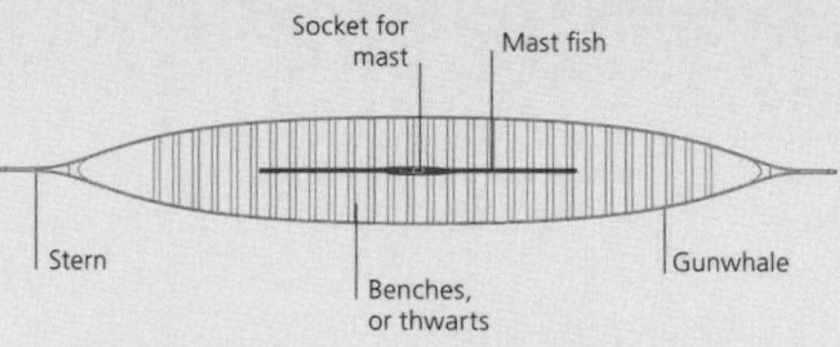

Longship profile
The long, narrow shape of the longship was designed for speed. *Skuldelev 2* was approximately 30m (98ft) long but only 12 ft 6 in (3.8 m) wide. It could sail in water less than 3 ft 3 in (1 meter) deep.

"NEVER BEFORE HAS SUCH TERROR APPEARED ... NOR WAS IT THOUGHT THAT SUCH AN INROAD FROM THE SEA COULD BE MADE."

ALCUIN ON THE SACK OF LINDISFARNE, 793

Landfall
Vikings waited for a favorable wind before setting sail on a raid. They would get hardly any sleep on the gruelling voyage from England from Denmark, but could make it in about two days.

Shield
Vikings used their shields as a defense as they rowed to land on a hostile shore, but it is not known how they were attached to the side of the ship.

Clinker construction
The overlapping planks, or "strakes," are fixed with iron nails. The white objects are the locks sealing the oar ports. Only materials available to the Vikings were used in the linseed-oil paint.

Sail power and oar power
The rope fastened to the cleat *(left)* is one of the sheets that controls the yard (the wooden spar that carries the sail). When the ship was under sail and the oars not in use, the oar ports *(right)* were sealed with a special lock so that they would not let in water.

Oar port and frame timber
Oar ports were designed so that the whole oar and blade could pass through them. Frame timbers *(center)* were fixed at intervals to the top three planks to reinforce the hull.

Weathervane
Many later Viking ships had a highly decorative weathervane, made of gilded bronze, attached to the prow.

Built for speed
Skuldelev 2 was the product of Viking shipbuilding technology at its most advanced. Its modern reincarnation, the *Havhingsten*, has been fitted with 1,200 sq ft (112 sq m) of sail. With this and its superbly streamlined hull, it is thought that, given a favorable wind, the ship will be able to attain a speed of 20 knots.

Oars
The pine oars are about 15 ft (4.55 m) long with blades just 6 in (15 cm) across. It has been found that this width is the most effective for rowing long distances at sea.

Blowing horn
The Vikings used blowing horns to call their ships together. They could be heard from long distances and would have been especially useful at night and in foggy weather.

Mast and mast fish
The mast slotted into the keelson, a block of wood in the bottom of the boat, and the "mast fish," seen here at the center of the ship at deck level.

Seating arrangements
The narrow benches may look uncomfortable, but they allowed the oarsmen to shift position regularly on a long journey. There was enough space between them for a man to lie down and rest.

Rowing for the shore
Vikings fixed their shields to the ship's gunwhale as a defense against spears and arrows. The warlike appearance of the ship must have intimidated any watching enemy.

OTHER WARRIORS OF THE VIKING ERA

Viking raids and settlement were just one element in a period of widespread insecurity throughout Europe and the Mediterranean zone after the splintering of the Western Roman Empire. By the 7th century even the Byzantine successors of Rome in the east were not wealthy enough to pay and equip a large standing army. The Anglo-Saxons were not unusual in relying upon a small band of full-time warriors supported by a much larger number of self-equipped levies—men forced into service. In the 8th and 9th centuries the Franks created a substantial, if fragile, empire in western Europe through the effectiveness of their heavy cavalry, but it was the Normans, French-speaking descendants of the Vikings, who proved the most formidable fighters of the era.

THE ANGLO-SAXONS

Taking over control of England from the 5th century CE, the Anglo-Saxon rulers initially led personal warbands in the Germanic tradition. By the time King Alfred (ruled 871-899) was fighting the Danes, he was leading an army of levies, known as the "fyrd." They were raised on a regional basis. A local nobleman or "thegn" was obliged to present himself when required with the appropriate number of men drawn from among the lower ranks of the free population. They had to come equipped with basic armor and a weapon. The fyrd not only supplied troops for the king to lead in battle but also maintained and manned fortified "burghs" as centers of local defence. In the 11th century Anglo-Saxon kings also had a standing professional force of "housecarls"—a system copied from the Danes. Funded from taxation, these formidable fighters acted as the king's escort and companions, and were the core of his army in battle.

Most Anglo-Saxon soldiers traveled on horseback, but they always dismounted to fight. The housecarls were armed with swords or with formidable two-handed axes—originally a Viking weapon. Most of the fyrd carried spears, the easiest weapon for a local blacksmith to make and the simplest for an untrained man to use. Archers formed a normal part of Anglo-Saxon forces, although few were present at the battle of Hastings in 1066. On the battlefield, the Anglo-Saxons stood in tight formation, creating a shield wall. Housecarls, who were often protected by a shield-bearer and a spearman, could chop down a horse with a single blow of their two-handed axes. Facing the Norman mounted knights near the village of Hastings, the Anglo-Saxons were still very effective fighters despite being exhausted from the long march south from Yorkshire, after defeating the Norwegian King Harald Hardrada. The result of the battle could easily have gone the other way.

Last stand
A scene from the Bayeux Tapestry shows Anglo-Saxon housecarls, clad in chainmail "byrnies," desperately resisting a Norman cavalry charge at the battle of Hastings in 1066.

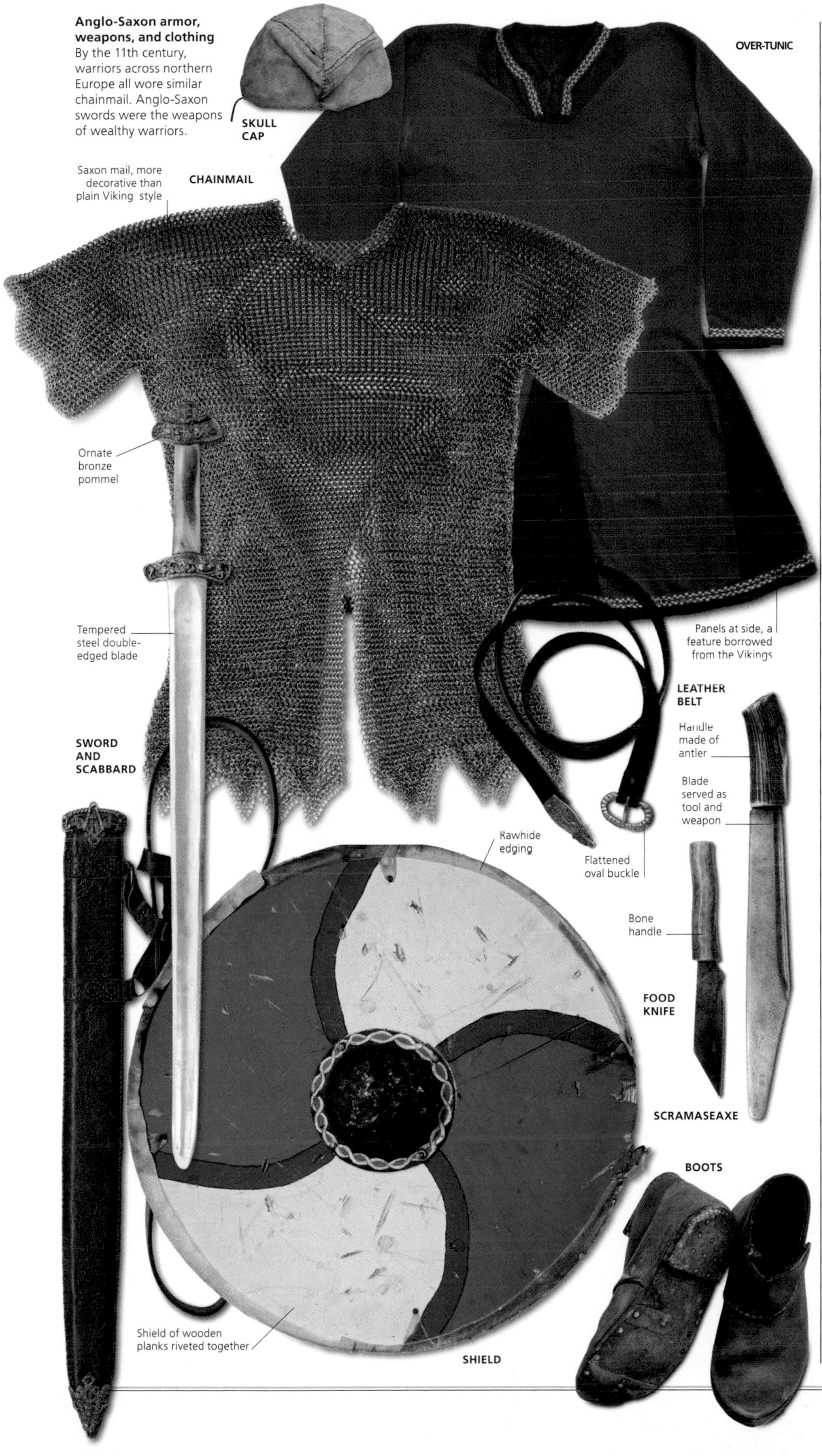

Anglo-Saxon armor, weapons, and clothing
By the 11th century, warriors across northern Europe all wore similar chainmail. Anglo-Saxon swords were the weapons of wealthy warriors.

SKULL CAP

OVER-TUNIC

CHAINMAIL

Saxon mail, more decorative than plain Viking style

Ornate bronze pommel

Tempered steel double-edged blade

SWORD AND SCABBARD

Panels at side, a feature borrowed from the Vikings

LEATHER BELT

Handle made of antler

Blade served as tool and weapon

Flattened oval buckle

Rawhide edging

Bone handle

FOOD KNIFE

SCRAMASEAXE

BOOTS

Shield of wooden planks riveted together

SHIELD

THE FRANKS

The Franks were a Germanic people who made a kingdom in Gaul after the fall of the Roman Empire in the west. During the reign of their greatest king, Charlemagne (ruled 771–814), the Franks conquered an empire that covered most of Christian western Europe, fighting Saxons, Danes, Muslims, and Avars in annual military campaigns around the borders of their lands.

The majority of the Frankish army of the 8th and 9th centuries was made up of levies. All free men who were judged to be sufficiently well-off to afford armor and a weapon had to present themselves for military service, led by their local count, whenever the king required. More important than these part-time soldiers were the trained warriors who formed the heavy cavalry. These consisted of the king's household troops and of the followers of nobles, who held their high position in the realm in return for military service. These aristocrats would be ordered to turn up at a certain time and place not only with a retinue of fully equipped horsemen but also with a supply train of carts carrying food and other necessities for three months' campaigning.

The Frankish cavalry wore the "byrnie," or mail coat, and carried shields. Their principal weapons were the lance or spear and the sword. According to Charlemagne's edicts the horsemen were also expected to be equipped with a bow. At the famous battle of Poitiers against Arab raiders in 732 the Franks fought on foot, but by Charlemagne's time they fought mounted, using stirrups and the high-backed saddle to provide a sufficiently stable platform for wielding their weapons. With this style of fighting they presaged the knight of the high Middle Ages.

Frankish cavalry
The charge with lance couchant – held horizontally as in a joust – was one way that the Frankish cavalryman fought; he also wielded the weapon overarm, using a stabbing motion.

THE BYZANTINES

The Byzantine Empire was the continuation of the Roman Empire in the east and its armed forces at first followed the Roman professional model. In the 7th century, however, when the empire came under threat from Muslim Arab forces, a new form of military organization emerged. The empire was divided into military districts known as "themes," each under the command of a general or "strategos." Soldiers were granted land to support themselves, as the empire could not afford to pay them.

From the 8th century, Byzantium put more reliance upon the "tagmata," cavalry and infantry regiments in the direct employ of the emperor. There was also an increasing use of foreign auxiliaries and mercenaries, including the famous Varangian Guard. The crack troops were armored cavalry, the cataphracts. These differed from West European knights in carrying bows as well as swords and lances; they also lacked the special social status that went with knighthood. The cataphracts typically made repeated lance charges in waves supported by a rain of arrows, wearing down the enemy rather than attempting to break through in a single mass charge. By the start of the 11th century, when Basil II, known as the Bulgar-slayer, was emperor, the Byzantine army was one of the world's most effective fighting forces. It never fully recovered, however, from defeat by the Seljuk Turks at Manzikert in 1071.

Byzantine cataphracts
Like other medieval heavy cavalrymen, when not fighting Byzantine cataphracts carried their shields slung over their backs. Horses were sometimes armored as well as the riders.

THE NORMANS

A Viking warband commanded by Rollo settled in northern France in 911, with the agreement of the Frankish king, Charles the Simple. Rollo's descendants became the Dukes of Normandy. Because of intermarriage with other inhabitants of France, by the 11th century the Normans' Scandinavian blood was much diluted, but the warrior spirit of their intrepid ancestors remained very much alive.

Norman conquests were wide-ranging. In the Mediterranean, the Norman adventurer Robert Guiscard and his brothers took over southern Italy and Sicily after defeating the forces of the Holy Roman Emperor Henry III at Civitate in 1053. They were repeatedly victorious against the Byzantine Greeks and threatened to attack Constantinople in the 1080s. Normans were also prominent in the First Crusade, which captured Jerusalem from the Muslims in 1099. Robert Guiscard's son Bohemond founded and ruled the Norman principality of Antioch, situated in northwest Syria. But the Normans' most famous conquest was undoubtedly that of England, accomplished by Duke William the Bastard and his followers after a cross-Channel invasion from Normandy in 1066.

Riveted bands reinforcing top of helmet

Reinforcement of rim

Nose guard

Norman helmet
The Normans wore a conical helm made of sheet iron. While offering some protection, it would not have been strong enough to withstand a direct blow with a sword or ax.

FIGHTING METHODS

A Norman army always included considerable numbers of foot soldiers. These comprised armored infantry with spears and bowmen—light archers with simple bows and a lesser number of crossbowmen. But it was heavy cavalry that constituted the cream of the Norman forces. These horsemen did not yet have the social status of the medieval knight; they were simply professional fighting men who could afford to own a warhorse. A Norman knight would join the entourage of a nobleman in the hope of reward through victory in war. It was only after the conquest of England that a full-blown "feudal" system developed, with knights owing service to their overlord—and ultimately the king—in return for land ("fiefs").

Crusading knight
This knight armed with a spear wears a Norman helmet and carries a Norman shield. The distinctive long, kite-shaped shield is emblazoned with a cross that indicates that the knight is a crusader.

The Normans were skilled at war because they practised it constantly. Normandy was the site of endless low-level warfare involving raids and sieges that kept the fighting men actively occupied. They were expert castle-builders, although until the 12th century these were usually forts of earth and wood rather than stone structures. The Normans built castles as part of an offensive strategy, regarding them as military bases from which mobile forces would sally forth to exercise control over a conquered region.

The invasion of England offers a prime example of how the Normans waged war. Assembling a fleet of more than 700 vessels to carry around 10,000 men, 3,000 horses, and all the necessary equipment across the Channel showed exceptional organizational ability. At Hastings the Norman tactics were initially to soften up the Anglo-Saxons with a rain of arrows and then launch a cavalry charge against the shield-wall with lances, riding straight-legged in long stirrups on their short, sturdy horses. Later in the battle they feigned a retreat to draw the Anglo-Saxons out of formation, after which the knights could get among them with swords. The Normans' subjection of England after their victory at Hastings showed a ruthless will to power.

Sicilian stronghold
Some of the most enduring monuments to the military power of the Normans are to be found in Sicily, such as this castle perched high on a clifftop at Erice in the west of the island.

“SHIELDS, HELMETS, AND COATS OF MAIL WERE SHIVERED BY THE FURIOUS AND IMPATIENT THRUSTS OF HIS SWORD; SOME HE DASHED TO THE EARTH WITH HIS SHIELD ...”

ORDERIC VITALIS DESCRIBING WILLIAM FIGHTING AT THE BATTLE OF HASTINGS

The battle of Hastings
Chainmailed Norman foot soldiers advance to attack the Anglo-Saxon line in a spectacular modern re-enactment of the battle.

The battle of Hastings
Normans and Anglo-Saxons clash in this dramatic reenactment of the Norman invasion of Britain in 1066. Led by William the Conqueror who defeated the armies of King Harold II, it remains the last successful military conquest of England.

1000 – 1500

MEDIEVAL KNIGHT

WHAT IS THE FUNCTION OF KNIGHTS? TO GUARD THE CHURCH, TO FIGHT UNBELIEVERS, TO VENERATE THE PRIESTHOOD, TO PROTECT THE POOR FROM INJURIES, TO POUR OUT THEIR BLOOD FOR THEIR BROTHERS ... AND IF NEED BE, TO LAY DOWN THEIR LIVES.

THE EUROPEAN KNIGHT was a formidable warrior, an armored horseman equipped with lance and sword who—in principle if not always in practice—dominated the medieval battlefield with his superior fighting skills. The knight also represented a cultural ideal of Christian manhood whose honor, valor, and virtue were celebrated in the epic poetry of the period. In practice, as professional fighting men, knights were of necessity immersed in the inglorious reality of medieval warfare, besmirched by countless episodes of plunder and massacre.

The medieval knight emerges obscurely into the pages of history from the heavy cavalry employed in the realms of the great Frankish ruler Charlemagne and his successors in the 9th and 10th centuries. These were mounted fighting men with a key role in warfare but no special status or prestige, serving a local lord or the king. From around the middle of the 11th century, however, knights began to be recognized as elite warriors of notable social standing. The crusader movement against Muslim control of the Holy Land highlighted the image of knights as specifically Christian warriors and defenders of the Church. Knights' prestige rose so rapidly that, by the 12th century, every nobleman was happy to describe himself as a knight, although most knights were not noblemen.

BECOMING A KNIGHT

The special status of knights was confirmed by public ceremonies and symbols, as well as being protected by laws and decrees that attempted to guarantee its exclusivity. Heraldic emblems, used to decorate banners, shields, and surcoats so that helmeted knights could be readily identified at tournaments or in battle, developed into a system of symbols identifying each warrior's place in the knightly caste. Over time the lowborn were explicitly forbidden from becoming knights and knightly status became largely hereditary. Boys of appropriate social standing would serve first as pages and then as squires in the household of a knight who ensured their education in horsemanship and the use of the sword and lance. When they were old enough and were judged fit to be knights, knighthood was formally conferred with the ceremony of the "accolade," a girding with a sword or touch of sword or hand on the shoulder. In the case of a royal prince or the son of a nobleman this would be the occasion for elaborate festivities.

COSTLY ROLE

Kings increasingly assumed the exclusive right to confer knighthoods and used this as a means of raising revenue, charging a hefty fee for the privilege. By the 14th century, many qualified by birth to be knights tried to avoid the expense and onerous duties it involved. As well as the cost of the accolade, there was a substantial outlay for equipment and mounts. A knight needed at least two horses when on campaign—a palfrey, or saddle horse, for ordinary travel and a splendid destrier, or warhorse, for combat. Full plate armor, which gradually replaced the mix of chainmail and plate, was very expensive, shaped to offer protection against missiles and sword blows, yet light and well balanced enough to be comfortable when fighting on foot. The knight would also need a lance, a sword, a shield, and probably a mace, war-hammer, or poleax.

Many young men with military ambitions were prepared to pay for the horses and gear but baulked at the cost of a knighthood, or lacked the requisite birth qualification. They remained squires or sergeants, fighting alongside the knights and largely indistinguishable from them on the battlefield. A squire or sergeant might hope to receive an accolade on the battlefield in recognition of some spectacular feat of arms, though such on-the-spot knightings were not common.

Knights, squires, and sergeants were collectively known as "men-at-arms".

ITALIAN "HOUNSKULL" BASINET

Knights in combat
The knights of Edward III of England and Philip VI of France do battle at Crécy, in northern France, in August 1346 *(above)*, one of the first major clashes of the Hundred Years' War. A knight was always well equipped when on campaign; he took with him a minimum of two mounts and a squire, and was heavily laden with armor and weapons. The basinet helmet *(right)* has a distinctive pointed visor (nicknamed a "hounskull").

Heraldry
Heraldic devices, such as the shields displayed by this 15th-century knight in the *Codex capodilista*, were both a military status symbol and a mark of social standing.

Knights broadly fitted into the system of personal loyalty and mutual obligation that shaped medieval society. They might, for example, owe military service as vassals or liegemen to a lord or king in return for a grant of land held as a fief—the classic pattern of the "feudal" system. But in the later Middle Ages monetary arrangements progressively came to the fore. Whether knights lived on their own land or as retainers in a noble household, by the 14th century they would expect to be paid for their services, even though the service was recognized as a feudal obligation. By the same token, they could often pay money in lieu of service—shield tax or "scutage."

CHIVALRY AND GLORY

Medieval society thoroughly encouraged young males of social standing to seek glory in war. They were provided with role models both in fiction—as in the Arthurian legends or the French "chansons de geste"—and in tales of the feats of contemporary real-life heroes such as England's Black Prince or Bertrand du Guesclin, the constable of France. The Church sanctified the practice of war, at least if directed against "infidels" or in some other just cause, and the code of chivalry established principles of conduct that a knight should follow.

Chivalry incorporated many of the usual principles of warrior morality, such as loyalty to your leader or to your brothers-in-arms, together with Christian-derived values such as respect for the poor and needy. But the chivalric code was also a practical arrangement between knights to limit the risks of warfare. Being of the same rank and often related by blood or marriage, opposing knights had an interest in avoiding a fight to the death. If they were facing defeat, they could usually surrender in the confident expectation of being treated well as prisoners and eventually ransomed – although there were exceptions to this rule, as when the English King Henry V ordered the killing of French prisoners at Agincourt in 1415.

Ransoms could be considerable sums of money, so there was obviously a profit motive at work in the preservation of prisoners' lives. However much knights might be inspired by the prospect of honor and glory, they usually also had material goals in sight. Many knights were far from wealthy. They might hold fiefs that were small plots of land similar to those worked by peasant families, or they could be younger sons with no expectation of an inheritance. Skill in the use of arms gave a man a chance to better himself. He could forge a distinguished military career, as Bertrand du Guesclin did from unpromising provincial origins, or win lands through participating in conquest, as happened during the Crusades.

PRINCIPLES AND PROFIT

Some knights joined military orders, swearing allegiance to the master of the order and fidelity to their companions. These orders, often an elite among the knighthood, were either religious like the Templars, Hospitallers, or Teutonic Knights—

Horse armor
The warhorse was the knight's most expensive—and vital —piece of equipment. Horse armor, such as this 15th-century German shaffron (head plate), helped protect mounts in battle or during jousts.

EVOLUTION OF THE KNIGHT

The evolution of European knights' helmets and body armor from the 11th to the 16th century reflected advances in the technology of metalworking, but also the changing status of the knight. At the start of the period he was a rough-and-ready fighting man in the service of a great lord or ruler; by its end the knight had a prestige and self-importance that generally outweighed his practical function on the battlefield.

The basic armor of the knight in the 11th century was the hauberk, a coat of chainmail—knee-length, short-sleeved, and with a hood (or coif) to protect the head and neck. Over this hood the knight wore his helm, a cone of iron with a nosepiece as the sole protection for the face. The limitations of mail are evident in the fact that knights still carried shields to ward off blows.

In the following centuries, sections of plate were added to the chainmail, spreading from vulnerable points such as the lower legs, arms, and shoulders to cover the entire body, including the feet, by around 1400. The head received maximum protection, with a steel cap worn under the mail coif and over it a flat- or round-topped helmet with a visor covering the face. The anonymity of this outfit was countered by wearing identifying plumes on helmets or cloth surcoats—the latter also serving to cool the metal in hot sun. From the 15th century onward, plate armor was at its most elaborate. Metalworkers in Milan and Augsburg produced engraved suits of armor that were luxury works of art, intended primarily for tournaments. Meanwhile the battlefield function of knightly armor was undermined by the spread of firearms and disciplined pike-wielding infantry. Both knights and their armor became increasingly decorative and decreasingly effective.

10th-century helm
This Wenceslas-style helm is forged from a single piece of iron with an added nasal guard. Body armor of the period would be mainly chainmail.

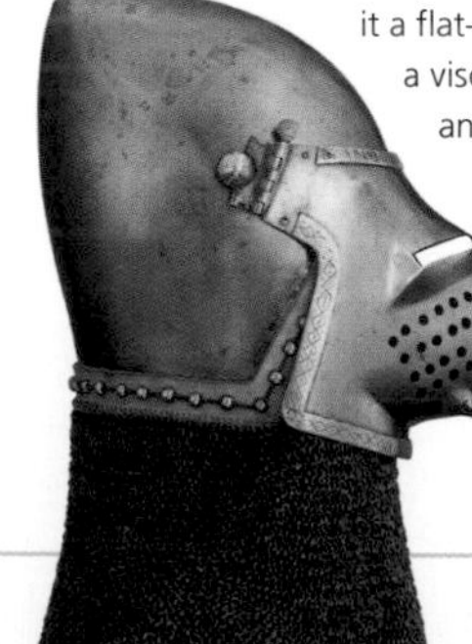

14th-century basinet
Full plate armor only gradually replaced chainmail. This Italian basinet combines a mail collar with a removable conical plate visor.

16th-century Armet
Helmets and armor reached the height of their magnificence in the 16th century, fashions growing increasingly elaborate as the knight's battlefield role declined.

> WHEN THE TOURNAMENT WAS IN PROGRESS KNIGHTS ... FELL IN SUCH NUMBERS, SOME DEAD, SOME PERMANENTLY DISABLED, THAT IT SEEMED THE SPORT NOT SO MUCH OF MEN AS OF DEMONS.
>
> **THOMAS OF CANTIMPRÉ** DESCRIBING A TOURNAMENT AT NEUSS, 1241

dedicated to following a monastic rule—or secular like the Order of the Golden Fleece in Burgundy, the Order of the Star in France, or the Order of the Band in Castile. But knights were not always so lofty in their pretensions. Others became outright mercenaries, leading "free companies" that were in effect private professional armies, selling their services to cities and states, none of which could afford to maintain permanent standing armies. Thus the force that a medieval king led off to war would be far from homogenous. It might include his own household knights, his barons or lords and their feudal followers, contingents provided by the military orders, and mercenaries led by their own chiefs.

At worst, during times of disorder and social breakdown, knights might degenerate into brigands, using their skills to carve out a dishonest living through robbery, plunder, and pillage.

TOURNAMENTS

Once the warrior caste of knights had been created, they needed a constant supply of pretexts for fighting, so they could fulfill their ambitious pursuit of glory and profit. There were normally wars to be found, if not in a knight's home country then around the periphery of the Christian world where crusades were more or less permanently in progress against Muslims or pagans. But an outlet for martial energies and ambitions was also to be found in the tournaments that became popular throughout Western Europe from the 12th century onward. Although these did function as practical military training exercises, they were primarily sport—a source of competitive fun but also a public arena in which talented combatants could seek fame and fortune.

Jousting helm
This late 15th-century German helmet features sloping sides to deflect an opponent's lance and steel attachments to lock the helm to the body armor.

Initially tournaments were the occasion of mock battles fought between two sides ranging over a wide area of countryside. As in real battles, knights were often taken prisoner, forfeiting their horse and equipment to their captor—a valuable prize. Deaths and serious injuries were common, with over 60 knights reportedly killed in one exceptionally costly tournament at Neuss in 1241. A substantial amount of damage was also done to property in the combat zone. By the 14th century, these hugely destructive free-for-alls had largely been replaced by strictly formalized combat fought with blunted weapons and under strictly enforced rules. Jousting became a central feature of tournaments in which individual knights charged one another with couched lance and completing their duel with swords on foot. Under the influence of chivalric romance, knights fought as the champions of ladies, whose tokens they wore. Participation in the jousts was vetted by heralds, who rejected from competition any candidates deemed not to be true knights. The adoption of special tournament armor, heavier than that worn for war, further reduced the risk of serious casualties. While in the 13th century, tournaments had often been denounced as a futile waste of life, by the 15th century they were being lampooned as gutless displays of vanity.

MAKING WAR

Medieval knights were committed to an ideal of warfare in which mounted warriors fought one another at close quarters in a fair contest of courage, strength, and skill. But the reality of warfare was often very different.

Jousting tournament
The pomp and pageantry of the later medieval tournament is well captured in this scene from a 15th-century edition of Froissart's *Chronicles*.

Siege warfare
An illustration from the *Chronicles of Charles VII* showing a group of knights and other men-at-arms under the banner of the Dauphin Louis spearheading an assault on the bastille at Dieppe in 1443.

As professional soldiers, knights often conducted campaigns in which such noble passages at arms were rare. Pitched battles were uncommon in medieval warfare. Instead, siege warfare occupied center stage. Since the building of castles and fortified towns was highly developed, sieges were as prolonged as they were frequent. Knights occasionally performed heroics in assaulting castle walls, but more often their role was marginal, since specialists were employed to operate siege engines or to to dig mines under defenses. There was little but boredom and hardship to be found in camping for months in unhealthy conditions outside the walls of a town, or in being one of the besieged defenders, and it was not unknown for knights from the opposing sides to agree to stage a tournament to alleviate the tedium. If a town held out until it was taken by storm, the rules of war permitted the victors to relieve their frustrations by subjecting its population to pillage and slaughter. This was a right of which knights took full advantage, as when crusaders massacred the citizens of Jerusalem in 1099 or when the Black Prince ordered the systematic slaughter of the people of Limoges in 1370.

CLOSE COMBAT

Apart from sieges, warfare consisted largely of raiding and laying waste to enemy territory, a messy business that imposed maximum cost upon local populations with

Knights of Christ
A line of crusader knights charge their opponents at Ascalon, near Jerusalem, in 1099. The impact from a group of well-ordered mounted knights moving at speed could be immense, particularly against less heavily armored opposition.

PITCHED BATTLE TACTICS

The mounted element of a medieval army would consist of groups of 30 or 40 men-at-arms, each behind their leader's banner. A number of such groups, combined with foot soldiers, would form a "battle," the basic all-arms division. Two or three battles typically made up an army in the field. Drawing up his forces on the battlefield, an experienced commander would try to position them so they had the sun and wind at their backs. The more confident side would hope to win the battle through the shock effect of a charge by its mounted knights and other men-at-arms.

CHARGE AND COUNTER-CHARGE

A commander who intended to stand on the defensive would exploit natural obstacles such as hedges, ditches, or soft ground to block the enemy charge. Alternatively, his soldiers would create artificial obstacles, digging trenches or making palisades. After some preliminary skirmishing, especially by bowmen, the knights on one side would launch their charge, surging forward on horseback or on foot to engage their opposite numbers with lance, mace, ax, and sword. If the initial advance was halted, the men-at-arms standing on the defensive would advance on foot to engage the opposing knights in a mêlée or might mount to deliver a counter-charge.

"WHEN BATTLE IS JOINED, NO NOBLE KNIGHT THINKS OF ANYTHING OTHER THAN BREAKING HEADS AND ARMS."

BERTRAN DE BORN, FRENCH BARON AND TROUBADOUR (C.1140–1215)

minimum knightly combat. Nonetheless, heavily armored, mounted knights were a formidable force whenever battle was joined in open field. At battles such as Bouvines in 1214 and Poitiers in 1356, knights formed up in their full splendor carried out classic charges and fought one another in savage mêlées mounted and on foot.

Well-made armor offered excellent protection and gave a knight full mobility to wield his lance, sword, or ax, in the saddle or out of it. The shock of close-quarters combat was, of course, intense and put a premium upon physical strength and endurance, especially if hot weather made the weight of the armor hard to bear. But fortified by their code of personal honor and duty, knights rarely flinched once combat was joined. Their chief weakness lay in the intemperate aggression and quarrelsomeness of hot-headed individuals bent upon glory. Chronicles of medieval warfare tell time and again of groups of knights unwisely breaking ranks to charge a superior enemy in a self-conscious show of competitive bravery, often in defiance of a battle plan agreed in advance. The knights' discipline rarely matched their valor.

LIVING ON

Even in the 14th century, the battlefield dominance of knights was challenged by lightly armored foot soldiers at Courtrai and Bannockburn and by archers at Crécy. From the second half of the 15th century, gunpowder weapons were increasingly effective, as were disciplined infantry armed with pikes. But armored cavalry was not driven from the battlefield by arrows, cannon or arquebuses. In something close to its medieval form it remained an important element in battles into the late 16th century. By then, however, the social and cultural basis of knighthood had declined with an increase in central state power and the inexorable rise of professional soldiering.

Tournament armor
During the 16th century, specialist armor for use in tournaments became common. This ornate German suit features heavier protection along the more vulnerable left arm and shoulder, while ventilation holes are kept to the right-hand side of the visor.

European swords
Early medieval swords were broad and heavy, used to hack through mail. As plate armor improved, swords grew longer and more sharply pointed for thrusting.

KNIGHT'S ARMS

Full plate armor came into use in the 15th century. While heavy and time-consuming to put on, a well-made suit distributed the weight evenly around the body, allowing reasonable mobility. The wearing of surcoats lapsed so owners could show off their expensive armor. The helmet was curved to deflect blows and had a moveable visor for better airflow. Plate armor gave such good protection against swords that percussive weapons such as hammers and maces grew in popularity.

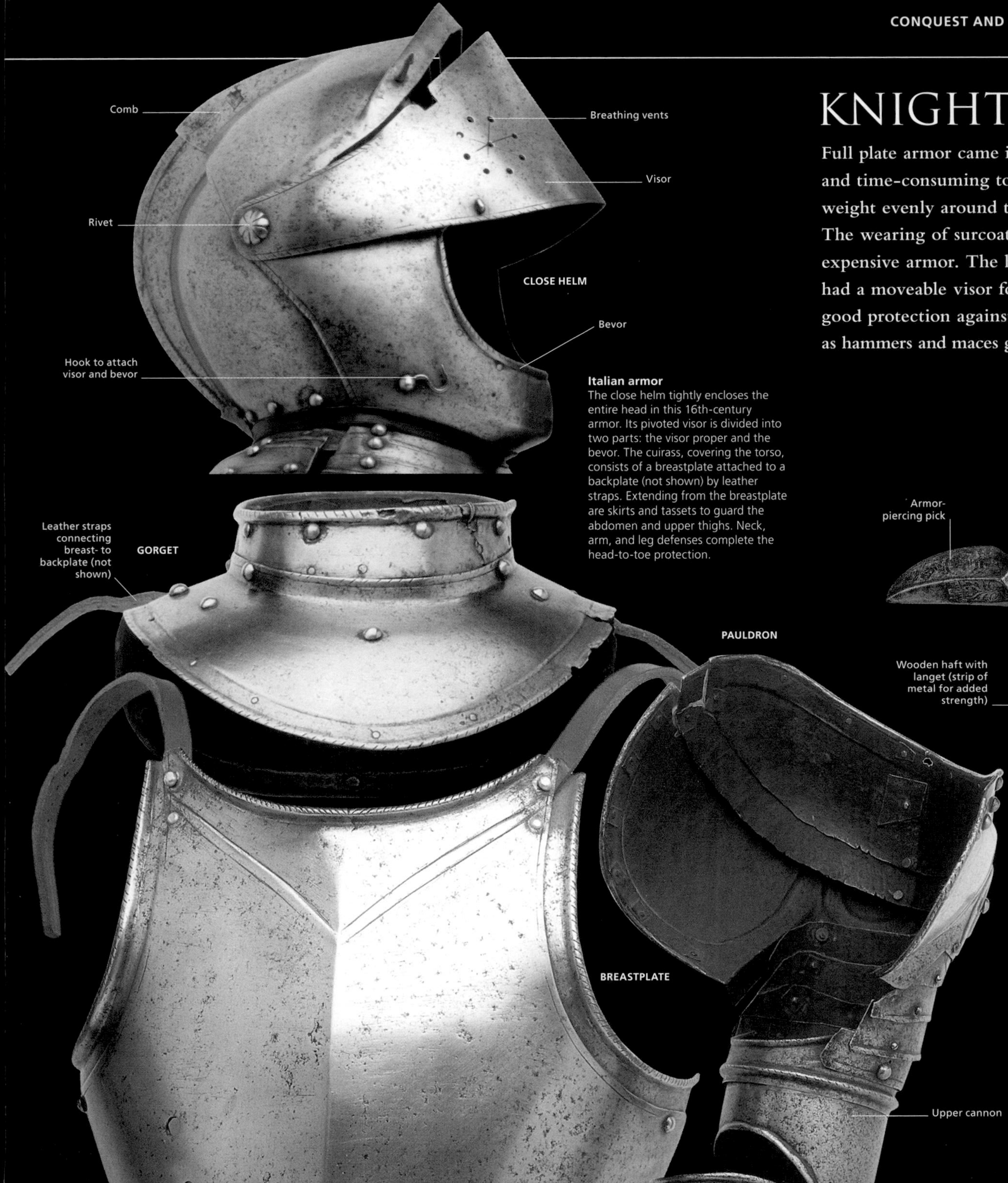

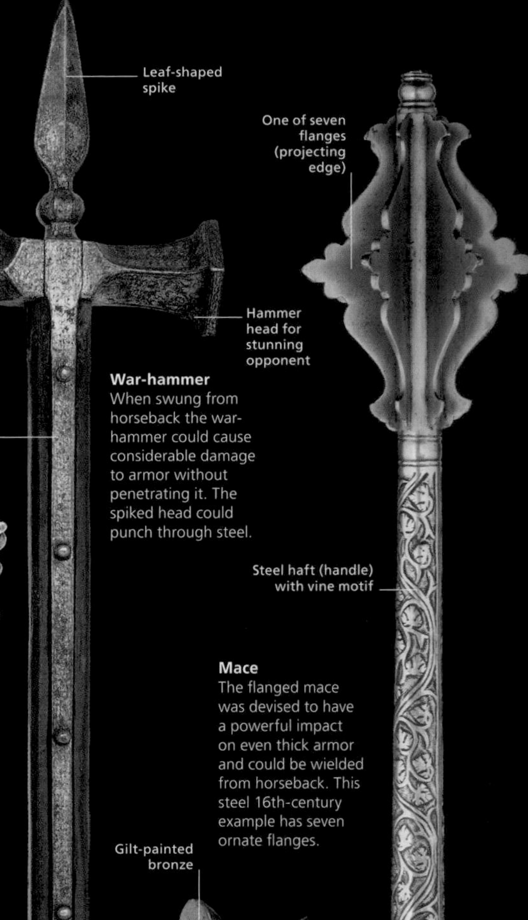

War-hammer
When swung from horseback the war-hammer could cause considerable damage to armor without penetrating it. The spiked head could punch through steel.

Mace
The flanged mace was devised to have a powerful impact on even thick armor and could be wielded from horseback. This steel 16th-century example has seven ornate flanges.

Comb
Breathing vents
Visor
Rivet
CLOSE HELM
Bevor
Hook to attach visor and bevor
Leather straps connecting breast- to backplate (not shown)
GORGET
PAULDRON
BREASTPLATE
Upper cannon

Italian armor
The close helm tightly encloses the entire head in this 16th-century armor. Its pivoted visor is divided into two parts: the visor proper and the bevor. The cuirass, covering the torso, consists of a breastplate attached to a backplate (not shown) by leather straps. Extending from the breastplate are skirts and tassets to guard the abdomen and upper thighs. Neck, arm, and leg defenses complete the head-to-toe protection.

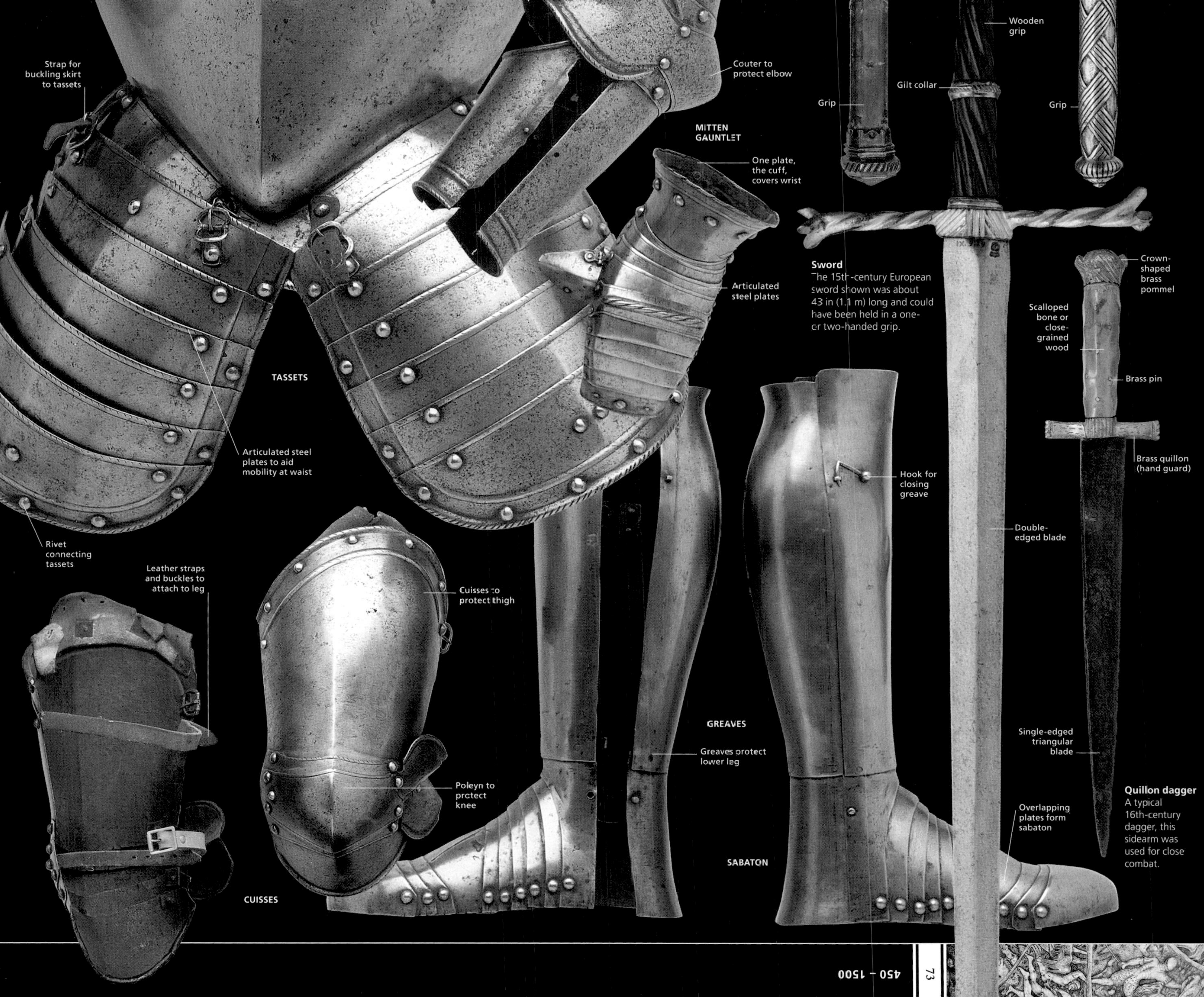

Sword
The 15th-century European sword shown was about 43 in (1.1 m) long and could have been held in a one- or two-handed grip.

Quillon dagger
A typical 16th-century dagger, this sidearm was used for close combat.

Armor in transition
The knights in this bloody encounter, from a 14th-century French manuscript, wear a combination of mail and plate armor. Each knight has a visored helmet over an aventail, a chainmail collar, and a chainmail hauberk under a colored cloth surcoat.

MEDIEVAL CASTLE

Fortifications were ubiquitous in medieval Europe, from the high walls and citadels that protected major towns to the castles that served as military strongpoints and administrative centers. Bodiam Castle in southern England, constructed during the Hundred Years' War, is an example of a fortified individual dwelling—the residence of a wealthy knight, Sir Edward Dallingridge, who believed his home was at risk from attack by the French.

Castle design evolved continuously through the medieval period. Originally European castles were built of wood and earth. The adoption of stone as a construction material from the 11th century made them more expensive to build but far more enduring and prestigious structures, immune to fire and rot. The earliest stone castles consisted of a central tower, or "keep," which was encircled by a defensive wall. By the time Bodiam was built in 1385, however, towers had been integrated into the walls and the gatehouse had become the most strongly defended position in the fortifications. A castle was a visual statement of the wealth, power, and prestige of its owner. But it was also a practical military structure, skillfully designed to give its defenders the best chance of holding off an enemy. Its walls and towers had to be resistant to stone-throwing siege engines, and difficult for tunnel-digging engineers to undermine. The increasing use of cannon in the 15th century eventually made the high, thick stone walls of the medieval castle obsolete, for they could not withstand the battering of such powerful projectiles.

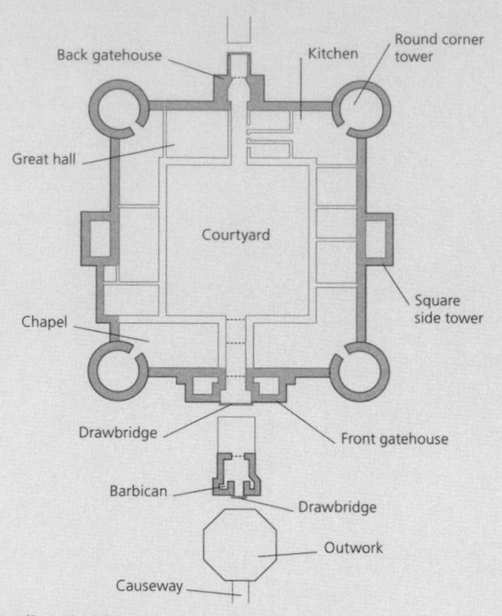

Bodiam Castle
Built around a courtyard, Bodiam Castle had round towers at each corner, square towers on each side, and fortified gatehouses at both the front and the back.

Knight in armor
A castle was stocked with armor and weapons. Full plate armor and visored helmets of sophisticated shape came into use in the 15th century.

> "AT BODIAM, NO TRACE OF THE MODERN WORLD APPEARS TO INVADE THE ANCIENT AND SOLITARY BEAUTY OF THE SCENE."
>
> **LORD CURZON OF KEDDLESTON**, 1859–1925

Siege engine
The torsion-powered ballista was inherited by medieval Europe from the Roman Empire. It was, in effect, a powerful crossbow.

Water obstacle
An aerial view shows how the moat would force any attacker to advance up the narrow causeway at the front of the castle.

Castle gate
The main gate was a potential weak point, since it could succumb to a battering ram. The gate would be protected during a siege by lowering the iron portcullis.

Stone shields
Heraldic shields carved above the castle gates were meant to impress visitors with the owner's status. Many owners, however, were in fact minor knights grown rich on plunder.

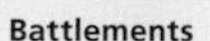

Battlements
Corbels support the battlements, which have crenels (gaps) used by archers.

Great hall
The castle was the fortified manor house of a wealthy man, and as such had its hall designed in the finest contemporary fashion, with Gothic arched windows.

Sturdy walls
Window embrasures reveal the impressive thickness of the castle's outer walls. The needs of defence dictated that outer openings be kept small, making for a somber interior.

Fine ceiling
The castle's inner chambers boasted elaborately vaulted ceilings. Such decoration was another display of the owner's wealth and refined taste.

Stone interior
The castle buildings were hard to heat. The stone floors were strewn with rushes, straw, or herbs and tapestries bedecked the walls.

Fairy-tale castle
Aesthetics were as important in the design of Bodiam as military considerations. It was consciously built to fulfil the ideal of a beautiful castle as described in medieval romances.

Machicolations
Openings known as machicolations between the corbels of a projecting battlement allowed the defenders to drop missiles onto an enemy beneath. These machicolations are in the gatehouse.

Loophole
The walls are dotted with loopholes and arrow-slits to allow defenders to shoot outward. This one is in the lower gatehouse wall.

Round tower
The corner towers were an excellent vantage point from which to observe the surrounding countryside. Their curved surfaces deflected missiles hurled by siege engines.

Inner chambers
Smaller structures within the castle walls provided accommodation for the knight's household and storerooms for weapons and armor.

MEDIEVAL MOUNTED WARRIORS

The state of military technology in the medieval period ensured that, under most circumstances, the armored fighting man on horseback was a decisive figure in warfare. But these heavy cavalrymen, although all fighting with lance and sword, were varied in their military organization. In the course of the Crusades, which established and sustained Christian kingdoms in the Muslim-dominated eastern Mediterranean from 1098 to 1291, orders of warrior-monks were founded to fight a holy war. Their Muslim enemies were equally inspired by religious enthusiasm, as well as by more practical motives. At the other extreme, bands of mercenaries led by faithless knights fought cynically for personal profit, at times laying regions of Europe to waste.

KNIGHT TEMPLAR

Founded by crusader knights based in the Temple of Solomon in Jerusalem in 1119, the Templars were the first monastic military order. Like monks, they lived by a rule of poverty, chastity, and obedience, but they also developed into an elite military force. Numbering around 300 "brother knights," the Templars were recognized as the best disciplined element in the crusader armies. They were also the wealthiest, thanks to the pious donations they received from all over Christian Europe. This allowed them to build impressive castles and employ substantial numbers of foot soldiers. The Templars fought courageously in defense of the crusader states to the very end. Their Grand Master, William of Beaujeu, was among those killed when the port of Acre, the last crusader stronghold in the Holy Land, fell to the Egyptian Mamluks in 1291.

The Templars' wealth eventually proved their undoing. In 1307 the impecunious French King Philip IV arrested all the Templars within his lands, charging them with heretical and obscene practices. Pope Clement V suppressed the order in 1312 and the last Templar Grand Master, Jacques de Molay, was burned at the stake in 1314.

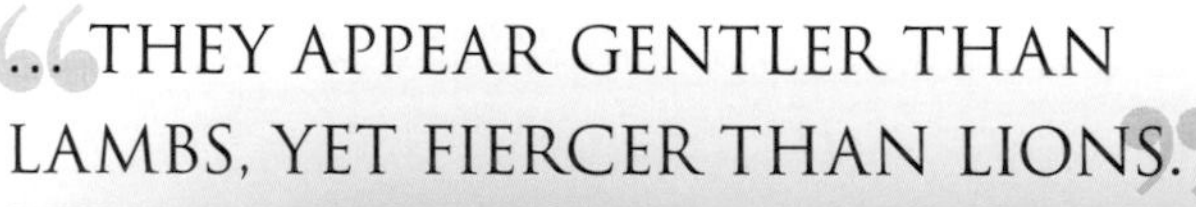

"... THEY APPEAR GENTLER THAN LAMBS, YET FIERCER THAN LIONS."

ST. BERNARD OF CLAIRVAUX PRAISING THE TEMPLARS IN THE EARLY YEARS OF THE ORDER

Crusader helmet
The flat-topped "pot helm," with a hinged visor covering the face, was the standard headgear of Christian knights in the Crusades.

Templar castle
In Portugal the Order of Christ took over the Templar headquarters at Tomar, where it preserved the tradition of warrior-monks.

TEUTONIC KNIGHT

The military order of the Teutonic Knights was founded by German crusaders at Acre in the Kingdom of Jerusalem in 1198. It is most famous for its crusades in Europe. From 1226 the order waged a long, brutal war to subjugate the pagan Prussians, establishing its own state in Prussia. In the 14th century its annual campaigns against pagan Lithuania were joined by knights from across Europe. The order was also at odds with its Catholic neighbors, the Poles. When the Lithuanians, now Christianized, and the Poles united against the Teutonic Knights, they crushed them at the battle of Grunwald in 1410. The order never recovered from this defeat and gradually lost all its Baltic territories, although it survived—in name at least—until 1809.

Rondel dagger
This style of dagger was popular with knights across northern Europe.

THE CONDOTTIERI

In the 14th and 15th centuries, the wars fought in northern Italy were dominated by companies of mercenaries led by commanders known as "condottieri"—from the "condotta" or contract of service that they would negotiate with their employers. The condottieri provided armed forces for city states such as Milan, Florence, Venice, and Genoa, which had grown rich on trade and manufacture but had no substantial military forces of their own. The first of these condottieri were rootless knights from outside Italy, hailing from countries such as Germany, Spain, Hungary, and England. They were later supplanted by Italians, similarly seeking to make their fortunes through the profession of arms.

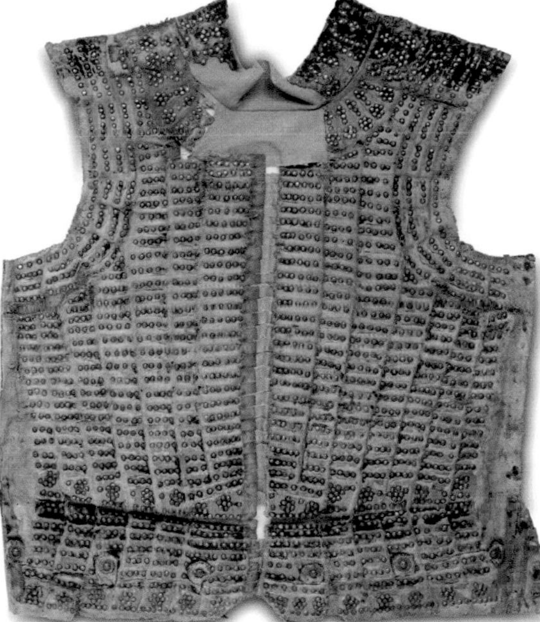

Brigandine
Worn chiefly by the foot soldiers in condottieri bands, the brigandine was a light sleeveless body armor of canvas and steel plates faced with rich material, in this case crimson velvet, which has all but perished.

BUSINESS IS BUSINESS

The condottieri were entrepreneurs with a wholly cynical attitude to their profession. The mercenary companies that they assembled—typically consisting of a few thousand knights and foot soldiers—would fight for whoever paid them and were notorious for changing sides at short notice. All, at times, fought against cities that had previously employed them. Although they liked to make a good show on the battlefield, wearing superb suits of armor, they avoided any hint of a fight to the death. They could be vicious in the massacre of civilians, but backed off from serious clashes with other mercenaries that might cost their men's lives. They tended instead to bribe the opposition to give way—or, preferably, to be bribed themselves.

Italian sallet
This fine example of a sallet, a style of helmet that came into fashion in the mid-15th century, was made in Milan around 1480.

Yet some condottieri won great renown. The English knight Sir John Hawkwood, leader of the White Company, died a wealthy man in Florence in 1394 and had his equestrian portrait painted as a fresco in the city's cathedral. Some of the leading condottieri developed political ambitions, the most successful founding ruling dynasties. Thus Francesco Sforza, himself the son of a mercenary captain, fought in a dizzying series of wars for and against the Pope, Milan, Florence, and Venice (among others) before establishing himself as Duke of Milan in 1450.

From the late 15th century onward, much of Italy was fought over by the armies of France and Spain, assisted by Swiss and German mercenaries. These forces showed up the military deficiencies of the Italian condottieri bands, so that by the mid-16th century the tradition had died out.

MUSLIM WARRIORS

The invasion of Palestine by Christian armies at the end of the 11th century was a shock to the Islamic world. It provoked a revival of the spirit of *jihad* (religious war) in a series of counter-offensives through the following two centuries. The Kurdish-born ruler of Egypt, Saladin, recaptured Jerusalem for Islam after decisively defeating a Christian army at Hattin in 1187. Only the arrival of forces from Europe led by King Richard the Lionheart of England and Philip Augustus of France enabled a crusader presence to survive in the Holy Land.

Divisions between the neighboring Muslim states gave the Christians a reprieve until the Mamluks, slave soldiers of Turkish origin, overthrew their masters and seized power in Egypt in 1260. Under their inspired general Baybars, the Mamluks inflicted a series of crushing defeats upon the Christians, as well as triumphing over the Mongols at the battle of Ain Jalut. The crusaders were effectively beaten well before the fall of Acre in 1291 brought their presence in Palestine to an end.

Muslim armies used broadly the same military technology as their Christian opponents, but their tactics were completely different. Unlike European knights, they had no special liking for the cavalry charge or close-quarters combat, tending to avoid pitched battle until their opponents had been fatally weakened or lured into an encirclement. They made great use of mounted archers fighting as skirmishers, who would inflict losses from a distance, then make their escape if the Christian knights attempted to charge. Muslim cavalrymen wore significantly less armor than the Christians and were thus better adapted to fighting in a hot climate. In general, prosperous Muslim states such as Egypt, fighting near to home, were able to assemble far larger armies than the Christians could ever field, ensuring their victory in the longer term.

Saladin's army
Despite religious enmity, the crusaders recognized Muslim warriors as worthy and chivalrous opponents. They were represented by many European artists as dignified and pious.

1300 – 1450

ENGLISH LONGBOWMAN

“THEN THE ENGLISH ARCHERS STEPPED FORTH ONE PACE AND LET FLY THEIR ARROWS SO WHOLLY AND SO THICK, THAT IT SEEMED SNOW—THE SHARP ARROWS RAN INTO THE MEN OF ARMS AND INTO THEIR HORSES, AND MANY FELL.

FRENCH CHRONICLER **JEAN FROISSART** DESCRIBING THE BATTLE OF CRÉCY, 1346

THE LONGBOW has been accurately described as "an ordinary wooden bow." Yet the outstanding skill of English and Welsh archers transformed this rather primitive weapon into a decisive battle-winning technology. It became the key to the military power of English kings in the 14th and 15th centuries, allowing them to defeat "the flower of French chivalry" at Crécy, Poitiers, and Agincourt. The archers were recognized as an elite force, although without the social status to match their importance to the English crown.

The effective use of massed archers armed with longbows emerged during warfare in Britain in the late 13th and early 14th centuries. Some historians have asserted that the English learned the power of the longbow from the Welsh, who allegedly employed it to deadly effect against the armies of Edward I (reigned 1271–1307). Although this theory is disputed, southern Wales was certainly an area where archery flourished. Both Welsh and English longbowmen were present in Edward's army when he defeated the Scots at Falkirk in 1298. But true credit for developing the effective deployment of archers as a source of mass firepower must be accorded to Edward III (reigned 1327–77). Fighting the Scots at Halidon Hill in 1333, he made the English knights fight dismounted with bodies of longbowmen positioned on their flanks. Chroniclers tell us that arrows flew "as thick as motes in a sunbeam." According to one contemporary source, the Scots "were able to sustain neither the force of archers, nor the arms of the knights"; another source tells us simply that the Scots "were beaten by the English archers." After this success, Edward and his successors went on to deploy massed bowmen in a series of wars against French kings between 1337 and 1453, known conventionally as the Hundred Years' War.

MASS AND SKILL

The great advantage of the longbow compared with the crossbow—a considerably more powerful and complex weapon—was its far greater rate of shot. An experienced archer was expected to shoot around 12 arrows a minute, if he was only required to aim in the general direction of the enemy. The English sought to put thousands of archers in the field. By the 15th century there were at least three bowmen to every one knight in the English army, and the ratio may have risen at times to ten to one. Collectively this mass of archers would deluge the enemy in a dense shower of arrows almost comparable to modern machine-gun fire. At the battle of Agincourt in 1415, it is thought that the English longbowmen may have had the capacity to loose 60,000 arrows a minute.

A medieval state inevitably found it a challenge to supply weaponry and ammunition on such a scale. In 1341 Edward III scoured his kingdom to collect 7,700 bows and 130,000 sheaves of arrows, which were then stored in the Tower of London and other armories. It was said that in the 1350s not an arrow was to be found in the whole of England, since the king had taken them all for his campaign in France.

The problem of supplying bows and arrows was nothing, however, compared with the difficulty of assembling sufficient numbers of archers. Shooting a longbow was a specialized skill, requiring lifelong practice—boys typically learned the use of the bow from the age of seven. The archer had to develop considerable physical strength. Archers' skeletons of the period have been found with deformed left arms and shoulder bones, and badly twisted vertebrae, as a result of the repeated effort of drawing the 6 ft (1.8 m) bow. Aware of the need to maintain a pool of bowmen from whom the best could be selected for service, the English monarchy took active steps to encourage the practice of archery.

BARBED ARROWHEADS

The power of the bowman
The reputation of the English longbowman grew significantly during the Hundred Years' War. At the battle of Najera in April 1367 *(above)*, the bow again proved decisive as the English forces, led by Edward the Black Prince, routed dismounted Franco-Spanish troops. The broad-barbed iron arrowheads *(right)* were typical of those used in the 14th century. They could cause a deep, wide wound, and were difficult to extract, but were not ideal for penetrating armor.

Longbows in action
At the battle of Aljubarrota in 1385 *(right)* English longbowmen helped the Portuguese defeat the French and Spanish forces. Here, as in many medieval illustrations, most of the archers are shown firing their arrows from the wrong side of the bow. A modern re-enactor *(far right)* demonstrates how the bow should be drawn.

Tournaments were mounted to showcase archers' skills, and statutes were proclaimed banning or limiting other sports and pastimes that might compete with archery. In the 1360s, as well as banning the export of bows and arrows, the king forbade archers to leave England without his express permission, presumably through fear that they might join the armies of his enemies.

CALL TO ARMS

The use of missile weapons, especially bows and arrows, was generally denigrated in medieval European warfare. Knights affected to despise a style of combat that allowed a man to kill from a distance, denouncing it as cowardly and base. As a result, the nobility and gentry did not fight as archers. Bowmen were typically drawn from the middling ranks of society, the small freeholders or "yeomen"—although at times plenty of poorer, less respectable folk undoubtedly filled out the ranks. As well as south Wales, most forested areas of England were major sources of bowmen, as the traditional basic use of archery was for hunting. Since there was no standing army in medieval England, archers were not full-time soldiers but men who undertook to serve for a particular campaign. In an attempt to ensure their quality, royal officials known as commissions of array were entrusted with selecting the best men from those mustered by local sheriffs in the shires. Later in the period, archers were more likely to be enrolled as indentured members of forces that noblemen contracted to supply to the king. On campaign archers were commanded by officers known as centenars, who commanded companies of 100 men, and vintenars who commanded 20. They were paid twice as much as ordinary foot soldiers, so we can assume that they were conscious of a special elite status. Like all other medieval soldiers, they would expect to augment their pay by pillaging or by the ransom of prisoners. Archers would not benefit from being ransomed themselves if captured on the battlefield, however. Despised

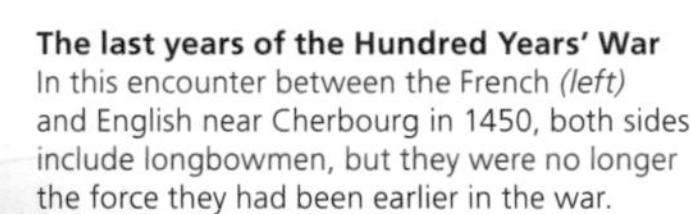

The last years of the Hundred Years' War
In this encounter between the French *(left)* and English near Cherbourg in 1450, both sides include longbowmen, but they were no longer the force they had been earlier in the war.

> "THE ENGLISH ARCHERS ISSUED FROM BEHIND THEIR STOCKADE, THREW AWAY THEIR BOWS … THEN TOOK THEIR SWORDS … AND OTHER WEAPONS, AND KILLED THESE FRENCHMEN WITHOUT MERCY."
>
> FRENCH CHRONICLER **JEHAN DE WAVRIN**, DESCRIBING THE BATTLE OF AGINCOURT

both for their cowardly style of waging war and for their low social status, they would probably be mutilated, tortured, or killed out of hand.

IN BATTLE

In preparing for battle, a bowman would equip himself with about 60 arrows. So these could be accessed at maximum speed, they would not be carried in a quiver but stuffed in his belt or stuck into the ground at his feet—the latter having the added advantage of soiling the points and thus infecting any wounds caused. Some archers wore a helmet and a form of mail coat, but many had virtually no body protection. They depended upon the armored men-at-arms to defend them, as well as on natural or artificial battlefield obstacles—hedges, ditches, or, as at Agincourt, sharpened stakes set point upward in the ground between them and the enemy horsemen. As well as shooting arrows, the archers fought as light infantry. For this purpose they were armed with daggers, axes, and lead "mauls" (hammers or mallets). When their arrows had reduced charging cavalry to a chaos of thrashing fallen horses and half-stunned, unhorsed knights, the archers would rush forward to slaughter the enemy with their edged weapons—as well as to retrieve arrows that could be reused, since ammunition could quickly be exhausted.

Armored bowman
This English longbowman from the end of the 15th century wears light armor and a helmet and carries a sword and buckler. Archers from the golden age of Crécy and Agincourt would not have been so well armed.

The historic reputation of the longbowmen rests above all on three memorable English victories over the French. The first was at Crécy in 1346. As French knights charged impetuously towards the outnumbered English, the English archers, in the words of French chronicler Jean Froissart, "let fly their arrows so wholly and so thick, that it seemed snow."

After this débacle the French nobility might have learned their lesson, but at Poitiers in 1356 the scenario was repeated. According to Froissart once more, the English men-at-arms and archers were in a position "at the end of a hedge among vines and thorn bushes, where no man can go nor ride." The archers shot at the French knights at a point where their charge was compressed into a narrow gap in the hedge, concentrating their fire on the horses rather than the riders, whose armor was hard to penetrate. Fallen horses caused chaos and an English counterattack won the day after fierce hand-to-hand fighting in which the archers' axes and daggers saw plentiful use. Finally at the Battle of Agincourt in 1415 an English force of around 6,000 men, probably including some 5,000 archers, defeated a French army as much as four times its size.

LONGBOWMEN ON THE BATTLEFIELD

The English deployed archers defensively, relying on their enemies to attack first. How exactly the archers were positioned is a matter of dispute between historians, and may well have varied considerably according to the terrain and the number of troops on each side. On some occasions they were massed on the flanks of the army, or on the flanks of each "battle" into which the army was subdivided. But at Agincourt they were probably deployed in front of or in between the men-at-arms, protected against the enemy's cavalry charge by sharpened stakes laid out in a checkerboard pattern. The archers would generally be by far the most numerous element of the English army. Their shower of arrows was intended to halt and disorganize the advancing enemy. Men-at-arms fighting on foot and the archers themselves would then rush forward to finish them off.

DECLINE OF THE LONGBOWMAN

The English archers were by no means universally victorious, however. Indeed, after Agincourt they were almost always on the losing side, especially when the French began to make effective use of cannon in the closing stages of the Hundred Years' War. Whether the longbow was rendered obsolete by the rise of gunpowder weapons is not clear. Its virtual disappearance from the battlefield in the 16th century certainly coincided with the introduction of the arquebus and the musket. But it would be another 300 years before any firearm could match the longbow's performance, firing 12 times a minute and consistently hitting a target 218 yards (200 m) distant.

Perhaps the most convincing explanation of the military decline of the longbow lies in the disappearance of the extensive pool of skilled archers on which it depended, itself partly caused by a long period during which England was relatively at peace. It was no longer possible to employs massed bows because there were simply not enough people capable of shooting them.

Longbow and arrows
The greatest archaeological hoard of English longbows and arrows was found aboard the *Mary Rose*, the Tudor warship that sank in 1545 and was raised from the seabed in 1982. The bows ranged between 6ft 1 in and 6ft 10 in (1.87 m and 2.11 m) in length.

Flight, usually of goose or swan feathers
REPLICA ARROWS
Nock (notch)
Wood chosen for its elasticity, combining different properties of heartwood and sapwood
LONGBOW FROM THE MARY ROSE
Single stave of yew

LONGBOWMAN'S GEAR

Some well-equipped archers, usually those retained by a nobleman, wore mail coats and helmets. Others wore padded, quilted coats, but many wore no protective clothing at all. A longbowman's job was to rain down death from a distance and when the fighting got too hot for him, he usually ran for safety or relied on the protection of the men-at-arms. If, however, they had to fight, longbowmen often carried a short sword such as a falchion and a small round shield or buckler. When there were spoils for the taking on a battlefield strewn with the bodies of enemy knights, they were quick to plunder their weapons and belongings.

Liripipe hood
No man at this time ever went bare-headed, so any archer without protective headgear would have worn a hat of some kind. A popular style in the 14th century was the hood with a liripipe, a long tubular extension of the tip.

Liripipe—could be wrapped around the neck as a scarf or used to carry valuables

Hood of fine-quality wool

Leather fastening to button up hood at neck

Horn extension to protect tip of the bow and make stringing easier

Bowstring, usually made of hemp

Undershirt
This plain white linen undershirt is of a kind worn by all classes of society in the 14th and 15th centuries.

Barbed arrowhead

Bodkin arrowhead, with square pyramid-shaped point for piercing chainmail

Drawing the longbow "to the ear"

Preparing to fight with a sword and buckler

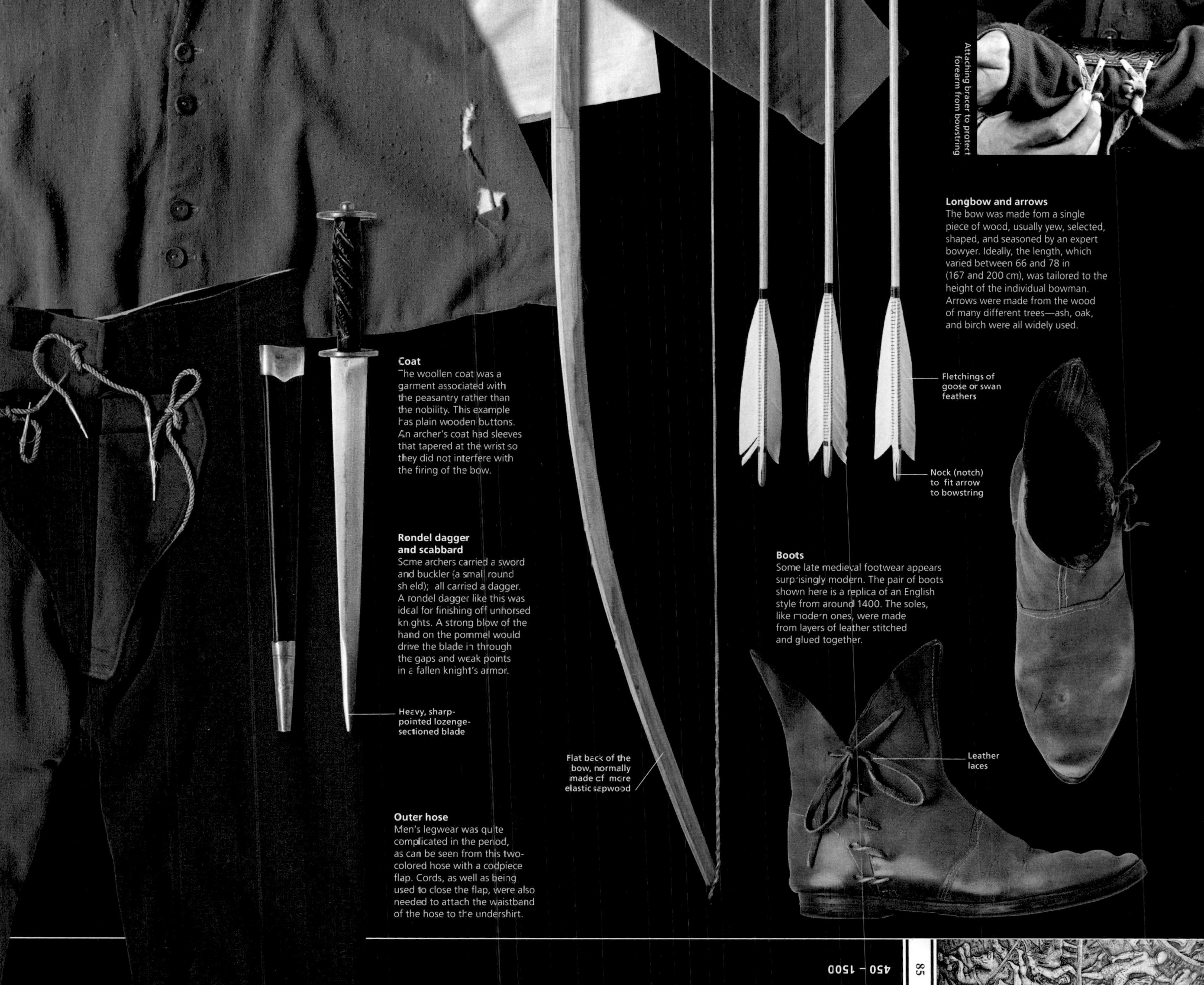

Attaching bracer to protect forearm from bowstring

Longbow and arrows
The bow was made fom a single piece of wood, usually yew, selected, shaped, and seasoned by an expert bowyer. Ideally, the length, which varied between 66 and 78 in (167 and 200 cm), was tailored to the height of the individual bowman. Arrows were made from the wood of many different trees—ash, oak, and birch were all widely used.

Coat
The woollen coat was a garment associated with the peasantry rather than the nobility. This example has plain wooden buttons. An archer's coat had sleeves that tapered at the wrist so they did not interfere with the firing of the bow.

Rondel dagger and scabbard
Some archers carried a sword and buckler (a small round shield); all carried a dagger. A rondel dagger like this was ideal for finishing off unhorsed knights. A strong blow of the hand on the pommel would drive the blade in through the gaps and weak points in a fallen knight's armor.

Boots
Some late medieval footwear appears surprisingly modern. The pair of boots shown here is a replica of an English style from around 1400. The soles, like modern ones, were made from layers of leather stitched and glued together.

Outer hose
Men's legwear was quite complicated in the period, as can be seen from this two-colored hose with a codpiece flap. Cords, as well as being used to close the flap, were also needed to attach the waistband of the hose to the undershirt.

MEDIEVAL FOOT SOLDIERS

Medieval knights tended to despise foot soldiers as a lowborn rabble. Their presence on the battlefield was a necessity, but it was a regrettable one. On many occasions, however, infantry armed with pikes, clubs, and other simple weapons proved their effectiveness against armored cavalry when resolute and properly organized. Armed with missile weapons, whether with longbows, crossbows, or early forms of cannon, foot soldiers could more easily subvert the social order. Knights especially resented these men who fought at a distance, an action they considered not only cowardly, but unfair, at least when used against them. In general no quarter was given to foot soldiers when they were taken prisoner—after all, they were not in a position to pay a ransom.

FLEMISH FOOT SOLDIER

In 1302 France sent a substantial army, including a large body of knights, to crush a rebellion in Flanders. The Flemish fielded a force composed almost entirely of foot soldiers. They were a well-drilled urban artisan militia, led by a small number of noblemen. Their distinctive arm was the "goedendag," a long pole with a spearhead at one end and a mace head at the other. At Courtrai on July 11, they took up a position on ground criss-crossed by streams, to which they added ditches of their own. This gave them some protection from the French cavalry charge, which they brought to a halt by stubbornly holding their lines. Flemish soldiers then surrounded and picked off the stalled knights one by one.

Battle of Courtrai
Although the armor and weapons of the Flemish are not accurately portrayed in this painting, it shows how they halted the knights and methodically unhorsed and killed them.

SCOTTISH SCHILTRON

In its war against England in the 13th and 14th centuries, the core of Scotland's forces were the infantry schiltrons. The schiltron was a phalanx-like formation of pikemen standing shoulder-to-shoulder, often organized in a circle. The majority of the foot soldiers were levies who, depending on their wealth, were expected to turn up either simply with a pike, or with additional equipment such as a sword, helmet, quilted body armor, and protective gloves. The armored men were placed in the front rows. Bristling with pikes, the schiltron was a highly effective defensive formation against a cavalry charge, but could also be used offensively as it was at Bannockburn in 1314. But in their packed formation the Scottish infantry were vulnerable to the arrows of the English king's longbowmen.

HUSSITE SOLDIER

Hussites were the radical followers of a strict form of Christianity in 15th-century Bohemia. Declared heretical by the papacy, they had to defend themselves against a crusade. Under the leadership of Czech squire Jan Žižka, a band of peasant farmers, artisans, and traders was turned into a disciplined force, obeying written statutes that laid down rules for punishments, camp life, and the division of booty. United by their beliefs, the Hussites marched to battle singing hymns. They devised innovative tactics, employing new and old weapons side by side. Many of their soldiers were armed with simple flails or pole arms, and they employed mounted crossbowmen. But they also built battle wagons, reinforced with iron, in which they installed cannons and men with firearms. These could be used as mobile fire platforms, driving in columns through enemy lines. The Hussites' most famous victory was at Kutná Hora in 1421.

Hussite encampment
The Hussites formed defensive encampments by circling their wagons. Defended by cannons, arquebuses, and crossbows, these laagers almost invariably thwarted any attackers.

"YE WHO ARE WARRIORS OF GOD AND OF HIS LAW, PRAY TO GOD FOR HELP ..."

HUSSITE BATTLE SONG

GENOESE CROSSBOWMAN

During the First Crusade, an expeditionary force from the Italian city of Genoa landed at Jaffa in 1099, then joined the crusaders at the siege of Jerusalem. Like the other maritime republics, Venice and Pisa, Genoa had developed crossbow contingents for naval warfare—they were used to shoot from galley to galley in close engagements. The performance of the Genoese crossbowmen during the siege was impressive enough to establish a durable reputation.

RENOWNED ACROSS EUROPE

It is said that one advantage of the crossbow, compared with the longbow, was that it required little training or experience to use. Even so, European armies showed a healthy respect for professional expertise when it came to employing crossbowmen. The reputation of the Genoese enabled them to find many customers for the services of a company several thousand strong, armed by a guild of crossbow-makers. In fact, the crossbowmen were not primarily recruited from the city itself, but from the surrounding mountainous Ligurian countryside. They practiced their shooting in the fields outside the city walls—a source of some complaint from landowners in the area. The company fought in defence of Genoa when required, but otherwise sold its services to the highest foreign bidder.

Experienced crossbowmen were accurate enough to act as snipers during sieges. On the battlefield they were usually deployed offensively, sent out in front of the army to soften up the opposition before the main charge was delivered. To span their bows they normally used a hook on their waist belt: the bowman bent forward, hooked the bowstring and stood up, spanning the bow with the strength of his back. Apart from the bow, their equipment consisted of a helmet, some body armor, a dagger, and a large shield, the pavise. They sometimes fought in teams, with the bowman sheltered by a servant holding the pavise and possibly backed up by another assistant loading a second bow while he shot the first.

Genoese crossbowmen continued to play a key role on European battlefields, even after the advent of hand-held firearms in the 15th century.

It is unfortunate that their most memorable appearance on the historical stage, at the battle of Crécy in 1346, was a fiasco. Employed by the French, they advanced toward the English lines but were ineffectual, apparently because the cords of their bows had slackened through damp. Retreating under a deluge of arrows fired by the English longbowmen, they were trampled underfoot by the charging French knights.

Stirrup for holding bow with foot while drawing bowstring

Composite tiller made of strips of horn, sinew, and wood

Steel pin to which spanning lever is attached

Groove where bolt is inserted

Rotating nut with notch to hold bowstring when bow is spanned

Crossbow and bolts
This late 15th-century bow required a lever to crank the bowstring back to its firing position, hooked over the central rotating nut. The bolt was then placed in the groove. Pressing the trigger on the underside of the bow rotated the nut to release the string.

BODKINHEAD CROSSBOW BOLT

TRIANGULAR-HEADED BOLTS

Flight, made of wood or paper

Pavise
This form of shield was most useful when crossbowmen were shooting at defenders on ramparts during a siege. They would crouch down behind it to reload.

> WHATEVER THESE DARTS CHANCE TO HIT, THEY DO NOT FALL BACK, BUT THEY PIERCE THROUGH A SHIELD, THEN CUT THROUGH A HEAVY IRON CORSELET.

ANNA COMNENA DESCRIBING BYZANTINES' FIRST EXPERIENCE OF CROSSBOWS IN THE *ALEXIAD*, WRITTEN C.1148

1200 – 1300

MONGOL HORSEMAN

“HIS WARRIORS ARE AS BRAVE AS LIONS, SO NONE OF THE FATIGUES OR HARDSHIPS OF WAR CAN INJURE THEM. THEY KNOW NEITHER EASE NOR REST. WHEN THEY EFFECT A CONQUEST, THEY LEAVE NOTHING ALIVE EITHER LARGE OR SMALL.”

REPORT ON **GENGHIS KHAN**'S ARMY MADE TO THE **SHAH OF KHWARIZMIA**, 1218

Nomadic horsemen from the Asian steppe, the Mongols established one of the world's largest ever land empires in the 13th century. After the traditionally warring steppe tribes united under the leadership of Genghis Khan, they launched campaigns of conquest westward into the Middle East and Europe, and eastward to China's Pacific coast. The armies of the settled civilizations of Eurasia were overwhelmed time and again by the speed of movement, aggression, and fighting skills of the all-conquering Mongols.

Before the rise of Temujin, later known as Genghis Khan, the Mongols were merely one among many Turkic tribes living in the tough environment of the steppe north of the Gobi desert. These tent-dwelling horsemen had mostly entered recorded history as raiders and invaders threatening the towns and cities of northern China. The steppe tribes were constantly at war with one another until, in 1206, they recognized Mongol leader Temujin as their khan (Genghis Khan means "lord of the earth"). Genghis and his successors were able to direct the energies of the tribal horsemen outwards and transform raiders into conquerors.

TOUGH FIGHTERS

The Mongols lived all their lives in a close relationship with their tough horses. It was said that a Mongol boy learned to ride before he could walk. As well as a horseman, every Mongol male was a hunter and a warrior. From an early age he was taught the use of the composite bow, a powerful weapon made of horn, wood, and sinew. He took part in the large mounted hunting parties that the steppe tribes employed to encircle and kill game, thus acquiring practice in coordination and maneuver that would serve him well in later battles. The Mongol warrior honed his fighting skills in local tribal wars and his survival skills in the hard life of the steppe.

Composed of such men, Genghis's armies were highly mobile, campaigning over distances of thousands of miles. They were capable of living off the land for long periods even in the most inhospitable terrain, and so were not slowed down by a supply train. The horsemen existed on a diet of dried meat and fermented mare's milk, augmented at times by fresh horse's blood. Since each warrior had a string of four or five mounts, he could continually change horses and thus keep moving over long distances day after day. Rivers were no obstacle to a Mongol campaign: the men would undress, stow their clothes in a waterproof bag, and swim across with their horses. The warrior's weaponry was usually light. Most were mounted archers who would carry two or three bows and a couple of quivers of arrows. A thoroughly self-reliant man, the warrior carried a sharpening stone for his weapons and a needle and thread for making repairs to his clothing and leather armor.

RUTHLESS VICTORS

The Mongols used their great mobility to find, fix, and destroy enemy forces. They were ferocious fighting men, but in no sense a disorganized horde. Each warrior belonged to a group of ten (an *arban*), itself part of a group of 100, 1,000, and 10,000. The army was well officered, with higher appointments made by the khan and lower officers chosen by their men. In practice this amounted to promotion by merit. Small units could operate with great independence, but the Mongol commanders were also capable of coordinating large-scale forces on the battlefield, using smoke signals, trumpets, and banners to communicate orders.

NOGAI HORDE HELMET

Fearsome mounted archers
14th-century Mongol horsemen depicted in battle *(above)* with their composite bows and tough, sturdy mounts. Mongol helmets were often peaked, a variation on the Steppe nomad's peaked felt cap. This late Mongolian-period Nogai Horde helmet *(right)* is from the Caucasus Mountain region, a remnant of the Mongol invasion of Eurasia.

When victorious, the Mongols were totally ruthless in their treatment of enemy combatants and often of whole civilian populations. Their reputation for terror grew with their conquests. Genghis invaded northern China in 1211 and had seized what is now Beijing by 1215, although rich and populous southern China remained for the time under the rule of the Song dynasty. In 1218 the Mongols attacked the powerful Kwaresmian Empire in central Asia, apparently after its shah offended Genghis by killing two traders who enjoyed the khan's protection. The campaigns that followed laid waste the famous cities of Samarkand and Bokhara, and many other historic cities, some of which would never recover their former glory.

GENGHIS'S LEGACY

The death of Genghis in 1127 did not check the course of destruction and expansion. In the 1230s Genghis's son Ogetai sent his armies further west. The Mongol general Subotai overran Russia, sacking Moscow in 1238. In 1240 it was the turn of the Ukraine, with the destruction of the venerable city of Kiev—a European traveler visiting Kiev five years later found "an enormous number of skulls and bones of slaughtered men lying on the plain" and "barely 200 houses standing." In 1241 Subotai led his Mongol forces into Poland and Hungary, defeating armies of European knights at the battles of Liegnitz and Mohi. Since the heavily armored Christian cavalry had proved incapable of coping with the speed of maneuver of the Mongol horsemen, nothing stood in the way of a Mongol conquest of western Europe. The Mongols were approaching Vienna when, by what Christian Europe regarded as a miracle, news arrived of the death of Ogetai. The Asian horsemen turned back, heading home to take part in the selection of a new leader. They never progressed as far westward again.

Decorated quiver
Mongol warriors were taught the use of the composite bow from an early age. A quiver was a crucial part of their armory.

"A SAVAGE PEOPLE, HELLISH OF ASPECT, AS VORACIOUS AS WOLVES IN THEIR HUNGER FOR SPOILS ... BRAVE AS LIONS..."

QUEEN RUSSUDAN OF GEORGIA DESCRIBING THE MONGOLS

CHANGING METHODS

The Mongols' relationship to the countries they subjugated was not, however, a purely destructive one. They benefited from the skills of states with a higher level of technological development. From the time of his very first campaign in China, Genghis became aware of the limitations of his tribal horsemen. Faced with the fortified defenses of Chinese cities, they needed to acquire the techniques and machinery for siege warfare. It was almost certainly through employing Chinese expertise and personnel that the Mongol army was able to deploy rams and mangonels—heavy stone-throwing catapults—in the successful siege of Beijing in 1214-15. From that time onward a siege train was often attached to Mongol forces, and Chinese or Muslim engineers regularly put their specialized skills at the service of the khans.

BAGHDAD MASSACRE

It was thanks to this proficiency in siege warfare that in 1258 a Mongol army led by Hulegu was able to capture Baghdad, the seat of the Islamic Abbasid Caliphate. Almost the entire population of the city was massacred, including the Caliph himself. To the delight of Christian Crusaders, who were at that time struggling to keep a presence in Palestine, this victory seemed to open up the Muslim Arab world for Mongol conquest. Syria fell to Hulegu in 1259, which left only the Mamluks of Egypt to defy Mongol power. But the Mongols

Born warriors
As most Mongol warriors fought as horsemen they wore leather body armor for ease of movement. Warriors formed a close bond with their horse, which was important in the heat of battle.

were thwarted in this goal: the following year, once again the death of the great khan obliged Hulegu and a large proportion of his army to return to Mongolia. The remnants of his forces were defeated by the Mamluks, commanded by Baibars, at Ain Jalut—the only occasion when the Mongols were decisively beaten in battle.

MONGOLS IN CHINA

In China the Mongol style of warfare eventually underwent an almost total transformation. From 1260 Genghis's descendant Kublai Khan, ruling from Beijing, launched a war of conquest against the Song dynasty that still controlled southern China. His army employed sophisticated Chinese weaponry, ranging from powerful crossbows, or ballistas, to varieties of gunpowder weapon, including bombs flung by catapults, primitive flamethrowers, and early antecedents of the handgun. The Mongols also learned from the Chinese how to conduct river and seaborne operations. Kublai's final victory over the Song, which made him undisputed emperor of China, was a naval battle fought in the South China Sea.

No doubt buoyed by this success, Kublai went on to attempt a seaborne invasion of Japan, which was launched from Korea. After a reconnaissance-in-force by a fleet of around 900 vessels in 1274, a full-scale invasion involving more than 4,000 warships was launched seven years later. The encounter with the Mongols was certainly a shock for the Japanese samurai, who had never experienced anything like their massed bowmen or gunpowder bombs. But a combination of stout Japanese resistance and a devastating typhoon made the Mongol expeditions costly failures.

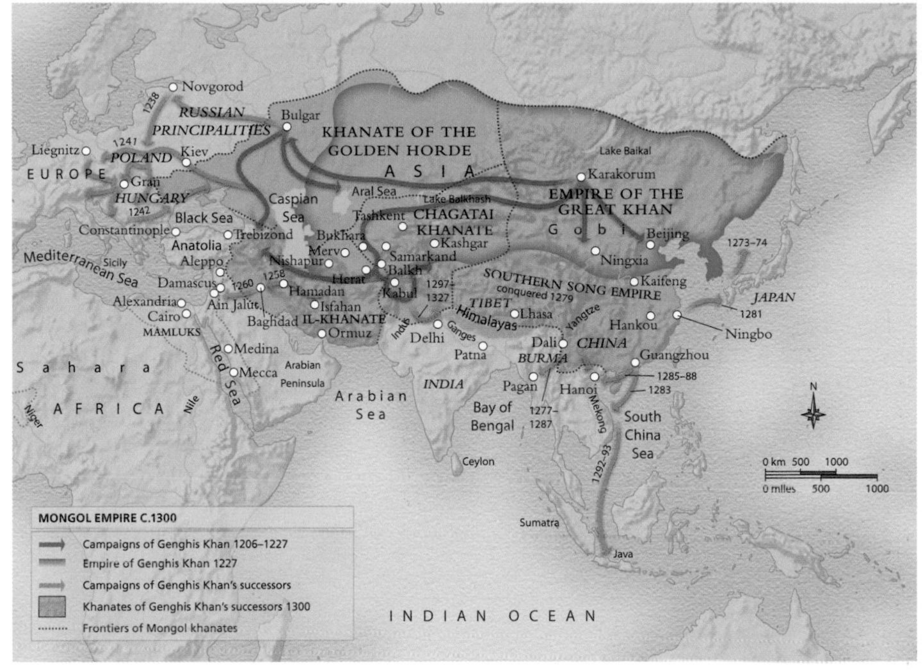

The Mongol Empire
The Mongols ruled an area stretching from modern-day Korea to the eastern edge of Europe. By 1300 the Mongol territories were divided into four khanates: one centred on China; the Chagatai Khanate in central Asia; the Il Khanate in Iran and Iraq; and the Khanate of the Golden Horde in Russia.

OLD HABITS

The Mongols remained essentially true to their roots. Even as Emperors of China, they continued to delight in hunting and value horsemanship above all other skills. They also never escaped from the bad habit of fighting each other over the succession to leadership. By the late 13th century Mongol rule extended from Russia to China and Korea, but this area was divided into four separate khanates. It was because they remained at heart steppe warriors that they could not found a durable empire. After Kublai's death in 1294, Mongol power went into rapid decline.

Mace, spear, and bow
This 14th-century depiction of Mongol warriors, led by Genghis Khan (with mace), accurately portrays their weaponry, but their small, sturdy horses were very different from these steeds.

MOBILITY AND FIREPOWER

The Mongol horsemen typically went into battle spread out in a dispersed formation. The majority of them were trained to fight as hit-and-run skirmishers. Their weapon was the composite bow, which existed in two versions: a light bow was shot from horseback, while a heavy bow was shot by a dismounted man. At the start of a battle the archers would advance to within range of the enemy and inflict a steady drain of losses by shooting arrows into their midst. At the same time they would avoid any efforts by the enemy to join battle, swiftly withdrawing in the face of counterattacks.

CUNNING WARRIORS

The Mongols delighted in battlefield trickery and would take pleasure in luring unwary opponents into a headlong pursuit by simulating flight, only to turn swiftly and trap their disorganized forces. When the enemy was at length worn down, frustrated and exhausted by the arrows of the skirmishers, the Mongols would bring in their elite armored horsemen. Charging forward armed with lance, sword, and mace, they would engage the enemy at close quarters to finish them off. The horsemen on the wings of the Mongol line would by then have advanced at speed to complete an encirclement, leaving the enemy with no avenue of escape when the final attack was launched.

MONGOL ARMS

Most Mongol mounted archers were simply equipped, but the minority of elite warriors, carrying lances and other close-quarters weapons, were more elaborately equipped. In 1246 a papal ambassador to the Great Khan described the Mongol lancers as having "helms and cuirasses of leather ... made of strips about a palm broad, sewn together so that they overlap." Mongols adopted richly decorated weaponry, largely influenced by civilizations they conquered, especially China.

Leather lacing

Padded roll of leopardskin

Helmet and armor
Armor was worn by the Mongols' elite warriors who were expected to engage the enemy at close quarters. Like the armor of Japanese samurai, it was made of hardened leather plates sewn together. This lamellar armor offered a high degree of protection relative to its weight, allowing full mobility. The Mongols' helmets were most often made of iron, but, as here, could also be of leather.

Silver blade

TWIN DAGGERS

Ivory handle

Elaborate decoration on head

IRON MACE

Close-quarters weapons
The elaborate decoration that adorns the 14th- century mace *(left)* suggests that it would have served a warrior of high status, almost certainly a member of a khan's personal entourage. The two small daggers, featuring silver blades and ivory handles, were also luxury products. A dagger might be employed to finish off a wounded enemy, but would also have many everyday uses.

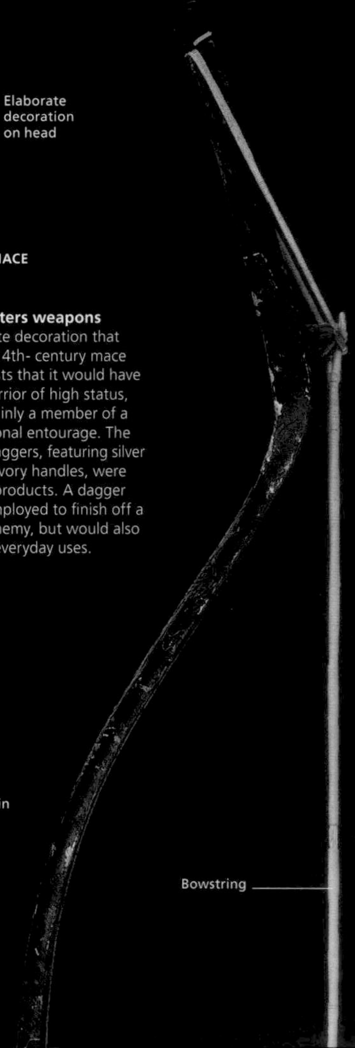

Wooden shaft covered with polished rayskin

Bowstring

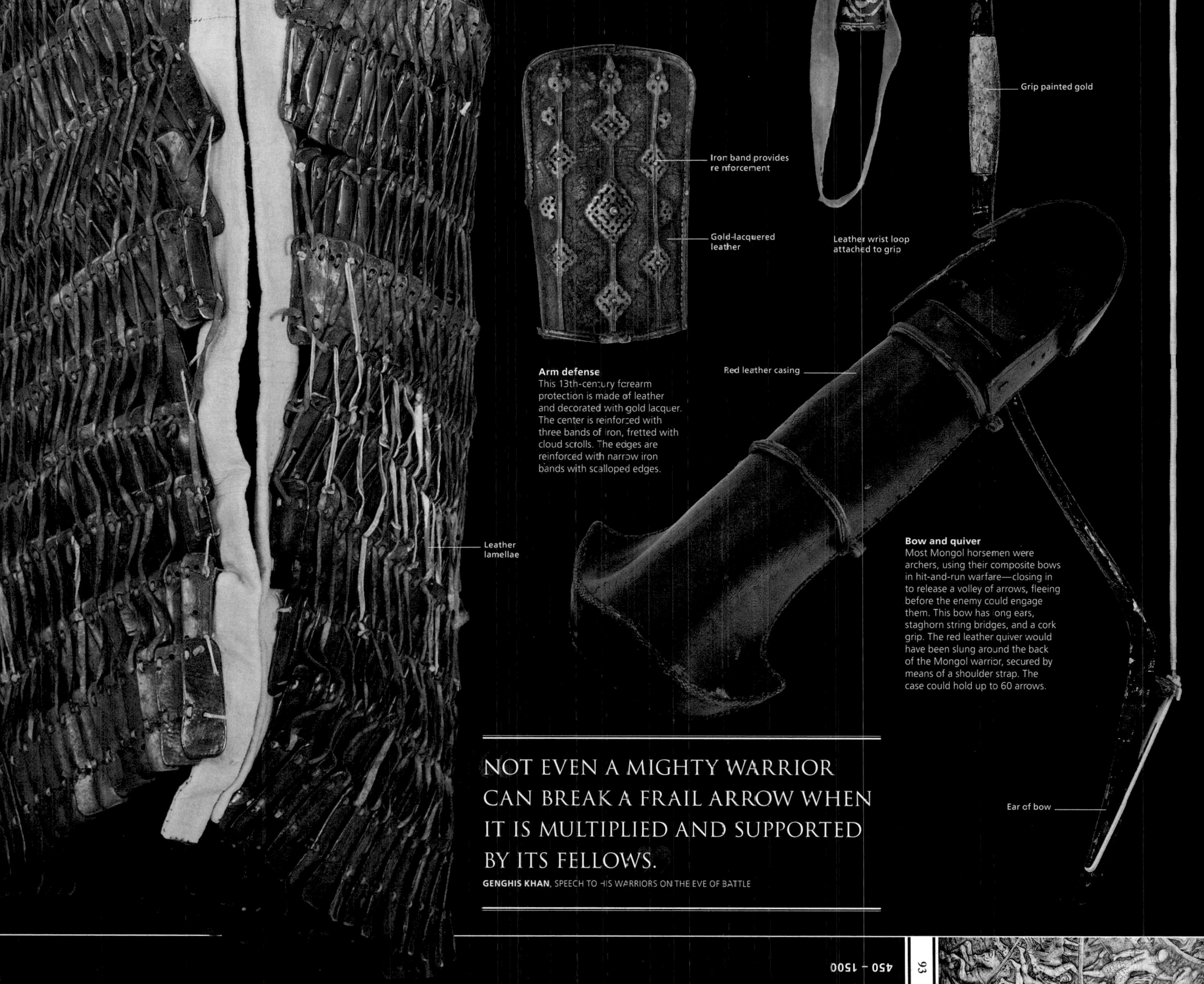

Arm defense
This 13th-century forearm protection is made of leather and decorated with gold lacquer. The center is reinforced with three bands of iron, fretted with cloud scrolls. The edges are reinforced with narrow iron bands with scalloped edges.

Bow and quiver
Most Mongol horsemen were archers, using their composite bows in hit-and-run warfare—closing in to release a volley of arrows, fleeing before the enemy could engage them. This bow has long ears, staghorn string bridges, and a cork grip. The red leather quiver would have been slung around the back of the Mongol warrior, secured by means of a shoulder strap. The case could hold up to 60 arrows.

NOT EVEN A MIGHTY WARRIOR CAN BREAK A FRAIL ARROW WHEN IT IS MULTIPLIED AND SUPPORTED BY ITS FELLOWS.

GENGHIS KHAN, SPEECH TO HIS WARRIORS ON THE EVE OF BATTLE

1150 – 1650

SAMURAI

"AS LONG AS IT IS MY DUTY TOWARDS MY LORD, I WOULD LIKE TO DIE IN BATTLE IN FRONT OF HIS EYES. IF I DIE IN MY HOME, IT WILL BE A DEATH WITHOUT SIGNIFICANCE."

OKUBA TADATAKA, 1622

Charging into battle
A mounted samurai warrior charges into battle with an enemy clan, supported by foot soldiers *(above)*. A samurai's armor and weaponry took many forms. The *zunari bachi* (head-shaped) helmet *(right)* features a gold-lacquered frontal plate. The sword accompanying it typically had a blade 24 in (60 cm) in length.

THE SAMURAI WERE MOUNTED armored warriors who enjoyed elite status in medieval Japanese society—in a sense, the Japanese equivalent of the European knight. Their code of chivalry, known as *bushido*, was based on the principle of absolute loyalty to the master they served. From the 12th century, samurai clans were the effective rulers of Japan under figurehead emperors. Samurai armies fought one another in interminable civil wars until the pacification of Japan under the Tokugawa shogunate in the 1600s.

The samurai originated as servants of the emperor, probably as early as the 8th century CE. They functioned as palace guards and upheld the emperor's authority in the provinces. Over time the samurai evolved into an aristocratic elite based on birth rather than function. The samurai warrior's true allegiance shifted from the emperor, whom he nominally served, to his own clan, or extended family. In the Gempei Wars (1180–85)—a turning point in Japanese history—two samurai clans fought for supreme power. The Minamoto family emerged triumphant, defeating their rivals the Taira. Minamoto Yoritomo was declared shogun, or military ruler, of Japan.

At the time of the foundation of the shogunate, the bow, rather than the sword, was the samurai's most prestigious weapon. It appears that the elite warriors regarded war as above all an opportunity to demonstrate individual fighting skill and courage. When opposing armies were drawn up on the battlefield, leading samurai would dismount and step forward to recite their ancestry and previous feats of arms. The two armies would then shoot their bows in a general exchange of arrows, after which samurai would seek out a suitable opponent to engage in single combat—it would be dishonorable for a samurai to fight a warrior of lesser standing than himself. This, at least, was the ideal to which samurai warriors aspired.

At times battles were far more complicated, involving the use of both trickery and surprise. At Kurikara in 1183, the Minamoto army reportedly trounced the Taira by sneaking around their defensive position in a mountain pass and attacking them from the rear, while simultaneously driving a herd of oxen into their ranks from the front.

BUSHIDO AND SEPPUKU

Samurai of the 12th and 13th centuries were acutely aware of their elite status. A warrior was expected to show both literary and artistic refinement, as well as military virtues. A samurai's training was often accomplished by the bonding of a young warrior to a veteran, a relationship in which homosexual love played its part. The samurai code of behavior—initially formalized as *kyuba no michi* (the way of horse and bow) and later as *bushido* (the way of the warrior)—emphasized self-control, restraint, and the avoidance of ostentation. Some of the customs that were observed in samurai warfare were a mixture of the savage and civilized. For instance, it was considered normal for a warrior to cut off the head of any man he killed in battle as evidence of his prowess. The severed head would then be washed, groomed, and prettified with cosmetics, before being mounted on a spiked board. If the head belonged to a warrior of high standing, it would be considered honorable to return it to his family.

SAMURAI HELMET AND SWORD IN SCABBARD

Samurai weapons and armor
A group of samurai warriors march in a procession during the Jidai Matsuri Festival of Ages in Kyoto, Japan *(right)*. A *katana*, the *tsuka* (handle) of which is clearly visible, lies among a collection of samurai clothing *(far right)*.

AN HONORABLE DEATH

The samurai's distinctive attitude to death was an essential part of the search for a heroic but aesthetically refined mode of existence. According to existing accounts of the Gempei Wars—which hover between legend and history—the Japanese tradition of *seppuku* (ritual suicide) was invented by the veteran warrior Minamoto Yorimasa in 1180. Defeated by the Taira at the battle of Uji, Yorimasa took refuge in a nearby temple.

There he wrote an elegant poem on the back of a fan before calmly slitting his abdomen with a dagger. The belly cut, or *hara-kiri*, became the accepted form of suicide for any samurai facing defeat or dishonor, although other modes of death are recorded. At the end of the Gempei Wars, the Taira committed suicide *en masse* by drowning. In a later period, one samurai, Miura Yoshimoto, took this ritual to the extremes of self-decapitation. Of course the Japanese had no monopoly of the practice of suicide as an honorable death for the defeated—to fall on your sword was considered a noble act, for instance, for losing generals in Ancient Rome. But the tradition of the samurai was notable for its extreme emphasis upon making a good death rather than achieving military success.

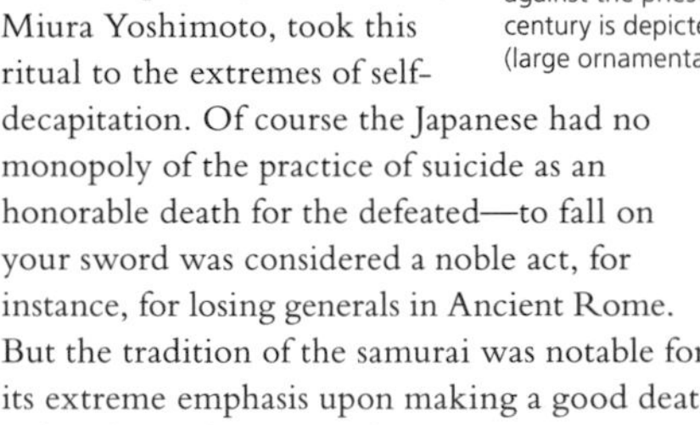

Yoshitsune and Benkei
The young Minamoto Yoshitsune fighting against the priest Benkei in the 12th century is depicted in this ivory *okimono* (large ornamental carving).

The semi-ritualized character of samurai warfare was possible to sustain only because the samurai almost exclusively fought one another. When the Mongol ruler of China, Kublai Khan, mounted seaborne expeditions to Japan in 1274 and 1281, the samurai were initially wrong-footed by an enemy who ignored invitations to single combat—partly because it was not Mongol custom, and partly because they did not understand the Japanese language. The samurai nonetheless successfully resisted the Mongols, with a great deal of help from a typhoon, the *kamikaze* (divine wind). Japanese forces did not fight a foreign enemy again until their unsuccessful invasion of Korea in the 1590s, but by then samurai warfare had undergone a radical transformation through the means of social change and imported technology.

In the 14th century major advances were made in the development of the sword—soon to become the samurai's principal weapon. A blacksmith called Masamune Okazaki is credited with producing a dual structure of soft and hard steel that provided much improved cutting power and endurance for swordsmen. Masamune's technique resulted in Japanese swords (*katana*) being recognized as some of the most potent hand weapons of preindustrial East Asia. Many swords made using this technique were exported across the East China Sea, a few making their way as far as India. Before coming into the possession of samurai, new sword blades were tested by cutting through the bodies of corpses or condemned criminals. Test results were often recorded on the *nakago* (the metal piece attaching the sword blade to the handle).

In the Sengoku period, beginning in the second half of the 15th century, general disorder reigned in Japan. As the old noble clans declined, many samurai emerged from the lower classes and carved out careers for themselves through their fighting prowess. Samurai with no master to claim their allegiance, known as *ronin*, roamed the country in search of military employment.

THE DAIMYO WARS

Self-proclaimed samurai leaders, the *daimyo* or warlords, attracted a following of fighting men and established themselves in control of areas of the country. Wars between *daimyo* forces tore Japan apart for 150 years. The samurai who fought in these conflicts rarely aspired to the refinement of their predecessors. They were professional soldiers occupying a place in substantial armies. Skill with the two-handed sword, not the bow, was now the mark of a great warrior. Samurai swordsmen were accompanied by large bodies of peasant foot soldiers, the *ashigaru*, to provide them with a degree of disciplined support in battle.

In the second half of the 16th and early 17th centuries, a string of major battles and sieges were contested as *daimyo* fought one another for control of Japan. Although Japanese chroniclers often dwelt upon individual combat between named samurai that apparently took place in the midst of these encounters, battles were clearly in fact decided by a combination of forces used in a tactically sophisticated manner. At Nagashino in 1575, the great general Oda Nobunaga deployed 3,000 *ashigaru* armed with muskets.

Wakazashi
The *wakazashi*, shown here with accompanying scabbard, was a sidearm often used by the samurai to perform *seppuku* (ritual suicide).

Iron *tsuba*
This *tsuba* (metal guard) for a sword is carved and inlaid with a depiction of a samurai under a flowering prunus tree. It dates from the Edo period (1603–1876).

They were protected from the mounted samurai of Takeda Katsuyori by a fence of stakes and by other *ashigaru* armed with long spears. Fired in volleys, the muskets cut down Takeda's horsemen, exposing the Takeda forces to a deadly counterattack.

FOSSILIZED TRADITION

Instead of fading from the limelight with the advent of the gunpowder age, Japanese samurai were preserved and mythified. Toyotomi Hideyoshi, the *daimyo* who rose to dominance in Japan after the death of Nobunaga in 1582, passed decrees restoring the link between samurai status and noble birth. He also gave the samurai a monopoly of bearing arms. Under the Tokugawa shogunate, which pacified Japan in the 17th century, firearms were largely withdrawn from use and as a result the cult of the samurai sword and swordsmanship grew. The *bushido* tradition was codified and glorified as Japan moved into an era of peace. With no enemies to fight, the samurai were elevated to the status of a national treasure, while losing all practical function. The samurai class was finally abolished in 1876 after the Meiji restoration, the Emperor ending their right to be the only armed force in Japan in favor of a modern, Western-style conscripted army. However, the values attributed to the samurai lived on as an essential element in the culture of modern Japan.

> "EVEN IF A MAN HAS NO NATURAL ABILITY HE CAN BE A WARRIOR ... GENERALLY SPEAKING, THE WAY OF THE WARRIOR IS RESOLUTE ACCEPTANCE OF DEATH."
>
> **MIYAMOTO MUSASHI,** *GO RIN NO SHO* (THE BOOK OF FIVE RINGS)

Ritual beheading
A detail of samurai beheading a member of an enemy clan from a scroll painting of *The Burning of the Sanjo Palace.*

SAMURAI ARMOR

The design of Japanese samurai armor centered around two principal functions—to be strong enough to provide adequate protection in battle, and light and flexible enough to permit the free movement needed by a sword-fighter. The style of armor, which has its roots in the Asiatic tradition of *lamellar* (scaled) armor, consists of lacquered plates of metal or leather bound together by silk or leather lacing. This reached a heightened level of sophistication in the *tosei gusoku* (modern armor) style from the 16th century onward, the focus eventually shifting toward decoration.

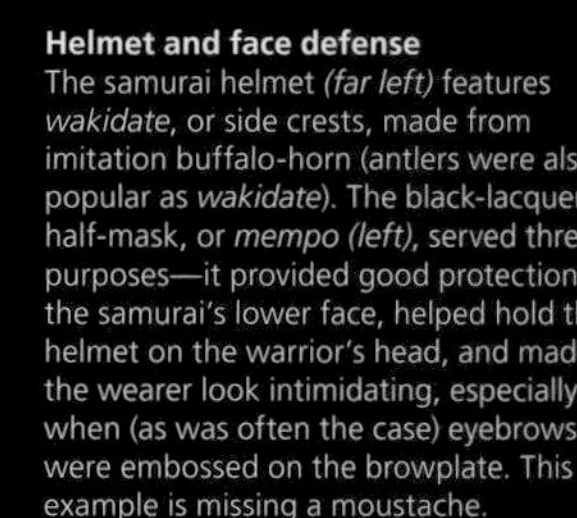

Helmet and face defense
The samurai helmet *(far left)* features *wakidate*, or side crests, made from imitation buffalo-horn (antlers were also popular as *wakidate*). The black-lacquered half-mask, or *mempo (left)*, served three purposes—it provided good protection for the samurai's lower face, helped hold the helmet on the warrior's head, and made the wearer look intimidating, especially when (as was often the case) eyebrows were embossed on the browplate. This example is missing a moustache.

Tosei gusoku (modern armor)
Samurai body armor (*tosei gusoku*) was largely constructed from bamboo, cloth, and metal. Unlike medieval armor, the Japanese example was much lighter, which provided for ease of movement but compromised protection. The armor had to be lightweight because the samurai would often engage in hand-to-hand combat, requiring fast and precise movements. The chest plate is one piece of metal while the arms and neck armor are composed of small pieces of metal bound together with strings.

SAMURAI WEAPONS

Samurai swords were manufactured by a complex process to create a blade of outstanding strength and cutting power. Fighting without a shield, the samurai held the sword two-handed, using his weapon for defense and attack. He blocked enemy blows with the face or back of the sword, which were tempered for resilience and strength. Standing square-on to his opponent, he attacked with a downward slash of the brittle, curved, cutting edge, tempered for extreme hardness.

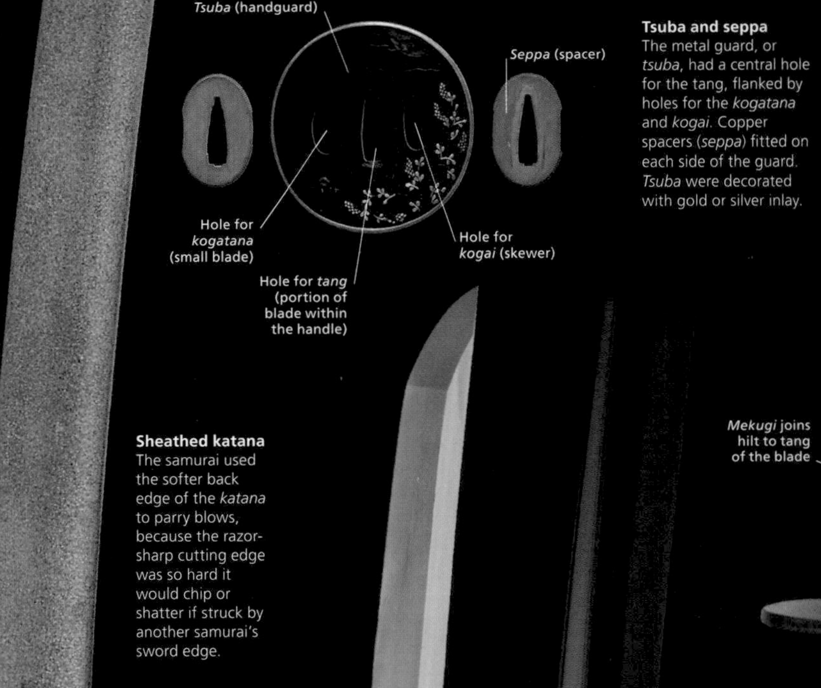

Tsuba and seppa
The metal guard, or *tsuba*, had a central hole for the tang, flanked by holes for the *kogatana* and *kogai*. Copper spacers (*seppa*) fitted on each side of the guard. *Tsuba* were decorated with gold or silver inlay.

Yari
The *yari* was a straight-headed spear. They measured anywhere from 3 ft (1 m) to 20 ft (6 m). The longer versions were called *omi no yari* while the shorter ones were known as *mochi* or *tae yari*. The longest versions were carried by foot troops, while samurai usually carried the shorter versions.

Mosaic decoration on handle

Katana
In the Edo period, the longer sword *(katana)* was worn exclusively by samurai, whereas the *wakazashi* could be carried by merchants and by townsmen. In combat a samurai typically held the *katana* in a two-handed grip, for which the *tsuka* (handle) allows plenty of room.

TANTO

Sheathed katana
The samurai used the softer back edge of the *katana* to parry blows, because the razor-sharp cutting edge was so hard it would chip or shatter if struck by another samurai's sword edge.

Yakiba (hardened edge)

Saya (scabbard)

Mekugi joins hilt to tang of the blade

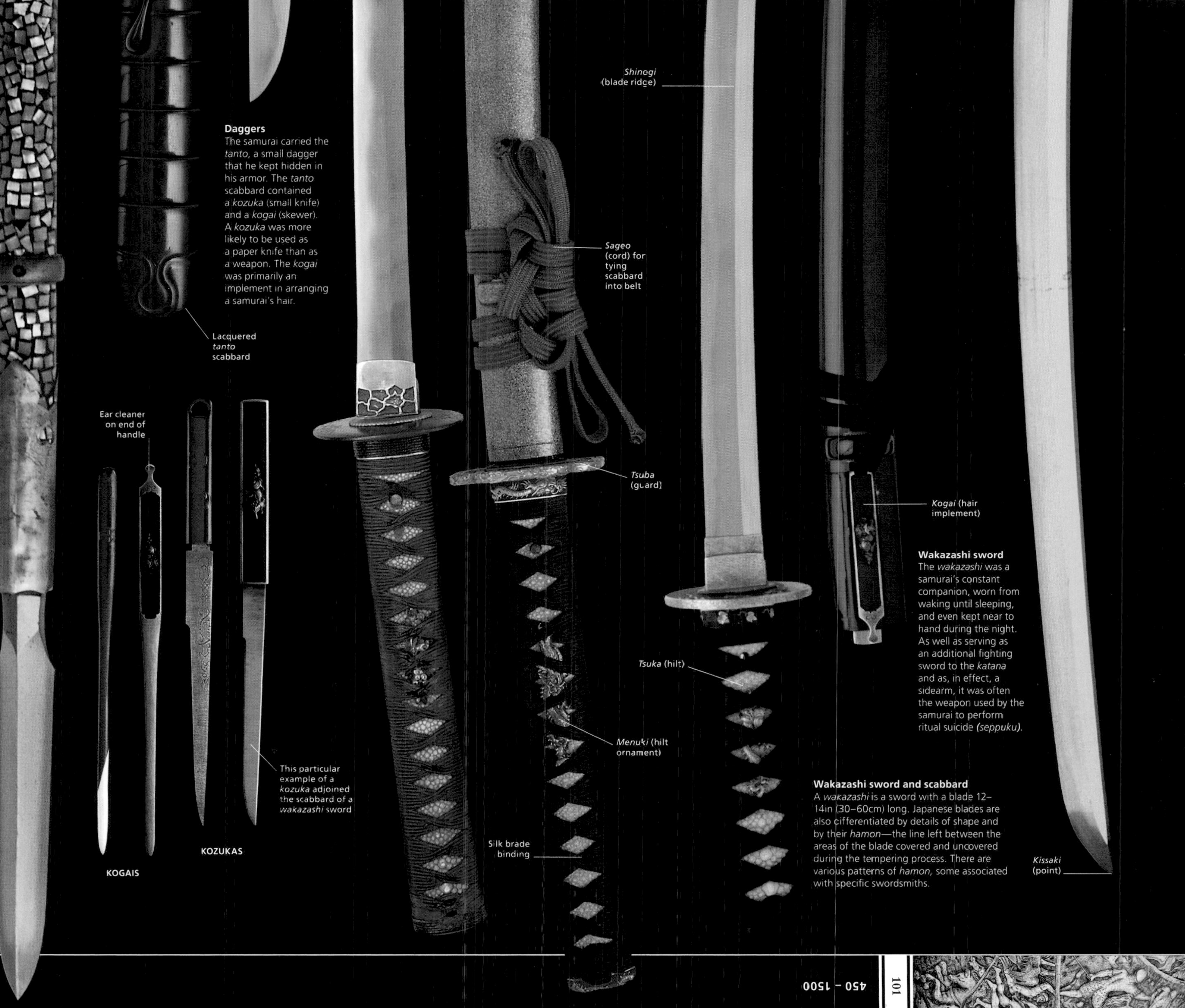

Daggers
The samurai carried the *tanto*, a small dagger that he kept hidden in his armor. The *tanto* scabbard contained a *kozuka* (small knife) and a *kogai* (skewer). A *kozuka* was more likely to be used as a paper knife than as a weapon. The *kogai* was primarily an implement in arranging a samurai's hair.

Wakazashi sword
The *wakazashi* was a samurai's constant companion, worn from waking until sleeping, and even kept near to hand during the night. As well as serving as an additional fighting sword to the *katana* and as, in effect, a sidearm, it was often the weapon used by the samurai to perform ritual suicide *(seppuku)*.

Wakazashi sword and scabbard
A *wakazashi* is a sword with a blade 12–14in (30–60cm) long. Japanese blades are also differentiated by details of shape and by their *hamon*—the line left between the areas of the blade covered and uncovered during the tempering process. There are various patterns of *hamon*, some associated with specific swordsmiths.

Last great samurai battle
Samurai fought in their thousands during the second siege of Osaka Castle in 1615, after the Toyotomi clan broke their treaty with the shogun, Tokugawa Ieyasu. This mural shows samurai armed with bows galloping to meet the enemy.

PRE-COLUMBIAN WARRIORS

Before the arrival of Europeans at the end of the 15th century, the peoples of the Americas had a culture of warfare that had developed independently across thousands of years. In the absence of the horse and of any form of artillery, pre-Columbian forces consisted exclusively of infantry. Weapons were primarily of wood and stone. In many societies a warrior aristocracy commanded on the battlefield, dressed in elaborate decorative costumes. One of the principal aims of warfare was the taking of prisoners for use as slaves or as victims of religious sacrifice. Some states, notably the Aztecs and Incas, assembled substantial armies which enabled them to exert political and military control over large areas that had previously been independent chiefdoms.

THE INCAS

In the second half of the 15th century the Incas established an extensive empire in western South America stretching from northern Ecuador to central Chile. The creation of the empire was largely due to the military skills of the Incas' tenth ruler, Topa Inca (reigned 1471–93) who led campaigns of conquest both before and after ascending the throne. His military operations showed a rare degree of organizational skill. On one occasion, for example, the south of the empire was threatened by the Calchaqui people from northern Argentina crossing the mountains to the Pacific coast. Topa Inca marched his forces 600 miles (1,000 km) down the Andes from his capital at Cuzco in Peru. Engineers went ahead of the army building mountain roads and bridges, while supplies of weapons and food were carried south by sea on balsa rafts. Resupplied on reaching the coast, the Inca army threw itself upon the Calchaqui and defeated them in battle.

At its height the Inca empire was a thoroughly militaristic state. From the age of 12, boys were toughened up with a routine of strenuous games and exercise. Then, from the age of 15 to 20, they had to perform compulsory military service. A minority of young conscripts stayed on to make a career in the army and a few achieved high position as a reward for conspicuous bravery. The Inca bureaucracy ensured that the army was well fed and clothed. The most common weapons were the slingshot and the stone-edged spear or ax. Members of the Inca clan, who constituted the nobility of the empire and made up the higher command of the army, sometimes carried axes of bronze. On campaign they would march alongside their ruler, who was carried on a litter. The Inca army was accompanied by a baggage train of llamas, and of women bowed down under their enormous loads. A large part of the Inca army was made up of contingents from subject peoples, some of doubtful loyalty. It was dissension within the empire, and civil war between members of the ruling Inca clan itself, that exposed the empire to European conquest in the 16th century. Nonetheless, it took the Spanish 50 years, from the 1520s to the 1570s, to fully subdue the Inca people.

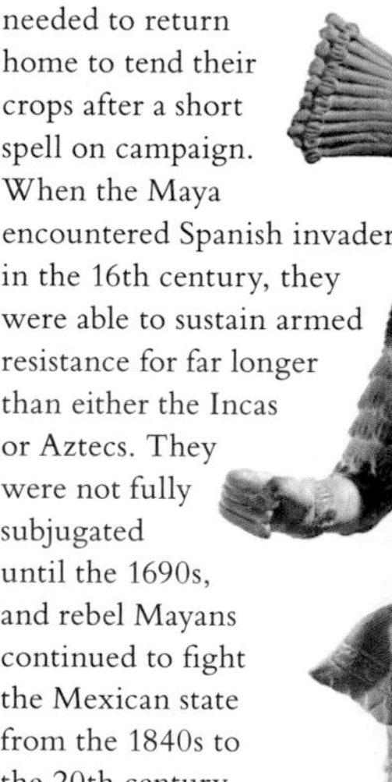

Inca warrior
Elaborate feathered headdresses were part of the war costume of many American peoples, serving as symbols of warrior status.

> "COME LET US EAT, AND COME LET US DRINK ... LET US EAT AND DRINK OF THE BLOOD AND THE BONES OF OUR ENEMY." INCA WAR CHANT

THE MAYA

The Maya civilization of eastern Central America, which reached its peak in around 250 to 900 CE, was once thought to have been averse to warfare. But in recent years historians have revised their opinions, concluding that the Maya fought wars of conquest and took prisoners to use as slaves and for ritual sacrifice.

The bulk of their forces were probably peasant militia led by warriors drawn from royal and noble families. Temple wall paintings show armies with splendid regalia—warriors decked out in masks and plumes, carrying standards and shields decorated with religious symbols. More prosaically, soldiers were equipped with quilted jackets as armor and carried a range of edged and missile weapons, including spears, stone-bladed wooden axes, throwing sticks, slingshots and bows. It is assumed that conflicts were brief, if bloody, since the peasant militia would have needed to return home to tend their crops after a short spell on campaign. When the Maya encountered Spanish invaders in the 16th century, they were able to sustain armed resistance for far longer than either the Incas or Aztecs. They were not fully subjugated until the 1690s, and rebel Mayans continued to fight the Mexican state from the 1840s to the 20th century.

Tomb fighter
This terracotta warrior comes from a Maya tomb on Jaina island, off Yucatan.

THE AZTECS

In the 15th century the Aztecs were the most powerful people in Mesoamerica, dominating over other city-states in a large area around their capital, Tenochtitlan. Their army, organized into legions 8,000 strong, was frequently on campaign, engaged in wars to extend the empire or suppress rebellion among the tributaries.

When no practical motive for warfare presented itself, the Aztecs arranged "flower wars." A tributary state was obliged to present its forces for battle at a specified time and place, to give the Aztecs practice in fighting and provide a fresh supply of prisoners. Taking prisoners was essential to Aztec life because it provided victims for human sacrifice. It also allowed an Aztec warrior to achieve promotion. His status depended on the number of enemy fighters he captured. Thus Aztec warriors struck at the legs of their opponents, seeking to disable them, rather than killing them with a blow to the head. The most successful warriors joined the elite orders of jaguar or eagle "knights." The Aztecs were not always victorious in pre-Columbian times. For example, in 1478 they lost a battle with the neighboring Tarascans. But they were fierce, courageous fighters.

> "PONDER THIS, EAGLE AND JAGUAR KNIGHTS, THOUGH ... CARVED IN JADE, YOU WILL BREAK."
>
> FROM A POEM BY **KING NEZAHUALCOYOTL** OF TEXCOCO, 15TH CENTURY

Strings of feathers

Pieces of obsidian

Wood

Feathered shield and war club
Aztec warriors often carried round shields decorated with jaguar skin and feathers. Their wooden war clubs were edged with razor-sharp pieces of volcanic glass.

Aztec downfall
Cortez, the leader of the Spanish conquistadors, battles the Aztecs for the causeway to their island capital Tenochtitlan in 1520.

1500 – 1775

PIKEMEN AND MUSKETEERS

During the period 1500–1775, the nature of warfare in Europe changed radically with the development of gunpowder weapons. Firearms evolved from the slow and unreliable arquebus and the equally unwieldy matchlock musket to the far superior flintlock. Artillery improved in its variety, mobility, and rate of fire. The pike was eventually to be supplanted by the bayonet. Even more significant than these technological developments, however, were the fundamental changes in the methods with which European armies were recruited and organized, and in their battlefield tactics.

MERCENARIES TO REGULARS

In the 16th century, standing armies were only a small part of European forces. The most typical fighting man was the mercenary, part of a company that sold its services to a monarch preparing for war. Mercenary bands of Swiss pikemen and German Landsknechts fought on the same battlefields, and broadly with the same tactics, as Spanish *tercios*, which were formations of regular soldiers, containing both pikemen and musketeers, in the permanent employ of the king of Spain. It was often impossible to tell the difference between mercenaries and regulars whether on or off the battlefield. Both were liable to mutiny when their payment failed—as it frequently did—and turn to the plunder and massacre of civilians.

Pikemen on the defensive
English Civil War soldiers form a lethal hedge of pikes. One of the duties of the pikemen, who wore breastplates and helmets, was to defend the unarmored musketeers from attack.

Change in the 17th century was slow at first. Despite the efforts of Dutch ruler Maurice of Nassau (1567–1625) and Swedish king Gustav Adolf (1594–1632) to improve army organization, it was only through the second half of the century that regular armed forces, permanently employed by the state and fitted with standard uniforms, gradually became the norm. Mercenary captains and aristocratic cavalrymen were transmuted into officers in the standing army, and received a defined rank. Mercenaries continued to be employed only in the form of companies of foreign soldiers hired from their ruler, rather than from private entrepreneurs. Perfected in the Prussian army of Frederick the Great (1713–86), draconian discipline and rigorous drill sought to make the infantryman, recruited from the lowest levels of society, into an automaton capable of holding firm on the battlefield regardless of his personal qualities. More regular pay and supply reduced the plunder and looting previously associated with military operations.

INFANTRY TACTICS

From the start of the 16th century and well into the second half of the 17th century, infantry tactics in Europe were based upon the use of tight squares of pikemen flanked by soldiers with firearms. At first, the firearms were used as an ancillary to the all-important pikes, but over time the number and effectiveness of musketeers grew, while the significance of the pikemen diminished. In the last decades of the 17th century the introduction of the flintlock musket and of socket bayonets led to the disappearance of the pike from the battlefield. By the early 18th century, European infantry were formidable, disciplined bodies, trained to fire in volleys and march unarmored into cannon and musket fire.

VARIED CAVALRY

The cavalry, seen as more prestigious, remained the standard place for the aristocracy, even if the increasing size of European armies meant that its lower ranks had to be opened to commoners. Horsemen struggled to find the most effective battlefield tactics, however, in the face of increasing firepower. The full armor and lance of the medieval knight had been abandoned by the end of the 16th century, but heavy cavalry still remained decisive shock troops—Gustav Adolf, the king of Sweden, was killed leading a cavalry charge at Lutzen in 1632. Along with a sword, cavalrymen adopted firearms such as pistols or carbines—the famous elite French musketeers were mounted troops.

Armored dragoons, riding to battle but dismounting in order to fight with their firearms, became an important element of European armies. So too did light cavalry, used for reconnaissance, skirmishing, and raiding. The example for these dashing horsemen was set by the impressive Polish winged hussars and the Russian Cossacks.

Mughal battle
The forces of Mughal emperor Akbar (reigned 1556–1605) fought with curved, slashing *talwar* swords in the warrior spirit of Islam, but combined these traditional weapons with up-to-date artillery.

OUTSIDE EUROPE

The surprisingly easy victories of the Spanish conquistadors over the large armies of Central America and Peru in the 16th century could give a false impression of European military superiority over the rest of the world. In fact, for much of this period there were armies outside Europe equal or superior in their organization, technology, and tactics. In the 1520s, when Hernán Cortés and his followers were crushing the Aztec Empire in Mexico, Muslim Ottoman forces shattered a Christian Hungarian army at Mohács and laid siege to Vienna, the capital of the Habsburg Empire.

Gunpowder weapons were successfully adopted in both Africa and Asia. Moroccan forces used muskets and cannon on military expeditions south of the Sahara in the 1590s. The Manchu armies that conquered China in the mid-17th century deployed large cannon to decisive effect. In Japan, arquebusiers firing in volleys gave Oda Nobunaga victory at the battle of Nagashino in 1575. The creation of the Mughal Empire in India is partly attributable to skilful employment of cannon by the empire's founder, Babur, at the battle of Panipat in 1526.

The major Islamic states of the Mughals, the Ottomans, and Safavid Persia at best effectively combined the virtues of a traditional warrior ethic with up-to-date weaponry. The Ottoman army had skirmishing light horsemen fighting in a long-established Central Asian style, heavy cavalry based on a semi-feudal system, high-quality disciplined infantry (the janissary slave-soldiers), and varied artillery. The decay of the once excellent Ottoman forces, well under way by the 1650s, reflected not so much specifically military failings as an irreversible institutional decay within the Ottoman Empire.

By the end of the 17th century there were already clear signs that European armies were gaining a lead over their extra-European rivals. Armies of the Muslim world were slow to replace the matchlock musket with the flintlock, while the Chinese, the original inventors of gunpowder weapons, came to depend upon European experts to maintain their artillery. Asian armies began to look unwieldy and disorganized compared to the disciplined, uniformed standing armies of 18th-century Europe—formidable forces on an open battlefield. Discipline and firepower opened the way for the age of European world domination.

1486 – 1550

LANDSKNECHT

“WE TOOK ROME BY STORM, PUT OVER 6,000 MEN TO THE SWORD, SEIZED ALL THAT WE COULD FIND IN CHURCHES ... AND BURNED DOWN A GREAT PART OF THE CITY, TAKING APART AND DESTROYING ALL.”

PAUL DOLSTEIN, LANDSKNECHT, ON THE SACK OF ROME, 1527

GARISHLY-DRESSED LANDSKNECHT mercenaries were a constant presence on the European battlefields of the late 15th and 16th centuries. Fighting as dense formations of pikemen supported by firearms, they were at their best exceptionally tough foot soldiers in combat. Out of battle, however, they could be a danger to all and sundry, especially if their employer failed to keep them adequately paid and fed. Quarrelsome and resistant to authority, the Landsknechts earned a fearsome reputation for plunder and massacre.

The first Landsknecht bands were raised in 1486, at a time when significant changes were taking place in European warfare. The breakup of the medieval social order was leaving rulers ever more dependent upon mercenary troops, rather than forces assembled on the basis of feudal loyalty or obligation. In France and Burgundy, mercenaries had been taken into permanent employment to form regular armies. At the same time, tactical innovations were questioning the role of heavy cavalry as the shock offensive force on the battlefield. At the battles of Murten and Nancy, in 1476–77, Swiss infantry armed with long pikes won notable victories through attacking their enemy in tight, massed phalanxes. Lacking both a regular army and pike wielding infantry, German Emperor Maximilian I felt threatened by these military developments. His response was to pay for the formation of Landsknecht ("land servant") bands. These were to be infantry paid as mercenaries, but ready to fight for the emperor when required.

FORMING UP

The soldiers who formed and led mercenary companies had to be both military leaders and ambitious entrepreneurs. A mercenary captain would contract with the emperor to provide a certain number of soldiers and receive the payment for their services, hoping to cream off a handsome profit. Landsknechts were mostly recruited from German-speaking areas of central and northern Europe, such as the Rhineland, Swabia, and Alsace. Men could be attracted from far afield, however, with even Scotland providing volunteers. The immediate lure was the promise of four guilders a month in pay—a reasonable income for the day and immensely tempting to anyone down on his luck. Beyond this there were all the traditional benefits of contemporary military life on offer, from the chance to indulge in looting and pillage to the amusements of a vagabond life rich in adventure and general hellraising.

A potential recruit had to present himself equipped with, at minimum, a 16–20 ft (5–6 m) long pike. Since such a weapon could be purchased for one guilder—a cheapness that goes a long way to explain the popularity of the pike as an infantry arm—most men were capable of fulfilling this obligation. The better-off might turn up with swords, armor, or even an arquebus. A candidate was traditionally subjected to a simple fitness test, being required to jump over an obstacle made of three pikes or halberds. This done, he was considered fit for service and his name was entered in the roll.

Given these less-than-stringent entrance requirements, the Landsknechts must have been of uneven quality. A successful mercenary captain needed a sharp eye for the individual qualities of his men. Deploying pikemen in battle in a tight mass formation had the considerable advantage of allowing him to hide inexperienced soldiers. As long as the front ranks advanced boldly into combat, and the back row were stout characters who would not turn and run, the men in the middle had no choice but to hold their position and go along with the crowd. The boldest, fiercest fighters were rewarded with double pay—hence their name *doppelsöldner*, which translates as "double-pay men"—and deployed independently to attack with double-handed broadsword or halberd.

CEREMONIAL BROADSWORD

Renaissance mercenaries
Dressed in a flamboyant style that typified the Renaissance era, the Landsknechts were the German answer to the Swiss soldiers of the day. The majority were pikemen, but the elite *doppelsöldners (above)* wreaked havoc with their halberds and double-handed broadswords *(right)*.

Battle of Marengo
Swiss and Landsknecht mercenaries clash at Marengo in 1515. A short *katzbalger* sword can be seen raised in the foregound; it proved highly effective at close quarters.

The Landsknechts also formed elite *blutfahnen* (blood banner) units that made near-suicidal attacks on especially well-defended enemy positions. The arquebusiers who provided the Landsknechts' firepower did not need to be especially well trained. Indeed, one of the advantages of firearms was that almost anyone could be taught to use them, whatever their personal qualities; a pike or halberd, by contrast, required considerable strength to use.

> "IT WAS SO HOT THAT THE ARMORED MEN NEARLY SUFFOCATED ... AND WHEN ONE WENT TO HELP THE OTHER BY LOOSENING THE ARMOR HE WOULD BURN HIS FINGERS ON THE METAL."
>
> **NIKLAUS GULDI**, LANDSKNECHT SOLDIER, ON THE TUNIS EXPEDITION, 1535

STYLE AND VIOLENCE

Exactly how the Landsknechts developed their distinctive swaggering style of dress is not clear, although it seems to have been based on the costume of their greatest rivals, the Swiss Confederates, only greatly exaggerated. As well as favoring broad flat hats crowned with large feathers and jerkins sporting puffed sleeves, the Landsknechts adopted hose with the legs of different colors and developed the custom of slashing their doublets open and pulling "puffs" of shirt through from underneath. A look that expressed arrogance and nonconformity, it became a major influence on Renaissance fashion.

Landsknecht captain
A mounted captain, holding a spear used for directing troops, addresses his bodyguard before battle.

Whether the Landsknechts were any wilder or more ungodly than the general run of fighting men in their period is hard to say. They were certainly much given to hard drink and gambling, which occupied the dead time out of combat. Many are known to have been killed in fights with their comrades rather than with the enemy, with luck at dice and cards often the source of the discord. Like all mercenary bands, they were liable to cause trouble when there was no war to provide them with an outlet for their energies and legitimate sources of plunder at the expense of the enemy. It was the failure of employers to pay them that provoked the most serious Landsknecht disturbances. The most infamous example was the sack of Rome in 1527. Unpaid Landsknechts mutinied from the army of Charles V, the Holy Roman Emperor, and went on the rampage, seeking to make up what they were owed through pillage. With other imperial troops (some 35,000 in all), they attacked and laid waste the city during a reign of terror that lasted nine months. The mercenaries refused to leave the city until they were paid their arrears of wages.

FIGHTING REGIMENTS

As fighting forces, the Landsknechts were at their peak in the early 16th century. From 1508, under the leadership of a German knight, Georg von Frundsberg, Emperor Maximilian I's Landsknechts were organized into a regiment more than 10,000 strong, which fought with distinction in a series of campaigns in Italy. But in these Italian wars there were often Landsknechts also fighting on the other side. Officially the Landsknechts were

Steel skull cap
This light, close-fitting skull cap was worn by a Landsknecht soldier c.1510. Secured with a chinstrap, it afforded all-round vision as well as essential protection.

not permitted to fight for the emperor's enemies, but finding imperial pay inadequate or insufficiently reliable, companies sought a different master. The French king, François I, was able to buy the services of a "Black Band" regiment of renegade Landsknechts at least similar in numbers to the imperial mercenaries.

In 1515, François I led an army across the Alps into Italy to fight the Swiss for possession of Milan. At Marengo, on September 13–14, the confident Swiss pikemen, considered the supreme infantry force in Europe, attacked the French king's lines full tilt. But the Landsknechts absorbed the momentum of the charging phalanx and the two forces of pikemen swayed back and forth in a deadly pushing contest. An eventual French victory, after some 28 hours of intermittent butchery, depended as much upon François' cavalry and artillery as upon the foot soldiers. But the defeat of the Swiss inevitably sent the Landsknechts' stock soaring. In 1525, when the army of the new emperor, Charles V, took on the French at Pavia, the Landsknechts were at the heart of the combat on both sides. The imperial pikemen made a vital contribution to a crushing victory for Charles' forces, but the Black Band earned the greater fame by fighting to the last man after the rest of the French army had fled the field.

LATE DECLINE

The Landsknechts never performed with this level of commitment again. Fighting as "lansquenets" during the French Wars of Religion in the second half of the 16th century, they were sometimes disparaged even by those who employed them. Spain's general, the Duke of Alva, entrusted with suppressing the Dutch revolt, claimed that he bought the Landknechts' services not because they were any use in battle, but so that they could not appear fighting on the other side. Whatever their later decadence, however, the Landsknechts had left an enduring legend as the quintessential Renaissance mercenaries.

LANDSKNECHT TACTICAL FORMATIONS

The Landsknechts' battle tactics were primarily designed for symmetrical combat against the opposing army's pikemen. Unlike the Swiss, the Landsknechts do not seem to have used their pike phalanx for a shock charge into the enemy line. Instead they typically stood on the defensive or advanced at a steady grinding pace. As two dense pike-wielding phalanxes approached one another, arquebusiers or crossbowmen on the flanks of the Landsknecht phalanx would fire into the enemy ranks, hoping to weaken and disrupt their formation. At the same time the fearsome Landsknecht *doppelsöldner* would advance ahead of the mass of pikes, attacking the enemy pikemen with blows from their halberds and massive two-handed swords. If the Landsknechts retained formation, their pikemen were invulnerable to all but missile weapons, their pikes forming an unbreachable barrier. Once the formation was disrupted, however, the pike was a clumsy weapon. Most Landsknechts carried a short sword, the *katzbalger*, for close-quarters combat.

Gevierte ordnung

Adopted from the Swiss, this *gevierte ordnung* (square order) formation was typically made by a single *fähnlein* (company) of 400 men. It was often preceded by an advance party, or "forlorn hope," of criminals, prisoners, and volunteers seeking promotion. A regiment consisted of ten *fähnleins*.

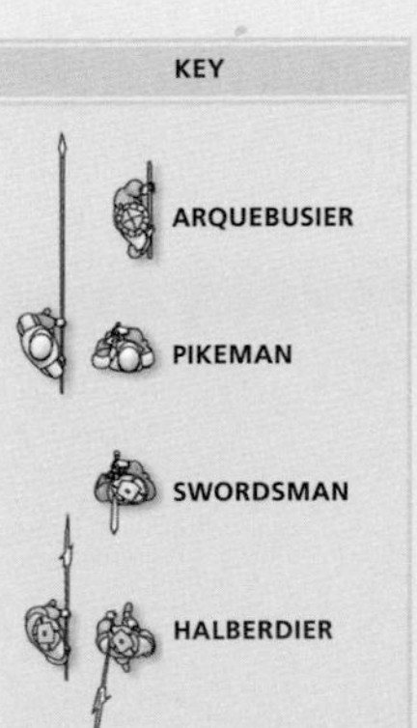

Defensive igel

When attacked by cavalry, the *fähnlein* would form a defensive *igel* (hedgehog). Arquebusiers retreated to the third row, while pikemen came forward with pikes extended in all directions. (The numbers shown here are greatly reduced.)

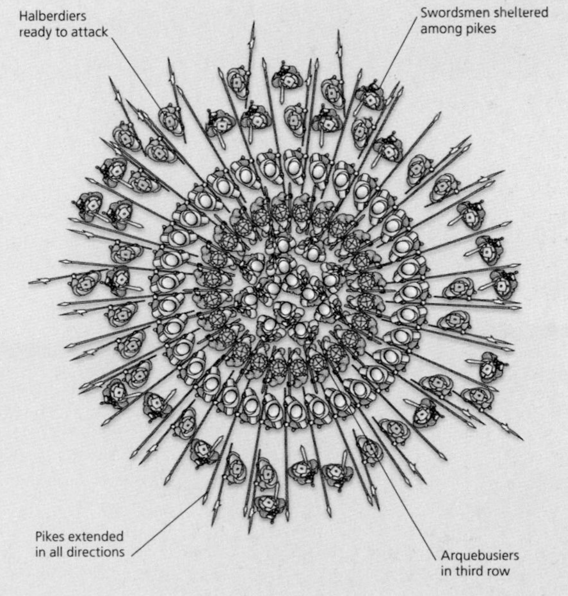

LANDSKNECHT ARMS

As always in the history of warfare, status was an important consideration in the weapons and armor of a Landsknecht. To own body armor or a two-handed sword was to be a man of considerable standing. The halberd, however, had intermediate status, and became a symbolic attribute of junior officers. The pike was most basic of all, but without it a man could not become a Landsknecht. Firearms generally had low status as the soldiers who fired them did not fight in close combat.

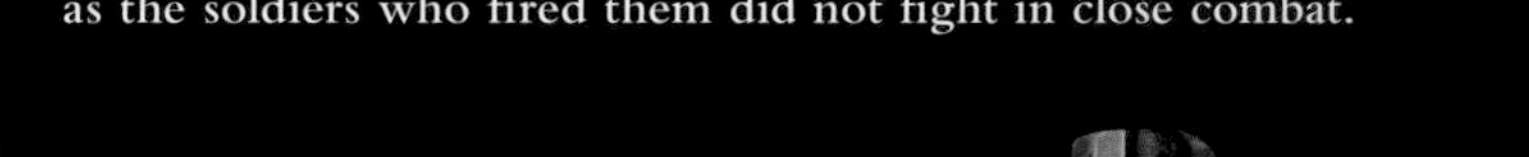

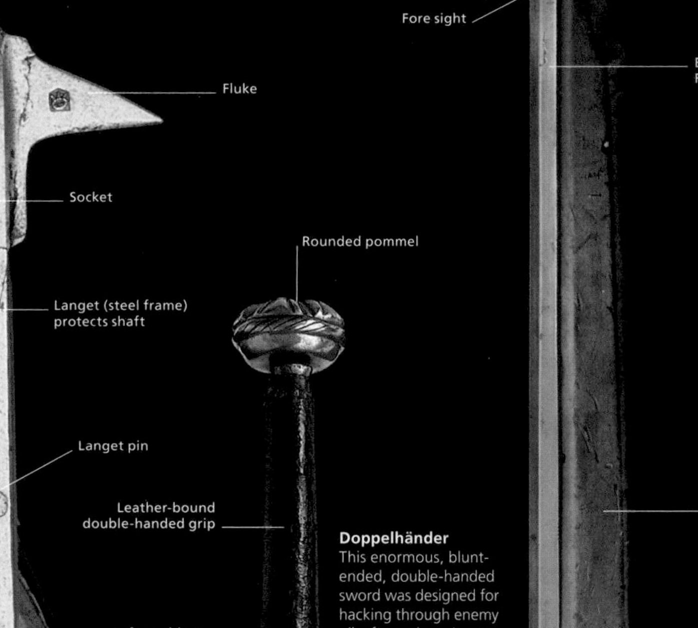

Pike
Between 14 and 18 ft (4 and 5 m) long, the pike was the principal weapon of the Landsknecht. The steel head was mounted on a shaft of ash.

Halberd
Developed by the Swiss in the 13th century, the halberd was chiefly a slashing weapon, although its spike could be used for thrusting. This Landsknecht version dates from 1500.

Doppelhänder
This enormous, blunt-ended, double-handed sword was designed for hacking through enemy pike formations. It was also used for executions.

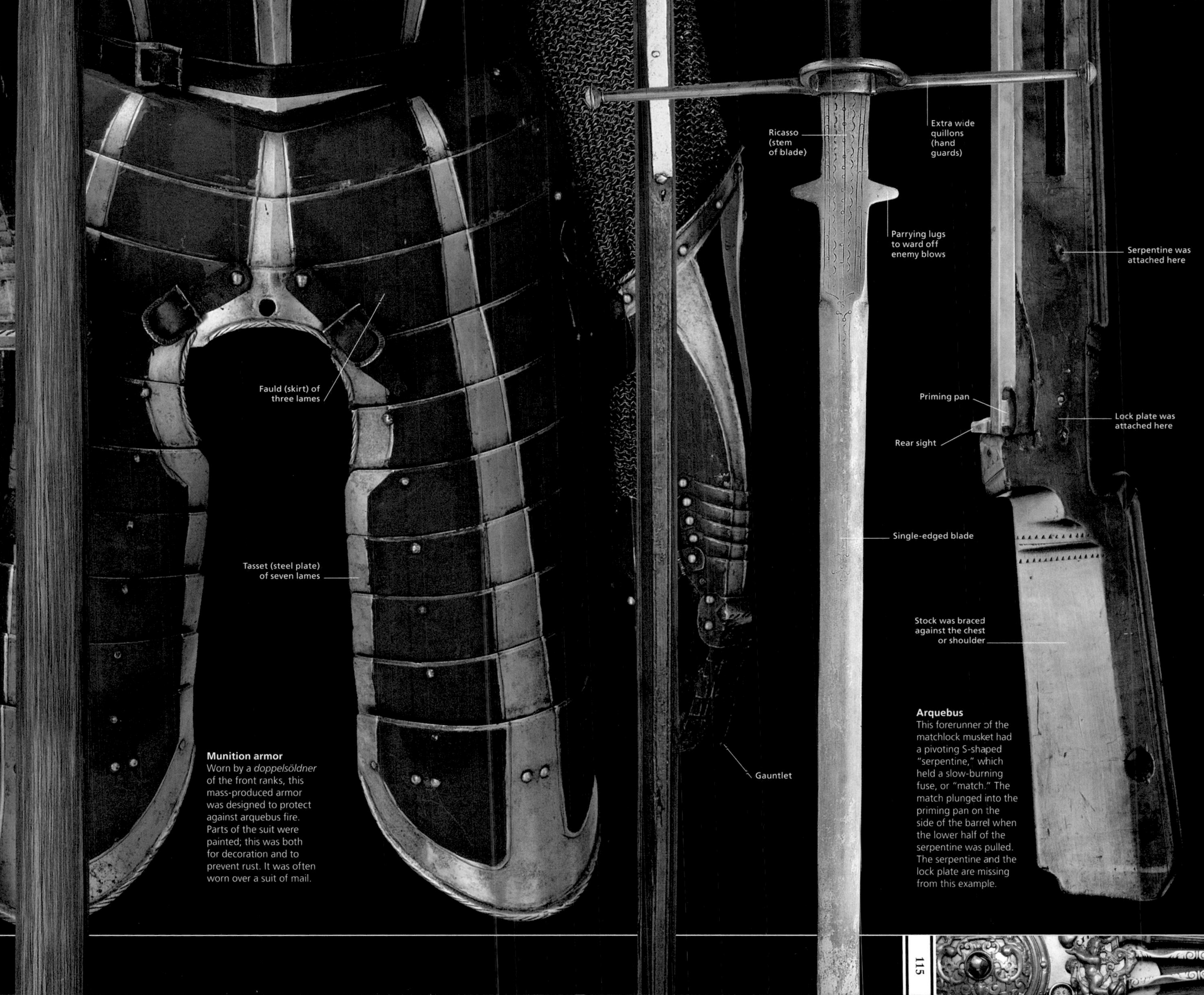

Munition armor
Worn by a *doppelsöldner* of the front ranks, this mass-produced armor was designed to protect against arquebus fire. Parts of the suit were painted; this was both for decoration and to prevent rust. It was often worn over a suit of mail.

Arquebus
This forerunner of the matchlock musket had a pivoting S-shaped "serpentine," which held a slow-burning fuse, or "match." The match plunged into the priming pan on the side of the barrel when the lower half of the serpentine was pulled. The serpentine and the lock plate are missing from this example.

FOOT SOLDIERS OF THE RENAISSANCE

The Renaissance was a period when new technologies, in the form of firearms and cannon, had a profound impact on war. Yet simultaneously Europeans sought to learn from the classical world in warfare, as well as in art and architecture. The study of Ancient Greece and Rome convinced military thinkers that disciplined infantry were the key to success in battle, although attempts to recreate the order and discipline of the Roman army foundered upon the financial and organizational weaknesses of European states. Soldiers remained diversely clad, cynically mercenary, and dangerously prone to plunder and mutiny. Forces that successfully combined firearms with pike formations similar to the Greek phalanx had the edge on the battlefield.

SWISS PIKEMAN

The pikemen of the Swiss Confederation won an immediate name for themselves in 1476, when they trounced the mighty Burgundian army at the battles of Grandson and Murten. The Swiss foot soldiers were militia called up for service by their cantons (self-governing districts), and their style of fighting expressed the solidarity of their egalitarian society. Forming dense columns armed with pikes or halberds, they attacked shoulder-to-shoulder at a trot, overrunning their enemies before their cannon or cavalry could mount an effective riposte.

After their victories over the Burgundians, the Swiss were in great demand as mercenaries. From the 1490s they were either hired out en masse by a canton to a foreign employer, or served in independent mercenary bands. Garishly dressed in striped hose and puffed sleeves, they always sought to take the offensive, depending on the momentum of their massed columns to steamroller the opposition. A few crossbowmen or arquebusiers might accompany the pikes and halberds, but their role was peripheral.

GERMAN COMPETITION

In the course of the Italian Wars of 1494 to 1525 the Swiss scored some notable successes, especially the defeat of the French at Novara in 1513. But other forces imitated their dense pike formation, particularly the Landsknecht mercenaries, who became the Swiss soldiers' bitterest enemies. And the limitations of Swiss tactics were revealed as armies learned how to combine pikes with a sophisticated use of firepower. At the battle of Bicocca in 1521 the Swiss ranks were decimated by fire from arquebuses and cannon after their initial "push of pike" had been blocked by field fortifications.

The Swiss, however, put in a lackluster performance on the losing side at the battle of Pavia in 1525, which effectively ended their period of ascendancy among European infantry. They continued to fight as mercenaries in the service of the French monarchy, however, throughout the religious wars in the second half of the 16th century.

16TH-CENTURY SWISS HALBERD

Swiss triumph at Grandson, 1476
The battle turned when the Burgundian knights were surprised by the opportune arrival of a second force of well-disciplined Swiss pikemen and fled in disarray.

SPANISH TERCIOS

After the unification of Spain had been completed with the conquest of Granada in 1492, the Spanish monarchy created a standing army to protect its interests abroad. The first infantry companies *(capitanias)* were sent to fight in Italy in 1496; they were organized into 12-company *tercios* in 1534.

HARDENED PROFESSIONALS

Whereas the majority of the soldiers serving Spain were foreign, the *tercios* consisted entirely of Spanish volunteers. They were an elite force, thoroughly trained and organized by the standards of their time. Service was in principle for life, so a core of veterans built up with experience of garrison duties in Italy, expeditions to Muslim North Africa, and sustained warfare against the Dutch in Flanders. On the battlefield, the *tercios'* heavily armored pikemen fought in dense squares, flanked by soldiers with firearms. They were also capable of operating in small units, with groups of skirmishing arquebusiers harassing the enemy, supported by soldiers with halberds.

The *tercios* suffered from the limitations of their time. In practice, pikemen often had little or no armor. Although soldiers were supposed to receive monthly wages, pay was often in arrears, leading to mutinies and to the sacking of cities in pursuit of payment in kind. About ten percent of soldiers deserted every year, disgruntled over harsh discipline and irregular pay. Yet the *tercios* remained the most effective infantry in Europe until defeat by the French at Rocroi in 1643 marked the end of their dominance.

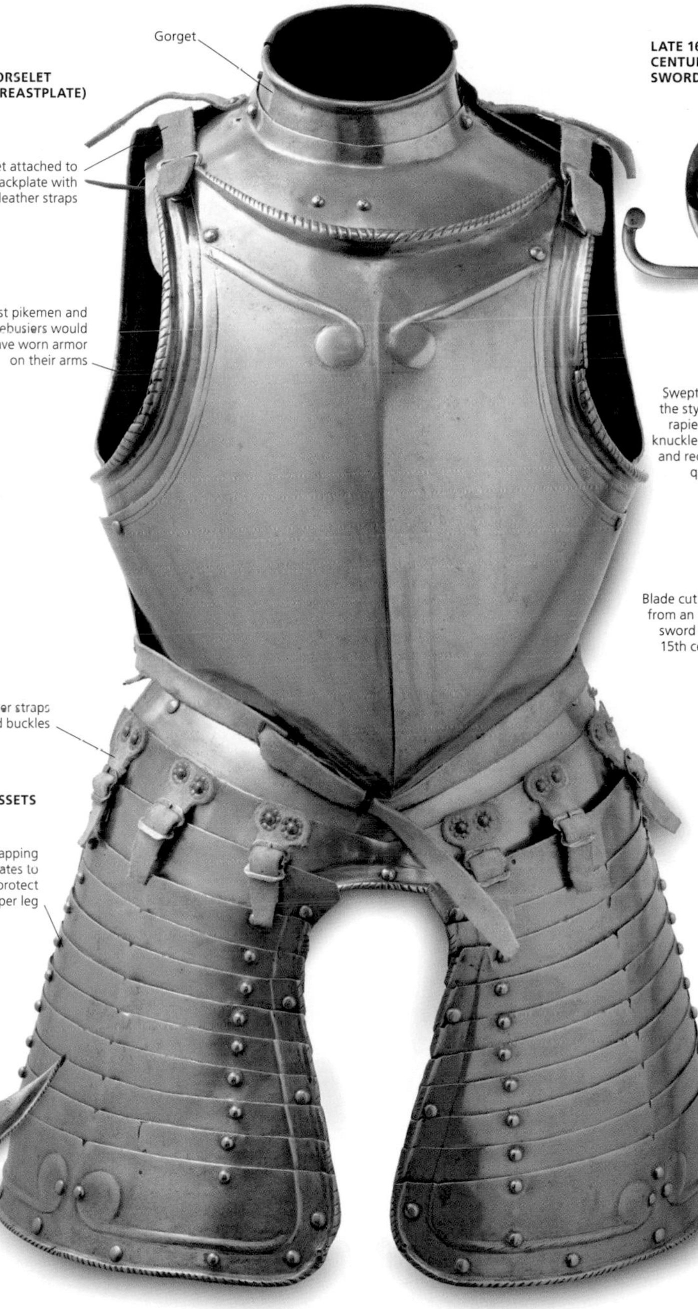

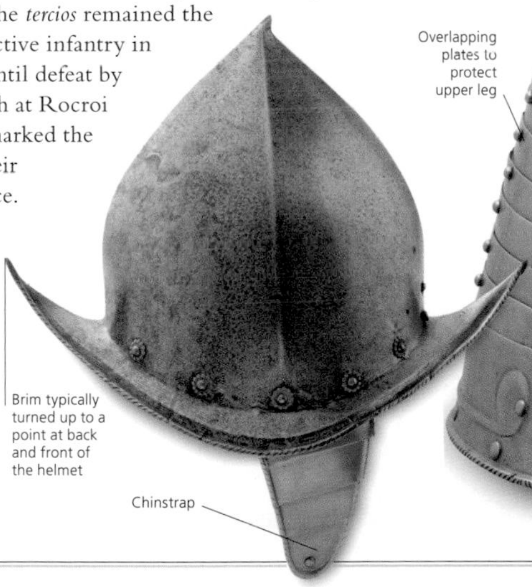

Spanish armor
Only in a very well-equipped *tercio* would all the men have been issued with half armor and a "morion" helmet. The armor was often made in Italy, where Spain had extensive possessions. A small number of the pikemen would also have carried swords.

> "AS THEIR VALIANCE WAS TO BE MUCH COMMENDED, YET CAN I MUCH DISCOMMEND THEIR BARBAROUS CRUELTY."
>
> **GEORGE GASCOIGNE**, EYEWITNESS TO THE SACK OF ANTWERP BY SPANISH TROOPS, 1576

1300 – 1700

OTTOMAN SOLDIER

ALL THROUGH THE DAY THE TURKS MADE A GREAT SLAUGHTER OF CHRISTIANS. BLOOD FLOWED LIKE RAIN WATER IN THE GUTTERS AFTER A SUDDEN STORM, AND CORPSES FLOATED OUT TO SEA LIKE MELONS ALONG A CANAL.

NICOLO BARBARO ON THE FALL OF CONSTANTINOPLE, 1453

Ottoman expansion
Suleyman the Magnificent (1494–1566) at the Battle of Mohacs in 1526 *(above)* and a 17th-century Ottoman helmet *(right)*. Under Suleyman's leadership, the Ottoman Empire reached its Golden Age and became a world power. He led Ottoman armies to conquer Belgrade, Rhodes, and most of Hungary, laid the Siege of Vienna, and annexed much of the Middle East.

AT THE START OF THE 16TH CENTURY the army of the Turkish Ottoman Empire was probably the most effective fighting force in the world. It was a unique mix of different kinds of fighting men, well rewarded and organized, and with high morale as a result of an unbroken string of victories. The most famous element in the Ottoman army were the janissaries, slave-soldiers trained from a young age who formed an infantry elite, but cavalry and artillery played just as important a role in the sultan's wars against Christian and Muslim powers.

The Ottomans originated as a band of a few hundred Turkish ghazis—fierce Muslim tribal warriors—who established control over an area of Anatolia during the 13th century. They were neighbors of the Byzantine Empire, still a major state but by then entering an advanced stage of disintegration. Under Osman (who ruled 1281 to 1326) and his successors, the Ottomans exploited Byzantine weakness to infiltrate into Europe, taking over the Balkans in the course of the 14th century. They finally seized the Byzantine capital, Constantinople, in 1453 and made it the center of their empire. In the 16th century their armies penetrated Christian Europe up to the walls of Vienna, while they also battled the Persian Safavids and the Egyptian Mamluks, taking control of North Africa and much of the Middle East. These extraordinary wide-ranging conquests were achieved by a military system that exploited the best of a number of different fighting traditions and technologies.

GOOD LEARNERS

Initially, the Ottomans fought in the style of steppe horsemen. They were mounted archers using the composite bow as their main weapon and generally avoiding close-quarters combat. Swift-moving, missile-armed cavalry would remain an important element of Ottoman forces throughout the peak years of their empire, but they could not have achieved the success they did without developing highly effective heavy cavalry, infantry, and artillery, as well as creating their own navy. One of the most striking aspects of Ottoman rule in the 15th and 16th centuries was the readiness with which they adapted to new ways of making war. A European observer commented that "no nation has shown less reluctance to adopt the useful inventions of others." The Ottomans mimicked Christian Europe in the adoption of firearms, progressing from the arquebus, via the matchlock musket, to the flintlock (although they never created Euopean-style bodies of pikemen). They were similarly swift to equip their army with cannon, initially by purchasing the skills of European experts. Mehmed the Conqueror famously employed a Hungarian, known as Urban, to found the great guns with which he battered the walls of Constantinople in 1453. Although the Ottomans became renowned for their use of extra large cannon in siege warfare, they did not neglect lighter field artillery, which always formed an effective part of their armies.

COMPLEX FORCES

The forces of the mature Ottoman Empire centered around a standing army of household soldiers in the direct pay of the sultan. These permanent forces included the sultan's elite infantry bodyguard, the janissaries, who at least until the late 17th century were slave-soldiers, and non-slave cavalry. When the sultan embarked on a military campaign, this relatively small regular army was augmented by provincial forces raised through the *timar* system, which was in some ways akin to European feudalism. Horsemen known as *sipahis* were given the right to raise rent from an area of land in return for military duties. They were required to present themselves for service along with a certain number of their followers, equipped for war, at the bidding of the sultan.

RAWHIDE CHICHAK (HELMET) WITH COPPER GILT

Ottoman campaigns
The Siege of Belgrade in 1456 led by Sultan Mehmet II "The Conqueror" *(right)* and the typical arms and armor of an Ottoman soldier *(far right)*. The siege eventually escalated into a major battle, during which John Hunyadi led a sudden counterattack that overran the Turkish camp, ultimately compelling the wounded Sultan to retreat.

"... THEN EACH [WARRIOR] WAS ORDERED TO KILL HIS OWN PRISONERS, AND FOR THOSE WHO DID NOT WISH TO DO SO THE KING [BAYEZID] APPOINTED OTHERS IN THEIR PLACE."

JOHANN SCHILTBERGER DESCRIBING THE CRUSADE OF NICOPOLIS, 1396

Other cavalry were recruited as *akinji*. They were ambitious young warriors with a horse and a taste for adventure who viewed warfare as a chance to make their way in the world. The *akinji* served as light cavalry—scouting and raiding ahead of the main army. They profited from plunder and might hope, if their valor attracted official attention, to one day be granted a *timar*. At the bottom of the army hierarchy were the *azabs*. They served as manual laborers and as foot soldiers, and were regarded as dispensable cannon fodder. Finally, an important contribution to Ottoman forces was made by countries owing allegiance to the sultan that provided national contingents under their own commanders—for example, the Serbs from the late 14th century.

SLAVE-SOLDIERS

Like most Muslim states, the Ottomans employed slaves both in high administration and to form elite troops in the armed forces—the Mamelukes in Egypt were a prime example. The janissary corps was raised through the *devshirme*, a selective conscription of boys from the Christian communities of the Balkans that came under Ottoman rule in the 14th century. Ottoman press gangs toured the Balkans every year, taking the children that looked the most promising military material. Removed from their Christian families, the boys were taken back to Constantinople and raised as Muslims. When they came of age they entered the sultan's service, either as janissaries or as civilian administrators. Forbidden to marry or own property and definitively separated from their families, the slave-soldiers were regarded as the ideal faithful servants of the sultan because they had no other attachments or personal ambitions. What the system failed to allow for was the inevitable development over time of the janissaries' loyalty to their own corps, which in the end would make them devoted less to the sultan than to their own interests as a military elite. However, in their golden age before self-interest took hold, they were fine infantrymen, disciplined, ascetic, fearless, and skilled in the use of firearms. They were the troops expected to storm the walls of a besieged fortress or hold the line on the battlefield in the face of charging enemy cavalry.

Warrior's cuirass
This example of Ottoman body armor would have provided superb protection, featuring several large plates and shoulder guards.

EFFECTIVE FIGHTERS

Although large and variegated, the Ottoman army was noted for the good order of its military operations, with camps clean and well organized and the off-duty behavior of soldiers less drunken

Ottoman weapons
A miquelet rifle and a *gurz* (mace)—both 18th century. Although Ottoman forces readily deployed firearms in battle, they rejected the use of the bayonet, seeing it as an "infidel weapon."

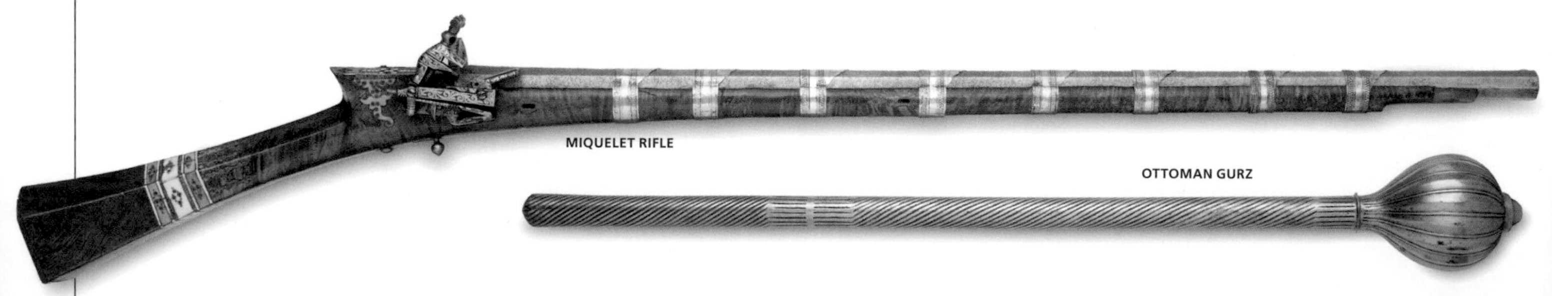

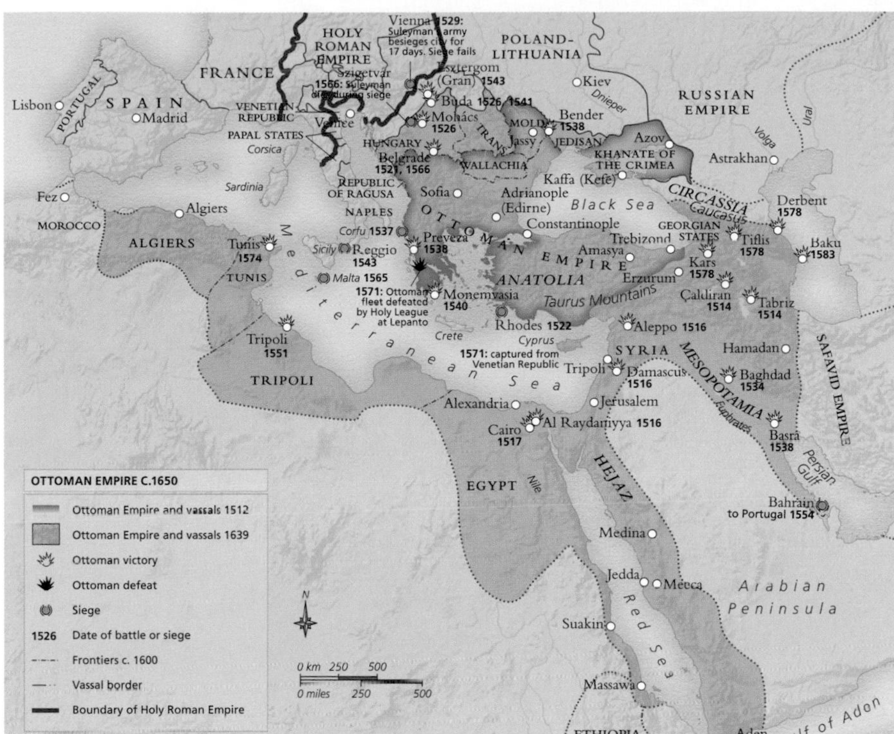

Ottoman expansion
In the course of 150 years, the Ottoman Turks grew from a small band of holy warriors, settled on land in northwest Anatolia, into rulers of an empire straddling Europe and Asia. The scale of their expansion, as illustrated, is extraordinary. They won almost 20 key battles in the 16th century alone, but by the end of the 17th century their empire was in decline.

and disruptive than was common among their contemporaries in the Christian world. Their highly decorated weaponry and noisy military band gave the Ottoman forces an air of great splendor, but they were thoroughly practical fighting men skilled in the deployment of their different arms and capable of disciplined battlefield maneuvers. In comparison to this efficiency, their enemies often seemed fatally naïve. At Nicopolis, for example, in 1396, a body of Christian crusader knights launched a hasty cavalry charge against an army led by sultan Bayezid without first establishing the size or disposition of the Ottoman forces. After scattering the "*azabs*," who had been placed in forward positions as sacrificial pawns, the knights found themselves exposed to a counterattack by Bayezid's far more numerous cavalry and were duly massacred. At Mohacs 130 years later, Christian knights suffered a similar fate on a battlefield where gunpowder weapons were present. Facing the usual enthusiastic charge by armored Christian knights, the Ottoman *sipahis* feigned flight, drawing the knights straight into the devastating fire of artillery and of disciplined ranks of janissaries armed with arquebuses. Also harassed by the flanking attacks of the Ottoman light cavalry, the knights were finally swept away by a counter-charge launched by the sultan's heavy cavalry armed with swords and spears.

The Ottomans were equally successful against Muslim opponents. Their defeat of the Egyptian Mamelukes at Marj Dabik, in Syria, in 1516 owed much to the possession of gunpowder weapons, which the Egyptians did not have. When the Mamelukes deployed their own hastily assembled cannon at Raydaniya in Egypt the following year, they were nonetheless defeated again, the skilful Ottoman cavalry executing nimble flanking attacks that nullified the firepower of the Egyptian forces.

FAIR-WEATHER FIGHTERS

If the Ottoman army had a major weakness, it was the sheer numbers of its soldiers and horses. With only limited logistic support, this host had mostly to live off the country and could not survive a winter on campaign in central Europe. Thus when Suleyman the Magnificent (ruled 1520-66) put Vienna, the capital of the Habsburg Empire, under siege in 1529, he had to withdraw after only a month in order to have time to complete the long march back to Constantinople before the weather worsened. In the European theater, the Ottoman forces were only a summer army.

Ottoman drums
Janissaries are shown here with the drums that were used to urge soldiers into battle. Janissaries lived in their barracks and served as policemen and firefighters in peacetime.

DECLINE AND FALL

Through the 17th and 18th centuries the Ottoman army gradually fell into a decadence that reflected problems experienced by the whole of Ottoman society. There was a failure to keep up with technological advances that were prevalent throughout Western European and a declining economy that undermined the resources available for military campaigns. The timar system began to decay and was eventually abandoned.

Especially sad was the fate of the janissaries. During the 17th century they ceased to be slaves recruited by the *devshirme*, instead being drawn from free-born Muslims eager to join a privileged military set. The janissary corps swelled in numbers, from around 20,000 at the time of Suleyman to well in excess of 100,000 by the end of the 18th century. This bloated body ceased to have any effective military function, degenerating into a pampered social elite and blocking efforts to reform and modernize the armed forces. It was finally suppressed, with considerable bloodshed, in 1826—known as "The Auspicious Incident." By then Ottoman Turkey had declined, now little more than a ramshackle military power clinging precariously to the remains of its empire.

OTTOMAN ARMS

The armed forces of the Ottoman Empire in the 15th and 16th centuries were extremely diverse. Armored cavalry equipped with saber and shield were an essential element, alongside light horsemen, infantry with firearms, and artillery. The armor and weaponry shown here—such as mail-and-plate coats, curved swords, and round shields—are broadly similar to that found at the same period across a wide area of the Islamic world, including Safavid Persia and Mughal India.

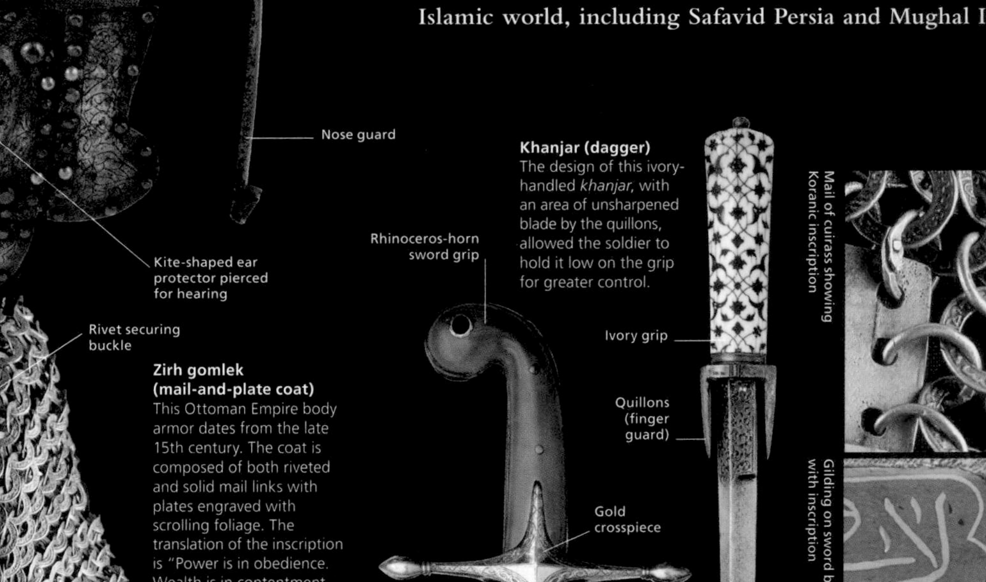

Chichak (helmet)
Made entirely of plates—with additional face, neck, and ear protection—this 16th-century *chichak* afforded the Ottoman Empire cavalryman excellent protection. The inner-skull, ear pieces, and peak all retain the lining of wadded and quilted red fabric. The central band and neck guard are engraved with Koranic text.

Riveted pointed peak

Nose guard

Concave neck guard

Chain mail

Kite-shaped ear protector pierced for hearing

Rivet securing buckle

Zirh gomlek (mail-and-plate coat)
This Ottoman Empire body armor dates from the late 15th century. The coat is composed of both riveted and solid mail links with plates engraved with scrolling foliage. The translation of the inscription is "Power is in obedience. Wealth is in contentment. May the end be to the best."

Buckles and straps secure armor at front

Khanjar (dagger)
The design of this ivory-handled *khanjar*, with an area of unsharpened blade by the quillons, allowed the soldier to hold it low on the grip for greater control.

Ivory grip

Quillons (finger guard)

Rhinoceros-horn sword grip

Gold crosspiece

Koranic inscription

Gold inlay

Silver gilt overlay

Mail of cuirass showing Koranic inscription

Gilding on sword blade with inscription

Rear of *kalkan* showing hand grip

Kilij (sword) and scabbard
Ottoman edged weapons were feared by their enemies, for they could sever a head with a single stroke. The Ottomans are credited with generalizing the use of curved sword blades in the Muslim world. This Ottoman *kilij* with trademark curved blade was made in 1625. Its hilt is based on the style of the Egyptian Mamluk period (1250–1517). The scabbard is made of wood, overlayed with silver gilt.

Boots
Although uncomfortable and heavy—each weighed 6.2 lb (2.8 kg)—these 16th-century boots provided superb protection. The main section, covering the legs is made up of four plates fastened to each other by three columns of mail at the front, back, and right side. The mail-and-plate configuration continues on the sole to afford all-round protection to the soldier.

Kalkan (small shield)
This 17th-century *kalkan* is made from cane covered in colored silks, aside from the central boss, which is made of iron. The boss is attached to the main shield by four rivets. Six large brass washers retain loops inside for the hand grips.

1500 – 1750

MUGHAL WARRIOR

DURING THE SEVEN OR EIGHT DAYS WE LAY IN PANIPAT, OUR MEN WENT CLOSE TO IBRAHIM'S CAMP A FEW AT A TIME, RAINED ARROWS DOWN ON THE RANKS OF HIS TROOPS, CUT OFF AND BROUGHT BACK THEIR HEADS.

BABUR, ON THE BUILD-UP TO THE FIRST BATTLE OF PANIPAT, 1526

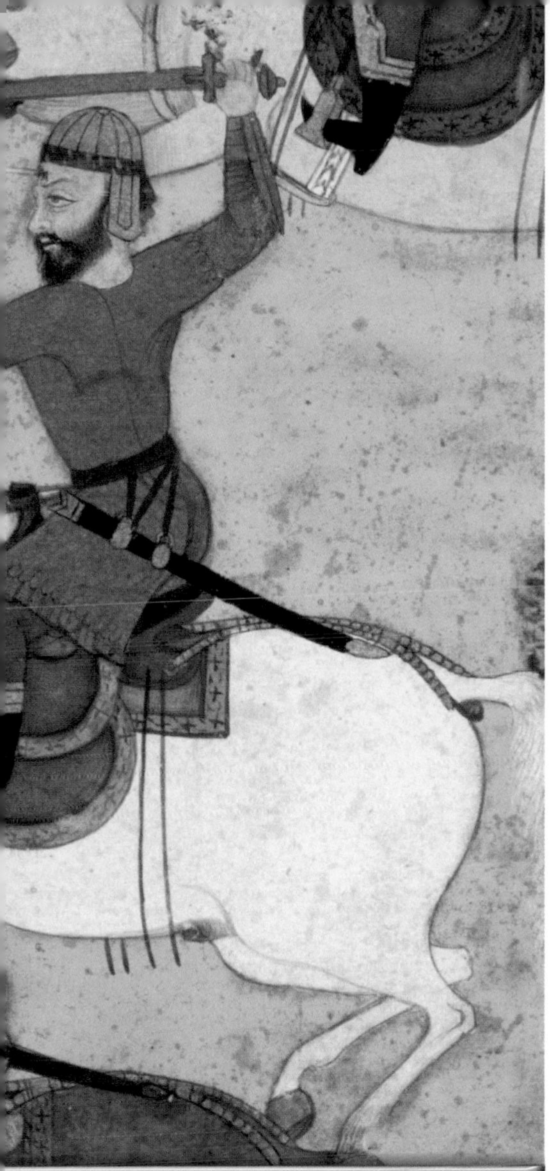

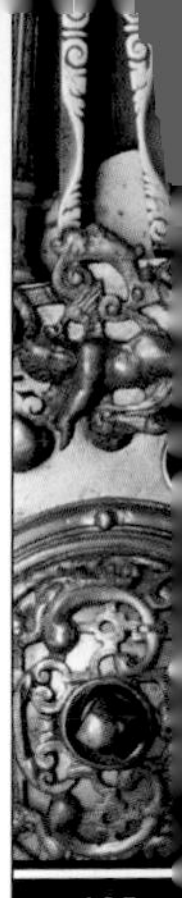

The invasion of India
Mughal cavalry ride into battle during Akbar's invasion of India in the 1560s. The Mughals came originally from present-day Afghanistan, but the army that Akbar and subsequent Mughal emperors created incorporated warriors from across Central Asia and the Indian subcontinent.

AT THE HEIGHT OF THEIR POWER in the 16th and 17th centuries, the Mughal emperors of India commanded far larger armed forces than any contemporary European power could have mustered. Like their fellow Muslims, the Ottoman Turks, they combined the Central Asian cavalry tradition of the Mongols and Tartars with the use of cannon and firearms. Their weaknesses were a failure to appreciate the effectiveness of disciplined infantry and the lack of a coherent command structure to direct their unwieldy and multiethnic army.

Babur, the founder of the Mughal Empire, was a Turco-Mongol descendant of the much-feared conqueror Timurlane. As the chief of a band of Muslim warriors, or *ghazis*, he conquered Kabul in Afghanistan in 1504 and from 1516 began raiding south into India. His defeat of Sultan Lodi of Delhi at Panipat in 1526 allowed him to establish his rule in northern India. The empire was not settled on a solid basis, however, until the reign of Akbar (ruled 1556–1605). An active military campaigner, Akbar extended the area of India under Mughal control and integrated warriors from varied backgrounds, Muslim and Hindu, into a large-scale imperial army.

IMPERIAL ARMY

The army Akbar created kept contact with the Mughals' Central Asian roots. The emperor recruited nomadic warbands into his army, attracting them with the prospect of a share in the empire's wealth. They included large contingents of Turanis, originating from Central Asia. These were horsemen especially skilled in the use of the composite bow, who were bound to their warband leader by the simple principle of fidelity to the man whose food they ate. Iranis and Afghanis—the latter noted both for their fierceness and their unreliability – also came south to serve the empire. But Akbar and subsequent emperors also integrated into their forces the warriors of each area of India that they conquered. Thus for example the Rajputs, renowned Hindu military aristocrats, brought their followers into the service of the Mughals. The Rajputs espoused a chivalric code of honor that valued close combat man-to-man and despised missile warfare. They also stressed self-sacrifice and the choice of death rather than dishonor. The more pragmatic Mughals are reported to have felt the Rajputs "knew how to die but not how to fight," but they welcomed the cavalry and armed peasantry that Hindu warriors brought to the army.

AMIRS AND HOUSEHOLD FORCES

The warlords and nobles who brought their followers to serve the emperor were designated "amirs." As well as status in the court hierarchy, they received money from the Mughal treasury to pay their men and the right to raise revenue from provinces placed under their control. There were several hundred amirs at any given time, with around 100,000 to 200,000 retainers. As well as these troops, the emperor had household forces under his direct control. These consisted of a few thousand cavalry and musketeers, added to large quantities of artillery and a substantial number of war-elephants. Surprisingly, though, he did not have any soldier-slaves, a major feature of contemporary Muslim armies in Turkey, Egypt, and Iran.

The function of the Mughal army was to maintain and extend the emperor's rule in the Indian subcontinent. The emperor was never close to establishing a monopoly of armed force within his own domains. As one observer commented, with reference to the widespread distribution of matchlock muskets, "even the cultivator at the time of plowing has his loaded gun fastened to the plow, and his match burning." It has been calculated that in the late 16th century the Mughal Empire contained over four million armed men.

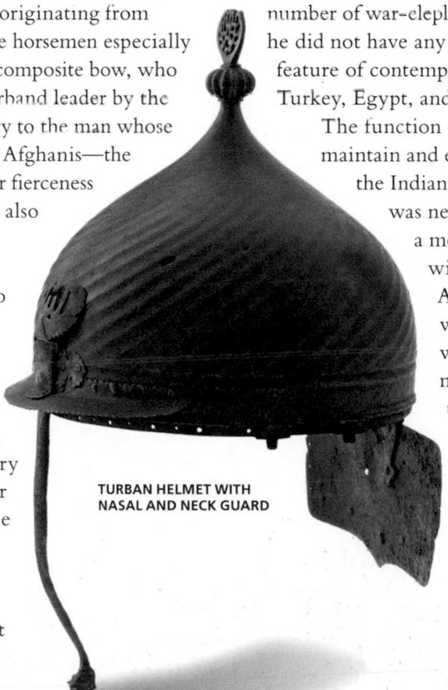

TURBAN HELMET WITH NASAL AND NECK GUARD

By maintaining such a large army, the emperor both reduced the number of potential soldiers available to those tempted to oppose him, by taking them into imperial service, and upheld the empire's prestige. Emperors spent much of their time moving around their lands in a vast mobile armed camp which, with military personnel and hangers-on together, may have numbered half a million people. It was the most practical way of demonstrating their wealth and prestige to their subjects and tributaries.

> "WHEN HE TRAVELS THROUGH HIS COUNTRY, THE EMPEROR TAKES FIFTEEN HUNDRED THOUSAND HUMAN BEINGS, HORSEMEN, SOLDIERS, OFFICERS, WOMEN, CHILDREN, WITH TEN THOUSAND ELEPHANTS, AND WITH A GREAT DEAL OF ARTILLERY."
>
> FRENCH TRAVELER **AUGUSTIN HIRIART**, C.1605

CAVALRY AND INFANTRY

As a fighting force, the Mughal army was centered upon the use of cavalry. The sheer number of horsemen was astonishing, at times almost certainly exceeding 100,000 men. The need to find mounts for cavalry on this scale—especially when every man would at least aspire to owning two horses—made horse-breeding a major activity in parts of India, notably the Punjab and Sind, but warhorses also had to be imported in bulk from Central Asia via Kabul. The majority of the cavalry were lightly equipped mounted archers, although there were also large numbers of heavy cavalry who wore substantial body armor—typically a helmet, plate cuirass, and coat of mail—and who had the sword as their main weapon. The horsemen were expected to win battles; but little was expected of the armed peasants who made up the infantry. They were men of low status conscripted into part-time military service, and made up the numbers at little cost to their employers, living off a meager diet of flour, rice, butter, and salt. Infantry might carry any of a variety of edged weapons, but their major arm was the matchlock musket.

Steel weapons
Many of the warriors depicted in the battle below are brandishing the type of distinctive curved sword, *talwar,* that was common in Mughal India.

GUNPOWDER WEAPONS

Although the Mughals cannot be credited with introducing gunpowder weapons into the Indian subcontinent—Francisco de Almeida defeated combined Arabian and Egyptian forces at the Battle of Diu, in February 1509, with ships' cannon—the first use of cannon and firearms there certainly dates from around the start of the Mughal period. Artillery and arquebuses played a crucial part in Babur's victory at Panipat in 1526. In that early period the Mughals depended heavily on foreign expertise in this area. The Ottoman Turks and various Europeans, especially Portuguese from Goa, carried out the transfer of technology, demonstrating how to found cannon and make firearms and gunpowder. Indian craftsmen were quick learners. By the end of the 16th century their matchlock muskets were better made than most European firearms and they were manufacturing light and heavy cannon of brass and bronze. Foreign experts were still employed to help with the aiming and firing of artillery pieces. When the Mughal army was on campaign, its heavy artillery was drawn

Ceremonial dagger
This extremely ornate 17th-century dagger with scabbard is typical of those from the Mughal period. Its ram-shaped hilt is studded with semiprecious stones. It would have been used for ceremonial purposes.

by oxen on carts or transported in pieces strapped to the backs of camels. The light artillery was pulled by horses. The very largest cannon, required for the siege of stubborn strongholds, would be manufactured on the spot. Although siege warfare was the primary use of artillery, its effectiveness was limited. The Mughals continued to resort to traditional tactics such as digging mines under fortress walls and simply starving the defenders into submission. The main impact of cannon seems to have been psychological, adding to the mounting pressure on besieged forces to agree surrender terms.

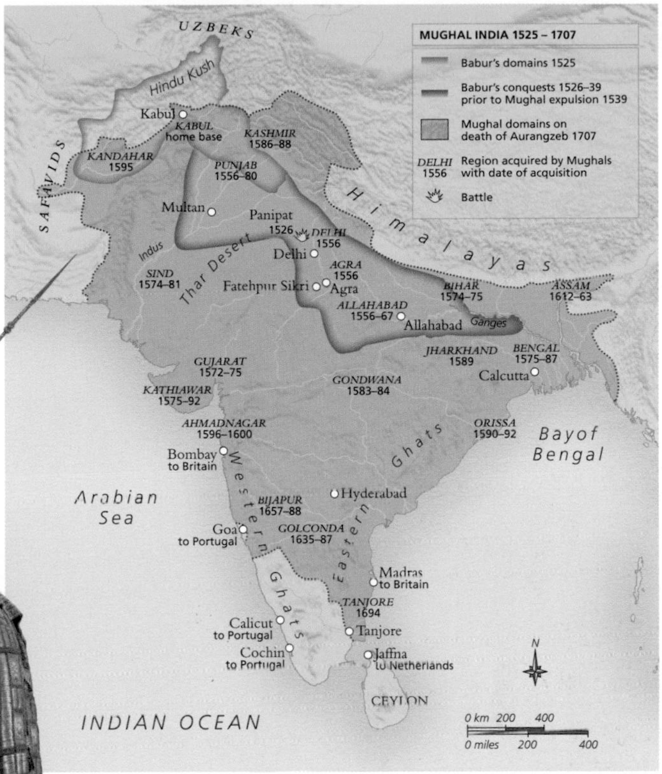

Mughals in India
Babur's defeat of Sultan Lodi of Delhi at Panipat in 1526 allowed him to establish Mughal rule in northern India. From this base, the Mughals expanded and consolidated territory to the south for almost a further 200 years, under successive rulers including Akbar and Aurengzeb.

MUGHAL INDIA 1525 – 1707
Babur's domains 1525
Babur's conquests 1526–39 prior to Mughal expulsion 1539
Mughal domains on death of Aurangzeb 1707
DELHI 1556 Region acquired by Mughals with date of acquisition
Battle

ON THE BATTLEFIELD

Mughal forces typically took form for battle with massed light cavalry on the flanks and heavy cavalry in the center. The artillery and the musket-armed infantry were deployed as a defensive block, with a line of war-elephants behind them. The presence of gunpowder weapons rendered elephants useless as an offensive force, since the noise and smoke made them panic uncontrollably. They functioned instead as command and observation posts, and as a last line of defense. The psychological impact of their towering presence was also significant.

The Mughals would usually start a battle by sending their mounted archers forward on the flanks to deluge the enemy with arrows. After this highly effective softening-up phase, the heavy cavalry would charge and engage the opposition in a general mêlée. An alternative battle plan, executed successfully against numerically superior forces at Panipat and in several other conflicts, was for the Mughal cavalry to feign a retreat, drawing the enemy into the fire of massed cannon and infantry firearms. The cavalry would then counterattack to devastating effect.

Animal army
Heavily armored elephants in battle were a fearsome sight for the Mughals' enemies. Furthermore, mounted warriors could exploit the animals' height to direct the battle.

MUGHAL WEAKNESSES

Although the Mughal Empire reached its zenith, territorially, under Aurengzeb (ruled 1658–1707), it was by then in military decline. Mughal armies suffered defeats at the hands of the Marathas in southern India from the late 17th century and had to make peace with them. They were also defeated by Persian and Afghan armies in the 1730s—led by Nadir Shah, ruler of Persia—well before the British takeover of India got under way. Shah invaded Delhi, carrying away many treasures, including the Peacock Throne in 1739.

The Mughal forces were in many ways highly sophisticated. Their engineers, for example, were skilled road builders who opened up routes for the army to use through otherwise impassable terrain. But they were limited in their adoption and use of new military technology. Their cavalry did not carry pistols and their infantry had neither pikes nor bayonets. They failed to move on from the matchlock to the superior flintlock musket, still employing the old-fashioned firearm into the 18th century. Despising infantry, they did not subject them to drill, so that foot soldiers were slow to load their muskets and could not fire in volleys.

The fragility of Mughal power was, however, largely a consequence of the army's fundamental structure, depending on warlords bringing their retainers to serve the emperor. This prevented the creation of any permanent hierarchy of command, since each warlord owed allegiance directly to the ruler and accepted orders only from him. Amirs were inevitably tempted to assert their independence in their provincial power base, rather than joining the imperial army. Professional soldiers would sell their services to another employer once imperial wealth and power waned. The Mughal Empire theoretically continued to exist until 1857, but by then it was a mere ghost of its former glory. However, the empire's legacy was long-lasting; many monuments of the Mughal period (most famously the Taj Mahal) are still in use today.

Indian kard (dagger) and scabbard
Brought to India through Mughal expansion, this straight-bladed, single-edged *kard* was in use across much of the Islamic world by the 18th century.

MUGHAL ARMS

Made up of warriors from diverse ethnic backgrounds and fighting traditions, the Mughal army was never remotely homogenous in armor or weaponry. The core of elite heavy cavalry, however, could be expected to wear mail-and-plate armor and carry a round shield of leather or steel. The armor was lighter, cheaper, and, crucially, cooler than its European equivalent. For engaging the enemy at close quarters they typically carried a sword—usually the curved *talwar*—and a percussion weapon such as a mace.

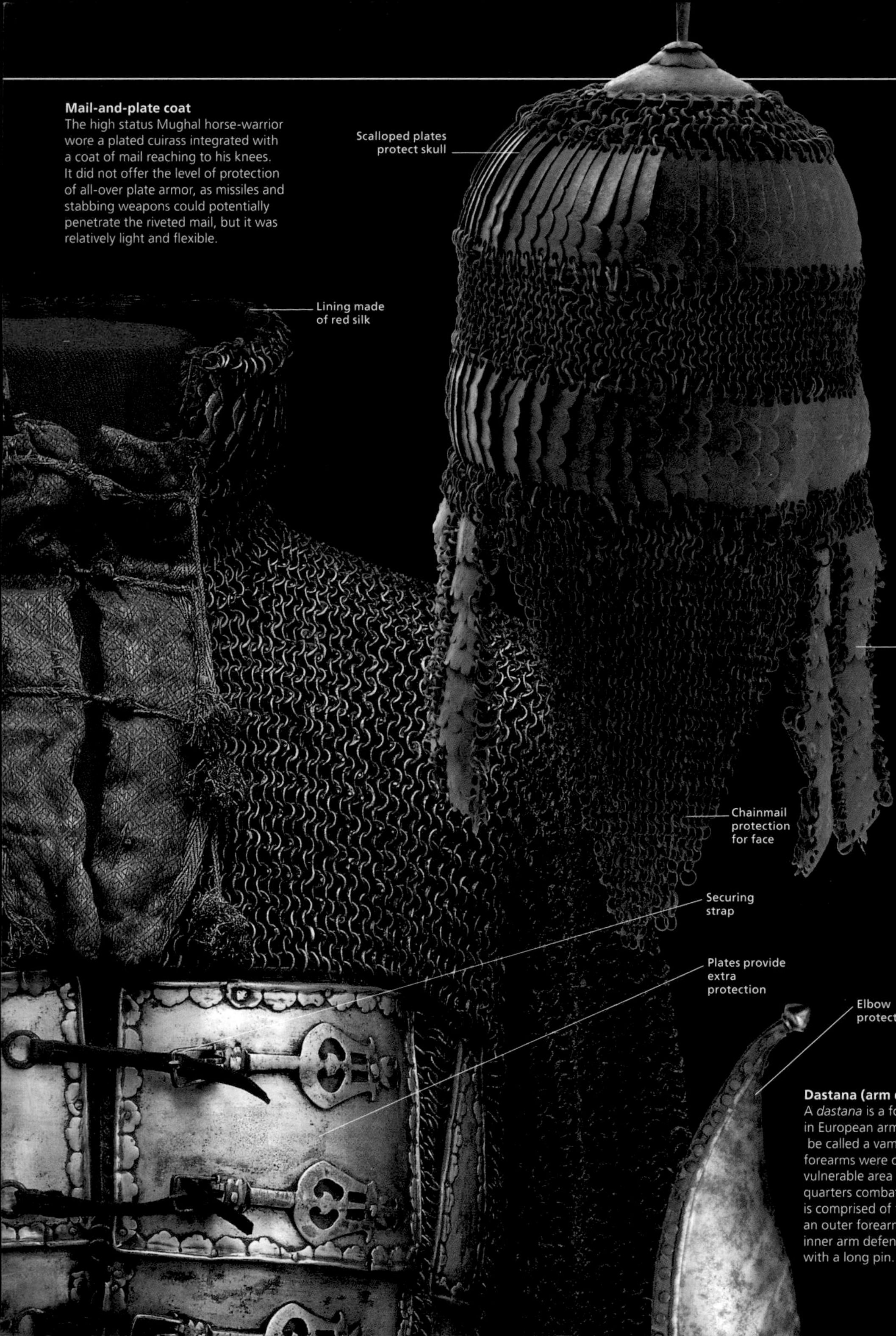

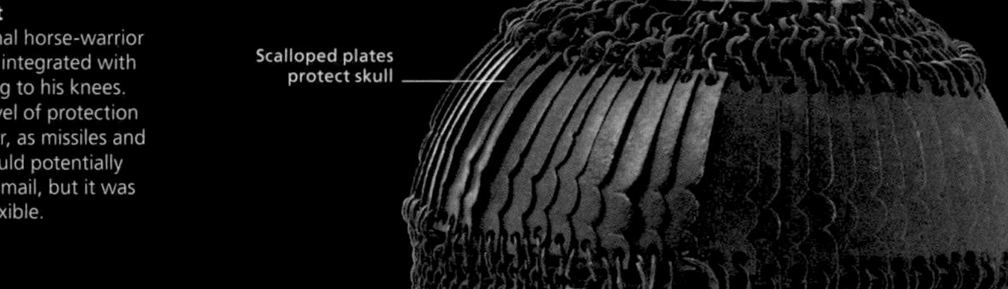

Mail-and-plate coat
The high status Mughal horse-warrior wore a plated cuirass integrated with a coat of mail reaching to his knees. It did not offer the level of protection of all-over plate armor, as missiles and stabbing weapons could potentially penetrate the riveted mail, but it was relatively light and flexible.

Lining made of red silk

Scalloped plates protect skull

Flaps protecting ears and neck

Chainmail protection for face

Securing strap

Plates provide extra protection

Helmet
Made mainly of mail this Mughal helmet (known as a "top") weighed a very manageable 1.75 lb (0.8 kg). The two horizontal rings of overlapping plates provided increased protection to the top of the head while the triangular section of mail was worn over the face.

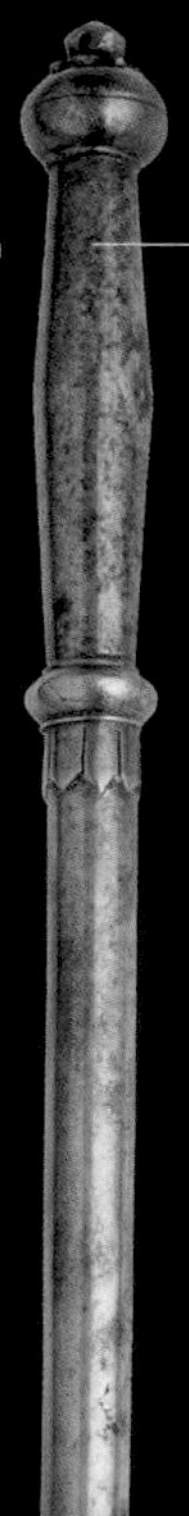

Mace
Simple solid iron maces, like this 16th-century weapon, were widely used by Mughal cavalry and infantry. They could deliver a powerful blow.

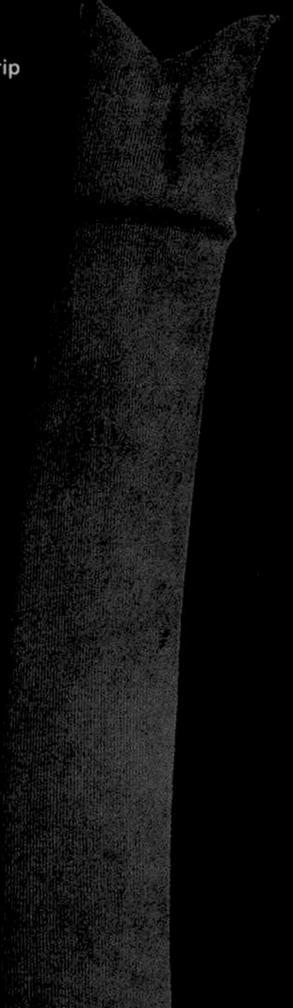

Grip

Elbow protection

Dastana (arm defense)
A *dastana* is a forearm guard; in European armor it would be called a vambrace. The forearms were obviously a vulnerable area in any close-quarters combat. This example is comprised of two pieces—an outer forearm and hinged inner arm defense—secured with a long pin.

SCABBARD

TALWAR

Disc pommel

Indo-Muslim hilt design

Elaborate gilding

Deeply curved blade typical of the Indian style in the Middle Ages

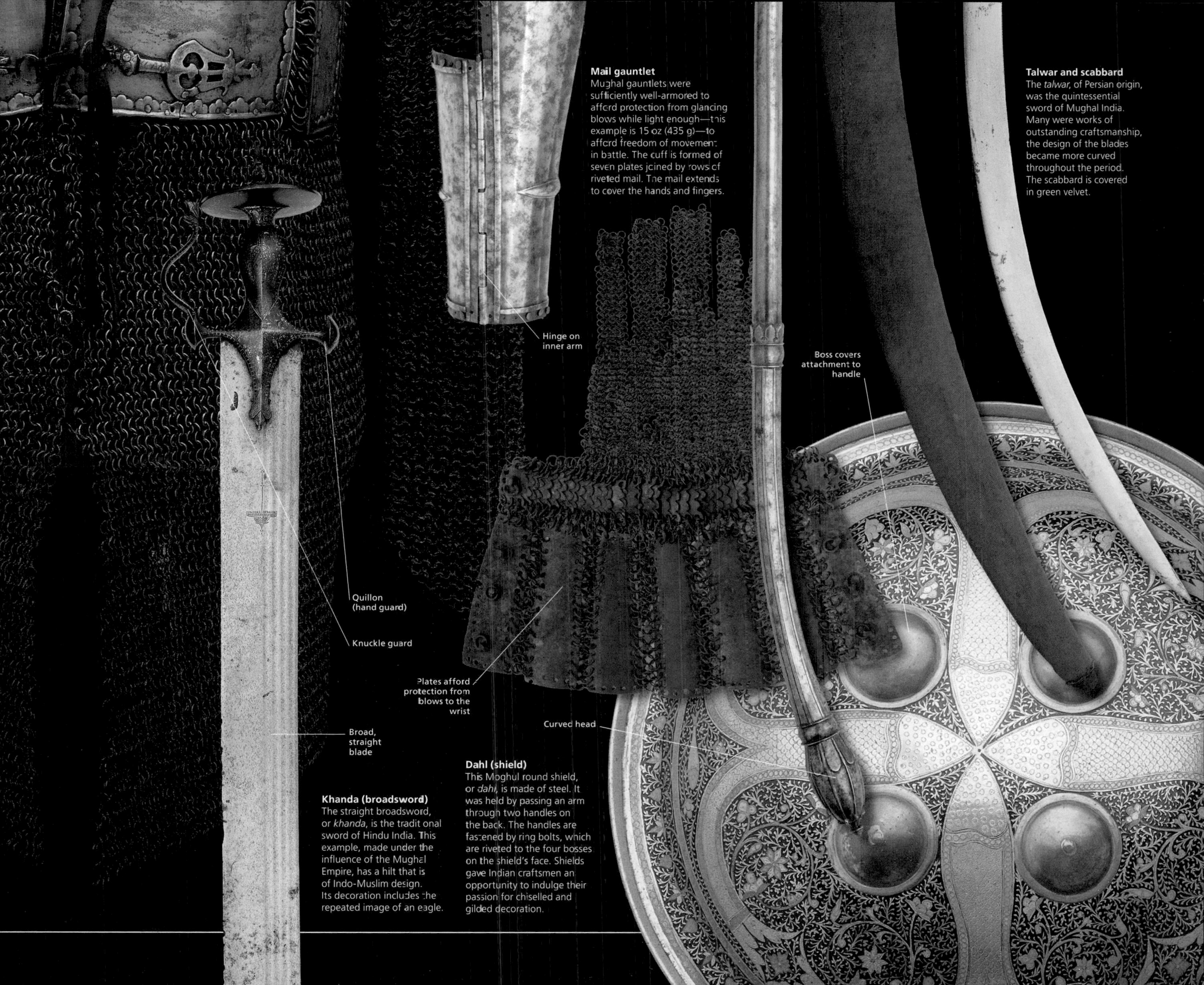

Mail gauntlet
Mughal gauntlets were sufficiently well-armored to afford protection from glancing blows while light enough—this example is 15 oz (435 g)—to afford freedom of movement in battle. The cuff is formed of seven plates joined by rows of riveted mail. The mail extends to cover the hands and fingers.

Talwar and scabbard
The *talwar*, of Persian origin, was the quintessential sword of Mughal India. Many were works of outstanding craftsmanship, the design of the blades became more curved throughout the period. The scabbard is covered in green velvet.

Dahl (shield)
This Moghul round shield, or *dahl*, is made of steel. It was held by passing an arm through two handles on the back. The handles are fastened by ring bolts, which are riveted to the four bosses on the shield's face. Shields gave Indian craftsmen an opportunity to indulge their passion for chiselled and gilded decoration.

Khanda (broadsword)
The straight broadsword, or *khanda*, is the traditional sword of Hindu India. This example, made under the influence of the Mughal Empire, has a hilt that is of Indo-Muslim design. Its decoration includes the repeated image of an eagle.

1642 – 1651

ENGLISH MUSKETEER

"WE WERE NOT A MERE MERCENARY ARMY, HIRED TO SERVE ANY ARBITRARY POWER OF A STATE, BUT CALLED FORTH TO THE DEFENCE OF OUR OWN AND THE PEOPLE'S JUST RIGHTS AND LIBERTIES.

LEVELLER PAMPHLET, *THE HUNTING OF THE FOXES*, 1647

THE ARMIES THAT FOUGHT in the civil wars in Britain between 1642 and 1651 were commanded by officers with experience of war in continental Europe. Their tactics and organization thus followed currently fashionable European models, in which well-drilled infantry armed with a mix of pikes and muskets were considered essential to battlefield success. But Britain had few men trained in the use of arms and it took years to create truly viable fighting forces, a process that reached its peak in the New Model Army.

At the heart of the complex series of conflicts that wreaked havoc in England, Scotland, and Ireland from 1642 onward was a political and religious confrontation between King Charles I and the English parliament. Many of those who fought in the civil wars were principled men with a sense of commitment to the royalist or parliamentarian cause. Yet from the outset there were also many soldiers who simply fought for whichever side happened to control the area they lived in; some fought for both sides at different times.

Bandolier
English musketeers carried measured powder charges in wooden flasks around their necks.

RAISING TROOPS

The bulk of the initial combatants in the civil wars were either volunteers or members of local militias (known as the "Trained Bands"). As the conflict dragged on, however, both sides had to raise levies to fill the ranks of their infantry, using a chaotic process of conscription that produced mostly poor quality troops from the lowest levels of society. Equipping and paying troops was a challenging task under the conditions of the time. With great effort, all soldiers in the civil wars were fitted out with basic weapons, shoes, and some kind of uniform. The uniforms were generally so diverse, however, that on the day of a battle soldiers would be issued with a special item to wear, such as a sash, to distinguish friend from foe. The soldiers' pay was normally heavily in arrears—a frequent cause of mutiny. Men often had to be paid some of the money they were owed before a battle or siege in order to get them to fight. Unpaid soldiers depended on pillage and the sacking of towns for the chance of gain.

A NEW ARMY

In 1645 the English parliament established the New Model Army in order to centralize the organization of its military forces, which had previously been raised and trained locally. It contained a strong core of ideologically committed officers and veterans who saw themselves as the "army of the Living God." It was unique in fitting out all its infantry in identical uniforms and it was also better than other civil war formations at paying its troops regularly. But it could not escape from the general conditions of armies of its day. As well as the dedicated core, the army contained many soldiers who had joined for the pay and adventure, or because as conscripts they had been given no choice. An officer, Colonel John Venn, complained that the levies he was sent were "men taken out of prison, tinkers, pedlars, and vagrants that have no dwelling." Such men had to be brought to the army under armed guard and many of them deserted at the very first opportunity. Nor did the new army always succeed in paying its troops on time, and its soldiers sought their own fortunes in traditional military fashion.

Slow and steady fire
A royalist regiment unleashes a volley of musket fire *(above)*. The uniforms and weapons of the two sides in the English Civil War were remarkably similar. Because the matchlock musket *(right)* was still very inaccurate and took a long time to reload, the musketeers always had to be protected by large bodies of pikemen.

MATCHLOCK MUSKET

Matchlock drill
In the first of these pictures from a Dutch illustrated drill manual, the match in the musketeer's left hand is already lit. In the second, he pours gunpowder from a flask from his bandolier. He then rams down a musket ball, before preparing to pour priming powder into the pan, keeping the smouldering match at a safe distance between the fingers of his left hand.

After their victory over the Royalists at the battle of Naseby in 1645, New Model Army foot soldiers plundered the battlefield and deserted in large numbers to carry off their booty.

ARMY LIFE

To the civilian population any civil war army on the march was like a plague of locusts. The soldiers did not carry tents, so when away from permanent camp the alternative to sleeping under the open sky was to commandeer space in houses or barns. As well as accommodation, a local community might be expected to provide food. As armies struggled to keep their men supplied with basics such as biscuits, cheese, boiled beef, and beer, they resorted to "free quarter"—imposing troops upon civilians with the promise of future payment for food and lodging. Free quarter easily slipped over into straightforward armed robbery, as soldiers took whatever they fancied or needed. The horses required for cavalry and transport, for example, were often stolen. When the New Model Army mutinied in 1647, one of the men's principal demands was that they be given immunity from prosecution for horse thefts committed while in uniform.

The puritanical commanders of the New Model Army made vigorous efforts to alter the behavior and attitudes of their soldiers. They tried to establish payment for provisions and put an end to looting. Preachers, who were considered a vital part of the army establishment, left men in no doubt of the future wrath God would visit upon the sinful. If this did not deter them, there were harsh punishments to focus their minds on virtue. For blasphemy, a man might have his tongue pierced with a red-hot iron. The punishment for desertion was hanging. Yet the New Model Army infantry continued to include, along with a solid core of committed, god-fearing men, a mass of unreformed reprobates. Suppressing the gambling, drinking, hunting, and whoring that made up the usual texture of camp life was an uphill struggle. Thousands deserted on the march, despite the death penalty, and the army readily employed deserters from the other side.

CAVALRY HELMET

Tough leather provided some protection against sword cuts

BUFF LEATHER COAT

Lobster-tail neck guard

Movable visor

BREASTPLATE

Armor gave some protection against muskets

New Model Army cavalry armor
While musketeers usually fought without armor, the soldiers most likely to be struck by musket balls, the cavalry, wore iron breastplates and backplates. New Model Army cavalry had distinctive "lobster-tail" helmets.

INFANTRY TRAINING

Out of often unpromising material, the armies of the English Civil War nevertheless succeeded in creating trained foot soldiers. One of the known advantages of a musket was that any fool could fire one with a little training; learning how to handle a pike was even simpler. The infantryman would belong to a company of perhaps 120 men at full strength, generally with two musketeers to every one pikeman. The soldier received systematic training—much of it recorded in contemporary drill books—in the handling of his weapon ("Posture"), and was taught how to operate in battlefield formation ("Motions" and "Evolutions"). Both muskets and pikes were collective weapons that made individual initiative worse than useless.Musketeers had to be disciplined to fight as a body, firing volleys as rapidly as possible in the general direction of the enemy. All foot soldiers were drilled to maneuver coherently in ranks and files.

> "MOSTLY YOUNG MEN AND BOYS ... WHO HAD LEFT THEIR TRADES TO FOLLOW WAR AND HAD BECOME ACCUSTOMED TO LEAD A LIFE OF DEBAUCHERY AND PILLAGE."
>
> **CONTEMPORARY EYEWITNESS** DESCRIBING CONSCRIPTS IN THE NEW MODEL ARMY

On the battlefield, a battalion would line up with its pikemen in the center and musketeers on each side. There would be cavalry on their flanks and reserves behind them. Some musketeers might also be formed into mobile companies to give fire support to the cavalry as it advanced. A sergeant with a halberd stood alongside each company organizing its movements and volley fire. A rank of musketeers had to "make ready," "present," and "give fire" as ordered by the sergeant—the whole process taking about 30 seconds with a matchlock musket—and then move out of the way for another rank to fire. When combat was joined at close quarters, the musketeers would use the butts of their weapons as clubs. Infantry could operate offensively, rushing the enemy to engage them in "push of pike," or stand on the defensive. If they were attacked by cavalry, probably the most unnerving experience for foot soldiers, the pikemen would form a bristling square. Since the cavalry had firearms, however, the reach of the 16 ft (5 m) pike was not necessarily decisive. Cool heads and good discipline were needed to make pike-and-musket infantry effective on the battlefield. Once their formation was broken, the foot soldiers were capable of nothing but a desperate mêlée.

VICTORIOUS ARMY

The creation of the New Model Army gave the Parliamentarian forces a distinct advantage over the Royalists, especially in terms of organization. Between 1645 and 1652 it was repeatedly victorious, subduing Royalists, Scots, and Irish. The civil authorities never liked it, because it was expensive to maintain and became a hotbed of political and religious radicalism. But it was a highly professional army by the standards of its day, led by dedicated, experienced officers, and with a core of veteran soldiers at its heart. It outlived the end of the wars but was eventually disbanded by Charles II at the Restoration in 1660.

Defending the musketeers
The musketeers were extremely vulnerable to attacks by cavalrymen or pikemen, especially while they were reloading. They were always drawn up on the battlefield accompanied by pikemen, who would come to their aid in the case of attack.

MUSKET AND PIKE TACTICS

In the 17th century European military commanders and theoreticians all agreed on deploying pikemen in close-packed phalanxes and on exploiting matchlock muskets fired in volleys. But differences arose over the numerical balance between pikemen and musketeers, the depth of formation, and the most effective system for firing. Through the first half of the century the proportion of musketeers tended to increase, from equality with the pikemen to double their number. The depth of ranks in the same period lessened, from around ten-deep to six-deep. There were two well known methods for using muskets. The countermarch system associated with Dutch leader Maurice of Nassau aimed to achieve a steady rolling fire. The other method, associated with King Gustav Adolf of Sweden, had three ranks of musketeers firing a simultaneous salvo. This had maximum shock effect, although it left the musketeers entirely dependent upon the pikemen for defense in intervals between volleys while they reloaded. Commanders in the English Civil War employed both systems of firing.

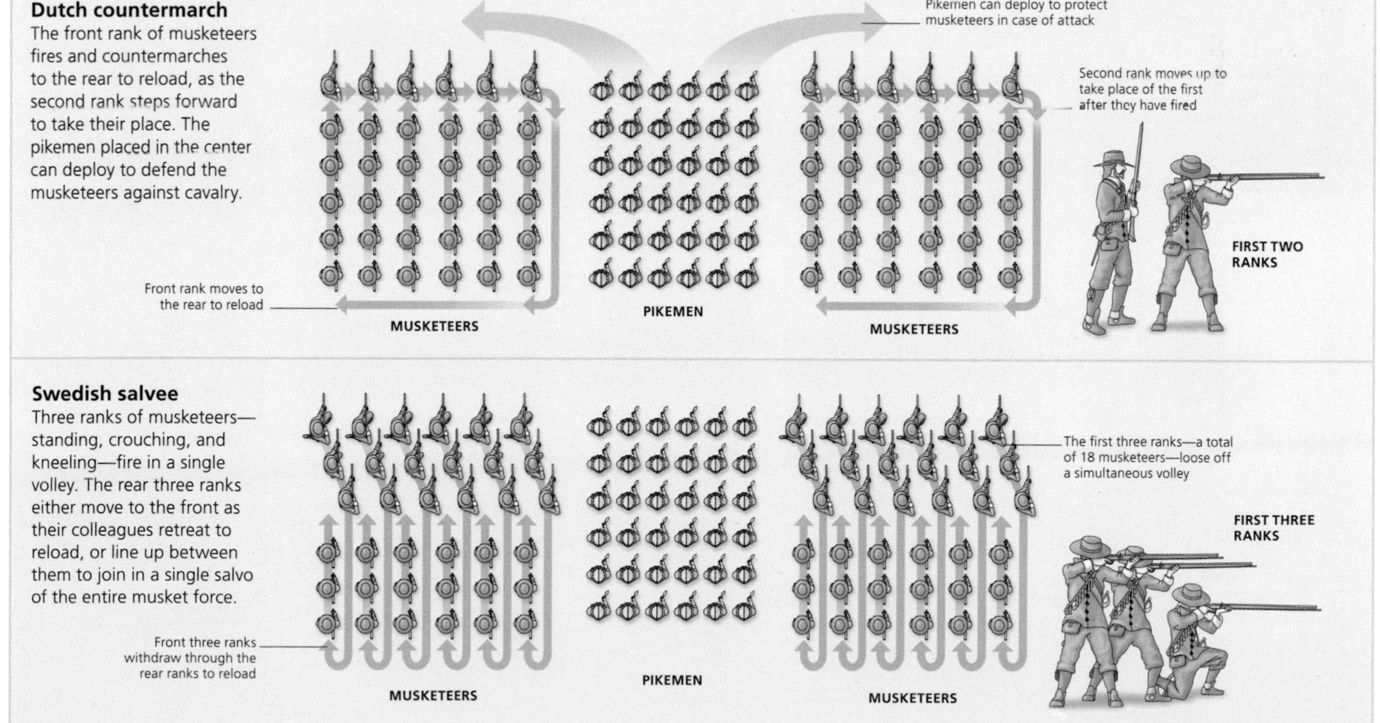

MUSKETEER'S GEAR

Because of a lingering prejudice against firearms, the musketeer ranked below the pikeman in English Civil War infantry. He was rarely issued even with a helmet for protection, while pikemen often had body armor. The muskets used in the Civil War were mostly clumsy matchlocks. More advanced flintlock muskets were given only to a few specialized infantry—for example, those guarding gunpowder stores, where sparks from a match might cause an explosion. Lighter than earlier models, the matchlock did not need to be leaned on a rest to fire.

Broad-brimmed hat
The hats worn by the foot soldiers in Cromwell's army were far from uniform, but were usually made of stiffened felt with a wide brim.

Soldier's red coat
The only item of uniform that was officially issued to the New Model Army was the red coat. The color of the lining, visible in the turned-back cuffs, indicated the soldier's regiment.

Muzzle

Scouring stick, for cleaning the barrel and ramming down charge and musket ball

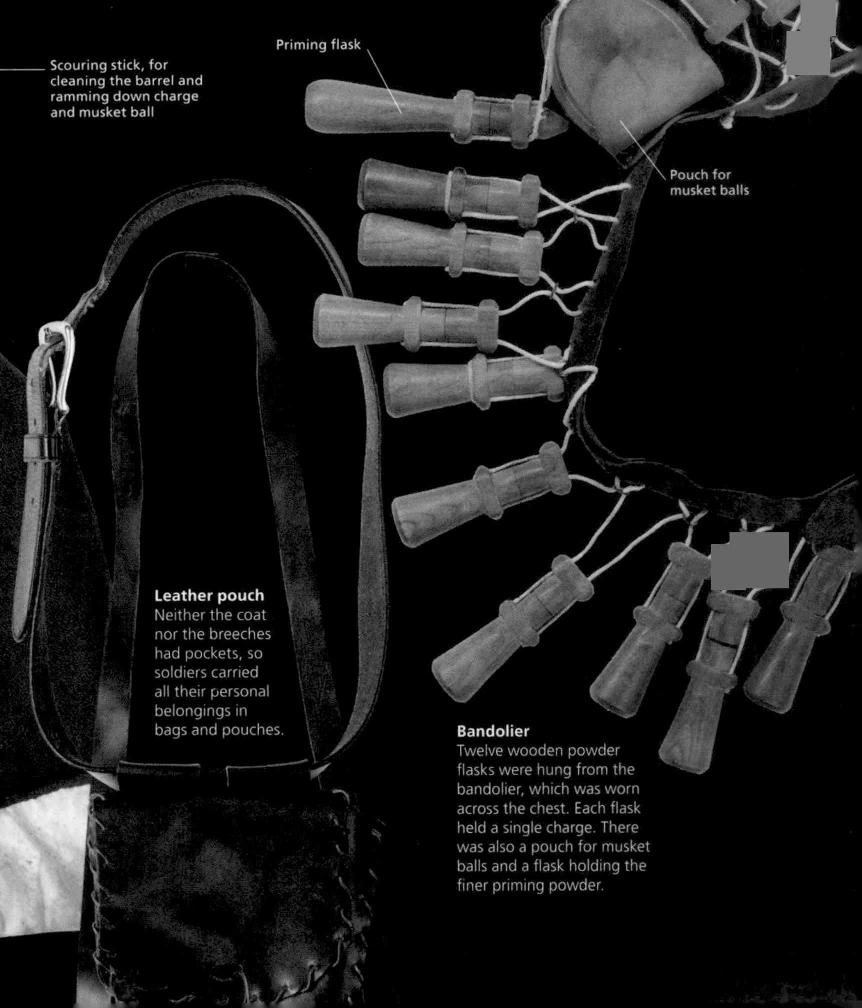

Priming flask

Pouch for musket balls

Leather pouch
Neither the coat nor the breeches had pockets, so soldiers carried all their personal belongings in bags and pouches.

Bandolier
Twelve wooden powder flasks were hung from the bandolier, which was worn across the chest. Each flask held a single charge. There was also a pouch for musket balls and a flask holding the finer priming powder.

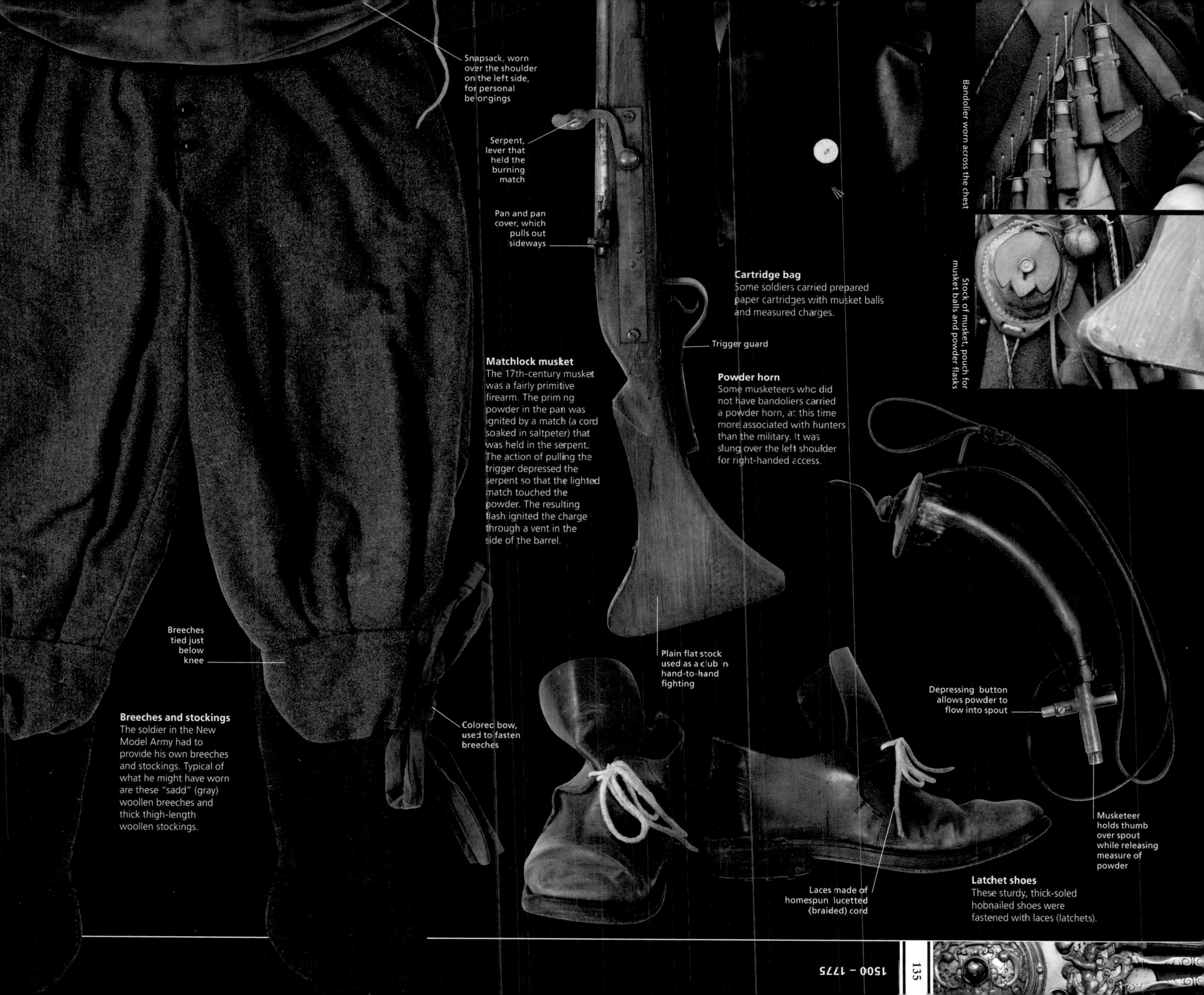

Bandolier worn across the chest

Stock of musket, pouch for musket balls and powder flasks

Cartridge bag
Some soldiers carried prepared paper cartridges with musket balls and measured charges.

Matchlock musket
The 17th-century musket was a fairly primitive firearm. The priming powder in the pan was ignited by a match (a cord soaked in saltpeter) that was held in the serpent. The action of pulling the trigger depressed the serpent so that the lighted match touched the powder. The resulting flash ignited the charge through a vent in the side of the barrel.

Powder horn
Some musketeers who did not have bandoliers carried a powder horn, at this time more associated with hunters than the military. It was slung over the left shoulder for right-handed access.

Breeches and stockings
The soldier in the New Model Army had to provide his own breeches and stockings. Typical of what he might have worn are these "sadd" (gray) woollen breeches and thick thigh-length woollen stockings.

Latchet shoes
These sturdy, thick-soled hobnailed shoes were fastened with laces (latchets).

Spanish squares

The Spanish *tercios* (units that were roughly equivalent to regiments) used the square to good effect during the early battles of the Eighty Years' War (1568–1648) against the Dutch. The Spanish square combined arquebusiers and pikemen.

17TH-CENTURY EUROPEAN SOLDIERS

The 17th century was a transitional period for European armies. Infantry began the century armed with pikes and arquebuses or matchlock muskets and ended it with flintlock muskets and bayonets. The wars of the first half of the century were mostly fought by mercenary forces raised by military entrepreneurs; in later decades, standing armies predominated, although rulers continued to employ large foreign contingents in their forces. Standards of discipline gradually improved, as did the quality of army administration. Soldiers who were regularly paid and fed became less likely to mutiny or wreak havoc upon civilians. Cavalry returned to fashion after its decline in the 16th century, diversifying into heavy and light horse and dragoons.

DUTCH FOOT SOLDIERS

In the late 16th century a Dutch army, consisting of a mix of local levies and foreign volunteers or mercenaries, was fighting for independence from the rule of the Spanish Habsburgs. The Dutch had usually had the worst of any confrontation with the Spanish *tercios*, but from the 1590s onward their performance improved under the direction of Maurice of Nassau (1567–1625). The supply and payment of the army became exceptionally reliable by the standards of the time, and the infantry were drilled and disciplined in a systematic fashion.

Maurice and his advisers evolved a more flexible battlefield formation than that of the *tercios*. The Dutch infantry took the field in battalions about 500 strong, with roughly equal numbers of pikemen and "shot"—soldiers with arquebuses or muskets. The armored pikemen deployed in a formation much broader than it was deep, usually in files of ten men from front to rear. The "shot," who flanked the pikemen, were drilled to maintain a rolling fire, each rank firing and then withdrawing to reload as the next rank fired. The pikemen held off the cavalry and provided the offensive "push of pike" to drive the enemy from the field at the decisive moment. Although the Dutch never truly got the better of the Spanish in battle, the Habsburg monarchy was eventually forced to recognize their independence formally in 1648. The Dutch system of fighting had widespread influence on European military thinking.

Plain, basic helmet, reinforced by projecting comb

PIKEMAN'S POT

BREASTPLATE AND TASSETS

Swivel hook for fastening shoulder straps

HALBERD

Tassets attached by hasps to studs on breastplate

SWORD, DATED 1633

Pierced shell guard is a decorative feature, but also gives protection

Dutch armor and weapons
The half armor, consisting of a breastplate, backplate, and tassets to protect the thighs, is typical of pikeman's armor in the early 17th century. So, too, is the pot helmet. The sword and decorative halberd would have belonged to an officer.

SWEDISH TROOPS

In 1620 Sweden introduced an Ordinance of Military Personnel, registering all men over 15 for military service. Some 10,000 were conscripted every year. Along with mercenaries hired from Protestant Germany, they allowed King Gustav Adolf to field a formidable army. Gustav built upon the Dutch infantry model, thinning the formation of pikemen to only six ranks and doubling the proportion of musketeers. The latter were trained to fire mass volleys in three ranks—kneeling, crouching, and standing. Gustav also made aggressive use of cavalry, charging with sabers drawn. The Swedish army intervened decisively in the Thirty Years' War, but at great cost. Of 230 conscripts recruited from one Swedish village, 215 died abroad.

FRENCH MUSKETEER

In 1622 French King Louis XIII equipped a light cavalry company of his royal household with matchlock muskets. Since this represented the latest in military technology, it helped give the musketeer company elite status. Its proximity to the king guaranteed that gentleman-soldiers would seek service in its ranks. In the 1660s two companies were created, known as the Grey Musketeers and the Black Musketeers from the color of their sleeveless surcoats. Despite their name, these units generally preferred the sword to the musket, which, having lost its aura of novelty, was despised by the aristocracy as an arm suitable only for lowly foot soldiers. The two companies remained in existence until 1776. Their reputation for panache and flamboyance was later immortalized in the novels of Alexandre Dumas.

17TH-CENTURY RAPIER

POLISH WINGED CAVALRY

The Polish army of the 17th century was predominantly a cavalry force—horsemen outnumbered foot soldiers by three or four to one, the reverse of the proportions found in other European armies. The army's elite force was the winged cavalry, or *hussaria*. Originally light skirmishing horsemen in the manner of the Hungarian hussars, by the 17th century they had evolved into a shock force of heavy cavalry.

Service in the *hussaria* offered prestige and privileges that attracted volunteers from the cream of the Polish aristocracy. The cavalryman not only had to provide his own powerful horses, he also had to equip himself with a full panoply of armor and weapons, including a cuirass and *zischagge* helmet, an armor-piercing saber known as an *estoc*, a pair of pistols, and probably a long *czekan* war hammer. The only equipment supplied by the state was the *hussaria*'s key arm, the *kopia*—a long hollow wooden lance with a steel tip.

A *hussaria* regiment was altogether a strange and imposing sight. Many of the cavalrymen wore gilded wooden "wings", decorated with eagle feathers, upon their backs. They also decked themselves in cloaks of leopard or tiger skin and hung long silk streamers on their lances. When they charged, the feathers and the streamers emitted a sinister hissing sound that reportedly had a psychological impact upon their enemies.

The practical effectiveness of the *hussaria* on the battlefield was demonstrated on many occasions. Operating in regiments of around 300 riders, they would charge at accelerating speed, opening and closing their ranks as they rode in order to evade musket fire. Their lances, which could outreach an infantry pike, were expected to shatter on impact. They would nonetheless serve to break up the defensive formations of the enemy's pikemen. The sabers and war hammers would come into use once the enemy was exposed; no armor was proof against them. Despite their armor and large mounts, the *hussaria* retained the speed and flexibility of their hussar origins, often making repeated charges that showed an ability to regroup and maneuver en masse unequalled by any other cavalry of the day.

Victories attributable to the Polish winged cavalry range from the crushing of the Swedes and Russians at the battle of Klushino in 1610 to the historic defeat of the Ottoman Turks outside Vienna in 1683 under Jan Sobieski.

"NO SOONER DOES A HUSSAR LOWER HIS LANCE THAN A TURK IS IMPALED ON THE SPIKE."

WESPAZJAN KOCHOWSKI DESCRIBING A CHARGE BY THE POLISH CAVALRY IN *THE SONG OF VIENNA LIBERATED*, 1684

Winged cavalry squadron
Today's Polish cavalry recreates the astonishing spectacle of 17th-century *hussaria* with their formidable lances and curious "wings" attached to the backplates of their armor. They were the pride of the Polish army, defending the country from attacks by the Russians, the Swedish, the Ottomans, and marauding Cossack bands.

18TH-CENTURY EUROPEAN ARMIES

Between 1700 and the French Revolution of 1789, the military commanders of the major European powers—France, Britain, Austria, Prussia, and Russia—aspired to an ideal of rational order. Regular armies were maintained by the state and supplied with standard equipment and uniforms. Infantry recruited from the lower classes were depersonalized by discipline and drill, so that in battle they would execute orders like automata. On campaign, armies were supplied from magazines (military storehouses) through an extensive supply train. This slowed their movements but reduced destructive foraging. Battles were fought on open ground, with artillery, cavalry, and infantry combining in aggressive maneuvers that often resulted in heavy casualties.

PRUSSIAN INFANTRYMAN

The Prussian army was the most admired force in 18th-century warfare, renowned for its discipline and drill. Mostly peasant conscripts, the men who formed Prussia's infantry were not inspired by any devotion to state or nation. They were trained like animals, by the building up of conditioned reflexes through repeated punishment. Any clumsiness on the parade ground, where they spent many hours every day, would instantly merit a blow with a cane or the flat of a sword. More serious infringements resulted in flogging or even execution.

The product of this system was a man who could execute the 22 actions required to fire a flintlock musket in around 30 seconds. He could deploy rapidly from marching column into battle line and, when ordered, would advance unarmored in tight formation across open ground in the face of musket and cannon fire. He was expected to have absolutely no individual will, carrying out every action on the command of an officer or NCO. This ideal of disciplined infantry was, needless to say, never achieved. On campaign, desertion was a constant problem, and on the battlefield, soldiers gripped by fear stopped loading their muskets properly, appearing to keep up with the volleys by firing primer powder only. Even so, Prussian infantry generally maneuvered quickly on the battlefield, had effective firepower, and were daunting advancing with bayonets fixed.

> "IF MY SOLDIERS WERE TO BEGIN TO THINK, NOT ONE OF THEM WOULD REMAIN IN THE ARMY."
>
> **FREDERICK II OF PRUSSIA**, WHOSE VICTORIES WERE THE ENVY OF OTHER EUROPEAN RULERS

Battle of Hohenfriedberg, 1745
Frederick II's Grenadier Guards advance across the battlefield directly into the fire of the Austrians. These aggressive tactics contributed to a famous victory.

Prussian uniform
The army built up by Frederick William I and used so effectively by his son Frederick II was always beautifully turned out. Most infantry regiments wore long, dark blue coats with red facings and lining.

Shorter barrel than infantry musket

Tricorne hat, worn by line infantry, in contrast to the tall mitres of the grenadiers

Flintlock carbine
The principal weapon was the standard flintlock musket of the day. Prussian muskets were well-made and generally reliable. This example is a rifled carbine, used by cuirassiers and dragoons, dating from 1722.

Striking steel attached to pan cover

Flint clamp

Lock plate stamped with name of armory

COSSACK

After the major European powers had created their strictly controlled 18th-century armies, they were forced to turn to the untamed ethnic groups that lived on the extreme margins of their territories in search of men who could act with individual initiative as scouts and skirmishers. Austria's Grenzer sharpshooters from Croatia and Slovenia were one example; Russia's Cossack horsemen were another.

The Cossack communities of the southern steppe seem mostly to have been founded by freedom-loving Slavs who fled the rapidly expanding kingdoms of Russia and Poland-Lithuania in the 15th and 16th centuries, preferring a hard but independent life to serfdom. Out of harsh necessity they became warrior bands, fighting as light horsemen in the traditional way of the steppe. Much of the time they would fight against both Russia and Poland, asserting their independence. At other times they acted as semi-independent frontier forces, raiding Ottoman territories in search of plunder, or fighting on behalf of the Tsars, guarding Russia from attack by the Tatars and helping to extend the borders of the Russian Empire further to the east.

SERVING THE STATE

In the course of the 18th century, tens of thousands of Cossack were integrated into the Russian imperial army as light cavalry regiments. In addition to their traditional swords and knives, their principal weapons were a musket or rifle, used chiefly for defense, and a long slender lance with which they would charge enemy positions in loose fast-moving lines. Their savage skill at harassing the flanks of an enemy on the march or running down fleeing infantrymen made them much feared and respected. In 1775, Russian Marshal Rumyantzev recognized the Cossacks' courage in war with the Ottoman Turks, describing them as "the first into the fire, distinguishing themselves with outstanding bravery."

Kindjal
This long, curved knife originated in the Caucasus, from where it was adopted by the Cossacks along with the shashka, a kind of saber. Russian troops were issued with kindjals of this type as late as World War I.

1775 – 1914

EMPIRES AND FRONTIERS

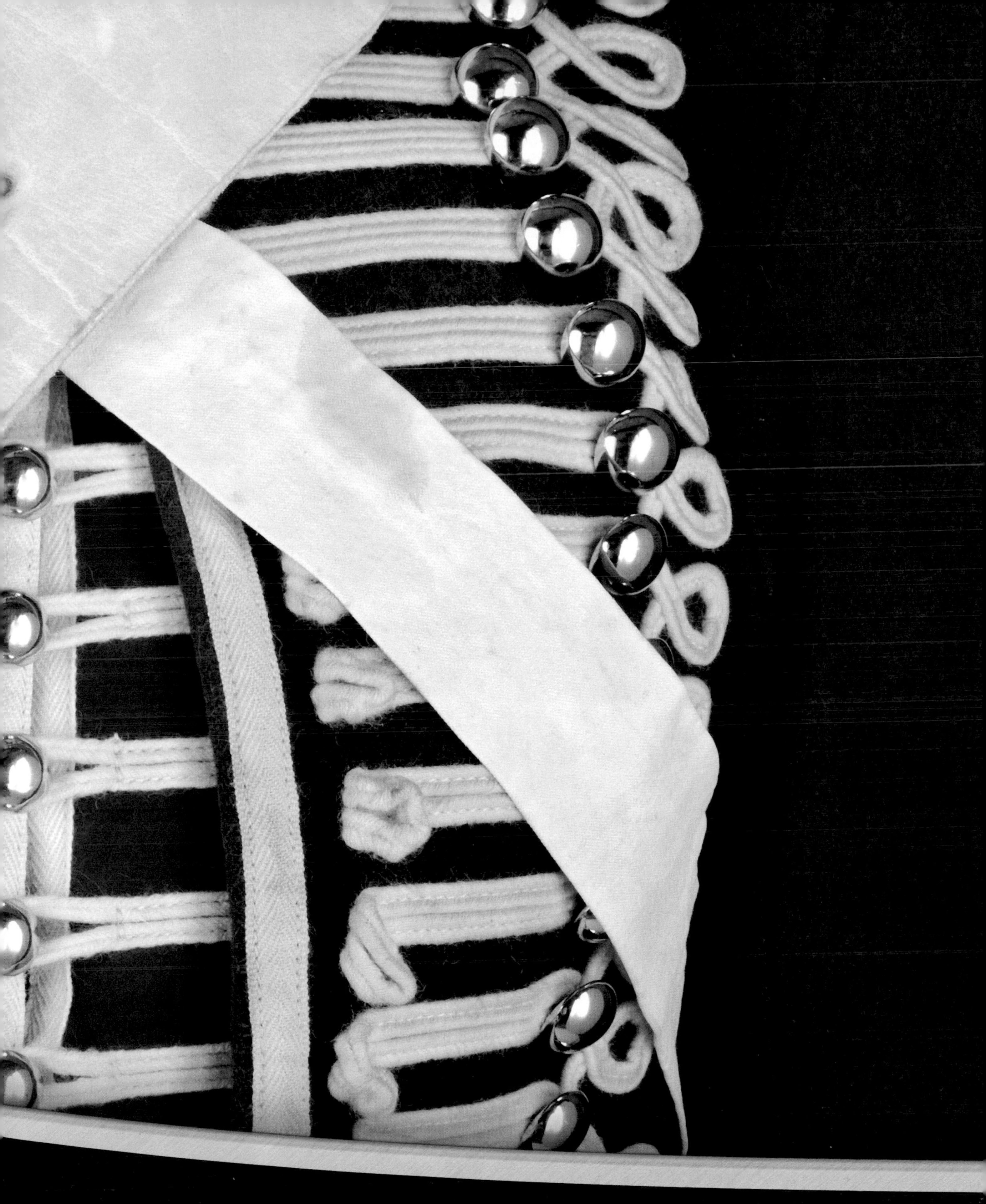

Through most of the 18th century there was little change in the accepted technology, organization, and tactics of European warfare. When Britain went to war with its North American colonies in 1775, the British "Redcoats" were a well drilled, strictly disciplined force of professional soldiers trained to fight in the open field with musket and bayonet. The American Continental Army employed a similar European style of fighting, and while the guerrilla tactics of American riflemen sometimes revealed the limitations of formal European fighting methods, the essentials of warfare remained the same.

MASS ARMIES

Radical changes that were to reshape the way wars were fought came with the French Revolutionary and Napoleonic Wars, between 1792 and 1815. In 1793 the French Republic, established following the overthrow of the king Louis XVI, declared a *levée en masse* or a mass conscription. The decree passed by the National Convention stated: "The young men shall fight; the married men shall forge arms and transport provisions ... the old men shall betake themselves to the public squares in order to arouse the courage of the warriors ..."

Although the army of the French Republic fell far short of this idealized vision, it did enforce the concept of the ordinary citizen owing a duty of military service as part of "the nation in arms". Linked to the beginnings of industrial-scale production of military equipment, there was a sharp growth in the size of European armies—more than half a million troops were engaged at the battle of Leipzig in 1813. It was Prussia that, in the wake of the Napoleonic Wars, first introduced a system of short-term peacetime conscription, without exemption either on grounds of social class or for payment, so that the mass of the male population would be trained and ready for call-up if a war should break out. Following the widespread adoption of this model, by the early 20th century, the major European powers, Germany, Austria-Hungary, Russia, France, and Italy were in a position to deploy armies numbering millions at very short notice.

STRATEGY AND TACTICS

Napoleon was the commander who, more than any other, established a new approach to warfare to suit the new age. He sought to bring his opponents to battle through the speed of maneuver of his mass armies and then crush them by the maximum use of force. On the battlefield, skirmishers were used to harass the enemy before the power of massed artillery,

British Redcoats
In their campaigns against Napoleon, the British infantry under Wellington usually fought defensively in a line, fighting off the enemy with volleys of musket fire. In the Peninsular War (1808–14) and at the Battle of Waterloo in 1815 their discipline won the day against the more aggressive tactics of the French.

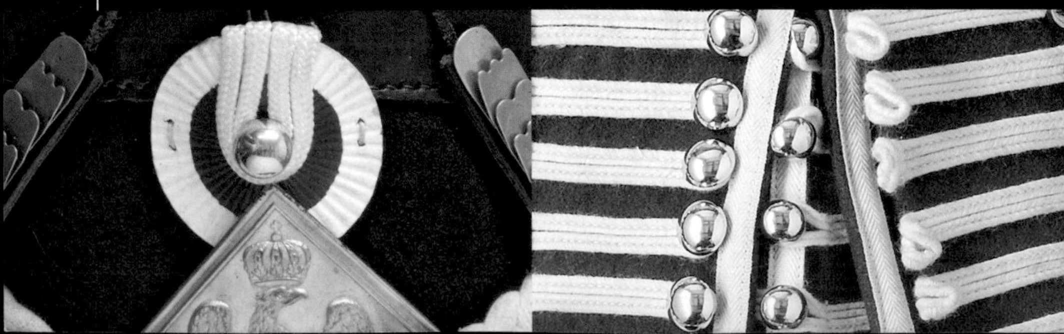

68

heavy cavalry, and infantry broke them down. Napoleon's approach on land was mirrored at sea by the British navy, dedicated to swift and decisive engagement with the enemy whenever feasible. The fact that Napoleon was ultimately defeated did nothing to tarnish the reputation of the methods with which he had won so many outstanding victories. European armies were dedicated to fighting large-scale battles to the death—ensuring massive casualties, as at Borodino in 1812, when more than 70,000 men were killed or wounded in a day.

TECHNOLOGICAL DEVELOPMENTS

The potential destructiveness of warfare was increased through the 19th century by rapid developments in many fields of technology. The accuracy, range, and rate of fire of infantry weapons were transformed as muzzle-loading muskets were superseded by breech-loading repeater rifles and then, from the 1880s, by fully automatic machine guns. Rifled artillery replaced smoothbore cannon and fired high-explosive shells at long range. Industrialized countries were able to produce such arms and munitions in unprecedented quantities. Meanwhile, the construction of railroads allowed large armies to move at unprecedented speed—although once away from the tracks they reverted to the pace of the march and the horse. The invention of the electric telegraph gave some help in controlling large-scale forces operating over wide geographical areas.

The American Civil War (1861–65) occurred before technological changes in weaponry were very far advanced. But even with muzzle-loading rifles and smoothbore cannon, the Union and Confederate armies amply demonstrated the potential for slaughter on battlefields where, counter to the aspirations of Napoleonic warfare, massed firepower was always likely to give the defense the upper hand. The cavalry charge in particular was shown to be outdated as it was simply unsustainable in the face of concentrated infantry and artillery fire.

While modern weapons technology was increasing the soldier's chances of dying on the battlefield, other manifestations of progress made his life substantially easier in many respects. The development of canned food, first issued to troops during the Napoleonic Wars, was a boon for men on campaign—opening cans became, for a time, the main use for bayonets. Mass production in general ensured that soldiers from industrialized countries were better clothed and shod than their rural ancestors.

In line with social reforms throughout the industrialized world, military punishments tended to become less harsh—flogging was officially abolished in the British and US armies in the 1860s. The pioneering activities of British nurse Florence Nightingale during the Crimean War (1854–56) and the founding of the International Red Cross in 1863 exemplified a new concern for the treatment of the war-wounded. Improvements in sanitation and in medical knowledge ensured that by the 20th century, for the first time in history, armies at war might potentially experience more deaths from actual combat than from the hardship and disease that accompanied any prolonged campaign.

US Civil War
A young drummer boy of the Union army poses in front of a cannon. Some drummer boys were as young as seven or eight. The most widely used artillery piece of the Civil War was the bronze 12-pounder field gun known as a Napoleon cannon. Most cannons of the Civil War were smoothbores with a range of only about 1 mile (1.6 km).

IMPERIAL POWER

With their industrial might, increasing populations, and aggressive attitude to military operations, 19th century Europeans and their overseas offshoots enjoyed a clear military superiority over non-European states. The Chinese government was forced to adhere to humiliating treaties through a series of military defeats, and the British took possession of India with piecemeal victories over local armies. European military expansion was certainly not wholly uncontested, and encounters between European armies and peoples with an indigenous warrior tradition were at times fought on surprisingly equal terms. The Maori in New Zealand, having transformed their traditional warfare by the adoption of firearms, at times outfought white settlers and a colonial army. The Zulu, one of many African peoples who resisted European imperial takeover in the late 19th century, were able on several occasions to bring the British infantry to close-quarters combat at which their spearmen excelled. In North America, the Plains Indians fought a guerrilla war against the US cavalry which was only suppressed with some difficulty. However, if an industrialized power had the will to devote all the necessary resources to a conflict, there could be no doubt as to the eventual outcome.

By the end of the 19th century, a wide technological divide had opened up between the world's major powers and the rest. The traditional warrior virtues of courage and aggression were of little use against the machine gun. At the battle of Omdurman in 1898, the British army lost a total of only 48 men while slaughtering some 16,000 followers of the Sudanese Mahdi. The English poet Hilaire Belloc was inspired to write the cruel couplet: "Whatever happens we have got/ The Maxim gun and they have not." But in 1914–18 the industrial powers would instead turn their destructive firepower upon one another, bringing the slaughter home to Europe.

1775 – 1783

AMERICAN RIFLEMAN

THE[illegible]E M[illegible]N HAVE B[illegible]N BRE[illegible] IN THE W[illegible]S T[illegible]

Battle of Kings Mountain
One of the greatest triumphs of the irregular frontier riflemen in the American Revolutionary War was their defeat of a force of well-trained Loyalist militia at Kings Mountain in 1780 *(above)*. The weapon that made them so successful as snipers and skirmishers was the long-barrelled rifle *(right)*, originally made for hunting.

EXPERT RIFLEMEN were the first companies of soldiers raised by the rebellious North American colonies to fight the British army and its Loyalist supporters at the start of the American Revolutionary War. At a time when inaccurate muskets were the standard military firearm, the accuracy of the American frontier marksmen's rifle fire inspired fear and awe. Although they were resistant to formal discipline, these tough and independent fighters proved impressively effective as sharp-shooting snipers and battlefield skirmishers.

The riflemen originated from the American frontier world of farmers and hunters—settlers carving out a life for themselves in the wild, gun in hand. Introduced to North America from Europe by German and Swiss immigrants, rifles were regarded principally as a hunting weapon. Americans developed the design of the European rifle to give it greater accuracy and range, creating what was later called the Kentucky rifle. With this long-barrelled, small-bore gun, farm boys and woodsmen learned to shoot with astonishing accuracy. They honed their skills in hunting, in skirmishes with Indians, and in shooting competitions, which became a favorite frontier pastime. Men would, for instance, compete to hit the head of a turkey—alive and moving—at a range of around 330 ft (100 m). Frontiersmen were also known for their hardihood and independent spirit, having learned the art of survival in virgin wilderness. They would consequently show endurance on the march and an ability to travel light, living off the land when required.

LONG RIFLE MADE IN PENNSYLVANIA IN THE 1750S

RIFLEMEN FOR THE REVOLUTION

The frontiersmen were not material from which regular soldiers could easily be made, but the leaders of the American colonies gathered in the Continental Congress were quick to recognize their military potential. Future US President John Adams expressed the opinion that they would make "an excellent species of light infantry" since they were "the most excellent marksmen in the world." Thus on June 14. 1775, Congress resolved that "six companies of expert riflemen be immediately raised in Pennsylvania, two in Maryland, and two in Virginia." The response in Pennsylvania was so enthusiastic that the state in fact provided nine companies. Volunteers initially enlisted for a year, with the promise of a gift of land to reward their services after victory. Each company typically had four officers, eight NCOs, and 68 men. Their immediate mission was to join the American forces besieging the British and Loyalists in Boston. The journey from the frontier regions to the New England coast had to be made on foot, a formidable march undertaken at a punishing rate. The riflemen from western Maryland, led by Michael Cresap, covered the 550 miles (990 km) from their recruiting point to Boston in three weeks—taking time en route to stage demonstrations of their marksmanship, including, in one instance, a rifleman firing at a target held between his brother's knees.

The arrival of the frontiersmen outside Boston caused a considerable stir. Their dress immediately marked them out as wild men: they wore fringed hunting shirts, moccasins, and hats decorated with feathers or animal tails, and many carried scalping knives and tomahawks as well as their rifles. Their accurate sniper fire soon began to take its toll of British sentries around Boston and even of officers who had the temerity to show themselves in the open.

Snipers and woodsmen
The incident at the battle of Saratoga in 1777 when Tim Murphy shot General Fraser soon became the stuff of legend. Here he is depicted high up in the pine tree on the right aiming at his distant target *(right)*. The appearance of the rifle companies, with fringed shirts and axes tucked in their belts *(far right)*, was in marked contrast to that of the British Army regulars.

At the same time, the frontiersmen revealed themselves to be a thoroughly undisciplined bunch, given to stealing from ordinary soldiers and disrespectful of all conventional authority. They would, by contrast, faithfully follow officers of their own ilk, such as the formidable Virginian Daniel Morgan, who in his earlier military career in the French and Indian War had survived having most of his teeth blown out by a bullet that passed through his neck and cheek.

The American commander-in-chief, General George Washington, was conviced that only a disciplined army trained and drilled on European lines could beat the British. But he appreciated the frontiersmen's fighting qualities and encouraged Morgan in particular to form and lead bodies of riflemen to act as snipers and skirmishing light infantry. Morgan thoroughly justified the confidence shown in him with a notable contribution to the defeat of the British at Saratoga in 1777. As General John Burgoyne's army advanced south down the Hudson Valley on September 19, their right flank ran into Morgan's riflemen at Freeman's Farm. Aimed fire directed from woodland across a clearing decimated the British advanced guard, in particular killing almost all of the officers. The riflemen were less successful in attempting to exploit the advantage thus gained, their ill-organized charges being repelled by the disciplined British bayonets. The battle was resumed after a lull on October 7, with a British assault on Bemis Heights. In a famous incident, American General Benedict Arnold called upon Morgan to get rid of one of the ablest British officers, General Simon Fraser, who was bravely riding in the open on a gray horse. One of Morgan's men, a legendary Indian fighter called Tim Murphy, obliged by shooting Fraser dead at a range of some 300 yards (275 m). This loss had a crushing effect on British morale, contributing to the failure of their attack and their eventual defeat.

> "MANY OF THEM AT 150 YARDS WILL HIT A CARD NINE TIMES OUT OF TEN."
>
> **BRITISH OFFICER** AT THE SIEGE OF BOSTON, 1775

Rifleman's haversack
Accustomed to hunting and living off his wits in the woods of the frontier colonies, the rifleman was much better equipped for most eventualities than any regular soldier.

UNFAIR TACTICS

The policy of sniping at individual officers was as controversial as it was effective. Morgan, who reputedly tested new recruits by asking them to shoot at a target in the shape of a British officer's head, was regarded by some of his opponents as in effect a war criminal. British Lieutenant William Digby, complaining of this "cowardly and cruel way of carrying on the war" called for snipers to be placed in "the hands of the hangman." The British equally objected to the riflemen's skirmishing style of warfare. The frontiersmen were expert at exploiting cover, firing at will from behind trees, rocks, or walls. They also did not hesitate to hide or run away when facing a counterattack. These tactics were viewed with contempt by British soldiers trained to fire muskets in volleys and stand up to their enemy in the open. One wrote indignantly of the riflemen: "Those people in fair action in open field would signify nothing." Naturally

Kings Mountain, 1780
The buckskin-clad rebel irregulars found the terrain much more to their liking than their Loyalist opponents, and made excellent use of the cover provided by the hill's wooded slopes.

the frontier fighters delighted in the irritation they caused the British and deliberately cultivated their "wild man" image to psychological effect. Morgan adopted a spine-chilling wild turkey gobble as a signal to his men and they frequently raised an Indian war cry when entering combat.

FRONTIER IRREGULARS

Morgan's riflemen were employed as light infantry skirmishers in Washington's Continental Army. But as the geographical scope of the Revolutionary War expanded into the back country of the South, many more frontiersmen were drawn into the conflict, who fought as irregular bands under self-appointed colonels. They harassed the British and Loyalists, using the classic guerrilla tactics of hit-and-run attacks and ambushes. The raiding of men such as Francis Marion of South Carolina, known as the "swamp fox," were a persistent nuisance to the British, and at times inflicted heavy losses.

The most famous victory by frontier irregulars was won at Kings Mountain in the Carolinas, in October 1780. A force of 1,000 Loyalist militia, led by British officer Colonel Patrick Ferguson—ironically himself a leading advocate of the use of rifles—was surrounded by a somewhat smaller force of rifle-armed backwoodsmen who "opened an irregular but destructive fire." Ferguson mounted bayonet charges to drive the riflemen off, but they simply withdrew, avoiding contact, and resumed their positions once the force of the charge was spent. After suffering more than 300 casualties, including Ferguson and 156 others killed, the entire Loyalist force surrendered.

WORLDWIDE INFLUENCE

Probably the finest hour of the American riflemen came at Cowpens in January 1781, when a mixed force of militia and Continental Army troops commanded by Morgan inflicted a humiliating defeat on the British under Sir Banastre Tarleton. The final British surrender at Yorktown in October 1781 was occasioned by the combined action of the American and French armies and the French navy—a reminder that, whatever their achievements, frontier riflemen could not themselves win a war. But their successes stimulated European armies to increase their use of rifle-armed light infantry and began a shift away from reliance on meticulously drilled formations armed with musket and bayonet.

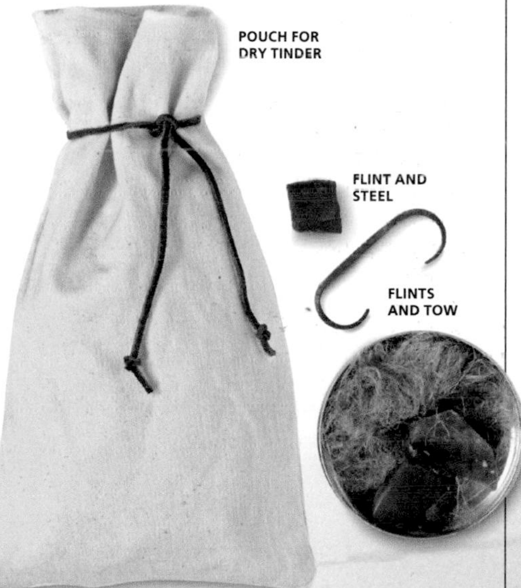

Fire-lighting kit
A rifleman would be able to light a fire at a moment's notice using tow (hemp or flax fibers) to catch the sparks he struck with his flint and steel. He often carried a pouch of dry kindling as well.

Battlefield of Cowpens
This was the scene of Daniel Morgan's greatest triumph. Skilful use of his sharpshooters caused havoc among the attacking British dragoons; he then ordered a sudden counterattack that led to the surrender of the British force.

RIFLEMAN'S GEAR

Many riflemen from Virginia and other frontier colonies who fought in the American Revolutionary War were incorporated into units of Washington's army and exchanged their fringed hunting shirts for more conventional uniforms. Others, such as Daniel Morgan's regiment that fought at the battle of Saratoga in 1777 retained their independent spirit along with their own clothing and equipment, fighting as skirmishers and skilled sharpshooters thanks to the accuracy of their long rifles.

Felt hat
The riflemen's flamboyant headgear reflected their life spent hunting. Instead of feathers, many riflemen decorated their hats with animal tails.

Dyed feather

Upturned brim, so rifle could be carried over the shoulder

Ramrod

Hunting shirt
Frontier riflemen did not have a uniform as such, but many favored this style of fringed linen shirt worn with a belt fastened around the waist. The shirts were often dyed in natural shades of brown or green that acted as camouflage.

Powder horn
Riflemen did not use paper cartridges, so had to measure out both the main charge, which was poured down the muzzle, and the small quantity of primer tipped into the pan. In addition to a powder horn, many carried a small measure that held the correct amount of powder for the main charge.

Wooden stopper

Ax blade is standard British military issue of the time

Hatchet
The rifleman was a skilled hunter and woodsman and usually carried a hatchet tucked into his belt for constructing shelters and making fires.

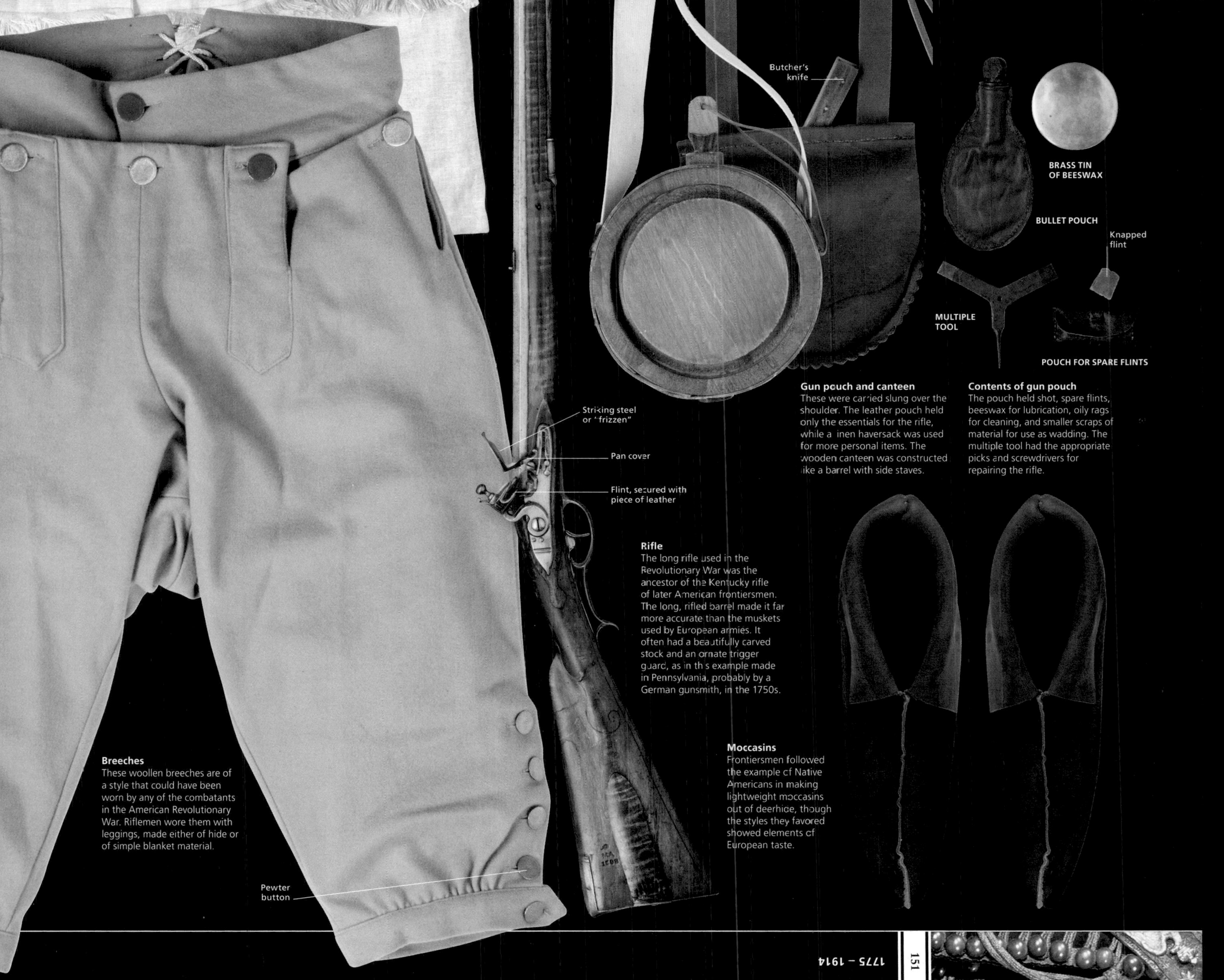

Gun pouch and canteen
These were carried slung over the shoulder. The leather pouch held only the essentials for the rifle, while a linen haversack was used for more personal items. The wooden canteen was constructed like a barrel with side staves.

Contents of gun pouch
The pouch held shot, spare flints, beeswax for lubrication, oily rags for cleaning, and smaller scraps of material for use as wadding. The multiple tool had the appropriate picks and screwdrivers for repairing the rifle.

Rifle
The long rifle used in the Revolutionary War was the ancestor of the Kentucky rifle of later American frontiersmen. The long, rifled barrel made it far more accurate than the muskets used by European armies. It often had a beautifully carved stock and an ornate trigger guard, as in this example made in Pennsylvania, probably by a German gunsmith, in the 1750s.

Moccasins
Frontiersmen followed the example of Native Americans in making lightweight moccasins out of deerhide, though the styles they favored showed elements of European taste.

Breeches
These woollen breeches are of a style that could have been worn by any of the combatants in the American Revolutionary War. Riflemen wore them with leggings, made either of hide or of simple blanket material.

AMERICAN REVOLUTIONARY WAR FORCES

The war that gave birth to the United States of America started as a small-scale encounter between British troops and American colonial militia and ended as a major international conflict. The British initially hoped that American loyalists would carry the main burden of suppressing rebellion, but they were disappointed. The deployment of a substantial British army, including mercenary forces from Hessen and other German states, failed to impose a decisive defeat upon the American Continental Army, which instead scored a notable victory at Saratoga in 1777. In the vast spaces of North America, the British could not bring their superior formal fighting skills to bear. In the end the intervention of the French army and navy tipped the balance decisively against Britain.

THE CONTINENTAL ARMY

The decision of the Continental Congress, the government set up by the 13 rebel American colonies, to form an army on June 14, 1775 was based on the belief that only a regular army, rather than a citizens' militia, could beat the British Redcoats. George Washington, the army's commander, had a low opinion of militias and aspired to create a disciplined European-style force, trained to fire musket volleys and advance in formation with bayonets fixed.

From the outset, the Continental Army ran into difficulties. The only troops initially available were New England militiamen, who signed on as short-term regulars, and undisciplined rifleman volunteers from the backwoods. At the start of 1776 even this rag-tag army threatened to disintegrate, because once they had served their term most of the militia went home, having farms and businesses to attend to. It was not until 1777 that a serious effort was made to raise a permanent national army, recruited on a quota basis from all 13 states, with men committed either to a three-year term of service or for the duration of the war. Bounty payments were offered to attract volunteers—initially $20 but rising sharply over time as recruits proved increasingly reluctant to come forward. Inevitably, quotas were filled from the lowest levels of society. Vagrants and criminals found themselves pressed into service, along with British and Hessian deserters and prisoners of war. Despite initial opposition from Washington, slave and free African Americans were allowed to enter the ranks. The states never managed to supply men in sufficient numbers, although some of the shortfall was made up by the conscription of state militiamen to serve one-year terms under Continental command.

It was probably just as well that the numbers of recruits always fell below planned levels, for it proved impossible for the fledgling republic to pay, feed, or clothe them adequately. Although some men were equipped with in uniforms by their state of origin, after a while on campaign many soldiers lacked

Uniform of 4th Maryland Independent Company
This was one of seven companies of 100 men authorized by the state of Maryland in January 1776. Later that year the men, armed with muskets and bayonets, marched north to join the Continental Army in the defense of New York.

"COULD WE GET A GOOD REGULAR ARMY, WE SHOULD SOON CLEAR THE COUNTRY OF THESE DAMNED INVADERS."

THOMAS NELSON WRITING TO THOMAS JEFFERSON, 1777

coats, blankets, or even shoes. When supply problems were at their worst, men were reduced to living off flour-and-water "firecakes." Camped for the winter at Valley Forge, Pennsylvania, in 1777–78, the army reached extremes of privation. Yet it was here that the army at last began to come together as a disciplined force, under the direction of Prussian mercenary officer Baron Friedrich Wilhelm von Steuben. He drilled the men daily, raised morale, cracked down on unruly behavior, and reduced disease by improving cleanliness and sanitation.

The problems of supply and payment were never solved. There was another major crisis in the winter of 1780–81 when those who had enrolled for three years in 1777 wanted to quit. Mutinies in the Pennsylvania and New Jersey regiments had to be suppressed in January 1781. But Washington succeeded in keeping his army in existence. A measure of the success of the Continental Army, despite all difficulties, is the admiration for American troops expressed by foreign observers. Baron von Closen, a member of the French expeditionary force sent to aid the American rebels, wrote: "It is incredible that soldiers composed of men of every age, even of children of 15, of whites and blacks, almost naked, unpaid, and rather poorly fed, can march so well and withstand fire so steadfastly." The British surrender at Yorktown in October 1781 was a triumph for an army once dismissed by British General John Burgoyne as a "rabble in arms."

Valley Forge
In the grim winter of 1777–78, Washington believed that his Continental Army must "starve, dissolve, or disperse, in order to obtain subsistence." But, in the end, it survived, all the stronger for the experience of shared hardship.

A disciplined volley
The ideal to which George Washington aspired—a disciplined, smartly dressed, European-style army—was never achieved by the whole army, although certain units did their leader proud.

MINUTEMEN

The Battle of Lexington
The first shots of the war were fired across the village green at Lexington, Massachusetts. A confused encounter watched by spectators standing along the road, it ended with eight of the American minutemen lying dead.

The only forces at the disposal of the American colonies at the start of their rebellion were militia. There was a long-established tradition that all male citizens had a duty to turn out with a weapon for the defense of their colony or local community when required. In 1774, in the colony of Massachusetts, the original focus of the rebellion, a proportion of the militia were designated "minutemen." Usually younger unmarried citizens, they elected officers for their companies and pledged to be available for action at a minute's notice. The first shots of the war, at Lexington and Concord in April 1775, were exchanged between minutemen and British soldiers. At Concord the minutemen got the better of a smaller force of British regulars and pursued them back to Boston.

THE ROLE OF THE MILITIAS

In all the rebel colonies, colonial militias turned into state militias under rebel control, with all loyalists expelled. At times state militias competed with the Continental Army for resources, but the militias also provided essential short-term draftees to bolster the army's ranks and auxiliary units to fight alongside the regulars.

Although militia training improved during the war, these part-time soldiers fresh from the workshop and the plow rarely stood up to British troops in open battle. Yet in spite of a reputation for running away when the fighting was hot, they performed invaluable service as security forces, ensuring the success of the rebellion at local level by manning garrisons and suppressing the activities of loyalists.

BRITISH REDCOATS

The red-coated British army was a typical European force of its day, splendidly uniformed, harshly disciplined, and drilled in the use of musket and bayonet. It was composed of regulars enlisted for life, but to raise extra troops for the American war short-term enlistments were introduced and eventually a virtual press gang was instituted. Most soldiers came from the lowest levels of British society and many were from potentially disaffected areas of Scotland and Ireland, but they generally fought with as much determination as any American patriot.

Shipped across the Atlantic, British soldiers entered a hostile and alien environment. The sniping and ambushes employed by rebel militia seemed outrageous to troops trained to fight in the open—one British ensign referred to it as "their skulking way behind hedges and walls." Americans derided the British for parading in bright colors when stealth and camouflage would have served them better. Yet the British were not inflexible in their tactics. They adapted as best they could to local conditions, employing light troops as skirmishers and making small adaptations such as shortening their jackets to prevent their coat tails becoming entangled in undergrowth.

LOGISTICS AND SUPPLY

The British unquestionably found American conditions hard. Campaigning on foot across vast tracts of wilderness tended to erode their forces through exhaustion and disease. A large part of their supplies were imported across the Atlantic, and they suffered shortages of everything from food to horses. The Americans proved expert not only at ambush in hilly, wooded terrain but also at field fortifications. In battles such as Bunker Hill in 1775 and Saratoga in 1777, British troops suffered morale-sapping losses in frontal attacks against determined American troops who skilfully exploited natural defensive positions, strengthened by entrenchment and stockades.

Volley fire
British troops were trained to fire in volley and deploy on the battlefield in formal line and square formations. Many were disconcerted by the American snipers and tactics.

Facing rebel activity that extended from Georgia in the south to Canada in the north, the British always had too few men to garrison areas they controlled and simultaneously campaign in strength. The British army that surrendered at Yorktown in 1781 was outnumbered two to one by its American and French opponents.

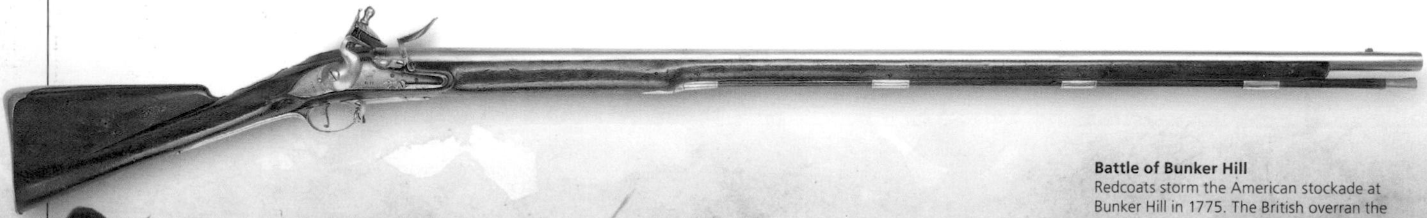

Brown Bess
The Long Land-Pattern flintlock musket, known familiarly as Brown Bess, was the standard British infantry arm from 1722 to 1838. The version shown here was issued in 1742.

Battle of Bunker Hill
Redcoats storm the American stockade at Bunker Hill in 1775. The British overran the fortified earthworks on their third assault, but suffered devastating losses in the process.

LOYALISTS

> GREEN IS ... THE BEST COLOUR FOR LIGHT TROOPS ... AND IF PUT ON IN THE SPRING, BY AUTUMN IT NEARLY FADES WITH THE LEAVES.
>
> **JOHN GRAVES SIMCOE,** COMMANDER OF THE QUEEN'S RANGERS 1777–83

Considerable numbers of Americans fought on the British side in the war. Some participated in provincial regiments of the British army—for example, the King's Royal Regiment created by Loyalist refugees in Canada in 1776, and the Caledonian Volunteers composed of Loyalist Scottish settlers. Some of these units, like the New York-based Queen's Rangers, proved to be tough fighting men capable of welding American rifle marksmanship and flexible tactics to British discipline. Others fought as militia or irregulars, often under British officers, waging partisan warfare against the rebels. Butler's Rangers, a mixed force of Loyalists and Indians, was responsible for a notorious massacre in Wyoming Valley in 1778. Tarleton's Raiders, operating in the Carolinas, also earned a fearsome reputation. Black slaves fought for the British in return for a promise of freedom, both as regulars in Lord Dunmore's Ethiopian Regiment, raised in 1775, and as guerrillas. At the war's end most Loyalist fighters, black or white, chose to leave the United States.

Green and white plume of the Light Company of the Queen's Rangers

Leather cap with crescent emblem

Hanoverian black cockade

Ruffled linen shirt with black neck stock

Short green jacket known as a "round jacket" with buttons marked QR

Canvas knapsack painted with regimental emblem

Cartridge box with brass flap showing initials GR (*George rex*)

White canvas breeches, worn with half garters

Queen's Rangers uniform
Founded in 1776 in New York, the Queen's Rangers was the first regiment in the British army to wear green uniforms for the purposes of camouflage.

HESSIANS

About a third of British forces engaged in the war were German mercenaries hired for the duration of the conflict. These "Hessians" came not only from Hessen-Kassel and Hessen-Hannau, but also from a number of other petty German princedoms that provided contingents of troops in return for a cash payment. Such mercenary service, contracted at government level, was standard practice in 18th-century European armies.

The Hessians were not notably inferior to British soldiers in battlefield performance or in their behavior towards civilians. Most were schooled in the standard musket-and-bayonet style of combat, but companies of *jäger*—light rifle-armed troops—made excellent skirmishers. Clad in green for camouflage, these German hunters on occasion outperformed the American rifleman as snipers and woodland fighters.

The American Congress and states attempted to bribe the Hessians with offers of land and livestock. Many did desert, but no more than was normal for a European army on campaign. Around 60 percent of the 30,000 Hessians eventually returned home. Combat losses were quite low, but many died of disease. The rest presumably made new lives for themselves in America.

1799 – 1815

FRENCH CAVALRYMAN

THE FRENCH CAVALRY OUTCLASSED ITS OPPONENTS SIMPLY BECAUSE, WHEN THE ORDER RANG OUT AND TRUMPETS CLARIONED “CHARGE !,” IT PUT IN ITS SPURS AND CHARGED ALL OUT, CHARGED HOME !

ARCHDUKE CHARLES, COMMANDER-IN-CHIEF OF THE AUSTRIAN ARMY FROM 1806 TO 1809

AS A GENERAL UNDER THE FRENCH REPUBLIC, and later as Emperor of France, Napoleon Bonaparte based his style of warfare on rapid movement of forces to bring the enemy to battle, and aggressive battlefield tactics to crush his adversary in the field. In his increasingly large armies, infantry, artillery, and cavalry all had their parts to play. Key functions of the cavalry included the mounting of decisive charges at crucial points in the battle and the pursuit of a routed enemy to complete an overwhelming victory.

The French Revolution of 1789 had a profound effect on the French army and other areas of French society. The cavalry had always been the most aristocratic element of France's armed forces. Many of its officers were hostile to the revolution and emigrated; others who would willingly have continued to serve their country were dismissed because the radical revolutionary government disapproved of their social origins. This was the fate of the Marquis de Grouchy, who was stripped of his rank in 1793, but he later rose to become one of Napoleon's most distinguished cavalry commanders. For some men of humble origin, however, the revolution provided unprecedented opportunity—Joachim Murat, son of a village postmaster, enlisted as a cavalry trooper in 1787 and was a colonel by 1795, while Michel Ney, the son of a barrel-maker, joined the hussars also in 1787 and was a general commanding a brigade by 1796.

RIDERS AND MOUNTS

But overall, despite the promotion of some talented individuals, the revolution played havoc with the French cavalry and it performed poorly in most of the battles of the Revolutionary Wars (1792–1801). Napoleon inherited a force short of horses, training, and confidence. As consul and then emperor, he set about reforming and upgrading the cavalry arm as a vital element in his rebuilding of the entire French army.

Of the two key components of an effective cavalry force—riders and horses—Napoleon found the human element easier to deal with. From 1799, when Napoleon took over the government as First Consul, annual conscription filled the army's ranks, bringing a constant flow of fresh recruits to serve alongside veterans of the army of the monarchy and of the revolutionary *levée en masse* (mass conscription) of 1793. Cavalry regiments were given magnificent new uniforms, with an emphasis on color and flamboyance, as part of a successful campaign to raise morale. Napoleon's regime inspired patriotic zeal, revolutionary enthusiasm, and the attachment of men who owed to it their advancement in life.

The shortage of horses was a problem that was much harder to remedy because it required years to breed sufficient numbers of the right mounts. When Napoleon's Grande Armée first assembled in 1805, dragoons fought on foot because of lack of horses. It was the victories at Austerlitz in 1805 and at Jena and Auerstadt in 1806 that effectively solved the problem by allowing the French to take large numbers of horses from the defeated Austrians and Prussians.

GLAMOR AND HARDSHIP

The cavalry service, with its dashing uniforms and its "death or glory" fighting tradition, naturally attracted adventurous young men with a taste for glamor and style. Napoleonic cavalrymen were famed for their hard drinking, their short tempers that easily flared into fights, and above all their relentless womanizing. But life in the cavalry was on the whole far from luxurious, even when not on campaign.

FULL DRESS SHAKO OF THE FIRST REGIMENT OF CHASSEURS

Vive l'empéreur
This late 19th-century painting of the charge of the 4th Hussars at the Battle of Friedland, 1807 *(above)* gives a somewhat idealized picture of the bravery and patriotism of Napoleon's troops. Hussars and other light cavalrymen cut even more dashing figures in their full dress uniforms. A chasseur on parade wore a splendid plume on his shako *(right)* instead of the pompom he wore on the battlefield.

Camped for the night
A group of hussars gather round a campfire on the eve of the battle of Austerlitz, December 1805. The lines of fires blazing on the hill beyond give some idea of the vast size of Napoleon's army.

> "WHEN I SPEAK OF EXCELLENT FRENCH CAVALRY, I REFER TO ITS IMPETUOUS BRAVERY, AND NOT TO ITS PERFECTION."
>
> **ANTOINE-HENRI JOMINI**, STAFF OFFICER IN NAPOLEON'S ARMY AND MILITARY THEORIST

Troopers slept two to a bed in barracks—the bed companions usually becoming close comrades in arms. Training was tough. It started with learning horsemanship by riding without saddle, bridle, or stirrups, progressing to the difficult art of using the sword or saber and carbine while mounted. New recruits were said to habitually lose a lot of weight during initial training, so stringent were its physical demands. Grooming horses was, of course, hard unglamorous work—the French cavalry were in fact often criticized for not looking after their mounts adequately.

Like those serving in the rest of Napoleon's army, cavalry troopers had to be treated as citizen soldiers deserving of their officers' respect. There was nothing like the harsh and arbitrary discipline of the Ancien Régime army. A thoroughly professional attitude to military life was encouraged, although cavalrymen continued to assert their individuality in various ways, such as wearing their hair in long, thin pigtails. Fiery young Frenchmen keen on winning glory were temperamentally ill-adapted to the boredom of barrack life, with its interminable routines of mucking-out and drill, and were always relieved to set out on campaign. With Napoleon in charge, there was never any lack of military action.

HEAVY AND LIGHT

The most distinctive feature of Napoleonic cavalry was the prominent role given to armored horsemen: the cuirassiers. Along with two regiments of carabiniers—also equipped with armor from 1809—the cuirassiers constituted the heavy cavalry. Armored horsemen had been considered an antiquated concept, looking backward to the age of the medieval knight, but Napoleon liked to use it as a shock force on the battlefield. The cuirassiers were large men mounted on large horses. They wore metal helmets and plate armor on their chest and back. For armament they carried a heavy straight saber and a pistol. Like armored soldiers through the ages, the cuirassiers found their metal shell hot and uncomfortable in summer; it was also very expensive. The cuirassiers were a self-conscious elite, forming the core of the cavalry reserve, which also included a number of dragoons. The reserve was only thrown into action after due deliberation, at what was considered a decisive

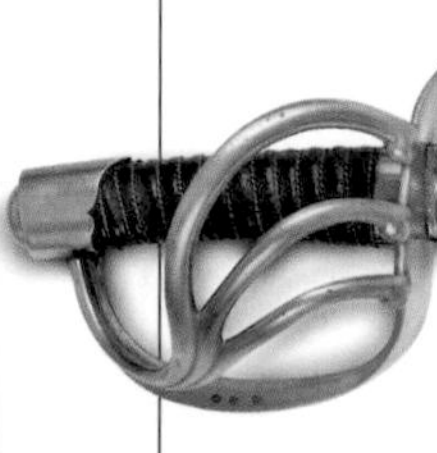

Heavy cavalry saber and scabbard
The cuirassier saber was a straight single-edged sword that could be used as a cutting weapon, but in a disciplined charge cavalrymen tended to use the point. Shown here is the An XIII (1810) model.

Dashing hussar
The hussars cultivated an image of reckless courage and death-defying boldness in action, always trying to outdo the rest of the French cavalry in feats of horsemanship.

moment in a battle. They were used in mass charges, a role that required discipline and horsemanship rather than dash and initiative.

The light cavalry, by contrast, were generally distributed among Napoleon's army corps—large formations in which they operated in collaboration with infantry and artillery. They consisted initially of hussars and chasseurs; these were later joined by increasing numbers of lancers. Hussars saw themselves as the most dashing of cavalry. Their attractiveness to women was legendary—they were said to be "hated by husbands and loved by wives". The hussars thought themselves far superior to the chasseurs, whose uniforms were cheaper and less splendid, and rivalry between the two was intense. Chasseurs carried carbines and on occasion fought on foot. Otherwise, the function of hussars and chasseurs was broadly identical. They acted as scouts, carrying out reconnaissance patrols and harassing raids, and screening the movements of the army from the enemy. Activities of this kind involved small groups operating independently and gave plenty of chance to show initiative. On the battlefield light cavalry would charge with their sabers held low to run infantrymen through. They were noted for their spirit of attack and speed in pursuit of a defeated enemy.

LANCERS AND DRAGOONS

One of the notable changes in military technology that took place during the Napoleonic Wars was the widespread use of lances as a light cavalry weapon. During the 18th century lancers were generally regarded as an exotic, marginal element in European warfare. The most famous lancers in Europe were the Polish cavalry known as Uhlans, who were renowned for their wild behavior and independent fighting spirit.

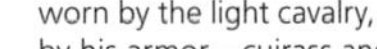

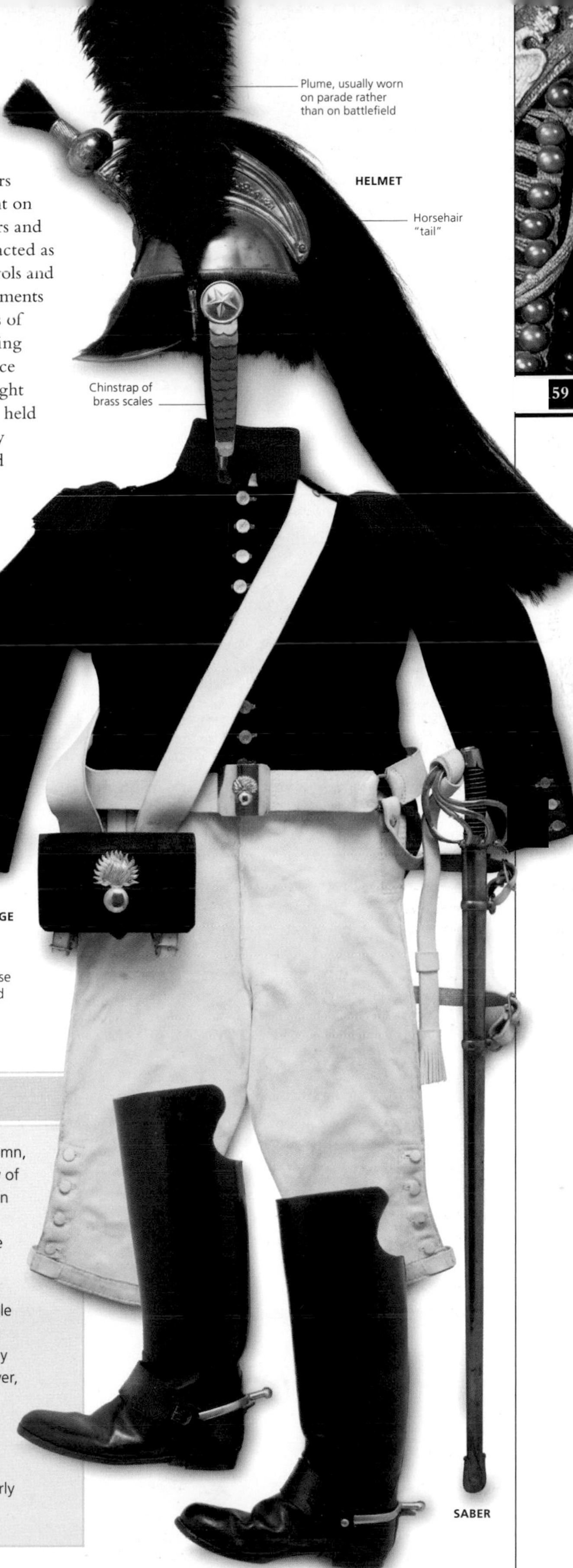

Plume, usually worn on parade rather than on battlefield

HELMET

Horsehair "tail"

Chinstrap of brass scales

CARTRIDGE BOX

SABER

Cuirassier uniform
The cuirassier's tunic was less spectacular than those worn by the light cavalry, but it was usually covered by his armor—cuirass and back plate. He made up for this with his magnificent plumed helmet.

HEAVY CAVALRY TACTICS

Napoleon's conception of the cuirassiers was as a force capable of delivering a mass cavalry charge of overwhelming power at a key point on the battlefield, if possible precipitating a general collapse of the enemy forces. In theory, there would be a preliminary artillery bombardment to weaken the enemy before the charge was launched, gradually accelerating from its start to the moment of encounter.

THEORY AND PRACTICE

Beginning at a trot, the cuirassiers were supposed to shift up to a canter and then, some 500 ft (150 m) from the enemy, break into a gallop, reaching full tilt over the last 150 ft (50 m). In practice, though, French commanders preferred to use the cuirassiers in a close formation that militated against such a headlong charge. They ordered the heavy cavalry to advance in a massive, tightly packed column, with men riding boot to boot. The difficulty of maintaining formation in the massed column made it virtually impossible to progress at any great speed, and of course deprived the individual cavalryman of any chance to use his initiative. But it did create a body moving with almost unstoppable momentum, capable of breaking enemy cavalry formations apart and beating down loosely organized infantry with hoof and saber. The cuirassiers, however, had no adequate tactics for penetrating infantry squares that held firm with bayonets fixed, as was demonstrated at the battle of Waterloo. When they charged in dense formation they were also particularly vulnerable to well-directed artillery fire.

It is not surprising, then, that first lancers in the Napoleonic cavalry were Poles. In 1811 a number of dragoon regiments were converted into lancers, as the usefulness of a weapon around 10 ft (3 m) long was becoming increasingly apparent. The lancers were potentially effective against infantry squares—immune to all other forms of cavalry attack—since their lances outreached the musket and bayonet. Lancers were also great skirmishers on the battlefield, marauding at will. In a cavalry mêlée, however, their long weapon was an unwieldy encumbrance and no match for the saber. To cope with this defect, not all the men in lancer regiments were armed with lances. Each group of riders that carried lances was supported by a number of comrades with sabers drawn.

The dragoons were numerically the largest element of the French cavalry. As they were armed with muskets and had originally been soldiers who rode to battle but fought on foot, Napoleon was tempted to use them in battle as infantry. They proved unsatisfactory in that role, however, not possessing the disciplined steadiness of true foot soldiers. At the same time, the distraction of infantry training tended to reduce their effectiveness in the saddle. Still, in the early battles of the Napoleonic Wars the dragoons frequently distinguished themselves fighting alongside the cuirassiers as a kind of ancillary semi-heavy cavalry. From 1807 they served chiefly in the Peninsular War in Spain. As well as fighting Wellington's army on many occasions, they were immersed in the cruel, dirty war of ambushes and reprisals against Spanish guerrilla fighters.

CAVALRY IN ACTION

The French cavalry won its reputation as a battle-winning force early on in the Napoleonic Wars. At Marengo in 1800, a charge by some 400 troopers commanded by General François Etienne Kellerman plunged into the flank of an Austrian infantry and cavalry column 6,000-strong, driving them from the field in panic and confusion at a moment when the French had been facing almost certain defeat. The Napoleonic cavalry reached its peak of effectiveness, however, in the period 1805 to 1812. Well mounted, thoroughly trained, decked out in splendid uniforms, and utterly self-confident, they were an elite that proved its worth in battle after battle. They made a notable contribution to the victories at Ulm and Austerlitz in 1805, but their most spectacular performance was probably against the Russians at Eylau in February 1807. At a desperate moment in the battle, Murat led the 10,000-strong cavalry reserve in a charge that swept through the Russian infantry, then reformed and charged through them a second time to regain the French lines.

Sabertache of the 8th Hussars
A distinctive leather satchel carried by cavalrymen, the sabertache hung from the sabre belt on the left flank of the horse. Originally holding writing and sketching materials, by Napoleonic times it was largely decorative.

Napoleon's invasion of Russia in 1812, however, brought catastrophe. Even at the start of the campaign, the lack of adequate forage for the massive cavalry force—the cavalry reserve alone was 40,000 strong—meant that many of the horses began to starve. "One saw their great emaciated bodies dragging themselves along," an eyewitness commented. "Every minute one would quiver and fall on its rider, who abandoned it." The Russian Cossacks proved superior to the French hussars and cuirassiers

> “YOU PERCEIVED IN THE DISTANCE WHAT APPEARED TO BE AN OVERWHELMING, LONG MOVING LINE ... ON CAME THE MOUNTED HOST ... WHILE THE VERY EARTH SEEMED TO VIBRATE BENEATH THEIR THUNDERING TRAMP.”
>
> **BRITISH INFANTRYMAN** DESCRIBING THE FRENCH CAVALRY CHARGE AT WATERLOO

The cuirassiers at Austerlitz
Napoleon considered Austerlitz his finest victory. He skilfully maneuvered his forces around the battlefield to gain local numerical superiority and then ordered attacks at crucial points and decisive moments. Here the cuirassiers wait their turn to charge.

at the murderous game of harrying and skirmishing. At the battle of Borodino in September the cuirassiers carried out one of their most famous actions, the capture of the formidably defended Grand Redoubt, but even this was achieved at heavy cost. The grim winter retreat from Moscow completed the destruction of the French cavalry. Most of the horses were slaughtered for food and the remnants of the army that survived the campaign could muster less than 2,000 mounts between them.

With desperate energy, the French cavalry was rebuilt in 1813, but most of the troopers were now ill-trained novices and horses were in short supply. Still, the spirit of the cavalry revived sufficiently for a heroic finale at Waterloo in 1815. Late in the battle, with the tide already turning decisively against the French, Ney threw massed cavalry forward in an attempt to break the British infantry squares. But, charging uphill over muddy ground onto the points of bayonets, the French cavalry were mown down by a combination of cannon and musket fire.

THE NAPOLEONIC WARS 1796–1815

- French territory ruled directly from Paris 1812
- Dependent state 1812
- French victory
- French defeat
- Egyptian campaign 1798–1801
- The War with Russia 1812

LESSONS OF WAR

In the last resort, Napoleon's faith in cavalry can be seen as excessive. The growth in the size of armies during the Napoleonic Wars meant that an adequate size cavalry arm required a greater number of suitable horses than could readily be found, and those horses needed an often impossible quantity of fodder. On the battlefield, the increasing firepower of artillery and the resilience of well-trained infantry with bayonets fixed tended to nullify the impact of the cavalry charge. By 1815 the bold death-defying cavalryman, with his dash and valor, was already on the verge of obsolescence.

Triumphs and disasters
From his first victories in Italy in 1796, through the glorious campaigns of 1805–1807, and even during the desperate defense of France in 1814, Napoleon's armies won many more victories than they suffered defeats. In the end, however, the continuous British naval blockade and the sheer number of his enemies—principally Britain, Austria, Prussia, and Russia —combined to bring Napoleon's dream to an end at Waterloo.

CHASSEUR UNIFORM

The appearance of Napoleon's cavalry regiments changed frequently between 1799 and 1815 and the uniform of each regiment and of each company within a regiment boasted its own particular distinguishing features. The one shown here is that of the 1er Chasseurs à Cheval de la Ligne, 2e Compagnie from around the year 1806. The matching red facings on the collar and cuffs indicate the regiment, the pale blue pompom on the shako the company. As well as his basic uniform, the chasseur always carried a dark green cape *(capote)* that was stowed away under his saddle cover *(shabraque)* when not needed.

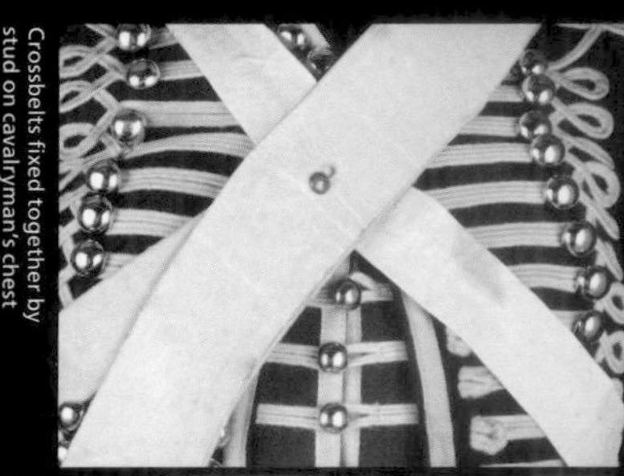

Pompom, worn in action rather than plume

Cockade in the red-white-and-blue of the French tricolor

Chinscales, tied behind shako when not in use

Cords and tassels, by this time purely decorative

Pewter buttons

Shirt and stock
The long white cotton shirt was worn tucked into the breeches and tied between the cavalryman's legs. The collar was fastened with an unobtrusive black stock designed simply to keep the neck looking smart and tidy.

Shako
The shako was adopted by many cavalry—and infantry—regiments across Europe at the end of the 18th century. This 1806 model worn by the chasseurs was made chiefly of felt and leather, with a waterproof top. It was secured under the chin by brass chinscales.

Dolman and waistcoat
The tight-fitting braided jacket worn by chasseurs and hussars was known as a dolman (originally from a Turkish word for a much looser garment). Dark green was the traditional color of the French chasseurs, who liked to swagger around with only the top four buttons of their dolmans done up in order to show off their splendid red *gilets* (vests).

Crossbelts fixed together by stud on cavalryman's chest

Saber, worn slung from a belt at the left hip

Cartridge box and bread bag carried over the shoulder

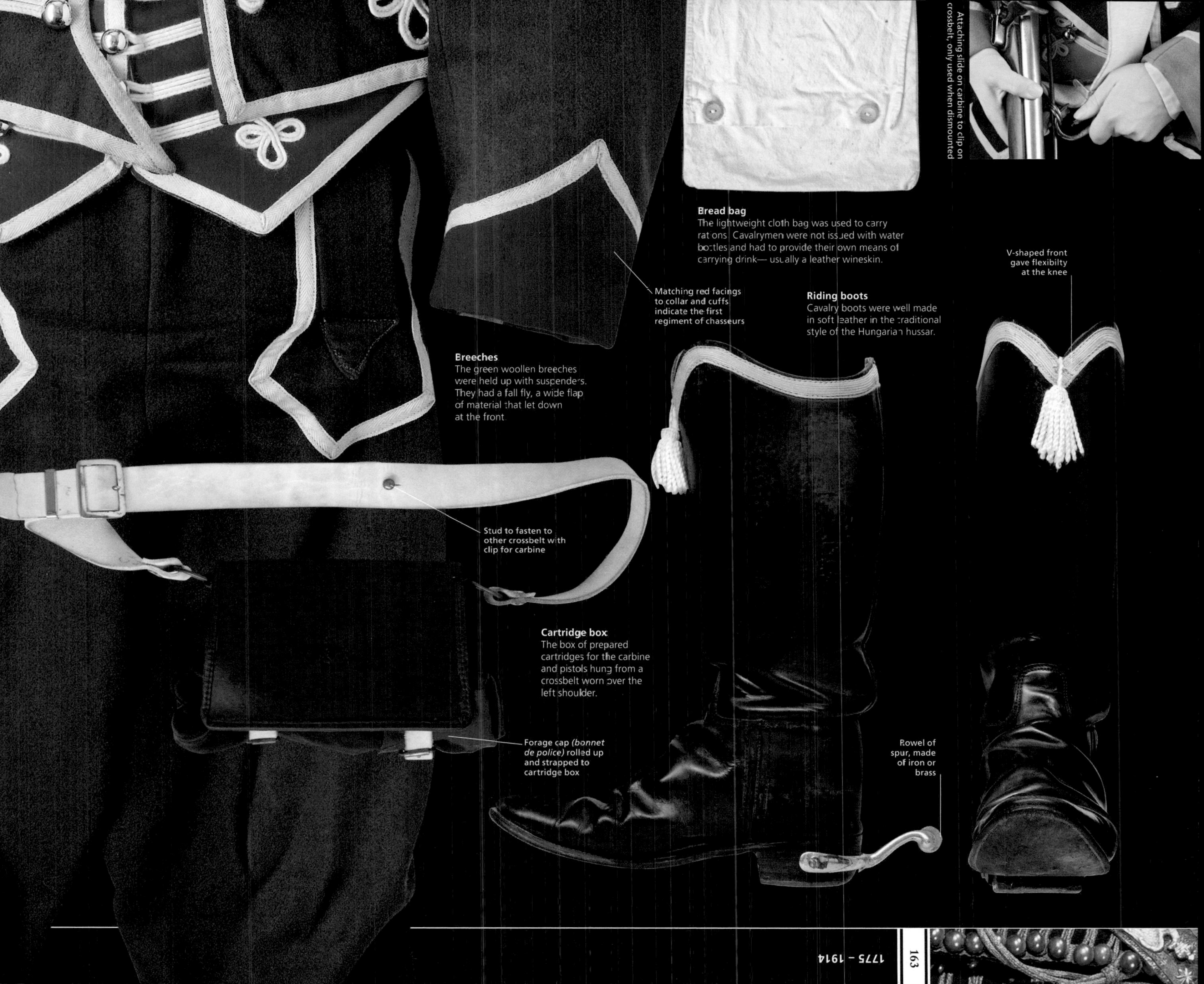

Bread bag
The lightweight cloth bag was used to carry rations. Cavalrymen were not issued with water bottles and had to provide their own means of carrying drink— usually a leather wineskin.

Riding boots
Cavalry boots were well made in soft leather in the traditional style of the Hungarian hussar.

Breeches
The green woollen breeches were held up with suspenders. They had a fall fly, a wide flap of material that let down at the front.

Cartridge box
The box of prepared cartridges for the carbine and pistols hung from a crossbelt worn over the left shoulder.

Attaching slide on carbine to clip on crossbelt, only used when dismounted

CHASSEUR WEAPONS AND EQUIPMENT

A chasseur on patrol carried a range of weapons, including a cavalry saber, a carbine, and sometimes a pair of pistols. His principal weapon was the saber—firearms were of real use only in an emergency as they would take too long to reload in a serious encounter with the enemy. While the cavalryman's weapons obviously played an important part in his role as a skirmisher and a scout, his horse and his tack were also crucial.

Carbine
The cavalryman's carbine was a smoothbore flintlock. This is the An 1X model (made in year nine of the Revolutionary calendar, that is 1801) manufactured at Charleville, the French government armament factory on the Meuse in northeastern France.

Saber and scabbard
French light cavalry liked to thrust with the point of the blade as well as deliver swinging cuts. As a result, their sabers had narrower blades than their British counterparts. This is an An XI model, introduced in 1802–03. The iron scabbard is tougher than earlier brass and leather examples.

Bridle
All French light cavalry used the same tack—in black leather as opposed to the British light tan. The light cavalry used a combination of headcollar and double bridle. The bridle shown here is only part of the whole.

Pair of pistols
In the chasseurs, the hussars, and the dragoons, whose functions within the army were broadly similar, officers, trumpeters, and NCOs usually carried a pair of flintlock pistols. These are a pair of dragoon's pistols of a late 18th-century model.

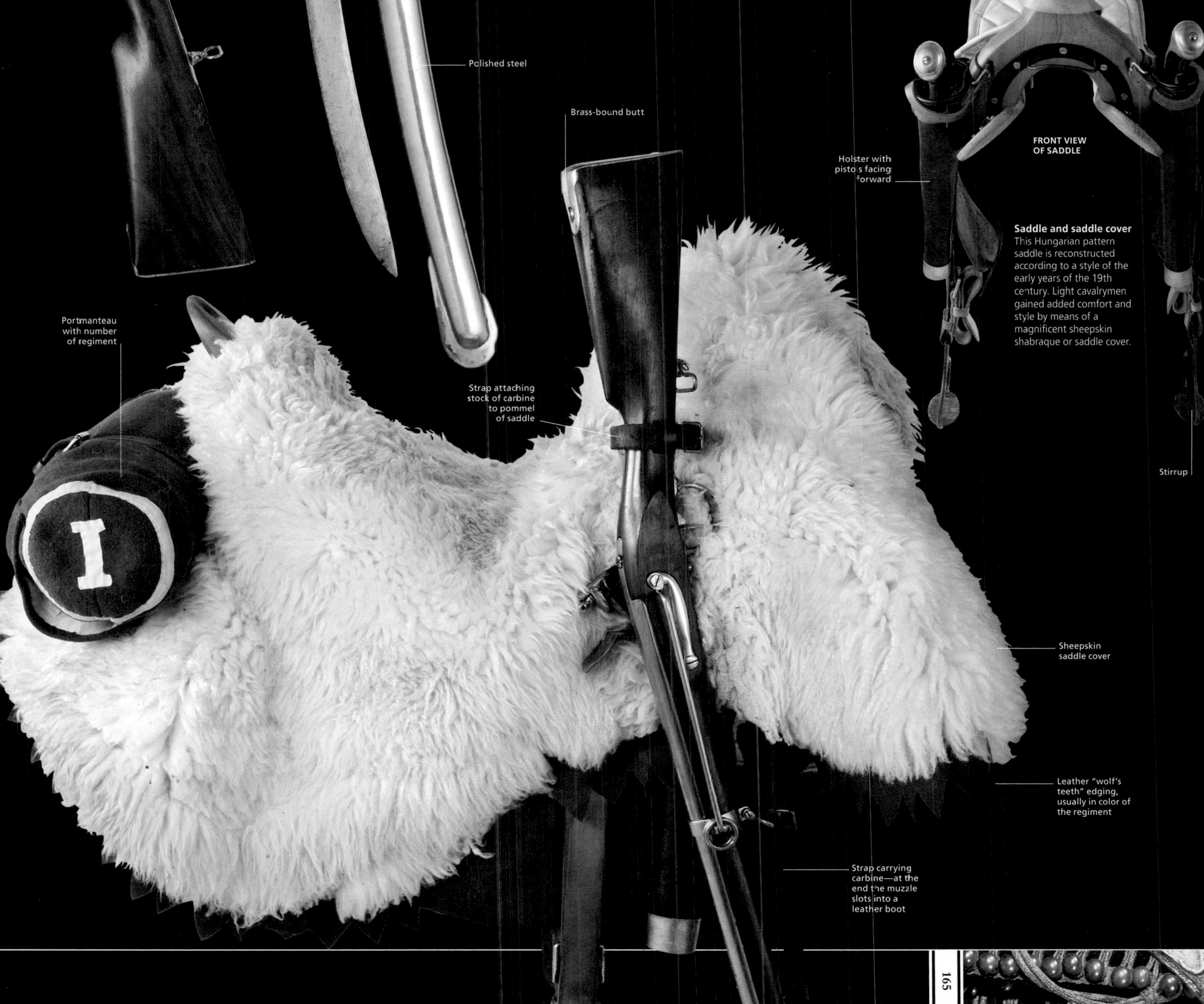

Saddle and saddle cover
This Hungarian pattern saddle is reconstructed according to a style of the early years of the 19th century. Light cavalrymen gained added comfort and style by means of a magnificent sheepskin shabraque or saddle cover.

OTHER SOLDIERS OF NAPOLEON'S ARMY

In forming his Grande Armée, Napoleon built on the inheritance of the French Revolution, with its emphasis on the "citizen-soldier," but created a force motivated by duty, honor, and the lust for glory, rather than by revolutionary enthusiasm. Around 1.6 million men of French birth and over 700,000 born in Italy, Poland, and other parts of Europe eventually served in the ranks of Napoleon's army. More than a million are reckoned to have died, many in combat but far more of hardship or disease, expiring in military hospitals, foreign prisons, or simply by the roadside. Yet, inspired by devotion to their great military leader, Napoleon's soldiers showed consistent courage, discipline, and endurance, even in the face of steadily worsening odds after the disastrous Russian campaign of 1812.

THE INFANTRY

In 1804 the infantry of Napoleon's Grande Armée numbered some 350,000 men, divided into line infantry and light infantry regiments. At that early stage in the Napoleonic adventure the foot soldiers were superbly trained and capable of executing rapid and precise maneuvers on the battlefield. The constant pressure of war and the attrition of veterans ensured that the Emperor's troops would never attain the same quality again. From 1805 onward, fresh recruits received only the most basic training, being expected to learn soldiering from more experienced colleagues.

The average infantryman was a conscript, and in many cases not a willing one. The annual call-up was the occasion for widespread draft evasion. The better-off paid substitutes; others simply hid or deserted after enrollment. Yet the morale of the infantry regiments were generally high. The army very quickly became the conscript's home, group solidarity ensuring low desertion rates once men were integrated in their regiments.

Napoleon's style of warfare, involving forced marches punctuated by pitched battles, placed daunting demands upon the infantry. They were expected to march 15 miles (25 km) a day for weeks on end. Once outside French territory they supplied themselves by pillaging the area through which they marched. When the population was actively hostile and the countryside poor, as in Russia and Spain, this was a hazardous mode of operation. Wear and tear left the foot soldiers a ragged body of men as a campaign went on.

On the battlefield, the infantry were usually expected to take the offensive. Preceded by a swarm of skirmishers—the "voltigeurs"—massed infantry columns marched, with bayonets fixed, into the enemy musket volleys, seeking to engage at close quarters or make the enemy break and flee. Casualties were expected to be heavy; soldiers were forbidden to stop to help wounded comrades. Even after the destruction of a generation of soldiers in the Russian campaign of 1812, the ever more inexperienced infantry never ceased to fight with enthusiasm and aggression.

Siege of Ratisbon
French troops use scaling ladders in the siege of Ratisbon (Regensburg) during Napoleon's campaign against Austria in 1809.

Infantry uniform and weapons
Like the redcoats, French infantry fought chiefly with musket and bayonet. Unlike their British counterparts, most French infantrymen also carried a sword.

The Polish Vistula Legion
The Poles were especially enthusiastic in their support for Napoleon as he liberated many of them from Russian and Austrian rule. The Vistula Legion fought in the Peninsular War and marched with the Grande Armée to Moscow.

THE ARTILLERY

Even in the pre-Revolutionary army, the French artillery was a technocracy in which men of ability were able to rise through their own merits. Napoleon's innovations were primarily tactical. He concentrated cannon in large batteries at decisive points on the battlefield and deployed horse artillery aggressively in forward positions.

Napoleonic artillery was very professional. A team of gunners could fire a 12-pounder cannon three times a minute. They were supported by teamsters who looked after the horses and carriages, and by artisans who maintained and repaired equipment. Firing the guns was tough work. After each shot the crew had to run the cannon back, load, and re-aim. Their arms and faces quickly became black with powder, while targets were often obscured by thick smoke. At the battle of Wagram in 1809, French artillery fired 96,000 cannonballs in two days. The horse artillery was no less impressive: galloping into range of the enemy, they were able to detach their guns, sight, and fire in under a minute.

The quality of artillery personnel remained high, even though officer training time was cut dramatically from 1807. By 1814, however, there were chronic shortages of both powder and shot. Napoleon never achieved the ratio of five cannon to every thousand soldiers he thought optimal.

THE IMPERIAL GUARD

Originally formed as the Consular Guard in 1799 and renamed in 1804, the Imperial Guard was at first a relatively small force serving as Napoleon's personal bodyguard. In 1804 it consisted of some 5,000 infantry, 2,000 cavalry, and an artillery contingent. By 1812, it had swelled into a large army corps with over 100,000 soldiers.

Imperial eagle
The Napoleonic eagle and imperial crown figured prominently on the uniforms and kit of all branches of the Imperial Guard.

At the core of the Imperial Guard were the hand-picked veterans of the Old Guard. To join this elite, a soldier needed to have served in at least two campaigns, have a minimum of four years service, and be at least 5 ft 5 in (1.65 m) tall. The senior infantry regiment within the Old Guard were the Grenadiers, nicknamed *les grognards* ("the grumblers")—because they alone dared complain to the Emperor's face. All the Imperial Guard enjoyed privileges. They had better pay, food, equipment, and medical treatment than line infantry. Guard ranks rated one step above their line equivalent—so a corporal in the Guards was equivalent to an ordinary sergeant. The Middle Guard, selected between 1806 and 1809 had a high percentage of non-French troops and never equalled the Old Guard in status. The Young Guard, recruited from the best of each year's intake of conscripts from 1809, barely constituted an elite force at all.

Always in full dress uniform on campaign, the Guards were an imposing sight, especially the Grenadiers in their tall bearskins. Napoleon was, however, reluctant to commit his Old Guard to battle, keeping them as his last reserve. They were notably held back from the slaughter at Borodino in 1812, earning them the ironic nickname "the immortals." When the Old Guard broke in the face of British and Dutch volleys at the battle of Waterloo in 1815, Napoleon was finished.

The Guard at Waterloo
As word spread that the Imperial Guard had been forced to retreat, the news was a crushing blow to morale in the rest of the French army.

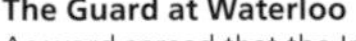

Redcoats in square
At the Battle of Quatre Bras, June 16, 1815, the 28th Regiment of Foot held off repeated French cavalry charges by "forming square." This four-deep hedge of bayonets, similar to a Renaissance pike formation, proved highly effective.

1808 – 1815

BRITISH REDCOAT

"WE GAVE THEM ONE VOLLEY AND THREE CHEERS—THREE DISTINCT CHEERS. THEN ALL WAS STILL AS DEATH. THEY CAME UPON US CRYING AND SHOUTING, TO THE VERY POINT OF OUR BAYONETS."

CAPTAIN THOMAS POCOCKE AT VIMEIRO, 1808

Redcoats in line
During the Napoleonic Wars, the British army often fought defensively, maintaining two-deep lines of infantry against the advancing French columns. A company of light infantry *(above)* formed one end of each battalion's line (grenadiers forming the other), and were often detached for skirmishing. They wore green-plumed shakos *(right)* to distinguish them from center companies.

THE BRITISH TROOPS who fought the armies of Napoleon in the Iberian Peninsula in 1808–14, and at Waterloo in 1815, were mostly recruited from among the lowest strata of society. Their commander, the Duke of Wellington, famously stated: "We have in service the scum of the earth as common soldiers." Yet the red-coated British infantry proved hardy and determined fighters, whether storming a breach in fortress walls or standing up to the test of French firepower and cold steel in open battle.

The vast majority of the men who filled the ranks of the British army during the Napoleonic Wars were volunteers either enlisted for life (in practice, 25 years) or for shorter periods of service permitted in wartime. Wellington described his soldiers' motives for signing up in the most disparaging terms: "Some of our men enlist from having got bastard children—some for minor offences—and many more for drink." There is no question that some soldiers did join the army as a refuge from prison or from other personal difficulties. Men due to stand trial for petty crimes such as poaching might enlist to avoid prosecution. Debtors found shelter in the ranks from the pursuits of their creditors. Sheer poverty drove many to enlist, especially among the half-starving Irish, for whom the prospect of regular food was a compelling motive.

THE KING'S SHILLING

Yet the positive attractions of military life also drew eager and ambitious young men to "take the king's shilling." When actively recruiting, a local regiment would put up posters advertising the advantages of a soldier's life, leaving no cliché unused in their appeal to men whose "hearts beat high to tread the paths of glory." A recruiting party—probably an officer, a couple of NCOs (non-commissioned officers), and a drummer—would then set up in a public place to receive volunteers. John Shipp, who enlisted in 1797, later recalled how he was attracted by a vision of a "merry life, muskets rattling, cannon roaring, drums beating, colours flying, regiments charging and shouts of victory!" At the same time, potential recruits were liberally plied with alcohol, and many woke up with a hangover and a lifetime commitment to serve king and country that they wished they had not made.

PATHS OF GLORY

During the Napoleonic Wars, the army expanded so rapidly (forcing many regiments to create new battalions) that recruits were in desperately short supply. As a result, substantial bounties were paid as an inducement to enlist, with the princely sum of 12 guineas (£12.60) on offer in 1805. When even this failed to fill the ranks, large numbers of soldiers were recruited from the militia, a process that came very close to conscription, while preserving the voluntary principle. The militia was a citizen home defense force composed of men selected by ballot and from which transfer to the army was highly desirable; the former afforded all the hardships of military life but none of the adventure found in the army proper.

By these various means Britain was able to raise an army of around 300,000 men by 1813, compared with a peacetime strength of about 50,000. The prolonged period of warfare also created a great demand for officers. These were mostly drawn from the minor aristocracy or the gentry—sons of clergymen made up about a tenth of officer numbers. Although men of some social standing, officers were not necessarily at all wealthy, but the man without money or social connections was unlikely to make a brilliant career. Commissions were obtained mostly through a mix of purchase, patronage, and seniority. An officer's career might start with his parents buying him a place as an ensign, the most junior

GREEN-PLUMED LIGHT INFANTRY SHAKO

Trotter packs
The infantry knapsack or "Trotter pack" (*right*) was a deeply resented burden. One soldier complained, "I am convinced that many of our infantry sank and died under the weight of their knapsacks." It was worn even into battle (*far right*), seen here on the Light Companies of the First Guards as they repel fierce French attacks at Hougoumont in 1815.

> "THE MEN ARE VERY PROUD OF [OFFICERS] WHO ARE BRAVE IN THE FIELD, AND KIND AND CONSIDERATE TO THE SOLDIERS UNDER THEM ... I KNOW FROM EXPERIENCE THAT IN OUR ARMY THE MEN LIKED BEST TO BE OFFICERED BY GENTLEMEN."
>
> **RIFLEMAN HARRIS**, *RECOLLECTIONS*, 1808

commissioned rank, for some £500. As vacancies occurred above him in his regiment, he could then buy further promotion. Free commissions, filled by strict seniority, cropped up from time to time, offering a slow path of advancement to officers without money. Either outstanding feats of valor or influential friends in the right places occasionally allowed a man to make more rapid progress up the promotion ladder without payment. Promotion from the ranks was not common, but it did occur. About one in 20 officers were former non-commissioned officers.

Officers could generally be relied upon to show courage in combat and, as experience of warfare accumulated in the long struggle against the French, increasing numbers of them became competent at leading their men. As in most armies, some of the officers were respected and admired by the soldiers underneath them and others were despised as ignorant and useless. In either case, officers were critically dependent on the performance of their sergeants and sergeant-majors, who were often the most experienced and professional members of a company. The sergeant-major would usually have started his career as an ordinary soldier and would certainly have been promoted on merit. His military ability had to be wedded to literacy and clerical skills, for he bore a heavy burden of paperwork in his administrative duties.

DRILL AND DISCIPLINE

Strict drill and draconian punishments were still seen as the keys to infantry performance in the British army of the Napoleonic Wars, as they had been throughout the 18th century. The use of the inaccurate flintlock musket, Brown Bess, as the main infantry weapon made disciplined volley fire essential—there was no place for individual initiative on the part of the ordinary soldier. But the assumptions of a decidedly unequal society also dictated the way that men were treated. It was taken for granted that, in the absence of corporal punishment, soldiers drawn from the common people would swiftly degenerate into a disorganized and cowardly rabble. Flogging was a common response to any resistance to authority or general disorder such as drunkenness—to which soldiers were certainly prone. The aim of the system was to create infantrymen who were unquestioningly obedient to commands, who when it came to battle would maneuver coherently and operate their flintlock muskets with minimum harm to their comrades and themselves, and inflict maximum harm on the enemy.

By the 1800s, however, the old ways of the army had important critics, and reforms were under way. In the light infantry ("light bobs") and the rifle regiments—which proved a valuable ancillary to the line infantry in the Peninsular War—individual initiative was not totally discouraged and a tentative effort was made to lead men more on the principle of mutual respect than of fear of punishment.

For most soldiers, in any case, there were more complex reasons to commit to a creditable performance, including the usual peer pressure and loyalty to friends and comrades found in all fighting formations. Soldiers identified strongly with their regiment and its traditions – men often fought to the death to defend the symbolically vital regimental colors. Loyalty to king and country was also present as a motivating force. Yet the Irish, serving in their own regiments or as individual soldiers in English regiments, on the whole proved outstandingly loyal and reliable,

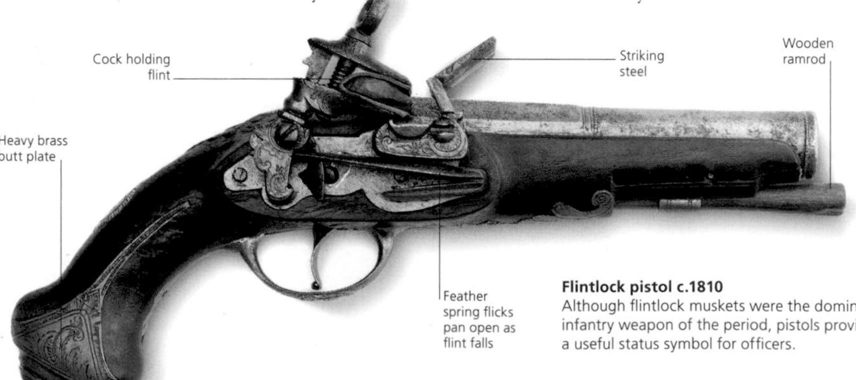

Flintlock pistol c.1810
Although flintlock muskets were the dominant infantry weapon of the period, pistols provided a useful status symbol for officers.

Musket drill
The British Redcoat was renowned for his steadiness in the face of enemy fire—the product of strict drilling, discipline, and long practice of battlefield maneuvers.

despite mostly being Catholics in the service of a Protestant king and coming from a country simmering with revolt against British rule.

CAMPAIGNING ARMY

The army that Wellington led on campaign in the Peninsular War was a complex and in some ways unwieldy entity. It was a multinational force, including not only Scots and Irish but also large numbers of troops from outside the United Kingdom, notably the King's German Legion. Infantry regiments fought alongside cavalry and artillery regiments but were not integrated with them. The infantry itself included different kinds of troops—"center companies" of line infantry, and "flanking companies" of light infantry, riflemen, and grenadiers—each of which had its own uniform and fighting methods. There were surgeons of often dubious qualification, chaplains, vets, bandsmen and drummer boys, pioneers for digging trenches and tunnelling during sieges, and commissary's men arranging supplies. A great train of transport, animals, and hangers-on moved with the army on the march. The men were accompanied, for example, by large herds of cattle, with some 300 of the beasts being slaughtered every day to feed the troops in the campaigns of 1813. The hangers-on included prostitutes, but also army wives and, indeed, whole families—one regiment is recorded as taking 48 wives and 20 children along with troops when embarked for Spain.

Marching and counter-marching across Portugal and Spain in the complex campaigns that swayed back and forth year after year was a trial of endurance, especially in the heat of summer. An ordinary soldier carried a load of around 60 lb (25 kg) and was expected to march around 15 miles (25 km) a day. On some occasions men marched for 30 consecutive days from sunrise until dark. Rifleman Harris' account of the British retreat to Corunna and Vigo in 1809 provides a vivid impression of the hardships this occasioned: "Our knapsacks too were a bitter enemy on this prolonged march. Many a man died, I am convinced, who would have borne up well to the end of the retreat but for the infernal load we carried on our backs." Until 1813 tents were not issued and soldiers either built rough-and-ready huts out of any materials they could find or slept in the open. Throughout the Peninsular War, British soldiers suffered a terrible death rate from fevers and exhaustion.

INTO THE BREACH

The spirit of the Redcoat—and his defects—were shown at their starkest in the siege warfare that formed an important part of the Peninsular campaigns. The fortresses of Ciudad Rodrigo, Badajoz, and San Sebastian were all taken by storm after lengthy preparations. A lieutenant observed that none of the soldier's other duties was "so galling or so disagreeable as a siege." For weeks the men would be forced to occupy trenches under the enemy walls, a constant prey to sniping and mortar fire, while gunners and engineers contrived to make a breach in the fortifications. Once a breach was made, they

The storming of Badajoz
An assault party prepares to storm the garrison at Badajoz in April 1812. Around 3,000 English and Portuguese troops were killed in the final successful assault.

> THE ENGLISH REMAINED QUITE SILENT WITH SHOULDERED ARMS, AND FROM THEIR STEADINESS THEY APPEARED TO BE A LONG RED WALL ... THEY BEGAN TO FIRE. THE ENEMY'S STEADY, CONCENTRATED VOLLEYS SWEPT OUR RANKS.
>
> **THOMAS BOUGEAUD**, FRENCH INFANTRY OFFICER IN THE PENINSULAR WAR

faced the hazardous prospect of fighting their way through the heavily defended opening. The assault on the breach was headed by a junior officer who led a group of volunteers known by long tradition as the Forlorn Hope. Instead of it being difficult to find volunteers for this exceptionally dangerous mission, there was keen competition to take part, especially among officers who could hope for a promotion if they survived.

The assault took place under cover of darkness, but the Forlorn Hope was inevitably under heavy fire by the time the party rushed the rubble-filled breach, which had often been booby-trapped by French engineers. One Forlorn Hope during the siege of Badajoz lost some 180 of its 200 men. The assault parties following behind, some carrying ladders, could also expect substantial losses, advancing over the bodies of the fallen. The existing rules of war were that if a fortress failed to surrender once its walls were breached, the attackers had the right to pillage the place once taken. At Ciudad Rodrigo, Badajoz, and San Sebastian, Wellington's soldiers indulged this right to the full. Civilians were the victims of an orgy of murder, rape, and robbery as British soldiers took their revenge for the risks and hardships of the campaign.

ON THE FIELD OF BATTLE

When facing the French in open battle, the British infantry were radically different creatures from the drunken rabble that sacked Badajoz. Their most striking characteristic was "steadiness," a quality especially admired by those who had experienced at first hand the sheer terror of the Napoleonic battlefield. Unarmoured men had to stand firm in the face of cannon fire, muskets, bayonets, lances, and sabres. Casualties were inevitably high. When British infantry faced a French onslaught at Albuera in 1811, around two-thirds of their men were killed or wounded, and yet they held the field. A soldier wrote proudly that "men were knocked about like skittles, but not a step backwards was taken."

During the Peninsular campaigns, Wellington began by exploiting the ability of his troops to hold a defensive position, in particular occupying the lines of Torres Vedras outside Lisbon in 1810–11. But later his army, with its Portuguese and Spanish allies, had opportunities to show true offensive spirit, especially at the battle of Salamanca in 1812. In this engagement, British infantry boldly marched forward in columns and then deployed in line—a textbook maneuver—to attack French forces that had allowed themselves to become overextended.

Waterloo medal
Awarded to soldiers present at the battles of Ligny, Quatre Bras, and Waterloo, this was the first medal to be given to all ranks. Veterans were also credited with two years' extra service.

Infantry squares
French cuirassiers charge the 42nd Highlanders at Waterloo in 1815. Drawn up in square formation, infantry battalions were almost impervious to attack by cavalry, who were unable to penetrate the massed ranks of men and bayonets.

The British cavalry—despised by Wellington as undisciplined poseurs "galloping at everything"—for once distinguished themselves greatly by their valor and aggression. The French army suffered a near-rout, with around 7,000 casualties and as many soldiers again taken prisoner.

WATERLOO

For all their draining effect upon French resources and manpower, however, the campaigns of the Peninsular War were never more than a side show. It was in taking on Napoleon at Waterloo in 1815 that the mettle of the Redcoats was tested to the limit, providing them with their finest hour. The effect of the famed Napoleonic artillery was limited as Wellington's men made use of the cover provided by the reverse slope of a hill and lay down whenever possible. The British and their Dutch allies repulsed an onslaught by massed French infantry columns with the grapeshot and canister fired by their field artillery and the musketballs of infantry formed up in line. As Wellington once commented: "I do not desire better sport than to meet one of their columns en masse with our line." When the French cavalry charged, the British infantry formed squares and held firm, the horsemen surging around them like "a heavy surf breaking on a coast." The arrival of the Prussian army in support of the British settled the outcome of the day's fighting, in the course of which Wellington's army had suffered 15,000 casualties.

At the start of the Napoleonic Wars, the British infantry were at least a match for the French, but by the end of the conflict in 1815 they had become tough, battle-hardened fighters, capable of standing up to anything the enemy could throw at them. Wellington's "scum of the earth" could claim to be the men who won the war.

REDCOAT BATTLE TACTICS

All infantrymen in the Napoleonic period were taught to execute battlefield maneuvers such as deployment from column (the ideal formation for coordinated movement) and into line (the best formation for firing musket volleys). The power of the French artillery, firing solid shot, shells, and canister, forced the infantry to use concealment when possible. Wellington liked to keep his men out of sight of the guns on the reverse slope of a hill until ready to confront the enemy. If no cover was available, soldiers might be ordered to lie down, although they had to stand to deliver their volleys.

The British infantry line was drawn up two ranks deep. Riflemen, acting as skirmishers, would deploy in loose order between the line infantry and the enemy. Officers and NCOs busied themselves around the line. With one rank firing while the other reloaded, infantry could deliver around six volleys a minute—an impressive volume of fire for an enemy to march into.If attacked by cavalry they formed a square with bristling bayonets. This made them more or less impregnable unless cannon fire broke up the square, letting the cavalry in.

Battalion in column

A battalion was composed of ten companies, each comprising around 50 soldiers. It deployed onto the battlefield in column, then wheeled into line to face the enemy. The two flanking companies (light infantry and grenadiers) were often detached for skirmishing.

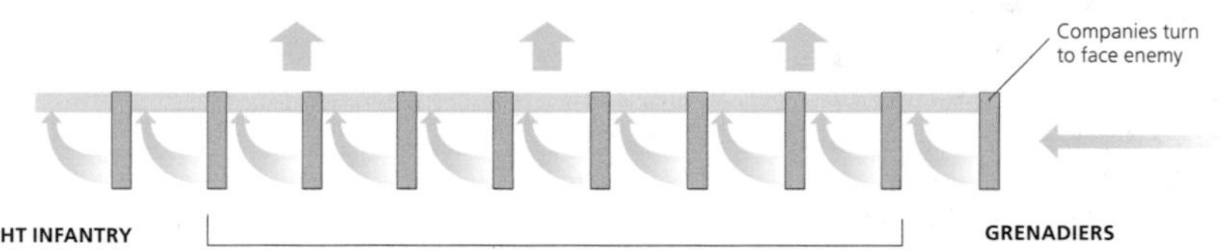

Companies in line

Arranged two-deep, soldiers in line fired in volleys, each loading up to three times a minute. This presented some 1,500 rounds per minute, per battalion, to the enemy, a barrage that destroyed French columns. The volleys were followed by a bayonet charge.

LINE IN PROFILE

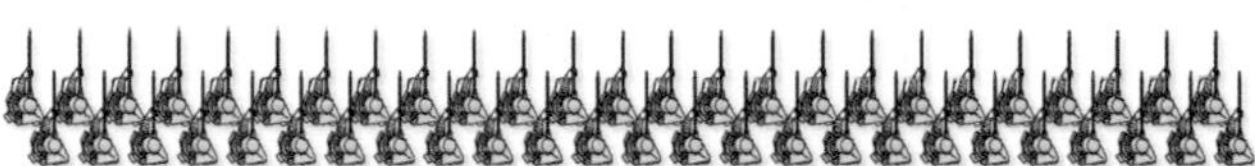

SINGLE COMPANY IN LINE FORMATION

Companies in square

Descended from the pike formations that ended the dominance of cavalry on the late-Medieval battlefield, the infantry square formed a four-deep wall, bayonets pointing outward to provide protection from all directions. The front ranks held position; the rear ranks fired in volleys.

SQUARE IN PROFILE

COMPANY IN SQUARE FORMATION

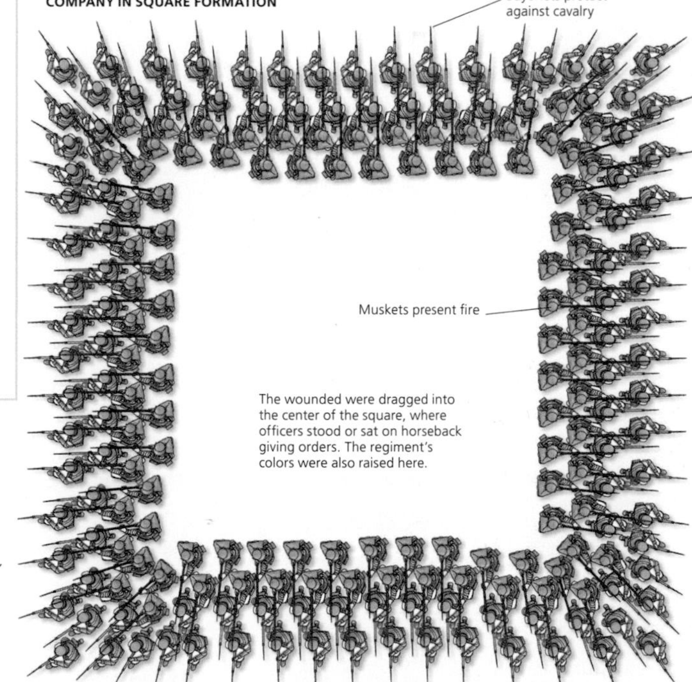

REDCOAT UNIFORM

This is the uniform of the British light infantry (the "light bobs") at the time of the Napoleonic Wars. Like the line infantry, they wore bright red jackets, which made sense when battles were fought on a field that would be heavily obscured by gunpowder smoke, making identification of friend or foe difficult. Concealment was not considered desirable, even for light troops who might be employed as skirmishers. The "stovepipe" shako was adopted as British infantry headgear in 1801–02.

I DON'T KNOW WHAT EFFECT THESE MEN WILL HAVE ON THE ENEMY, BUT BY GOD, THEY TERRIFY ME.

DUKE OF WELLINGTON, PENINSULAR WAR, 1809

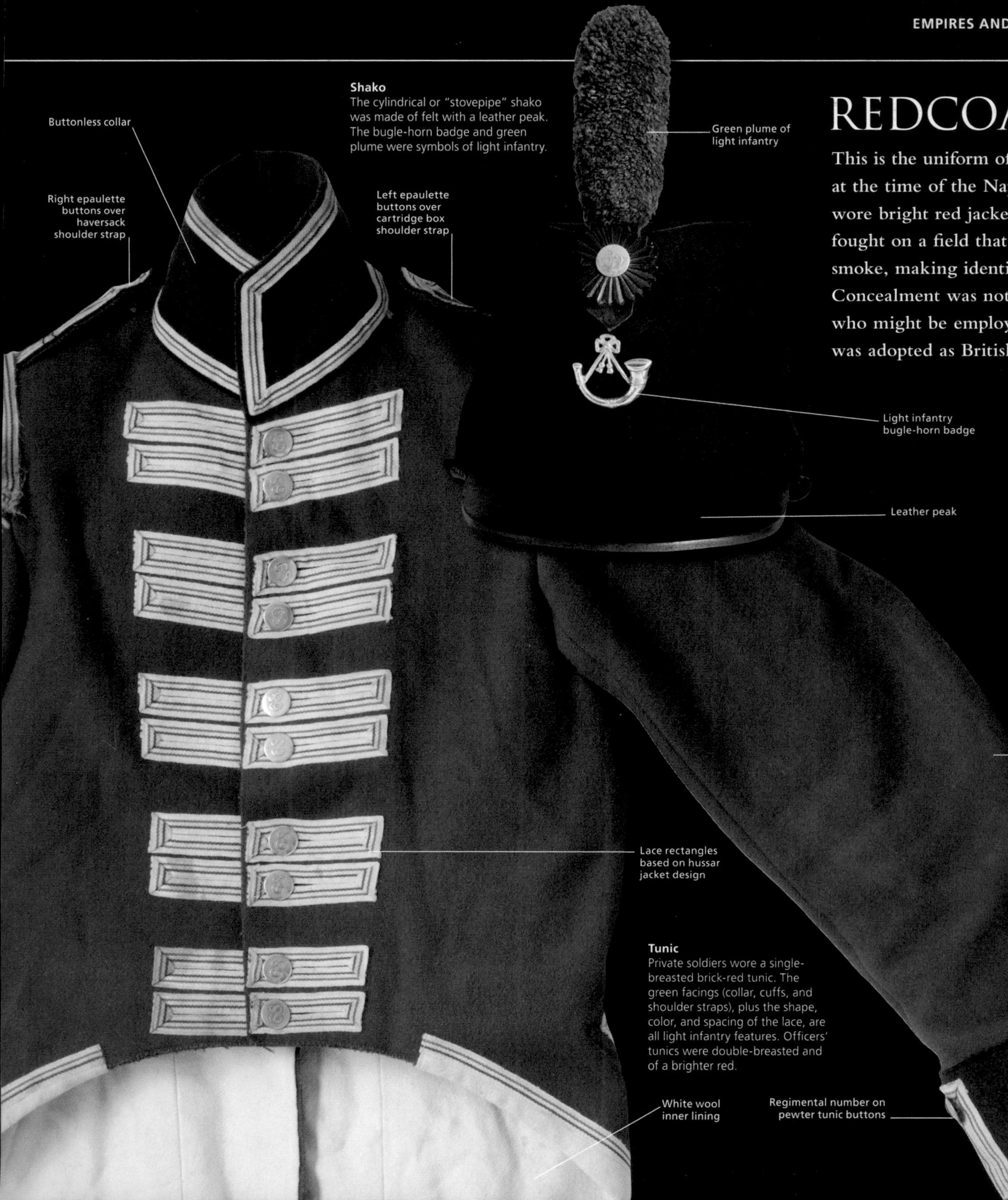

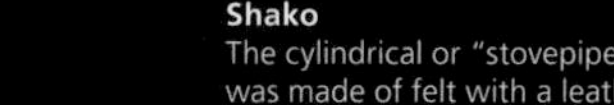

Shako
The cylindrical or "stovepipe" shako was made of felt with a leather peak. The bugle-horn badge and green plume were symbols of light infantry.

Buttonless collar

Right epaulette buttons over haversack shoulder strap

Left epaulette buttons over cartridge box shoulder strap

Green plume of light infantry

Light infantry bugle-horn badge

Leather peak

Red became the standard color for infantry during the English Civil War

Lace rectangles based on hussar jacket design

Lace colors specific to 68th Light Infantry

Tunic
Private soldiers wore a single-breasted brick-red tunic. The green facings (collar, cuffs, and shoulder straps), plus the shape, color, and spacing of the lace, are all light infantry features. Officers' tunics were double-breasted and of a brighter red.

White wool inner lining

Regimental number on pewter tunic buttons

Shoulder straps crossed at chest

Light infantry shoulder wings

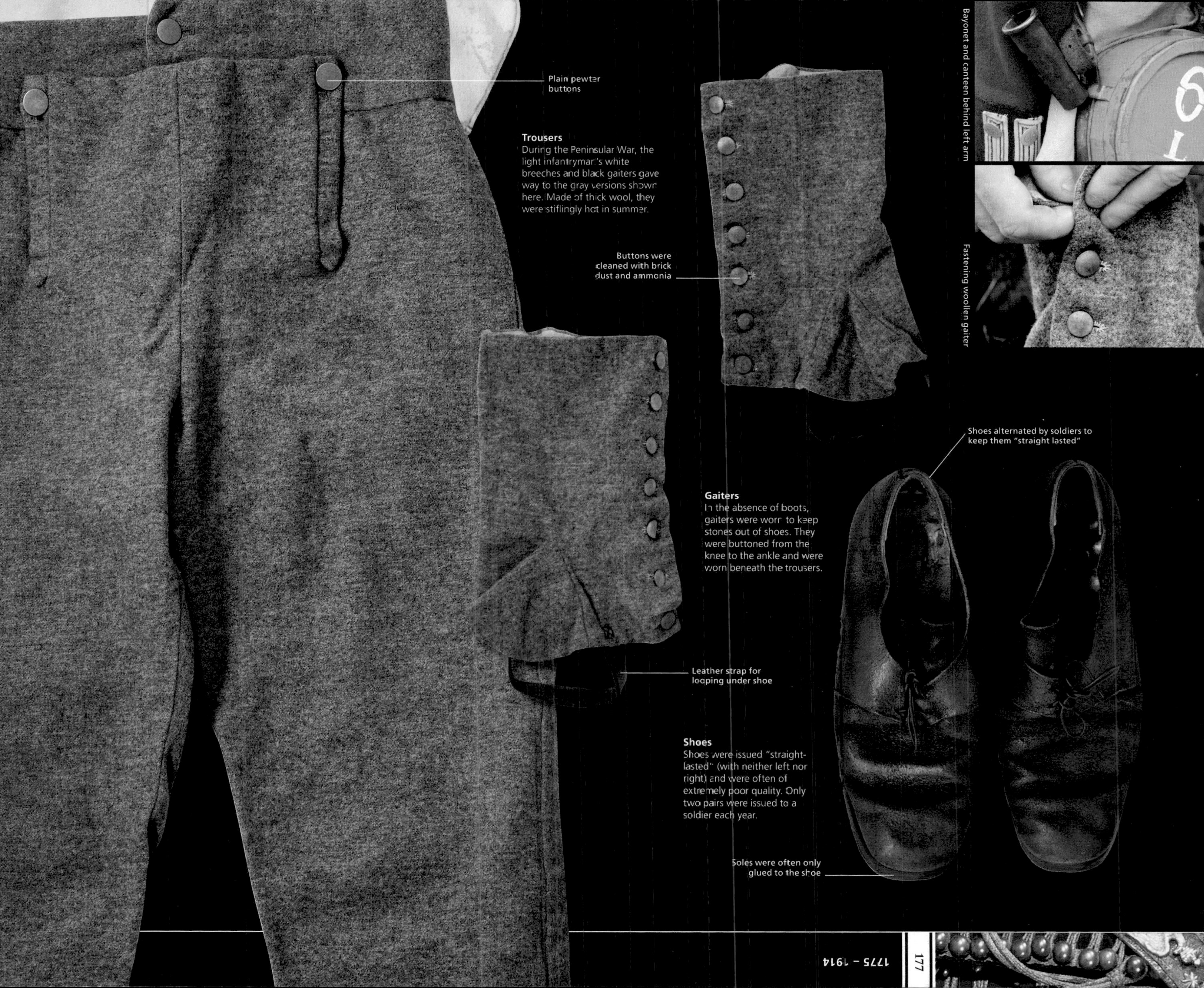

Trousers
During the Peninsular War, the light infantryman's white breeches and black gaiters gave way to the gray versions shown here. Made of thick wool, they were stiflingly hot in summer.

Gaiters
In the absence of boots, gaiters were worn to keep stones out of shoes. They were buttoned from the knee to the ankle and were worn beneath the trousers.

Shoes
Shoes were issued "straight-lasted" (with neither left nor right) and were often of extremely poor quality. Only two pairs were issued to a soldier each year.

Bayonet and canteen behind left arm

Fastening woollen gaiter

REDCOAT EQUIPMENT

A British soldier's most important piece of equipment was his personal weapon, the flintlock musket known as Brown Bess. But he also had to carry an overcoat, blanket, haversack, kettle, food bag, water canteens, and ammunition. On marches of around 15 miles (25 km) a day, this added up to a heavy burden. Benjamin Harris, a foot soldier who served in the Peninsular campaign, wrote: "I am convinced that many of our infantry sank and died under the weight of their knapsacks alone."

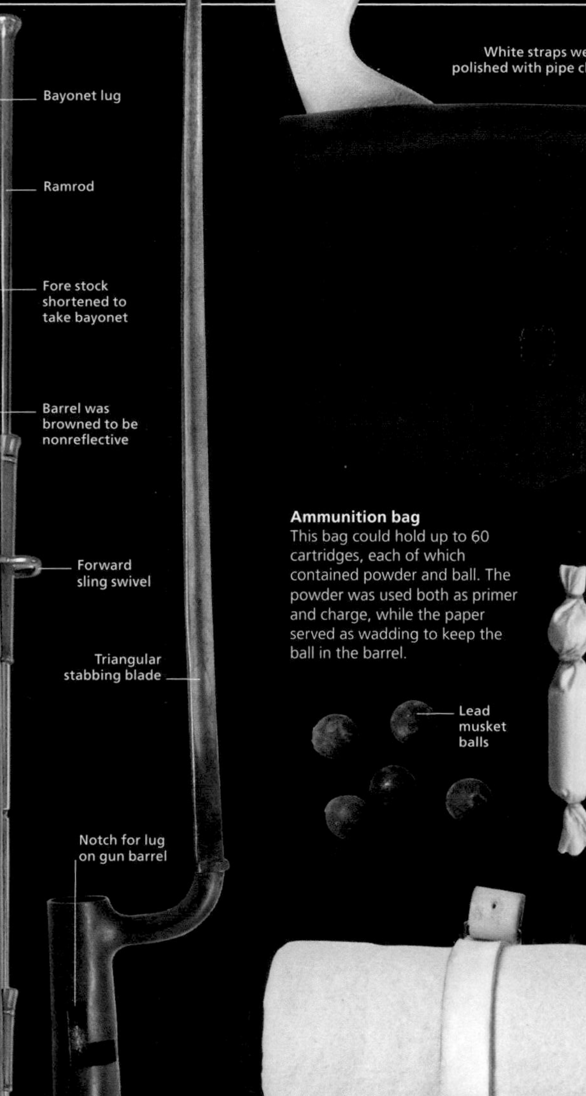

Bayonet
The musket's fore stock is cut back to take a 17 in (43 cm) socket bayonet. A lug on the barrel fits into a notch in the bayonet head, turning the musket into a short pike.

Ammunition bag
This bag could hold up to 60 cartridges, each of which contained powder and ball. The powder was used both as primer and charge, while the paper served as wadding to keep the ball in the barrel.

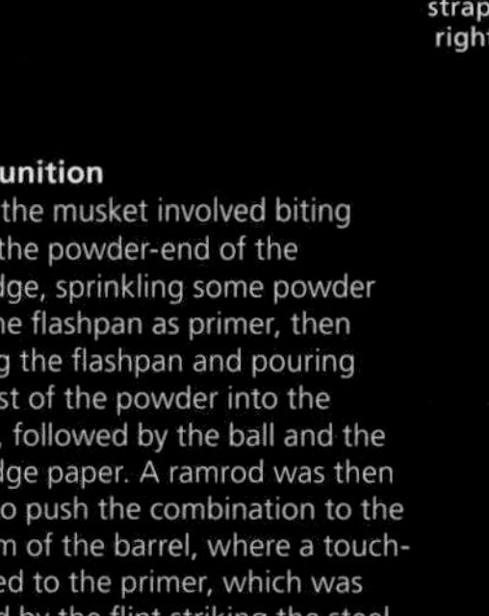

Ammunition
Firing the musket involved biting open the powder-end of the cartridge, sprinkling some powder into the flashpan as primer, then closing the flashpan and pouring the rest of the powder into the barrel, followed by the ball and the cartridge paper. A ramrod was then used to push the combination to the bottom of the barrel, where a touch-hole led to the primer, which was ignited by the flint striking the steel.

Canteen
This wooden canteen bears the regimental (68th) and battalion (2nd) numbers, and letters standing for "light infantry." It contained two quarts (2.3 liters) of water.

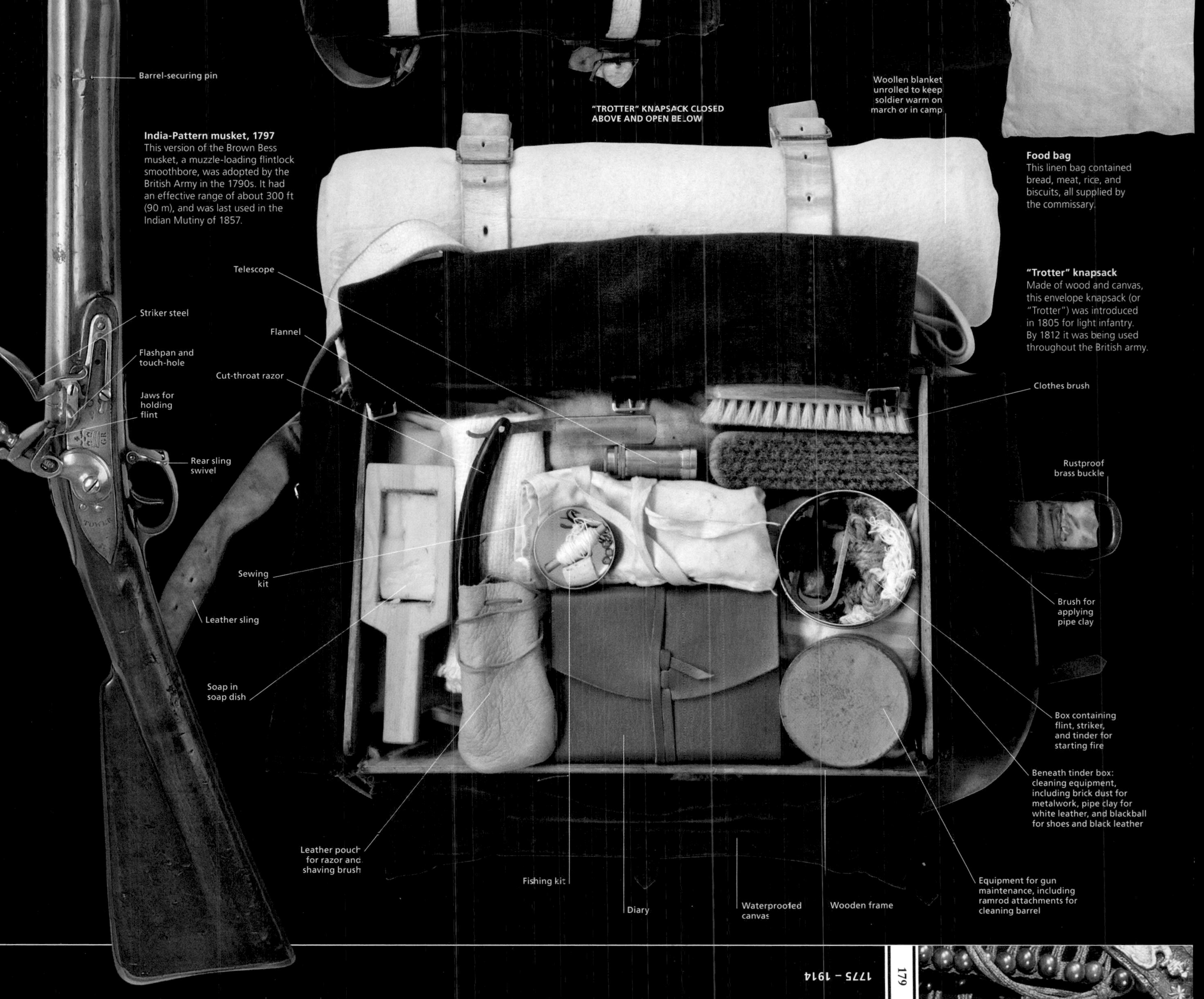

India-Pattern musket, 1797
This version of the Brown Bess musket, a muzzle-loading flintlock smoothbore, was adopted by the British Army in the 1790s. It had an effective range of about 300 ft (90 m), and was last used in the Indian Mutiny of 1857.

Food bag
This linen bag contained bread, meat, rice, and biscuits, all supplied by the commissary.

"Trotter" knapsack
Made of wood and canvas, this envelope knapsack (or "Trotter") was introduced in 1805 for light infantry. By 1812 it was being used throughout the British army.

1793 – 1815

BRITISH SAILOR

"OFTEN DURING THE BATTLE WE COULD NOT SEE FOR THE SMOKE WHETHER WE WERE FIRING AT A FOE OR FRIEND, AND AS TO HEARING, THE NOISE OF THE GUNS MADE US DEAF, THAT WE WERE OBLIGED TO LOOK ONLY TO THE MOTIONS THAT WERE MADE."

DURING BRITAIN'S WARS AGAINST FRANCE between 1793 and 1815, the Royal Navy was outstandingly successful, scoring a series of major victories against equal or superior enemy forces. Its performances in battle were the product of a well-established system for nurturing seamanship and fighting skills at all levels from ordinary sailor upward. At the same time, it must be admitted that the sailors, many of whom were "pressed" into service against their will, led a notoriously hard life, subject to draconian discipline.

Horatio Nelson, Britain's most famous admiral, began his naval career in 1771 at the age of 12, joining a ship captained by his maternal uncle. In this there was nothing exceptional. The officer class of the Royal Navy was mostly composed of the sons of respectable families—Nelson's father was a celergyman—who had joined the service at least by the age of 14. They would have found a place through the influence of some relative or patron, or through a personal connection with a ship's captain. Although the hazards of seagoing life were severe, the navy offered a tempting career. As a midshipman the boy would learn the complex business of operating a warship, including the intricacies of navigation, and hopefully pass the exam for promotion to lieutenant after six years afloat. If he had the right patronage, or sufficiently impressed his superiors, he might be a post-captain with his own ship by the time he was 21, assured that if he survived long enough he would one day become an admiral by simple right of seniority. There was the chance not only of promotion but also, in time of war, of making one's fortune, for the admiralty paid prize money to the officers and crew of ships that captured enemy vessels. A captain who had the luck to take a number of heavily laden enemy merchantmen could become a rich man.

In peacetime, most of the lower ranks of the navy also joined the service at an early age. Children from the poorest strata of society—some saved from the streets by the charitable Maritime Society—became ship's boys at the age of 10 or 11. They did the lowliest jobs on board, from acting as servants for the officers to looking after the animals that were carried on voyages as a source of fresh food. Gradually they would develop the muscles and the skills to be sailors. They would learn to move nimbly barefoot on the pitching deck and in the rigging, and acquire the broad-shouldered, barrel-chested physique of a sailor, the product of years of heavy lifting and pulling on ropes. Such long-term volunteers formed the core of the navy.

THE NAVY AT WAR

In wartime the number of sailors expanded rapidly—from 45,000 men at the start of the French Revolutionary War in 1793, for example, to 120,000 in 1799. Such numbers could not be supplied without the use of the infamous press gangs. The Impress Service scoured ports for experienced seamen—for example, men serving on merchant ships or river boats—and "pressed" them into the king's service. Men were also pressed at sea, a warship stopping a merchantman and forcibly taking the pick of her crew. Press gangs were highly unpopular and at times their methods were little better than kidnapping, but they provided a practical method of rapid selective conscription. The Quota System, introduced in 1805, was worse. Every local authority was ordered to supply a certain number of men to the navy; to fill their quota, they usually ended up by emptying the prisons, thus manning ships with petty criminals who were landsmen and often carriers of typhus.

VOLLEY GUN

The battle of Trafalgar
As Nelson lies wounded on the deck of the *Victory*, the well-drilled crew continues with its appointed tasks *(above)*, the sailors firing carronades (short-barrelled cannons), supported by red-coated marines. An unusual weapon of the period was the multi-barrelled volley gun *(right)*, used to fire on enemy boarding parties.

Boarding party
British sailors, armed with cutlasses, and marines, firing muskets, make a hazardous attempt to board a French warship.

TEAM AFLOAT

Once aboard a warship, voluntarily or not, a man took his place as part of a complex, enclosed society over which the captain ruled with almost absolute power. The character of the captain was the key to a happy or unhappy ship. He could make life unbearable for everybody on board, but a captain who cared for his officers and men, while maintaining good discipline and order, could form a crew into a highly motivated team in which each man willingly played his part. The sailors were organized into two watches, alternating at their stations to keep the ship manned 24 hours a day. As well as a watch, each sailor belonged to a "mess" of eight to ten men, who ate together and usually formed a bonded group within the crew. Sailors were assigned specific tasks depending on their skills—for example, topmen were those sufficiently nimble and assured to work high on the masts.

LIVING CONDITIONS

A ship was a hard place to live and work. Operating a sailing ship in all weathers exposed men to the constant risk of accidents, which cost many their lives. Cramped living conditions encouraged the spread of disease even on a ship kept spotlessly clean. Disease always killed far more men than combat, especially in unhealthy regions such as the West Indies. Sailors, however, were not badly fed by the standards of their day, with basic rations of salted meat, peas, and dry biscuits ("hard tack"), plus an ample supply of beer and watered rum ("grog"). The tack was unfortunately liable to infestation with weevils and larger grubs known as "bargemen." On a well-run ship sailors would also have some fresh fruit and vegetables and lemon juice to avoid scurvy. Officers ate better than the men because they paid for their own extras supplies.

At sea as ashore, corporal punishment was the means by which order was maintained. In the navy this ranged from "starting"—casual blows with a rope or cane administered to men thought not to be working hard enough—to flogging with the cat o'nine tails and even hanging. Starting was much resented by sailors and was formally abolished in 1809. Flogging was the punishment for a range of offenses from drunkenness to sleeping on duty. It was a ritualized procedure carried out by the bosun's mates in front of the whole crew and widely, though not universally, accepted as necessary. Its use could be abused by a sadistic officer, but this was the exception rather than the rule. Hangings were rare. They were the punishment for mutiny, treason, and sodomy— the latter rare on board ships that afforded no privacy. Men's grievances, as expressed in the mutinies of Spithead and the Nore in 1797, tended to focus on issues such as pay being in arrears, the unequal distribution of prize money, the poor quality of food, and the lack of shore leave. But a mutiny was above all likely to be provoked by the irrational and unjust behavior of a specific captain.

COMBAT STATIONS

In the age of Nelson, the quality of Royal Navy sailors was demonstrated time and again. Many operations, such as the blockade of the French ports, were unshowy feats of seamanship calling for the maintenance of vessels at sea for long periods in all weathers. Actual battles were rare events, but they were ones for which all crews were well prepared. As two opposing warships vied for position in relation to the wind and one another, the guns were manned by their crews and other sailors issued with weapons in order to form or repel a boarding party. The marines, meanwhile, assembled with their muskets, some climbing aloft to act as snipers. Once the captain considered the position right, gun crews would follow a sequence of orders—remove tampions; load and ram; fire; run back the guns—to fire a broadside about once a minute. A ship would continue to engage an enemy even while broadsides fired at close range scattered deadly splinters of wood through the ship like shrapnel, and the surgeon, operating under dreadful conditions below decks, amputated limbs at terrifying speed.

Far from avoiding contact with the enemy, Royal Navy ships sought it, driven by the thirst for glory and prize money. Almost absurd risks were taken to cut out enemy ships in defended harbors or undertake one-on-one actions against heavily gunned opponents. From the boys who carried the cartridges to the guns (hiding them under their jackets so a spark would not ignite the powder and burn their face off) up to the captain who stood on deck amid shot, shell, and falling spar, these were fighting men whose pulses quickened at the scent of battle. By the late period of the Napoleonic Wars they had enabled the Royal Navy to establish an unprecedented dominance of the world's oceans.

The horror of naval warfare
At the battle of the Nile in 1798, the French flagship, *L'Orient (left)*, blew up, killing almost the entire crew. Both sides were so shocked by this catastrophe that they stopped firing for a few minutes.

NAVAL TACTICS IN THE AGE OF NELSON

Royal Navy warships often departed from the formal tradition of fighting in line of battle—when two hostile fleets sailing in the same direction formed up abreast of each other to exchange broadsides (volleys fired by all the guns on one side of the ship). Nelson and captains who followed his ideas preferred to cut through the enemy line to fight in what Nelson called a "pell-mell" fashion. They could do this because of the high standard of their seamanship. In a sea battle, the ship's guns could be loaded with various kinds of shot: large round shot (the traditional cannonball) to inflict damage on the enemy's hull, chain shot (two smaller projectiles linked by a chain) for attacking a ship's rigging and spars, and canister (a container of small shot used as an antipersonnel weapon).

Broadsides

The classical form of naval engagement throughout the 18th century was based on the line of battle. The attacking fleet bore down on the enemy to fire broadsides. Well-trained gun crews could time the moment of firing a broadside, using the rolling motion of the ship on the waves to direct their fire at the enemy hull or upward at its sails and rigging.

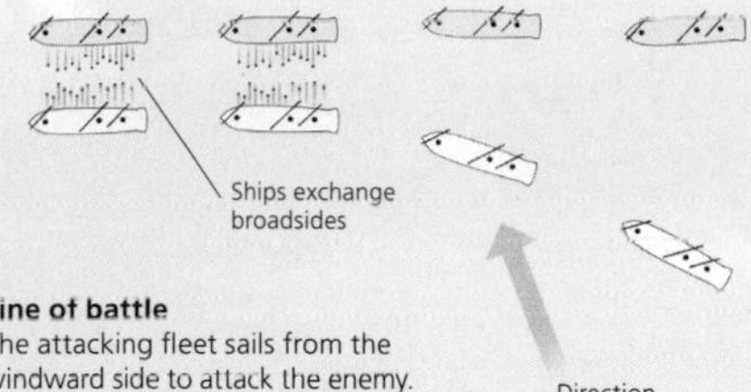

Line of battle
The attacking fleet sails from the windward side to attack the enemy. Each ship singles out one of the enemy with which to engage.

Firing on the downward roll
This tactic was used by captains keen to win the encounter. Round shot was directed at the enemy's hull, causing destruction and death on the gun decks.

Firing on the upward roll
When a captain wanted to disable the other ship so it could not give chase, he directed chain shot and canister upward to damage the sails and rigging

Cutting through the line

This tactic was employed with spectacular success by Nelson at Trafalgar. The British fleet bore down on the Franco-Spanish line in two columns and one by one the ships, led by HMS *Victory*, sailed through the line.

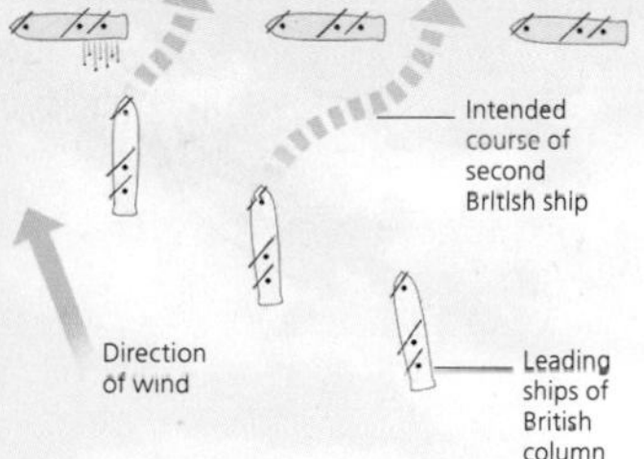

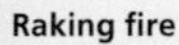

Column reaches enemy line
As the attacking fleet sails toward the enemy line, it places all its ships in grave danger as they are in no position to return fire.

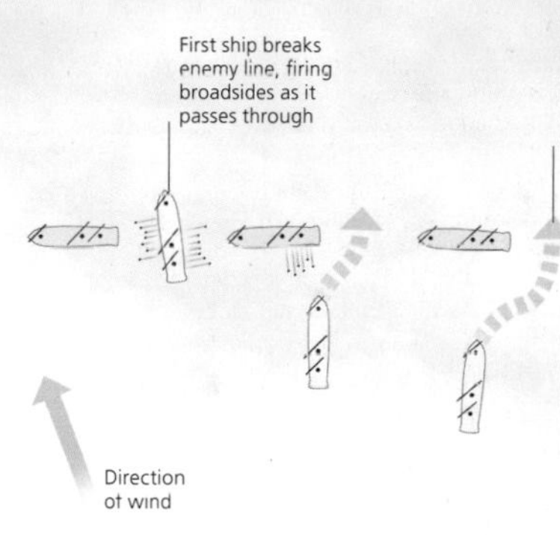

Cutting the line
As more and more ships cut the line, the battle becomes a mêlée, a confused, pell-mell engagement, where skillful maneuvering is at a premium.

Raking fire
As a ship cuts through the enemy line, it can unleash a broadside in either direction while the enemy is unable to return fire.

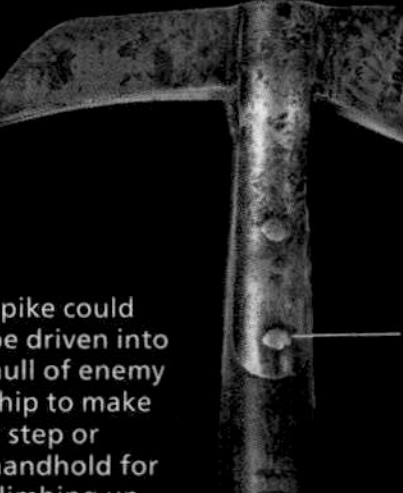

BRITISH SAILOR'S GEAR

The "Jack Tar" in the age of Nelson was not issued with a uniform as such. Traditions in regard to dress were, however, so strong that the sailor's customary outfit of checked shirt, vest, and short jacket made him instantly recognizable. Most of the sailors' duties revolved around sailing and maintaining the ship or firing its guns, so it was only when they boarded an enemy ship or their own ship was boarded that they were issued with cutlasses, pistols, and other weapons.

Jacket
Jackets were short with no tails and usually, but by no means always, blue. Sailors often bought material or clothes from the same outfitter or from the ship's purser, so there was considerable uniformity in their appearance.

Round hat
Sailors sported a great variety of headgear. Straw hats, popular in sunny latitudes, were often tarred to make them waterproof. The "round hat" had a tall crown rather like a top hat.

Brim, usually narrow

Shirt and neck cloth
Checked shirts were very popular and very much the hallmark of the sailor, whether serving in the Royal Navy or in the merchant marine. Equally emblematic was the neck cloth. This might double as a bandanna tied around the head to keep the sweat out of one's eyes when working in the intense heat of the lower decks.

Vest
A colorful waistcoat (vest) was another more or less standard piece of clothing for British sailors. Being skilled at repairing sails, many of them were accomplished needleworkers, making and mending most of their own clothes.

Cutlass
The model 1804 naval cutlass was a no-frills cut-and-thrust weapon. There was no call for sophisticated swordsmanship when fighting at close quarters or slashing away the enemy's rigging.

Plain iron grip, painted black to protect it from corrosion

Guard consisting of two discs of thin iron

Almost flat, straight steel blade

Spike could be driven into hull of enemy ship to make a step or handhold for climbing up

Axhead nailed to handle

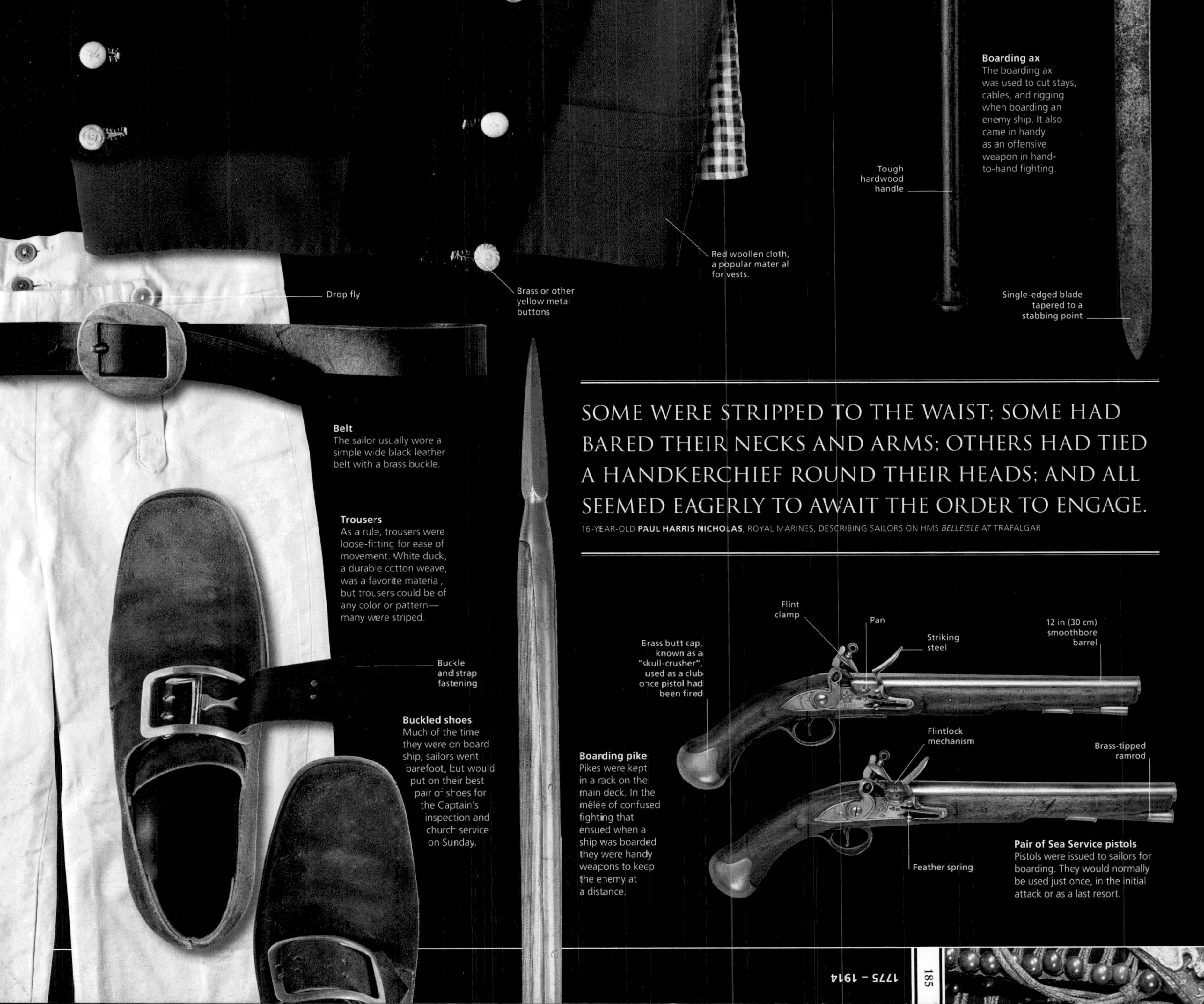

Boarding ax
The boarding ax was used to cut stays, cables, and rigging when boarding an enemy ship. It also came in handy as an offensive weapon in hand-to-hand fighting.

Belt
The sailor usually wore a simple wide black leather belt with a brass buckle.

Trousers
As a rule, trousers were loose-fitting for ease of movement. White duck, a durable cotton weave, was a favorite material, but trousers could be of any color or pattern—many were striped.

Buckled shoes
Much of the time they were on board ship, sailors went barefoot, but would put on their best pair of shoes for the Captain's inspection and church service on Sunday.

SOME WERE STRIPPED TO THE WAIST; SOME HAD BARED THEIR NECKS AND ARMS; OTHERS HAD TIED A HANDKERCHIEF ROUND THEIR HEADS; AND ALL SEEMED EAGERLY TO AWAIT THE ORDER TO ENGAGE.

16-YEAR-OLD **PAUL HARRIS NICHOLAS**, ROYAL MARINES, DESCRIBING SAILORS ON HMS *BELLEISLE* AT TRAFALGAR

Boarding pike
Pikes were kept in a rack on the main deck. In the mêlée of confused fighting that ensued when a ship was boarded they were handy weapons to keep the enemy at a distance.

Pair of Sea Service pistols
Pistols were issued to sailors for boarding. They would normally be used just once, in the initial attack or as a last resort.

SHIP OF THE LINE

HMS *Victory* was a "first rate" ship of the line, mounting 104 guns and requiring a crew of around 850 men. It was an extremely expensive capital investment, costing £63,175 to build—equivalent to perhaps US $25 million in today's money. At least 6,000 trees, mostly oak, were felled for its construction. The ship won immortal fame as Nelson's flagship when the Royal Navy defeated the Spanish and French at the battle of Trafalgar in 1805.

HMS *Victory* was launched at Chatham dockyard on May 7, 1765, but it was not commissioned until Britain went to war with France in 1778. During the French Revolutionary Wars (1792–99) it became the Royal Navy's flagship in the Mediterranean and led the action that destroyed the fleet of France's ally Spain at the battle of Cape St. Vincent in 1797. After this triumph the aging *Victory* was declared "defective" and relegated to service as a hospital ship. But from 1800 it underwent a major rebuilding and returned to service as Nelson's flagship in 1803. Two years later, on October 21, 1805, it played a prominent role in the famous action at Trafalgar, losing 57 men killed, including its admiral.

Victory was known as a three-decked warship because it had three gun decks. The heaviest of the ship's guns, the 32-pounders, were on the lower gun deck, the 24-pounders on the middle gun deck, and the 12-pounders on the upper gun deck. As well as the three gun decks, however, there were three upper decks—the forecastle, the quarterdeck, and poop—as well as the orlop deck and hold below the waterline.

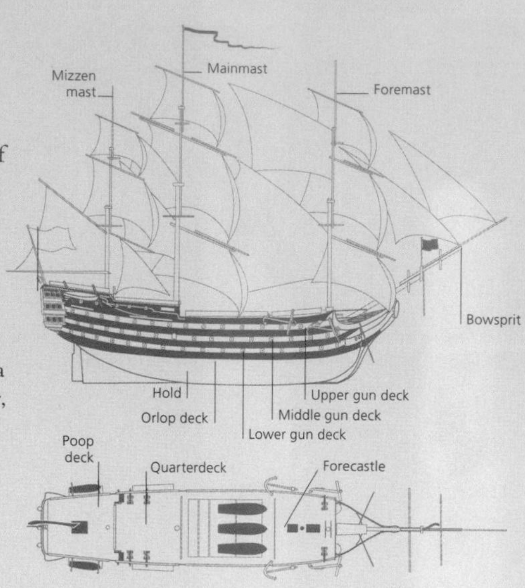

Side and aerial view of HMS Victory
The gun decks were 186 ft (57 m) long and the ship was 52 ft (16 m) wide at its broadest point. The masts and spars supported a total of 37 sails.

On the poop deck
Re-enactors take the roles of Admiral Nelson, the captain of the ship, and some of the officers standing on the poop deck surveying the action on the quarterdeck below.

"EVERY GUN WAS GOING OFF ... THERE WAS THE FIRE FROM ABOVE, THE FIRE FROM BELOW ... THE GUNS RECOILING WITH VIOLENCE ... THE DECKS HEAVING AND THE SIDES STRAINING."

LEWIS ROTELY, MARINE 2ND LIEUTENANT, ABOARD HMS *VICTORY*, OCTOBER 21, 1805

Powder horn
Each gun captain carried a cow horn filled with powder to prime the gun.

Stern windows
Behind the three rows of windows in the stern were the cabins of the admiral, the captain, and the other officers.

High lanterns
The high stern lanterns, fueled by whale oil, helped the ships of the fleet to maintain formation at night.

Gun port
This long gun has been run out of the gun port but the tampion would have to be removed from the muzzle before it could fire.

Rigging
A mass of rigging controlled the ship's vast expanse of sail – around 4 acres (16,000 sq m) in total.

Block and line
Experienced sailors had complete mastery of the the ship's complex cordage.

High climb
The main mast reaches 220 ft (67 m) above sea level at its tip. Fatal falls were common as men climbed on the yard arms to set or furl sails.

Jeer blocks
Under the top (platform) on each mast the lower yard is held in place by four huge pieces of wood called jeer blocks.

Victory restored
HMS *Victory* has been restored to its condition before the battle of Trafalgar and now stands in dry dock at Portsmouth, on the south coast of England. It is the oldest ship in the world that is still officially commissioned in naval service.

Heavy anchors
It required the effort of 144 men, pushing on the bars of two linked capstans, to raise the largest anchors, which weighed more than 4.5 tons.

Ship's figurehead
The figurehead had two cupids supporting the royal coat of arms. Fitted in 1803, it was much simpler than the original figurehead of 1765.

Forecastle
The fore- and mainmasts were controlled from the forecastle. The ship's bell in the center of the deck was rung every half hour. On the left are two carronades, powerful short-barreled, short-range guns.

THE LOWER DECKS

Most of the ship's crew slept in hammocks slung from the beams of the gun decks. Each man had 21 in (53 cm) of sleeping space. At meal times the crew messed in the same area at tables that were also suspended from the beams. The gun ports provided the only natural light and fresh air, but these were often shut to keep out the waves. The areas below the water-line were even more dank and gloomy, but they were actually the safest place in a battle and thus suitable for storing gunpowder. The ship's surgeon had his dispensary on the orlop deck below the lower gun deck and this was where wounded men were brought to be operated on.

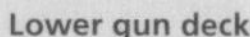

Lower gun deck
The recoil of each gun was controlled by a thick breeching rope. It allowed the gun to move back enough to be in-board of the gun port, so it could be reloaded.

Middle gun deck
The wide low gun decks not only housed the guns but also provided the eating and sleeping space *(below)* for most of the ship's crew.

On-board food
The ship's galley, with the cast-iron Brodie stove, was on the middle gun deck. The sailors ate their rations, including dry "hard tack" biscuits, from wooden bowls or their own plates.

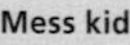

Mess kid
This was a kind of bucket made by the ship's cooper. It was used by one member of a mess to collect the food for his messmates from the galley.

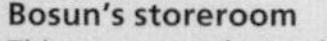

Bosun's storeroom
This storeroom housed stores to repair the rigging. The bosun was in charge of the deck crew and responsible for the cordage and anchors.

Carpenter's storeroom
The upkeep and repair of the wooden fabric of the ship was a daily activity on board. The carpenter's storeroom was well forward in the hold.

Sick berth
The sick were moved to this light, airy part of the ship forward on the upper gun deck.

Round shot
The ship's cast-iron cannonballs weighed up to 32 lb (14.5 kg).

Dispensary
The surgeon had a small dispensary forward on the orlop deck, below the lower gun deck. The cockpit, on the same deck, served as his operating theater.

Ship's hold
The hold is here almost empty, containing gravel for ballast and a few water barrels. However, when full it could store supplies for a six-month voyage.

Wheel and compasses
Aft on the quarterdeck, the double wheel was operated by four men in calm weather but could need the muscle of eight in a storm. In front is the binnacle, holding two compasses.

THE SHIP'S COMMAND CENTER

The quarterdeck, behind the mainmast, was the site of the commanding officers' cabins, which also served as their offices, and the ship's wheel. Along with the poop deck, which provided a roof for the cabins and a navigation and observation platform, it constituted the command center of the ship where senior officers were habitually found. Off-duty crew were restricted to the forecastle at the other end of the ship. It was on the quarterdeck that Nelson was shot by a French marine sniper at Trafalgar.

Captain's day cabin
At the stern of the quarterdeck the admiral and the captain both had light and spacious cabins that provided separate areas for sleeping, dining, and working.

1861 – 1865

UNION INFANTRYMAN

"WE WERE ... ALL HAPPY AND ALL EXPECTED TO COME HOME AFTER THE WAR WAS OVER ... LITTLE DID WE CARE FOR WHAT THERE WAS AHEAD OF US. WE WAS NOW ON THE ROAD SOUTH TO DO OR TO DIE."

JEFFERSON MOSES, WRITING IN HIS DIARY ON JOINING UP, 1862

Red Badge of Courage
Union soldiers take aim in a scene from the film of Stephen Crane's 1895 Civil War novel, *The Red Badge of Courage*. Rifled muskets and more effective cannon gave Civil War armies a greater rate and range of firepower than in earlier conflicts, and soldiers learned to take up defensive positions behind field fortifications and entrenchments.

THE AMERICAN CIVIL WAR, fought between the secessionist Confederacy and the northern Union forces from 1861 to 1865, was primarily a foot soldiers' war. Around 80 percent of those who fought were infantry. Career soldiers were few and far between on the Union side below the highest levels of command. Men fresh to war learned how to fight the hard way—on campaign. The Union soldiers developed tenacity and endurance in the harsh conditions of a conflict that cost one in four of them their lives.

President Abraham Lincoln first called for volunteers to fight to defend the Union after the Confederate attack on Fort Sumter in April 1861. Initially men were invited to sign up for 90 days' service—the time optimistically considered sufficient to suppress the rebellion—but this was soon extended to a more realistic three years. As a torrent of war fever swept the northern states, the volume of volunteers far exceeded the number that could be taken on. Around 300,000 were recruited by the first winter of the war, but far more would-be soldiers had by then been turned away. Young men naively enthusiastic for the experience of battle were desperate to see action before the expected short conflict ended. Many felt a vague but powerful patriotic devotion to the integrity of the United States; very few were inspired by the notion of fighting against slavery.

Forage cap
The insignia on the cap denotes the 124th New York Infantry, a Union volunteer regiment.

AN EVOLVING ARMY

America's small regular army was only marginally involved in the creation of the Union forces. Most regiments were formed from scratch, set up by a prominent local citizen who would later be confirmed as the regiment's colonel. When enough volunteers had been attracted, they set up a regimental camp and elected officers and NCOs. In practice, higher ranks were filled by the colonel's appointees, but those aspiring to be junior officers had to canvas for votes from the men they would then command. Whether appointed or elected, the officers rarely had military experience, and neither did their men. Some of the first recruits were members of local militias, but even these were no more than civilians who had enjoyed meeting up to parade in uniform.

Provision of uniforms and equipment was chaotic, depending upon local initiative as federal organization failed to cope. Regiments selected their own outfits, so the Union army first entered combat decked out in a wide range of uniforms, including Zouaves attired in a flamboyant imitation of French African troops, complete with a fez. After skimpy training, these diversely clad soldiers were carried by train to camps near the war front. Not surprisingly, their initial performance was mixed, courage only partly compensating for lack of skill, experience, and leadership. Defeat at Bull Run (Manassas) in July 1861 shocked the North into building a more professional-style army for a longer war.

SPRINGFIELD MODEL 1861

By 1862 the factories of the North were gearing up to supply the expanding army with standard uniforms and equipment, which were soon in far better supply for the Union soldier than for the Southerner. Improved training and daily drill gave the troops a more soldierly look. The election of officers was gradually phased out and many inefficient commanders were fired. Yet discipline often remained poor compared with contemporary European armies. Most Americans had no natural sense of obedience to authority. Soldiers were conscious of being citizens with rights—or were just downright obstinate. One private complained bitterly of officers seeming to "consider themselves as made of a different material from the low fellows in the ranks."

SOCIAL ORIGINS

The Union soldier was most likely to be from a farming background or an urban artisan. Mostly in their twenties, the troops reflected the diversity of Northern society. One in five Union soldiers was of German origin, with the Irish the next largest ethnic group. Around ten percent of the army were recent immigrants from Europe.

African Americans were initially banned from enlistment, but mounting manpower shortages necessitated a change of policy during 1862—though they were not granted equal pay until June 1864. Black soldiers were used first in labor battalions, but were then formed into "colored" regiments under white officers. Mostly escaped slaves—known as "contrabands"—the black soldiers encountered vicious prejudice from many Union troops, as well as especially harsh treatment from the Confederates. But their performance eventually won them a grudging respect and substantially influenced white opinion in the North in favour of emancipation. By the end of the war, African-American soldiers constituted around ten percent of the Union army.

African-American soldiers
The band of the 107th US Colored Infantry poses at Fort Corcoran, Virginia in 1865. African-American soldiers suffered disproportionately high casualties in the Civil War: approximately one-third of black Union soldiers lost their lives during the conflict.

EXPERIENCE OF WAR

During the first two years of the war the Union forces suffered many defeats and setbacks, but in July 1863 victories at Gettysburg in the eastern theater and Vicksburg in the west shifted the balance decisively against the Confederates. From then onward the South could only fight to prolong the conflict, rather than to win it.

The Civil War has sometimes been described as the first "modern war," with emphasis on innovations such as the use of trains for transport and the telegraph for communications. But for the ordinary soldier the experience of military life had nothing especially modern about it. Once away from a rail depot he moved on foot, often over substantial distances. Inevitably a soldier had a heavy pack and weapon to carry, a burden he was always seeking to lighten—the route of a march was usually littered with discarded blankets and other gear. Unless strict discipline was enforced, stragglers would fall by the wayside in droves. Although food supplies in the Union army were

Camp life
A Union encampment at Cumberland Landing on Virginia's Pamunkey River in 1862. Soldiers usually slept under canvas in conical Sibley tents or, as the war dragged on, in smaller wedge tents.

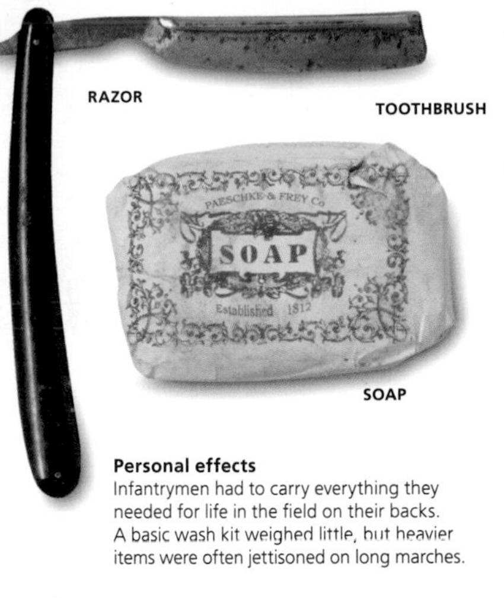

Personal effects
Infantrymen had to carry everything they needed for life in the field on their backs. A basic wash kit weighed little, but heavier items were often jettisoned on long marches.

generally adequate, soldiers often indulged in foraging and pillage. Since the war was mostly fought on Confederate territory, this was tolerated or even encouraged by commanders, most notoriously during the March to the Sea across Georgia in 1864.

Life in army camp was a variant on age-old military traditions. Soldiers followed a routine of drill and fatigues regulated by bugle calls or the beating of the drum. Punishments for indiscipline could be crude and severe, ranging from hanging by the thumbs to the excruciating "bucking"—tying the arms and legs together around a rifle.

Disease was ever-present and more soldiers died of diarrhea and dysentery than lost their lives in combat. As the war went on, improved medical services and tighter discipline—leading to better cleanliness—cut the death rate. Whenever warfare became static, though, as in the sieges of Vicksburg or Richmond, epidemics flared up. The worst lot was to be taken prisoner; thousands died in the awful conditions at Andersonville, Georgia, and in other Confederate camps.

CHANGING ARMY

Combat may have caused numerically smaller losses than disease, but the level of casualties in pitched battles mounted alarmingly as the war grew in intensity. At Antietam in September 1862 the Union forces suffered 12,000 casualties in a single day's fighting. In the decisive battle of Gettysburg the following year there were around 23,000 Union casualties, and their Confederate opponents suffered even heavier losses.

Mounting casualties and the prolongation of the war increased the Union army's manpower requirements while simultaneously blunting popular enthusiasm to volunteer. When the offer of bounty money failed to attract enough recruits, the Federal government introduced conscription in 1863. This sparked riots in New York and a stampede of draft evasion. The well-off bought their way out of service, making a commutation payment or paying a substitute to take their place, while many poorer folk hastily volunteered and grabbed the bounty money. Only a small minority of Union soldiers actually served as conscripts.

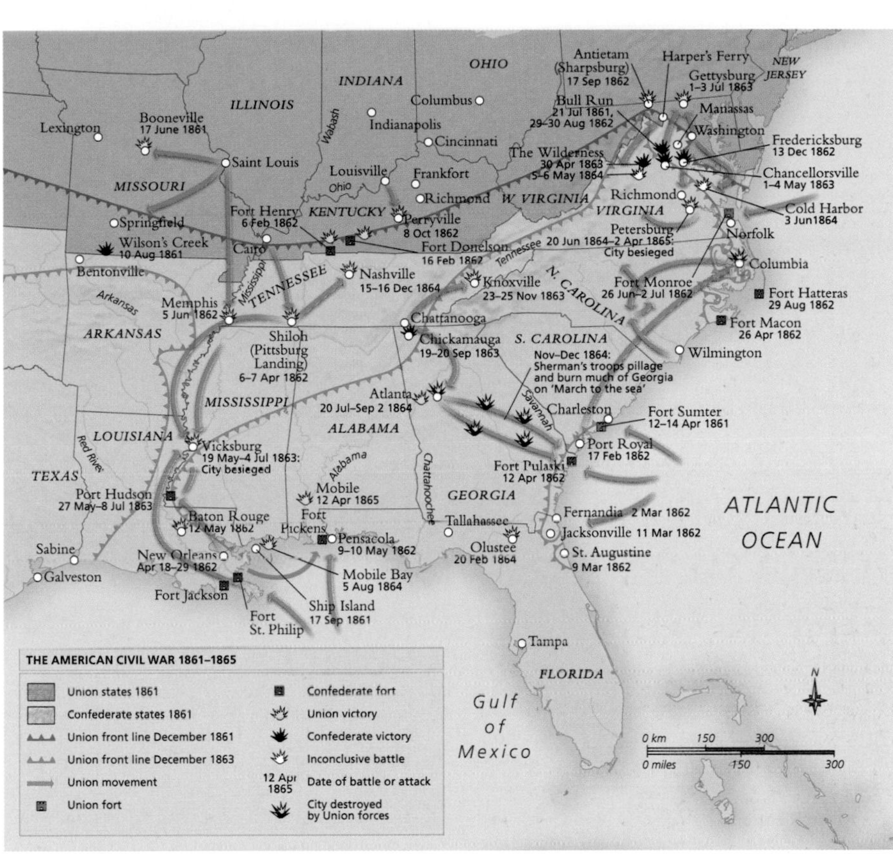

Progress of the war
The war developed into a struggle on two fronts. In the eastern theater the Union's Army of the Potomac fought in a relatively restricted area of Virginia, Maryland, and Pennsylvania. In the western theater, the fighting eventually ranged from Kentucky and Mississippi across to the coast of Georgia and the Carolinas.

Gettysburg
Union casulties lie on the field of battle near Herbst woods in Gettysburg, Pennsylvania. The battle of Gettysburg was one of the largest and bloodiest of the war. After three days of fighting, around 50,000 Union and Confederate soldiers lay dead.

Infantry and specialists
The increasing emphasis on trenches and other field fortifications during the Civil War meant specialists such as these engineers from the 8th New York State Militia (*right*) played a vital role in both Union and Confederate armies. A regular Union infantryman in forage cap (*far right*) sips water from his canteen during a Civil War reenactment.

> "I HAVE A MORTAL DREAD OF THE BATTLEFIELD ... I AM AFRAID THAT THE GROANS OF THE WOUNDED AND DYING WILL MAKE ME SHAKE, NEVERTHELESS I HOPE AND TRUST THAT STRENGTH WILL BE GIVEN ME TO STAND AND DO MY DUTY."
>
> **PRIVATE EDWARD EDES,** LETTER TO HIS FATHER BEFORE FIRST ENTERING COMBAT, APRIL 1863

At the same time as introducing conscription, the government set about encouraging the volunteers of 1861 to stay in the army when their three-year term was up. War-weariness was rife among the men—many of whom had had no home leave since enlisting—but with the aid of the promise of a 30-day leave of absence, some 200,000 were induced to extend their service to the war's end.

A gulf separated these proud "Veteran Volunteers" from the later recruits, bounty men and substitutes, generally dredged from the poorest sectors of society by the lure of cash. A private, Frank Wilkeson, described them as "conscienceless and cowardly scoundrels" whom "clean-minded American and Irish and German volunteers would not associate with." Desertion rates had always been high in the Union army, men drifting away to cope with difficulties back home or discouraged with the soldiering experience. But the bounty men or substitutes were notorious for disappearing as soon as they received their lump sum. General Ulysses Grant complained in September 1864: "The men we have been getting in this way almost all desert."

BATTLING THROUGH

Yet whatever their changing nature—from the naive volunteers of 1861 to the mix of hardened fighters and poor-quality recruits of the latter stages of the conflict—the Union infantry were the men who ultimately won the war. Cavalry performed a useful function as scouts and raiders. Artillery inflicted a high percentage of combat casualties. But battles were decided by the success or failure of waves of infantry advancing in the face of withering defensive fire.

Soldiers on both sides used the Springfield or Enfield rifle-musket, a muzzle-loading firearm which was fired by using a percussion cap. This was a step forward from the unrifled flintlock musket of the Napoleonic era in rate of fire, range, and accuracy. Since cannon were also significantly more effective than those used at Waterloo, infantry out in the open were certain to take heavy casualties. In the course of the war, soldiers learned either to take up defensive positions that exploited existing cover such as stone walls or ditches, or to construct earth

Tobacco
Licensed vendors known as sutlers traveled with the army in the field, selling everything from writing paper to whiskey and tobacco. The pipe bowl shown here is hand carved—a popular pastime for bored soldiers.

FIGHTING IN THE TRENCHES

The intensification of infantry and artillery firepower as the Civil War went on increasingly led armies to resort to field fortifications. In the static warfare around Vicksburg in 1863 and around Petersburg in 1864–65, these developed into extensive trench systems—at Petersburg the trenches stretched for some 30 miles (50 km). Inevitably in retrospect the Civil War trenches are seen as pointing forward to the stalemate on the Western Front in World War I.

SAPPERS AND MINERS

Entrenchment had been a familiar feature of siege warfare since the 17th century and before. Civil War armies deployed traditional siege weaponry, including mortars and grenades. Also in the siege tradition, Union engineers dug a tunnel under the Confederate lines outside Petersburg and exploded four tons of gunpowder in it, creating a vast crater which, however, Union soldiers were unable to exploit. Trench warfare was demoralizing for both sides. Soldiers were subject to boredom, disease, and the steady attrition of sniper and mortar fire.

Trench warfare
A re-creation of a Civil War-era trench system, complete with wooden supports (revetments), of the type used at Spotsylvania in 1864. The trenches around the "bloody angle of Spotsylvania" were the scene of savage close-quarters bayonet fighting.

parapets as field fortifications. But there was really no hiding place once battle was joined. If on the defensive, men had to hold firm, firing steadily, in the face of the seemingly unstoppable advance of enemy infantry, and pull back in good order if instructed to do so. On the offensive, they often had to march forward in lines across open ground, despite the relentless depredations of explosive shells and rifle fire. Then would come the order for the final charge with bayonets fixed, through a hail of bullets and grapeshot.

Inevitably, not everyone's nerve held. Some individuals crept away and hid from the mayhem. Mass panics took place in the Union ranks at battles such as Shiloh and Fredericksburg, alongside displays of solid courage and individual heroism. In the heat of battle, even determined soldiers botched the procedures needed to load and fire their weapon—which involved ripping open the paper cartridge with their teeth, ramming ball and powder down the barrel, and placing a percussion cap in the firing mechanism. Rifles were fired with the ramrod in the barrel or failed to fire because no percussion cap was fitted. Some battles were contested in heavily forested terrain where the fighting soon disintegrated into a savage mêlée.

VICTORY OF ATTRITION

Infantry-on-infantry encounters at close range were a terrifying but exhilarating experience. The same could not be said for the trench warfare that predominated in the final stage of the war. Union infantry discovered trenches at the siege of Vicksburg in 1863 but this style of conflict reached its apogee in front of Petersburg in 1864–65. A daily attrition through the explosion of mortar shells and the sniping of enemy sharpshooters replaced the wild slaughter of pitched battle, while soldiers became as adept at the use of pick and spade as of their firearms. By then, precious little was left of the glamour of war that had enthused the volunteers of 1861. For most, the war had become a grim, arduous task that had to be carried through to its conclusion.

Victory came to the Union side in April 1865, but at a price. Some 360,000 Union soldiers died in the conflict, about one in eight of those who served. Those who survived could return home with the satisfaction of having achieved, at their best, an impressive combat performance. When battle-hardened and properly disciplined, Billy Yank exhibited, in the words of one officer, "implicit obedience to orders, undaunted courage, and great endurance." The Confederates may often have fought with more fiery passion, but the Union infantryman ultimately proved to be a stubborn and cool-headed fighter.

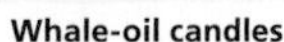
Whale-oil candles
Candles were an important piece of equipment for soldiers in camp. Candle tins with polished metal surfaces were used to increase illumination and avoid fires while under canvas.

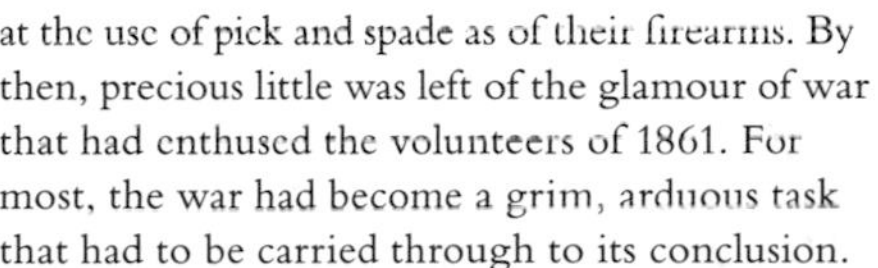

Union artillery
Federal ordinance stands at a depot ready for deployment during the siege of Petersburg, 1864–65. Artillery played a major role in the entrenched warfare around the city.

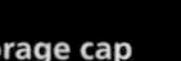

UNION UNIFORM

Uniforms were standardized by War Department orders after the first Battle of Bull Run in 1861. The Union government took over responsibility for supplying clothing and equipment from the individual states, harnessing the potential of its factories for mass production. As a result, while the Confederacy struggled to equip its troops with any kind of uniform, the Union soldier was well shod and clothed.

Forage cap
This was made of wool broadcloth with a rounded, flat top, cotton lining, and visor. The men would sew in their corps badge (in this case "I") and attach brass numbers that specified their regiment (124th New York) to the top of the cap.

Corps badges either red, white, or blue

Leather chin strap

Fatigue blouse
The Union soldier's dark-blue fatigue blouse was made of lightweight wool and featured an inside pocket and four brass buttons on the front. Like all Union army gear, it was produced in a range of standard sizes to facilitate mass production.

Short collar

Four evenly spaced US eagle buttons

Domet (cotton warp and wool weft) flannel ensured greater warmth

BILLY YANK HAD LITTLE GROUND FOR COMPLAINT AS TO THE QUALITY OF CLOTHING RECEIVED FROM THE QUARTERMASTER.

J. G. RANDALL *THE CIVIL WAR AND RECONSTRUCTION*

Fixing the bayonet to the rifle-musket

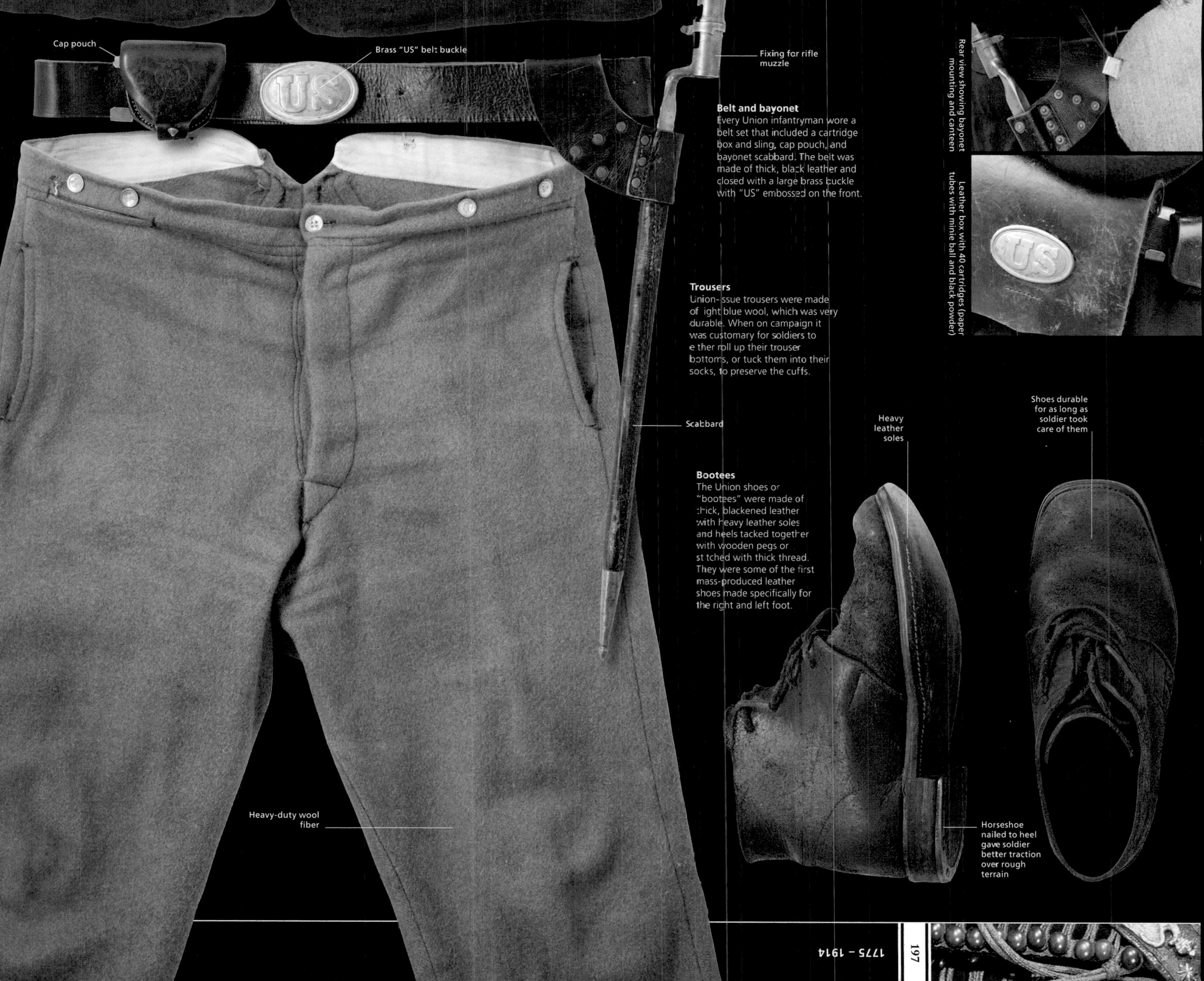

Rear view showing bayonet mounting and canteen

Leather box with 40 cartridges (paper tubes with minie ball and black powder)

Belt and bayonet
Every Union infantryman wore a belt set that included a cartridge box and sling, cap pouch, and bayonet scabbard. The belt was made of thick, black leather and closed with a large brass buckle with "US" embossed on the front.

Trousers
Union-issue trousers were made of light blue wool, which was very durable. When on campaign it was customary for soldiers to either roll up their trouser bottoms, or tuck them into their socks, to preserve the cuffs.

Bootees
The Union shoes or "bootees" were made of thick, blackened leather with heavy leather soles and heels tacked together with wooden pegs or stitched with thick thread. They were some of the first mass-produced leather shoes made specifically for the right and left foot.

UNION EQUIPMENT

The Union infantryman's equipment pack—containing up to 80 rounds of ammunition, three days' worth of rations, rifle, clothing, shelter, and personal effects—could weigh up to 50 lb (23 kg). New soldiers quickly learned what was necessary for them to carry and what was less important. Campaigns in the early spring always began with full knapsacks, but the roads were soon littered with overcoats, blankets, extra clothing, and shelter tents that had been tossed aside to lighten the load.

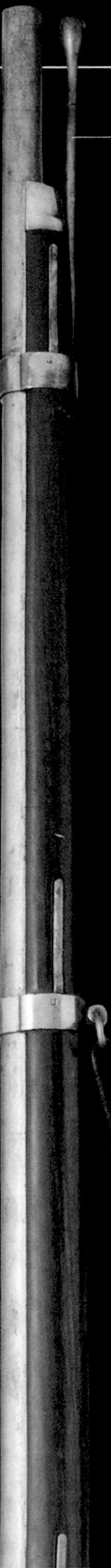

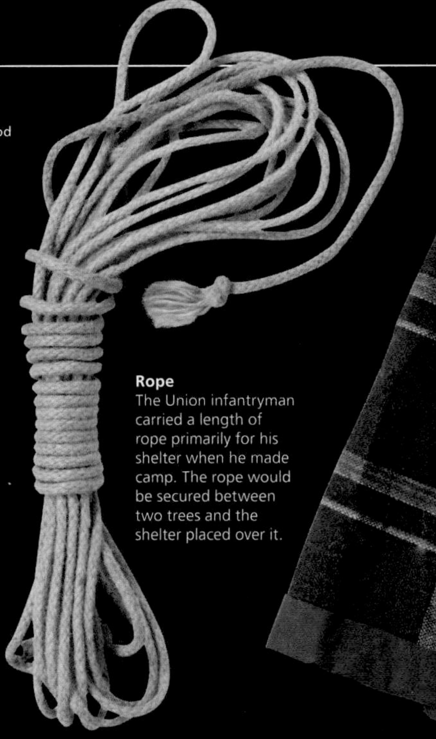

Ramrod

Rope
The Union infantryman carried a length of rope primarily for his shelter when he made camp. The rope would be secured between two trees and the shelter placed over it.

Sleeping cap
Personal items such as this sleeping cap would have provided the raw Union recruit with a semblance of comfort (keeping his head warm at night) in what were otherwise highly oppressive conditions.

Blanket

Rawhide straps

Springfield 1861 rifle-musket and bayonet
The Springfield was the most widely used US army weapon during the Civil War, favored for its long range (some 2,000 ft, or 600 m), accuracy, and reliability. It used the percussion cap system that had superseded the flintlock in the 1840s. The musket came with a three-sided spike bayonet.

Shoulder sling

Three-sided spike

COFFEE ESSENCE POWDER

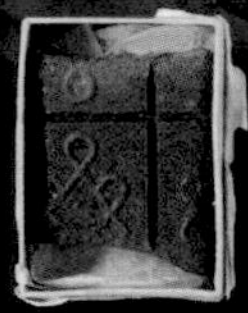

BLOCK OF TEA

WOODEN-HANDLED KNIFE AND FORK

Loop of wire to hang mug over fire

TIN DRINKING MUG

WATER-BOILING CONTAINER

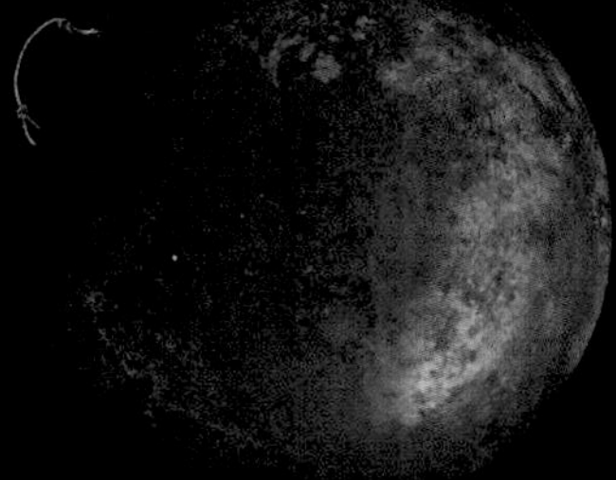

IMPROVISED FRYING PAN

Painted canvas

Eating and cooking kit
The Union soldier's mess kit was predictably basic but the inclusion of coffee essence and tea did provide some flavor to hot water. Typically, the infantryman would carry three days' rations at a time (usually salted pork) but would invariably consume it all on the first day, thereafter subsisting on berries.

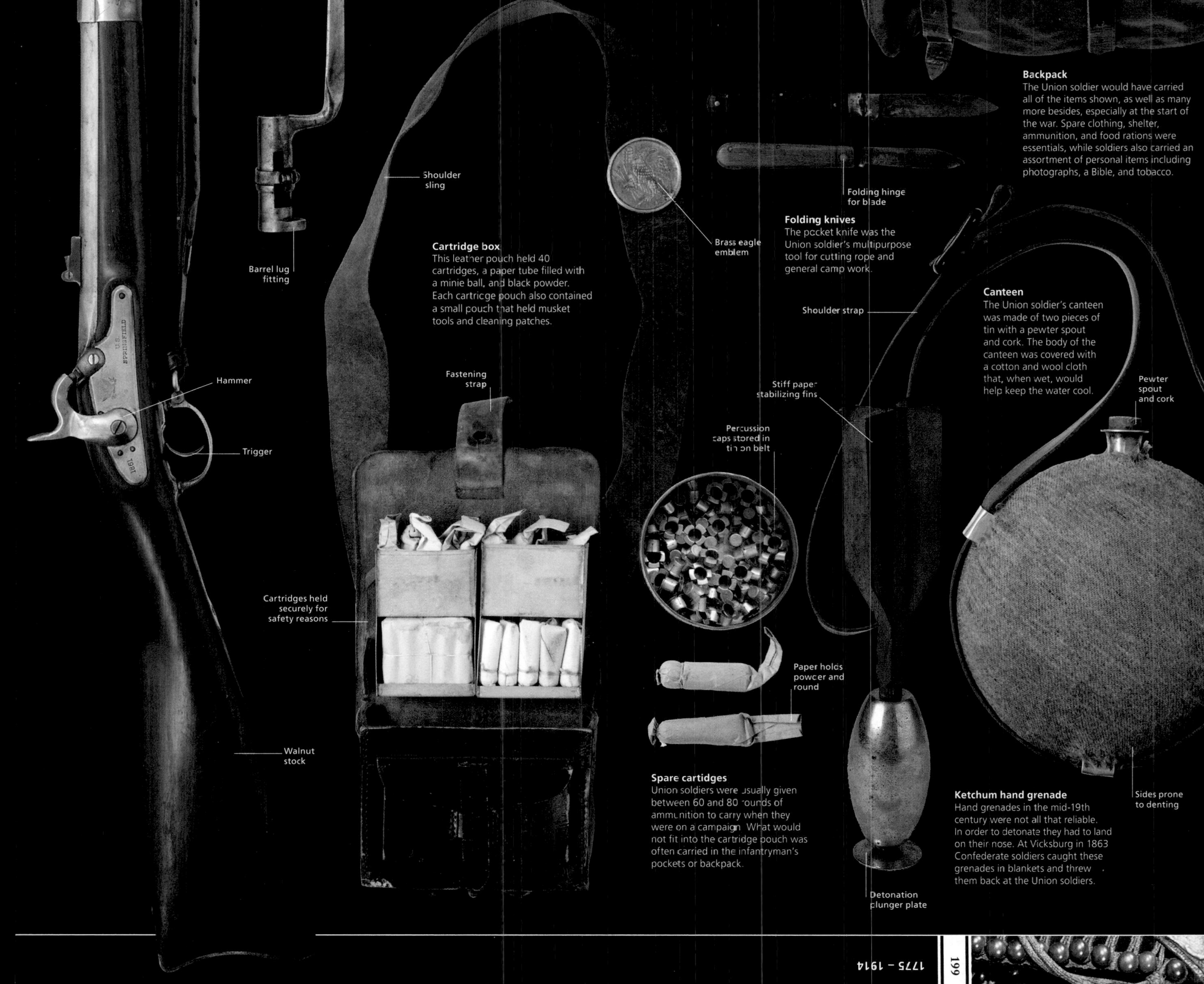

Cartridge box
This leather pouch held 40 cartridges, a paper tube filled with a minie ball, and black powder. Each cartridge pouch also contained a small pouch that held musket tools and cleaning patches.

Backpack
The Union soldier would have carried all of the items shown, as well as many more besides, especially at the start of the war. Spare clothing, shelter, ammunition, and food rations were essentials, while soldiers also carried an assortment of personal items including photographs, a Bible, and tobacco.

Folding knives
The pocket knife was the Union soldier's multipurpose tool for cutting rope and general camp work.

Canteen
The Union soldier's canteen was made of two pieces of tin with a pewter spout and cork. The body of the canteen was covered with a cotton and wool cloth that, when wet, would help keep the water cool.

Spare cartidges
Union soldiers were usually given between 60 and 80 rounds of ammunition to carry when they were on a campaign. What would not fit into the cartridge pouch was often carried in the infantryman's pockets or backpack.

Ketchum hand grenade
Hand grenades in the mid-19th century were not all that reliable. In order to detonate they had to land on their nose. At Vicksburg in 1863 Confederate soldiers caught these grenades in blankets and threw them back at the Union soldiers.

CONFEDERATE INFANTRYMAN

The American Civil War was an unequal contest, the Confederacy fighting at a great disadvantage in terms of manpower and resources. But at least for the first two years of the conflict, despite undergoing privations and hardship, the Southerners often outfought the Union forces, showing aggression, commitment, and superior leadership. By the end of the war, over a million soldiers had served in the Confederate ranks. Some 260,000 of them died in combat or of disease—almost one in four of those who took part. The Confederates' outstanding general, Robert E. Lee, was unstinting in his praise of his men's fighting qualities, stating: "Their courage in battle entitles them to rank with the soldiers of any army and of any time."

The Confederate army was created virtually out of nothing, in much the same manner as the Union forces. Volunteers stampeded to enlist, inspired by dreams of glory and convinced of the rightness of their cause. Some 200,000 soldiers were enrolled in the first four months of the war. As in the North, companies and regiments were mostly formed on a local basis under the leadership of individuals of wealth and standing, and company officers and NCOs were initially elected by the men. The Confederacy benefited, however, from a substantial leaven of regular army officers who resigned from the US forces to fight for secession.

> "CONFEDERATES HAD GONE DOWN AS THE GRASS FALLS BEFORE THE SCYTHE."
>
> JOURNALIST **CHARLES COFFIN** DESCRIBES THE AFTERMATH OF THE BATTLE OF ANTIETAM, SEPTEMBER 17, 1862

COMMITTED REBELS

Given its shortage of manpower, the Confederacy, in 1862, was forced to resort to conscription, but they succeeded in making the draft work better than the Union ever did. All white males aged between 18 and 35 were liable for military service and no one could pay for a substitute to take his place. Confederate soldiers were predominantly farmers or farm hands, and unlike the Union troops, very few were foreign-born.

It was widely agreed that the Southern soldiers fought with greater dash and enthusiasm than the stubborn, pragmatic Northerners. Their shrill "rebel yell" struck dread into hearts of their enemies during an attack. The Confederate soldier generally felt a greater commitment to the war than the average Union soldier. Confederates felt they were fighting in defense of home and family, and of their entire way of life. Lee expressed the feelings of most of his men when, in 1864, he declared: "If victorious, we have everything to hope for; if defeated, nothing will be left for us to live for." In the last two years of the war, with defeat looming, the Confederate army was swept by religious revivalism, with many soldiers engaging enthusiastically in prayer meetings and hymn-singing.

Holding the Line at All Hazards
Confederate soldiers, despite being outnumbered for much of the time, held their positions heroically.

Many were struck by the contrast between the rebels' ragged appearance and their courage. A woman who saw the Confederate Army of Northern Virginia on the march in late summer 1862, described the "gaunt starvation that looked from their cavernous eyes" and commented: "That they could march or fight at all seems incredible." Yet these were the soldiers who checked the Union forces at Antietam.

A HOPELESS CAUSE

The Confederate soldier's experience of war was of a shortage of everything: boots, clothes, blankets, tents, food, cartridges, pay. Many were reduced to marching barefoot unless they could "liberate" some Union footwear. Faced with the North's overwhelming superiority, the South had little choice but to rely upon the attacking spirit of its soldiers. It cost them dearly and could not win the war. But the Confederate soldier emerged with honor, if little else.

Confederate weaponry
The standard infantry weapon was the rifle-musket. The Enfield was imported in large numbers from manufacturers in Britain.

> "A MOTLEY-LOOKING CREW, BUT THEY FIGHT LIKE DEVILS."
>
> **UNION SOLDIER** ON HIS CONFEDERATE ENEMIES

Confederate uniform
Infantrymen fought in a huge variety of different colors, including gray, blue, and "butternut," shown here in this replica of a uniform of 1862.

Trench warfare
As the American Civil War progressed, both sides made greater use of earthworks and trenches to protect their troops. Here Union soldiers of the Army of the Potomac wait in a trench before launching an attack during the second battle of Fredericksburg, May 1863.

1800 – 1870

MAORI WARRIOR

"THEN, OH MY CHILDREN BE BRAVE! THEN OH MY FRIENDS BE STRONG! BE BRAVE THAT YOU MAY NOT BE ENSLAVED AND THAT YOUR COUNTRY MAY NOT BECOME THE POSSESSION OF STRANGERS."

The haka
The *haka* (literally meaning "dance") was originally performed by warriors before a battle, proclaiming their strength and prowess in order to intimidate the opposition. Today, the *haka* constitutes an integral part of formal welcome ceremonies for distinguished visitors or foreign dignitaries *(above)*. Facial tattoos, a Polynesian custom, indicated a warrior's ancestry, status, and fighting prowess. The carved jade *hei-tiki (right)* is a neck pendant worn by the Maori, who esteem jade highly for its beauty and resilience.

POLYNESIAN FARMERS AND SAILORS, the Maori settled in New Zealand some time between 800 and 1300 CE. Warfare was a central part of their traditional culture. They built fortified villages for defense and organized war parties every year to fight their neighbors. In the 19th century, contact with Europeans added muskets to the Maori's traditional wood-and-stone weaponry. Equipped with firearms, the Maori fought a series of costly wars—the Musket Wars—against one another, and the British army.

Much about the pre-colonial history of the Maori is a matter of dispute, including the causes and nature of their warfare. It would appear that, as in many societies before modern times, war was regarded as a normal activity to be engaged in at the appropriate time of year. Male Maori were trained up to be warriors, or *toa*, from boyhood. Since different Maori tribes lived in close proximity on well populated coastal farmland, motives for fighting with neighbors were never in short supply. Some anthropologists have argued that the Maori battled mainly over possession of scarce land, but less obviously rational motives seem actually to have predominated. The Maori were highly sensitive to any insult or injury, memory of which might be transmitted through generations. Military action was justified in pursuit of vengeance (*utu*) for whatever offense the tribal chief felt that he had suffered. Combat was also an end in itself, providing the *toa* with a chance to prove their valor and their chief with an opportunity to enhance his status.

RITUAL AND MASSACRE

Maori warriors would form a war party on their chief's orders; typically between 70 and 140 men constituted a warband—70 was the number that would fit in a war canoe, the usual mode of transport for warriors. Various rituals had to be observed before setting off, including the rehearsal of grievances against the enemy and the avoidance of certain foods. Ambushes and surprise attacks played a major part in Maori warfare, but inevitably opposing forces would sometimes confront one another in open combat. In preparation for battle, warriors would perform a dance (the *haka*); this was a combination of war chants and aggressive gestures with grotesque grimaces designed to intimidate the enemy.

The warriors would probably be naked but for a belt around their waist. They fought with wooden spears and clubs, given a sharp edge by incorporating pieces of stone, coral, bone, or shell. Despite ritualized elements that sometimes limited casualties, Maori warfare could be brutal and thoroughly deadly. If an enemy force tried to flee, for example, the fleetest warriors might pursue them, striking as many as possible to the ground with their spears without stopping. The injured men would then be overtaken by slower-moving warriors following on behind who ruthlessly slaughtered them with clubs and axes. Similarly, a warband that fell into an ambush could often expect to be killed to the last man. After a victory, some of the dead enemy would be eaten, for religious rather than nutritional reasons, and their embalmed heads exhibited around the village as trophies of battle.

The principle of vengeance could have led to wars of extermination, since if only some of the enemy were killed, the survivors would inevitably return to seek revenge. What usually prevented the total massacre or enslavement of tribes were their strong defensive preparations. The Maori built *pa* (fortified strongholds) on hill-tops, surrounded by palisades, ditches, and banks, and incorporating food stores that would enable them to survive a lengthy siege. Once withdrawn within these defenses, the Maori were unlikely to be overrun, even by a clearly stronger enemy.

JADE HEI-TIKI (NECK PENDANT)

MUSKET WARFARE

By 1800, the Maori had begun to have contact with Europeans, as whalers, sealers, and traders stopped off on the New Zealand coast. The Europeans brought with them flintlock muskets, which had an obvious appeal for Maori warriors. Initially, these inherently clumsy and inaccurate firearms had little effect on local warfare. In 1807, when the Nga Puhi tribe first used muskets in battle, they were trounced by their traditionally armed enemies, the Ngati Whatua. Quickly, though, tribes that equipped themselves with muskets began to establish their dominance. A substantial commerce developed in which the Maori exchanged potatoes, pigs, or flax for firearms and ammunition. They soon discovered that the products of war could also be traded for guns, since the Europeans would accept war captives as slaves and the embalmed heads of the slain as curios. Some Maori chiefs traveled to the Australian colonies and at least one, Hongi Hika, visited Britain, where he had an audience with King George IV in 1820. These contacts with the wider world encouraged the territorial ambitions of some Maori leaders, and provided new and improved military technology.

From the 1810s to the 1830s, the Maori tribes engaged in a series of highly destructive conflicts that have been called the Musket Wars. These conflicts were fought in ways that were broadly similar to traditional Maori warfare, with war parties attacking tribes against whom they had grievances, the enemy dead being eaten, and weaker groups taking refuge in forts. But the scale of the fighting was much greater than before. Led by Hongi Hika, the Nga Puhi sent out musket-armed war parties 800 or 900 strong on long-distance raiding expeditions. Other tribes such as the Ngati Toa, led by Te Rauparaha, imitated their example. Weaker tribes were massacred, enslaved, or driven off their lands. The conflicts petered out in the 1830s, partly because once all Maori had

War canoe
Waka taua were the Maori warrior's usual mode of transport. They were as long as 130 ft (40 m) and could hold up to 70 men. Two canoes were sufficient to transport an entire war party. A bailer *(below)* was essential gear in case the boat took on water.

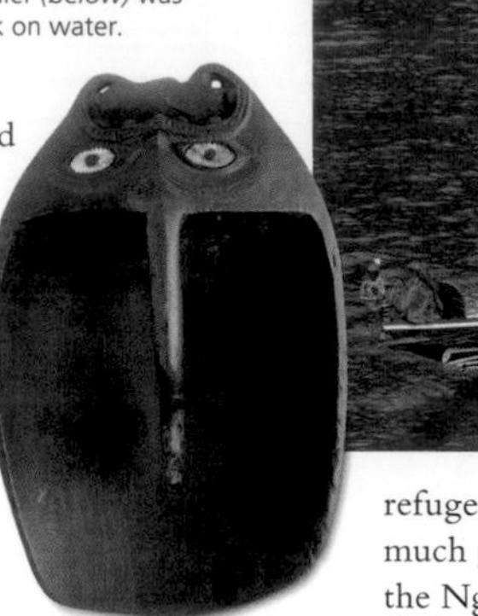

CANOE BAILER

“NOT ONE ESCAPED. SOME RAN AWAY FROM US, THESE WE KILLED AND OTHERS WE KILLED—BUT WHAT OF THAT? IT WAS IN ACCORDANCE WITH OUR CUSTOM.”

MAORI WARRIOR ON MASSACRE OF CHATHAM ISLAND POPULATION, 1835

Tribal gathering
The warrior culture survived long after the pacification of New Zealand in the mid-19th century. This photograph of a meeting of Maori warriors dates from around 1920.

muskets there were no easy gains to be made by any of the tribes. An estimated 20,000 Maori warriors died in the Musket Wars, possibly one in five of the entire population.

LAND WARS

In 1840 Britain took over New Zealand as a colony, after agreeing the Treaty of Waitangi with the Maori. Within five years the first of a string of conflicts had broken out in which Maori tribes contested the rule of the British authorities and resisted land grabs by European settlers. Although the Maori King Movement attempted to unify resistance from 1858, there were always Maori who fought on the British side (known as *kupapa*), mostly motivated by tribal rivalry. Yet despite their divisions, the Maori proved among the most effective opponents the British army faced in its 19th-century colonial campaigns. This was despite a lack of numbers—for a combination of British troops, settler militias, and *kupapa* could usually assemble a larger force than Maori rebels could field. Maori weaponry was also inferior; although they obtained rifle muskets, they often had no proper ammunition, resorting to homemade substitutes.

Maori warriors proved adept at guerrilla warfare, but they were also surprisingly successful at adapting their fortified strongholds to the demands of modern warfare. They created *pa* encircled with complex systems of earthworks and palisades, constructed to give entrenched defenders effective fields of fire against enemy infantry attempting an assault. Deep bunkers were dug inside the fort to allow the Maori to survive artillery fire. They invited the British to attack them in these fortified positions, which they would abandon once they had inflicted maximum casualties on the attackers. The strength of this system was demonstrated on April 29, 1864 at Gate Pa, Tauranga. Less than 250 Maori inside the fort faced 1,700 soldiers under General Duncan Cameron equipped with mortars, howitzers, and Armstrong guns. Cameron's artillery destroyed the fort's palisade, but his soldiers suffered heavy casualties in a failed attempt to storm the line of trenches. The Maori staged a strategic withdrawal from the *pa* with only slight losses.

Sacred feeding funnel
The *kumete* is a ceremonial food vessel used to feed a warrior after his face had been tattooed. His scars were so severe from tattooing that he was unable to chew for several days; his food was therefore pounded to a paste and taken through the funnel. The contents of the *kumete* were not to be touched by others.

Battle ready
A modern-day Maori in traditional costume performs the *haka*. He is armed with a *taiaha* (long staff) used for stabbing and striking, and a *wahaika* (short-range club), secured inside a war belt.

In the 1860s Christian-inspired prophet-led Maori movements erupted, whose followers waged a guerrilla war that seriously threatened the colonists' hold on North Island. In 1868, Titokowaru's forces won two victories defending forts against colonial militia and *kupapa*, and a warband led by Ti Kooti massacred settlers at Matawhero. Yet Titokowaru's rebellion disintegrated the following year, while Ti Kooti's band struggled on as isolated raiders until 1872.

ENDURING TRADITION

The Maori had proved that they could match the Europeans as fighters, but not in their capacity for large-scale economic organization and sustained campaigning. Altogether these colonial conflicts were far less murderous than the Musket Wars, costing the lives of around 2,000 Maori rebels and some 750 British soldiers, settlers, and *kupapa*.

The Maori warrior ethic was not entirely lost after the pacification of New Zealand. A Maori Pioneer battalion served in World War I and a volunteer battalion was organized to fight as part of the New Zealand Expeditionary Force in World War II. The Maori performed with distinction in the Mediterranean theater, including Greece, Crete, North Africa, and Italy. The men who fought in the desert at El Alamein and on the slopes of Monte Cassino were keenly aware of fulfilling the traditions of their ancestors.

MAORI WEAPONS

Before the wars of the mid-19th century brought the Maori people into contact with firearms, the Maori's principal weapons were short clubs, long staffs, and stone-headed spears, which they used to great effect in a series of long-running tribal conflicts. Their proficiency in hand-to-hand fighting can be traced to the ancient martial art of *Mau Rakau*, meaning "to grasp a weapon," which was taught to all young *toa* (warriors). The Maori fighting style was entrenched in religious symbolism and ceremonies such as the *haka* (war dance), often performed holding weapons aloft.

Heavy clubbed end

Decorative carving

Inlaid with haliotis shell

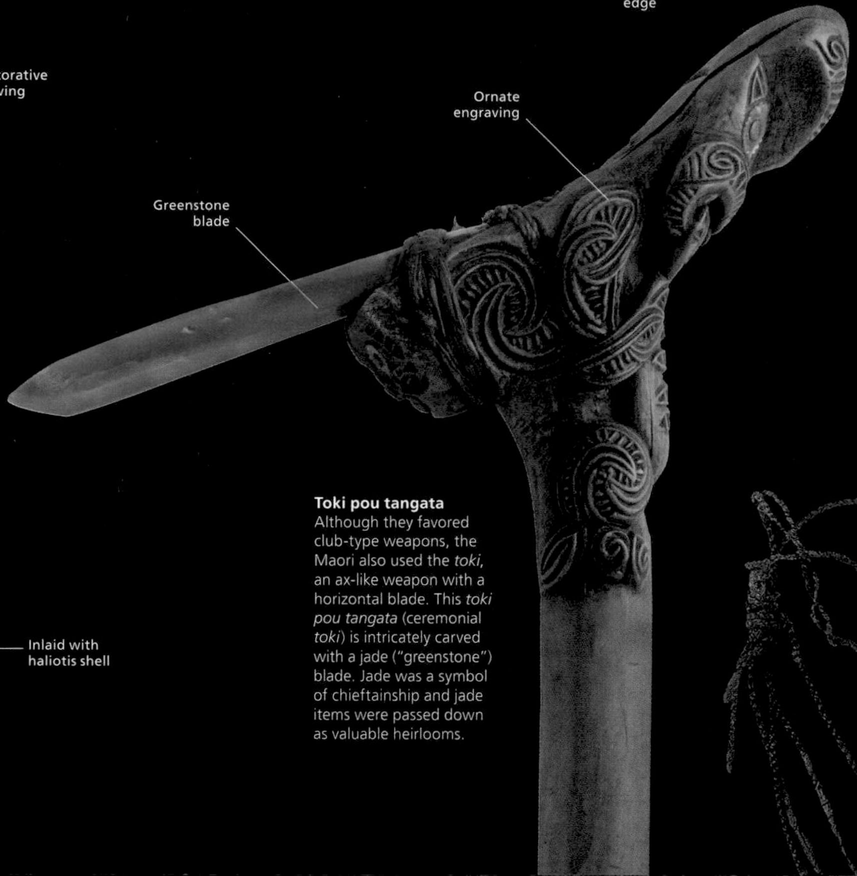

Greenstone blade

Ornate engraving

Toki pou tangata
Although they favored club-type weapons, the Maori also used the *toki*, an ax-like weapon with a horizontal blade. This *toki pou tangata* (ceremonial *toki*) is intricately carved with a jade ("greenstone") blade. Jade was a symbol of chieftainship and jade items were passed down as valuable heirlooms.

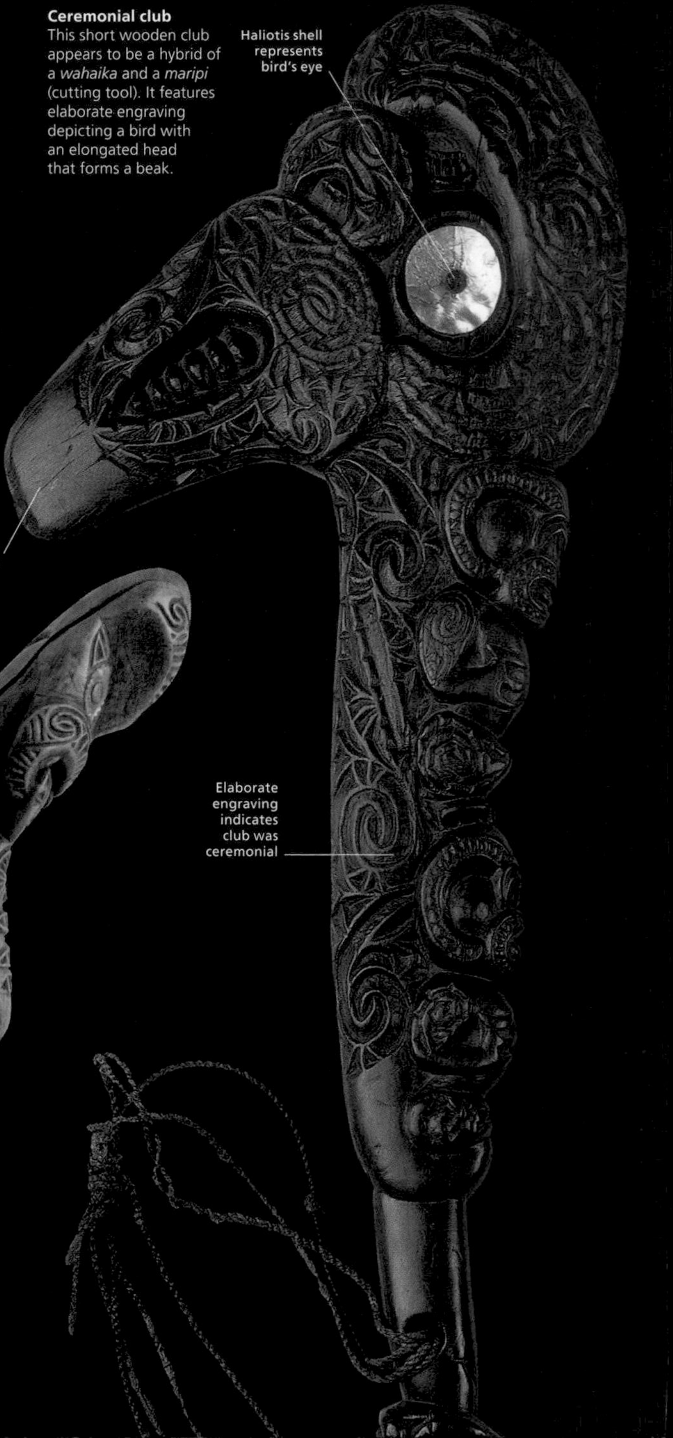

Ceremonial club
This short wooden club appears to be a hybrid of a *wahaika* and a *maripi* (cutting tool). It features elaborate engraving depicting a bird with an elongated head that forms a beak.

Haliotis shell represents bird's eye

Cutting edge

Elaborate engraving indicates club was ceremonial

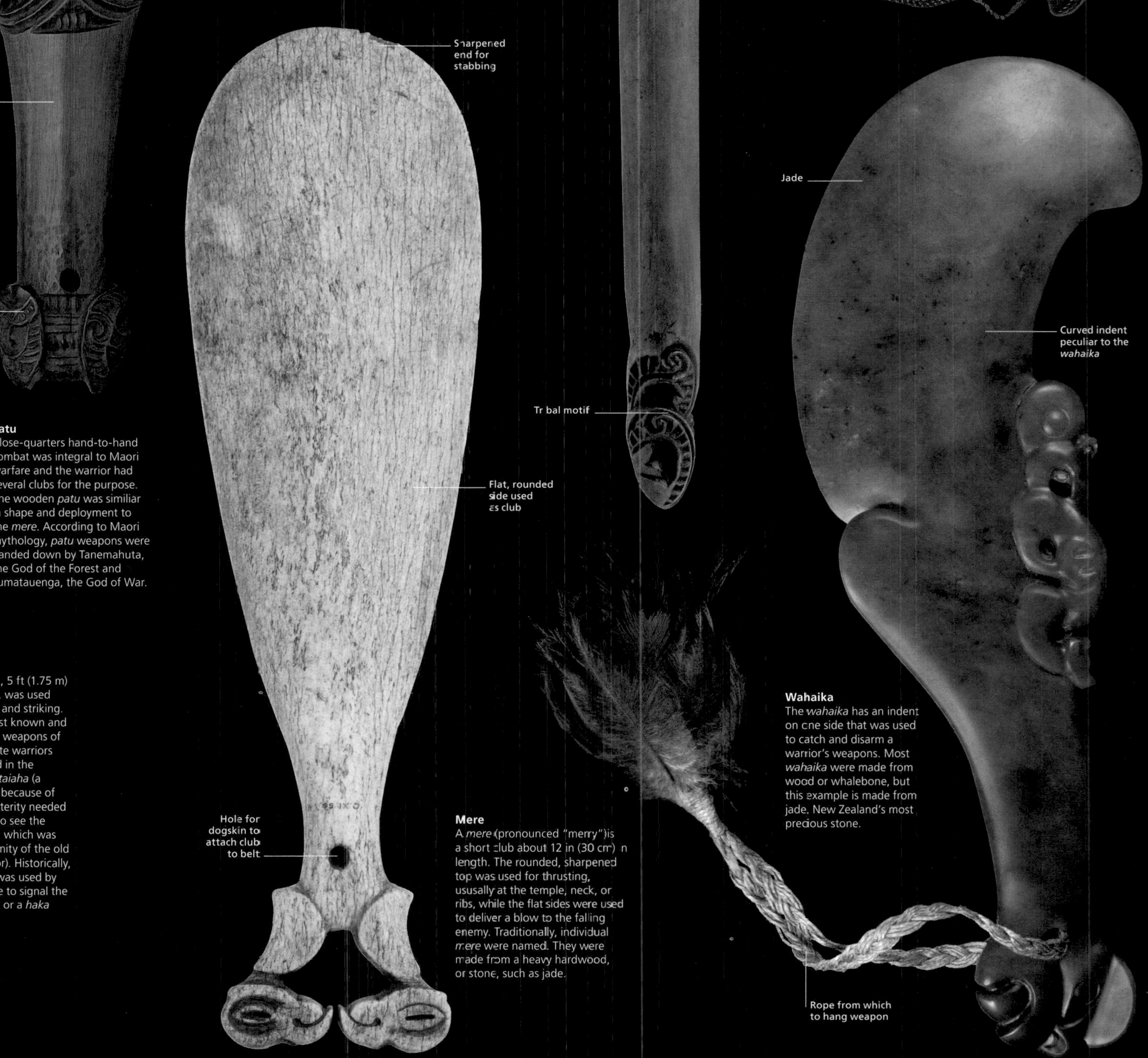

Patu
Close-quarters hand-to-hand combat was integral to Maori warfare and the warrior had several clubs for the purpose. The wooden *patu* was similiar in shape and deployment to the *mere*. According to Maori mythology, *patu* weapons were handed down by Tanemahuta, the God of the Forest and Tumatauenga, the God of War.

Tewhatewha
This staff weapon, 5 ft (1.75 m) or more in length, was used both for stabbing and striking. It is one of the best known and commonly taught weapons of the Maori. The elite warriors of old were skilled in the *tewhatewha* and *taiaha* (a similar long staff) because of the poise and dexterity needed to "get in close" to see the enemy eye to eye, which was the favored proximity of the old school *toa* (warrior). Historically, the *tewhatewha* was used by the chief of a tribe to signal the time for an attack or a *haka* (war dance).

Mere
A *mere* (pronounced "merry") is a short club about 12 in (30 cm) in length. The rounded, sharpened top was used for thrusting, ususally at the temple, neck, or ribs, while the flat sides were used to deliver a blow to the falling enemy. Traditionally, individual *mere* were named. They were made from a heavy hardwood, or stone, such as jade.

Wahaika
The *wahaika* has an indent on one side that was used to catch and disarm a warrior's weapons. Most *wahaika* were made from wood or whalebone, but this example is made from jade, New Zealand's most precious stone.

1800 – 1880

ZULU WARRIOR

"THE CHIEF WAS SHOT THROUGH THE FOREHEAD AND DROPPED DOWN DEAD, BUT THE UMCIJO RUSHED OVER HIS BODY AND FELL UPON THE SOLDIERS, STABBING THEM WITH THEIR ASSEGAIS AND DRIVING THEM RIGHT IN AMONG THE TENTS."

WARRIOR OF THE UMBONAMBI REGIMENT DESCRIBING THE BRAVERY OF THE UMCIJO REGIMENT AT ISANDHLWANA

Mobile warriors
Young Zulu warriors were extremely fit and hardy. At war, they could cover 20 miles (32 km) a day, which was double the speed achieved by the British army at that time. Although the Zulu carried throwing spears, clubs, and latterly firearms into battle, they relied chiefly on the cowhide shield and stabbing spear *(above and right).*

IN THE EARLY 19TH CENTURY, the Zulu developed an aggressive warrior spirit and disciplined fighting skills that made them a dominant military power in their region of southern Africa. Despite their low level of technology, they proved difficult opponents for the British army in the Anglo-Zulu War of 1879, achieving a notable victory at Isandhlwana. But their mode of warfare, based on the spear and the shield, could not ultimately prevail in the face of the overwhelming firepower of rifles and artillery.

Before 1816, when they came under the rule of the paramount chief Shaka, the Zulu were an insignificant pastoral people with no pretensions to military excellence. They participated in the traditional warfare of the southern African cattle-herding tribes, which consisted of ritualized fighting that minimized casualties. When opposing sides met for battle, typically to decide a dispute over grazing land, individual warriors would demonstrate their prowess by challenging an enemy to single armed combat. Otherwise, the two sides would limit themselves first to an exchange of insults followed by the throwing of missiles at a distance. If their flimsy throwing spears managed to cause any deaths, warriors had to break off from combat to carry out cleansing rites to appease the spirits of the dead. The weaker side accepted defeat without insisting on a fight to the finish.

The development of the Zulu into a militaristic society began in the early 19th century under clan chief Dingiswayo, but it was only after chief Shaka seized power in 1816 that their practice of war was transformed. Shaka abandoned the traditional reliance on *assegais* (throwing spears) as the main weapon, instead introducing the stabbing spear and encouraging his warriors to use it to deadly effect in close combat. Instead of ritualized fighting, Shaka sought to fix and destroy the forces of his enemy. In a series of exterminatory campaigns, known as the *mfecane* ("crushing"), he massacred neighboring peoples or forced them into submission. By the time of Shaka's death in 1828, the Zulu had spread almost as far north as Swaziland. The military machine, and style of warfare, that Shaka created remained broadly unchanged until the Zulu's disastrous encounter with the British Empire forces in 1879.

FORMING A WARRIOR

As young boys, future Zulu warriors picked up informal fighting skills by battling one another with sticks. They also learned to be hardy and self-reliant in their harsh natural environment, accompanying their elders as bearers on long cross-country journeys and hunting small game. Induction into the warrior class came between the ages of 18 and 20. Men of the same age group were assembled to form a regiment and set up a barracks. The warriors would remain with the same regiment—identified by the adoption of a particular color shield and other details of dress—for the next two decades. Obviously, this regimental system encouraged bonding and group identity.

Although in the time of Shaka's rule warriors were, according to reports, trained in forced marches and military maneuvers, there seems very little evidence at any later period for a tough training routine in the style of Western armies. In fact, the warriors' equivalent of parade-ground drill and weapons training appears to have largely consisted of performing complex rhythmic dances with shields, sticks, or spears.

COWHIDE SHIELD AND STABBING SPEAR

Zulu war dance
Zulu warriors in full battle dress, armed with cowhide shields, stabbing spears, and knobkerries, perform a war dance (*umghubha*). Ceremonial dancing and singing, performed before and after battle, was of great religious significance to the Zulu. Note the plumes of dust in the photograph, caused by the vigorous stamping of unshod feet.

Yet military life for the Zulu warrior was far from idyllic. Fights were constantly breaking out between individuals or rival regiments, who attacked one another with knobkerries (heavy sticks). These punishing duels were connived at by the officers (*izinduna*), who saw fighting as a useful toughening exercise for the warriors, although combat with spears was strictly forbidden. The food supplied to the regiments by the chief was often meager, at times a serious cause of discontent. Warriors were generally forbidden to marry, a regulation that became more irksome as men grew older. In practice, marriage was permitted after around 15 years of service. Warriors were released from their military duties at around the age of 40.

Cowhide shield
Shields needed to be both strong and lightweight. The distinctive coloring of the shield showed the regiment to which the warrior belonged, and his status within it.

ZULU WARRIOR SHIELD

FIGHTING METHOD

A Zulu warrior functioned as part of a mobile aggressive army dedicated to locating and then destroying an enemy force at close quarters. One of Shaka's reforms was to abandon the wearing of sandals, because he believed his warriors could move faster unshod. Thus the Zulu traveled barefoot—a European observer described the soles of their feet as hardened "like the hoof of a cow." Warriors advanced in columns at around 20 miles (30 km) a day, often accompanied by boys under 12 years old carrying their cooking pots, sleeping mats, and extra weapons. On occasion, cattle were brought along as a mobile food supply, but when maximum speed was required the warriors traveled light and survived by foraging. Scouts reported back on the enemy's location and strength, and acted as skirmishers, screening the movement of the army.

Although the Zulu always exploited speed of movement and knowledge of the country, they were in no sense guerrilla fighters. Their aim was to engage the enemy in pitched battle, deploying thousands of men at a time in a decisive attack. Before entering combat, a warrior would carry out various rituals, including anointing himself with a magic potion to guarantee his safety. With his regiment he would then take up his appointed position in the traditional "buffalo horn" battlefield formation. Younger regiments formed the "horns" on each flank, which were to encircle the enemy. The center, or "chest," would be composed of experienced fighters, since it was expected to bear the brunt of the battle on a frontal charge. The "loins," a body of older veterans, was held in reserve.

Movement on the battlefield was directed by the *izinduna* using hand movements or messengers, although Zulu armies rarely departed from standard tactics with which all were familiar. The warriors would advance toward their enemy at a steady jog, sometimes beating their shields rhythmically with their spears. Once within suitable distance, they rushed forward in a last full-tilt dash, launching their throwing spears when about 100 ft (30 m) from the enemy. At close quarters the stabbing spear and shield were put to deadly use. The Zulu never took prisoners, massacring their enemy to the last man and ripping open the bodies of the dead to release their spirits.

EFFECT OF FIREARMS

The Zulu first experienced the power of European firearms when fighting Dutch-speaking Afrikaner settlers, known as the Boers. At Blood River in 1838, the firepower of a few hundred Boers defeated a Zulu army possibly numbering 10,000 men. Zulu leaders subsequently obtained firearms for their warriors, but failed to make any radical change in tactics. They continued to practise massed infantry assault, which against rifle-armed troops in a prepared position was bound to cost them heavy casualties. The Zulu did learn to make good use of cover in approaching the enemy position and attacked in

> "WE WILL GO AND EAT UP THE WHITE MAN AND FINISH THEM OFF. THEY ARE NOT GOING TO TAKE YOU WHILE WE ARE HERE. THEY MUST TAKE US FIRST."
>
> **ZULU ARMY**, ADDRESSING **KING CETSHWAYO** AT THE BATTLE OF ULUNDI, 1879

far looser formation than had been customary in Shaka's time. But they employed their rifles merely as an adjunct or alternative to the traditional throwing spear, shooting a scattered volley of bullets in the general direction of the enemy as a prelude to the final charge.

The Zulu empire was arguably already in decline before conflict with Britain brought about its downfall. Zulu chief Cetshwayo was nonetheless able to field some 40,000 warriors in an effort to repel the invasion of his territories by the British army in January 1879. The enemy was numerically inferior but armed with breech-loading rifles, field artillery, and Gatling guns.

Boldly seizing the initiative, on January 22, a force comprising around half of the entire Zulu army fell upon 800 British soldiers and their African auxiliaries camped in a defensively ill-prepared position at Isandhlwana. Despite suffering heavy losses, the Zulu pursued their attack, urged on by the *izinduna*. Even when the Zulu reached the British lines, they found their red-coated enemies formidable fighters with the bayonet. One Zulu later recalled that warriors hurled their spears or fired their rifles at the British rather than closing to stab them: "They avoided the bayonet; for any man who went up to stab a soldier was fixed through the throat or stomach." By sheer weight of numbers, however, the British were ultimately overrun and slaughtered. An almost simultaneous attack on a small British outpost at Rorke's Drift was repulsed, although fighting was at times again engaged at close quarters with bayonet against spear.

Glory at Isandhlwana
The Zulu were largely no match for the British army's artillery in 1879, but at Isandhlwana on January 22, they survived heavy losses to triumph.

Militaristic pretentions
Utimuni, nephew of chief Shaka Zulu, in ceremonial dress. Shaka transformed the Zulu into an aggressive fighting force during his rule (1816–28).

DECLINE OF POWER

The scale of the loss of fighting men in these and subsequent battles was more than the Zulu could sustain. Ironically, when dispersed Zulu warriors mounted an uncoordinated harassment of British forces in defense of their homes, they had a large measure of success in this low-level guerrilla warfare. But Cetshwayo remained committed to pitting the magic-impregnated flesh of his warriors against British bullets in open battle, even though he knew victory was impossible. A final bloody defeat at Ulundi in July brought the brief flourishing of Zulu military power to an end. The British annexed Zululand; Cetshwayo was captured and taken to England, where he was feted as a celebrity by the patronizing victors.

ZULU BATTLE DRESS

The Zulu warrior's main equipment consisted of a heavy stabbing spear and a large cowhide shield, although the Zulu also carried throwing spears, knobkerries (clubs), and, by the second half of the 19th century, muskets or rifles. Details of dress and decoration of equipment were used to signify status and allegiance. The war shield in particular symbolized the warrior's commitment to his king's service—one Zulu commander referred to the shield as "the love charm of the nation."

Headdress
The warrior's headpiece, to which was attached elaborate feather decorations, was generally a leopard- or otterskin band, set over a monkey skin cap that had neck and ear flaps. This 19th-century example was used for ceremonial purposes.

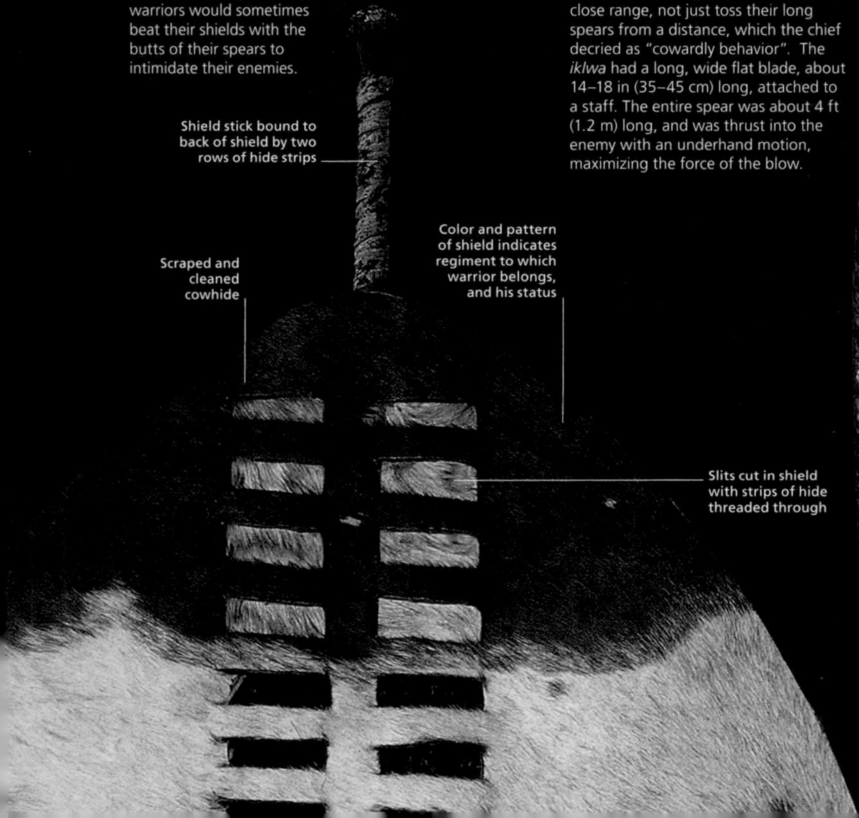

Feather decoration

Zulu war shield
War shields were made from the hides of cattle from the king's herd. The hide was scraped, cleaned, and buried in the soil for several days before being cut to shape. When advancing to attack, warriors would sometimes beat their shields with the butts of their spears to intimidate their enemies.

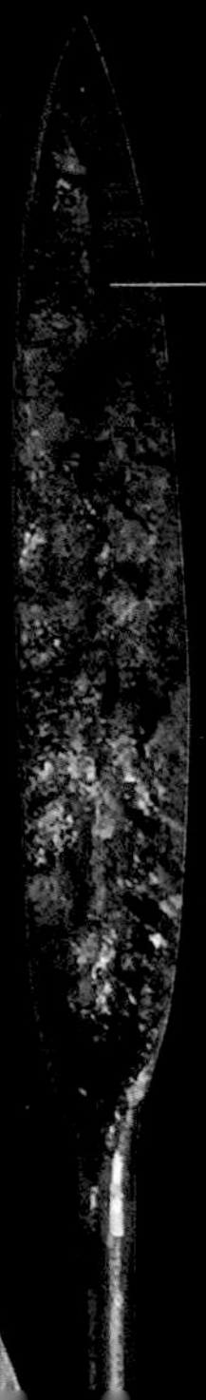

Shield stick bound to back of shield by two rows of hide strips

Scraped and cleaned cowhide

Color and pattern of shield indicates regiment to which warrior belongs, and his status

Slits cut in shield with strips of hide threaded through

Iklwa (stabbing spear)
The most devastating Zulu weapon was the *iklwa*, or stabbing spear, said to be named for the sound it made when drawn from a body. The *iklwa* is traditionally said to have been developed by Chief Shaka, who wanted his warriors to engage their enemies at close range, not just toss their long spears from a distance, which the chief decried as "cowardly behavior". The *iklwa* had a long, wide flat blade, about 14–18 in (35–45 cm) long, attached to a staff. The entire spear was about 4 ft (1.2 m) long, and was thrust into the enemy with an underhand motion, maximizing the force of the blow.

Broad flat blade

Hardwood end produced a deadly blow

Decorative carving made each tribe's knobkerrries unique

> WE KILLED EVERY WHITE MAN LEFT IN THE CAMP AND THE HORSES AND CATTLE TOO.
>
> **GUMPEGA KWABE**, ZULU WARRIOR, ON MASSACRE OF BRITISH AT NTOMBE RIVER, MARCH 1879

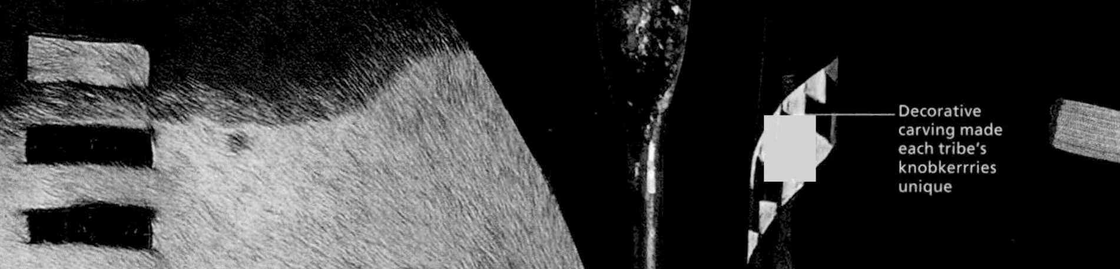

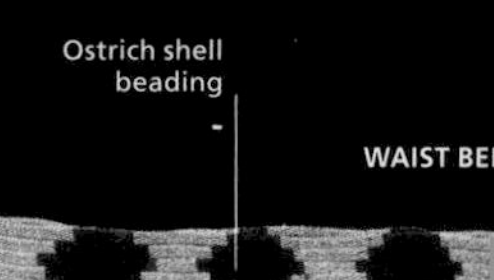

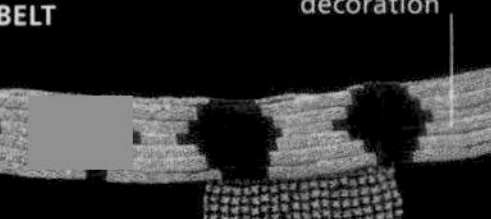

WAIST BELT

Ostrich shell beading

Fur strips and feathers were hung from belt as decoration

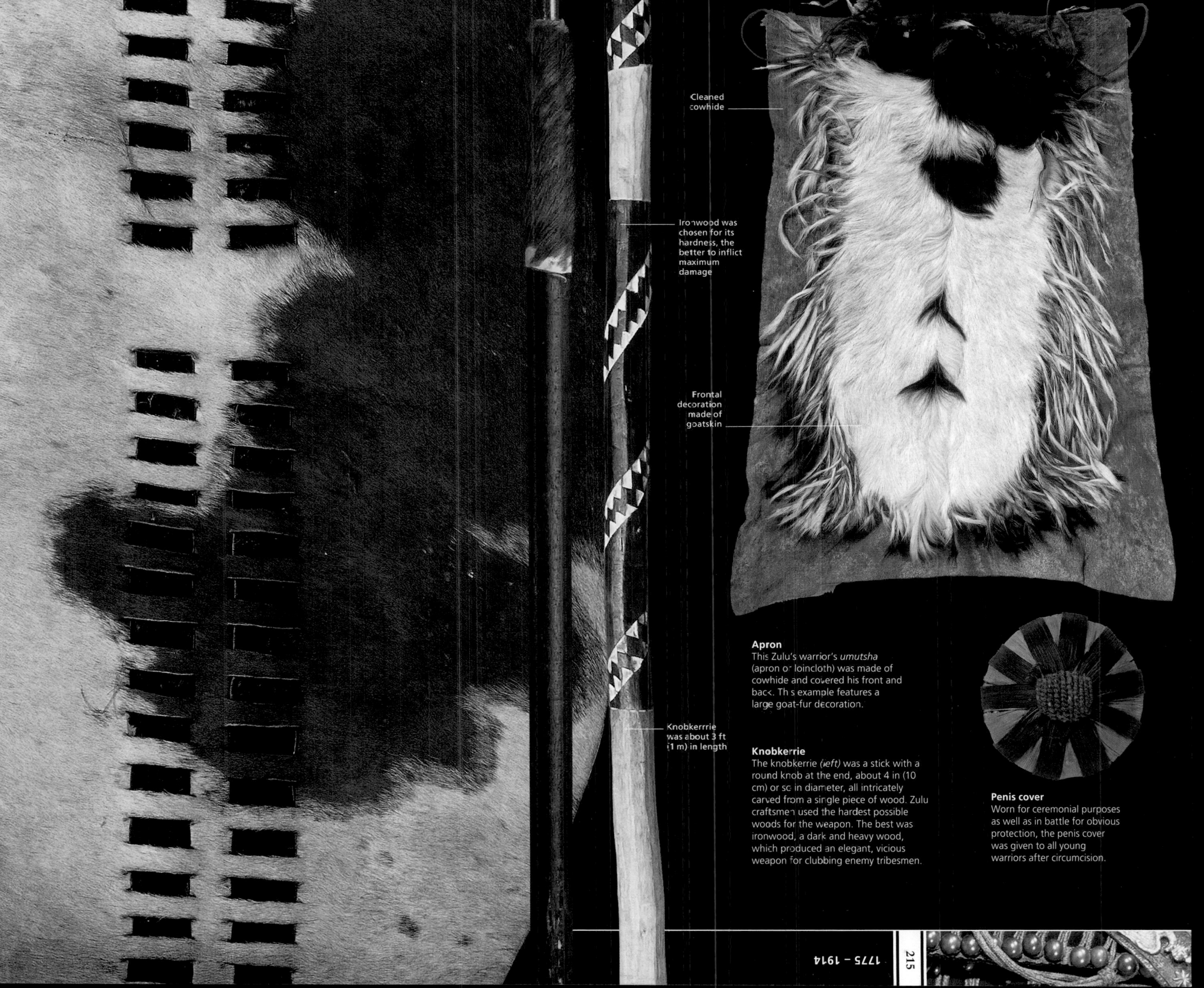

Apron
This Zulu's warrior's *umutsha* (apron or loincloth) was made of cowhide and covered his front and back. This example features a large goat-fur decoration.

Knobkerrie
The knobkerrie *(left)* was a stick with a round knob at the end, about 4 in (10 cm) or so in diameter, all intricately carved from a single piece of wood. Zulu craftsmen used the hardest possible woods for the weapon. The best was ironwood, a dark and heavy wood, which produced an elegant, vicious weapon for clubbing enemy tribesmen.

Penis cover
Worn for ceremonial purposes as well as in battle for obvious protection, the penis cover was given to all young warriors after circumcision.

1860 – 1890

SIOUX WARRIOR

"I WAS HOSTILE TO THE WHITE MAN ... WE PREFERRED HUNTING TO A LIFE OF IDLENESS ON OUR RESERVATIONS. AT TIMES WE DID NOT GET ENOUGH TO EAT AND WE WERE NOT ALLOWED TO HUNT. ALL WE WANTED WAS PEACE AND TO BE LEFT ALONE.

FROM THE 1860S TO THE 1880S the Sioux tribes, along with other nomadic buffalo-hunting Plains Indians such as the Cheyenne and the Arapaho, fought a guerrilla war against the US Army in a last-ditch attempt to block settler encroachment on their hunting grounds. They evolved a form of warfare based on their skills as horsemen, hunters, and raiders. Although they had no chance of ultimate success, given the willpower and resources of their opponents, they proved superior in combat on their own terms.

For the men of the Sioux nations, fighting was a way of life. Warfare was central to the social and economic existence of the tribe. But it was also crucial to personal ambition, for it was through combat that an individual warrior could prove his courage and martial skills, and thus hope to rise in the warrior hierarchy of his society. The practical objectives of warfare were many and various. Tribes raided their neighbors to steal horses or to take women and children captives—thus increasing their own population. They fought for control of hunting grounds and for control of trade. But warfare was also likely to be provoked by some insult or misdeed that the honor of the tribe required be avenged.

The Plains Indians' traditional form of warfare was what Europeans once called "the skulking way of war." It consisted of raids and ambushes carried out by stealth. Raiding parties typically numbering no more than 30 or 40 warriors would embark on a combat mission, usually returning after a single fight with the chosen enemy. Fighting was generally not very destructive. Minimizing one's own casualties was an important principle, for Plains Indian peoples had low birth rates and the lives of their warriors were a precious resource. Mostly there was also no attempt to inflict heavy losses on the enemy tribe. Combat had ritualistic elements bringing it close to sport. Men would be awarded "points" for certain achievements—such as the total of horses stolen—which would contribute to their grading as warriors.

A Sioux warrior would get more points for the courageous act of touching an enemy with a "coup stick"—the willow rod used for this ritual strike—than for killing one with an arrow at a distance. Yet it must not be imagined that Sioux warfare was a bloodless game. The scalping of dead enemies was a well-established practice, apparently designed to prevent the fallen warrior from entering the afterlife, where he might have pursued revenge against his killer. This practice was encouraged when white traders proved ready to pay good money for scalps as curios.

TRADITION AND INNOVATION

Adopted as recently as the 17th century, after being introduced to the Americas by Spanish invaders, horses were the Sioux's most prized possessions, vital for both hunting and war. Mostly small, thin, hardy, and fast-moving, they were accumulated by successful tribes in large numbers. Every warrior needed second-string ponies for traveling distances and a specially-prized mount as his warhorse. The Sioux were exceptional horsemen, capable of tricks such as hanging over one side of a galloping horse to keep its body between them and an enemy. But they did not always fight on horseback, more often dismounting when combat was joined.

Remembering Bighorn
Modern-day Sioux gather at the Little Bighorn river, Montana, *(above)* for a re-enactment of the famous battle in 1876 in which Sioux and Cheyenne warriors annihilated part of General Custer's 7th cavalry. Steel knives *(right)* were traded with the Sioux by European settlers, usually in return for furs. They were far more effective than the Sioux's traditional stone implements.

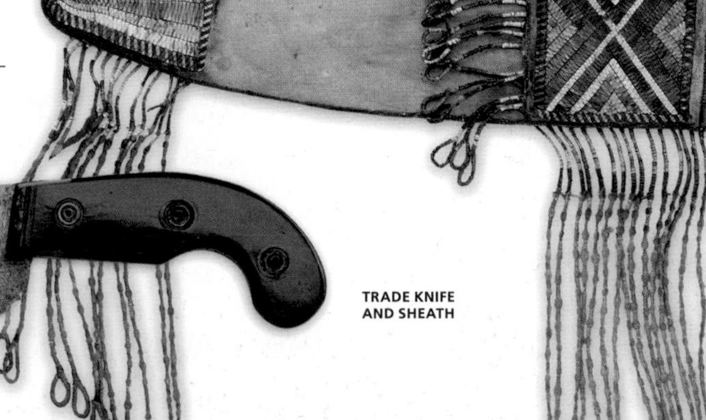

TRADE KNIFE AND SHEATH

> "WE MUST ACT WITH VINDICTIVE EARNESTNESS AGAINST THE SIOUX, EVEN TO THEIR EXTERMINATION, MEN, WOMEN, AND CHILDREN."
>
> **GENERAL SHERMAN,** 1866

Decorated defense
Shields were very important to the Plains Indians, not only because of the obvious physical protection they provided, but also because of spiritual associations. This hunting shield is painted with a silhouette of a bison and decorated with feathers.

The Indians' traditional key weapon was the composite bow, made of wood backed with sinew. A Sioux warrior was trained in shooting a bow from childhood and could deliver arrows onto a target with speed and accuracy. His other traditional weapons were a long lance and a knife that was used for finishing off the wounded and for scalping. Tomahawks were ceremonial objects rather than weapons of war. The equipment that the Sioux used was constantly evolving, especially under the impact of contact with European settlers and traders. By the second half of the 19th century Sioux were as likely to ride their horses with stirrups and saddle as they were to ride bareback, while their arrows had metal tips, instead of the traditional flint. They also owned large quantities of firearms, including rifles and Colt pistols, either captured or obtained by trade. The Sioux never achieved an effectiveness with firearms to match their skill with the bow.

Although a Plains Indian warrior saw warfare as a chance to prove his individual prowess, he was used to fighting as part of a disciplined group. The discipline was imposed by a number of warrior societies within the tribe.

WARRIOR SOCIETIES

Made up of men who had proved their courage and ability, these societies acted as a kind of police force upholding collective rules against the impulsiveness of unruly individuals. The warrior societies had an especially important task in the hunting season, when success in killing bison was essential to the tribe's survival. They would severely punish any junior warrior who menaced the overall success of the hunt by stepping out of line. This discipline could also be applied to warfare. When the Sioux found themselves engaged in a life-or-death struggle with the US Army and white settlers, the organization and direction provided by the warrior societies was crucial to coping with such an unprecedented challenge.

War between various Sioux nations and the United States was almost inevitable as their territory lay across the path of US westward expansion. From the early 1860s, the Indian peoples responded to aggressive incursions by settlers and the US Army with raids against isolated outposts and settlements, using the hit-and-run tactics familiar from intertribal warfare. Transport and communication links were disrupted, with stagecoaches and supply trains ambushed and telegraph wires ripped down. Traveling faster and lighter than US troops, Sioux warriors could easily evade army columns sent to engage them.

THE BOZEMAN TRAIL

The most successful exercise in Indian guerrilla warfare was led by Chief Red Cloud of the Oglala Sioux in 1866 to 1868. The United States was determined to open up the Bozeman Trail, a route from the East to the Montana gold fields, passing through Sioux hunting grounds. In the summer of 1866 the US Army built three forts along the Trail to give security to travelers. Instead, Sioux attacks on wagon trains increased while the soldiers were trapped inside the forts by warbands that placed them virtually under siege. In December 1866, outside Fort Kearny, Colonel William J. Fetterman was lured into pursuit of a temptingly small party of Sioux warriors; they led him into an ambush by a far superior force that massacred Fetterman and the 80 cavalry and infantry with him. Unable to protect travelers, in 1868 the US government agreed to abandon the Bozeman Trail and evacuate the forts. Red Cloud had the distinction of being the only Indian leader to sign a peace treaty as a victor with the United States.

The Sioux's finest hour
Soldiers from General Custer's 7th cavalry make an unsuccessful attempt to resist the charging Plains Indians in June 1876. Although the Sioux are depicted here on horseback it is likely they attacked on foot.

The tragic climax of the Plains Indian Wars was precipitated by the penetration of US troops and gold miners into the Black Hills of South Dakota, which was the spiritual center of the Sioux world, from 1874. Inspired by leaders such as Crazy Horse and Sitting Bull, the warrior societies succeeded in organizing the Sioux and their Comanche and Arapaho allies for larger-scale operations to resist the US advancing cavalry.

LITTLE BIGHORN

There were probably more than 1,000 warriors involved in the famous victory over soldiers led by George Custer at the Little Bighorn River in June 1876. Although no truly reliable account of this battle exists, it appears that the Indians rapidly fired a large volume of unaimed arrows in a high trajectory to fall in a dense shower upon the US troops. They probably attacked on foot, creeping forward with maximum use of any protection afforded by the terrain and vegetation.

But even at Little Bighorn, the Indian warriors could not hold the field, being forced to retreat behind a grass fire smokescreen the following day to avoid encountering more US soldiers. Once the US was ready to devote resources ruthlessly to the Plains Indian Wars, the Indians had no answer to the destruction of their food supplies or attacks on their encampments. Crazy Horse and his assorted followers surrendered the following year, beaten by starvation and exhaustion. Sitting Bull initially took refuge in Canada, but returned to give himself up to the US authorities in 1881.

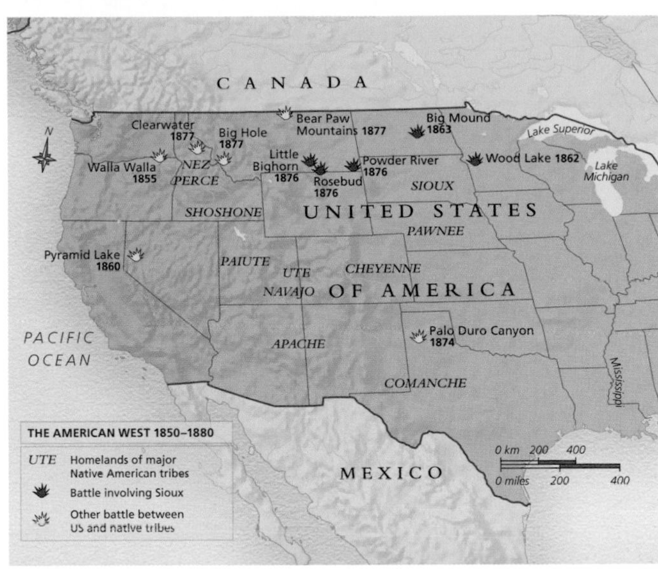

Battlegrounds and territories
As European settlers pushed westward, it was inevitable there would be conflict with Plains Indians. Many of the major battles and incidents in the American West between 1850 and 1880 involved the Sioux.

Ironically, the defeated Sioux warriors were instantly embraced by US popular culture as the noblest of savages. Sitting Bull became a celebrity, appearing briefly in Buffalo Bill's Wild West Show and making a substantial income from selling autographed pictures of himself. The reality of the Sioux's fate was, of course, grim. The Ghost Dance revival movement of 1890, ended by the infamous massacre at Wounded Knee, was a doomed last throw in a struggle the Indians knew at heart they were going to lose.

Better than bareback
Traditionally bareback riders, by the 1850s the Sioux used saddles and stirrups, bought from European traders.

Raiding party in battle dress
Sioux warfare typically consisted of raids and ambushes mounted by stealth involving 30–40 warriors.

SIOUX BATTLE DRESS

A raiding party of Sioux and other Plains Indian warriors was traditionally equipped with bows and arrows, shields, lances, clubs, and scalping knives. In the 19th century Sioux weaponry evolved under the influence of contact with Euro-American settlers and traders. Metal blades or tips replaced stone or bone on traditional weapons, while industrially produced implements were bought from traders and customized with decorative motifs. The Sioux also adopted firearms, although they were more effective fighters with the bow and arrow. Although the superior weaponry of European settlers made it hard for the Native Americans to take on the intruders in open battle, Indian weapons were effective in low-level guerrilla warfare.

WHOSE VOICE WAS FIRST SOUNDED ON THIS LAND? THE VOICE OF THE RED PEOPLE WHO HAD BUT BOWS AND ARROWS.

RED CLOUD OGALA SIOUX (1822–1909), ON THE ENCROACHMENT OF THE WHITE MAN

Headdress
The feathered headdress is often considered to be a significant feature of Native American dress in the 19th century, and is certainly the most recognizable. However, in reality, the headdress was worn (outside of tribal rituals) only by the Sioux tribes of the western plains. An eagle-feathered war bonnet such as this would have been the mark of an experienced and respected warrior.

Quiver and bowcase
Plains Indians, who always traveled on horseback when fighting and hunting, used a combined bowcase and quiver to carry their bow and arrows. Made of animal hide, it was slung across the rider's back, suspended on a strap. Arrows were traditionally tipped with stone, but following contact with Europeans, iron was increasingly used instead.

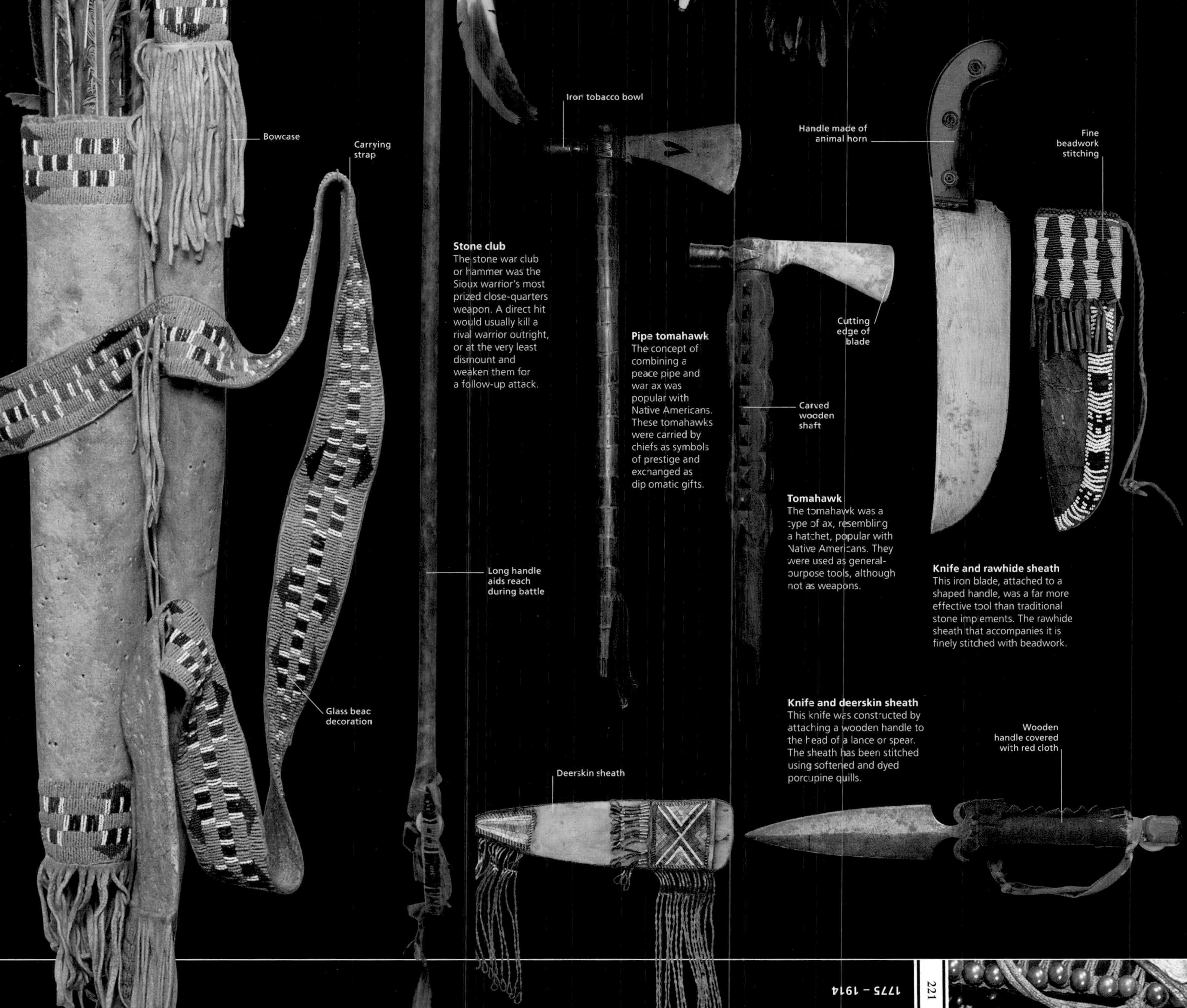

Stone club
The stone war club or hammer was the Sioux warrior's most prized close-quarters weapon. A direct hit would usually kill a rival warrior outright, or at the very least dismount and weaken them for a follow-up attack.

Pipe tomahawk
The concept of combining a peace pipe and war ax was popular with Native Americans. These tomahawks were carried by chiefs as symbols of prestige and exchanged as diplomatic gifts.

Tomahawk
The tomahawk was a type of ax, resembling a hatchet, popular with Native Americans. They were used as general-purpose tools, although not as weapons.

Knife and rawhide sheath
This iron blade, attached to a shaped handle, was a far more effective tool than traditional stone implements. The rawhide sheath that accompanies it is finely stitched with beadwork.

Knife and deerskin sheath
This knife was constructed by attaching a wooden handle to the head of a lance or spear. The sheath has been stitched using softened and dyed porcupine quills.

FIGHTERS OF THE INDIAN WARS

The westward expansion of the United States in the second half of the 19th century brought white settlers into conflict with Native American peoples, who defended their territories by carrying out hit-and-run raids and ambushing travelers. The US army sought to drive the Indians off their lands and hunted down bands that refused to submit. These campaigns rarely came to pitched battle. US forces typically found themselves tracking an elusive enemy across hundreds of miles of wilderness. Foot soldiers proved of little use and by 1877 the US army contained almost 11,000 cavalrymen, compared with only 10,000 infantry. The Native Americans fought with no real hope of victory but great skill and courage. By 1890 their resistance had been pitilessly crushed.

US CAVALRY

The cavalry force with which the United States fought the Sioux, Apache, Nez Percé, and other Native American mounted warriors was largely created at the end of the American Civil War. Its higher ranks were staffed from the large surplus of Union officers available when the Civil War armies disbanded. The enlisted men it attracted were a rag-bag of footloose adventurers, those in trouble with the law, fresh immigrants from Europe who spoke little English, and even a fair number of former Confederate officers. Two regiments of white-officered African-American cavalry, nicknamed "buffalo soldiers" by the Kiowa people, performed with great credit.

Cavalry troopers faced a hard life, garrisoning remote forts, escorting travelers through disputed territory, and mounting campaigns against Indian warbands. The US cavalry were slower-moving than their highly mobile enemies. In the early years a trooper typically carried 50 lb (22 kg) of equipment, including a 5 lb (2 kg) sword, and 15 lb (7 kg) of grain for his horse. Gradually they learned to imitate Indian tactics. In 1876 troopers pursuing Crazy Horse were ordered to carry only a tin cup, a carbine and ammunition, and four days' rations, while their horses fed on grass, not grain. Extensive use was made of Indian scouts, whose skill at tracking and speed of movement were invaluable. The counterinsurgency war conducted by the cavalry was often vicious and included massacres of women and children, but as fighting men they showed skill and tenacity in taking on a skillful enemy in difficult terrain.

Henry Model 1860
The Henry rifle was one of the first practical repeating rifles, which saw some army use in the 1860s. Other cavalry firearms included the Colt pistol and the Spencer rifle and carbine.

Little Big Horn
A contingent of the US 7th Cavalry was surrounded and massacred by Sioux and Cheyenne warriors at Little Big Horn in 1876, the worst cavalry defeat of the Indian wars.

APACHE

In the 19th century, the six Apache tribes lived in the mountains and deserts of present-day western Texas, New Mexico, Arizona, and northern Mexico. Until the 1840s their great enemies were the Mexicans and they welcomed the takeover of the southwest by the United States in 1848. The Apache maintained an uneasy peace with the United States until the 1850s, but the often violent intrusion of American settlers and the US army into Apache territory soon embittered relations.

Tough, courageous, ruthless fighters who excelled in raids and ambushes, the Apache mounted a campaign of attacks on settlers and mail coaches intended to drive the whites off their land. From 1862, while the Civil War raged further east, federal troops and settler volunteers launched an offensive against the Apache. Union officer Colonel James Carleton ordered that Indian men were "to be slain whenever and wherever they can be found." In 1863 Mangas Coloradas, leader of the Bedonkohe Apache, met with US military commanders to negotiate for peace. He was arrested, tortured, and shot, supposedly while attempting to escape.

The Apache responded with guerrilla war. Their resistance was initially led by Cochise, a chief of the Chiricahua Apache; after his death in 1874, the leadership of the Apache passed to Goyathley, known to whites as Geronimo. After many exploits and narrow escapes, by the mid-1880s Geronimo's rebel force had been reduced to just 17 warriors and their families. This small band was pursued by 5,000 US troops, plus thousands of militia and Mexican volunteers. Geronimo surrendered in September 1886. He was held as a prisoner of war up to his death in 1909.

APACHE WAR CLUB

Decorated cap
Apache warriors wore buckskin caps that were decorated with feathers and with colorful beadwork in elaborate individual designs.

APACHE BUCKSKIN CAP

NEZ PERCÉ

The Nee Me Poo, named Nez Percé by French-Canadian trappers, lived by fishing and hunting on the Columbia Plateau in the northwest United States. They had generally good relations with the whites until the 1860s, when gold prospectors penetrated their lands. In 1863 the United States took most of the Nez Percé reservation to open up the area for mining. The leader of the Wallowa band, known to whites as Chief Joseph, organized peaceful resistance to the land seizure. In June 1877, however, clashes broke out between the US army and Nez Percé bands. Numbering less than a thousand people, including women and children, the Nez Percé knew that they could not stand and fight. Instead they conducted a fighting retreat across 1,200 miles (2,000 km) of mountain and plateau towards the Canadian border, pursued by several thousand US troops and their Indian auxiliaries.

The Nez Percé repeatedly outfought and outmaneuvered their enemies, winning the praise of General William Sherman for their "almost scientific skill" in warfare. But in October 1877 they were surrounded near the Bear Paw mountains in Montana, 40 miles (65 km) short of the border. After a five-day siege in which many Nez Percé were killed, Chief Joseph surrendered, declaring: "My heart is sick and sad. From where the sun now stands I will fight no more forever." A few warriors slipped through the army lines and escaped to Canada. The rest of the survivors were exiled to disease-ridden reservations far from their ancestral lands.

Bow and quiver
The bow was the basic weapon of all Native American warriors. It was typically made of wood reinforced with sinew on the side facing away from the archer.

Nez Percé brave
A warrior poses with ceremonial headdress and lance. The Nez Percé were renowned for their skill in breeding horses, and kept their best mounts for warfare.

1914 – 1945

TRENCHES AND DOGFIGHTS

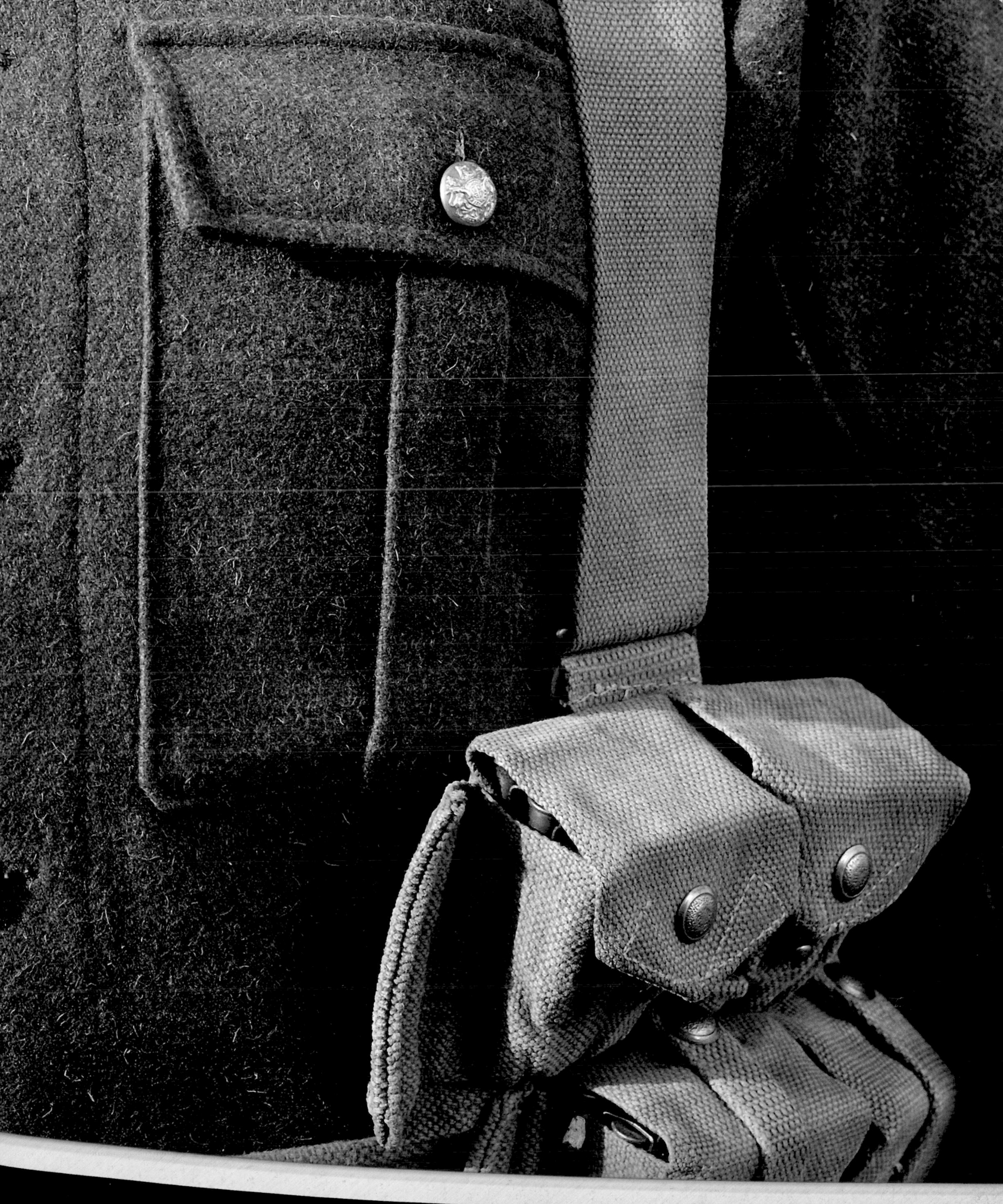

The world wars of 1914–18 and 1939–45 were almost certainly the most costly conflicts ever fought. Their combined death toll may have exceeded 80 million. The massive number of casualties was the result of "total war," the devotion of the entire resources of modern industrial states to warfare and the exploitation of every possible means of attacking the enemy without limit or scruple, including the systematic massacre of civilians and the destruction of cities. The typical fighting man in these wars of mass destruction was a civilian hastily thrust into uniform through conscription or the large-scale recruitment of volunteers.

Whatever the political system under which he served, the civilian was in principle a citizen-soldier, fighting for the society to which he belonged, and motivated primarily by feelings of patriotism. A state that could no longer count on the active support of the mass of its people for the war effort—as was the case for Tsarist Russia by 1917—was doomed.

OVERWHELMING FIREPOWER

In the line-up of powers, the two world conflicts were remarkably similar. In both, Germany fought Britain, France, Russia, and the United States, although the struggle in Asia and the Pacific between Japan and the United States, Britain, and China added an extra dimension to World War II. But the nature of the fighting in the two wars was strikingly different. From the outset of World War I the

Men and machines
Soviet soldiers advance alongside a T-34 tank. The resources—both human and industrial—that the Soviet Union could call on in World War II brought victory, but at appalling cost.

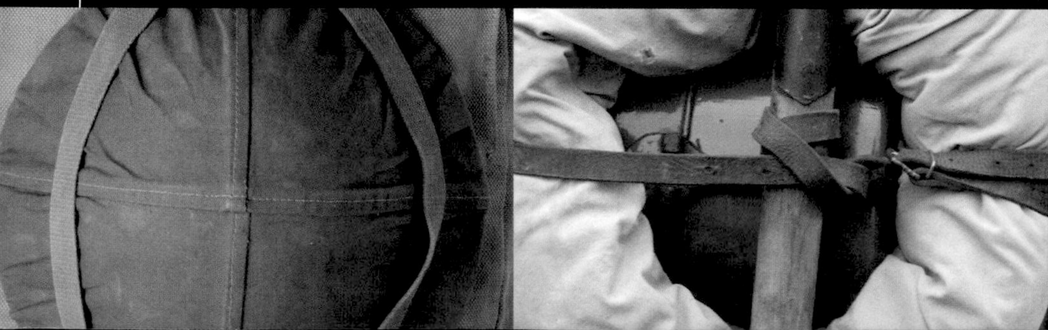

Death from above
German Stukas (Ju-87s) return to their base in Northern France after attacking a British convoy in the English Channel. The Stuka divebomber played an important part in the German successes of 1940, combining with tanks and fast-moving motorized divisions in the "blitzkrieg" invasion of France.

sheer quantity of firepower available, from rapid-fire rifles and machine guns to heavy artillery batteries, ensured massive losses in clashes between armies committed to victory at any cost. Soon, at least on the crucial Western Front, firepower triumphed over mobility. Largely static trench systems remained in place for more than three years because, with cavalry rendered ineffectual and few motor vehicles available, no offensive could advance fast enough to avoid being blocked by a counter offensive. Infantry attacks across the no man's land between the trenches were often near-suicidal, and although a degree of mobility was restored in the last year of the war, casualties in offensives remained punishingly high.

MECHANIZED WAR

World War II was a more fluid and varied contest. Tanks and aircraft, marginal in their impact during World War I, became the determining factors in most of the campaigns of World War II. The Germans at first used them most successfully, having experimented with new fighting tactics during their military intervention in the Spanish Civil War (1936–39). Between 1939 and 1941 they conquered much of Europe in a series of lightning "blitzkrieg" campaigns, in which mechanized divisions and aircraft were used in combination to decisive shock effect. Japan made similar dramatic gains in Asia and the Pacific in 1941–42, with seaborne airpower playing a crucial role. The long fight by the Allies to press the war back in the opposite direction was a slower, gruelling process, in which ever greater quantities of weaponry were deployed. The tank battles fought between German and Soviet forces were large-scale attritional warfare, just as the trench battles of World War I had been. Allied bomber aircraft were used in thousands to devastate German and Japanese cities. Yet, as ever, there was no substitute for the courage and skills of individual fighting men, whether advancing from building to building in Stalingrad, jumping into action by parachute at Arnhem, making an opposed landing on a beach in the Pacific, or flying a bomber in broad daylight through German air defenses.

AIR POWER

The use of aircraft was the biggest single innovation of warfare in this period. From early on it was realized that pilots had opportunities for individual heroism not possible on the land battlefield. High above the mass carnage of the trenches, the fighter pilots of World War I fought duels in which the outcome was decided by their sheer daring and skill in handling their aircraft. The most successful were hailed as "knights of the air," lionized by the press and in some cases accorded state funerals if they died, which many of them did.

The Spitfire and Hurricane pilots who defended their country in the Battle of Britain in 1940 were also glamourized as the "few" to whom so much was owed. But although individual skills were often at a premium in air combat, fliers generally fought a war of attrition in which their losses were proportionally as heavy as those in land fighting at its worst. Allied bomber crews flying over Germany in 1943 had a similar life expectancy to an infantryman at the battle of the Somme in 1916.

INFANTRY ELITES

Inevitably, the mass conscript armies of the two World Wars emphasized quantity over quality. In reaction, the idea of elite forces expected to outperform the average conscript infantryman came into being . Special "stormtrooper" units were created by the German army in World War I to spearhead offensives using specialized "infiltration" tactics. In World War II the US Airborne and Marines were promoted as special infantry formations with especially rigorous training and an aggressive attitude to combat.

DOOMED WARRIORS

In spite of attempts to keep traditional warrior virtues alive, they became problematic in this age of industrialized warfare fought by millions of civilians in uniform. Most nations went to war in 1914 inspired by notions of patriotic self-sacrifice and the glory of dying on the battlefield. But for many the spectacle of mass slaughter in the trenches permanently discredited any ideas of heroic warfare.

In the 1920s and 1930s the Japanese militarists, the Fascists in Italy, and the Nazis in Germany sought to revive a warrior ethic. The Nazi authorities certainly knew how to put on a magnificent military parade, yet there were no demonstrations of popular enthusiasm in Berlin to greet the oubreak of war in 1939 as there had been in 1914. The 1914–18 war was called "the war to end war," but this was something it signally failed to do. The dropping of atom bombs on the Japanese cities of Hiroshima and Nagasaki, which ended World War II in August 1945, however, suggested a future in which wars would simply be too costly to fight.

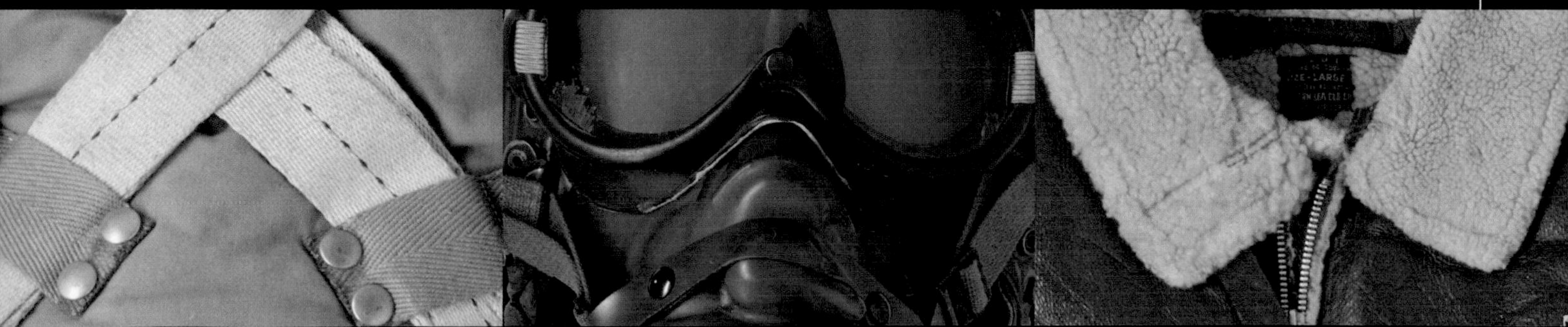

1914 – 1918

BRITISH INFANTRYMAN

“WE WERE NEVER HIT, BY THE GRACE OF GOD, FOR THE DEEP MUD WAS OUR SALVATION, THAT MUD WHICH WE CURSED AND IN WHICH WE STUCK AND STAGGERED, SLIPPED AND SLID, TUGGING OUR BOOTS OUT OF IT EACH TIME WE MADE A FRESH STEP.”

About four million British soldiers served on the Western Front during World War I, manning a sector of the Allied trenches between the Channel and the Somme River. The majority of them were either volunteers or conscripts, who left their factories, offices, or fields to take up arms in their country's cause. More than 1.7 million of them were killed or wounded, yet they stuck to their task with dogged perseverance in the face of artillery bombardment, toxic gas, and machine-gun fire, and ultimately prevailed over their enemy.

Alone among the major powers that went to war in August 1914, Britain did not have a mass conscript army. The British Expeditionary Force, sent to the Western Front at the outbreak of war, consisted of professional soldiers of the small regular army; most were wiped out in the first five months' desperate fighting. Lord Kitchener, the secretary for war, was one of the few men who from the outset anticipated a prolonged conflict. Having little faith in the territorials—prewar part-time soldiers—as a source of manpower, he set about raising a new mass army from scratch. The appeal for volunteers (with the slogan "Your Country Needs YOU") brought a flood of patriotic young men to join long lines outside recruitment centers. By the end of September 1914 about 750,000 men had come forward. Although enthusiasm began to wane in the following year, a total of 2.6 million had volunteered to fight by the time conscription was belatedly introduced in 1916.

In order to encourage men to volunteer, they were allowed to sign up on the understanding that they would serve with others from their own locality or occupational group. Thus were formed the famous "Pals' Battalions." There were battalions of stockbrokers, of artists, and of football (soccer) players—sometimes including fans as well as players; there were also battalions that were based on schools, such as the "Grimsby Chums" from Wintringham Secondary School; but mostly they were drawn from specific towns or villages, while major cities provided several battalions. In Ireland, elements of the Ulster Volunteer Force, formed by Protestants to resist the granting of Home Rule, were permitted to enlist together and formed the 36th (Ulster) Division. Numbers of Irish Catholics also volunteered in large groups, including one of 350 rugby players and a company of Dublin dockworkers. The unforeseen result of the establishment of Pals' Battalions was local tragedy when a formation later suffered heavy casualties—as when the "Accrington Pals" had 584 out of 720 men killed or wounded in the space of half an hour at the battle of the Somme.

TO THE FRONT

Although many early volunteers were rejected as medically unfit for service, those accepted at first far exceeded the numbers that could be trained and equipped. They were sent to makeshift tented camps, many equipped with "Kitchener blue" uniforms for lack of khaki material, and, in the absence of weaponry, they drilled with broomsticks. It was only gradually through 1915 that the men received proper uniforms and equipment, citizens began to turn into soldiers, and the New Army took shape. Toughened up by route marches and bonded with their comrades, morale was generally high by the time they embarked for France.

LEWIS GUN

Trench warfare
The drudgery of trench life was punctuated by moments of terror, but also by periods of light relief. Here, an officer shares a story from a newspaper with his men *(above)*. As well as rifles and grenades, British infantry employed the Lewis light machine gun *(right)*. By mid-1918, infantry battalions had 36 Lewis guns each.

Soldiers old and new
Soldiers wait in a town in northern France for transportation to the front in August 1914 *(right)*. By the end of the year many of these regulars had been killed or wounded, to be replaced in 1915–16 by Kitchener's volunteers. By then the nature of war had changed considerably, as is evident from the gas mask holder hanging round the soldier's neck *(far right)*.

Toughened up by route marches and bonded with their comrades, the men's morale was generally high by the time they embarked for France. But apart from being trained in the use of the rifle and bayonet, they were inevitably ill-prepared for the experience of trench warfare.

Ferried across the Channel and then carried by train toward their sector of the front, a fresh division would generally have a long march before it finally reached the trenches. On a number of occasions new arrivals were thrown straight into action. This was the fate of two New Army divisions that reached the front at Loos on September 26, 1915. Having marched for two days along cobbled roads in heavy rain, the men—completely exhausted and with no combat experience—were ordered forward into the fire of German machine-guns. As a result, some 8,000 out of 10,000 soldiers were killed or wounded on their first day at the front. Fortunately, cases of such instant slaughter were rare. If they were fortunate, fresh soldiers would arrive in a quiet sector of the front and have time to learn from experienced troops the secrets of survival in trench warfare.

TRENCH LIFE

Newcomers to the front-line trenches were inevitably horrified by the extraordinary spectacle they presented. Winston Churchill, arriving to serve at the front in November 1915, described the scene in a letter to his wife: "Filth and rubbish everywhere, graves built into the defences … feet and clothing breaking through the soil, water and muck on all sides; and about this scene in the dazzling moonlight troops of enormous rats creep and glide." Yet in this strange world men made themselves at home.

Observing the enemy
Periscopes were essential for observing activity in the German trenches and no man's land. Some were simple metal tubes with a mirror at either end, others were more sophisticated.

> "CERTAIN PLATOONS OR COMPANIES FOUGHT SHOULDER TO SHOULDER TILL THE LAST MAN DROPPED."
>
> **PRIVATE STEPHEN GRAHAM** ON THE SACRIFICES OF THE BRITISH INFANTRY

The life of a soldier at the Western Front was governed by a daily routine and by the longer-term rhythm of rotation between service in the front line and spells in reserve and at rest. The day in the front line hinged around the fixed points of stand-to at dawn—usually with a tot of rum—and stand-down at dusk. Time was filled with a busy routine of chores, from maintaining and improving the fabric of the trenches to keeping rifles clean and in perfect order, plus special tasks such as observation duties, of obvious importance since the enemy was only a few hundred metres away. Rations were adequate if unexciting. Cigarette smoking was more or less universal. There was a constant struggle against lice infestation and against the rats that thrived among the unburied bodies and discarded food. The soldiers' morale depended in considerable measure upon the physical quality of their trenches, which varied greatly. A good, dry dugout was a godsend. Where the ground became waterlogged, as in Flanders, sodden trenches surrounded by a shell-churned sea of mud made daily life almost unbearable.

The level of danger a soldier faced depended on how active a sector he was in. In some parts of the front an unspoken truce prevailed. In other parts trench mortar fire, shelling, and sniping caused a steady attrition of men.

Daily routines such as bringing up rations from the rear became a perilous activity when artillery regularly bombarded the zone behind the front line. Soldiers were inevitably shaken by the sudden death of a comrade, a sniper's bullet opening a hole in his forehead or a mortar shell blowing his body apart. Many preferred active fighting to a monotonous routine in which death was an ever-present possibility. There was rarely any lack of volunteers to take part in night raids on enemy trenches or night patrols in no man's land, even though the percentage of casualties in such small-scale operations was high.

OFFICERS AND MEN

Officers shared the hardships and dangers of the trenches and suffered high casualty rates—58 British generals were killed in action in World War I, a far higher toll than in World War II. Subalterns—junior officers with the rank of lieutenant or second lieutenant—who led from

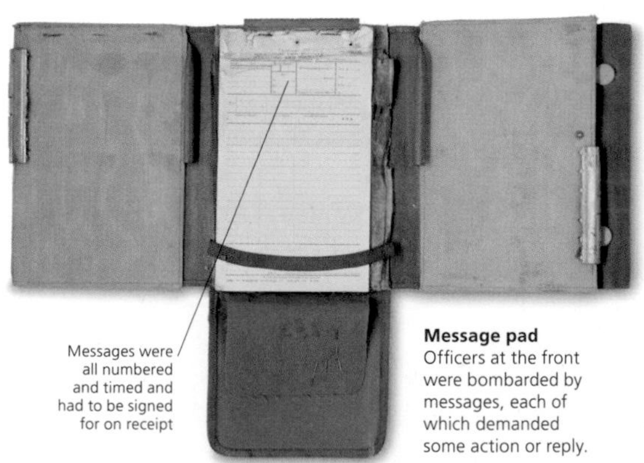

Message pad
Officers at the front were bombarded by messages, each of which demanded some action or reply.

the front, had a higher death rate than any other group. The attitude of ordinary soldiers to their officers varied depending on personal factors, but respect was more common than hostility, despite an inevitable social class divide. The working class predominated in the ranks and set the tone for the ordinary soldier, even though many individuals of higher social standing dutifully served as privates. Officers were generally from the middle or upper class. At the start of the war, men from a public school background were able to step straight into commissions on the grounds of having served in their school cadet corps. This did not, of course, mean that they were necessarily poor officers or out of touch with the experience of their men, though some were both. Yet promotion from the ranks was in fact not unknown even in the prewar British army—the head of the Imperial General Staff, Field Marshal Sir William Robertson, had started his army career as a private. From 1916 onward the majority of newly commissioned officers were men who had served in the ranks.

DISCIPLINE AND PUNISHMENT

The strains of trench life inevitably led to disciplinary problems. The odd foray by British soldiers into French villages often resulted in drunkenness and disorder; although the men had little money to spend on their pleasures, many of them still managed to contract venereal diseases. As well as drunkenness, common forms of indiscipline leading to punishment included insolence to a superior and various forms of sloppiness in dress or conduct. In some of the more traditionalist regiments officers and NCOs were especially punctilious about minor regulations, but the excessive enforcement of such rules could attract adverse attention from the press—as when the court martial of a young officer for shaving off his mustache was quashed after a public outcry. Although flogging had long been abolished, there were brutal old-fashioned army punishments—such as being tied to the wheel of a heavy artillery piece for public humiliation—that were still administered. Many soldiers objected to such practices as inappropriate for a citizen-army. For the gravest offences, such as striking an officer and desertion, the death penalty was available. It was rarely applied, some 260 men being executed for military crimes, mostly for desertion, in the course of the war.

A war of attrition
Between late 1914 and the summer of 1916, the front line barely moved. Even after that, as the Allies gradually wore down German resistance, progress was painfully slow. At the Armistice in November 1918 the Germans still occupied most of Belgium and significant areas of France.

WESTERN FRONT 1914–18
Allied powers
Germany
Neutral states
Front line Dec 1914–Jul 1916
Front line at Armistice 11 Nov 1918
Major battle 1914–16
Major battle 1917–18

Occupying a captured trench
Moments like this when men could relax after a successful advance were rare. The trench now had to be refortified quickly in preparation for the inevitable German counterattack.

"DULLY, I HAULED MYSELF OUT OF THE MUD AND GAVE THE SIGNAL TO ADVANCE, WHICH WAS ANSWERED BY EVERY MAN RISING AND STEPPING UNHESITATINGLY INTO THE BARRAGE."

LIEUTENANT EDWIN CAMPION VAUGHAN, AT THE THIRD BATTLE OF YPRES, 1917

Since 5.7 million British soldiers served in the conflict, it was clearly not fear of the firing squad that kept them at their posts or drove them loyally to follow their officers "over the top" when an attack was ordered.

OVER THE TOP

Some infantrymen never experienced a major offensive and most only participated once or twice in full-scale operations. It was possible to spend years in the trenches without going "over the top" at all. But when an offensive did happen, it was certainly an experience that no surviving participant ever forgot. At the start of the battle of the Somme, on July 1, 1916, inexperienced soldiers marched forward with full packs straight into machine-gun fire and uncut German wire, and 58,000 men were killed or wounded in a day. But such futile butchery was exceptional. Usually a soldier had a sense of taking part in a fierce battle, rather than being herded to slaughter. Carrying a rifle, essential rations, and digging tools, plus possibly grenades, he would move into position before dawn. The first wave would advance across no man's land as close as possible behind a creeping artillery barrage, hopefully finding the enemy wire cut by shelling or by a preparatory infantry raid. Fighting might be joined at close range, with difficult assaults on concrete machine-gun posts and the clearing of German front-line trenches with grenade and bayonet. It would usually fall to supporting troops to pass through a captured trench and advance against the next line of enemy defenses. Attacks became increasingly difficult to sustain as they stretched further from the starting point. As enemy artillery fire rained down on soldiers who had fought their way forward to exposed positions and German infantry mounted counterattacks, the advance would come to a halt or be forced back.

The awesome casualties suffered were a function of the vast destructive power of mass-produced artillery shells and machine guns, but also of the sheer duration of battles fought with utter tenacity on both sides. The Somme offensive, begun at the start of July 1916, continued until mid-November; the offensive at Ypres the following year, infamous for the appalling mud

Field telephone
Communication between the artillery and the infantry was crucial to the success of an offensive. In the absence of radios, the infantry had to rely on the portable field telephone.

Joining an offensive
British infantrymen thread their way along a sap—a narrow trench extending forward from the front line—and then out through the barbed wire before advancing across no man's land.

in which it was fought, lasted only a month less. Since the advances achieved in many weeks of costly fighting were a few miles at best, the war's reputation for futility is understandable.

EXPERIENCE OF WAR

Morale was often low in the later stages of the war. The idealism and patriotism so plentiful in the early days came to be in short supply. Soldiers cursed staff officers for their blunders and were horrified by the losses suffered. The experience of sitting passively under prolonged artillery bombardment shook men to the core. Gas attack was also traumatic, often more psychologically disturbing than militarily effective. Some men were reduced to a catatonic or incoherent state and identified as victims of "shell shock." They were few compared with the victims of terrible physical injuries. In the absence of antibiotics, yet to be invented, amputation was often the response to a wounded limb. But even a serious injury was sometimes welcome, for a "Blighty" wound would get you home and might save your life.

Yet despite all this, Britain's citizen-soldiers, mostly young conscripts by 1918, stuck to the fight and rarely wavered. Most took pride in the military skills they gradually learned and believed the war had to be won. They developed a feeling of comradeship with their fellows that many looked back on as the closest bonding in their lives. The courage and endurance of men taken out of civilian life and thrown into the most destructive battles the world had ever seen ultimately brought victory in November 1918. Many soldiers, disillusioned with the peace that followed, were later to look back on the war as a waste of young men's lives. But at the time most were quietly proud of their performance, regarding it as a hard job well done.

BREAKTHROUGH TACTICS

Frustrated by static trench warfare, the British army repeatedly sought a decisive breakthrough, to be achieved by punching a hole in the German line and pouring troops through it. By 1917 breakthrough tactics were well thought-out. A brief but ferocious preparatory bombardment was followed by the advance of infantry behind a creeping barrage. This curtain of fire moved forward at a prearranged speed equal to the expected rate of progress of the troops. By "leaning on the barrage"—keeping at most 55 yd (50 m) behind it—infantry could often reach the German front trench, which would be lightly held. Penetrating further through the trench lines was much harder. Forward observers tried to keep artillery coordinated with the infantry, but communications usually broke down. Counter-barrage fire rarely succeeded in silencing the German guns, which shelled advancing troops. Even if a hole was eventually punched in the German defense-in-depth, exploiting an initial success proved impossible because movement was too slow.

Launching an attack

By 1917 a British attack on German trenches required precise cooperation between waves of infantry and artillery firing high-explosive, shrapnel, smoke, and gas shells. The guns kept enemy defenses suppressed while the infantry crossed no man's land.

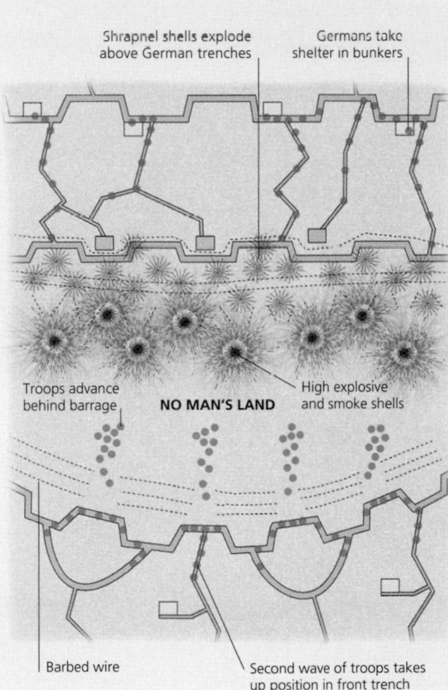

Dawn attack
The first wave of infantry climb out of their trenches under cover of darkness and lie on the ground ready to attack at dawn. At a prearranged time, the infantry begin to advance across no man's land, while the artillery lays down a creeping barrage ahead of them.

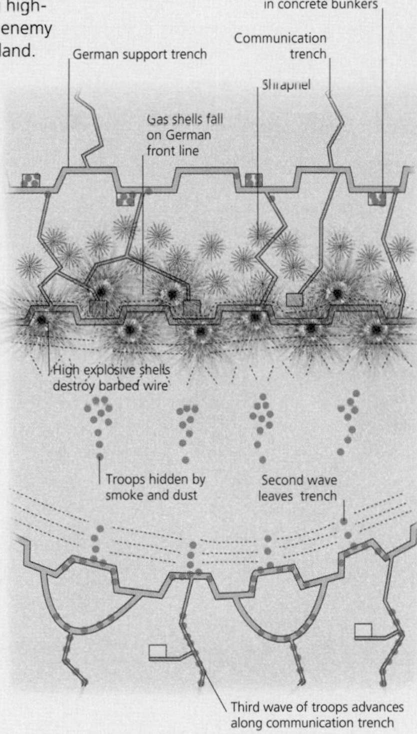

Creeping barrage
The barrage forces German troops to shelter in bunkers, allowing the British infantry to approach their trench largely unscathed. By the time the barrage passes on and the German defenders emerge to take up their positions, the first wave of British infantry is upon them.

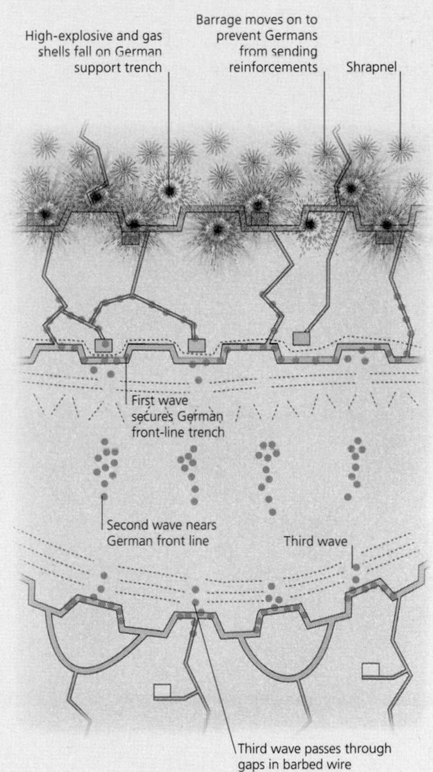

Advancing in depth
After close-quarters combat the first wave secures the German front-line trench. The artillery now moves on to the second line of trenches, attempting to prepare the way for the second wave infantry, who will pass through the first wave and continue the advance.

INFANTRY UNIFORM

The British infantryman's uniform in World War I owed its khaki color to the experience of troops in India in the 19th century and in the Boer War of 1899–1902. Effective as camouflage in the hot, dry plains of southern Africa, it was retained in the muddy trenches of Flanders. Its color was not as important to a soldier's safety as not showing his silhouette above ground. The one important change in the uniform in the course of the war was the introduction of the steel helmet in 1916.

Hats, caps, and helmets
The men who went to war in August 1914 wore a variety of headgear according to their regiment. Most common was the standard service cap *(below)*. As casualties mounted, all the combatants realized the need for steel helmets. The Brodie helmet (or "tin hat") became standard issue in 1916.

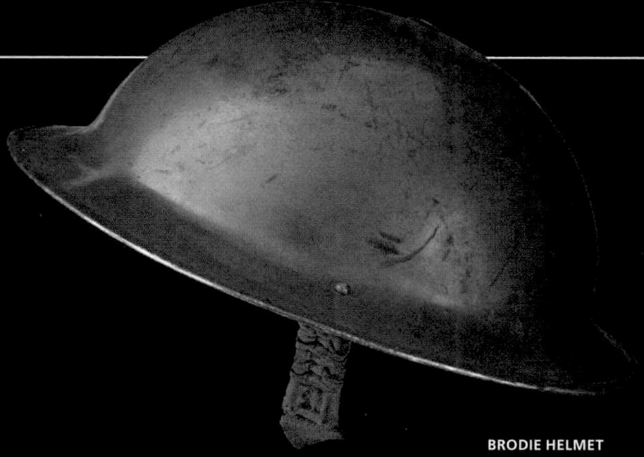

BRODIE HELMET

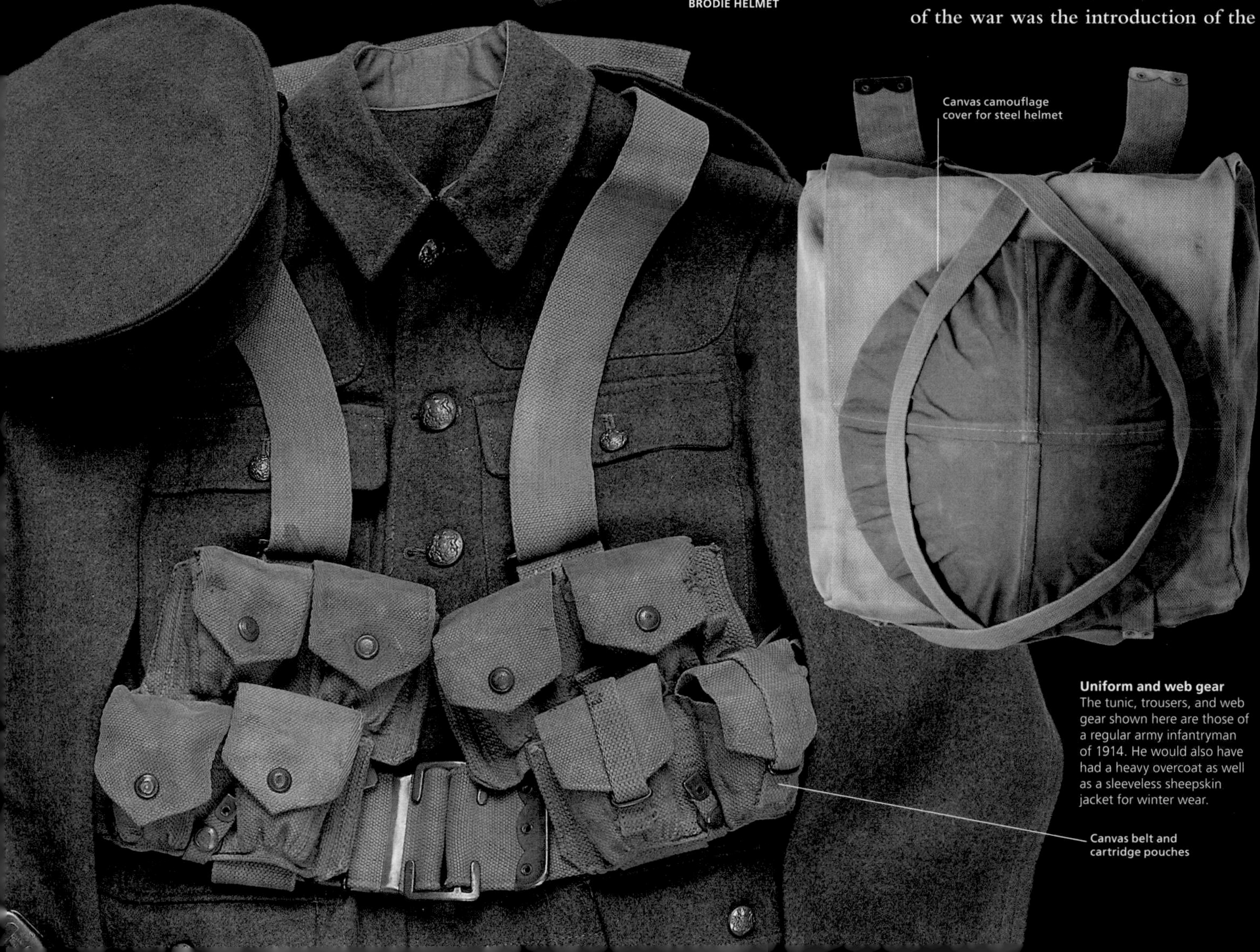

Canvas camouflage cover for steel helmet

Backpack and helmet
The pack, in which a soldier kept his overcoat, other spare clothes, and personal effects was part of the standard 1908 pattern webbing. He would often have left it behind the lines when serving a stint in the front line trench. He could never be without his steel helmet when within range of enemy artillery.

Regimental badge on shoulder

Uniform and web gear
The tunic, trousers, and web gear shown here are those of a regular army infantryman of 1914. He would also have had a heavy overcoat as well as a sleeveless sheepskin jacket for winter wear.

Canvas belt and cartridge pouches

Clips stored in ammunition pouch

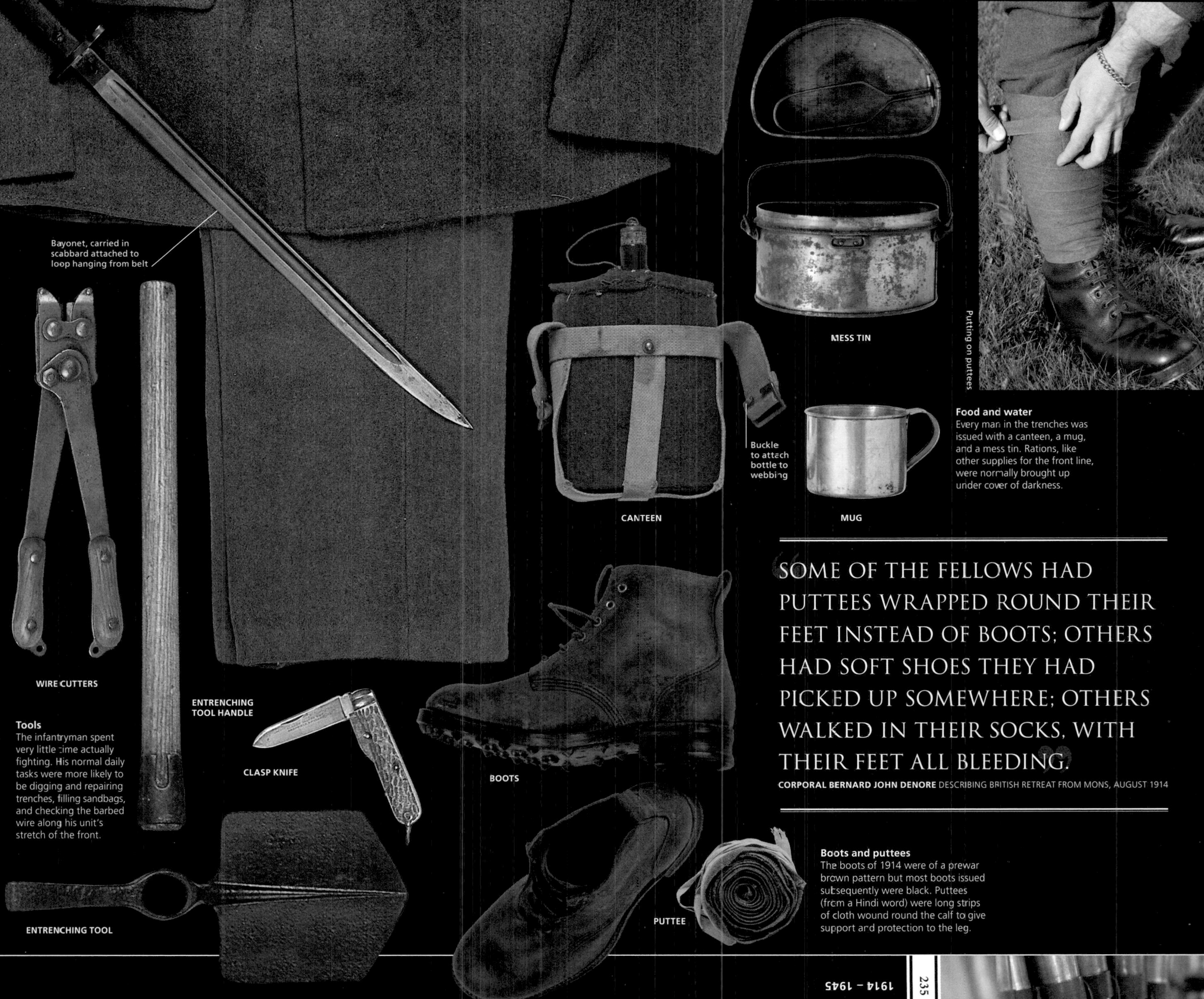

Putting on puttees

Tools
The infantryman spent very little time actually fighting. His normal daily tasks were more likely to be digging and repairing trenches, filling sandbags, and checking the barbed wire along his unit's stretch of the front.

Food and water
Every man in the trenches was issued with a canteen, a mug, and a mess tin. Rations, like other supplies for the front line, were normally brought up under cover of darkness.

> "SOME OF THE FELLOWS HAD PUTTEES WRAPPED ROUND THEIR FEET INSTEAD OF BOOTS; OTHERS HAD SOFT SHOES THEY HAD PICKED UP SOMEWHERE; OTHERS WALKED IN THEIR SOCKS, WITH THEIR FEET ALL BLEEDING."
>
> **CORPORAL BERNARD JOHN DENORE** DESCRIBING BRITISH RETREAT FROM MONS, AUGUST 1914

Boots and puttees
The boots of 1914 were of a prewar brown pattern but most boots issued subsequently were black. Puttees (from a Hindi word) were long strips of cloth wound round the calf to give support and protection to the leg.

INFANTRY WEAPONS

At the start of World War I most British infantrymen fought with nothing more than rifle and bayonet, backed up by a scattering of heavy machine guns. Trench weaponry gradually improved and diversified. Grenades, used by the Germans from the start of the war, were soon adopted by the British. The infantry also acquired its own artillery in the form of the trench mortar. Trench raiding spawned equipment that ranged from wire cutters to primitive weapons for hand-to-hand fighting.

Protected fore sight

Cleaning rod

Single-edged blade

Firing pin

Safety lever, released as grenade left the cup

Detachable base plate

NO. 36 GRENADE

Impact fuse

Fragmentation casing

Arming mechanism

Clip to attach grenade to rifle muzzle

Rod—inserted into rifle barrel

Clips to attach discharger to rifle muzzle

DISCHARGER CUP

Rifle grenades
Various devices were used to deliver grenades into the opposing trenches. This version of the No. 36 model of the Mills bomb could be fitted into a discharger cup attached to the rifle. A blank was fired, which struck the base of the grenade and activated it. The fuse was set for a longer time than on a normal hand grenade. A special blank was also used to fire the Hales No. 3 "stick" grenade. This had a longer range, but had a more complicated and less reliable device for arming the grenade in flight.

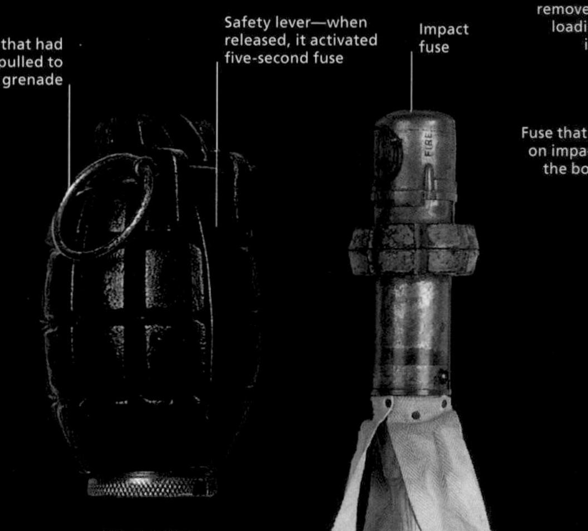

Ring that had to be pulled to activate grenade

Safety lever—when released, it activated five-second fuse

MILLS BOMB

Impact fuse

NO. 1 GRENADE

Hand grenades
The British army experimented with many designs for hand grenades, some with impact fuses, others with time fuses. The early No. 1 grenade had a tail of streamers designed to ensure that the head of the grenade hit the ground first. In the end grenades with time fuses proved more successful and from 1916 one of the most widely used was the classic pineapple-shaped Mills bomb, which continued in use through World War II.

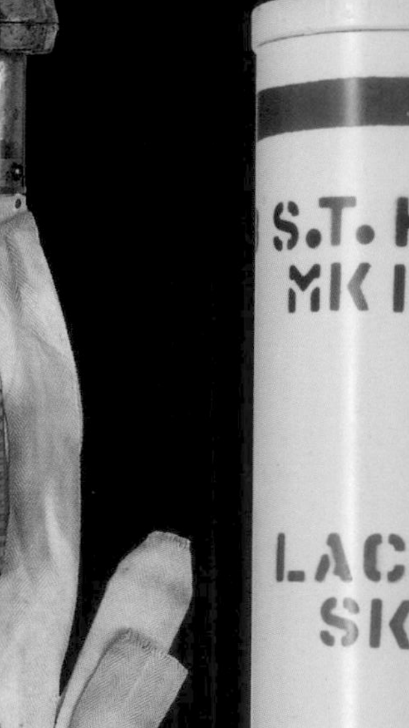

Safety ring—removed before loading bomb in mortar

Fuse that detonated on impact however the bomb landed

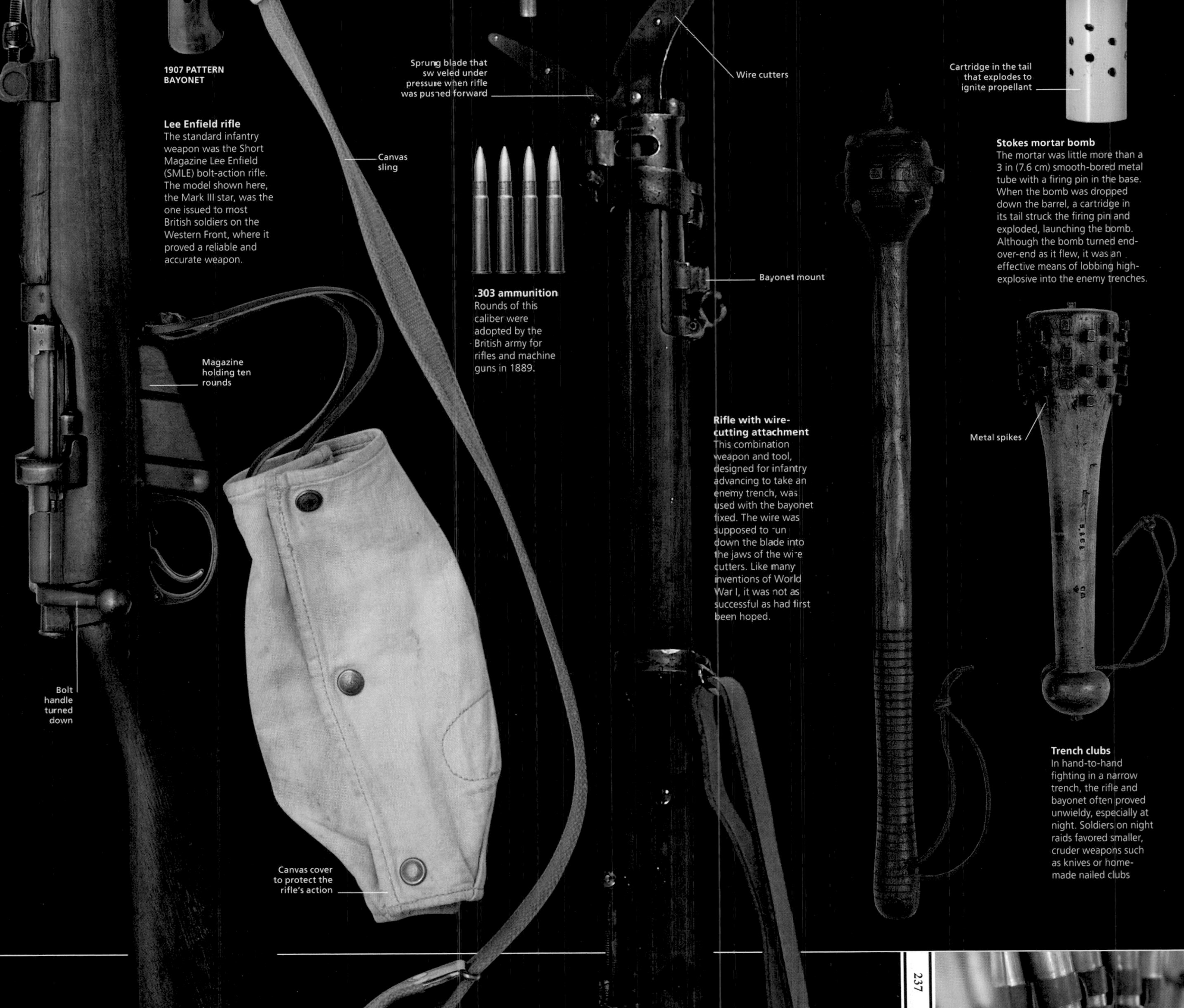

Lee Enfield rifle
The standard infantry weapon was the Short Magazine Lee Enfield (SMLE) bolt-action rifle. The model shown here, the Mark III star, was the one issued to most British soldiers on the Western Front, where it proved a reliable and accurate weapon.

.303 ammunition
Rounds of this caliber were adopted by the British army for rifles and machine guns in 1889.

Rifle with wire-cutting attachment
This combination weapon and tool, designed for infantry advancing to take an enemy trench, was used with the bayonet fixed. The wire was supposed to run down the blade into the jaws of the wire cutters. Like many inventions of World War I, it was not as successful as had first been hoped.

Stokes mortar bomb
The mortar was little more than a 3 in (7.6 cm) smooth-bored metal tube with a firing pin in the base. When the bomb was dropped down the barrel, a cartridge in its tail struck the firing pin and exploded, launching the bomb. Although the bomb turned end-over-end as it flew, it was an effective means of lobbing high-explosive into the enemy trenches.

Trench clubs
In hand-to-hand fighting in a narrow trench, the rifle and bayonet often proved unwieldy, especially at night. Soldiers on night raids favored smaller, cruder weapons such as knives or home-made nailed clubs

1914 – 1918

GERMAN STORMTROOPER

“WE ARE GOING LIKE HELL, ON AND ON … WE ARE GLAD IF RATION CARTS AND FIELD KITCHENS CAN GET UP TO US AT NIGHT. NOW WE GO FORWARD, PAST CRATERS AND TRENCHES, CAPTURED GUN POSITIONS, RATION DUMPS, AND CLOTHING DEPOTS.”

DIARY OF **RUDOLF BINDING**, CAPTAIN IN THE GERMAN ARMY, DESCRIBING THE **KAISERSCHLACHT** OF MARCH 1918

Although Germany was defeated in World War I, the performance of German infantry was generally excellent, at least until morale began to waver in the final months of the conflict. Enduring the horrors and hardships of trench warfare on the Western Front, German soldiers showed not only courage and resolution but also skill in the adoption of flexible battlefield tactics. This was especially true of the elite stormtroopers, who spearheaded the mighty German offensive of March 1918, the "Kaiserschlacht" (Kaiser's battle).

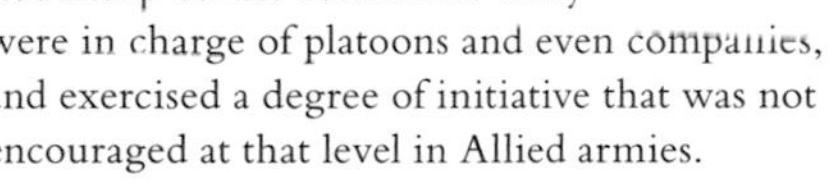

The overwhelming majority of German soldiers in World War I were conscripts and reservists, products of a system of universal conscription that even in peacetime made every male between the ages of 17 and 45 liable to some form of military service. The strength of universal conscription was its perceived fairness—men from all classes mixed in the ranks—and the sheer numbers of trained men it could deliver to the army. Reservists were often rusty in their military training, and the quality of the performance of the citizen-soldiers depended heavily upon the German army's highly professional NCOs. Generally better educated than their Allied opposite numbers, they instilled discipline and ensured a high level of training. They also provided leadership on the battlefield. They were in charge of platoons and even companies, and exercised a degree of initiative that was not encouraged at that level in Allied armies.

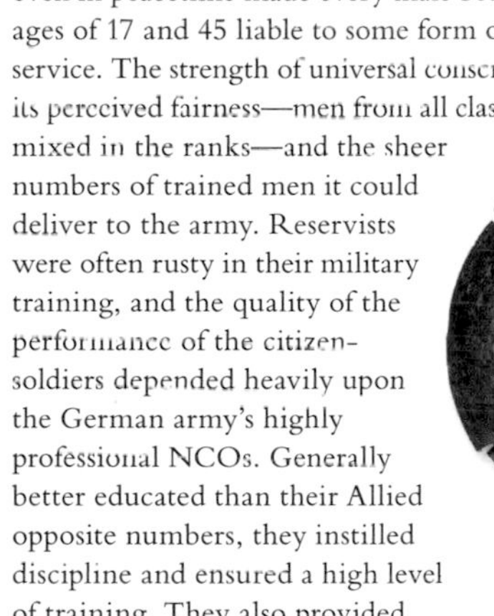

Discus grenade
This grenade was in general use in the German army in the early years of the war.

A DEFENSIVE WAR

The German soldiers were initially highly motivated, inspired by the belief that they were fighting in defense of their homeland. Although some demoralization was inevitable among the carnage of the Western Front, their commitment remained to the end more solid than that of the German home front, buoyed by the usual group bonding of comrades fighting shoulder-to-shoulder in the front line.

The Germans were the first soldiers to begin digging trenches on the Western Front and settled into trench systems more easily than their enemies. This was partly a result of their strategy, which from mid-1915 to spring 1918 dictated a broadly defensive stance on the Western Front. Mostly, German soldiers benefited from dry iron-and-wood-lined trenches, sometimes with deep concrete bunkers for protection against heavy artillery. In places they enjoyed electric lighting, piped water, and ventilation systems for underground bunkers. But not all German trench systems were of high quality and many soldiers spent their tours of duty in the front line sheltered by little more than hollows dug into the side of a trench wall. A policy of mounting counterattacks at all costs to regain any ground lost ensured that even in defensive battles casualties were massive. It was not only Allied soldiers who advanced across open ground into heavy machine-gun fire. Exposed to prolonged artillery bombardments, poison gas attacks, and mass infantry offensives, it often seemed to German soldiers that they were holding on in vain against a materially superior enemy.

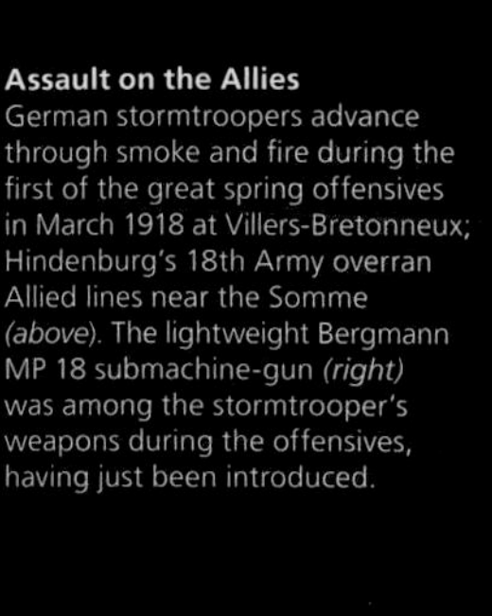

Assault on the Allies
German stormtroopers advance through smoke and fire during the first of the great spring offensives in March 1918 at Villers-Bretonneux; Hindenburg's 18th Army overran Allied lines near the Somme *(above)*. The lightweight Bergmann MP 18 submachine-gun *(right)* was among the stormtrooper's weapons during the offensives, having just been introduced.

BERGMANN MP 18 SUBMACHINE-GUN AND 32-ROUND MAGAZINE

STORMING FORWARD

Hundreds of thousands of Germans died in the great blood-lettings of Verdun and the Somme in 1916, and in the Allied offensives of 1917. As the war went on, a gulf opened up in the German ranks between battle-hardened troops who had survived this carnage and the ageing reservists or fresh young conscripts who were required to make up the numbers at the front. The best soldiers were grouped into elite formations of "stormtroopers" and used to spearhead counterattacks and offensives. The stormtrooper concept was traceable to an assault unit created in March 1915 by Captain Willy Rohr of the Prussian Guards Rifles. Through 1916 and 1917 storm battalions became common, along with smaller stormtrooper detachments in standard infantry regiments. They were created either by the conversion of units of riflemen (Jäger) or by hand-picking the best soldiers from conventional infantry. Stormtroopers received intensive training and they were encouraged to regard themselves as the "princes of the trenches." A storm battalion might consist of three or four infantry companies armed with rifles and hand grenades, a machine-gun company, a trench mortar company, a battery of light infantry guns, and a flamethrower section. They were expected to operate on their own initiative, punching holes through the enemy's trench systems without stopping. The concept of the stormtrooper represented a bold attempt to exploit the fighting skills of superbly trained infantry in a war paralyzed by the brute attritional impact of massed firepower. Its drawback was that standard infantry units were stripped of their best men, who were then thrown into the forefront of every costly counterattack or offensive. Inevitably, the stormtroopers took heavy casualties, so that German losses were concentrated among their finest, most experienced soldiers.

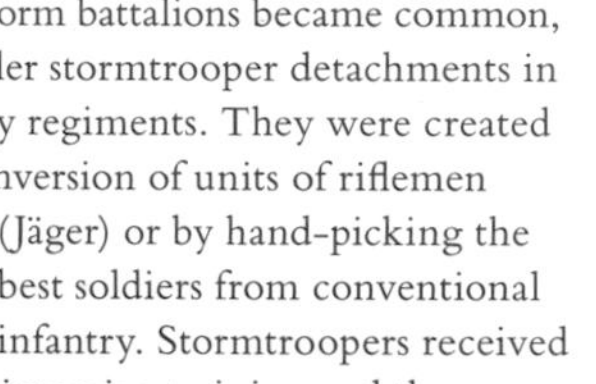

Trench ax
Although used primarily as a general purpose tool in the trenches, the ax was useful for close-quarters fighting during trench-raiding missions.

Enlightened warfare
Magnesium flares, known as star shells, were fired into the air by a flare pistol to send prearranged signals. Some shells had parachutes that slowed their descent. Star shells were also used to illuminate No Man's Land and reveal enemy activity.

KAISERSCHLACHT

The acid test of the effectiveness of stormtroopers came with the Kaiserschlacht offensive of March 1918. This was a desperate gamble by the German High Command, who threw the resources released by victory over Russia on the Eastern Front into a massive offensive in the West, hoping to win the war before American troops were ready to fight. On March 21, the full force of the German onslaught fell upon the British Third and Fifth Armies. After being subjected to a ferocious

> "I TRIED TO CONVINCE MYSELF OF WHAT WOULD HAVE HAPPENED TO ME IF I HADN'T ... THRUST MY BAYONET INTO HIS BELLY FIRST."
>
> **STEFAN WESTMANN**, 29TH DIVISION GERMAN ARMY

Over the top
German stormtroopers laden with equipment advance over open but broken ground during the spring offensive of 1918. The enemy know of their approach because of a preliminary barrage.

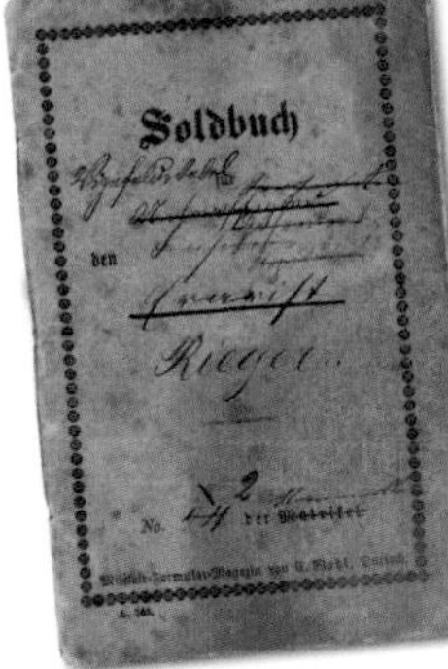

German paybook
A *Soldbuch* was carried by every member of the German army. It contained a record of the soldier's pay and home leave, unit information, equipment issued, and medical records.

artillery bombardment for four hours, British front-line troops were overrun by German stormtroopers as they emerged out of thick morning fog. Once the Germans were at close quarters, there was no resisting their flamethrowers, grenades, and submachine guns. In some places, stormtroopers advanced 10 miles (16 km) in a day's fighting and 40 miles (65 km) by the end of a week, an achievement unprecedented since the trench lines had solidified in late 1914. But in other parts of the front the German offensive failed or made little progress. The Kaiserschlacht gained the Germans territory but not overall victory, and completed the exhaustion of their army.

BITTER DEFEAT

As a result of the conscription of farm workers and farm horses, Germany was desperately short of food by 1918, and German soldiers could not be insulated from these shortages. At Easter, one soldier complained that his day's rations had consisted of half a loaf of bread and a chunk of roasted horsemeat. The March offensive was disrupted when German soldiers overran Allied stores brimming with food and drink, which they stopped to plunder and enjoy. Their poor diet left them very susceptible to the deadly flu epidemic that erupted in the second half of 1918.

Worse than hunger and sickness for the German soldiers, however, was the certainty that they could no longer win the war as American troops arrived in force. When the Allies drove them back in a series of well-planned offensives from the late summer, German soldiers began to surrender. Most never gave up, however, and they remained on foreign soil at the armistice. Many Germans could not accept they had been defeated after such a titanic struggle, which had cost around two million soldiers their lives. While most ex-servicemen became staunchly anti-war as a result of their experiences, a substantial minority recreated the comradeship of the trenches in nationalist paramilitary organizations. The memory of the stormtroopers was later perverted by the Nazi Party in search of a warrior myth to justify aggressive militarism.

INFILTRATION TACTICS

The Germans sought to end the dominance of defense on the World War I battlefield by tactics designed to penetrate enemy lines rapidly and in depth. First used to full effect by General von Hutier at Riga in September 1917, infiltration tactics dispensed with a prolonged preliminary bombardment of enemy trenches. Instead, a "hurricane" artillery barrage of great intensity, but short duration, was followed by the advance of heavily-armed stormtroopers. Bypassing strongpoints, these elite troops would overrun weaker points in front-line trenches with the force of their shock attack. They then pressed on swiftly through second- and third-line trenches to threaten enemy artillery and communications. Assault infantry would follow immediately behind them cleaning up pockets of resistance such as machine-gun nests. Although infiltration tactics often succeeded in their objective of punching a hole in enemy lines, they did not solve the problem of exploiting the opportunity thus presented. In the absence of motor vehicles, any advance soon slowed to a crawl because of insuperable logistical and transportation problems.

Stick grenade
The *Stielhandgranate*, or stick grenade, was synonymous with the stormtroopers' rapid assaults on enemy lines.

Last line of defense
Almost deserted, this German soldier stands in his trench about to deal one last attack on the advancing enemy.

Gas mask
The German army's means of protection from gas attacks was more sophisticated than the Allies' goggles and cotton wadding. This mask features a cylindrical screw-fitted air filter.

Plastic goggles

Tin container for safe keeping

STORMTROOPER GEAR

As assault troops, who launched near-continual raids on Allied trenches during the spring of 1918, German stormtroopers were constantly on the move. Everything about their gear and weaponry was designed to facilitate rapid mobility, ease of use, and ready access in the heat of battle—from the crowded utility belt and assault pack (which contained everything from food and water to ammunition and temporary shelter) to the grenade bag and specially shortened Mauser KAR98AZ carbine.

Helmet
All armies were obliged to equip infantry with steel helmets in the course of World War I. The German "Stahlhelm" was introduced in 1916. Its distinctive "coal-scuttle" shape protected the back of the neck.

World War I soldiers were among the first to use camouflage on a widespread basis.

Ribbon from iron cross – second class

Tunic
This standard-issue stormtrooper tunic provided great warmth but would have been very heavy, especially when wet. Many stormtroopers covered their epaulettes with a strip of cloth, so the enemy would not see their regimental badge.

Shovel blade for trench digging

Assault pack
Worn as a backpack, this compact kit featured a shovel, a *zeltbahn* (a large rain poncho that could also be used as a tent), and a container of cooking utensils, the lid of which doubled as a frying pan—all bound together tightly with leather straps.

Badge indicating soldier had been wounded

Iron cross – first class

Zeltbahn (rain poncho)

The assault pack, as worn around the back for ease of transportation

The Mauser KAR98AZ, the stormtrooper's principal weapon

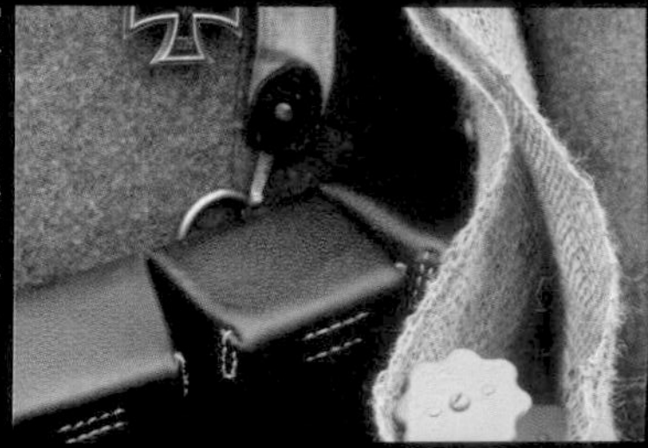

Equipment pouches and canvas sack for holding grenades

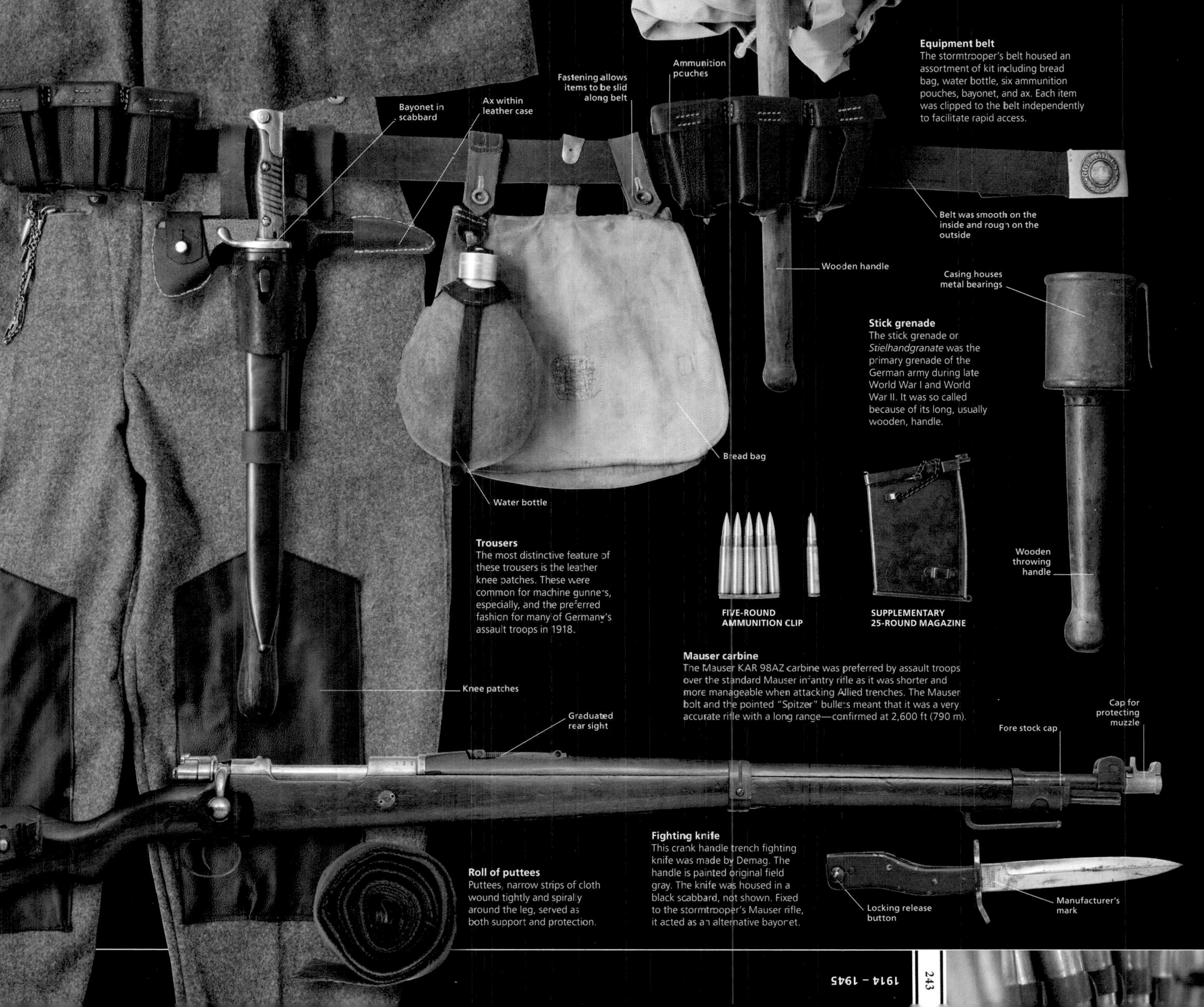

Equipment belt
The stormtrooper's belt housed an assortment of kit including bread bag, water bottle, six ammunition pouches, bayonet, and ax. Each item was clipped to the belt independently to facilitate rapid access.

Stick grenade
The stick grenade or *Stielhandgranate* was the primary grenade of the German army during late World War I and World War II. It was so called because of its long, usually wooden, handle.

Trousers
The most distinctive feature of these trousers is the leather knee patches. These were common for machine gunners, especially, and the preferred fashion for many of Germany's assault troops in 1918.

Mauser carbine
The Mauser KAR 98AZ carbine was preferred by assault troops over the standard Mauser infantry rifle as it was shorter and more manageable when attacking Allied trenches. The Mauser bolt and the pointed "Spitzer" bullets meant that it was a very accurate rifle with a long range—confirmed at 2,600 ft (790 m).

Roll of puttees
Puttees, narrow strips of cloth wound tightly and spirally around the leg, served as both support and protection.

Fighting knife
This crank handle trench fighting knife was made by Demag. The handle is painted original field gray. The knife was housed in a black scabbard, not shown. Fixed to the stormtrooper's Mauser rifle, it acted as an alternative bayonet.

GERMAN TRENCH

Through most of World War I, a line of field fortifications stretched for over 450 miles (700 km) along the Western Front from Nieuport in Belgium to the Swiss border. The first trenches, improvised in the autumn of 1914, were intended as temporary structures, but these hastily-dug ditches gradually evolved into permanent in-depth defensive systems incorporating concrete bunkers and strongpoints, protected by dense belts of barbed wire.

The opposing lines of trenches were typically separated by a "no man's land" some 220–330 yards (200–300 m) wide, although in places they could be as close as 28 yards (25 m). The nature of the trenches varied depending on the terrain. In the dry, firm chalk of Artois and the Somme, soldiers could dig deep and create safe, comfortable shelters. But in the wet, soft terrain of Flanders, where the Bayernwald trench, featured here, was dug, deep structures flooded and earth walls crumbled unless shored up with timber or wicker. Life for soldiers in these shallow trenches was often a miserable struggle against mud and damp. The Germans at least had the advantage of having chosen their position to dig in at the outset, selecting the higher ground that was drier and less exposed to enemy fire.

At minimum, a trench needed a wall facing the enemy that was taller than a man, for snipers picked off anyone whose head showed over the top of the parapet. Construction and repair work had to be carried out under cover of darkness. Keeping the trenches solid and dry used up much of soldiers' energies through the war.

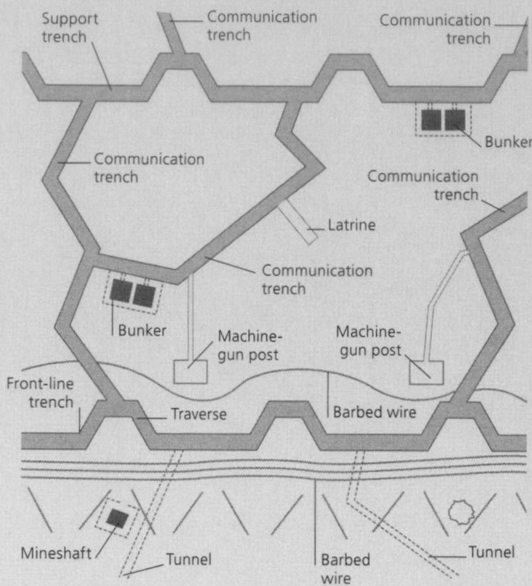

Simplified German trench system
After 1916 the Germans kept their front-line trenches lightly manned. They were linked by a network of communication passages to support and reserve trenches to the rear.

Pride in their work
German officers and men pose in a newly constructed trench of unusually high quality. It is far too wide to be a front-line trench.

"ATTACKS ALTERNATE WITH COUNTERATTACKS AND SLOWLY THE DEAD PILE UP IN THE FIELD OF CRATERS BETWEEN THE TRENCHES."

ERICH MARIA REMARQUE IN HIS NOVEL *ALL QUIET ON THE WESTERN FRONT*

Grenade launcher
The Germans were quicker than the Allies to produce specialized weapons for trench warfare such as this grenade launcher.

Winding line
Trenches were never dug in a straight line. Turnings prevented blast or shrapnel raking the whole length of the trench and also blocked the line of fire of any enemy units that broke into the trench.

Firestep
A wooden A-frame provides a firestep, enabling a soldier to step up and fire over the parapet. In drier areas firesteps would be dug out of the wall of the trench.

Entrance to mineshaft
Mines were dug in an effort to tunnel under enemy lines and plant explosives, as the British did at nearby Messines in 1917.

Looking down a mineshaft
Two mineshafts 55 ft (17 m) deep survive at the site. It must have been a soul-destroying job digging them as they would often have flooded.

Servicing the trench
The length of timber spanning the trench could serve various purposes, such as carrying telephone wires or rigging a hose to pump out water.

Wicker and sandbags
The wet ground in this sector meant trenches had to be shallow with a builtup parapet of earth-filled sandbags.

Precast concrete
There were originally ten bunkers at Bayernwald, of which two have survived. Built in 1916, most were made of precast concrete blocks brought up to the front by narrow-gauge railroad.

Two-room bunker
Inside, each bunker consisted of two rooms with ceilings only 4 ft (1.2 m) high. A tube through the ceiling could be adapted as a flue for a stove or as a periscope.

Uninviting shelter
The soldiers were allowed to use the bunkers only during heavy artillery bombardment. They were made cramped and uncomfortable for fear men might lose the will to come out and fight.

OTHER INFANTRYMEN OF WORLD WAR I

The experience of war in 1914–18 was in many ways common to the infantry of all nations. Whatever their country of origin and to whichever front they were posted, soldiers had to endure artillery bombardment and gas attack, advance in the face of machine-gun fire, and fight the squalid daily struggle in the trenches against rats, lice, and mud. Casualties in offensives were always high and gains frustratingly small in proportion to the losses suffered. That civilians, rushed into uniform, coped so well with the demands of modern warfare at its most destructive is a tribute to both their courage and commitment. Many of them not only endured, but developed from poorly trained amateurs into skilled, hard-bitten fighting men.

FRENCH POILUS

The French "poilu"—infantry conscript—was the product of a system designed to make every Frenchman into a trained soldier. In peacetime all male French citizens did two years' national service (raised to three in 1913), then passing into the army reserve. They were taught to regard service in the army as a source of patriotic pride. Mobilization at the outbreak of war put more than three million of these citizen-soldiers in the field within weeks. Inadequately armed and wearing bright uniforms that made excellent targets, they were thrown away in offensives that collapsed in the face of overwhelming German firepower. The French army rallied to defeat the Germans at the First Battle of the Marne, but by the end of three months about a million French soldiers had been killed or wounded. After these shattering losses the French settled in to the demoralizing attrition of trench warfare. On the whole their conditions were worse than those of either British or German troops, with poor quality trenches, monotonous food, and inadequate rest facilities when out of the front line. French morale survived the slaughter at Verdun in 1916, but futile offensives in early 1917 brought widespread mutinies. The authorities were forced to improve food and leave, and be less wasteful of men's lives. Morale recovered sufficiently for the French infantry to make a major contribution to victory in 1918. Out of some 8.3 million French soldiers who served in the course of the war, almost 1.4 million were killed.

Uniform and weapons
The conspicuous uniform of 1914 was changed in 1915 to a pale blue overcoat and trousers plus the Adrian steel helmet.

LEBEL RIFLE (1893 MODEL)

LEGION D'HONNEUR

Desperate measures
French troops use rocks as well as rifles to dislodge German soldiers from hillside trenches in eastern France.

US INFANTRY

When the United States entered World War I in April 1917 it was in the process of expanding its regular army to 140,000 men and creating a volunteer reserve of 400,000, incorporating the National Guard. These numbers were, however, wholly insufficient for the mass army needed for the European war. The government decided to create a new "national army" raised entirely by conscription. Despite traditional hostility to the draft, conscription went ahead smoothly, but it was a slow process assembling and transporting troops to Europe. The American Expeditionary Force numbered over 500,000 by June 1918, when it first entered combat on the Western Front. Nicknamed "doughboys," the conscripts impressed jaded Europeans as physically fit, mentally fresh young men, their optimism contrasting sharply with the cynicism of the war-weary British and French.

The US troops' inexperience, and that of their officers, cost them dearly in early engagements. Their supply system was often poorly organized and troops at times went hungry in their trenches. Apart from rifles, most of their fighting equipment had to be supplied by the British and French. But the doughboy proved his fighting worth, most notably in the St. Mihiel offensive in September 1918.

US forces were totally racially segregated. Some 200,000 African-American conscripts were sent to Europe, but only a fifth of these were allowed to serve in a combat role, in separate all-black divisions. By the end of the war there were two million US troops in Europe. Around 50,000 US soldiers died in combat; a similar number were killed by influenza between 1918-19.

Americans on the Western Front
Men of the 23rd Infantry Regiment fire a 37-mm gun at a German position during the successful St. Mihiel offensive of September 1918, the first major US operation of the war.

US equipment
The Americans added a few new touches to the weaponry of the war, such as shotguns used to clear enemy trenches.

CAMOUFLAGED HELMET

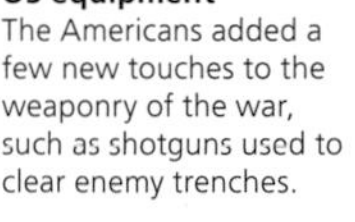
WIRE CUTTERS

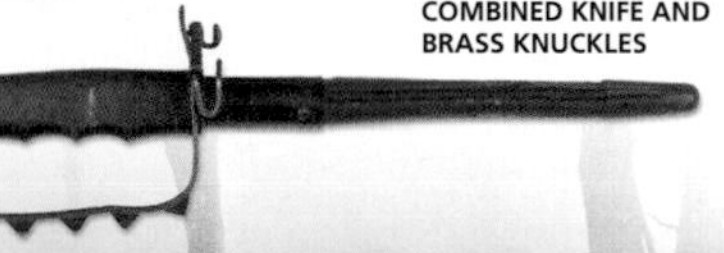
COMBINED KNIFE AND BRASS KNUCKLES

PUMP-ACTION SHOTGUN

CANADIAN INFANTRY

Canada had only a few thousand men in its regular army when the war began. Unhesitating in its support for Britain, the dominion invited volunteers to create a Canadian Expeditionary Force. Some 600,000 Canadians enlisted, of whom 418,000 served overseas. Organizing an army almost from scratch was a formidable task, but a body of hastily trained Canadian civilians-in-uniform was ready to take its place in the front line at Ypres in April 1915—just in time to face the first chlorine gas attacks on the Western Front. As Canadian numbers grew, so did their exposure to the worst the war could show. Canadians suffered heavy casualties at the Somme in summer 1916 and in the mud of Passchendaele the following year. Their exceptional fighting qualities were universally recognized. The Canadian capture of heavily defended Vimy Ridge on April 9, 1917, charging up a steep slope in sleet and snow, was one of the great feats of arms in the war. More than 56,000 Canadian soldiers died in combat.

> "... ITS ASSAULT ONLY FAILED ... BECAUSE DEAD MEN CAN ADVANCE NO FURTHER."
>
> **GEN. BEAUVOIR DE LYLE**
> ON THE NEWFOUNDLAND REGIMENT AT THE SOMME

Canadian weapons and kit
The Canadians' khaki uniform was based on the British one, but they produced their own rifle, the Ross, which had an unusual short, stubby bayonet.

INFANTRY CAP

ROSS BAYONET

POCKET KNIFE

ROSS .303 MK III SNIPER RIFLE

THE ANZACS

On the outbreak of war, young men in Australia and New Zealand responded eagerly to their governments' call for volunteers to fight in support of Britain—about one in five male New Zealanders eventually joined up. Grouped together as ANZACs, Australian and New Zealand troops were initially stationed in Egypt for training. The Australians in particular soon gained a reputation as tough characters. Their indifference to military etiquette outraged British officers and their off-duty behavior appalled the Egyptians. Once in battle, however, ANZAC troops proved the most fearsome and effective fighters on the Allied side in the war. Their baptism of fire in the notorious Gallipoli campaign would have demoralized a less resolute body of soldiers, but they went on to fight at the Somme and Passchendaele. By summer 1918 the Australians had their own corps, which spearheaded the offensives that rolled back the German Army. Proportionally, the Australians suffered the highest casualty rate of any national army in the war, with 60,000 killed and 220,000 wounded out of around 320,000 sent for overseas service. New Zealand suffered 58,000 casualties, including 17,000 dead.

RUSSIAN TROOPS

Peasant conscripts formed the majority of the Russian army, with an admixture of workers from the major cities. Mobilization went very smoothly, but badly-led Russian forces suffered a catastrophic defeat at Tannenberg in late August 1914. From then on the Russians were beaten whenever they fought the Germans, although they sometimes inflicted defeats on the Austrians and the Turks. Discontent grew as lives were thrown away in futile offensives and conditions at the fronts worsened. Soldiers resented those exempted from conscription who made money out of the booming wartime economy and many also hated their arrogant and incompetent officers. In March 1917 soldiers in reserve units helped overthrow the Tsarist regime. Soldiers' committees (or "soviets") were set up and unpopular officers were ejected by their men. The new Provisional Government called on soldiers to continue to resist "the bayonets of conquerors," but the offensive of June 1917 revealed the limited appeal of continued fighting. It petered out and there were mass desertions. Nothing could stop the army's dissolution as peasant soldiers laid down their rifles and went home to join in land seizures. Some 1.8 million Russian troops had died in the war.

PAPAKHA SHEEPSKIN HAT

Badge in Romanov colors

MOSIN-NAGANT RIFLE

Russian uniform
The khaki tunic, introduced in 1907, was worn with more traditional items of clothing, such as the Cossack papakha.

> "WHAT'S THE USE OF US PEASANTS GETTING LAND IF I AM KILLED AND GET NO LAND?"
>
> **RUSSIAN PEASANT SOLDIER**, MAY 1917

ITALIAN TROOPS

Bersaglieri hat
The Bersaglieri, a crack rifle corps, wore distinctive plumed hats on parade.

Italy's belated declaration of war on Austria-Hungary in May 1915, motivated by territorial ambitions, was unpopular with much of the population. Having been unified only half a century earlier, Italy had built up only limited patriotic sentiment, and conscripts from Sicily and the south generally viewed the north of Italy as a foreign posting. The Alpine front to which Italian soldiers were sent was harsh and forbidding terrain. Weather conditions were often appalling and assaults on Alpine ridges, even if successful, only revealed another ridge behind to be taken. Only the elite Alpini had any special skills for coping with mountain warfare. Front-line troops often went short of food, clothing, and medical services. Soldiers were routinely mistreated by their officers.

The saving grace for the Italians was that the Austro-Hungarians were generally in a similar plight to themselves. The transfer of German forces to the Italian front precipitated disaster for Italy at Caporetto in October 1917. Demoralized, riddled with pacifist and defeatist sentiment, influenced by left-wing revolutionary ideas, and exhausted by too many costly offensives, Italian soldiers quit the battlefield almost as soon as the fighting began and fled as far and fast as they could. A defensive line was stabilized on the Piave River in winter 1917. After a period cautiously devoted to the restoration of morale, the Italians ended the war on the offensive, led by new assault troops, the Arditi. But overall the Italian soldier's experience of the war was disillusioning in the extreme. Almost half a million Italians died in the conflict.

ID TAGS

Mountain trenches
Repeated Italian attempts to break through the Austrian lines failed despite heavy bombardments and vicious hand-to-hand fighting.

FOLDING SHOVEL

THE AUSTRO-HUNGARIAN ARMY

The Austro-Hungarian army reflected the complexity of a multinational empire in which Austrian Germans and Hungarians dominated assorted other peoples—chiefly Czechs, Slovaks, Croats, Slovenes, Bosnians, Ruthenes, and Poles. The majority of officers were German speakers, while nearly half the conscripts were Slavs, many of whom spoke no German. The army, however, initially fought well and the infantry was supplied with good quality weapons for trench warfare, even if quantities were insufficient. But cracks in loyalty to the empire soon began to appear. The shock of the Russian Brusilov offensive in summer 1916 led to mass desertions by Czechs and Ruthenes. The exhausted army later came increasingly under the control of its German allies, a fact resented by many of the troops. By September 1918, with defeat inevitable, the army was disintegrating into its separate national components. Probably around a million Austro-Hungarian soldiers died in the war.

Mountain troops
The Austrians had specialized Alpine troops, whose skills were called on both in northeast Italy and in the Carpathian mountains against the Russians.

Schwarzlose machine-gun
This water-cooled machine-gun proved a very reliable weapon even in the freezing conditions of the Alps and the Carpathians.

TURKISH TROOPS

Kalabash hat

INFANTRY TUNIC

When it entered World War I as an ally of Germany in November 1914, the multinational Ottoman Empire was in the middle of a political upheaval that would eventually create the nation-state of Turkey. Its conscript army was largely recruited from the Turkish Anatolian peasantry. There were Kurdish and Arab units, but these could not be relied on, and Jews and Christians were only used in support roles. The Turkish Army had performed poorly in recent wars in the Balkans and against Italy. When Allied forces carried out the Gallipoli landings in April 1915, they were astonished by the resilience and motivation of the Turkish soldiers. A German observer attributed the troops' performance to "stubborn devotion and unshakeable loyalty to their Sultan and Caliph." For whatever reason, "Mehmedchik"—the equivalent of the British "Tommy"—was ready to die in desperate counterattacks to repulse the landings. Courage was no remedy for economic and administrative failings, however. As the war dragged on, Turkish troops ran short of food, as did the population at home. Medical services were minimal and disease took its toll. German troops, fighting alongside the Turks, occasioned great resentment because of their superior food supplies and equipment. By summer 1918, defeated in Iraq and Palestine, the Turkish army was in full disintegration. Troops deserted en masse, either returning to work their abandoned fields or resorting to banditry. Over half a million Turkish soldiers died in combat, with perhaps half as many again dying of disease.

FRAGMENTATION GRENADE

Turkish weapons and unifom
The Turks were issued with Mauser rifles—some new, some older models that the Germans no longer used. The style of their khaki uniform also showed the influence of their German advisers.

9.5MM MAUSER CARBINE (1887)

BAYONET

On the advance
German infantry prepare for the advance on Leningrad in World War II. Codenamed Operation Barbarossa, the 1942 invasion of the Soviet Union failed, arguably leading to the fall of the Nazi Regime.

FIGHTERS OF THE SPANISH CIVIL WAR

The failure of an attempted military coup in Spain in July 1936 led to a three-year civil war, in which right-wing Nationalists led by General Francisco Franco fought forces loyal to the Republican government. Nazi Germany and Fascist Italy intervened on the Nationalist side, while the Republicans received support on a smaller scale from Soviet Russia and from volunteer International Brigades. Apart from advanced experiments in the use of air power by the German Condor Legion, the war was mostly fought using World War I-era tactics and equipment. The Nationalists were ultimately victorious in a conflict that cost more than 500,000 lives, around a quarter of them civilians or prisoners massacred in cold blood.

NATIONALISTS

The core of the Nationalist forces was the Army of Africa, which occupied Spain's North African colony, Spanish Morocco. The elite of this force was the Spanish Foreign Legion, created in 1920 on the model of the French Foreign Legion, but recruited almost entirely from Spanish volunteers, at least until the civil war brought recruits from Portugal and elsewhere. The Army of Africa also included large numbers of tough Moroccan Riff tribesmen serving under Spanish officers. Unlike the troops on the mainland, who were mostly ill-trained conscripts, the Legion and Moroccan soldiers were hardened professionals.

After the Army of Africa, the most effective troops on the Nationalist side were the Catholic royalist militias known as the "requetés." Chiefly farmers from the Navarre region, these soldiers fought in a crusading spirit, "one hand holding a grenade, the other a rosary." The Nationalists also had the support of the militia of the fascist Falangist movement and of much of the Civil Guard, a paramilitary police force that was better equipped than the Republican army. At first the progress made by the Army of Africa promised an easy Nationalist triumph. Ferried to Spain aboard German and Italian aircraft, they advanced on Madrid massacring thousands along the way. But stiff resistance brought the colonial troops to a halt in Madrid's suburbs, condemning the Nationalists to a long war of attrition. The superior foreign support they enjoyed, and the disunity of their opponents, eventually gave Franco's men a hard-fought victory.

> "SPANIARDS! THE NATION CALLS TO HER DEFENCE ALL THOSE WHO HEAR THE HOLY NAME OF SPAIN."
>
> **FRANCISCO FRANCO** MANIFESTO OF JULY 19, 1936

SPANISH MAUSER MODEL 1893

The siege of Madrid
Nationalist soldiers attack an enemy position on the Madrid front. After three years of fighting, the city finally fell to Franco's forces in March 1939.

CONDOR LEGION

"Volunteers" from the armed forces of Germany and Italy supported the Nationalists throughout the civil war. The Italians were more numerous, but the Germans were more effective. Organized into the Condor Legion from November 1936, the German intervention force consisted primarily of Luftwaffe aircraft and pilots. There was also a contingent of light tanks and of 88mm artillery used in an anti-aircraft and antitank role.

Nazi leaders saw the war as a testing ground for new equipment and tactics. The Junkers Ju 87 Stuka dive-bomber and the Messerschmitt Bf-109 fighter were two aircraft blooded in Spain that would prove crucial in the opening phase of World War II. The Luftwaffe gained experience in air-to-air combat and in providing air support to ground forces. The Condor Legion was infamously responsible for the destruction of the Basque town of Guernica by aerial bombardment in April 1937. Personnel serving with the Legion were well paid by their government and returned to Germany as a combat-hardened elite.

Messerschmitt Bf-109D
Many Luftwaffe pilots and aircraft such as the Messerschmitt Bf-109D saw their first combat with the Condor Legion in Spain.

INTERNATIONAL BRIGADES

From late 1936 the Soviet Union organized International Brigades to fight against fascism in Spain. Enthusiastic volunteers from many countries, including France, Italy, Germany, Poland, Britain, and the United States, joined up in Paris and were moved clandestinely into Spain. The first Brigades were ready in time to play a crucial part in the defense of Madrid in November 1936. Through 1937–38 thousands lost their lives in futile frontal offensives. Others were executed by communist officers for deviation from the correct political line or for desertion. The Brigades were disbanded in September 1938, those who remained being integrated into the Republican People's Army. Out of 60,000 volunteers, 10,000 died in Spain.

LOYALISTS

At the start of the civil war the government had the support of loyal units of the regular army and of the majority of the paramilitary Assault Guards. But the Republic's survival depended upon the creation of people's militias by a variety of left-wing groups, chief among them the anarchist and socialist trade union movements. Seizing weapons from army depots, they secured major cities and mounted a defense against the Nationalist forces, while simultaneously trying to carry through a social revolution. The militias were run on strictly democratic lines, with the election of officers and a total lack of formal discipline. At times they performed with outstanding bravery, but the militias were probably too unreliable to fight a long war of attrition against Franco's regulars.

Perhaps surprisingly, no one considered mounting a guerrilla campaign against the Nationalists. Instead, the Republican government insisted on creating a conventional army to fight a conventional war. The People's Army integrated the popular militias, loyal pre-civil war troops, and fresh conscripts from Republican-controlled areas. It was watched over by political commissars who were almost exclusively communist. With the Soviet Union supplying the Republic with arms and specialist personnel, the influence of the communists, at first a minority, rapidly increased.

Infighting between left-wing groups within the army hampered its effectiveness. Although brave and stubborn, the troops were poorly led, often thrown away in overambitious offensives. It was a weary and demoralized army that finally surrendered in March 1939.

Propaganda poster
"1st win the war: fewer wasted words!" urges a 1937 poster—a reference to the infighting between left-wing groups that undermined the Loyalist cause.

Flash hider
Gas port
Cooling fins
Ammunition strip feedway
Optical sight
Gas cylinder
Pistol grip
Elevation wheel

Hotchkiss Mle 1914
The French-manufactured Hotchkiss machine-gun saw service with both sides in the Spanish Civil War.

> "A BATTLE IS IN PROGRESS NOT MERELY TO DEFEND A PEOPLE FROM A SAVAGE AGGRESSOR, BUT TO DESTROY SOMETHING THAT ... WILL ... CRUSH THE PEOPLE OF ALL DEMOCRATIC COUNTRIES."

BILL PAYNTER BRITISH INTERNATIONAL BRIGADES MEMBER, MAY 1937

1940 – 1945

RAF FIGHTER PILOT

"WE ARE GOING TO WIN THIS WAR EVEN IF WE HAVE ONLY ONE AEROPLANE AND ONE PILOT LEFT ... THE SPIRIT OF THE AVERAGE PILOT HAS TO BE SEEN TO BE BELIEVED. **FLIGHT LIEUTENANT RONALD WIGHT**, 213 SQUADRON

IN THE SUMMER OF 1940, Britain's RAF Fighter Command faced a sustained air offensive by bomber and fighter aircraft of the German Luftwaffe. Known as the Battle of Britain, this was the first battle fought exclusively in the air. It was a conflict for which the RAF had made some preparation, chiefly in the form of radar masts placed around the coast, but it remained a knife-edge contest. The defense of Britain depended upon a remarkably small number of pilots (around 1,500 at full strength) who fought to the limit of their endurance.

Before the war, the RAF attracted a stream of volunteers, some of whom were then assigned to the aircraft flown by Fighter Command. Young men were excited by the prospect of flying Britain's fast new monoplane fighters, the Supermarine Spitfire and the Hawker Hurricane. They were also aware that, as fighter pilots, they would be objects of male envy and female desire. One pilot described RAF fighter service as just "beer, women and Spitfires." In the class-bound British society of the 1930s, Fighter Command came to be regarded by some officers as an elite flying club. Some of them were recruited through socially exclusive organizations such as the Auxiliary Air Force and the Oxford University Air Squadron, bringing with them the public school ethos of the "stiff upper lip" and a bantering, self-deprecatory tone. But aspiring fliers from outside the privileged class also gained entry to Fighter Command, through the Volunteer Reserve. Most of these volunteers flew as sergeant pilots, rather than officers.

OVERSEAS PILOTS

About 20 percent of Fighter Command's pilots in the Battle of Britain were non-British. One in ten were provided by Commonwealth countries, with New Zealanders the most numerous single group. Commonwealth pilots were often better shots than the British, whose training put less emphasis on marksmanship. Other Fighter Command pilots were refugees from Occupied Europe, including Poles, Czechs, French, and Belgians. The Poles comprised the largest European contingent, and the most motivated; beaten by the Luftwaffe during the invasion of Poland in September 1939, they were hot for revenge. Whatever their origins, all fighter pilots were young—in principle no one over the age of 26 was allowed to lead a squadron, although the two greatest leaders in the Battle of Britain were exceptions—"Sailor" Malan and Douglas Bader—were both aged 30.

BATTLE COMMENCES

In the spring of 1940, Fighter Command took on the Luftwaffe in the battle for France and during the evacuation of the British army from Dunkirk. These early encounters showed that the Germans were better at air fighting than the RAF, with more experienced pilots and superior tactics. After clashes over the Channel through July, the German aerial onslaught on southern England began in earnest in the second week of August, with fleets of bombers, escorted by Messerschmitt fighters, attacking in daylight whenever the weather permitted. The aim of the Luftwaffe campaign was to establish air supremacy, thus opening the way for a seaborne invasion of Britain. Fighter Command chief Hugh Dowding intended to keep his fighter pilots and aircraft in existence as a viable defensive force, and husbanded resources to that end. The RAF squadrons based at airfields in southern England found themselves in the front line of the fighting, as the vast majority of Luftwaffe raids were launched across the Channel from bases in northern France.

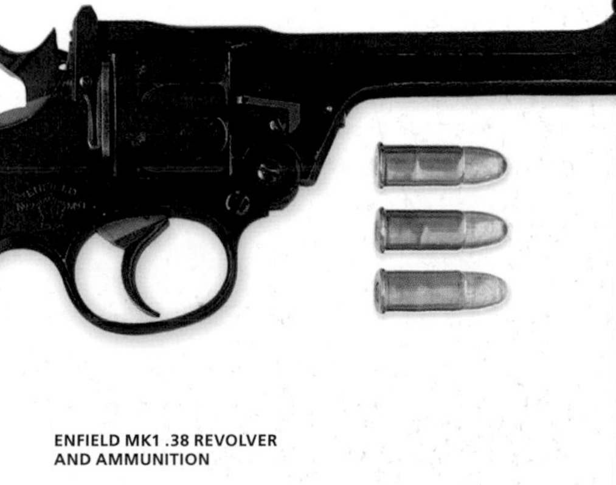

ENFIELD MK1 .38 REVOLVER AND AMMUNITION

Battle of Britain
An RAF fighter pilot sits in the cockpit of his Supermarine Spitfire after returning from combat over Britain in July 1940 *(above)*. Each pilot was issued with an Enfield Mk1.38 revolver in the event of being downed in enemy territory *(right)*.

Hurricane and Spitfire
A Hurricane fighter (foreground) flies with a Spitfire during World War II. Though the Spitfire is better known, the Hurricane was more numerous, and so had the higher strike record against the Luftwaffe.

Instead of mounting air patrols, the RAF pilots waited near their aircraft on the ground, ready to "scramble" at a moment's notice. Coastal radar stations alerted control centers to the approach of enemy aircraft; controllers ordered squadrons into the air. The fighters were then given radioed instructions to guide them towards the enemy.

GETTING AIRBORNE

Scrambling always had to be carried out with utmost speed, because every second of delay would translate into less altitude gained before meeting the enemy. At worst, squadrons stationed at airfields close to the south coast ran the risk of being caught on the ground. Consequently, pilots set off for their aircraft at a run. It typically took five minutes for a squadron to get airborne. There were cases of men caught unprepared taking off wearing flying gear over pajamas.

The pilot was squeezed into a tight cockpit under a Plexiglass hood, with his feet on the rudder bar, his right hand on the control stick, and his left hand on the throttle. There was virtually no space at all for body movement; to look around, the pilot could only turn his neck or his aircraft. In the air, he was expected to take his place in a tight V-shaped "vic" formation of three aircraft, which would usually be combined with other "vics" in a squadron of 12. For less experienced pilots, simply keeping formation was a demanding activity that left no time for watching the enemy. Although higher command insisted on this tight formation flying, experienced pilots increasingly took the initiative and abandoned the "vics." The better squadrons adopted a loose formation and acted on the principle of engaging the enemy as aggressively as possible whenever and in whatever way might work.

Eagle Squadron pilot
Due to a shortage of pilots after the Battle of Britain, the RAF recruited volunteers from overseas to make up their numbers. The Eagle Squadrons were made up of US recruits.

The Luftwaffe force typically consisted of a bomber swarm accompanied by Messerschmitt fighter escorts either in close attendance or at high altitude. The fighters had learned during the Spanish Civil War to base their formation on a pair of aircraft: a leader and a wingman. The leader was the senior pilot and the best shot; his wingman was supposed to guard his tail. Two such pairs would join together to make a loose "finger-four" formation. The four aircraft flew at slightly different altitudes and relatively spread out, so that they did not need to worry about the risk of collision. The looser formation also made the aircraft more difficult to spot.

The worst scenario for the RAF was to be "bounced" by the Messerschmitts. If they failed to spot the Luftwaffe fighters high above them, the latter would attack in a high-speed dive, picking on aircraft at the back of the British formation. It is reckoned that four out of five RAF pilots shot down never saw their attacker. Exploiting the momentum of the dive, the Messerschmitts could escape before any of the RAF fighters reacted. If the German fighters were spotted in time, the RAF pilots could turn to engage them and a "dogfight" ensued—a general mêlée with aircraft chasing one another in tight turns and firing in short bursts at any enemy in their sights. Dogfights were mostly brief but shatteringly intense and chaotic.

Inexperienced pilots were liable to fire at any aircraft they saw, friend or foe. Out-turning an enemy to get on his tail was the most successful tactic, but if a pilot turned his fighter too tightly he could pass out through excessive g-forces.

Attacking the mass of slower-moving Dornier, Junkers, and Heinkel bombers posed its own problems. The most effective tactic was to fly head-on toward the bombers, which could break up the formation. It was also incredibly risky and psychologically demanding. Most pilots settled for attacking bombers from the flank or rear. Bombers were relatively easy to hit but were hard to shoot down, absorbing a great deal of punishment. The fighter had to fire at close range to achieve any decisive effect, taking the chance of being himself hit by the bombers' well-trained gunners.

THE BEST AND THE REST

When aircraft flying at over 300 mph (480 kph) met in aerial combat, the speed at which events occurred required a pilot to possess very special qualities. In the pre-computer age, just controlling the aircraft was a refined skill, even without the need to maneuver in a crowded airspace and locate and fire on a target. It has been estimated that no more than one in 20 Battle of Britain pilots had the combination of flying skills, superb eyesight, instant reactions, situational awareness, and killer instinct to make a really effective fighter pilot. A small number of aces accounted for a large proportion of enemy aircraft shot down—men such as South African Adolph "Sailor" Malan, Czech pilot Josef Frantisek, and British Sergeant "Ginger" Lacey. At the other extreme, new pilots thrown into combat after around 12 hours flying time on fighter planes were quite likely to be killed on their first or second mission—especially as squadron leaders, keen to hold onto their experienced pilots, would often put the novices in the most vulnerable position at the rear of the formation. Pilot Hugh Dundas recalled being "close to panic in the bewilderment and hot fear" of his first dogfight. But at least "as the silhouette of a Messerschmitt passed by," he managed to fire his guns. There were many pilots who went through their first experience of air combat without seeing the enemy at all—everything simply happened too fast.

The performance of Fighter Command improved as experience built up in daily combat. Many second-rate squadron leaders were quickly replaced, and some outstanding figures emerged, such as Peter Townsend, in command of 85 Squadron, and Malan leading 74 Squadron. As the days passed, skilled fighters spread information about successful methods of combat, so that, for example, pilots learned the importance of only firing when close in to the enemy, setting their guns to fire in a cone converging at

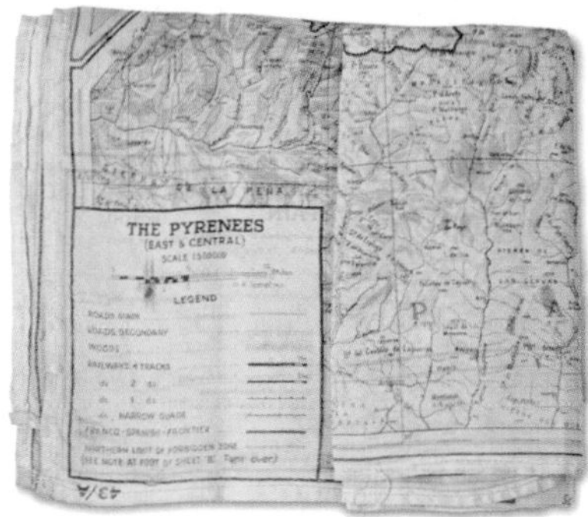

Silk map
This light, silk map was stitched into the pilot's jacket. It was needed if he was forced to bail out—in this case, over the Pyrenees.

> "THE BEST DEFENCE OF THE COUNTRY IS THE FEAR OF THE FIGHTER ... IF WE ARE WEAK IN FIGHTER STRENGTH ... THE PRODUCTIVE CAPACITY OF THE COUNTRY WILL BE VIRTUALLY DESTROYED."
>
> **SIR HUGH DOWDING**, AIR CHIEF MARSHAL

Hurricane squadron
Twelve pilots scramble for their Hurricane fighters during a peacetime exercise in 1939. Each wears a seat-type parachute over his flying suit.

“THE GRATITUDE OF EVERY HOME ON OUR ISLAND ... GOES OUT TO THE BRITISH AIRMEN WHO ARE TURNING THE TIDE OF WORLD WAR ... NEVER IN THE FIELD OF HUMAN CONFLICT WAS SO MUCH OWED BY SO MANY TO SO FEW.”

WINSTON CHURCHILL, PRIME MINISTER OF GREAT BRITAIN

250 yd (228 m) rather than the 400 yd (366 m) normal at the start of the conflict. There were always squadrons that fought by the book, however, entering combat and maneuvering in the rigid formations of the prewar years, often with disastrous consequences.

WAR OF ATTRITION

The RAF was aided by the fact that the Luftwaffe's campaign suffered from a certain lack of clarity. Radar stations and aircraft factories should have been top of the German target list, yet they were soon neglected in favor of raids on airfields. Then, German bombers and escorts were engaged by almost 700 RAF fighters.

Physical exhaustion became a serious problem as almost daily combat was sustained week after week. Pilots became so exhausted they fell asleep in their cockpits while returning from missions. At times there was little rest on the ground, as airfields were bombed and strafed by the Luftwaffe. The constant stress of battle was hard for anyone to cope with—Ginger Lacey may have been a fighter ace, but he always vomitted before taking off for combat. By mid-September most pilots in front-line squadrons had been shot down at least once. As the battle

Celebrating victory
Pilots from a Spitfire squadron celebrate with bottles of wine after fighting over France in 1944. Some Battle of Britain fighter pilots saw action through to the end of the war.

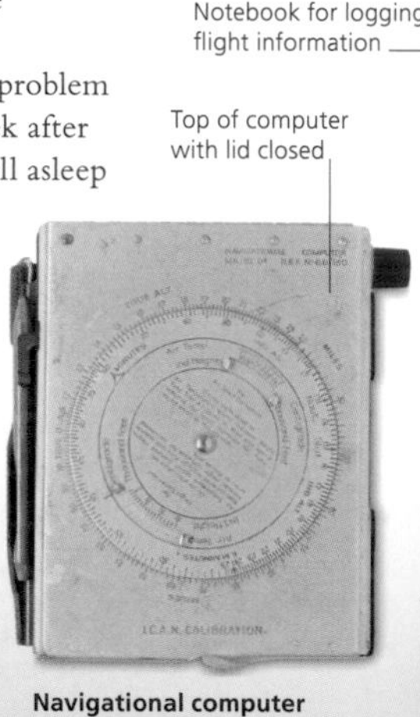

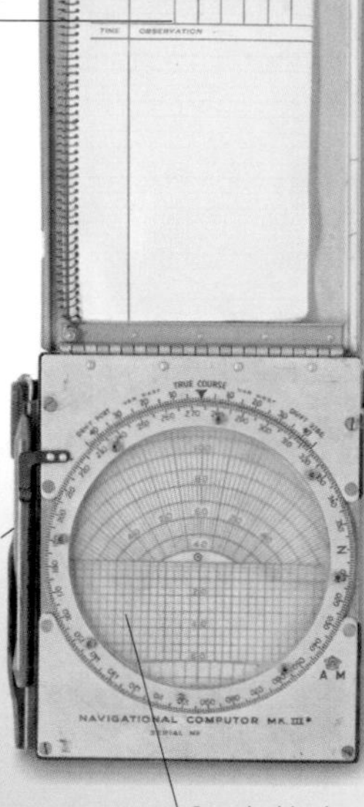

Notebook for logging flight information

Top of computer with lid closed

Speed, altitude, and direction readings

Navigational computer
For navigation, a pilot had a map and a computer strapped to his left and right leg respectively.

The Blitz
Dornier Do 17Z bombers of the Luftwaffe bomb London during the Battle of Britain, 1940. The Germans' decision to strike civilian targets relieved the airfields that had been taking the brunt of the offensive, and allowed the RAF to recover.

was being fought over England, they had a good chance of bailing out successfully and returning to their units unscathed. But hundreds were not so lucky. A pilot flew with an armored plate behind his seat and a reinforced windshield in front, but neither could provide protection against a Messerschmitt's cannon fired at close range. The worst anxiety for almost every flier was the risk of the aircraft catching fire. Pilots flew swaddled in clothing and goggles largely in the hope of finding some protection against burns if the fuel tank ignited. An unfortunate few, their faces destroyed by flames, survived to become experimental subjects for plastic surgery.

MORAL VICTORY

What kept the pilots going was partly the sheer joy in flying and fighting, the most exciting experience they would ever know. Many British fliers also bore witness to a motivating patriotism—the determination to defend their country against invaders. Pilot Douglas Bader expressed the indignation of many of his colleagues when he wrote: "Who the hell do these Huns think they are flying like this over our country in their bloody bombers covered with Iron Crosses and Swastikas?" For others, especially the Poles, there was a more savage and intimate hatred of the German enemy. Sustained by whatever belief or commitment, the RAF squadrons never faltered. Fighter Command's most important aim was to deny the Luftwaffe air supremacy, and in this they succeeded. The Luftwaffe was not beaten, but from October it was diverted to night bombing. There were around 1,900 Luftwaffe aircraft shot down in the Battle of Britain for around 1,000 RAF aircraft lost. It was by no means a clear-cut victory, but it was enough.

RAF FIGHTER TACTICS

Before the war, RAF Fighter Command trained to fly and fight in tight formations under strict control. Disciplined execution of well-drilled aerial maneuvers was viewed as the key to success against enemy bombers. The basic formation was the "vic"; three aircraft almost wing-tip-to-wing-tip in a flat V. A squadron practiced flying as four "vics," all tight to one another, and then deploying into line astern, line abreast, or some other shape for various forms of attack. When it came to combat, this formation flying proved totally unrealistic and positively harmful. Maintaining position and avoiding a midair collision absorbed attention that should have been devoted to looking for the enemy. The V-shape was hopelessly vulnerable to attack from behind. To alleviate this problem, one pilot was designated to fly behind the "vics" to guard their tails, but so many of these were shot down that the tactic had to be abandoned.

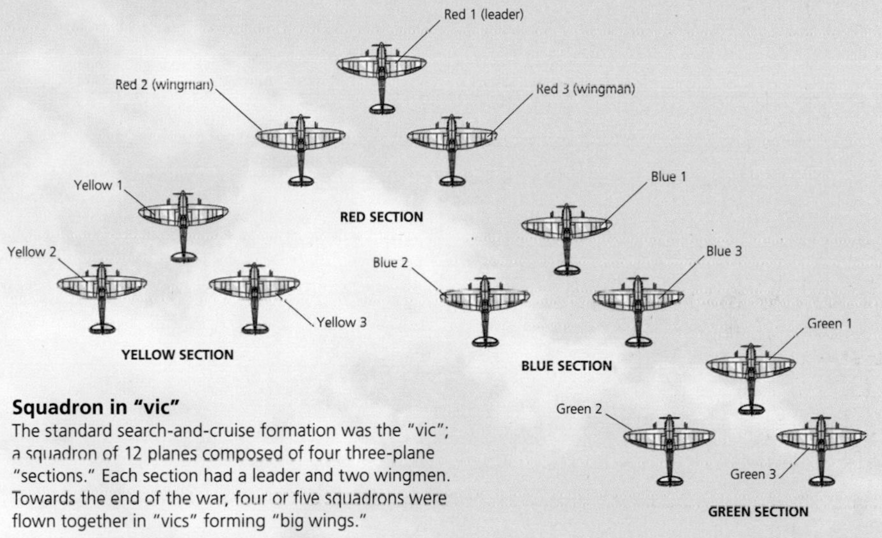

Squadron in "vic"
The standard search-and-cruise formation was the "vic"; a squadron of 12 planes composed of four three-plane "sections." Each section had a leader and two wingmen. Towards the end of the war, four or five squadrons were flown together in "vics" forming "big wings."

Section formations
Other than the "vic," fighters learned "line abreast," "line astern," and "echelon" flying. Abreast and astern were offensive and defensive formations, while echelon could deploy either way.

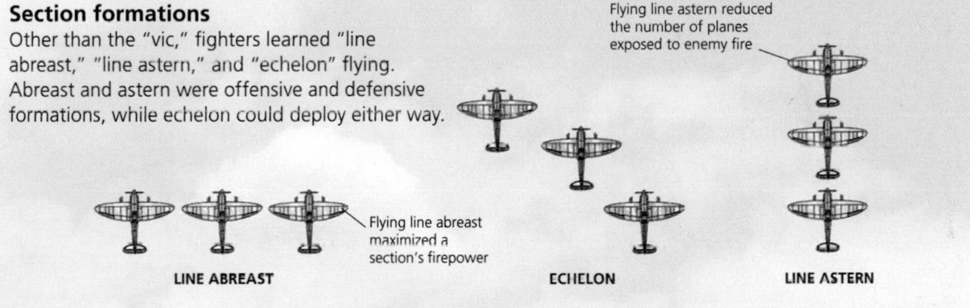

Battle of Britain
The Battle of Britain saw an end to the prewar tactics practiced by the RAF. When German bombers appeared escorted by Messerchmitt fighter planes, the RAF Spitfires and Hurricanes were forced to break formation and engage the enemy one-on-one. This often resulted in "dogfights," with enemy fighters trying to out-turn each other.

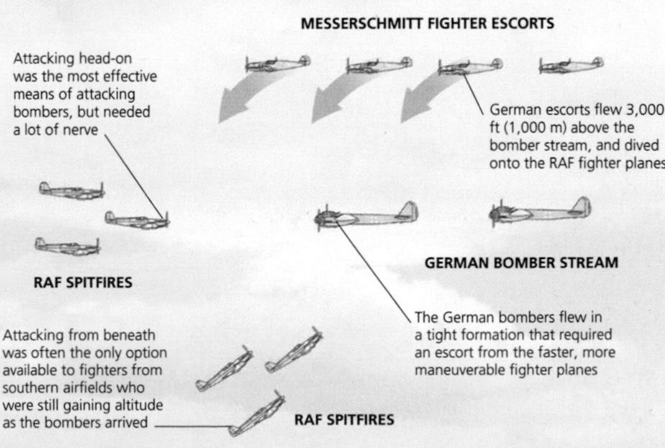

RAF PILOT'S UNIFORM

RAF fighter pilots generally wore as much as they could in flight because of fear of fire. If the fuel tank in front of the cockpit was hit and erupted into flames, a pilot could be disfigured for life in the seconds it took to slide back the canopy and exit the aircraft. Hence it was desirable to cover every inch of the body, with more than one layer if possible. On the other hand, when they had to "scramble" at short notice, pilots often flew in unlikely garb, for example with a jacket thrown over pajamas.

Peaked cap
This privately tailored peaked cap was part of an officer's service dress. It was usually worn to the aircraft and then put aside while the helmet and mask were worn. The brass and gold cord badge was unique to officers.

Officer-rank lace on epaulettes

Whistle needed if pilot was ditched at sea

Officer's badge

Battledress blouse and trousers
Introduced in 1940, this battledress was made of wool serge and partially lined with cotton drill. According to regulation, it was never worn when the pilot was off duty.

Pilot's brevet (badge)

Distinguished Flying Cross ribbon

Extra long gloves to cover wrists

D-type gauntlets
Introduced in 1942, these flying gauntlets could be worn with silk inner gloves and/or electrically heated insets. They were deliberately long to protect the wrists and hands in the event of a fire.

Fastening oxygen mask and microphone to flying helmet

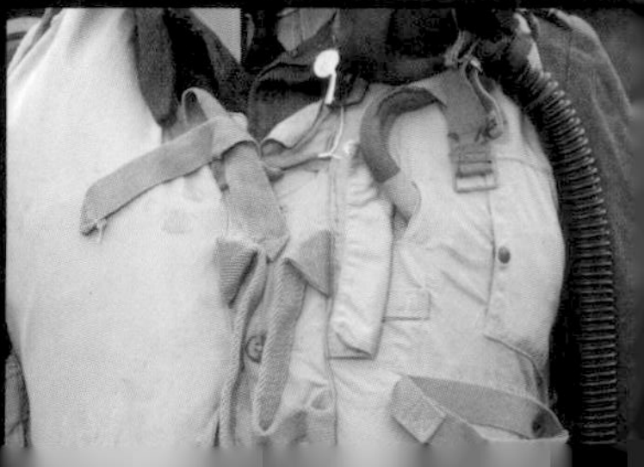

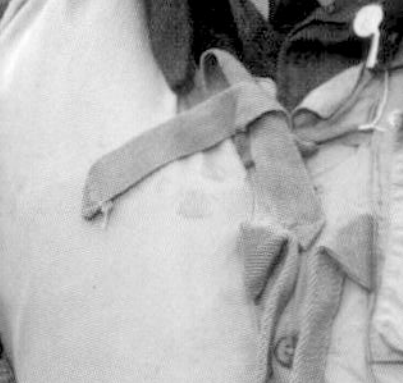

Three-buttoned life vest on top of battledress

Buckling escape boots over battledress trousers

Irvin flying jacket
Worn on top of the battledress, this flying jacket, made of sheepskin, kept the pilot warm at high altitudes. The large panels are characteristic of prewar designs, before shortages forced the production of multipanel variants. Though inferior in quality, the latter made better use of materials.

1943 escape boots
These 1943-pattern escape boots were made so that the leg section could be cut away if the owner came down in enemy territory. The remaining shoe section was of a civilian design to aid escape without detection. A knife was secreted in the leg.

RAF PILOT'S GEAR

VHF radio was central to RAF strategy in the Battle of Britain, since it allowed pilots to be controlled from the ground and to communicate with one another. Goggles, worn in earlier open-cockpit aircraft to protect the eyes against wind, were now mostly a defense against fire. More than half of RAF pilots shot down survived thanks to their parachutes. Ditching in the sea was still often fatal, for even with a life vest a pilot could only survive for a few hours in the water.

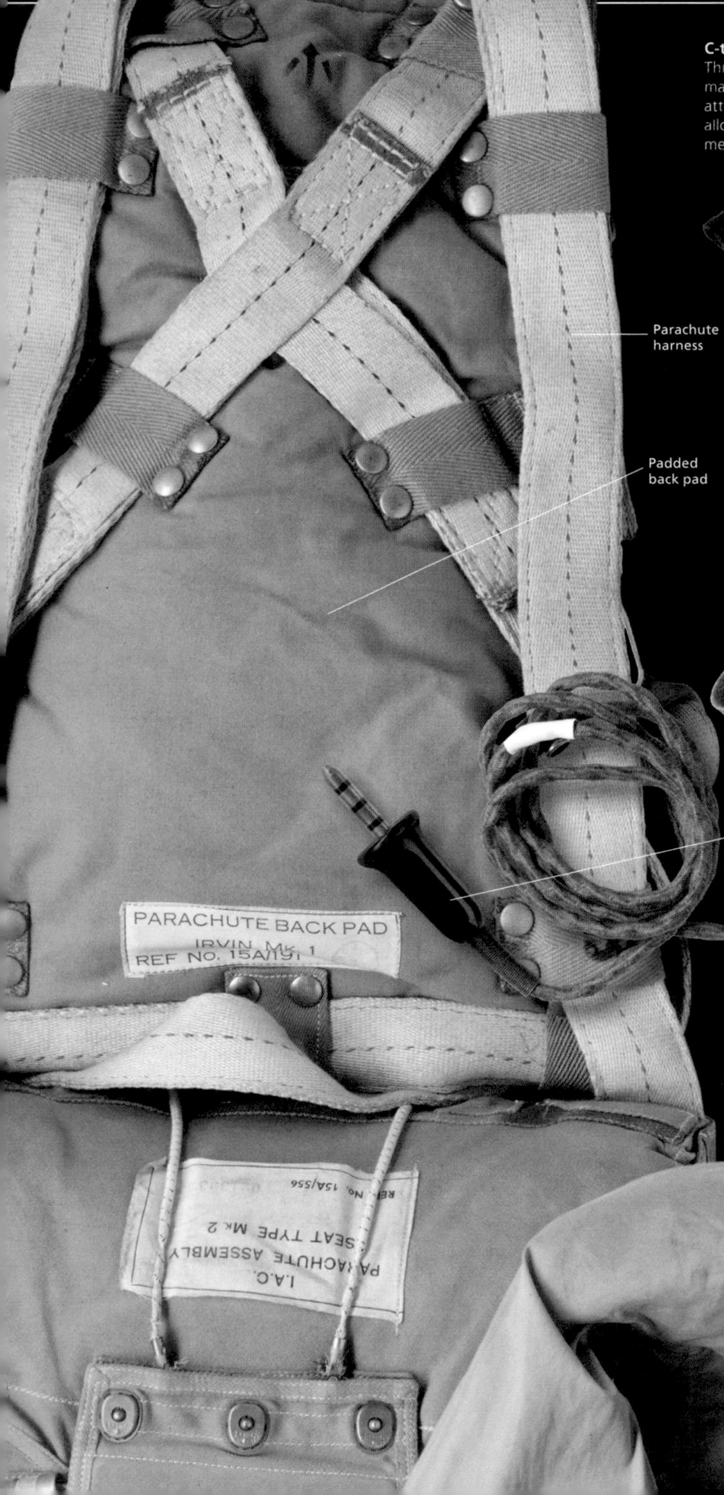

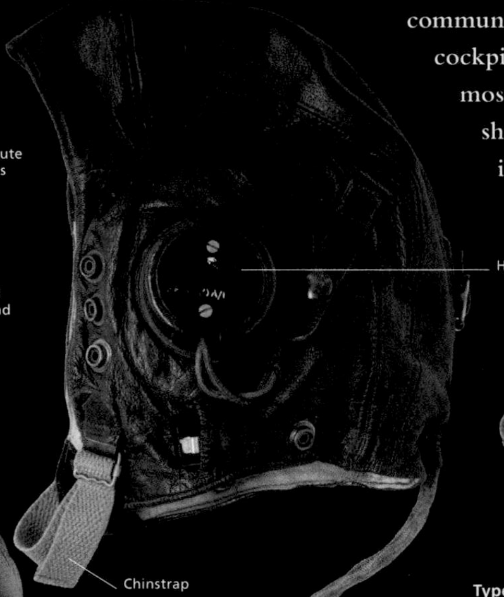

C-type flying helmet
This flying helmet fastened to the oxygen mask to which the microphone was attached. Receivers built into the earpads allowed the pilot to hear from other members of the squadron.

Parachute harness

Padded back pad

Headphones

Chinstrap

Headphone jack plug

PARACHUTE BACK PAD
IRVIN Mk 1
REF No. 15A/191

I.A.C.
PARACHUTE ASSEMBLY
SEAT TYPE Mk 2
REF No. 15A/556

Elastic head strap

Type VIII flying goggles
Introduced in October 1943, these goggles remained in service until the 1950s.

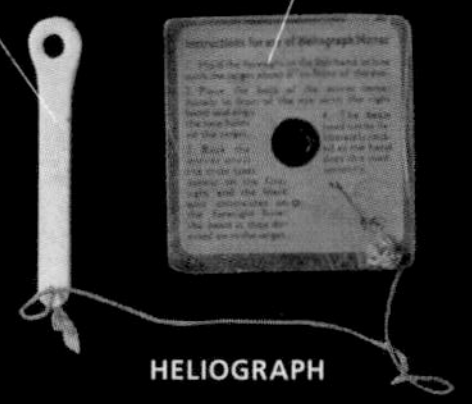

Bright, eye-catching cotton

Seat type parachute
This parachute assembly literally formed a seat that the pilot sat on, the top half forming the seat back. The lower half contained the parachute canopy, which was made of nylon, while the top half formed the harness. The canopy was released manually by pulling a rip cord.

Sighting arm

Mirror

HELIOGRAPH

SKULL CAP

Survival at sea
Carried in the pocket of the pilot's life vest, this bright yellow cap improved a pilot's chances of being spotted at sea. The heliograph was used to reflect sunlight to attract rescue aircraft.

HELIOGRAPH

HELIOGRAPH BAG

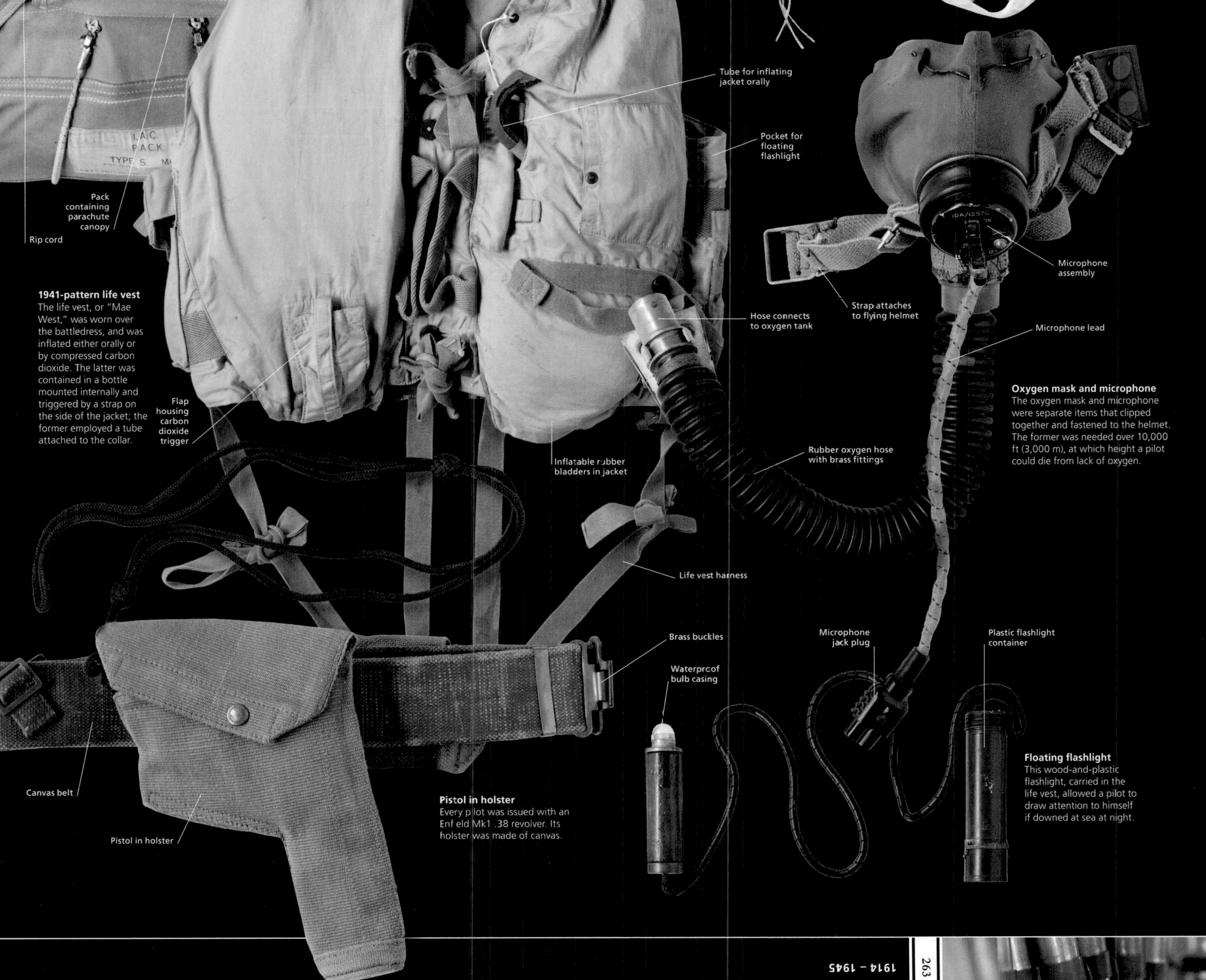

1941-pattern life vest
The life vest, or "Mae West," was worn over the battledress, and was inflated either orally or by compressed carbon dioxide. The latter was contained in a bottle mounted internally and triggered by a strap on the side of the jacket; the former employed a tube attached to the collar.

Oxygen mask and microphone
The oxygen mask and microphone were separate items that clipped together and fastened to the helmet. The former was needed over 10,000 ft (3,000 m), at which height a pilot could die from lack of oxygen.

Pistol in holster
Every pilot was issued with an Enfield Mk1 .38 revolver. Its holster was made of canvas.

Floating flashlight
This wood-and-plastic flashlight, carried in the life vest, allowed a pilot to draw attention to himself if downed at sea at night.

GERMAN U-BOAT CREW

When they were at the peak of their effectiveness, between 1941 and 1943, Germany's U-boats came close to cutting Britain's supply lifeline across the Atlantic. Commanded by captains of an independent, buccaneering spirit, they hunted across vast expanses of ocean, assembling in "wolf packs" to savage merchant convoys. In total, U-boats sank some 14 million tons of Allied shipping in the course of the war. Yet the U-boats were themselves the prey of Allied hunters, in the shape of escort warships and patrol aircraft. U-boat crews suffered probably the highest percentage casualties of any group of combatants in World War II. Some 1,000 U-boats were sunk and roughly two out of every three U-boat crewmen who served in the war lost their lives.

U-boat crews entered the war as a highly trained elite. Admiral Karl Dönitz, who masterminded the U-boat program, insisted that his men had five years training before they went operational, thus instilling a high degree of professionalism and team spirit. The Type VII, the most common U-boat, was crewed by four officers and 40 petty officers and seamen. Some crew members had their own specialities—for example, the personnel who maintained and fired the torpedoes or the radio staff with their Enigma encoding machine. Others performed general duties, such as standing watch or operating the guns.

ON PATROL

The routines of a patrol in the Atlantic were tough and demanding. The U-boat travelled on the surface—submerging was an emergency tactic only. Constant alertness was required to avoid being surprised by enemy aircraft or warships. Watch was kept 24 hours a day by four seamen, each surveying 90 degrees of the horizon, and a watch officer in the conning (or observation) tower. A four-hour watch could be a severe trial in bad weather, as freezing waves swept over the men on the rolling deck. Inside, conditions were cramped and claustrophobic. Some men shared bunks on a shift system. Only the captain had a curtain to give some privacy to his living space. On a patrol that would last weeks or even months, the crew were unable to bath or shave or change their clothes. Deodorant was issued to palliate the effects of enforced uncleanliness in a confined space.

> "A GIANT'S FIST SHOOK THE BOAT. IT SOUNDED LIKE THE DISSOLUTION OF THE UNIVERSE. I WAS CHOKING, THINKING IT WAS THE END."
>
> **WOLFGANG HIRSCHFELD** DESCRIBING A DEPTH-CHARGE ATTACK ON U-109 BY AN AMERICAN DESTROYER IN 1942

Returning to base
A German U-boat arrives at its base in Kiel in November 1939. Most of the crew are on deck, wearing their leather weather-protection gear.

ATTACK AND DEFENSE

In the early years of the war, U-boats attacked merchant convoys on the surface at night, exploiting their good surface speed and low profile to slip through the screen of escort warships and strike at the heart of the convoy. The watch officer on deck relayed targeting instructions to the torpedo crew through a voice tube. Later in the war, as the enemy's radar improved, U-boats were increasingly forced to attack submerged. Naturally, coming under attack themselves was the most nerve-racking experience for a U-boat crew. If spotted by an enemy warship, their best chance was to crash-dive, which took around 30 seconds. They would then hope to avoid detection by sonar or hydrophones, maintaining strict silence as their own hydrophones picked up the sound of an escort vessel drawing close. Being depth-charged was a severe test of the nerves. Even a near miss could cause leaks and other damage requiring all hands to the pumps. Cowering under the sea was such a demoralizing experience that, if attacked by aircraft, U-boat captains often preferred to take their chance on fighting back rather than diving.

Up to 1943, U-boat losses were low and sinkings of merchant ships were common. But times changed. As Allied anti-submarine warfare techniques improved radically, life became hell for the U-boat men. As losses mounted the elite veterans were killed off and new U-boats were rushed into service with hastily trained crews. Late in the war, the introduction of the Type XXI U-boat at last gave the Germans a genuine submarine—a vessel that could patrol at good speed under water for long periods. But it arrived too late and in too small numbers to affect the course of the war.

Matrose service suit
An ordinary seaman, or Matrose, was issued with a blue service suit. When at sea, U-boat crewmen often wore working suits or even informal checked shirts.

Engine room
A U-boat's engine room was a narrow passageway running between two diesel engines. The latter propelled the boat when it was on the surface; when it was underwater, it relied on relatively weak electric motors

1941 – 1945

SOVIET TANK CREWMAN

> “WHEN SHELLS HIT THEIR TARGETS DIRECTLY, TANKS GOING AT HIGH SPEED BLEW UP … TANKMEN GOT OUT OF BURNING TANKS AND ROLLED ON THE GROUND TO EXTINGUISH THE FLAMES.

FROM HITLER'S INVASION of the Soviet Union in June 1941 to the conquest of Berlin in May 1945, the soldiers of the Soviet Red Army fought a titanic struggle against Nazi Germany, enduring the heaviest losses ever seen in the history of warfare; over eight million Soviet soldiers were killed. That this struggle should have ended in victory for the Soviet Union was in large part due to the performance of its tank crews, whose T-34s took on and eventually beat the formidable German panzers.

Adolf Hitler intended his invasion of the Soviet Union to produce a swift and spectacular "blitzkrieg" victory over opponents he despised, both on racial grounds because they were Slavs and on political grounds because they were communists. At first the course of the fighting seemed to fulfill the German dictator's expectation. In a string of military disasters, the poorly led Red Army lost millions of men, killed or taken prisoner, and was driven back to the outskirts of Moscow. But even while inflicting defeat after defeat upon their enemy, the Germans were struck by the extraordinary fighting spirit and almost fatalistic readiness for self-sacrifice exhibited by Soviet troops. This was true not only of the infantry but also of Soviet armored forces, which were decimated by their experienced German opponents. "Crews in burning tanks kept up fire for as long as there was any breath in their bodies," one German officer wrote.

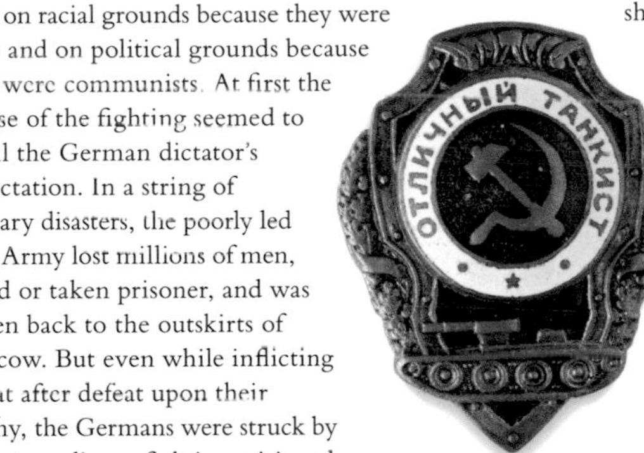

Excellent Tanker badge
This badge was awarded to crewmen who distinguished themselves in battle. A Soviet tank is depicted.

THE T-34 ENTERS THE SCENE

It was in the midst of this military catastrophe that, in fall 1941, the T-34 tank made its first appearance on the battlefield. It was a roughly finished, noisy machine that made no concessions to the comfort of its four-man crew. The driver, seated at the front with the tank's machine-gunner alongside him, could only see directly forward and steered mostly on instructions shouted by the tank commander into an intercom. Sitting with the loader in the turret, the commander himself lacked all-around vision. In combat he aimed the gun with his face pressed to the rubber eye guard of his sight, while the loader fetched the ammunition to his orders. This was no simple task, as most of the rounds were stored in bins under the rubber matting of the turret floor. The scene in the turret was often chaotic, with commander and loader dodging the recoil of the gun while hot shell cases flew into a half-dismantled tangle of shell bins and matting. Inevitably, inexperienced commanders tended to lose all sense of the battlefield situation around them, especially as none of the tanks had radios.

Yet tank crews quickly found much to praise about the T-34. It was a rugged and reliable fighting machine capable of traveling over ice or boggy ground that would stop other tanks dead. It was also quick and nimble: a German tank sergeant commented that "the Russian tanks … will climb a slope or cross a piece of swamp faster than you can traverse the turret."

"To Berlin!"
The goal of the Soviet army's long counter-offensive against Germany is emblazoned on the side of a T-34 tank *(above)*. The T-34, the most effective tank of the war, was armed with an 85mm turret gun *(shells right)* and two 7.62mm DT machine-guns.

85MM TANK SHELLS

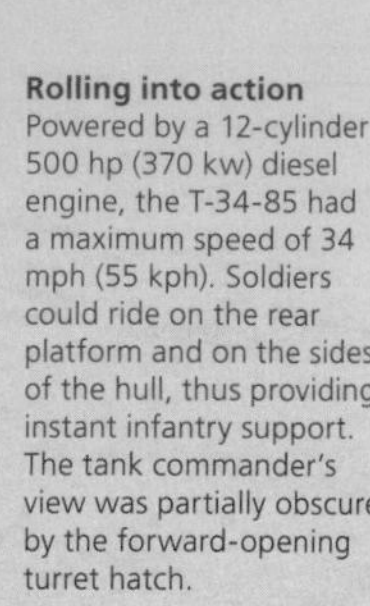

Rolling into action
Powered by a 12-cylinder 500 hp (370 kw) diesel engine, the T-34-85 had a maximum speed of 34 mph (55 kph). Soldiers could ride on the rear platform and on the sides of the hull, thus providing instant infantry support. The tank commander's view was partially obscured by the forward-opening turret hatch.

LEARNING CURVE

The Soviets took a long time to learn how to use their tanks effectively against the German invaders. They typically advanced together in a rigidly drilled formation, groping their way short-sightedly around the battlefield, blundering into German antitank guns and preyed upon by the more flexible panzers, which, in the words of a German tankman, prowled around them "like leopards stalking a herd of bison."

By early 1943, however, the Red Army had sorted out its armored organization and tactics, finding leaders such as General Pavel Rotmistrov, the commander of 5th Guards Tank Army, who knew how to use armor effectively. The Soviet Union also had ever increasing numbers of tanks pouring out of its factories. Although a core of battle-hardened tankmen had developed, survivors of the fearful losses of the previous two years, many of the crew for the expanding tank arm were inevitably hastily trained draftees, who would have to use courage as a substitute for experience. The armored warfare they were to undertake from 1943 to 1945 had little in common with the dashing mobility of the earlier "blitzkrieg" era, when German panzers had hammered effortlessly through infantry lines and raced across country in sweeping encircling maneuvers. Tanks were now to fight in grinding attritional battles that pitted massed armored formations not only against one another, but also against antitank guns, artillery, infantry antitank weapons, tank-busting aircraft, and mines. This was a context in which tanks were powerless without infantry and artillery support, and in which doggedness, perseverance, and sheer numbers were likely to score over flair and initiative.

Soviet victory
Members of a Soviet tank battalion are greeted by people in Lodz, Poland, after the German withdrawal in 1944. A T-34 tank stands in the background.

SHOWDOWN AT KURSK

The largest tank battle of World War II took place at Kursk in July 1943. The Germans assembled around two-thirds of their entire Eastern Front armored forces to the north and south of a bulge, or salient, in the front. They intended to cut the neck of the salient, trapping the Red Army forces inside. Aware of the German plan, the Soviets turned the salient into a fortress defended by minefields, trenches, artillery, and massed armored formations. The Germans launched their offensive on July 5. In the north the panzers were fought to a standstill by Soviet antitank guns and tanks in fixed emplacements. But in the south an armored thrust spearheaded by SS Panzer divisions penetrated to Prokhorovka, 20 miles (30 km) behind the Soviet defensive line.

On July 7, Rotmistrov's 5th Guards Tank Army, in reserve more than 217 miles (350 km) from the fighting, was ordered to advance to Prokhorovka and counterattack. Traveling by day and night in unbearable heat, the massive armored column threw up a cloud of gray dust that coated the crews' sweat-soaked skin and choked their parched throats. In a feat of endurance

УДОСТОВЕРЕНИЕ

ЗА УЧАСТИЕ В ГЕРОИЧЕСКОМ ШТУРМЕ И ВЗЯТИИ БЕРЛИНА

Старший сержант

Жарков

Михаил Герасимович

УКАЗОМ ПРЕЗИДИУМА ВЕРХОВНОГО СОВЕТА СССР от 9 июня 1945 года НАГРАЖДЕН МЕДАЛЬЮ

„ЗА ВЗЯТИЕ БЕРЛИНА"

От имени ПРЕЗИДИУМА ВЕРХОВНОГО СОВЕТА СССР МЕДАЛЬ ВРУЧЕНА

7 ноября 1945 года

Командир 328 артполк

(должность, воинское звание и подпись лица,

М. П. Краснознаменного полка

(Пятов)

Tankman's award
This is the front page of the standard commendation that accompanied a medal presented to a Soviet tankman for his part in the taking of Berlin in 1945.

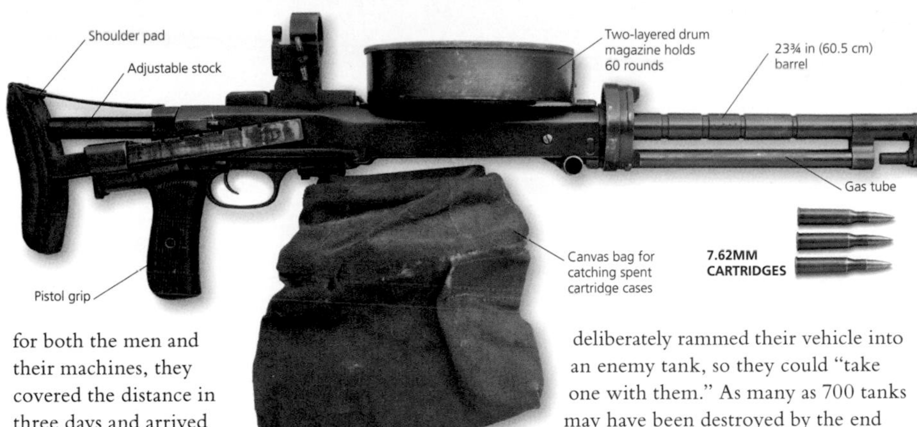

7.62DT machine-gun
The T-34 tank was fitted with two 7.62DT machine guns. One, which was static, used tracer rounds to guide the main turret gun.

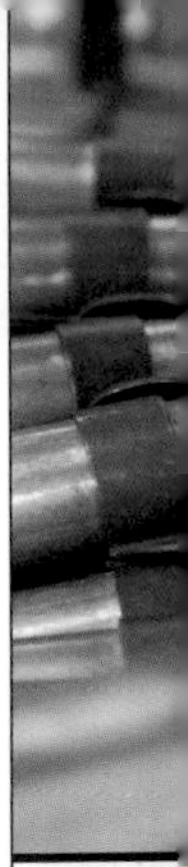

for both the men and their machines, they covered the distance in three days and arrived exhausted but in good order at the battlefield. On the morning of July 11, some 850 Soviet and 600 German tanks advanced to attack one another, clashing in an area measuring around 3 sq miles (7.5 sq km). A German officer described the T-34s as "streaming like rats all over the battlefield." Outgunned by the German Tigers and Panthers, the Soviet tanks aimed to drive close in to their enemies, so their lighter guns would have maximum effect. Soon the tank forces were so intermingled that neither side could use its artillery or ground-attack aircraft. The fighting lasted for eight hours, a colossal armored mêlée conducted amid intermittent thunder storms. The T-34 crews fought without a thought for survival. Tanks that had lost tracks or wheels went on firing until destroyed by enemy shells, exploding in flames, their turrets spinning through the air. When they ran out of ammunition, commanders deliberately rammed their vehicle into an enemy tank, so they could "take one with them." As many as 700 tanks may have been destroyed by the end of the day, more of them Soviet than German. The Soviets could cope with the scale of the losses, however; the Germans could not.

COSTLY VICTORY

The long advance of the Red Army from Kursk in July 1943 to the streets of Berlin in April 1945 was never easy and cost heavy casualties, though far fewer than in the battles of 1941–42. The readiness of the Soviet tank crews, like all other Red Army soldiers, to endure almost unimaginable losses and hardship was in the end the key to their victory. In a sense they were given no choice. Discipline in the Red Army was ferocious, enforced by the Stalinist political police, the NKVD. Any soldier or officer deemed to have shown cowardice or failed to execute orders to the letter would either be shot immediately or placed in a punishment battalion—almost equal to a death sentence, since such battalions were given tasks such as marching across minefields to clear a path for soldiers behind them. Yet there is no question that most Red Army soldiers were genuinely motivated to fight—by patriotism, by hatred of the invaders and their atrocities, and also in some cases by enthusiasm for the Soviet revolution.

> "ONE WOULD THINK WE WERE ON AN ISLAND IN A SEA OF FIRE. IT WAS SENSELESS TO STAY ANY LONGER."
>
> **LIEUTENANT-GENERAL DRAGUNSKY** DESCRIBING THE BATTLE OF KURSK, JULY 8, 1943

Tank column
A column of T-34 tanks moves west during the long offensive that began at Stalingrad, in the Caucasus, and ended in Berlin.

T-34 TANKMAN'S GEAR

The Red Army tankmen fighting the Nazi invaders in what Russians call "the Great Patriotic War" were equipped in solidly utilitarian fashion. They were consistently better supplied with clothing for fighting in freezing weather conditions than were their enemies. From 1943 insignia of rank, which had been abolished in the egalitarian spirit of the Russian Revolution of 1917, were reinstated, taking the traditional Russian form of *pogoni* (shoulder-boards).

NEVER HAVE I RECEIVED SUCH AN OVERWHELMING IMPRESSION OF RUSSIAN STRENGTH AND NUMBERS AS ON THAT DAY.

GERMAN SOLDIER, DESCRIBING THE BATTLEFIELD AT PROKHOROVKA ON JULY 12, 1943

Schuba
This winter sheepskin overcoat, or *schuba*, was issued to Soviet armored crews. It is without insignia, but could be fitted with shoulder boards. Worn instead of the *telogreika*, it is still used by crewmen today.

Tanker's helmet
For reasons of economy, this 1941-model helmet was made of canvas. Its predecessor, of 1939, was made of leather.

Chinstrap

Brass button

Red piping for armored division

Sergeant's stripes

Pogoni (shoulder board)

Leather head strap

Goggles
Made of non-shatterproof glass, Red Army goggles were of a universal model shared by tankers, aircrew, and motorcyclists.

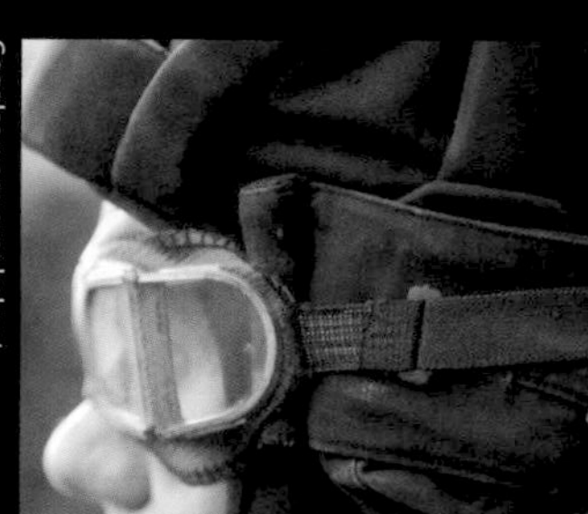

Goggles worn over helmet

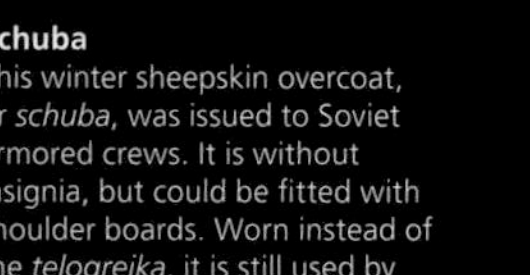

Strap for provisions bag

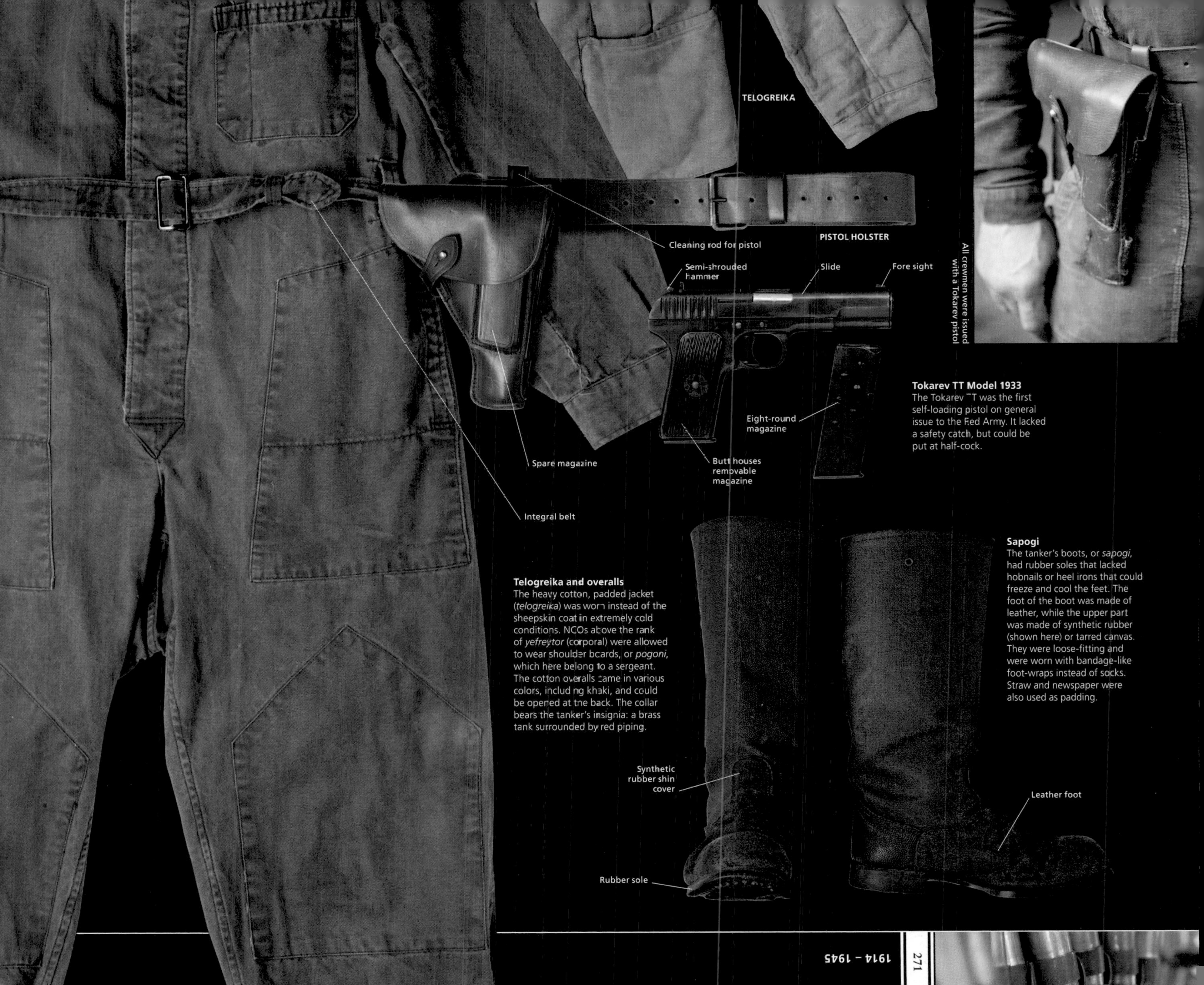

All crewmen were issued with a Tokarev pistol

Tokarev TT Model 1933
The Tokarev TT was the first self-loading pistol on general issue to the Red Army. It lacked a safety catch, but could be put at half-cock.

Telogreika and overalls
The heavy cotton, padded jacket (*telogreika*) was worn instead of the sheepskin coat in extremely cold conditions. NCOs above the rank of *yefreytor* (corporal) were allowed to wear shoulder boards, or *pogoni*, which here belong to a sergeant. The cotton overalls came in various colors, including khaki, and could be opened at the back. The collar bears the tanker's insignia: a brass tank surrounded by red piping.

Sapogi
The tanker's boots, or *sapogi*, had rubber soles that lacked hobnails or heel irons that could freeze and cool the feet. The foot of the boot was made of leather, while the upper part was made of synthetic rubber (shown here) or tarred canvas. They were loose-fitting and were worn with bandage-like foot-wraps instead of socks. Straw and newspaper were also used as padding.

T-34 TANK

The Soviet T-34 is considered by many experts to be the best-designed tank of World War II. Although by the end of the war there were German tanks that outclassed it in firepower and armor, they were heavy, sophisticated machines that could not be produced in such quantities as the relatively straightforward T-34, and never achieved the same ease of operation. Almost 40,000 T-34s were built in the course of the war.

The T-34 was designed by Soviet engineer Mikhail Koshkin, using a suspension developed by the American inventor J. Walter Christie. Entering production in summer 1940, the T-34 initially mounted a 76mm main gun—hence the designation T-34/76. It had a crew of four, with the tank commander doubling as the main gunner. The top speed of 32 mph (51 kph) was impressive for an armored vehicle, while its relatively light weight and wide tracks were excellent for traveling cross-country over mud and snow. In combat, the high-velocity gun proved effective at armor penetration, and the T-34's own sloped armor, at around 4 in (100 mm) thick, offered good protection.

The T-34 was definitely not a glamorous vehicle, but it was hardy, easy to repair, and ideally suited to mass production. In 1944 the up-gunned T-34/85 came into service. As well as mounting an 85mm main gun, it had a turret with space for three men, allowing the functions of gunner and commander to be separated. In this version, the T-34 remained in service with some armies into the 1990s.

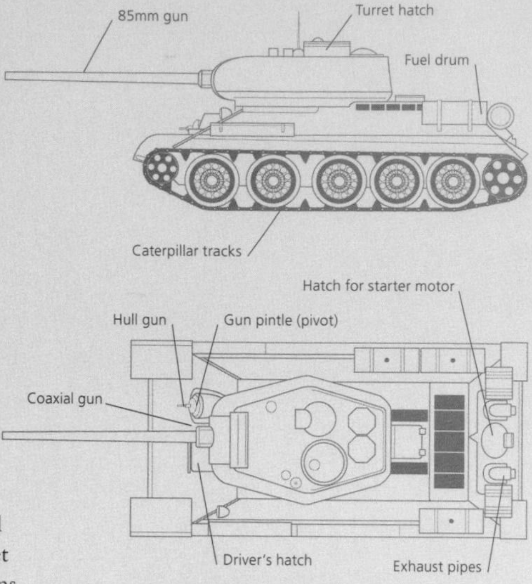

Russian T-34/85
The T-34/85 had a different profile to its predecessor, the T-34/76. Its turret was flatter, making it a more difficult target, and its main gun was longer.

"THE T-34 WAS THE BEST EXAMPLE OF AN OFFENSIVE WEAPON IN WORLD WAR II ... WE HAD NOTHING COMPARABLE."

FRIEDRICH VON MELLENTHIN, GERMAN GENERAL

Gunner in action
The gunner here operates the elevation control on the main gun; the traverse wheel is to his left. He was also responsible for firing the coaxial machine gun alongside the main gun.

Repair kit
A very basic set of tools was kept inside the tank to meet the need for running repairs.

Hull gun
The lower machine gun was mounted on a pintle that gave it a traverse denied to the static, coaxial gun above it. The gunner sighted through a hole above the barrel.

Driver's hatch
The driver could climb into his seat through a small hatch at the front of the hull. The tank was usually driven with the hatch open to give the driver a better view.

Towing rope
This metal eye was at the end of a wire hawser (large rope) running along the side of the tank. It was used for tasks such as hauling disabled vehicles from the battlefield.

Steel wheel
An all-steel wheel and metal track made the T-34 a noisy vehicle, but its suspension gave it good speed.

Driving seat
The driver sat with the hull gunner squeezed in to his right. The interior of the tank was cramped and made no concessions to the crew members' comfort.

Gun sight
While aiming the main gun *(left)* the gunner pressed his head on the rubber guard above the optical sight. He could fire the gun by pulling the red wooden toggle on the right.

Ammo drums
Ammunition for the gunner's coaxial machine gun lay ready to hand *(above)*. The coaxial gun was usually loaded with tracer rounds, often fired as range finders for the main gun.

Troop carrier
Soviet infantrymen ride into battle on the back of a T-34/85. The hole for the tank's coaxial gun can just be seen on the right-hand side of the turret, beside the main gun.

Cleaning can
A can containing cleaning fluid for the gun was kept inside the vehicle.

Loader's seat
The loader sat on a detachable seat that was suspended from the inside of the turret and the gun. It was a precarious perch, since the seat would twist as the gun traversed.

Back view
At the back of the tank, a hatch between the exhaust pipes gave access to the starter motor. The exhausts tended to emit impressive clouds of smoke, especially when starting up.

Extra fuel
Three drums containing spare diesel fuel were carried on the outside of the tank. They obviously constituted a fire hazard, but were usually empty when entering combat.

Spare track
Spare pieces of caterpillar track were carried in case repairs to the running gear were needed. Hooked onto the turret, they also provided extra protection against enemy fire.

OTHER TANKMEN OF WORLD WAR II

In 1940, tanks seemed to be the most glamorous of military vehicles. Nazi propagandists portrayed tankmen as modern-day knights, welding the latest technology to an aggressive warrior ethic. Yet the reality was often closer to the ironic British view of tank crews who "cheerfully went to war in tin cans, closely surrounded by a lethal mixture of petrol and ammunition." Early in the war, tanks promised a revolution in land warfare, allowing decisive victories to be won by shock effect and rapid maneuver. But by the end of 1942 attrition was back. Infantry learned to stand up to armor, while massed tanks fought one another in vast slogging matches. Mass production, rather than dash and flair, became the key to victory in a war that took a heavy toll of tank crews' lives.

US TANK CREWS

In the interwar years, US senior commanders viewed tanks as primarily an infantry support weapon. They were therefore fortunate in being able to watch the success of the German blitzkrieg in 1940 before themselves becoming committed to participation in World War II. The US 1st Armored Division was established in July of that year, and was soon followed by other divisions.

The US possessed an outstanding tank commander in the flamboyant General Patton, who did much to prepare US tank forces for their entry into combat in North Africa in 1942. Inevitably, it took the crews time to accustom themselves to real fighting, but by the time the invasion of Sicily was undertaken in 1943, Patton was able to lead his armor with verve, showing an instinctive understanding of the importance of maintaining the momentum of an attack.

The overwhelming majority of American armored units were equipped with the Sherman tank, which was quick but inadequately armored and was armed with a 75mm gun that could not damage a German Tiger tank from the front. But it had the supreme advantage of quantity through mass production. In the breakout from Normandy in 1944, American tank crews, especially those in Patton's Third Army, showed what they could do, sweeping across France full tilt until supply problems halted their progress. The swift reaction to the German counterattack at the Bulge in winter 1944–45 was another of the finest moments in US armor's notable contribution to the defeat of the Reich.

Fall of Munich
Tanks from General Patton's Third Army advance along the Dachauerstrasse in Munich to occupy the city in May 1945.

BRITISH TANK REGIMENT

The British invented the tank, but by the outbreak of World War II the Royal Tank Regiment had fallen behind the Germans in the development of armored tactics. Britain had large slow tanks for infantry support, light tanks for reconnaissance, and "cruisers" to engage enemy tanks in running battles. Yet none of this worked against German forces in the battle of France in 1940. The 7th Armored Division (the "Desert Rats") overwhelmed the Italians in Libya, but the German Afrika Korps' arrival in 1941 soon put this success in perspective. The defects of British tanks early in the war were many. The Matilda heavy tank's top speed was only 8 mph (13 kph); the Crusader, a cruiser, was fast but thinly armored, under-gunned, and unreliable. Tactically, the British had no answer to the German 88mm antitank guns, which they were often reduced to charging as disastrously as World War I infantry against machine-guns. Later in the war the US-supplied Sherman and the British Cromwell were better— but the Germans called all these tanks "Tommy cookers" due to how often their crews roasted in flames.

Yet the British tankman never lacked grit and resolution. The tank crews drove Rommel out of Africa, slogged their way through Normandy, and had the satisfaction of ending the war in the heart of Germany. The Royal Tank Regiment lived up to its motto, "Fear Naught," and its men wore the regimental black beret with pride.

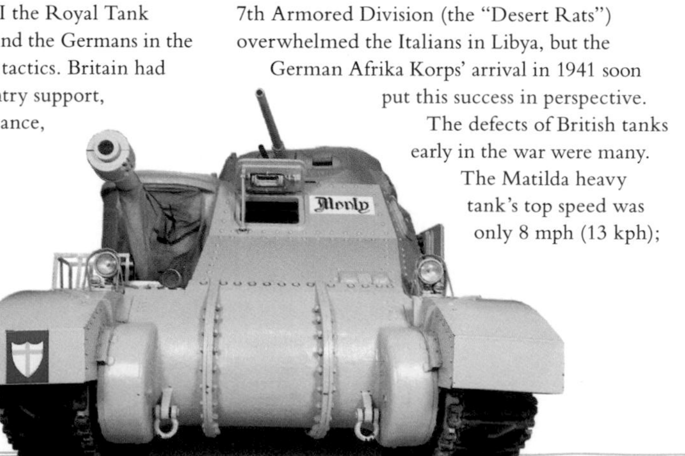

Desert warfare
The British Eighth Army made extensive use of US Grant and Lee tanks in North Africa. This Grant M3A3 was used by General Montgomery for forward observation.

GERMAN PANZER CREWS

The mastermind behind Nazi Germany's panzer divisions was General Heinz Guderian. In the 1930s he evolved the tactical approach that would become known as "blitzkrieg." He envisaged massed tank formations, supported by motorized infantry and artillery, punching through weak points in the enemy defenses and pressing on at speed to exploit the opening in depth. "If the tanks succeed," General Guderian wrote in 1937, "victory follows." Unlike many proponents of armored warfare Guderian won government backing for his plans—Hitler was an enthusiastic believer in the shock effect of maximum force.

BLITZKRIEG AND ATTRITION

In the early years of World War II Germany had fewer armored vehicles than its enemies, and the tanks that it did have were not technologically superior. Germany's tank commanders and crews, however, were unequalled in their skill and initiative. Scything across northern France in the summer of 1940, Guderian's panzers initially produced the lightning victory he had predicted. After Rommel took command of the Afrika Korps in January 1941, he repeatedly outmaneuvered and outfought the British tanks in the desert war. It was the same story in the Soviet Union in 1941–42. Gradually, however, the panzers were overwhelmed on all fronts by the sheer weight of numbers opposing them.

In the later years of the war, the Germans introduced the Tiger and Panther tanks, machines matched only by the Soviet T-34 for the power of their guns and the protection afforded by their armor. In the slogging battles fought in Normandy in July 1944, where speed and maneuverability were negated by hedges and banks, they took a terrible toll on Allied tanks. One Panther is credited with destroying nine Shermans in a day. But on the Eastern Front these sophisticated machines, supplied in too small numbers and with an alarming tendency to break down, had no chance of reversing the tide of defeat. Unlike the Luftwaffe, the German panzers never suffered a degradation in the quality of personnel. Fighting without air cover and short of fuel, they often outfought their opponents to the bitter end.

Panzer driver's uniform
Panzer crewmen wore short, close-fitting jackets suitable for the cramped conditions inside a tank. Panzer crews who were members of the Waffen SS (the combat arm of the SS) carried SS victory runes on their uniforms as well as rank and divisional markings.

> "THE ENGINE OF THE PANZER IS A WEAPON JUST AS THE MAIN GUN."
>
> **GENERAL HEINZ GUDERIAN**

1942 – 1945

US BOMBER CREWMAN

AS Y[illegible]U [illegible]ET CL[illegible]ER T[illegible] THE TAR[illegible]ET Y[illegible]UR HEAR[illegible]

B-17 bomber crew
The crew of a B-17 bomber returns to its base in England after a bombing raid over Germany *(above)*. Each crew member was issued with an inflatable life vest *(right)* in the event of being downed at sea; pulling the cords released carbon dioxide into the jacket's inner tubing.

THE US BOMBER CREWS who flew B-17 Flying Fortresses and B-24 Liberators on daylight missions over Germany and Occupied Europe suffered some of the highest combat losses of any US forces in World War II. Flying daylight missions, initially without fighter escorts, they were vulnerable to anti-aircraft fire and to attack from German fighter aircraft. In order to hit their assigned targets deep inside hostile territory, the bomber formations had to "shoot their way in and shoot their way out again."

All US Army Air Force fliers had volunteered for service in the air. Mostly in their late teens or early 20s, they came from every part of the US and every occupational background, from stockbrokers to farmhands—although virtually all were white, as a consequence of the determination of senior air force commanders to keep blacks out of aerial combat. Bomber crews received extensive training at American bases before being sent abroad to fight. A B-17 crew had four officers—a pilot (the senior-ranking officer, often a captain), who was the flight commander, a co-pilot, a bombardier, and a navigator. It also had six NCOs, namely a radio operator, a flight engineer, two waist gunners, a tail gunner, and a ball-turret gunner. Each officer or enlisted man was taught the specialized skills corresponding to his role in the aircraft. The pilots, in particular, had to master flying in close formation, which led to quite a few fatal training accidents. A crew might have around 360 flying hours under its belt before completing training, but nothing could prepare them adequately for what they faced when they arrived in the European theater.

STRATEGIC BOMBING

The USAAF mounted its strategic bombing campaign from bases in England, North Africa, and, later, Italy. Air force commanders believed that their fast, heavily armed bombers could carry out precision raids on targets such as factories or sources of fuel supplies. The bombers would attack in daylight, flying at high altitude in mass formation. In theory, a combination of speed, altitude, and overwhelming firepower would ensure their survival—and use of the new, sophisticated Norden bombsight would allow their bombardiers to deliver the payload on the target.

THEORY AND PRACTICE

But combat did not work out as planned. Accurate bombing proved an elusive ideal. The weather in Europe was completely different than the clear blue skies of the southern or western United States where the bomber crews had trained. Targets were liable to be obscured by cloud, and, in any case, under combat conditions few bombardiers were capable of operating their complex bombsights successfully. The Americans soon opted for a system in which only the lead bomber in the formation used the bombsight; the rest dropped their bombs when the leader did. Worse than the lack of accuracy was the problem of survival. Losses in the first phase of the bombing campaign in 1943 were staggering. When 376 B-17s raided factories at Schweinfurt and Regensburg on August 17, 1943, for instance, 60 bombers were shot down and another 11 so badly damaged they had to be written off.

For crews at a US air base in eastern England in 1943, the day of a combat mission started early. Woken at around 3 a.m. by an operations officer snapping on the lights in the crowded hut where they slept, they would stumble through the darkness to a briefing room, where the day's mission was outlined.

US ARMY AIR FORCE LIFE JACKET

Strategic bombing
A group of B-17s from the 398th Bombardment Group fly a bombing run to Neumunster, Germany, on April 8, 1945. By that stage of the war, Luftwaffe fighters had ceased to pose a serious threat to the Flying Fortresses.

> “THE TERROR STARTS ON THE NIGHT BEFORE THE MISSION ... ANXIETY, DREAMS ... EXCUSES NOT TO FLY ... LOOSE BOWELS, SHAKING AND SILENCE.”
>
> **HOWARD JACKSON**, BOMBARDIER, USAAF 15TH AIR FORCE

A chorus of groans and curses greeted the announcement of a target deep inside Germany. While ground crews prepared the aircraft, the airmen tucked into breakfast, if they had the stomach for it. Take-off was usually at around dawn, the B-17s lifting off at 30-second intervals, using the full length of the runway burdened with a maximum load of bombs and fuel. The bombers then had to climb to the assembly point and take their place in the formation (no simple matter) before heading towards the coast of Occupied Europe. The tail gunners and ball-turret gunner did not occupy their positions until after take-off. The ball-turret gunner had the most unenviable post in the aircraft. Squashed into a fetal position underneath the belly, he did not even have room to wear a parachute. But no one had a comfortable flight.

Traveling in an unpressurized aircraft at 25,000 ft (7,600 m), men were exposed to temperatures as low as -49°F. Survival on flights lasting many hours depended on wearing oxygen masks and electrically heated flying suits. There were casualties from frostbite and deaths when the oxygen supply failed.

Once they traveled beyond the range of their fighter escorts, the bombers came under attack from swarms of Messerschmitts and Focke-Wulfs flown by Luftwaffe pilots. One advantage of flying in tight formation was that the enemy fighters were exposed to the collective fire of the entire formation's gun turrets—however, it also meant that when under fire themselves, pilots were unable to take evasive action.

Boredom and discomfort were instantly replaced by fear and adrenaline-soaked excitement as the gunners strove to hit their fast-moving adversaries. Many would forget their training, opening fire at too long a range, or failing to use their sights correctly. The waist and top turret gunners would soon be standing in heaps of spent cartridge cases. Some German fighters attacked from directly ahead, where the bomber's only defense consisted of hand-held guns operated by the bombardier and navigator. B-17s began to fall from the sky in flames with parachutes blossoming as airmen jumped for their lives. Approaching the target through heavy flak was the most nerve-racking part of the entire mission. In the lead aircraft of the formation the bombardier took control of the aircraft, using his Norden bomb-sight linked to an autopilot.

Flak helmet
This steel flak helmet was worn to protect against enemy fire. It had a special coating that prevented the crewman's fingers freezing to the metal at high altitude.

The whole formation had to fly straight and steady for the bomb run, making a perfect target for the German anti-aircraft gunners below. When the B-17 lurched upward as the bombs were released, every member of the crew would feel a surge of relief. But getting home was, of course, not necessarily any easier than the outward journey. The pilot was often nursing a damaged aircraft with wounded or dead personnel on board. As survivors landed back at base around mid-afternoon, losses were tallied and the wounded carried off for treatment.

COPING AND SURVIVAL

A bomber crew's standard tour of duty initially consisted of 25 combat missions, although this was subsequently increased to 35. The received wisdom was that a man had a one in three chance of surviving his tour. In some unfortunate formations, though, the odds were far worse. One squadron flying out of East Anglia in 1943 had lost seven of its nine original crews by the

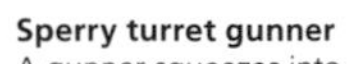

Sperry turret gunner
A gunner squeezes into the ball turret under the belly of a B-17E, watched by fellow crew members. The gunner never entered his position before take-off, instead climbing down into the turret from inside the aircraft once in the air.

Gunner and bombardier
Bombardier Lt. William Witt sits in the nose of a B-17 returning from a mission over Germany. As well as his vital role in guiding the aircraft on its bomb run, the bombardier operated the chin gun against enemy fighters making head-on attacks.

end of 25 missions. The tension experienced by men approaching their last one or two missions was almost unbearable. Superstition flourished, men putting their faith in a treasured love letter or a lucky coin always carried with them into combat. All traces of the dead were eradicated immediately, the accepted opinion being that they were best never mentioned and treated as if they had never existed. While the ground crew remained the same month after month, air personnel changed all the time as new recruits replaced those who had failed to return. For most fliers, the bomber crew they belonged to was their major source of support and comradeship.

WINNING THROUGH

Although the strategic bombing campaign was never easy, things did improve over the course of the war. The introduction of the chin gun on B-17s, in the second half of 1943, helped to stem the losses incurred by frontal attacks. From the start of 1944, long-range escort fighters, especially the P-51 Mustang, transformed daylight bombing missions. Capable of accompanying the bomber formations to targets deep inside Germany, they imposed unsustainable losses on German fighters. In the final year of the war, German industrial production, communications, and, above all, fuel supplies were crippled by the Allied bombing campaign. But success was achieved at a heavy cost. Eighth Air Force, which operated out of England from 1942 to 1945, had one in eight of its 210,000 airmen killed; its total losses, including those wounded and taken prisoner after bailing out, were 53,000, more than one in four of its airmen. Ninth Air Force (which transferred from Italy to England in 1944) and Fifteenth Air Force also suffered heavy casualties. The men who flew in the face of such severe punishment showed outstanding courage and commitment.

COMBAT BOX FORMATION

A typical B-17 formation was based on a group of three squadrons, each consisting of six or seven bombers. The "lead" squadron flew with a "high" squadron above and to its right, and a "low" squadron below and to its left. All the aircraft were at different altitudes to allow their gunners a free field of fire. Three groups combined to make a "wing" of 54-plus aircraft, the groups also arranged as "lead," "high," and "low." It was impossible to avoid problems at the trailing edges of this "combat box," where the rear units would be relatively exposed to attack by enemy fighters. A group of three squadrons is shown below.

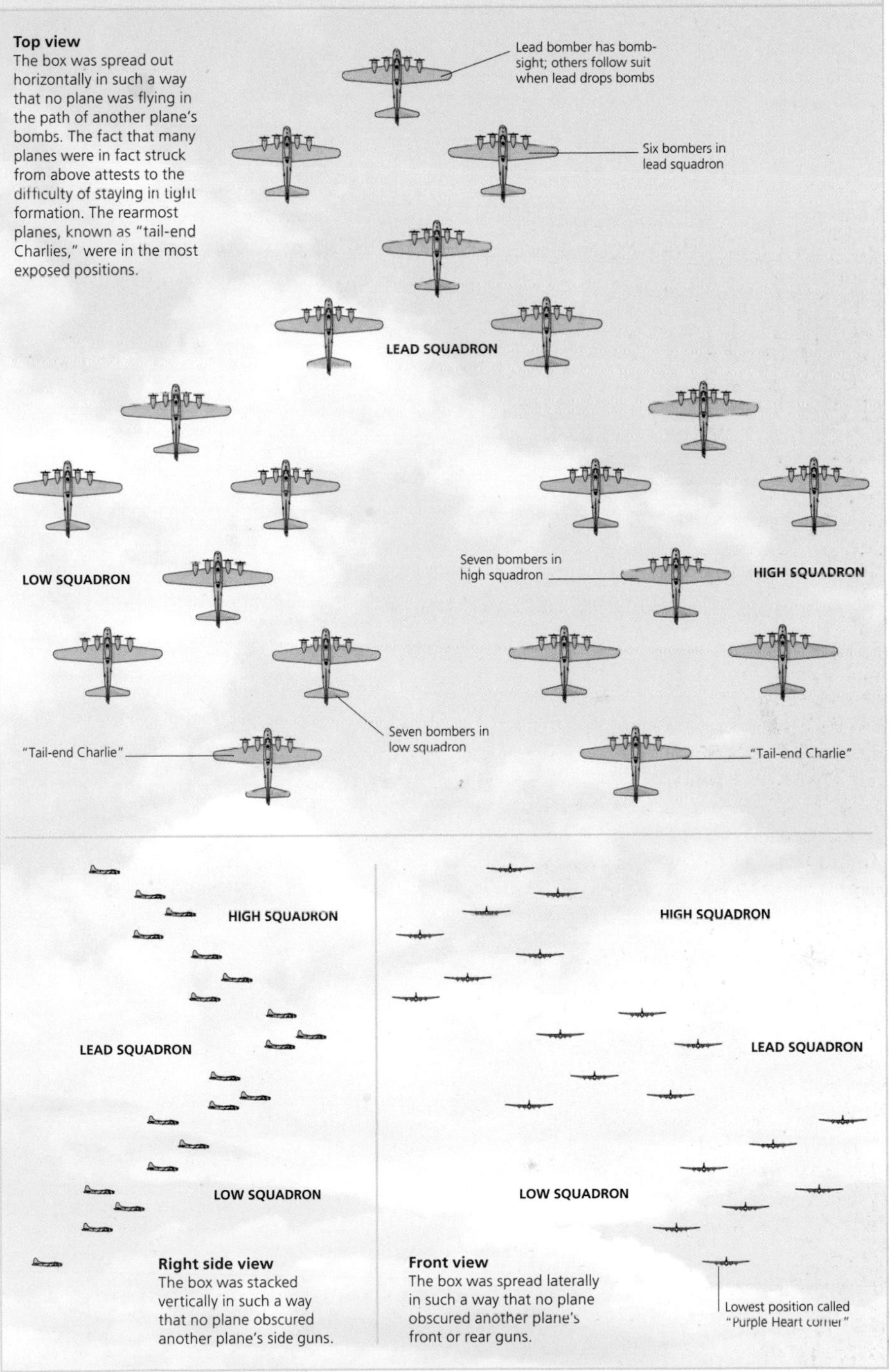

Top view
The box was spread out horizontally in such a way that no plane was flying in the path of another plane's bombs. The fact that many planes were in fact struck from above attests to the difficulty of staying in tight formation. The rearmost planes, known as "tail-end Charlies," were in the most exposed positions.

Lead bomber has bomb-sight; others follow suit when lead drops bombs
Six bombers in lead squadron
LEAD SQUADRON
LOW SQUADRON
Seven bombers in high squadron
HIGH SQUADRON
Seven bombers in low squadron
"Tail-end Charlie"
"Tail-end Charlie"

HIGH SQUADRON
LEAD SQUADRON
LOW SQUADRON

Right side view
The box was stacked vertically in such a way that no plane obscured another plane's side guns.

HIGH SQUADRON
LEAD SQUADRON
LOW SQUADRON

Front view
The box was spread laterally in such a way that no plane obscured another plane's front or rear guns.

Lowest position called "Purple Heart corner"

B-17 CREW UNIFORM

Bomber crews were fitted out to survive the rigors of high-altitude operations. Clothing had to keep the men warm when temperatures inside the aircraft could drop well below zero. Electrically heated suits were introduced as an alternative to thick clothing, but crew tended to favor leather and fleece regardless. In the thin upper air, an artificial oxygen supply was essential—if it failed a man would lose consciousness in minutes. The crew also had to be prepared for bailing out at any time.

B10 flying jacket

Flying jacket
The B10 flying jacket was made of tightly woven cotton lined with alpaca. It featured a fur collar and knitted wrists and waistband for body warmth retention. It was initially introduced in 1943 and became a template for flying jacket designs. The D1 jacket was of an earlier design, but saw service up until the Korean War.

D1 flying jacket

A11 helmet
The A11 helmet was standard for all aircrews and had integral earphones and snaps to cover the A14 oxygen mask. The B8 goggles had a chamois lining for extra comfort in the cold, and came with clear, amber, red, or green lenses to cope with various light conditions.

B8 goggles

A14 oxygen mask

Hose connects to oxygen tank

Fastening oxygen mask to helmet

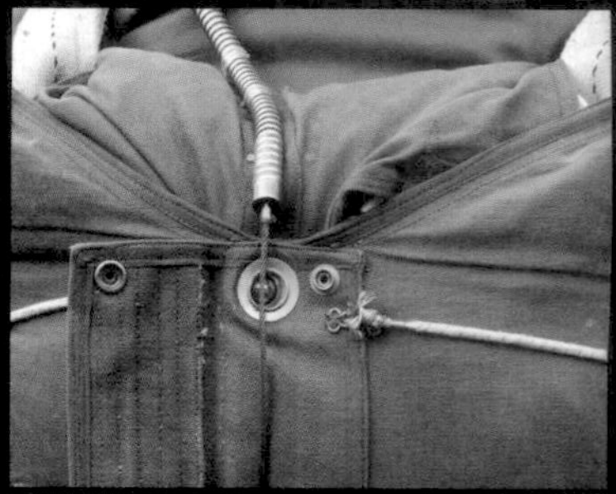

Rip cord at back of parachute

Front of harness, with rip cord to right

Armored front of vest

braces

Fastening harness to waist

A10 gloves
For ease of movement, gunners preferred gloves to thick, padded mittens. Rayon inserts were supplied for greater warmth.

A3 trousers
The A3 trousers were made of shearling sheepskin oversprayed with an acrylic lacquer.

B8 backpack parachute
The B8 parachute deployed manually via a rip cord attached to the front of the harness. When bailing out at high altitude a man had to use an emergency oxygen bottle to avoid blacking out on the way down.

Shoulder strap

Rip cord

Fastened back of parachute

M3 flak vest
Made of olive-green cotton duck canvas, the M3 flak vest was armored on the front only. It was used by crewmen whose seats had armored backs, like the pilots and the ball-turret gunner.

SERVICE SHOES

Footwear
Flying boots were designed to be worn over regular service shoes, which were essential if a crewman bailed out over difficult terrain. The A6 flying boot had an improved tread and a zipper instead of buckles.

A6 FLYING BOOTS

B-17 BOMBER

When the Boeing B-17 bomber first flew as the Model 299 prototype on July 28, 1935, it was immediately dubbed "the Flying Fortress" by journalists, a nickname that stuck. The B-17 belonged to a new generation of all-metal monoplane aircraft with enclosed cockpits. Large and fast by the standards of its time, the four-engined bomber became a mainstay of America's strategic bombing force of World War II.

The B-17 went through radical modifications between the prototype stage and the entry of the US into World War II. The first mass-produced version, the B-17E, emerged in September 1941, and B-17Fs and B-17Gs were introduced in 1942. Around two-thirds of all B-17s built were the G version. The B-17G had up to 13 machine guns (hence its nickname), and its maximum speed was 287 mph (462 kph) at 25,000 ft (7,600 m), although the normal operational speed flying in mass formation was a more modest 180 mph (290 kph).

On a short-range flight the aircraft could lift a 17,600 lb (7,983 kg) bomb load, but the need to carry large amounts of fuel for long-range sorties meant that in practice the payload was typically between 4,000 and 6,000 lb (1,814 and 2,724 kg). The B-17 was never a comfortable aircraft to fly in, but it was popular with its ten-man crews because of its legendary ability to survive heavy punishment. Nonetheless, losses were severe; around 4,750 B-17s were lost on combat missions in the course of the war, more than a third of the total of 12,761 built.

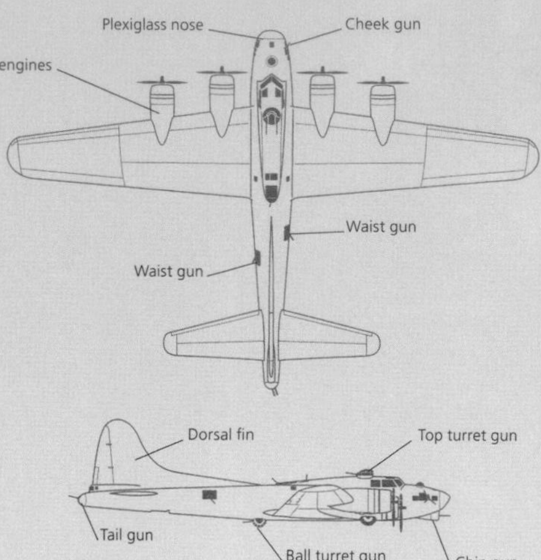

Bomber profile
The B-17 had a wingspan of 103 ft 9 in (31.62 m) and measured 74 ft 9 in (22.78 m) from nose to tail. The massive dorsal fin gives it its distinctive profile.

> WE LIVED, SLEPT, ATE, WORKED, AND PLAYED TOGETHER. WE WOULD SHARE OUR LIVES UNTIL DEATH OR THE WAR'S END.
>
> **LIEUTENANT ROLAND PEPIN**, B-17 NAVIGATOR

Flying boots
Aircrew wore sheepskin-lined rubber-soled boots to keep their feet warm at high altitude. They also had electrically-heated flying suits that they could plug in on board the aircraft.

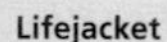

Lifejacket
A "Mae West" inflatable jacket was among the array of life-saving equipment provided for aircrew.

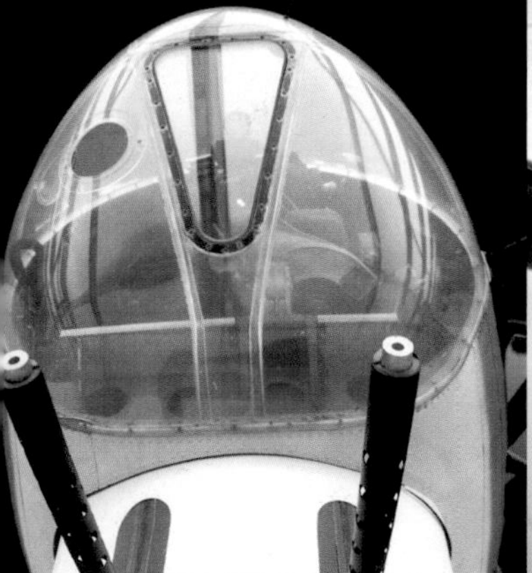

Aircraft nose
The Plexiglass nose of the B-17 provided a view for the bombardier, who guided the aircraft to its target.

Chin gun
This is one of the remote-controlled chin guns operated by the bombardier. They were introduced to counter head-on attacks.

Radial engine
Each of the B-17's four engines generated 1,200 hp. They were fitted with turbo-superchargers to improve performance at high altitude.

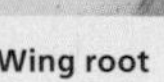

Wing root
The B-17 was mass produced and so construction methods were kept as simple as possible. Riveted aluminum sheets were a major component.

Top turret
Operated by the flight engineer, the hydraulically powered top gun turret could sweep the sky in a full circle.

Machine-gun
The B-17 was equipped with 0.5in Browning machine guns, a ubiquitous American weapon of World War II. Here it is mounted in the waist window.

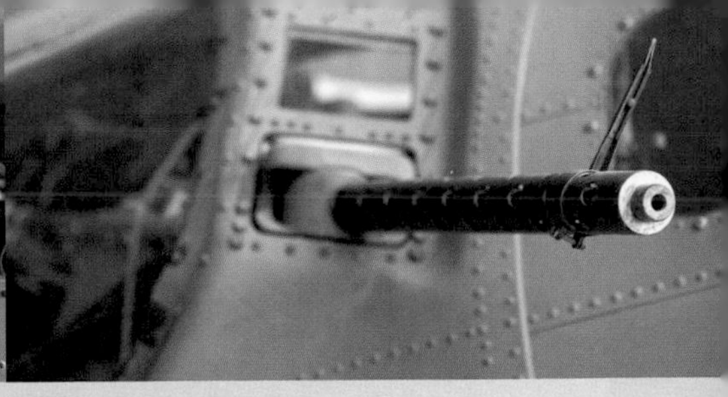

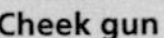

Cheek gun
This 0.5in Browning is one of the flexible cheek guns that were sometimes mounted on each side of the Plexiglass nose. It was operated by the navigator.

Constant manufacture
A B-17 flies over Europe in 1945. For every one of the aircraft shot down by the Germans during the war, two more were produced by US factories. For this reason there were more B-17s in service during the last months of the war than at any time previously.

Strong wheels
Hydraulic suspension helped the undercarriage take the strain of operational flying.

Sperry ball turret
The Sperry ball turret could swivel 360 degrees horizontally and 90 degrees vertically. It was suspended on a gimbal from a tube attached to the fuselage ceiling.

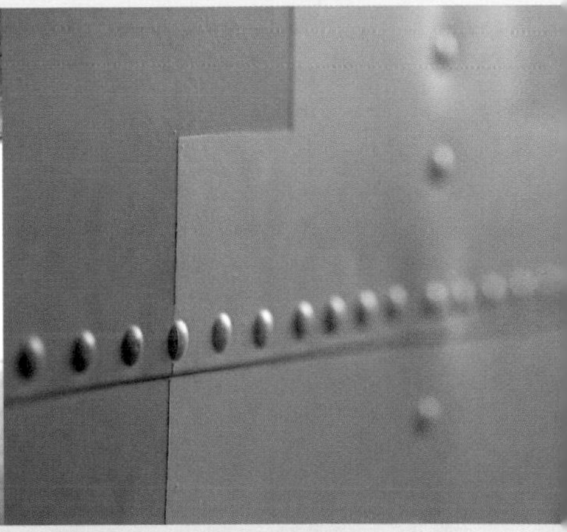

Aluminum skin
The fuselage was made of aluminum alloy rings fastened with longitudinal aluminum strips and covered with an aluminum skin.

INSIDE THE B-17

Packed with bombs and fuel, the B-17 had limited space for its crew. The bombardier and navigator had to crouch to reach their seats in the nose of the plane, although once there they enjoyed a superb view. The pilot and copilot sat on the flight deck, with the flight engineer above and behind them. The radio operator's room, separated from the flight deck by the bomb bay, was the only place where a man could stand fully upright. The ball-turret gunner occupied a notoriously cramped seat under the fuselage and the tail gunner had to crawl into his remote position.

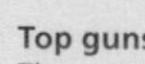

Top guns
The gun positions on the top of the B-17's fuselage were manned in combat by the radio operator and the flight engineer.

Manual controls
The controls of a B-17 were complex enough to require the collaboration of pilot and copilot if the aircraft was to be flown with any ease.

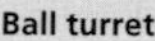

Norden bomb-sight
The Norden bomb-sight was installed behind the Plexiglass nose of the aircraft, in front of the bombardier's seat. Top-secret devices, the bomb-sights were removed from the aircraft between missions and kept under guard.

Parachute log
This log was used for recording each time the parachute was packed, used, and repaired.

Ball turret
The ball-turret gunner climbed into his cramped position after takeoff. He had to sit with his knees drawn up to his chest and could not wear a parachute; he donned one rapidly in an emergency.

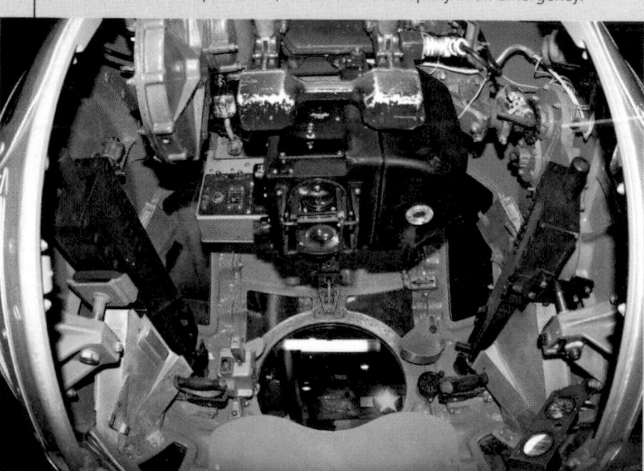

Bomb bay
The bomb bay, immediately behind the flight deck, had a walkway only some 8 in (20 cm) wide. The bombers typically carried some 6,000 lb (2,700 kg) of bombs, a mix of high explosive and incendiary munitions.

Oxygen regulator
Each crew member had an oxygen hose at his position. If he needed to move around in the aircraft, he grabbed a walk-around oxygen bottle.

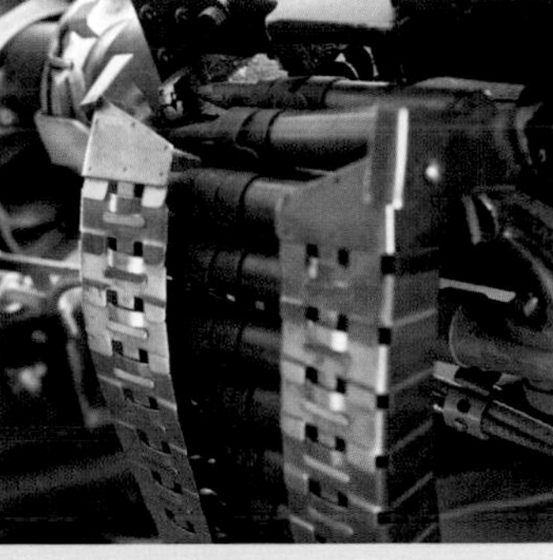

Sight and ammunition
The waist guns had sophisticated sights to aid the gunner. In theory, a gunner could use up an ammunition belt in half a minute, although in practice he naturally fired much shorter bursts.

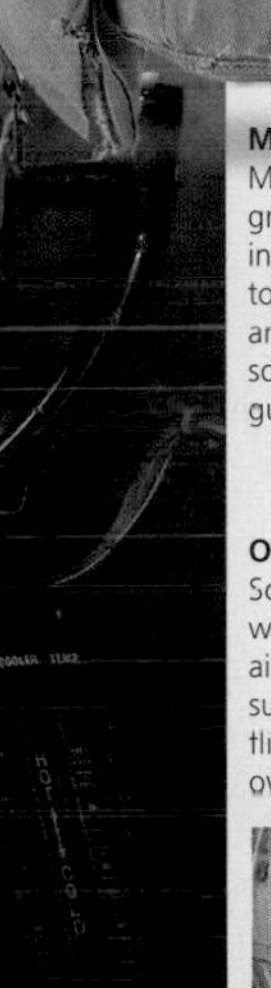

M4 flak helmet
Made of steel covered with green cloth, this was issued in late 1943. It was designed to be worn with headphones and had been slimmed down so it could be worn by gunners in their turrets.

Oxygen bottles
Some 18 bottles of oxygen were carried on board the aircraft. They were essential supplies since operational flights were made at altitudes over 25,000 ft (7,600 m).

Waist gun
The waist gunners, between the radio operator's position and the tail gun, fired out of each side of the aircraft, exposed to the freezing air. Spent shell cases covered the floor of the aircraft once the gun was in use.

Tail turret
The rear gunner knelt in his position on padded knee-holds. Since attack from behind was the obvious tactic for fighter aircraft, these hydraulically-controlled twin guns were crucial to the bomber's defense.

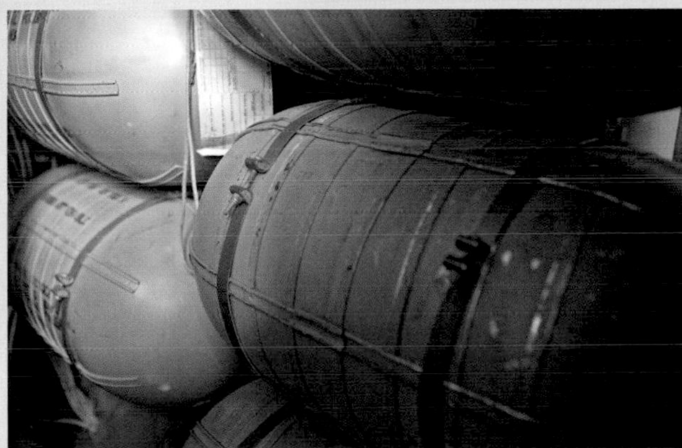

Flight deck
The pilot and copilot sat on each side of the control yokes, the pilot on the left-hand side, and the copilot on the right. The cockpit afforded excellent visibility.

Elevator wires
Control cables ran along the ceiling from the cockpit to the tail and wings of the aircraft to manipulate the rudder and wing flaps.

Fuselage interior
This is the view forward along the fuselage toward the radio operator's position, and, beyond that, the bomb bay. The aluminum rings of which the fuselage structure was made are visible. The black column supports the ball turret beneath the fuselage.

B-17 waist gunners
The B-17 Flying Fortress was armed with up to thirteen 0.50in Browning machine guns. The waist gunners, photographed here in England in 1943, were non-commissioned officers with specialist training in gunnery. Bombers were also launched from North Africa and Italy.

WORLD WAR II FIGHTER PILOTS

Being a fighter pilot was the most glamorous job in World War II. Young men in all combatant countries competed for a chance to fly the most advanced fighter aircraft in the world. Those few individuals who possessed the ideal combination of fast reaction times, sharp eyesight, and a killer instinct were able to have an exceptional impact on the air war. It has been estimated that the top five percent of pilots were responsible for 40 percent of kills. For this reason, the balance of air combat would turn decisively against any country that was forced by heavy losses to field too many inexperienced pilots. This is what happened to both the Germans and the Japanese in the later stages of the war—a blow from which neither country recovered.

US ESCORT FIGHTER PILOTS

The United States' B-17 and B-24 bombers were designed to attack in daylight without fighter escorts, and their speed, altitude, and firepower would supposedly make them immune to enemy fighters. But heavy losses in 1942–43 proved they needed fighter cover. At the outset, American fighter groups in Europe mostly flew Spitfires, which had inadequate range, or P-38 Lightnings, which had poor maneuvrability. The Republic P-47 Thunderbolt was an improvement, but still it could not accompany bombers all the way into the heart of German territory. It was the arrival of the North American P-51 Mustang in early 1944 that transformed the situation. The Mustang could outperform any existing German fighter—its top speed was an impressive 435 mph (700 kph)—and with drop tanks it could fly anywhere that the bombers could reach.

US escort fighter pilots had the quality to match their machine. By 1944 many had lengthy combat experience, but intensive training sessions were still run to keep everyone at their peak. Some of America's most famous pilots flew escort in Mustangs, including future sound-barrier breaker Chuck Yeager, who shot down five German aircraft in a single day in October 1944. Like the bombers, the fighter groups flew mostly from bases in England and Italy. There was competition between different groups to be the safest for bombers to fly with. Especially keen was 332nd Fighter Group, all of whose pilots were black. These "Tuskegee airmen" had struggled long and hard against racial prejudice for the right to fly fighters in combat and they had plenty to prove. Escorting bombers against the toughest targets, including Berlin and the Ploesti oilfields, they claimed, perhaps with slight exaggeration, never to have lost a bomber under their protection. The Luftwaffe fighters adapted their tactics to meet the challenge of the Mustang. They hit the bombers with rapid mass attacks, hoping to disappear before the escort fighters could react. They also introduced the Me 262, the first jet fighter to enter combat, which was 100 mph (160 kph) faster than the Mustang. But nothing availed to stem their losses, especially after the Americans began roving away from the bomber streams to hunt down Luftwaffe fighters and attack their bases. By the end of the war, Mustang-equipped fighter groups had shot down some 5,000 German fighters, and destroyed over 4,000 on the ground.

P-51 Mustang
The Mustang is widely regarded as the supreme fighter aircraft of World War II. It combined an American airframe with a British Rolls Royce Merlin engine.

Tuskegee airmen
The black pilots of the 332nd Fighter Group, trained at Tuskegee Institute in Alabama, became African-American heroes.

GERMAN FIGHTER PILOTS

In the early years of World War II, German fighter pilots were superior to their opponents in training, tactics, and combat experience. The Luftwaffe operated as a meritocracy with an anti-authoritarian ethos. Status was based on flying experience and combat record (those who had served in the Condor Legion during the Spanish Civil War, for example, expected to be treated as a privileged elite), and "score chasing" was encouraged. As the war developed, however, the Luftwaffe's position radically changed. The fighter pilots who had flown as bomber escorts over England in the Battle of Britain were split between homeland defense against Allied bomber fleets and air support for the army fighting the Soviet Union on the Eastern Front. Although the home defense units performed magnificently in both day and night fighting, they were subject to steady attrition that turned into massive losses once the US long-range fighter escorts appeared over Germany. On the Eastern Front losses were even heavier, although German pilots ran up vast kill-tallies against the massed Soviet aviation—Erich Hartmann shot down 352 aircraft, making him the highest-scoring air ace in history. By the winter of 1944 the Luftwaffe was short of fuel and of experienced pilots. Many of the surviving fighter aces, such as Adolf Galland, ended up flying experimental Messerschmitt Me 262 jets as interceptors in a last-ditch air defense of Germany against overwhelming Allied numbers. By then there was nothing left to fight for but honor.

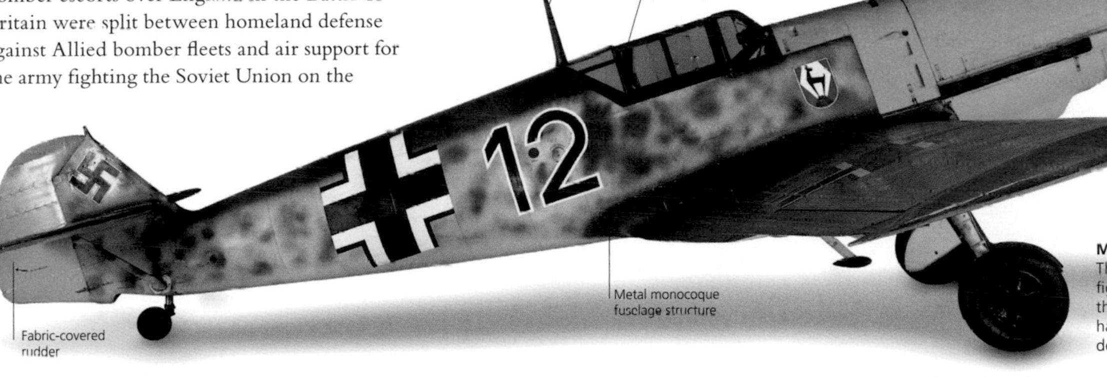

Messerschmitt Bf109D
The Bf109 was the Luftwaffe's key fighter aircraft in the early years of the war. However, it was tricky to handle in landing and take-off, a defect that killed many pilots.

JAPANESE NAVAL PILOTS

The Japanese pilots who caused devastation at the US naval base at Pearl Harbor, Hawaii, in December 1941, were part of the finest naval air force in the world. Not only were their aircraft, such as the Mitsubishi Reisen "Zero" fighter, of the highest quality, but the pilots themselves were superbly trained and battle-hardened, having fought in Japan's war against China since 1937.

Japanese naval aviators continued to hold their own against the US in the Pacific War in 1942 and 1943, but the number of experienced pilots fell sharply through battle casualties, while the performance of US pilots and their aircraft steadily improved. In the battle of the Philippine Sea in June 1944, the Japanese lost 300 aircraft in a single day and the entire Japanese carrier fleet was destroyed, leaving naval aviators to operate from shore. During the battle of Leyte Gulf in October 1944, the First Air Fleet, based on the Philippines, initiated suicide tactics. Kamikaze ("Divine Wind") pilots, as the Americans called them, packed their aircraft with explosives and tried to crash on the decks of US warships. They donned a *hachimaki* headband once worn by the samurai, a sign of their supposed status as elite warriors. But since the lives of experienced pilots were precious, the kamikaze role soon in practice devolved to barely trained youngsters. By April 1945, a mass "special attack" force of over 2,000 aircraft dedicated to suicide attacks had been formed. In total, kamikaze raids sank 34 warships and damaged 288 by the war's end.

Kamikaze attack
A Japanese Zero fighter crashes onto the deck of the USS *Missouri* during the wave of suicide attacks launched against the Allied fleet in 1944–45.

> "MAY OUR DEATH BE AS SUDDEN AND CLEAN AS THE SHATTERING OF CRYSTAL."
>
> **KAMIKAZE PILOT** WRITING BEFORE HIS MISSION

1940 – 1945

SOE AGENT

A NEW ORGANIZATION TO COORDINATE, INSPIRE, CONTROL, AND ASSIST THE NATIONALS OF THE OPPRESSED COUNTRIES ... WE NEED ABSOLUTE SECRECY, A CERTAIN FANATICAL ENTHUSIASM ... COMPLETE POLITICAL RELIABILITY.

Sabotage specialists
The SOE mounted one of its most successful sabotage operations in Nazi-occupied Norway. Norwegian commandos *(above)* were flown in to attack the Norsk Hydro plant at Rjukan, which was producing heavy water that could have been used by the Germans in the manufacture of nuclear bombs. The Webley & Scott 1907 automatic pistol *(right)* was favored by SOE personnel in many such operations.

BASED IN LONDON DURING World War II, the Special Operations Executive (SOE) sent secret agents into Nazi-occupied Europe to support and organize resistance groups, gather intelligence, and carry out sabotage and assassination missions. It was desperately dangerous work and many agents fell into the hands of the SS or the Gestapo. SOE ended the war with some notable successes to its credit, even if it never quite achieved the ambitious goal fixed by Prime Minister Winston Churchill, to "set Europe ablaze."

The Special Operations Executive was set up in July 1940, as an expression of Churchill's determination to take the fight to the enemy even under the most unfavorable circumstances. The defeat of the British and French armies had left Germany and its allies with undisputed military dominance of continental Europe. The British government envisaged nothing less than a continent-wide revolutionary uprising against the Nazis and pro-Nazi regimes. The Minister of Economic Warfare, Dr. Hugh Dalton, in whose political domain SOE was placed, foresaw the creation of movements similar to Northern Ireland's Sinn Fein or Mao Ze Dong's Chinese guerrillas and the fostering of "industrial and military sabotage, labour agitation and strikes, continuous propaganda, terrorist acts against traitors and German leaders, boycotts and riots" to thwart Hitler's menace.

RECRUITMENT AND TRAINING

SOE senior staff were recruited in typically British fashion via personal contacts—the "Old Boy" network of former pupils of the top public schools and graduates of Oxford and Cambridge Universities. This does not mean that they were unsuitable or incompetent, although they were sometimes criticized by the more established intelligence services. Colonel Colin Gubbins, for instance, put in charge of SOE training and operations, was an energetic man who had thought in depth about the tactics and strategy of irregular warfare. The organization set up its headquarters at 64 Baker Street, London, and took over country houses around Britain as training centers. Potential agents and other staff were recruited from all walks of life—one of the most effective female agents, Violette Szabo, was the half-French daughter of a south London car dealer. Because agents would have to merge into a foreign country during their missions, language skills were at a premium. Many recruits were, like Szabo, bilingual British citizens with one foreign parent, or foreign nationals, including members of the forces of Allied governments in exile. SOE sought special skills wherever they could be found. Burglars taught agents to pick locks and convicted forgers prepared their false identity papers. At its peak SOE probably employed around 13,000 people, some 5,000 of these as agents in the field.

Initial training concentrated on physical fitness and the use of basic weapons. Candidates were observed to assess their psychological suitability, with plenty of alcohol provided to see how drinking might affect their behavior. Those who made it through the initial stage were sent for commando training in the rugged Highlands of Scotland. There they learned skills such as parachute jumping, the use of explosives for sabotage, and how to kill an enemy with their bare hands—lethal single combat being taught by E. A. Sykes and W. E. Fairbairn, formerly of the Shanghai Municipal Police.

WEBLEY & SCOTT 1907 AUTOMATIC PISTOL WITH SILENCER

The final stage of training focused on the basic craft of an undercover agent. This included lessons in the identification of members of various enemy police and security agencies, the operation of a shortwave radio, the use of codes, and resistance to interrogation.

> "NO SOONER HAD A DUMMY, IMPELLED BY WIRES, LEAPED OUT OF BED TO TACKLE THE INTRUDER AND BEEN SHOT FOR HIS PAINS, THAN A TRAPDOOR OPENED, "MEN" EMERGED FROM BENEATH TABLES, BOTTLES AND CHAIRS CAME HURTLING DISCONCERTINGLY AT THE GUNMAN'S HEAD."

EWAN BUTLER RECALLS HIS SOE TRAINING AT THE HANDS OF E. A. SYKES

Secret air drops
The Lysander aircraft was capable of landing on very short airstrips and therefore was well suited to missions into Occupied Europe, dropping off SOE agents and supplies.

The quality of the training and equipment the agents received was mixed. For example, no one realized how quickly the Germans would track the source of shortwave radio broadcasts. Thus agents were not sufficiently warned to keep radio messages brief and avoid sending repeatedly from the same place. As a result, radio operators were often arrested almost as soon as they started their work. Agents' forged documents were generally excellent, but details, such as providing them with the right brand of cigarettes, were sometimes missed. SOE pioneered the use of plastic explosives, yet time was wasted on fanciful ideas such as stuffing explosives into the bodies of dead rats or making it resemble animal dung to be spread on roads. In general, the pressure for speedy action meant many agents went into Europe with preparation too skimpy for the demanding task that faced them.

INTO OCCUPIED EUROPE

SOE's original preferred method of inserting agents into Occupied Europe was by sea, either using fishing boats or fast motor patrol boats to land on isolated stretches of coast. The reluctance of the Royal Navy to cooperate and a battle for resources with the Secret Intelligence Service (SIS), which had the same idea, forced SOE to turn to the air. Flying by night, agents and supplies were dropped in by parachute or landed in aircraft such as the Lysander, which were capable of operating from short, rough landing grounds. An agent could typically expect to be met by a reception committee made up of members of resistance groups or fellow SOE operatives. They would arrange discreet lights to mark a landing strip or drop zone. Arrival in hostile territory and movement from the initial arrival point to safe housing were inevitably among the most dangerous phases of an agent's mission.

False identities
It was essential for all SOE agents to have impeccable documentation to support their covert lives, and thus avoid detection.

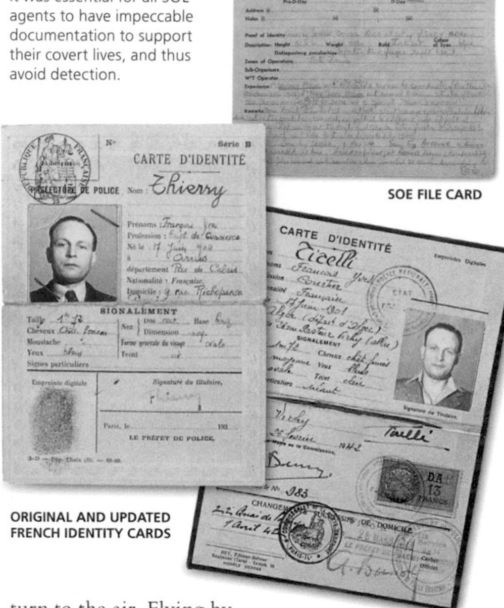

SOE FILE CARD

ORIGINAL AND UPDATED FRENCH IDENTITY CARDS

UNDERCOVER

SOE agents were assigned a variety of roles. The most responsible were organizers, entrusted with setting up and developing resistance networks. Like radio operators and sabotage specialists, these were almost always men. Women agents were generally employed as couriers, partly because it was felt they were less likely to attract suspicion when travelling around. Living under the cover of a false identity in hostile, heavily policed territory, agents had to cope with, in Gubbins' words, "a continual anxiety all day and

Behind enemy lines
Captain John Roper of the SOE in a wood near Savournon, shortly after parachuting into the Haute Savoie region of France.

every day." Arrest meant certain torture and almost certain death. To survive, they needed to play a role at all times, scrupulously monitoring every detail of their behavior to ensure they were not attracting attention to themselves as in any way unusual or foreign. To make anything happen they had to contact local people, but every contact brought the risk of betrayal— for opposition to the Nazi occupiers was nothing like as universal as SOE had naively assumed. Under pressure, some agents seemed to forget their common sense and much of their training. They wrote down codes or addresses that they were supposed to memorize, carried identity documents for two different aliases at the same time, or even spoke openly to one another in English in public places. On the other hand, some blended into their surroundings and sustained false identities even under suspicious cross-questioning.

Women at war
The SOE deployed many female agents during the war. Some were tasked with sabotage or radio operating duties *(left)*, but most were successfully used as couriers.

Covert communication
The Type 3 MK II suitcase radio was used by SOE agents in the field to communciate with HQ. Coded transmissions constantly evolved to avoid detection by the Nazis.

Headset

SUCCESSES AND FAILURES

Among SOE's most notable operations was the assassination of Reinhard Heydrich, deputy chief of the Gestapo. He was shot in Prague by two agents, Jan Kubis and Josef Gabcik, parachuted in by SOE in May 1942. In reprisal the Germans murdered some 5,000 Czech civilians; Kubis and Gabcik also died, betrayed by a fellow agent who had changed sides. A more clear-cut example of success was the sabotage of Norsk Hydro plant in occupied Norway in February 1943; it was producing heavy water, which could have been used by the Germans to make an atomic bomb. Norwegian SOE agents not only blew up the plant but also later sank a ferry carrying a consignment of heavy water destined for Germany.

Some SOE operations, however, were costly fiascos, none worse than the abortive effort to run a network in the Netherlands from 1942 to 1944. The first agents sent in were betrayed by a Dutch collaborator and German intelligence cracked their communication codes. An arrested SOE radio operator agreed to send messages for the Germans, carefully omitting security checks in order to alert his home section to the fact that he had been "turned". Inexplicably, senior SOE officers ignored the lack of security checks in the messages they were receiving and sent in agents and supplies to rendezvous fixed by the Nazis. More than 50 agents had fallen into German hands before the deception was discovered.

LARGE-SCALE RESISTANCE

By 1944 SOE was providing support and supplies for substantial resistance movements conducting rural guerrilla warfare in Yugoslavia, Greece, and the "maquis" of southern France. Although the SOE had not created these movements, the presence of SOE agents clearly raised morale, and the weaponry they supplied encouraged offensive operations that tied down large numbers of German troops. One of the SOE's finest hour's probably came with the Normandy landings in June 1944, when SOE agents and the French resistance succeeded in providing important intelligence on German defenses and sabotaging transport links to block the movement of German reinforcements to Normandy.

Hundreds of SOE agents died in Nazi torture chambers and concentration camps in the course of the war. Whether the organization's achievements were worth the cost is an impossible calculation. However, it is clear that SOE agents showed as much bravery as any soldier on the field of battle.

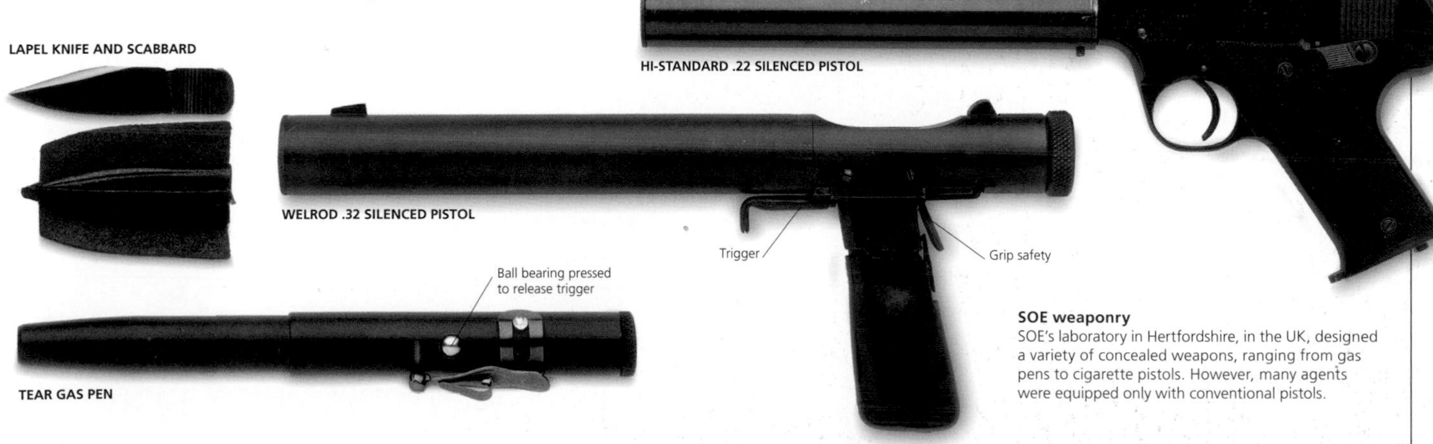

SOE weaponry
SOE's laboratory in Hertfordshire, in the UK, designed a variety of concealed weapons, ranging from gas pens to cigarette pistols. However, many agents were equipped only with conventional pistols.

SOE GEAR

The British Special Operations Executive (SOE) trained and equipped hundreds of secret agents. Many were parachuted into enemy-occupied territory, wearing the outfit shown, to support and coordinate local resistance groups. Aircraft carrying the agents were sometimes guided to safe dropping zones by agents on the ground equipped with a portable transceiver, the S-phone. Agents were also equipped with compasses and maps to find their own way if they for some reason failed to link up with a "reception committee" awaiting their arrival.

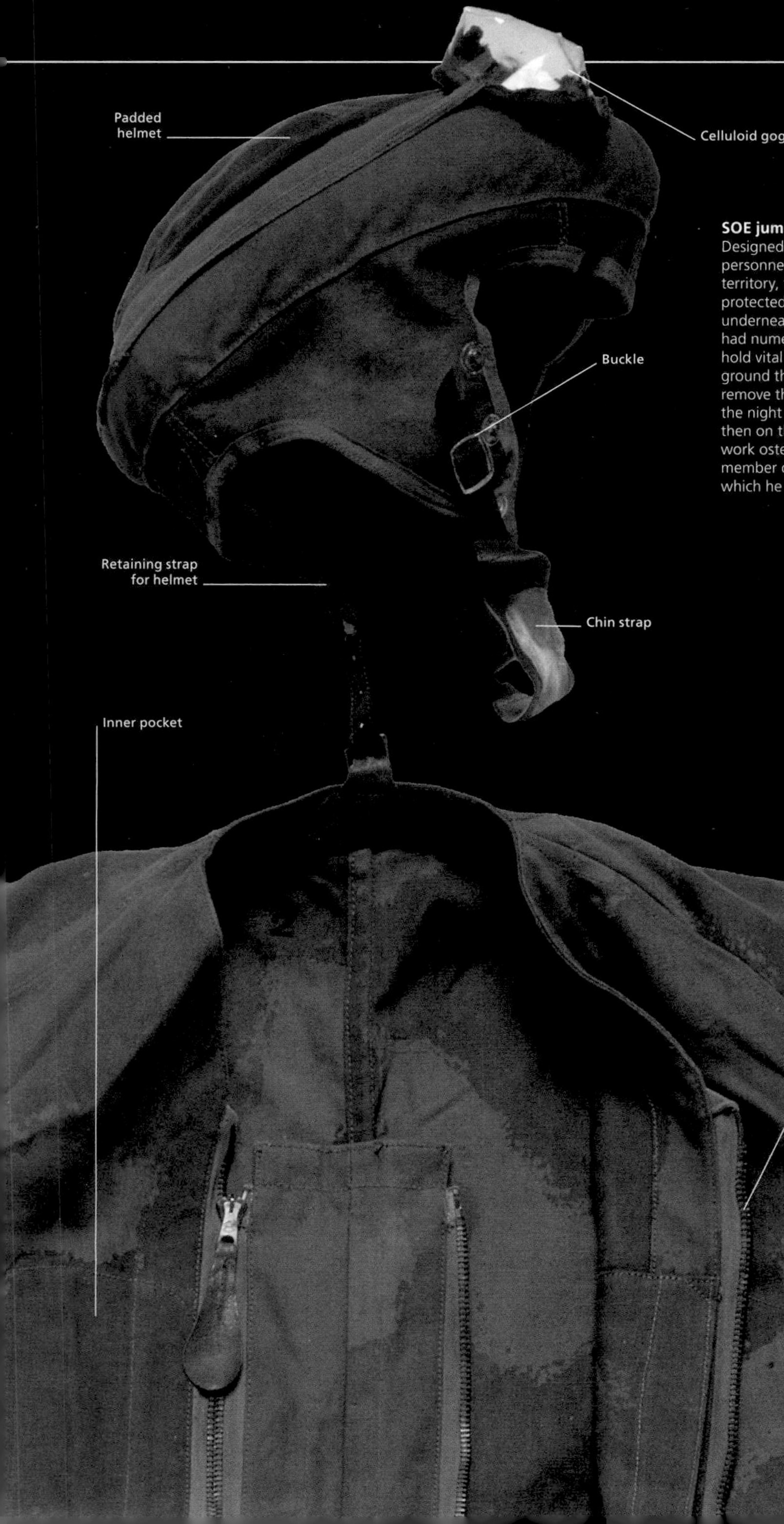

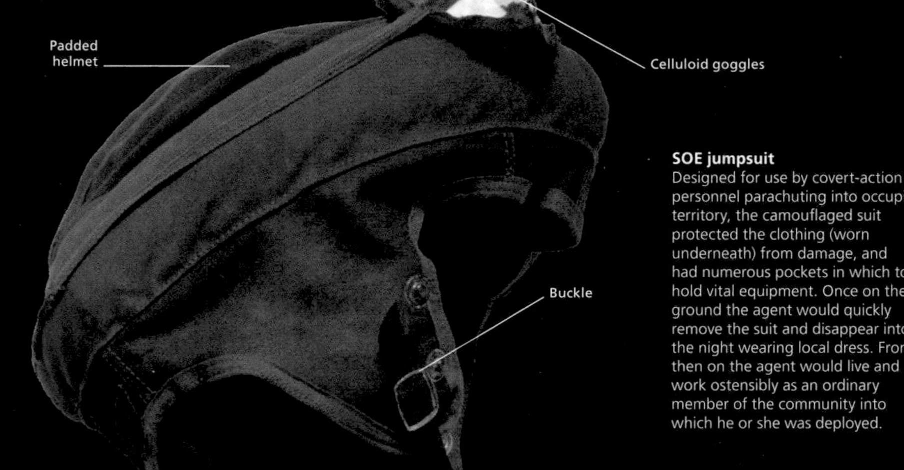

SOE jumpsuit
Designed for use by covert-action personnel parachuting into occupied territory, the camouflaged suit protected the clothing (worn underneath) from damage, and had numerous pockets in which to hold vital equipment. Once on the ground the agent would quickly remove the suit and disappear into the night wearing local dress. From then on the agent would live and work ostensibly as an ordinary member of the community into which he or she was deployed.

SOE SPECIAL FORCES BADGE

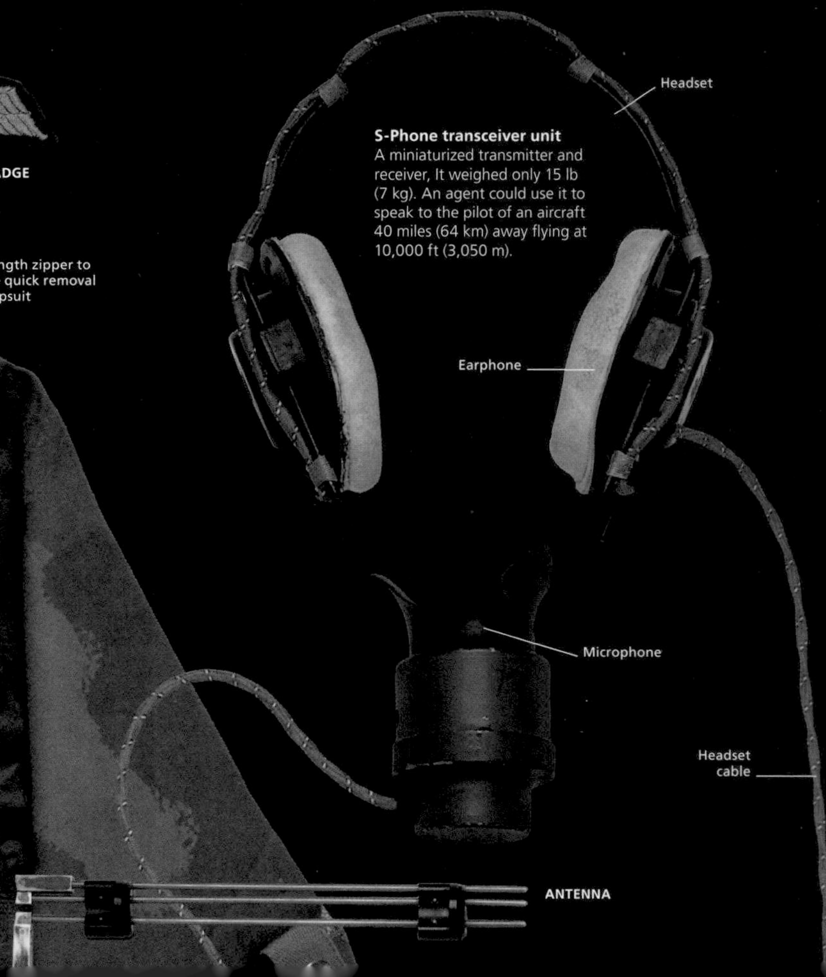

Headset

Earphone

Microphone

Headset cable

ANTENNA

S-Phone transceiver unit
A miniaturized transmitter and receiver, It weighed only 15 lb (7 kg). An agent could use it to speak to the pilot of an aircraft 40 miles (64 km) away flying at 10,000 ft (3,050 m).

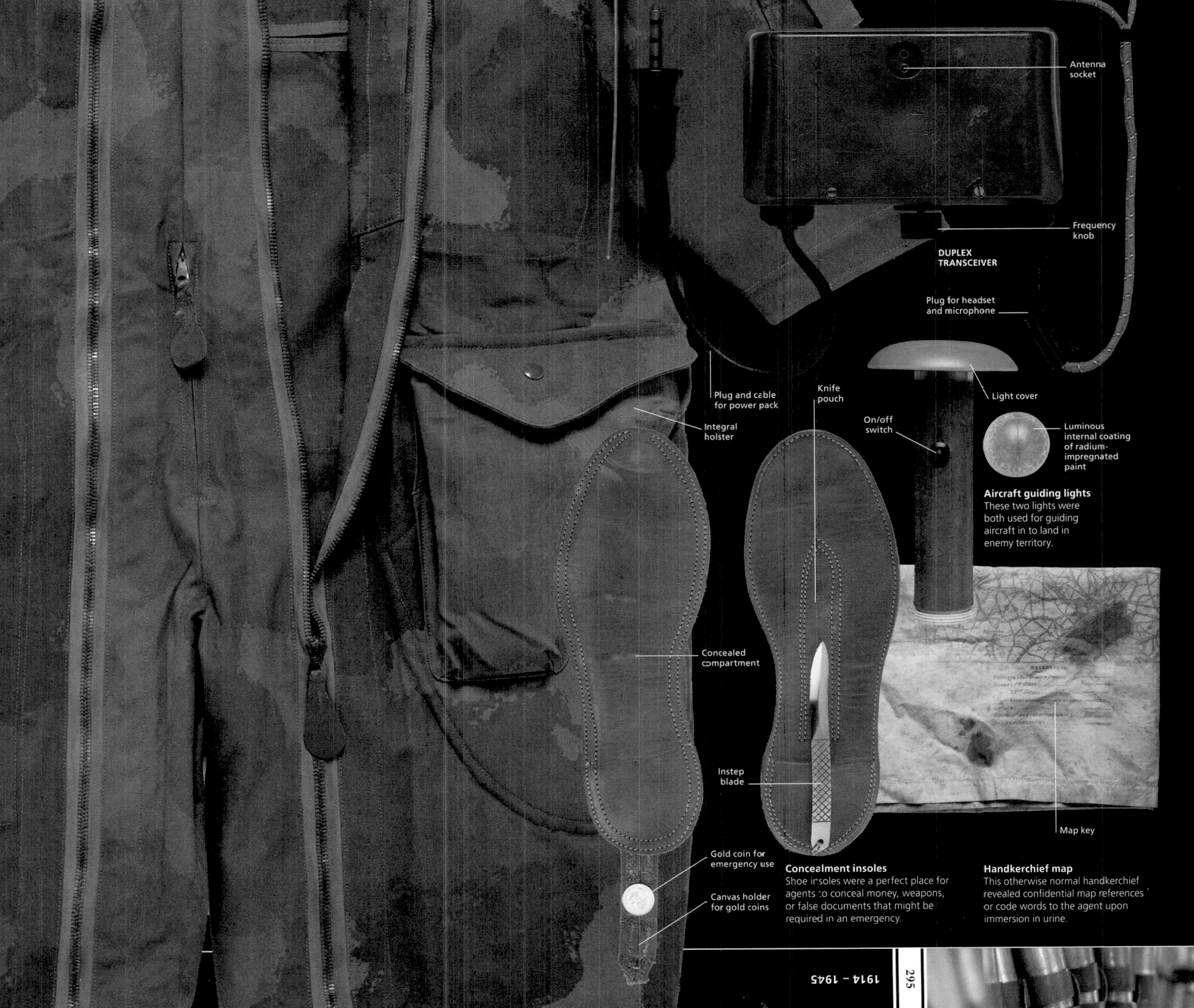

Aircraft guiding lights
These two lights were both used for guiding aircraft in to land in enemy territory.

Concealment insoles
Shoe insoles were a perfect place for agents to conceal money, weapons, or false documents that might be required in an emergency.

Handkerchief map
This otherwise normal handkerchief revealed confidential map references or code words to the agent upon immersion in urine.

SOE WEAPONS

A variety of ingenious weapons were available for SOE agents. Full-sized silenced pistols were common, and even crossbows were used, but many other weapons were designed by the SOE's laboratories in Welywn Garden City, near London, with the intention of concealment. Agents required weapons that were small enough to be hidden easily or disguised as everyday objects, from the relatively simple lapel knife and cigarette firing device to the more sophisticated belt pistol. Because these weapons were so small, they had a limited range—usually no more than 12 ft (3.7 m). Typically, though, this armory of weapons would only be called into action if the agent's cover was blown and he needed to evade capture.

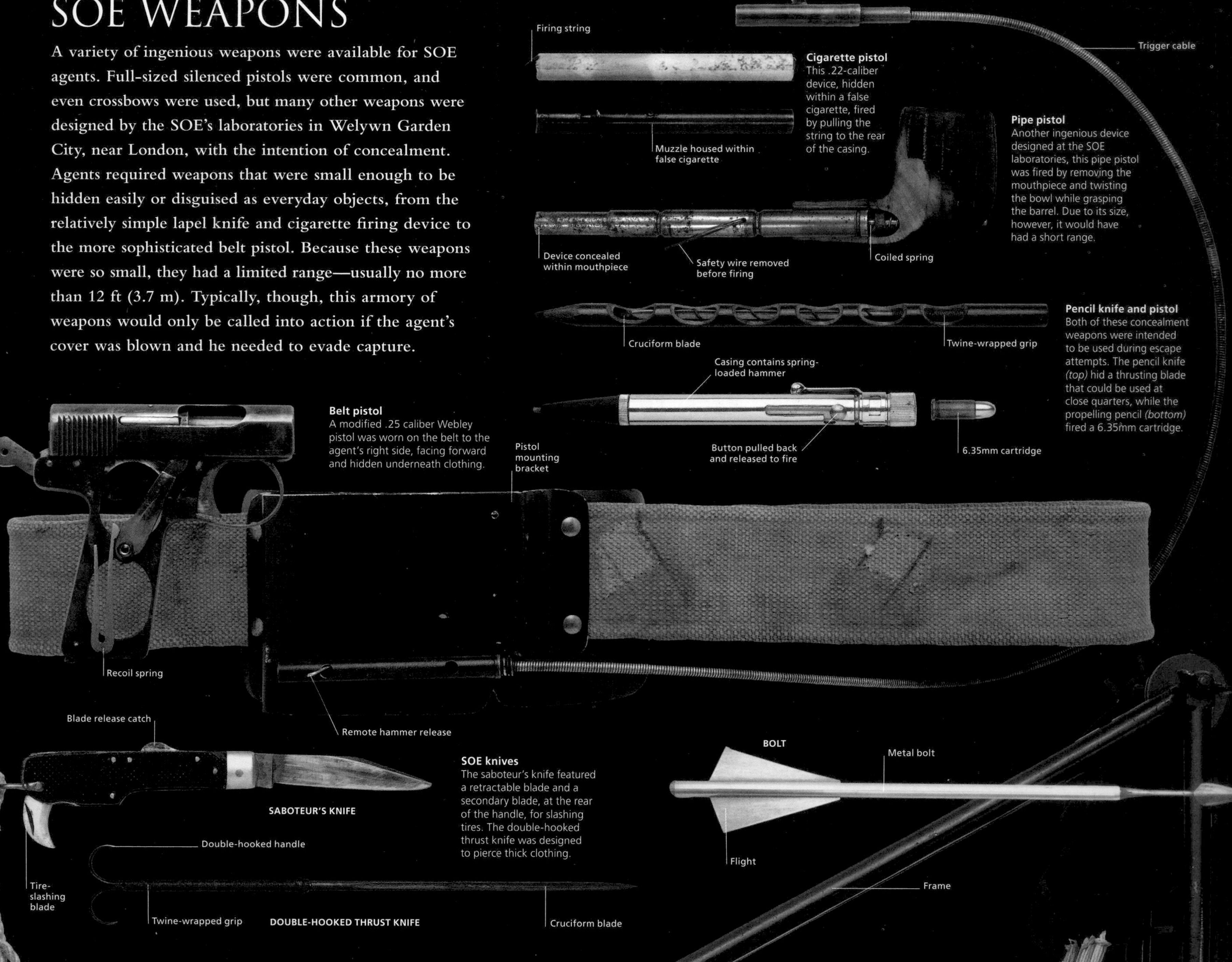

Cigarette pistol This .22-caliber device, hidden within a false cigarette, fired by pulling the string to the rear of the casing.

Pipe pistol Another ingenious device designed at the SOE laboratories, this pipe pistol was fired by removing the mouthpiece and twisting the bowl while grasping the barrel. Due to its size, however, it would have had a short range.

Pencil knife and pistol Both of these concealment weapons were intended to be used during escape attempts. The pencil knife *(top)* hid a thrusting blade that could be used at close quarters, while the propelling pencil *(bottom)* fired a 6.35mm cartridge.

Belt pistol A modified .25 caliber Webley pistol was worn on the belt to the agent's right side, facing forward and hidden underneath clothing.

SOE knives The saboteur's knife featured a retractable blade and a secondary blade, at the rear of the handle, for slashing tires. The double-hooked thrust knife was designed to pierce thick clothing.

Crossbow and bolt
This SOE crossbow was powered by rubber loops that were tensioned by a windlass handle before firing. The front frame and shoulder stock could be folded for easier transportation. The bolt *(above)* was made of metal.

Welgun submachine-gun
The Welgun was a light and compact experimental submachine-gun (SMG) developed for SOE use. It had a top-folding stock and was fed from a 32-round magazine.

Webley & Scott 1907
The 1907 was one of several pistols made by Webley & Scott in the early 20th century. This model, which equipped British agents in World War II, is fitted with a silencer.

Colt and holster
This SOE gun and its holster were designed to be concealed beneath a jacket.

1942 – 1945

US PARATROOPER

LIKE THE EARLY AMERICAN PIONEERS WHOSE

DURING WORLD WAR II the US created five airborne infantry divisions that were elite formations of outstanding fighting effectiveness. They were men not ultimately defined by use of a parachute or landing in a glider, but by their exceptionally high standard of fitness, training, initiative, fighting skills, and aggression. The 82nd Airborne "All American" Division and the 101st Airborne "Screaming Eagles" played a prominent part in some of the toughest fighting in Europe, including the D-Day landings in Normandy.

The US was comparatively slow to develop airborne infantry—the Soviet Union, Japan, Italy, Germany, and Britain all had trained paratroops before the Americans entered the field. It was in August 1942 that 82nd Infantry became the first US division with the Airborne designation. The 101st Airborne was next in seniority, with the 11th, 13th, and 17th Airborne following on in the course of 1943.

Airborne infantry insignia
This silver badge bearing the paratrooper's wings and parachute insignia was worn on the jacket pocket.

The vast majority of US soldiers who fought in World War II were conscript citizen-soldiers, not full-time, professional "lifers." But you could not be drafted into a parachute regiment; draftees were invited to volunteer to become paratroopers. It was an option that attracted the most ambitious and competitive draftees: men who wanted to make something positive of their time in the army and welcomed a chance to prove themselves. They were offered the lure of extra pay, but although welcome, this was a weak motivation compared with the attraction of joining an elite with its special standards and proudly-worn insignia. For this reason, the number of volunteers for paratroop service always exceeded the places available. Those who got through initial selection and the subsequent hard months of training had to be outstandingly healthy and determined. In the segregated US army all the volunteers were of necessity white, but otherwise they could reasonably be said to come from every part of the US and every area of society. The majority had lived hard lives growing up in the Depression era. The tough conditions they had to endure in training were less of a shock to them than they might have been to recruits from a more pampered generation. It has been said that these were men prepared to risk death for the right to wear silver wings on their pockets and to tuck their trousers into the top of their boots. Strangely, the soldiers of the glider regiments that formed an essential part of airborne divisions were not volunteers and did not receive extra pay, even though landing in gliders was much more dangerous than parachuting.

GOING AIRBORNE

From the start, the airborne divisions pushed physical training to record-breaking levels. A spirit of competition was encouraged between men and units on an extreme program of forced marches by day and night. Pushed to the limit of endurance, no volunteer ever wanted to surrender to exhaustion or fear—no one wanted to "wash out." The first airborne jump was always a crucial challenge in which the nerve of a fair number of soldiers failed.

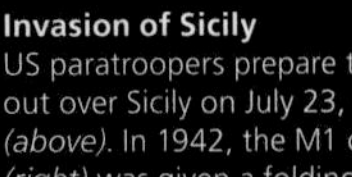

Invasion of Sicily
US paratroopers prepare to bail out over Sicily on July 23, 1943 *(above)*. In 1942, the M1 carbine *(right)* was given a folding butt stock especially for paratroop use.

M1 CARBINE WITH FOLDING BUTT STOCK

“THOUSANDS OF WHITE PARACHUTES DROPPED THROUGH AN INFERNO OF FLAK, WHILE ... GLIDERS RAMMED HIGH-TENSION CABLES IN SHOWERS OF BLUE SPARKS.”

FRENCH PILOT PIERRE CLOSTERMANN DESCRIBES AIRBORNE LANDINGS ON THE RHINE, MARCH 1945

The men also had to exhibit unquestioning instant obedience to their superiors. Fortunately officers were generally of high quality and won the respect of their men, as did NCOs promoted from the ranks of the parachute volunteers.

The airborne troops were trained to be dropped behind enemy lines, where they would have to be capable of fighting unsupported in small units. They had to learn to operate radios, carry out sabotage with high-explosives, fight at night, and survive for long periods without resupply. Having to carry with them all the equipment needed for light infantry operations, they were so encumbered that it was hard for them to board their C-47 transport aircraft, let alone jump out of them in the air. This was especially true of men attached to machine guns or mortars.

Service diary
A lightweight service diary was part of a soldier’s basic gear.

POSTED OVERSEAS

North Africa was the destination for the first US airborne troops sent overseas. On the night of July 9, 1943, units of 82nd Airborne made their first combat jump as part of the invasion of Sicily. The 82nd also participated in the invasion of mainland Italy at Salerno the following September. Most American airborne troops, however, were sent to Britain to prepare for the Normandy landings. These young men not only had no previous experience of war, but the vast majority had never been outside the US. Carried across the Atlantic on overcrowded troop ships, they arrived at bases in rural England, an environment radically different from any they had known. Released from the constraints of their homes, they were hell-raisers when off the leash. But in camp rigorous training continued to occupy all their energies.

In the Sicily landings, strong winds, the inherent problems of night flying, and enemy anti-aircraft fire had resulted in paratroopers landing scattered over a wide area. Despite this, a similar nighttime jump, with accompanying glider landings, was planned to accompany the invasion of Normandy in June 1944. Large-scale exercises in Britain in the run-up to D-Day did nothing to suggest that problems had been overcome, but 82nd and 101st Airborne were

Operation Market Garden
US paratroopers jump from troop transport planes to land in a Dutch field during Operation Market Garden, 1944. Allied glider troops have already assembled in the foreground.

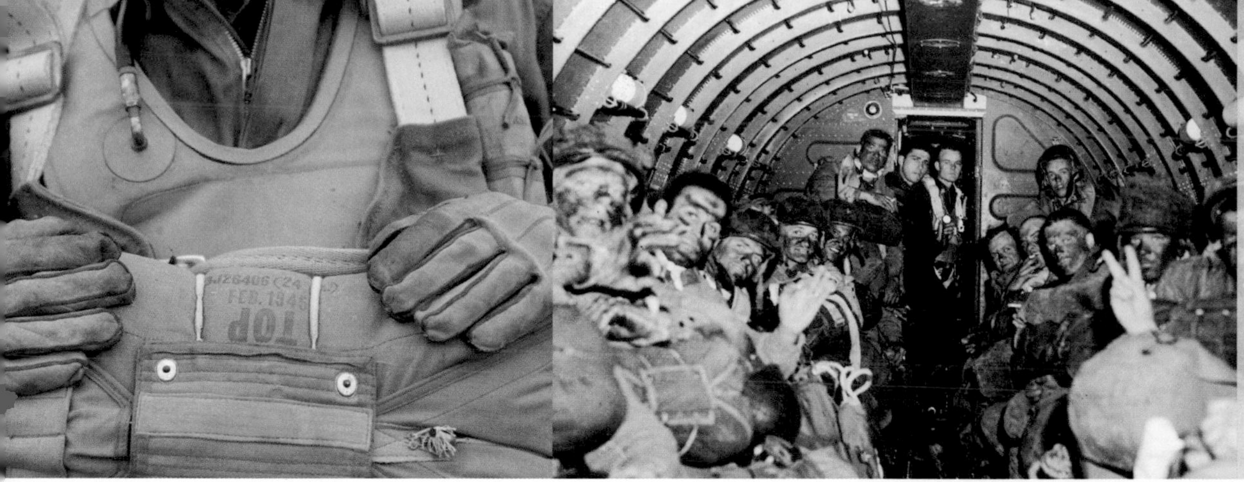

Invasion of France
Paratroopers of the 439th Troop Carrier Group aboard a Douglas C-47 just before taking off from an airbase in England. Secondary parachutes and life vests were worn in case of emergencies *(far left).*

none the less slated to seize and hold vital objectives inland from the invasion beaches. For the majority of paratroopers, who had not been in Sicily or Italy, D-Day was their first real experience of combat after two years of training. Since the drop was to take place in pitch darkness, they were issued with "clickers" to emit a sound that would hopefully allow them to find one another once on the ground, and with a password so they would not kill one another. Hyping themselves up for the operation, some shaved their heads and daubed their faces with war paint.

NORMANDY

An armada of transport aircraft and towed gliders lifted the airborne divisions off from British airfields on the night of June 5-6, but chaos ensued on arriving over the French coast. Confused by fog and dodging heavy flak, the aircraft dropped their parachutists over a wide area. Many men lost their equipment. Some drowned, landing in the sea or in marshland. It was a remarkable tribute to the quality of US airborne training that mostly unblooded troops, fighting with limited arms and in scattered units, succeeded as well as they did, spreading confusion behind German lines, seizing key gun emplacements, bridges, and causeways, and helping hold off German counterattacks against the US forces on Utah beach. Airborne soldiers remained in the thick of the fighting in Normandy for between three and five weeks, taking substantial casualties.

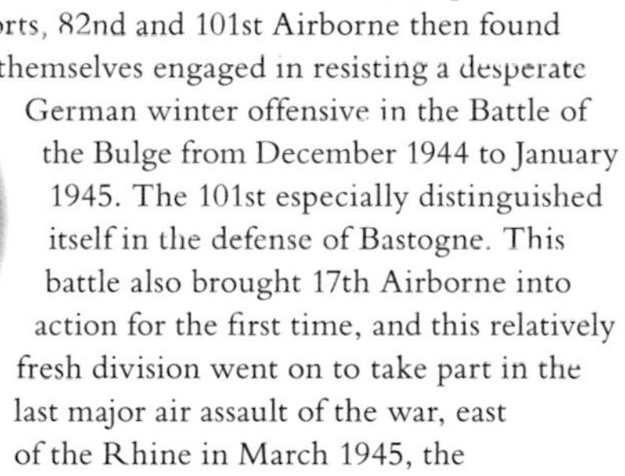

Garrison cap badge
The garrison cap bore a badge showing a white parachute against blue infantry piping.

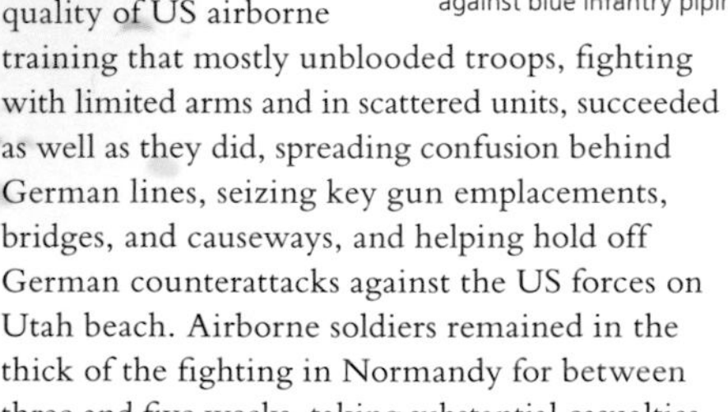

WAR TO THE END

After Normandy, the faith of Allied commanders in airborne operations was at its peak. This led to the immense gamble on Operation Market Garden in September 1944. Some 33,970 US, British, and Polish airborne troops, formed into First Airborne Allied Army, were to seize a series of bridges over the Maas, Waal, and Rhine rivers in the German-occupied Netherlands, and hold them until an armored column arrived. The 82nd and 101st Airborne were again the US divisions selected. The US troops achieved their objectives and fought off numerous German counterattacks, but the British only took one end of the Rhine bridge and overall the operation achieved little of value. Due some rest after superhuman efforts, 82nd and 101st Airborne then found themselves engaged in resisting a desperate German winter offensive in the Battle of the Bulge from December 1944 to January 1945. The 101st especially distinguished itself in the defense of Bastogne. This battle also brought 17th Airborne into action for the first time, and this relatively fresh division went on to take part in the last major air assault of the war, east of the Rhine in March 1945, the most wholly successful of the Allies' parachute and glider operations.

Washing equipment
Standard-issue washing equipment included a safety razor and blades, acid-neutralizing tooth powder and brushless shaving soap.

DISTINGUISHED SERVICE

Overall, World War II revealed the limitations of the concept of large-scale airborne operations. Parachute troops were extremely vulnerable to ground fire while floating down to earth. Large numbers of gliders were lost to accidents or anti-aircraft fire. Less than perfect weather and enemy fire often meant that men landed dispersed and far from their objectives. Surviving without heavy equipment in the face of counterattacks was costly. In short, parachuting had a limited future. But as elite light infantry, the Airborne Divisions had performed outstandingly. The 101st and 82nd had sustained more than 16,000 casualties, including 3,400 killed in action. A tradition had been established that could not be easily discarded. The 82nd Airborne was not demobilized at the end of the war and 101st Airborne was reactivated in 1954. Both remain elite forces within the US Army, although mass combat drops are no longer part of their tactics.

Heavy load
Paratroopers of the 82nd Airborne Division prepare to jump during the invasion of Normandy, on June 6, 1944. Their heavy loads included a reserve parachute and leg bags stuffed with gear.

US PARATROOPER UNIFORM

Initially the subject of contension, the differences between the Airbornes' uniform and that of standard infantry were established more to mark out these elite units than for any practical purpose. The right to wear special boots and to "blouse" their trousers—tucking the cuffs into their boots—were coveted Airborne privileges. Their distinctive dress led the 509th Infantry (Airborne) Regiment to be dubbed the "devils in baggy pants" by a German soldier at Anzio.

> I SHALL SHOW OTHER SOLDIERS ... BY MY NEATNESS OF DRESS, BY MY CARE OF MY WEAPONS AND EQUIPMENT, THAT I AM A ... WELL-TRAINED SOLDIER.
>
> EXTRACT FROM THE PARATROOPER CREED

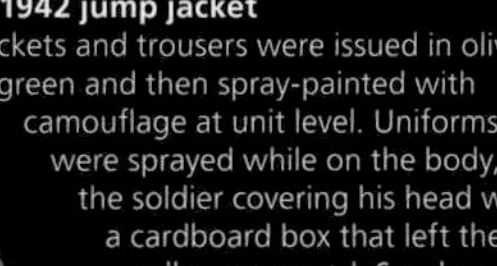

"Gingerbread Man" emblem

M2 paratrooper helmet
Issued in plain olive green, helmets were painted with camouflage by the owner. The "Gingerbread Man" was the emblem of the 509th Regiment.

Helmet sprinkled with dried cork to dull the surface

D-ring chin strap holder

Collar left unsprayed

Pocket with zippers on either side held M2 switchblade used to cut the soldier loose in emergencies

Badge kept covered when dropped at night

Camouflage applied by soldier

M1942 jump jacket
Jackets and trousers were issued in olive green and then spray-painted with camouflage at unit level. Uniforms were sprayed while on the body, the soldier covering his head with a cardboard box that left the collar unsprayed. Surplus bandoliers were chopped up and sewn inside the coat to make extra pockets.

Luminous disk to identify comrades in the dark

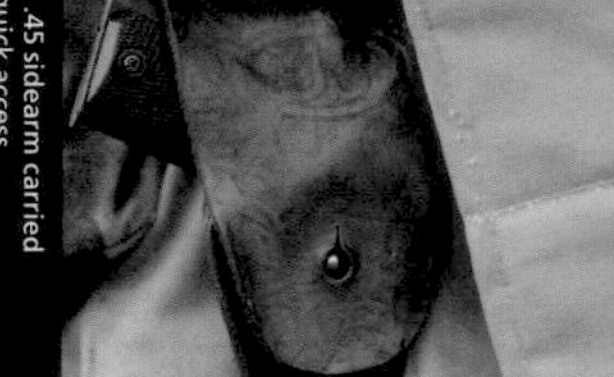

Colt .45 sidearm carried for quick access

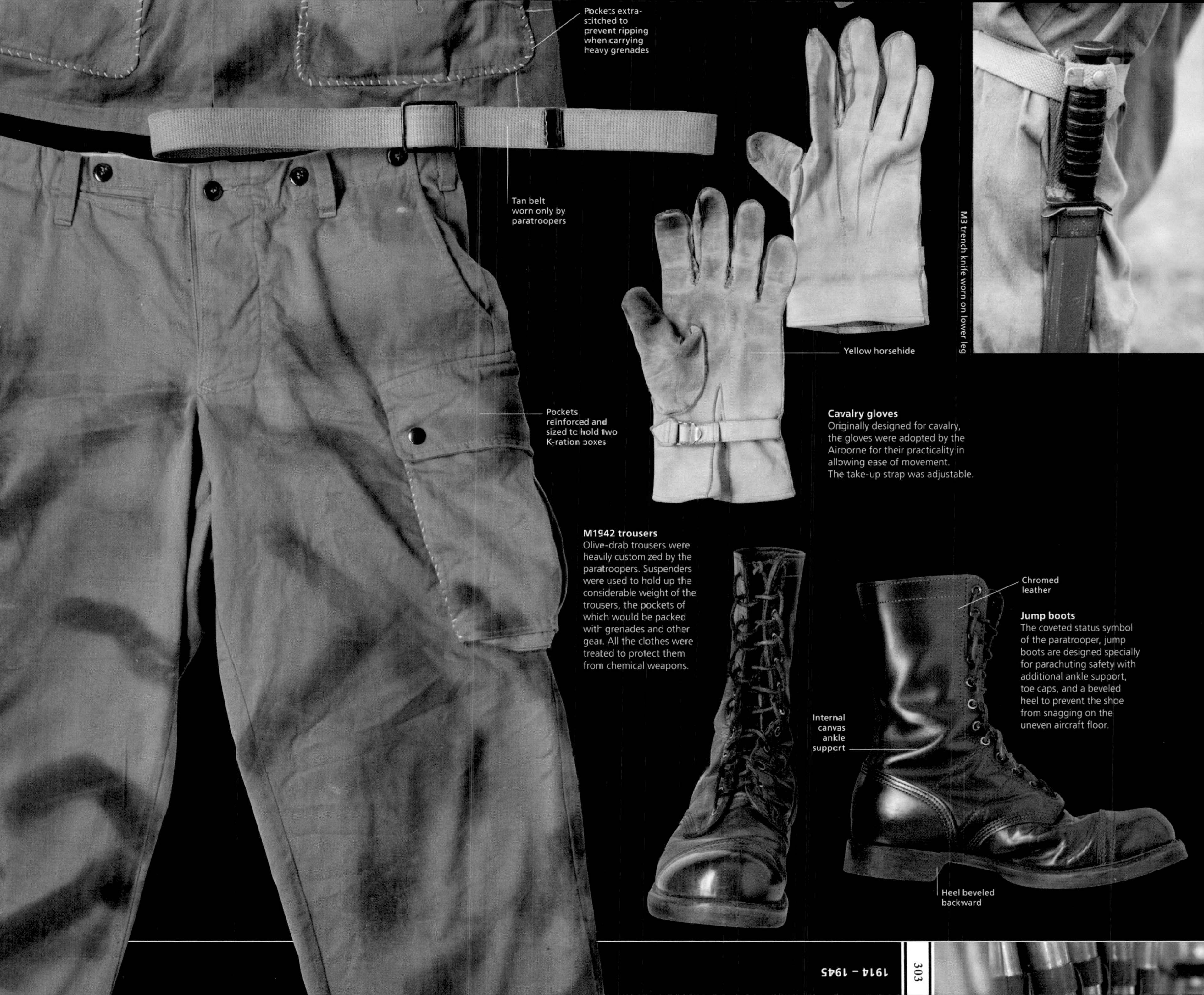

M3 trench knife worn on lower leg

Cavalry gloves
Originally designed for cavalry, the gloves were adopted by the Airborne for their practicality in allowing ease of movement. The take-up strap was adjustable.

M1942 trousers
Olive-drab trousers were heavily customized by the paratroopers. Suspenders were used to hold up the considerable weight of the trousers, the pockets of which would be packed with grenades and other gear. All the clothes were treated to protect them from chemical weapons.

Jump boots
The coveted status symbol of the paratrooper, jump boots are designed specially for parachuting safety with additional ankle support, toe caps, and a beveled heel to prevent the shoe from snagging on the uneven aircraft floor.

US PARATROOPER EQUIPMENT

US Airborne soldiers used much of the standard equipment of a World War II US infantryman, although with a bias toward items that were light and easily portable. K-rations, ideal for men who might have to survive behind enemy lines without resupply, were first tested by Airborne troops in 1942 before becoming general army issue. They could be supplemented by energy-rich D-rations. The MK3 fighting knife, for hand-to-hand fighting, was mass produced from 1943.

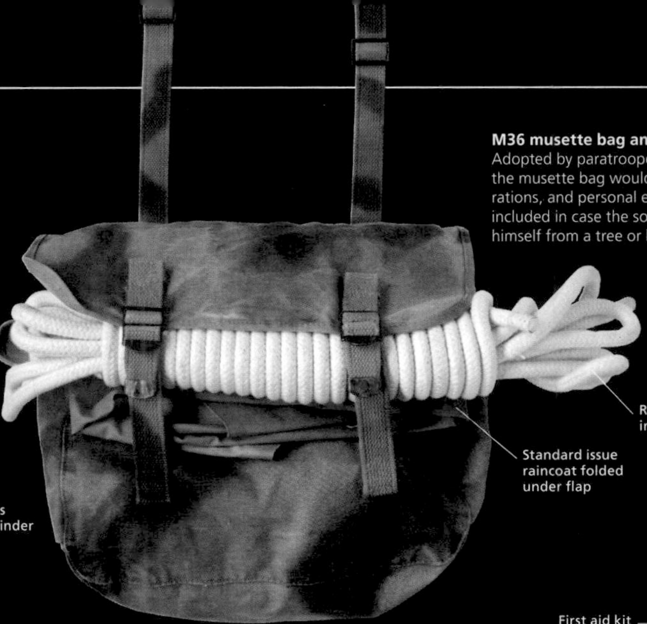

M36 musette bag and rope
Adopted by paratroopers for its versatility, the musette bag would have held ammunition, rations, and personal effects. The rope was included in case the soldier needed to free himself from a tree or building.

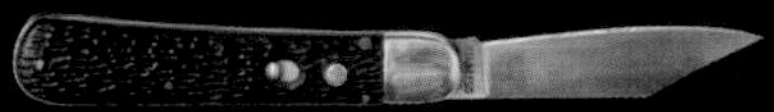

Rope 33 ft (10 m) in length

Standard issue raincoat folded under flap

Fore sight

Gas cylinder

M2 switchblade
The soldier used the knife to cut himself free of his webbing.

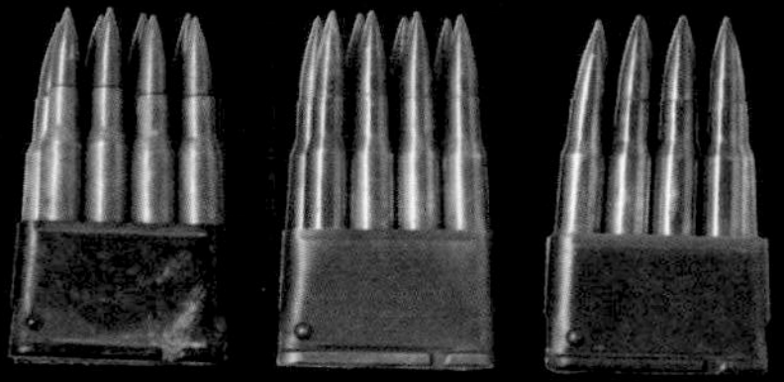

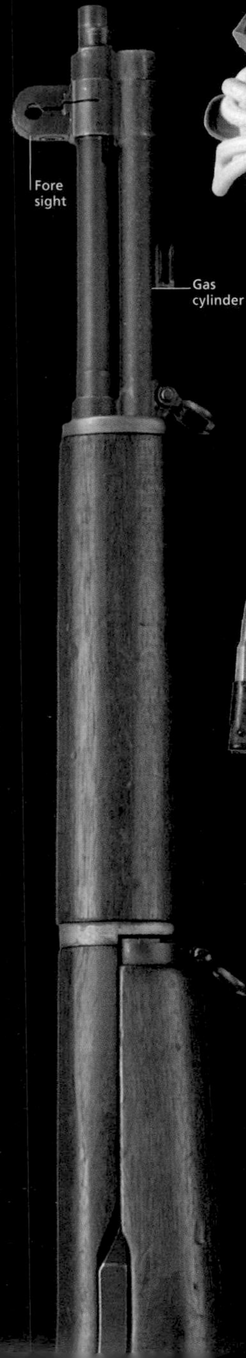

M1A1 Garand rifle and ammunition
The Garand was the standard US Army rifle of World War II. A semi-automatic, it was loaded by inserting an 8-round spring steel clip into the empty magazine. The empty clip was automatically ejected after the last round was fired. Soldiers had to watch out for the bolt snapping shut while reloading, or risk a case of "M1 thumb." The M1A1 carbine was also specific to the Airborne.

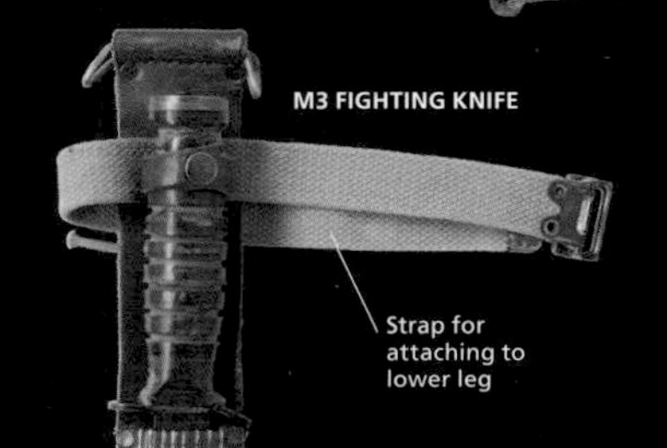

M3 FIGHTING KNIFE

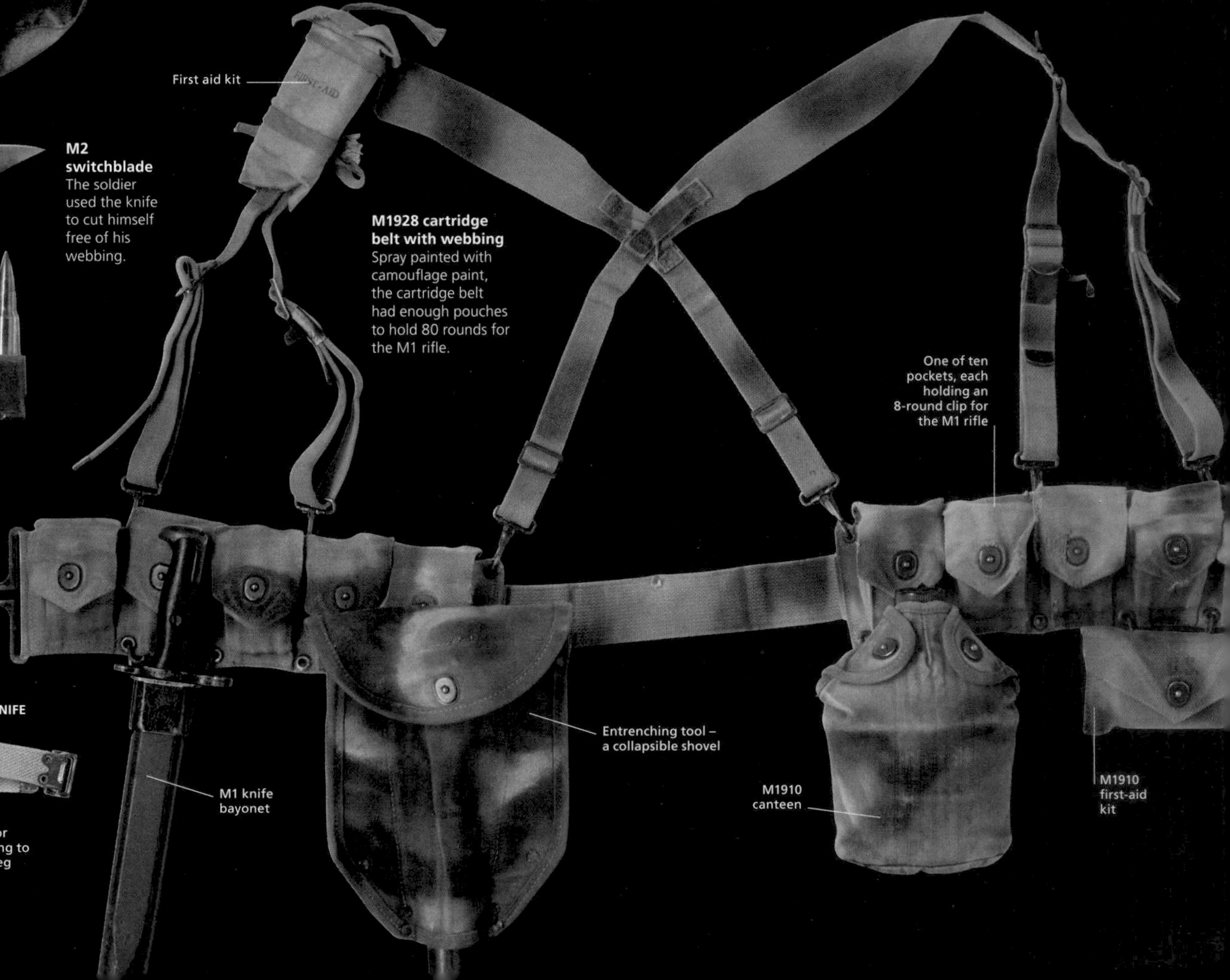

Strap for attaching to lower leg

First aid kit

M1928 cartridge belt with webbing
Spray painted with camouflage paint, the cartridge belt had enough pouches to hold 80 rounds for the M1 rifle.

M1 knife bayonet

Entrenching tool – a collapsible shovel

M1910 canteen

One of ten pockets, each holding an 8-round clip for the M1 rifle

M1910 first-aid kit

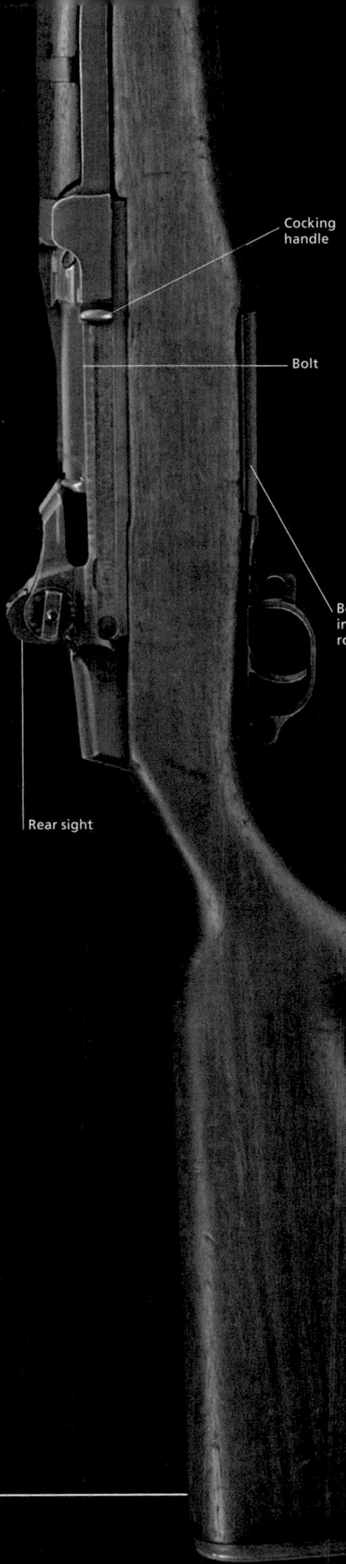

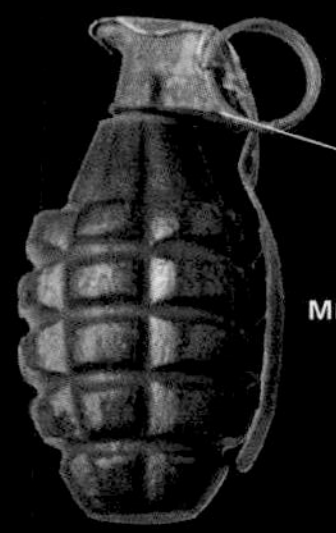

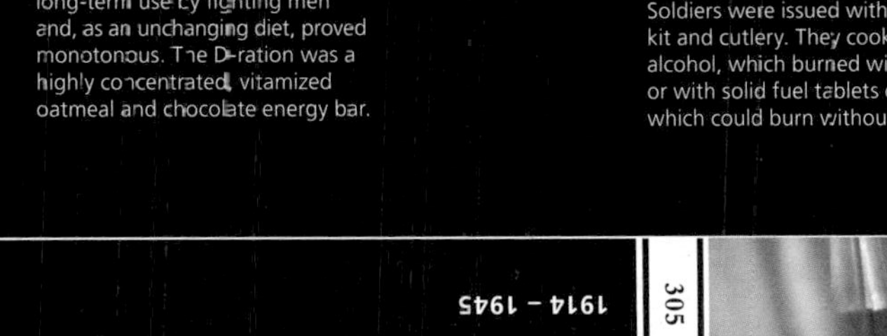

Cocking handle

Bolt

Rear sight

Bottom plate of internal eight-round magazine

Pin

MK II GRENADE

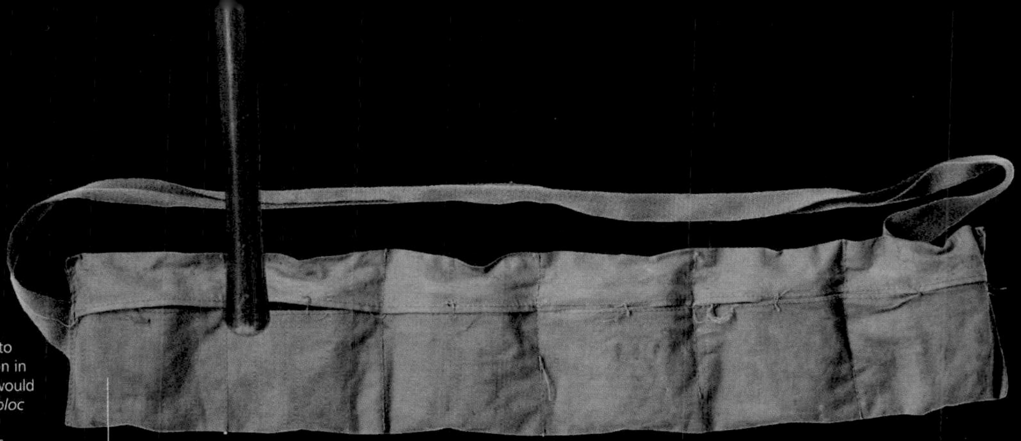

Bandolier
Worn across the chest to supplement ammunition in the cartridge belt, this would have contained six *en-bloc* (single unit) clips, each containing eight rounds of .30-06 ammunition.

Contained one *en-bloc* clip

K-RATIONS

D-RATIONS

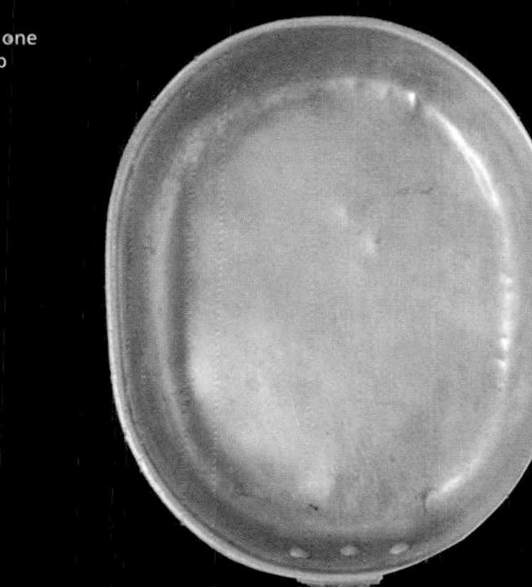

MESS KIT PAN

Rations
K-rations were eaten three times a day, with different breakfast, dinner, and supper packs. They contained non-perishable foods such as dry biscuits, canned ham and egg, sugar, fruit juice powder and coffee, as well as gum and cigarettes. Designed as an emergency ration, the food provided too few calories for long-term use by fighting men and, as an unchanging diet, proved monotonous. The D-ration was a highly concentrated, vitamized oatmeal and chocolate energy bar.

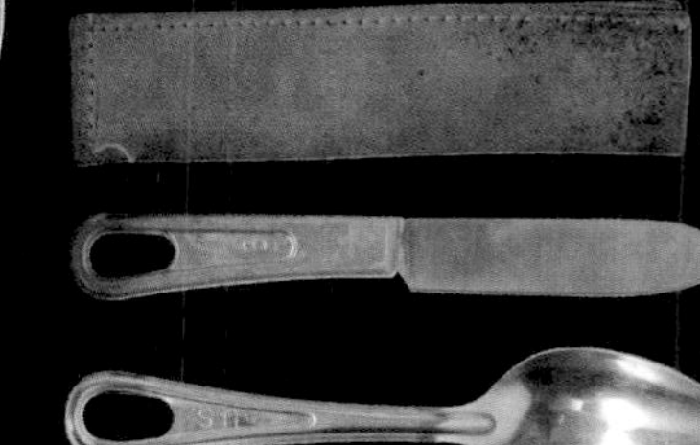

STANDARD ISSUE CUTLERY

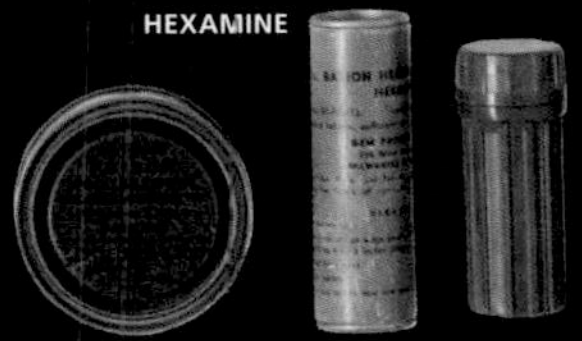

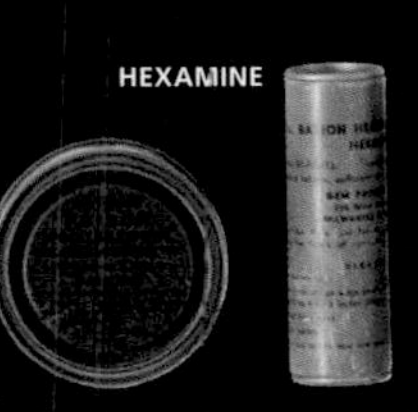

HEXAMINE

WOOD ALCOHOL

WATERPROOF MATCH CONTAINER

Cooking equipment
Soldiers were issued with a standard mess kit and cutlery. They cooked with wood alcohol, which burned with a hot flame, or with solid fuel tablets of hexamine, which could burn without kindling.

PARACHUTE

Despite the successes achieved by Airborne forces, parachutes had serious drawbacks as a means of delivering men into combat. It was difficult to achieve an accurate drop under fire, at night, or in adverse weather conditions. Paratroopers were vulnerable during the descent, being both highly visible and unable to maneuver. They were also easy prey immediately after landing while freeing themselves from their gear. The trooper risked having too much equipment for a comfortable jump, yet too little for effective infantry operation once on the ground.

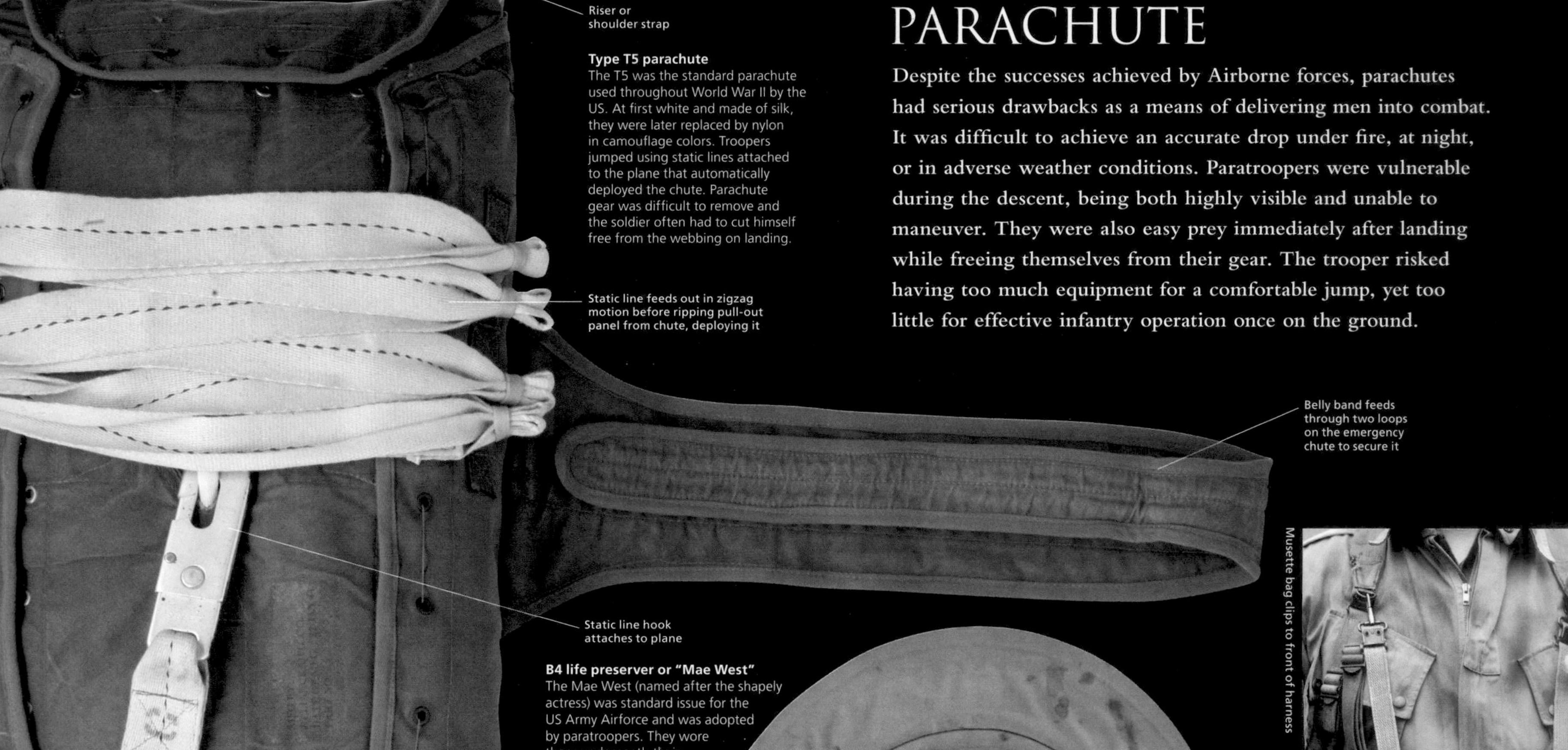

Type T5 parachute
The T5 was the standard parachute used throughout World War II by the US. At first white and made of silk, they were later replaced by nylon in camouflage colors. Troopers jumped using static lines attached to the plane that automatically deployed the chute. Parachute gear was difficult to remove and the soldier often had to cut himself free from the webbing on landing.

B4 life preserver or "Mae West"
The Mae West (named after the shapely actress) was standard issue for the US Army Airforce and was adopted by paratroopers. They wore them underneath their harnesses when being dropped near water. However, this was more of a psychological than practical advantage: the parachute harness had to first be removed before inflating the vest, and this was difficult to achieve in the water.

Musette bag clips to front of harness

Mae West worn beneath harness

Emergency chute showing release handle

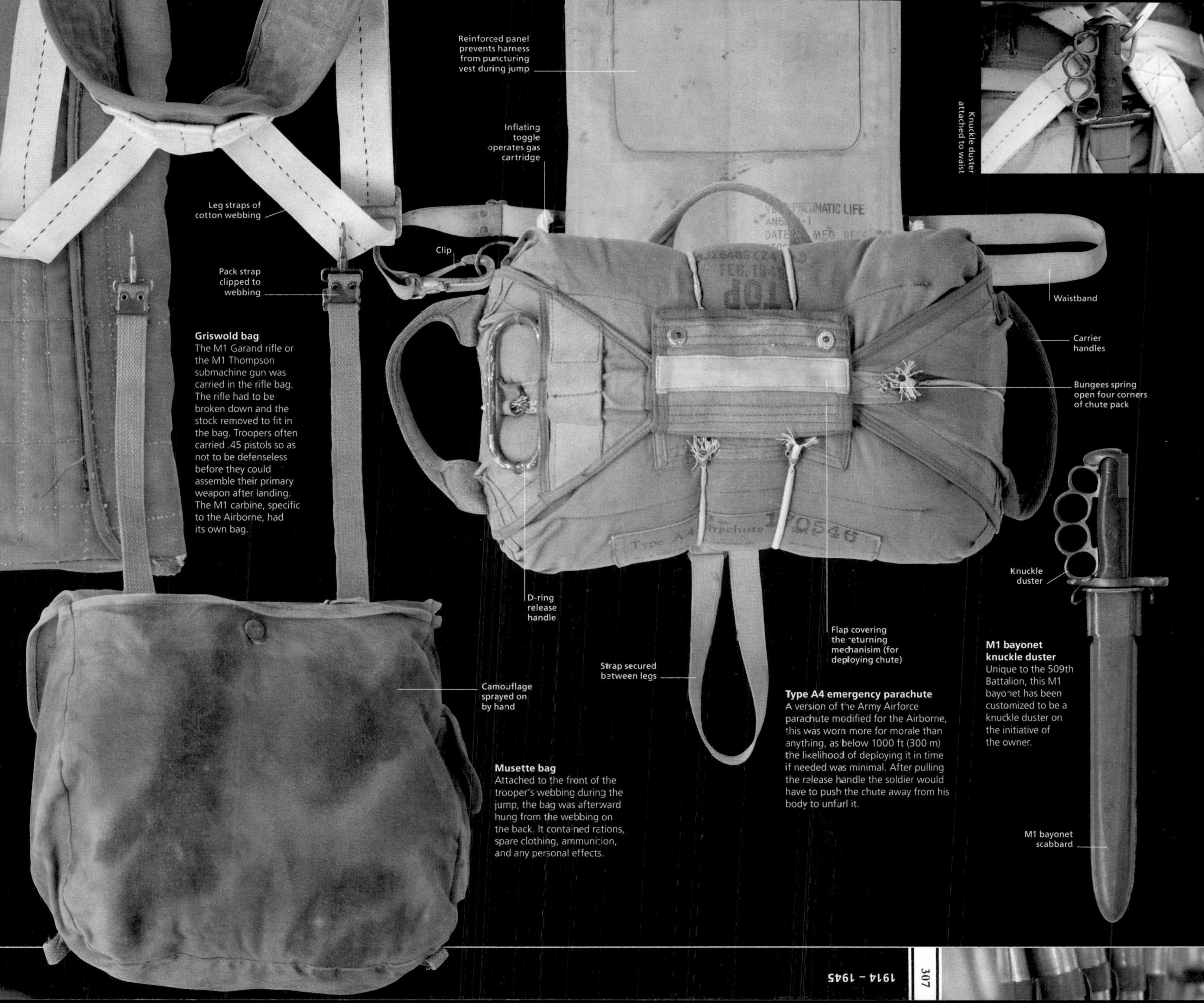

Knuckle duster attached to waist

Griswold bag
The M1 Garand rifle or the M1 Thompson submachine gun was carried in the rifle bag. The rifle had to be broken down and the stock removed to fit in the bag. Troopers often carried .45 pistols so as not to be defenseless before they could assemble their primary weapon after landing. The M1 carbine, specific to the Airborne, had its own bag.

Musette bag
Attached to the front of the trooper's webbing during the jump, the bag was afterward hung from the webbing on the back. It contained rations, spare clothing, ammunition, and any personal effects.

Type A4 emergency parachute
A version of the Army Airforce parachute modified for the Airborne, this was worn more for morale than anything, as below 1000 ft (300 m) the likelihood of deploying it in time if needed was minimal. After pulling the release handle the soldier would have to push the chute away from his body to unfurl it.

M1 bayonet knuckle duster
Unique to the 509th Battalion, this M1 bayonet has been customized to be a knuckle duster on the initiative of the owner.

1945 – PRESENT

GUERRILLAS AND COMMANDOS

Since World War II ended in 1945, there has not been a single day of global peace. At all times fighting has been going on somewhere in the world. Military theoreticians have repeatedly predicted the demise of the traditional fighting man, rendered obsolete by nuclear weaponry or by precision-guided munitions delivered from a safe distance. Yet even the most sophisticated armies with advanced electronic equipment, guided missiles, and remote-controlled aircraft have repeatedly found themselves forced to engage in face-to-face combat, whether in the streets of Iraqi cities or the jungle of Vietnam.

COLD WAR

The context for the first four decades of the postwar era was the global confrontation between two nuclear-armed superpowers, the United States and the Soviet Union. They avoided direct conflict through fear of the destructive power of each other's weaponry, but contested limited regional wars, either sending in their forces or supporting the armies of smaller powers. The largest of these wars was in Korea from 1950 to 1953—where the US and its allies intervened under the United Nations banner in support of South Korea against Soviet- and Chinese-backed North Korea—and in Vietnam from the mid-1960s. Those US formations that established an outstanding reputation in World War II, including the Marine Corps and Airborne divisions, were again called on to bear the worst of the fighting.

People's Liberation Army
Known as the Red Army up until 1946, China's PLA is the largest standing army in the world with 1.6 million active ground troops. In theory, all citizens have to serve in the PLA, but in practice, military service is voluntary.

Delta Force
Soldiers jump from a moving Humvee during a training exercise. Delta Force was created specifically for the purpose of counter-terrorism and national interventions operations, and forms the core of the unit hunting Osama Bin Laden. The US equivalent of the British SAS, Delta Force requires recruits to undergo a punishing selection course.

Apart from the use of helicopters for transport and fire support, nothing radically distinguished the combat experience of the infantryman in these conflicts from that of World War II.

FALL OF EMPIRES

The conflict in Vietnam was not only a limited war fought within the context of the Cold War, but also a war of national liberation fought as part of a worldwide process of decolonization. The European imperial powers, who had carved up much of Africa and Asia between them in the 1800s, were weakened financially, militarily, and psychologically by World War II. In the postwar era Europeans faced independence movements in their colonies which, in places, resorted to arms. In Latin America, liberation movements emerged that also saw themselves as essentially part of the anti-colonial movement, with the US cast as the imperial power.

The natural mode of combat for fighters taking on the forces of a colonial state was guerrilla warfare. Guerrillas were inspired by the example of Mao Zedong's victory in the Chinese Civil War in 1949, achieved by a graduated campaign building up from small-scale raids by rural-based guerrillas to eventual large-scale conventional warfare. The pattern was repeated in Vietnam in the 1960s and 1970s, when the US and the South Vietnamese government were defeated in a war that was started by Viet Cong guerrillas wearing rubber sandals and ended by soldiers of the North Vietnamese Army driving tanks.

On the whole, however, guerrilla forces remained relatively small, lightly equipped groups. Where they succeeded in taking power, they did so because their opponent's will to resist collapsed. Thus the triumph of Fidel Castro in Cuba in 1959 was dependent on the political breakdown of the Cuban government, rather than the military strength of Castro's guerrillas. But although revolutionary guerrilla movements often failed, or had success fall into their laps, the guerrilla fighter undoubtedly became one of the most widely admired warrior figures of modern times, glamourized in the heroic image of Ernesto "Che" Guevara.

CONVENTIONAL WAR

The colonial era was over by the end of the 1970s, but with no discernable reduction in the incidence of war. In the 1980s the US became a promoter of guerrilla war, backing irregular forces against the Soviet Union in Afghanistan, and against left-wing governments in Nicaragua, Angola, and Mozambique. At the same time, Western powers became increasingly interested in rapid reaction forces, ready for overseas intervention whenever required. The era of mass conscript armies seemed to be receding, with increasing reliance on well-trained professional soldiers. Special forces grew in importance both for use in conventional warfare and for countering guerrilla and other irregular forces.

Special forces found another use in countering the growth of international terrorism. Terrorist tactics such as assassination and bombings were always present as an adjunct of guerrilla warfare, but from the late 1960s onward terrorism developed an independent existence as the weapon of various groups opposed to the US-led capitalist world. Special forces trained for scenarios like airliner hijackings and hostage-taking, as strategists pondered how to counter an enemy operating almost below the military horizon. The use of conventional military force in a war on terrorism—as declared by President Bush in 2001—has been compared to using a pistol against a swarm of bees.

UNSTABLE WORLD

Much terrorist activity originated in the Middle East, a focus for war both before and after the ending of the Cold War in the late 1980s. Israel was founded and sustained by military prowess in a series of wars with its Arab neighbors, while Saddam Hussein's rule in Iraq triggered a succession of conflicts—with Iran, Iraq's Kurdish population, a UN coalition after the Iraqi invasion of Kuwait, and finally with a US and British invasion force in 2003. The disintegration of Iraq after Saddam's fall made it likely to join the many areas of the world where war had become a permanent state of affairs—Afghanistan, Congo, Colombia, and Sudan were other examples. The world was awash with weaponry and men were as ready to fight as they ever had been, for power, for profit, for ideals, or out of hatred and fear.

1945 – PRESENT

FOREIGN LEGIONNAIRE

EVERY OTHER LEGIONNAIRE IS YOUR BROTHER. IN COMBAT YOU ACT WITHOUT PASSION OR HATE BUT WITH RESPECT FOR YOUR VANQUISHED ENEMY. YOU NEVER ABANDON YOUR DEAD, YOUR WOUNDED, OR YOUR WEAPONS ...

CODE OF HONOR, FRENCH FOREIGN LEGION

THE FRENCH FOREIGN LEGION is a unique mercenary force that traditionally provided a no-questions-asked refuge for rootless misfits. The most dramatic period in its extraordinary history came after World War II, when it was in the forefront of France's losing struggle to maintain a colonial empire. Its heroic defeat at Dien Bien Phu in 1954 is the stuff of military legend. Nevertheless, the Legion has outlived the French Empire to go forward into the 21st century as one of the world's most respected elite military formations.

The Foreign Legion was formed in 1831 as a way of evading a ban imposed on employing foreigners in the French Army proper. Based at Sidi-bel-Abbès in Algeria, it soon established a reputation for toughness, implacable discipline, and a readiness to take on recruits from any country without inquiring into their identity or personal history. The Legion attracted French and foreign volunteers—adventurers, refugees, the unemployed, and the homeless, men with something to prove and men whose lives had taken a wrong turn, and no doubt some individuals who should have been in jail. After World War I, potential recruits were fingerprinted to weed out escaped convicts and criminals on the run, but the Legion remained a haven for many with pasts they would prefer forgotten. After Germany's defeat in World War II, the Legion actively sought recruits in French-run prisoner-of-war camps, some of them Waffen SS soldiers who might otherwise have faced prosecution for war crimes. Even today, part of the Legion's appeal lies in the opportunity it presents to start a new life from scratch. Potential legionnaires who present themselves at Legion recruiting offices in France now have to show a valid passport, or some other identity document, and their background will be checked for security reasons. But it is still normal to enlist under a pseudonym and acceptable to lie about marital status— officially all legionnaires are unmarried.

NCO's arm badge
This diamond-shaped arm badge bears the Legion's "flaming grenade" insignia.

TRAINING AND SELECTION

The chief barrier to acceptance into the ranks of the Legion lies in the high level of physical and mental fitness required of recruits. They are subjected to a barrage of medical and psychological tests, as well as gruelling exercises before being accepted into the ranks. This is just as well, since the training regime is traditionally one of the most rigorous of any force in the world, including pitiless forced marches carrying full equipment. The discipline and the austerity of life as a legionnaire, added perhaps to unsuitable motives for joining up in the first place, have made desertion a constant problem. Enlistment is initially for five years. A foreigner who re-enlists will qualify for French citizenship at the end of ten years' service; a full 15 years in the Legion earns the right to a pension. All NCOs are promoted from the ranks, but only 10 percent of officers, the rest being provided by the French Army.

Legionnaires on parade
French Foreign Legionnaires, bearing FAMAS assault rifles with bayonets attached, march along the Avenue des Champs Elysées, Paris, during the annual Bastille Day parade on July 14, 2006 *(above)*. The MAT 49 submachine gun *(right)* was used by the Legion in the 1950s and '60s.

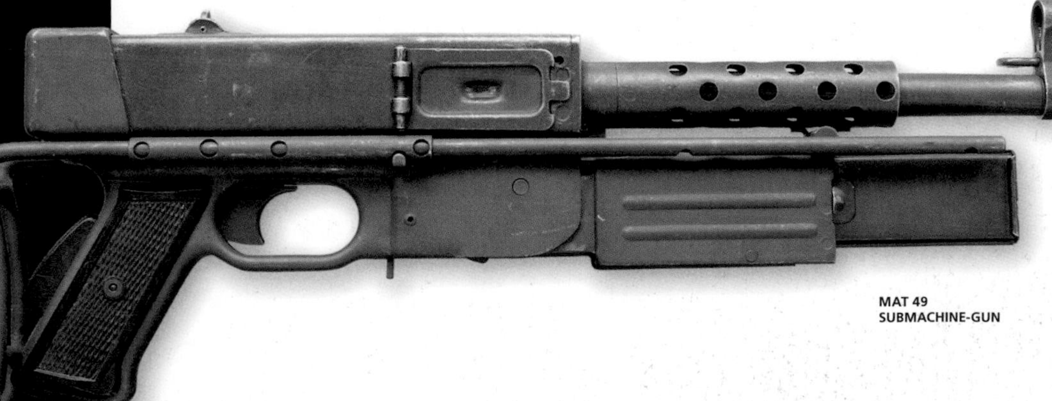

MAT 49 SUBMACHINE-GUN

Training and tradition Legionnaires head up the Approuague River to a training center deep in the jungle of French Guiana *(right)*. Their FAMAS assault rifles have a "bullpup" configuration; the barrel begins in the butt stock, which shortens the gun, and the magazine is placed behind the trigger. When standing at attention *(far right)*, the rifle is worn hanging across the chest.

> "YOU ARE A VOLUNTEER SERVING FRANCE WITH HONOR AND FIDELITY. EVERY LEGIONNAIRE IS YOUR BROTHER ... REGARDLESS OF NATIONALITY, RACE, OR RELIGION. YOU WILL DEMONSTRATE THIS BY THE STRICT SOLIDARITY WHICH MUST ALWAYS UNITE MEMBERS OF THE SAME FAMILY."
>
> **FRENCH FOREIGN LEGION CODE OF HONOR**

Since the language of command is French, recruits from France or Francophile countries have the best chance of promotion.

As a force drawn from many nationalities, legionnaires have traditionally been taught loyalty to the Legion, rather than to France—hence the motto *Legio patria nostra* ("the Legion is our homeland"). Legionnaires are inculcated with the history of more than 170 years of warfare, a story in which sacrificial zeal in defeat is celebrated with even greater enthusiasm than victory. The Legion's combat reputation was founded upon decades of desert warfare against Muslim tribesmen resisting the French presence in North Africa, from Abd al-Qadir to Abd al-Krim. Becoming France's favourite expeditionary force, it fought in the Crimea in the 1850s, in Mexico in the 1860s, in Indochina in the 1880s, and in Dahomey and Madagascar in the 1890s. The Mexican expedition was the occasion for the destruction of a Legion company in a famous action at Camerone. The Legion also served with distinction in Europe, from the battles of Magenta and Solferino in Italy in 1859 to the trenches of the Western Front during World War I. In World War II, after the defeat of France in 1940, the Legion was split between allegiance to the Vichy government and the Free French movement; legionnaries briefly fought one another in Syria in 1941. Yet units of the Legion performed outstandingly against Rommel's forces at Bir Hakeim in the Western Desert in 1942 and eventually participated in the liberation of France in 1944.

Paratrooper's badge This beret badge bears the parachute regiment's multi-winged dagger insignia.

END OF EMPIRE

Determined to hold on to its colonial empire, France certainly needed its Foreign Legion after 1945. For political reasons, the conscripts who made up the bulk of the French Army could not be thrown into the costly job of resisting anti-colonial uprisings. This task fell to French colonial forces and, above all, to the Foreign Legion. The Legion that entered this most controversial phase of its history was probably tougher than ever before or since. Its largest national contingent was from Germany, many of them, as has been mentioned, recruited directly from prisoner-of-war camps at the war's end. To call these men "battle-hardened" would be an understatement, since many had taken part in the almost unimaginable carnage and massacre of the war on Germany's Eastern Front. Another major source of new recruits were Frenchmen who had collaborated with the Nazis during the occupation of France, taking refuge in the Legion to avoid retribution. These were the sort of men who faced the communist-led Viet Minh movement in a brutal struggle for control of Indochina from 1946 to 1954. At any one time between 20,000 and 30,000 legionnaires were serving there. Faced with an elusive enemy using guerrilla tactics, they were ordered to build and defend formidable "hedgehog" strongpoints in contested territory. Since the Viet Minh

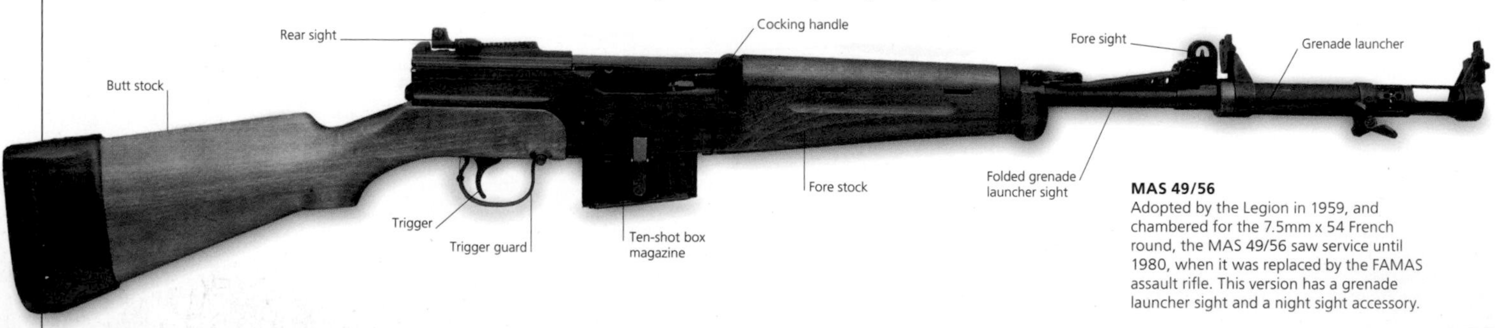

MAS 49/56 Adopted by the Legion in 1959, and chambered for the 7.5mm x 54 French round, the MAS 49/56 saw service until 1980, when it was replaced by the FAMAS assault rifle. This version has a grenade launcher sight and a night sight accessory.

proved lethally expert at ambushing forces traveling to supply or relieve these strongpoints by road, the Legion formed its first parachute battalions to airdrop men into the war zone. The Legion carried out 156 combat jumps in the course of the war. The brutal fighting, marked by massacre and atrocity on both sides, culminated in the decisive defeat of the French at the Battle of Dien Bien Phu in 1954. In total, some 10,000 legionnaires died in the Indochina War, with 30,000 more wounded or taken prisoner. It was a disaster for the Legion, and just as the war in Indochina came to an end, a new conflict opened in Algeria, the Legion's traditional home.

Foreign Legion insignia
This ringed, seven-flamed grenade was adopted as the Legion's insignia in 1963.

ALGERIA AND BEYOND

From 1954 a nationalist movement, the FLN, mounted a guerrilla and terrorist campaign to drive the French out of Algeria. Once more the Legion was at the core of France's military riposte. The 1st Régiment Etrangère Parachutiste (REP—Foreign Legion Parachute Regiment) played a leading role in the controversial Battle of Algiers in 1957, a ruthlessly effective crackdown on FLN terrorists operating in the city's casbah quarter, which was accomplished partly through the routine use of torture.

When in 1961 French President General de Gaulle decided to grant Algeria independence, 1st REP was prominent in supporting a coup attempt mounted by disaffected French generals. The coup was abortive, however, as most of the Legion, and of the French Army in general, refused to support it. The 1st REP was permanently disbanded in punishment for its act of rebellion.

On October 24, 1962, the Legion left Algeria for good, relocating to Aubagne, in the south of France. It might have appeared that the Legion had no future, but there was plentiful need for highly trained forces to project French power around the world. The 2nd REP, based in Corsica, established an impressive reputation as a rapid intervention force, and elements of the Legion were sent to fight against Iraq in 1991 and more recently against the Taliban in Afghanistan.

BATTLE OF DIEN BIEN PHU

In the winter of 1953–54, France flew in some 16,000 troops to construct and occupy a series of strongpoints around an airstrip at Dien Bien Phu, in a remote valley near the border between Vietnam and Laos. The Foreign Legion provided the majority of the soldiers, settling into their fortified positions with support facilities that included a well-staffed brothel. By March 1954, Viet Minh commander General Vo Nguyen Giap had encircled Dien Bien Phu with some 50,000 men, installing heavy artillery on the surrounding hills.

Defeat of the French

The French believed that they could keep their men supplied by air and that their firepower would destroy the Viet Minh. But Giap's artillery quickly put the airstrip out of action, and resupply by paradrop was made hazardous by anti-aircraft fire. Two outlying strong points, Beatrice and Isabelle, were overrun on March 13–14, but then the defense stiffened. Legion volunteers were paradropped in as reinforcements, some making their first ever parachute jump to come to their comrades' aid. Their courage was wasted, however. On May 7–8 the final French positions were overwhelmed. Almost half of the 4,000 defenders killed at Dien Bien Phu were French legionnaires.

Parachute drop into Dien Bien Phu
Legionnaires parachute into the fortified valley of Dien Bien Phu during the disasterous Indochina War, 1953.

FRENCH FOREIGN LEGIONNAIRE GEAR

Few military formations in the world are as attached to their traditions as the French Foreign Legion. Thus an item of equipment like the white *képi*, of little practical relevance, remains of symbolic importance to its wearer. The Legion has always been armed with the best available French infantry weaponry; the MAS-49 was, at the time of France's Indochina War, a technologically advanced rifle. Reliable and accurate, it continued in service through the war in Algeria.

Képi blanc
The *képi blanc* became the official headgear of the French Foreign Legion in 1939. The original model had a removable white cover, seen here with a neck curtain attached, while today's variants are made of white plasticized cloth. A green beret is standard duty headwear for the Legion, with the *képi* worn on parade and off-duty.

Removable cover

False chin strap

Protective neck curtain

Desert scarf used as turban during sandstorms

M1947 fatigues
These light cotton desert fatigues were worn by legionnaires of the *Compagnie d'Instruction* in the Algerian war of 1954–62. They were designed for ease of movement in the North African heat.

Gas cylinder

Fore sight between protective blades

MAS-49 rifle
Developed in 1949 by *Manufacture d'Armes St. Etienne*, the MAS-49 is a semi-automatic infantry rifle which employs a direct impingement gas operating system. It is chambered for the 7.5x54 French round and takes a 10-round detachable magazine. It was first used by the Legion in the Indochina War of 1946–54.

Fore stock

Leather webbing

Barrel band

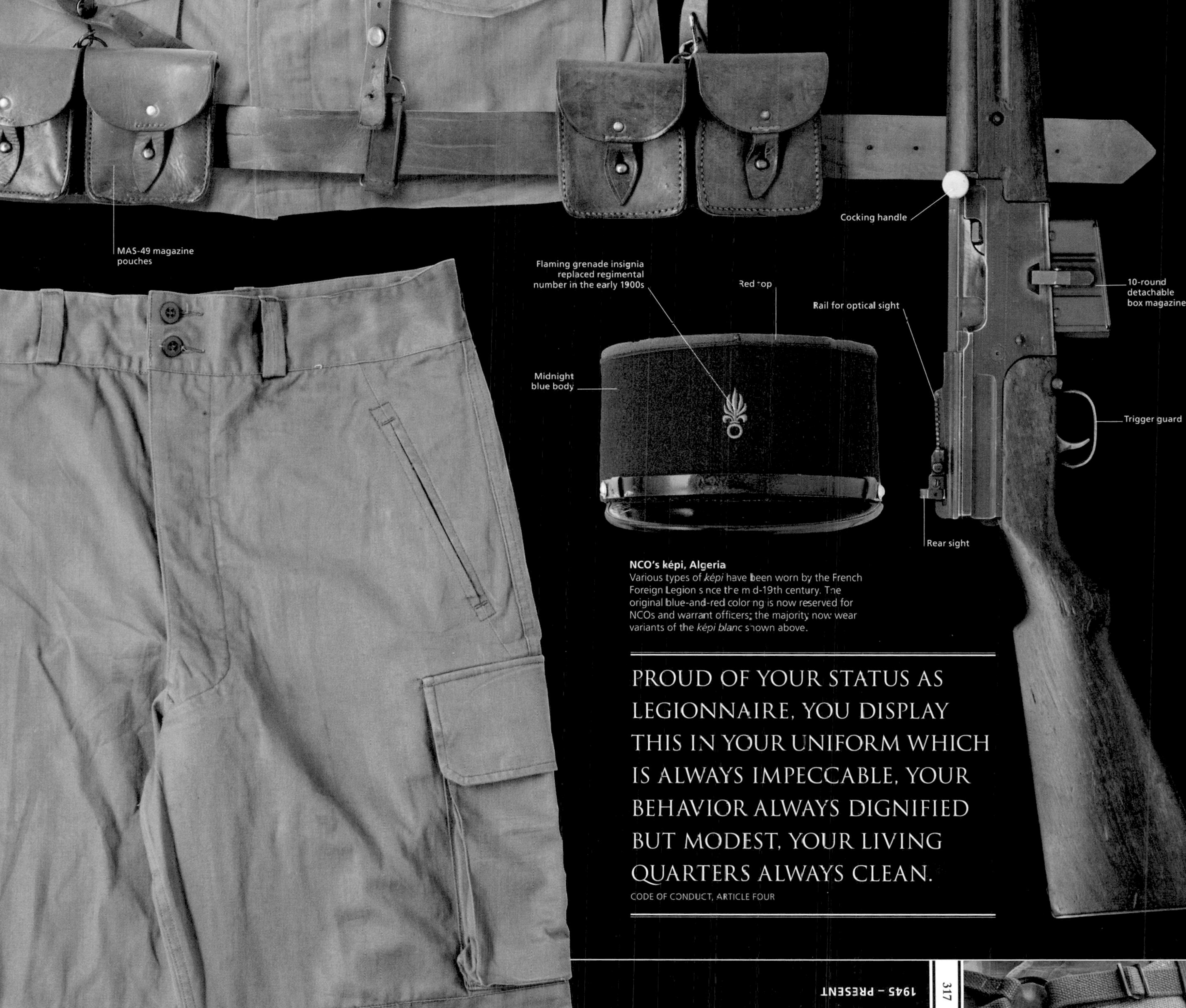

NCO's képi, Algeria
Various types of *képi* have been worn by the French Foreign Legion since the mid-19th century. The original blue-and-red coloring is now reserved for NCOs and warrant officers; the majority now wear variants of the *képi blanc* shown above.

PROUD OF YOUR STATUS AS LEGIONNAIRE, YOU DISPLAY THIS IN YOUR UNIFORM WHICH IS ALWAYS IMPECCABLE, YOUR BEHAVIOR ALWAYS DIGNIFIED BUT MODEST, YOUR LIVING QUARTERS ALWAYS CLEAN.

CODE OF CONDUCT, ARTICLE FOUR

1965 – 1971

US MARINE

ONLY THE UNITED STATES MARINE CORPS STANDS OUT AS AN ELITE FORCE IN AND OF ITSELF. MARINE IS A WORD OF RESPECT. WHENEVER THIS WORD IS USED IT EVOKES IMAGES OF SPARTANS, EXEMPLARY EXAMPLES OF AMERICAN EXCELLENCE. THE ELITE OF THE ELITE.

SERGEANT BILL M. BROWER, UNITED STATES MARINE CORPS, 1969—1972

Reconnaissance team
A platoon commander from the 1st United States Marine Division uses a radio during operations in Vietnam *(above)*. The Marines' chief machine gun was the general-purpose M60 *(right)*.

THE FIRST AMERICAN GROUND FORCES deployed in offensive combat operations against the Viet Cong and the North Vietnamese Army (NVA) were the US Marines who came ashore at Da Nang on the coast of South Vietnam on March 8, 1965. The choice of the Marines to spearhead US involvement in Vietnam reflected both their status as an elite fighting force and their traditional role as agents of US overseas intervention. The following six years of warfare were to test the Marines' endurance to the limit.

The US Marines who served in Vietnam were inheritors of a long and proud tradition. The Marine Corps traced its origins back to the two battalions of Continental Marines established in 1775 to serve as soldiers on board naval vessels during the American Revolutionary War. In the course of the 19th and early 20th centuries, the Marines developed a role as an overseas intervention force—one of their notable actions was to seize the harbor at Guantanamo Bay in Cuba during the 1898 Spanish-American War. They served with distinction in World War I, for which they were considerably better prepared than the US Army. By World War II, the Marines were developing techniques of amphibious warfare that were applied successfully during the island-hopping campaign against the Japanese in the Pacific from 1942 to 1945. The Korean War subsequently confirmed their claim to be the toughest American infantry force—a claim with which the US Army naturally did not agree.

TRAINING AN ELITE

The quality of the Marines as fighting men depended largely upon the quality of their training. At the time of the Vietnam War, the Marine Corps was, at it is today, a self-contained all-arms formation, with its own artillery, helicopters, and fixed-wing aircraft. But the infantry was the focus of Marine operations (Marine aircraft were intended primarily for close air support) and all Marine recruits had to undergo training as riflemen. The rigors of the 13-week Marine "boot camp" at the Parris Island Recruit Depot, and at the Corps' other initial training facility at San Diego, are legendary. Gruelling marches, push-ups, and runs are executed to the constant accompaniment of aggressively yelled orders and abuse from instructors. The process culminates in the "Crucible," a 54-hour field training exercise in which the recruit is allowed a maximum of eight hours' sleep. Successful recruits then go on to other camps for regular infantry training, with an emphasis on accurate shooting at long range, and to learn specialized skills. A sign at Parris Island proclaims: "The deadliest weapon in the world—a Marine and his rifle."

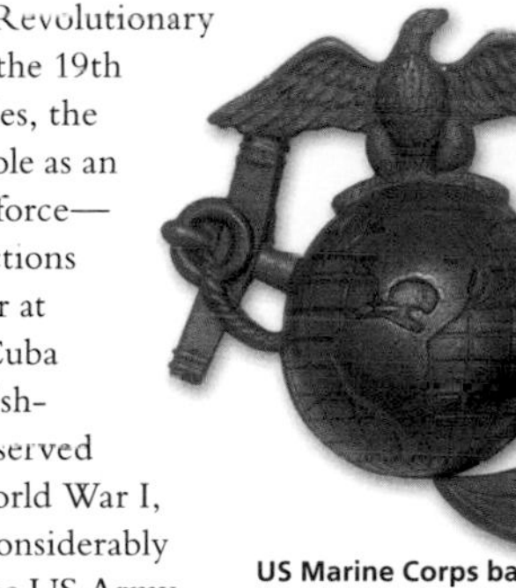

US Marine Corps badge
The eagle and anchor symbolize the Marine Corps' air and sea capabilities.

The Marine infantryman sent to Vietnam—the "grunt"—was typically no more than 18 to 20 years old. Recruits came from all over the US, although there was a tendency for more to hail from the rural Midwest and South. Fully racially integrated since the later stages of the Korean War, the Marines attracted many African-Americans, who found in the armed forces a better employment opportunity and relatively equal treatment at a time when civil rights were a hotly contested issue in the US.

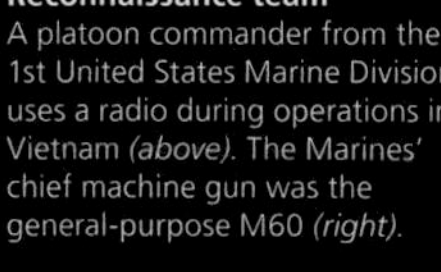

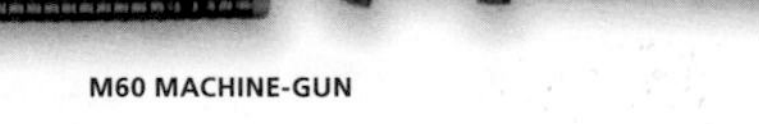

M60 MACHINE-GUN

Amphibious warfare
Amphibious landing techniques are a mainstay of Marine Corps training. Here a company disembarks from an LVTP5 amphibious armored personnel carrier in South Vietnam, 1965.

Canteen
This standard-issue canteen, still in use today, holds 1 US quart (95 ml) of water.

By 1968 just over one in ten Marines were black, although a significantly higher percentage would be found at the sharp end of the war, with less in safe technical or administrative jobs. Black officers were rare—less than one in a hundred in 1968. White or black, the grunts tended to belong to the less educated, most underprivileged strata of American society. They would make courageous soldiers, but not necessarily sensitive ambassadors for the American way of life.

INTO VIETNAM

The Marines were deployed in the northern sector of South Vietnam, in a region abutting the Demilitarized Zone (DMZ) that separated the US-backed South from communist-ruled North Vietnam. The area in which they had to operate comprised a densely populated coastal plain and, further inland, the wild jungle-clad mountains of the Annamese Cordillera.

Both the plain and the mountains were challenging, alien environments for the Marine soldier. Amid the villages and rice-paddies of the plain he was surrounded by a population with a culture and language he did not understand, and in which active supporters of the Viet Cong guerrillas were indistinguishable from genuine noncombatants. In the Highlands he had to seek out an elusive enemy among jagged ridges and ravines wreathed in mist, cutting a path through the tangled vines of triple-canopy forest with a machete, plagued by insects and battling with heat and humidity. Even on routine patrols in areas theoretically under the control of the South Vietnamese government, there was a steady drain of casualties from mines and booby traps (which the Viet Cong excelled at making), or sniper fire. Once away from an American base, no soldier could afford to relax—taking off your flak jacket because you were hot could cost you your life.

At first the Marines faced the challenge of Vietnam with good morale and adapted well to the difficult conditions. They even mounted an intelligent counterinsurgency effort in the villages known as the Combined Action Program. This involved putting small squads of Marines in "friendly" hamlets alongside local militia to keep out the Viet Cong. It was one of the few occasions when the American military chose to regard ordinary Vietnamese as potential friends and allies. But little of the Marines' time was devoted to winning hearts and minds. Their main function was to seek out and destroy the enemy, whether Viet Cong guerrillas or NVA soldiers, primarily in the thinly populated Highlands. US commanders believed that they could win the conflict through a combination of the mobility provided by helicopters and maximum use of the firepower available to American forces. To provide the firepower, Marines set up firebases in advanced positions from which their artillery could then support infantry advancing into enemy-controlled territory. Helicopters inserted Recon teams of six to eight Marines into hostile territory to track the movements of enemy formations, or ferried larger units into jungle landing zones (LZs) from which they could launch patrols in search of the enemy.

It proved an exhausting and costly way of waging war. Men advancing through forested mountains carrying 80 lb (36 kg) of gear—including an M16 rifle, grenades, ammunition, canteens, entrenching tool, machete, first-aid kit,

M79 "Blooper"
With a maximum range of 984 ft (300 m), the M79 grenade launcher fills the gap between the hand grenade and the mortar. Two were issued to each rifle squad.

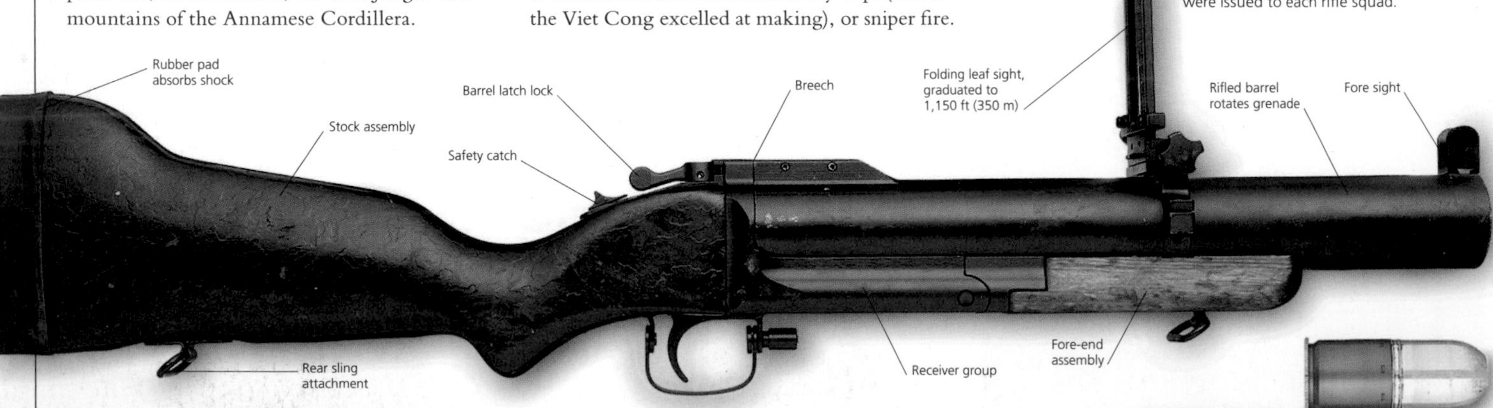

and flak jacket—might be lucky to make 1,650 ft (500 m) an hour. Even without enemy action, casualties were sustained from falls, snakebite, heat stroke, and other natural causes. "No-contact" missions were common. When firefights occurred, the Marines inevitably suffered losses to the well-trained, tenacious communist infantry. The availability of helicopters to evacuate the wounded saved many lives, although "medevac" missions were extremely dangerous; low-roving helicopters were prime targets for enemy mortar fire.

UNDER SIEGE

The Marines increasingly found themselves on the defensive as their firebases and outposts just south of the DMZ came under attack from NVA forces. The hill-top base at Con Thien was the object of a determined NVA infantry assault in September 1967. This was beaten off by the Marine garrison, but they then came under sustained artillery bombardment from NVA 130mm and 152mm guns sited inside the DMZ. Marine artillery and aircraft hit back at the artillery and at the NVA soldiers around the base. For the Marines sheltering in bunkers at Con Thien, the experience was reminiscent of World War I trench warfare. Once the monsoon rains started, the base became a quagmire of red mud in which men sank knee-deep. Around the flooded bunkers, artillery fire created a barren moonscape, scorched and pocked with craters. The siege of Con Thien was lifted at the end of October, but it was sign of things to come.

On January 21, 1968, NVA artillery, rocket, and mortar fire struck the Marine base at Khe Sanh in the foothills of the Cordillera. The Marines' ammunition dump exploded. For the Americans it was an inauspicious start to a siege that was to last for 77 agonizing days. The base was defended by some 6,000 men, mostly

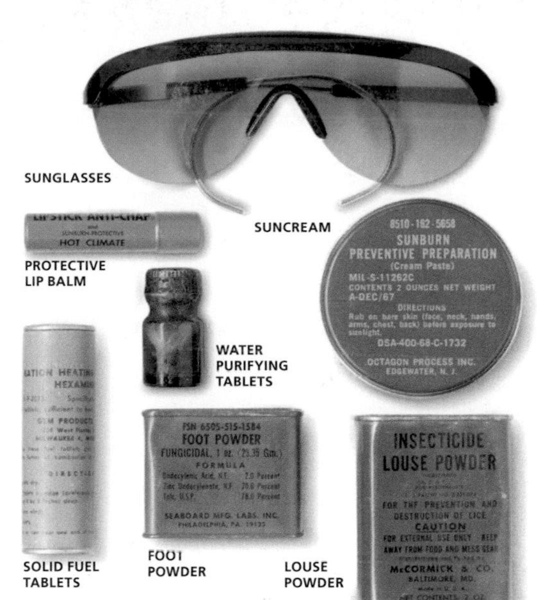

Jungle survival kit
An assortment of medications and preventatives was issued to each Marine. In the absence of kindling, hexamine fuel tablets were used for cooking.

> "THE CORPS—WE LOVE IT AND SHALL DIE FOR IT. IF YOU HAVE NEVER BEEN IN IT, YOU SHALL NEVER UNDERSTAND IT."
>
> **BRAD LEMKE**, US MARINE CORPS GUNNERY SERGEANT

Sea Knight
A CH-46 Sea Knight helicopter arrives at the Marine base of Khe Sanh. The helicopter provided all-weather, day/night transport for troops, equipment, and supplies.

SEARCH AND DESTROY TACTICS

US ground forces took the offensive in South Vietnam, aiming to "find, fix, and destroy" the enemy. Typically, a company would be airlifted by helicopter into a part of the jungle where communist troops were known to be operating. The area around the designated landing zone (LZ) would be "prepped" by air strikes or by artillery fire from the nearest firebase before the helicopters were sent in. Either alone or alongside other units in a wider sweep, the company would then move on foot through the forest seeking contact with enemy infantry.

AIR AND ARTILLERY SUPPORT

When a firefight began, the American infantry would call in artillery fire and air strikes to hammer the enemy position. Efforts to surround enemy formations generally failed. The agile communists were expert at filtering through any attempted encirclement, and at ambushing reinforcements moving up to join the combat. The awesome firepower at the Americans' disposal, especially from the air, ensured that many more Viet Cong and NVA troops died than US soldiers. On the other hand, the grunt on the ground frequently found himself fighting at a disadvantage, facing a numerically far superior enemy.

belonging to the 26th Marine Regiment. The NVA force that surrounded the base was probably 40,000-strong. The NVA dug trenches to within 100 yd (90 m) of the perimeter of sandbags and barbed wire but failed to take the base by assault. On the other hand, the Marines had severe difficulties keeping the garrison supplied by air. The base's airstrip was exposed to enemy mortar and artillery fire and anti-aircraft guns menaced the approaches to the base. Air operations were also rendered hazardous by persistent low cloud. The American nightmare was that the base would be overrun or forced to surrender, as had happened to the French at the hands of the Viet Minh at Dien Bien Phu in 1954. There was a tremor of anxiety when, during the siege, an American outpost at Lang Vei was overrun by the NVA using tanks. But the Marines held on at Khe Sanh and at their surrounding hill-top outposts until a relief column broke through on April 8. The Marines had lost 199 dead and 830 wounded in the siege.

US Army note pad
During the Vietnam War much of a Marine's equipment, despite rivalry, was US Army-issue.

While the siege of Khe Sanh was going on, the communists launched the Tet Offensive (during the Tet holiday celebrations) in which they attempted to seize control of cities and towns across South Vietnam. While most urban areas were held or swiftly retaken by US and South Vietnamese forces, the city of Hue was held by NVA soldiers for 25 days. The Marines played the leading part in wresting back control of the city. They fought from house to house and from street to street, at one point reportedly taking a casualty for every yard of ground gained. By the time NVA resistance finally ceased on February 24, the Marines had lost almost a thousand men killed or wounded.

CRISIS OF MORALE

At Khe Sanh and at Hue the grunts had shown all the qualities expected of US Marines. Many men had been driven to the limits of endurance; war correspondents described the "thousand-yard stare" of the soldier reduced to mental and emotional blankness by the stress of sustained

On patrol
Captain Charles Robb leads a group of Marines on patrol south of Da Nang in May 1968. Patrols were usually made in platoon (20-man) or company (100-man) strength.

Cooking equipment
Most of a Marine's food came in cans. After eating, cutlery was slid onto the pan handle through holes at their ends to keep them together while being washed.

TIN PAN FOR COOKING AND EATING

CUTLERY

> "THE STRENGTH OF THE PACK IS THE WOLF, THE STRENGTH OF THE WOLF IS THE PACK."

MOTTO, 3RD LIGHT ARMORED RECONNAISSANCE BATTALION

exposure to combat. Yet they had taken punishment from the enemy without cracking and had gone on doing the job they were employed to do. Morale in the Marines, as in the rest of US ground forces in Vietnam, was nonetheless seriously on the wane. As the number of Marines making their final journey home in a green rubber bodybag mounted, the ordinary grunt's focus inevitably fixed on surviving his 13-month tour of duty. Even without the persistent criticism of the war being expressed by journalists and the anti-war movement in the United States, men could see that the prospect of anything that could be called "victory" was remote. Maintaining commitment was especially hard for black Marines. After the assassination of civil rights leader Martin Luther King in April 1968, many African-Americans felt torn in their allegiance, unsure whether they were right to be fighting for the United States at all.

Urban combat
The Tet Offensive saw the city of Hue overrun by NVA troops. Under the constant threat of snipers, the Marines of Task Force X-Ray fought street-by-street for a month to regain the city.

AFTER VIETNAM

It was with relief that the Marines withdrew from Vietnam in 1971, leaving the war to be fought by the army alone. By then, they had long ceased to carry out offensive operations. Around 800,000 Marines had served in the war. Of these, 13,091 had been killed and 51,392 wounded in action. Overall, Marines accounted for about a quarter of all US combat deaths in Vietnam. Rebuilding the image and morale of the Corps was a task that took a decade, but the Marines have survived to play a prominent role in subsequent conflicts, including the invasion and occupation of Afghanistan and Iraq in the 21st century.

Purple Heart
The Purple Heart, or Badge of Military Merit, was instituted by George Washington (depicted) in 1782, when he was commander-in-chief of the Continental Army. It is awarded to soldiers either wounded or killed in battle.

US MARINE UNIFORM

When the Marines went into Vietnam in 1965, they suffered a shortage of gear suitable for their environment. Jungle fatigues (officially known as Tropical Combat Uniforms) were not issued until 1966–67, replacing previous standard olive-drab utilities (OG-107s). The hazards of patrols and sweeps in Vietnam, where booby-trap devices inflicted a heavy toll in casualties, meant that protection was a high priority— hence the wearing of flak jackets and the eventual adoption of reinforced footwear.

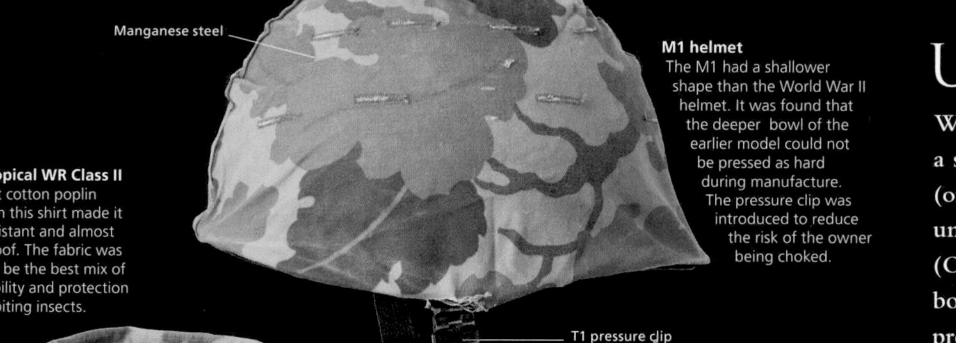

M1 helmet
The M1 had a shallower shape than the World War II helmet. It was found that the deeper bowl of the earlier model could not be pressed as hard during manufacture. The pressure clip was introduced to reduce the risk of the owner being choked.

Coat tropical WR Class II
The tight cotton poplin weave on this shirt made it wind resistant and almost waterproof. The fabric was found to be the best mix of breathability and protection against biting insects.

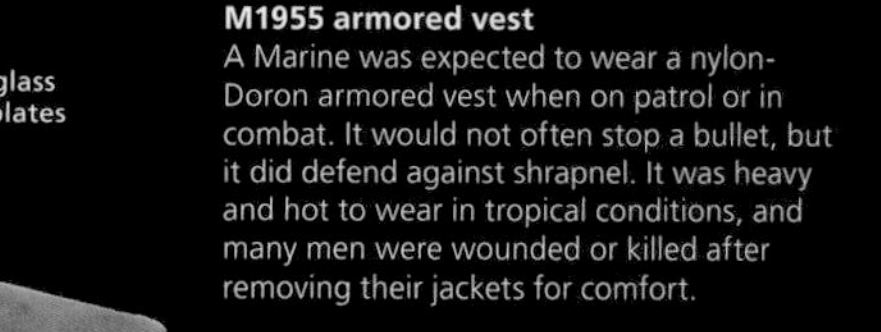

M1955 armored vest
A Marine was expected to wear a nylon-Doron armored vest when on patrol or in combat. It would not often stop a bullet, but it did defend against shrapnel. It was heavy and hot to wear in tropical conditions, and many men were wounded or killed after removing their jackets for comfort.

Mitchell pattern camouflage

Webbing secured around waist

M61 webbing
Webbing was worn like a jacket. Straps looped over the shoulders and equipment hung around the waist. The reverse of the webbing had more snaps for attaching rifle ammunition pouches.

BEING READY IS NOT WHAT MATTERS. WHAT MATTERS IS WINNING AFTER YOU GET THERE.

LIEUTENANT GENERAL V. H. KRULAK, USMC, TO A MARINE UNIT LEAVING FOR VIETNAM, APRIL 1965

Trousers tropical WR Class II
These standard issue camouflage trousers were worn by Marines and also the army. The ankles had drawstrings and were worn rolled up on the boot to prevent saturation with water.

Tropical combat boots
The most common of all boots issued to Marines, they were made of leather and canvas with the hard rubber sole directly molded on as stitching tended to rot in the tropical climate. From 1967 Panama sole boots were issued with an embedded steel plate to protect against punji sticks—booby traps of sharp stakes.

US MARINE WEAPONS

Much of the gear used by Marines in Vietnam was of World War II or Korean War vintage. The M14 rifle in use in 1965 was a direct descendant of the WWII M1 Garand, although it was largely replaced by the innovative M16 from 1967. Hand-launched parachute flares were employed when defending against night attacks. Insect repellant was an essential in the jungle.

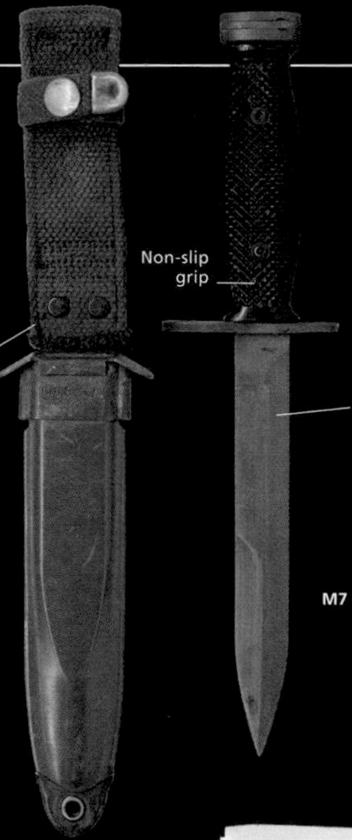

M7 knife and M8 scabbard
The M7 knife doubled as both a fighting knife and a bayonet. The M8 scabbard was used for a number of knife models.

Web carrying strap

M8 SCABBARD

Non-slip grip

Carbon steel blade sharpened both sides

M7 KNIFE

Canteen and cup
Aluminum canteens held a US quart (950 ml) of water and nested inside the canteen cup as shown. Cans were sometimes pierced to use as makeshift stoves.

MAP OF SAIGON BASE AREA

PARACHUTE FLARE

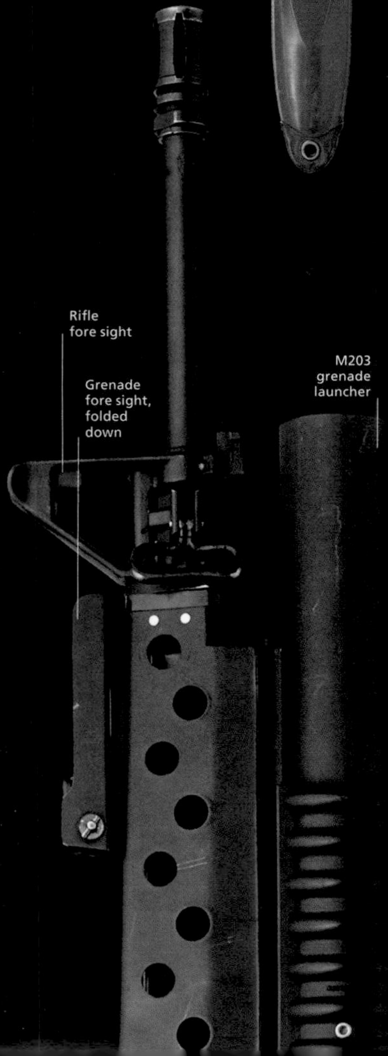

Rifle fore sight

Grenade fore sight, folded down

M203 grenade launcher

Loading/ ejector slide

ANGLE HEAD FLASHLIGHT

1941 pack
Part of a top and bottom pack system to hold rations and personal effects, the second pack could be worn underneath the first. The rolled piece of canvas or shelter-half formed half of a "pup" tent when snapped to a second piece.

Mitchell pattern camouflage issued only to Marine Corps

Rolled canvas shelter-half

M1943 folding entrenching shovel

Cotton bandolier
The bandolier shown held M16 magazines for the M16 rifle.

Claymore mine bag
After planting the antipersonnel mine the Marine would retain the bag as a musette (side bag)

M16 automatic rifle with M203 grenade launcher
The M16 became the primary infantry rifle of the US Army and Marines in 1967. Soldiers disliked it at first, claiming the rifle was unreliable and the 5.56mm round lacked stopping power. However, it remains in front-line service today.

Baseball grenades
Designed to fragment, the grenades contained high explosives and notched wire.

1943 jungle first-aid kit
Marines made use of World War II vintage kits that were used in tropical regions. Malaria was a threat and in addition to insect repellant Marines would have taken a weekly malaria tablet.

Carabiner
Used for rappelling or linking items, the sprung part of the metal ring releases easily but can't spring open unaided.

Under enemy fire
US soldiers of the 7th Marines wade ashore after arriving by landing craft at Cape Batangan, Vietnam, November 1965, following the start of Operation Piranha in September. The year 1965 saw US troops begin to arrive in large numbers in Vietnam.

1965 – 1975

VIET CONG GUERRILLA

“THE NIGHT ... BELONGS TO THE VIET CONG.

THE PEOPLE'S LIBERATION ARMED FORCES (PLAF), known to its American enemies as the Viet Cong, was a rural-based guerrilla army that fought against the US and the US-backed South Vietnamese government in the Vietnam War. Like the North Vietnamese Army (NVA) infantry who fought with them, the Viet Cong guerrillas were skillful and dedicated fighters. In combat they almost always suffered far heavier losses than their opponents, but they were sustained by comradeship and a clear sense of purpose.

The Viet Cong evolved from the communist-led Viet Minh guerrilla movement that fought against French colonial rule in Indochina. After the Viet Minh defeated the French in 1954, Vietnam was split, with the South coming under the control of the US-backed government of Ngo Dinh Diem and the North under communist rule. When the country was divided, tens of thousands of Viet Minh guerrillas from the South chose to relocate to the North; other former guerrillas resumed a peasant life in their Southern villages.

Diem's government proved to be corrupt and brutal, soon alienating much of the population of South Vietnam. By 1957, small-scale guerrilla warfare had resumed in many rural areas. Sensing that the time was ripe to resume the struggle for a unified communist-ruled Vietnam, in 1959 the North Vietnamese government sent tens of thousands of former Viet Minh guerrillas back to the South as "cadres" with the intention of organizing a full-scale insurgency.

During their time in the North, these men had undergone rigorous training in the theory and practice of revolutionary warfare. They had learned that the political and military struggles were inseparable. After the long, tough journey to the South through trackless jungle, they made contact with villagers, slipping into the hamlets at night to talk to local people and win their support for a guerrilla campaign. The South Vietnamese peasants were prepared to listen to the cadres as people of their own kind, who spoke about issues that concerned them, such as excessive government taxes and unpopular local landowners. The National Liberation Front (NLF), set up in 1960 as the political arm of the guerrilla movement, backed up the propaganda efforts of the cadres with clandestine radio broadcasts, posters, and news sheets.

GUERRILLA ARMY

Wherever the cadres found support among the local population, they recruited guerrilla soldiers. The most promising young men were encouraged to leave their village and become full-time guerrillas; women were also taken to serve in support roles. There were plenty of willing volunteers, although various kinds of pressure were applied, and in some cases recruits were conscripted at gunpoint. The full-time guerrillas were subdivided into regional forces, which carried out low-level operations around the guerrillas' home area, and main force soldiers, who received thorough infantry training at bases in sparsely inhabited country and were readied for full-scale combat in large military formations. The peasants who remained in the villages were organized into a part-time guerrilla militia. They had only the most basic military training but could, for example, provide intelligence, set booby-traps for government patrols, and dig tunnels to serve as hiding places for guerrilla troops and their equipment.

By early 1965, the Viet Cong had extended its control over three-quarters of South Vietnam, achieved mostly through small-scale guerrilla activity. Viet Cong units raided villages, killing government-appointed village leaders and slaughtering local pro-government militia.

DEGTYAREV LIGHT MACHINE-GUN

Female warrior
A female Viet Cong soldier poses with an RPG-7 rocket launcher in the Mekong Delta in 1968 *(above)*. Although figuring prominently as fighters in Viet Cong propaganda photos, women mostly served in support roles. The RPG-7, like the Degtyarev light machine gun *(right)*, was a Soviet-manufactured weapon supplied to guerrillas via North Vietnam.

Isolated military outposts were overrun. Roads were rendered unusable by a number of ambushes. In the cities, terrorist attacks were launched against the government's US military advisers, including bombings of American-frequented movie theaters and clubs.

Chinese compass
Much of the equipment used by the Viet Cong was provided by communist China. Compasses such as this were essential for orientation in the jungle.

FIGHTING THE AMERICANS

From 1965, the nature of the war changed radically. The United States sent in its armed forces to prevent the fall of the South Vietnamese government. At the same time, the North Vietnamese Army began sending troops into the South in large numbers. Although the guerrilla war of ambushes, booby traps, and assassinations continued, soon much of the war was being fought between US soldiers and North Vietnamese infantry or Viet Cong main force guerrillas in wild, largely deserted country. The Viet Cong proved to be a match for US ground forces as light infantrymen. Led by officers who shared their hardships, they moved swiftly across country, maneuvered skillfully to carry out ambushes, and hugged their enemy in firefights to inhibit close air support. US forces found them frustratingly elusive, filtering away before decisive defeat could be inflicted. But for the guerrillas, subject to bombing, shelling, napalm, and fire from fixed-wing and helicopter gunships, combat with the US forces was, above all, a gruelling ordeal in which they took heavy casualties.

FAR FROM HOME

The guerrilla's experience of war was characterized by fear, hardship, homesickness, and boredom. The jungle was no more a familiar habitat to peasants from the rice paddies than it was to the Americans. To the Vietnamese, the jungle-clad mountains were a place to be feared, inhabited as they were by ghosts and fearsome wild animals. They suffered terribly from malaria and from snakebites—the guerrillas' famous rubber sandals offered very poor protection against poisonous reptiles. Surviving on small quantities of rice, salt, and dried fish or meat, the guerrillas were often in a state of semi-starvation. They augmented their rations by eating jungle fauna, including monkeys, elephants, and large moths

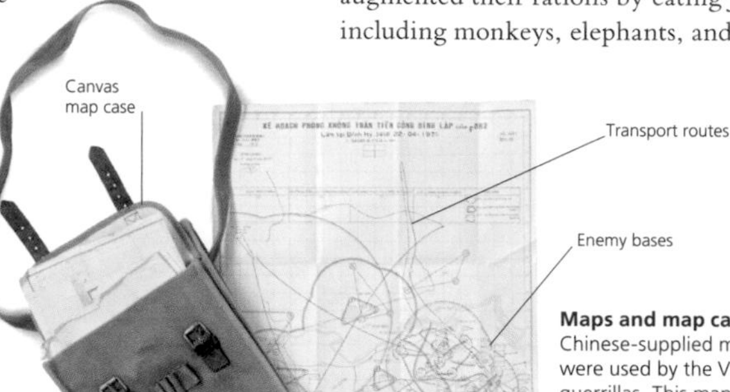

Maps and map case
Chinese-supplied map cases were used by the Viet Cong guerrillas. This map has marked on it detailed information about the location of enemy bases.

Guerrilla weapons
The Viet Cong used a wide variety of infantry weapons, many originating from the Soviet Union. Here guerrillas are equipped with a Korean War-vintage Goryunov 7.62mm heavy machine gun, Simonov rifles, and state-of-the-art AK47 assault rifles.

> "DURING THE DAY, THEY GENERALLY DISAPPEAR, SLEEPING AND HIDING BENEATH THICK JUNGLE CANOPIES, TAKING REFUGE IN HILLSIDE CAVES."

ARTICLE IN *TIME* MAGAZINE, JULY 21, 1967

that they barbecued in a flame. Guerrillas were paid 60 piasters (about $2) a month, which they used to order luxuries such as sugar, soap, and tobacco that supply officers would purchase in Cambodian markets. Amusements were rare. The guerrillas trained endlessly or sat through classes in which they were taught revolutionary slogans or updated on world news. An occasional visiting entertainment unit would be welcome despite its generally repetitious programs of uplifting patriotic films and songs. To counter homesickness, guerrillas were occasionally given leave, although traveling through a war zone to visit their families was hazardous.

Attack by a US search-and-destroy sweep or by aerial bombardment instantly replaced any boredom with fear. The men might have to flee at a moment's notice and then move through the forest for days on end, hiding desperately from the enemy by day and sleeping in a hammock slung between two trees at night. By general agreement, most terrifying of all was a B-52 bomber strike, in which a whole area of forest would erupt with a roar that tore eardrums and shook nerves to the core. Sheltering in tunnels, many of which contained kitchens, sleeping rooms, and makeshift hospitals, offered some protection, but there was always the fear that they might collapse and bury their occupants alive. Some guerrillas had to be hospitalized with shell shock after persistent bombing.

Vietnam War
The Vietnam War was a conflict between communist North Vietnam (backed by China and Russia) and the US-backed South Vietnamese government. It also spilled over into Laos and Cambodia.

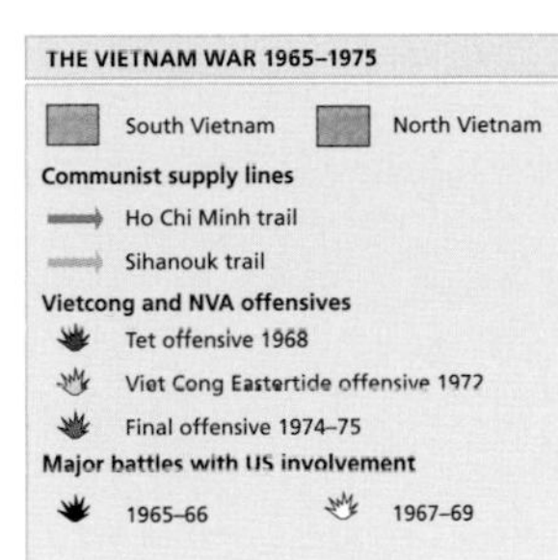

1965–69: Communist-controlled areas bombed by US

Aug 1964: North Vietnamese attacks reported on US destroyers. Gulf of Tonkin Resolution, commits US forces to war

1954: North-South Demarcation Line agreed at Geneva Conference

Mar 1965: First US ground forces arrive in Vietnam, ostensibly to protect air base

Mar 1968: Notorious massacre of 300-400 South Vietnamese civilians by US soldiers in My Lai

Apr 1975: North Vietnamese Army encircles city. US civilians are evacuated by helicopter from embassy rooftop. Final surrender

TET AND AFTER

In January-February 1968, the Viet Cong took advantage of the new year, or Tet, celebrations, when many South Vietnamese soldiers would be on leave, and occupied cities and towns across South Vietnam. Leading to the brief occupation of Saigon, the capital, the Tet Offensive, as it was known, dealt a fatal blow to America's will to continue the war, but at the cost of massive guerrilla casualties. There were many thousands of defections from the Viet Cong in the following year, as men found the tension and hardship of years of guerrilla life cumulatively unbearable. But desertions were never as numerous as from the government forces. A member of the Viet Cong political leadership, Truong Nhu Trang, wrote: "Although the guerrillas were short of food and often sick, they maintained the kind of esprit and comradeship that animates people who are fighting for a common purpose in which they believe with all their hearts. They got on, under horrendous conditions, through mutual support and a rough but genuine love for each other."

In the end, however, the defeat of the South Vietnamese government in 1975 was achieved by the North Vietnamese Army fighting a conventional war with conventional weapons, such as tanks and artillery. Militarily sidelined, many Viet Cong guerrillas were also disillusioned with the outcome of the war. Few of the rank and file had been communists and the harsh austerity of the reunified Vietnam was not what they had wanted, which was simply an end to foreign interference in their country and a better life for their families.

VIET CONG BOOBY TRAPS

Booby trap devices played a large part in the small-scale guerrilla war waged around the villages in Vietnam. One of the most effective—and most primitive—of these was the punji stick. Villagers sharpened pieces of bamboo, coated their tips with feces or some other infectious substance, and planted them upright in the ground under a covering of leaves or grass. If a soldier stepped on it, the stick would pierce the sole of his boot. Whole clearings were sometimes planted with punji sticks in an attempt to stop them being used as helicopter landing zones. When the Americans thickened their boot soles to resist punji sticks, the guerrillas invented a device made of two spiked panels that, when trodden on, penetrated the leg above the boot. Other booby trap devices included grenades attached to a tripwire made of fishing line and purloined US howitzer shells re-fused to turn them into remote-controlled mines. The guerrillas' use of booby trap weapons had a devastating psychological impact on US or South Vietnamese troops. They frequently resulted in amputation of limbs, if not death. Sometimes guerrilla snipers would cover the site of a booby trap, ready to add to the mayhem.

Spiked booby traps
Common Viet Cong booby traps were the spike plate and the grenade (here without its trip wire).

VIET CON[illegible]GEAR

The essence of the Viet Cong's strategy was to blend in with the civilian population, so the basic uniform consisted of a pair of black cotton pajamas, a black floppy hat, and a scarf. This outfit allowed their members, both male and female, to pass for local villagers. When on active operations they made skilful use of jungle camouflage, American parachutes providing a valuable source of material for shawls and helmet covers.

> "TWO PAIRS OF BLACK PAJAMAS, A COUPLE OF PAIRS OF UNDERPANTS, A MOSQUITO NET AND A FEW SQUARE YARDS OF LIGHT NYLON ... WERE ALL THAT A GUERRILLA OWNED."
>
> **TRUONG NHU TANG** *A VIET CONG MEMOIR*

Camouflage [illegible]
The Viet Cong [illegible] wore black cotton hats to [illegible] their clothes or the conical straw hats worn by local farmers. In combat, however, they might exchange these for camouflaged pith helmets or hats like this, similar to those worn by American troops.

Tube tied with scrap of cloth

Rice tube
The Viet Cong used a simple yet practical method of carrying provisions for their units—a long canvas tube filled with rice that was slung round the neck like a bandolier.

Male tunic
Both male and female guerrillas wore very similar black clothing, but the stitching on the tunics worn by women was slightly different.

Lightweight shovel
Digging played an important part in the Viet Cong guerrilla campaigns. As well as the famous underground tunnel systems that allowed them to move unseen through the jungle, they also constructed well camouflaged bunkers and strongpoints.

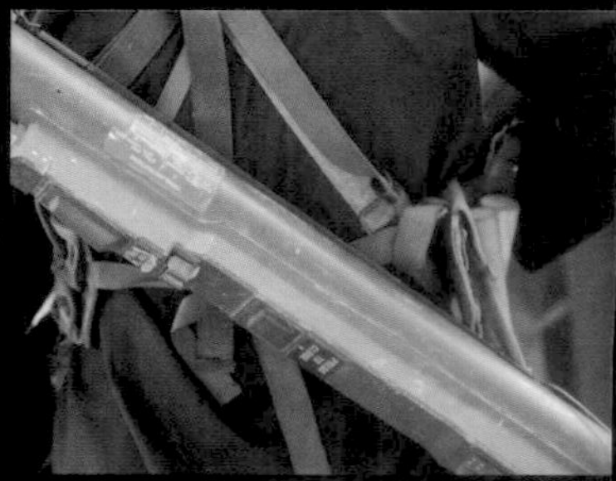

Canvas cover

Carrying a captured American light antitank weapon

Camouflage shawl and AK47

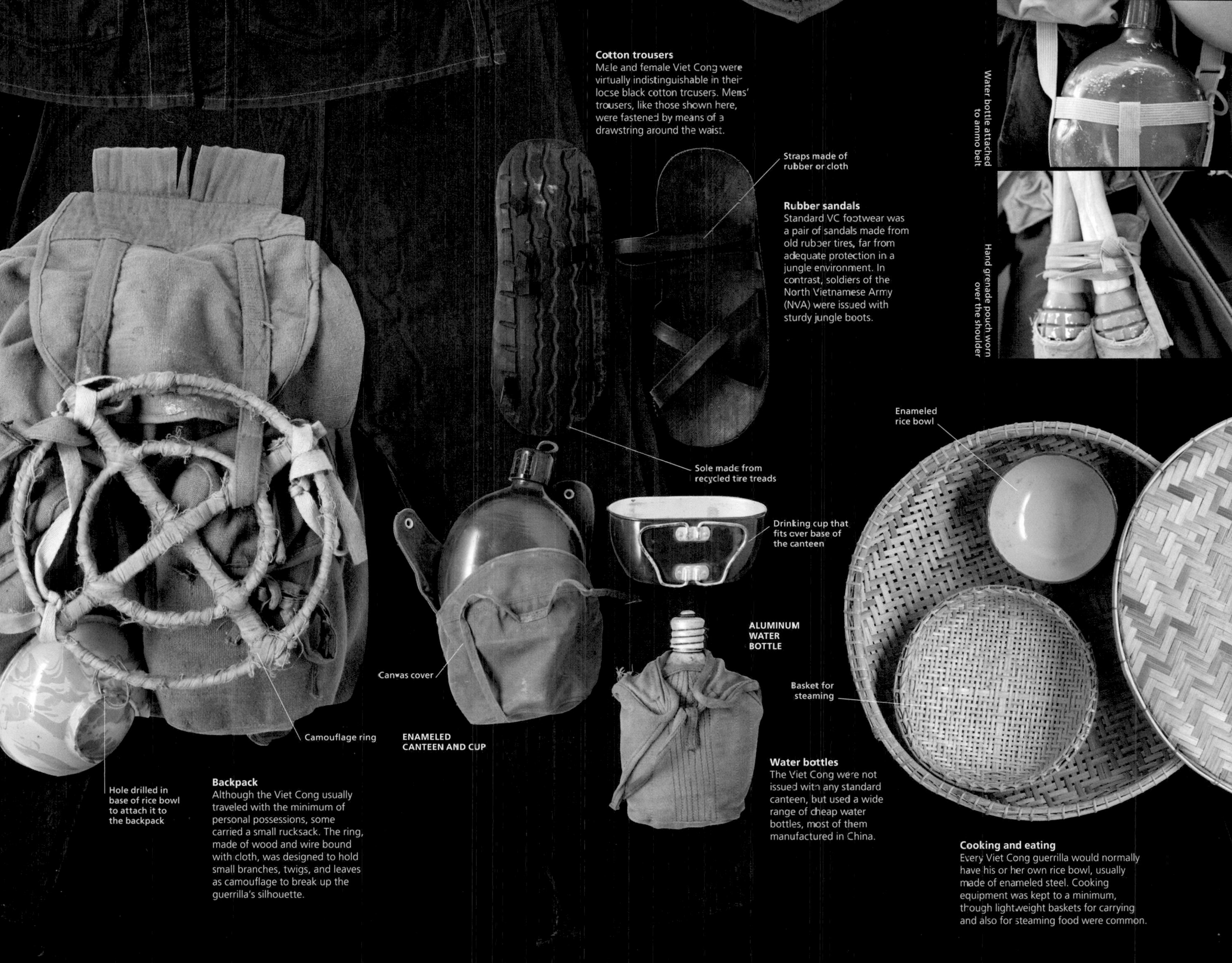

Water bottle attached to ammo belt

Hand grenade pouch worn over the shoulder

Cotton trousers
Male and female Viet Cong were virtually indistinguishable in their loose black cotton trousers. Mens' trousers, like those shown here, were fastened by means of a drawstring around the waist.

Rubber sandals
Standard VC footwear was a pair of sandals made from old rubber tires, far from adequate protection in a jungle environment. In contrast, soldiers of the North Vietnamese Army (NVA) were issued with sturdy jungle boots.

Backpack
Although the Viet Cong usually traveled with the minimum of personal possessions, some carried a small rucksack. The ring, made of wood and wire bound with cloth, was designed to hold small branches, twigs, and leaves as camouflage to break up the guerrilla's silhouette.

Water bottles
The Viet Cong were not issued with any standard canteen, but used a wide range of cheap water bottles, most of them manufactured in China.

Cooking and eating
Every Viet Cong guerrilla would normally have his or her own rice bowl, usually made of enameled steel. Cooking equipment was kept to a minimum, though lightweight baskets for carrying and also for steaming food were common.

VIET CONG WEAPONS

In the early years of the insurgency the Viet Cong used whatever arms they could lay their hands on, displaying great ingenuity in creating home-made weaponry. Later they received Soviet and Chinese machine guns, rifles, and grenade launchers along the Ho Chi Minh trail and from contact with the North Vietnamese Army. Their enemies were also a major source of supply, including arms and ammunition traded by South Vietnamese soldiers.

Machete
The Viet Cong were skilled at recycling the debris of modern warfare. Knives like this small multi-purpose machete were often fashioned from steel salvaged from wrecked US vehicles.

Pouch contains two or three ammunition clips of ten rounds

End pouch containing cleaning kit for the SKS

Ammunition belt
This light cloth belt was designed specifically for carrying ammunition for the SKS. With the strap passing around the neck, the belt was fastened at the back and the pouches worn across the stomach.

Integral bayonet that folds back along the barrel

Cleaning rod

SKS AMMUNITION STRIPPER CLIP

Folding bipod for firing from the prone position

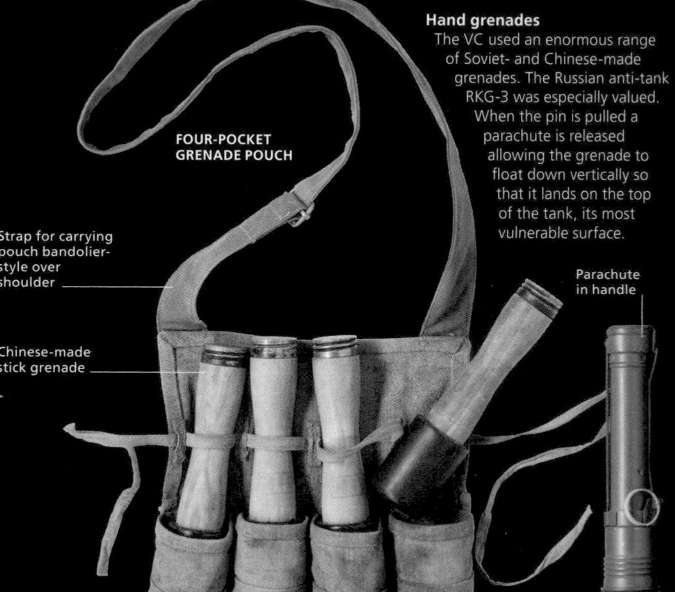
RPD CANVAS AMMO POUCH

Hand grenades
The VC used an enormous range of Soviet- and Chinese-made grenades. The Russian anti-tank RKG-3 was especially valued. When the pin is pulled a parachute is released allowing the grenade to float down vertically so that it lands on the top of the tank, its most vulnerable surface.

FOUR-POCKET GRENADE POUCH

Strap for carrying pouch bandolier-style over shoulder

Chinese-made stick grenade

Parachute in handle

RKG-3 ANTI-TANK GRENADE

Burning gas and smoke from rocket expelled here

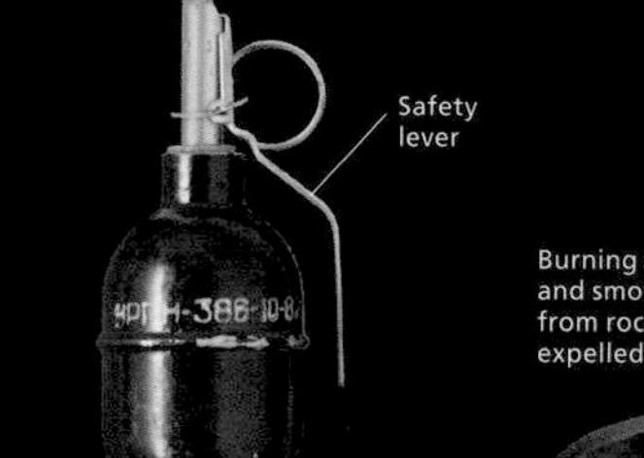

Safety lever

RUSSIAN RGD-5 GRENADE

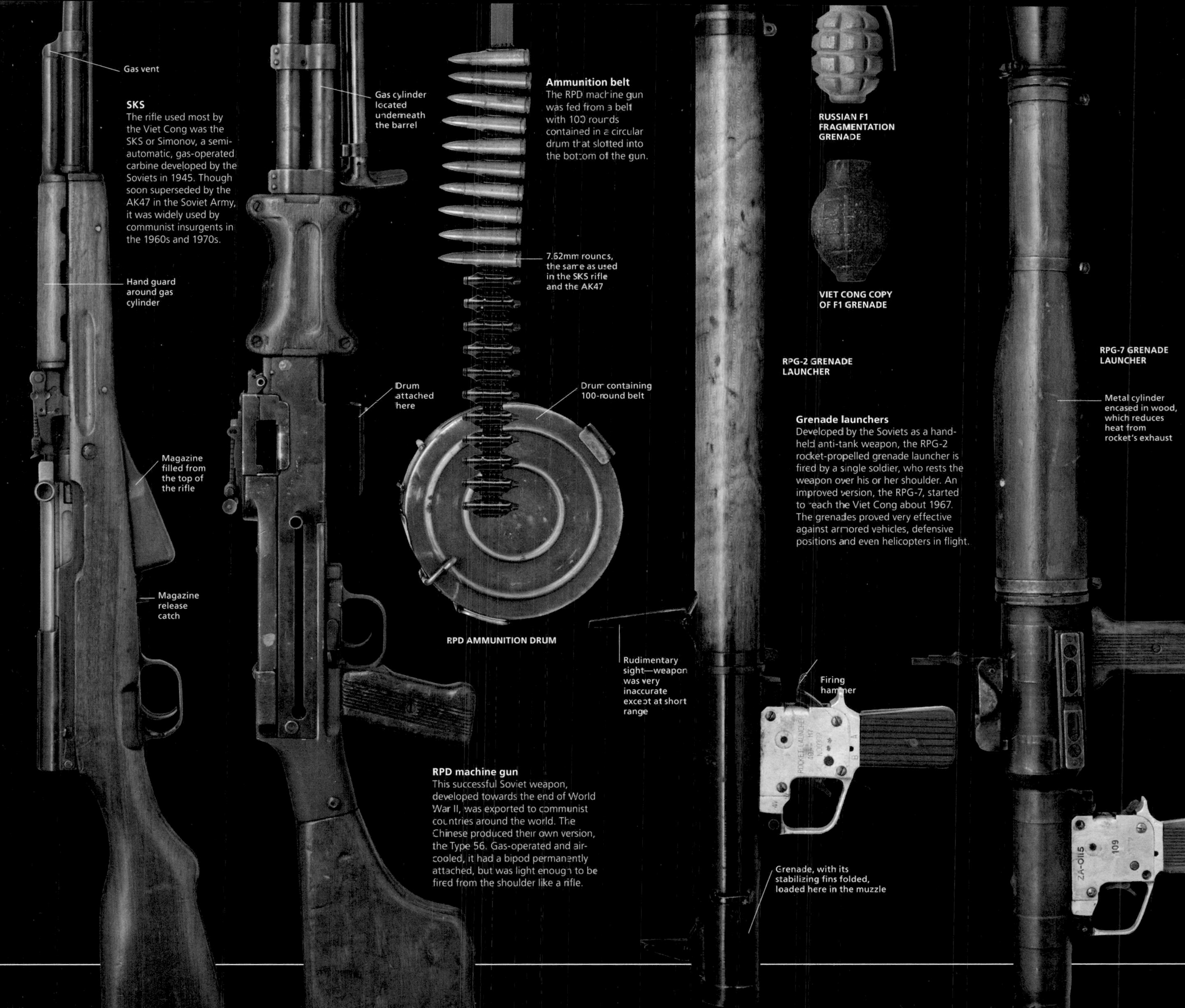

SKS
The rifle used most by the Viet Cong was the SKS or Simonov, a semi-automatic, gas-operated carbine developed by the Soviets in 1945. Though soon superseded by the AK47 in the Soviet Army, it was widely used by communist insurgents in the 1960s and 1970s.

Ammunition belt
The RPD machine gun was fed from a belt with 100 rounds contained in a circular drum that slotted into the bottom of the gun.

RPD machine gun
This successful Soviet weapon, developed towards the end of World War II, was exported to communist countries around the world. The Chinese produced their own version, the Type 56. Gas-operated and air-cooled, it had a bipod permanently attached, but was light enough to be fired from the shoulder like a rifle.

Grenade launchers
Developed by the Soviets as a hand-held anti-tank weapon, the RPG-2 rocket-propelled grenade launcher is fired by a single soldier, who rests the weapon over his or her shoulder. An improved version, the RPG-7, started to reach the Viet Cong about 1967. The grenades proved very effective against armored vehicles, defensive positions and even helicopters in flight.

MODERN GUERRILLA FIGHTERS

In the 1930s Mao Zedong in China formulated the theory of rural-based guerrilla war as the path to communist revolution. His triumph in China in 1949 and the subsequent defeat of France by Viet Minh guerrillas in Vietnam in 1954 was followed by victory for Fidel Castro's armed band in Cuba in 1959. By the 1960s the United States regarded counterinsurgency warfare as crucial to preventing the spread of communism in the Cold War. Yet from the late 1970s America itself backed guerrilla forces in wars against left-wing governments in Afghanistan, Angola, and Nicaragua. By the 21st century, guerrilla activity had in some countries degenerated into permanent warfare between armed gangs, existing in symbiosis with the international narcotics trade.

MUJAHIDEEN IN THE 1980S

In 1978 insurgent groups opposed to the pro-Soviet Marxist government of Afghanistan began training at bases in Pakistan. From the summer of 1979 these mujahideen (or "those who struggle") were backed by the American CIA as well as by Pakistani secret services. In December 1979 the Soviet Union sent troops into Afghanistan to counter the burgeoning insurgency. The guerrillas who took on the Soviet forces consisted mostly of local tribesmen operating in groups a few hundred strong. In the course of the war, links between guerrilla groups developed until they were able to mount operations involving as many as 10,000 men. The mujahideen maintained a campaign of hit-and-run raids in the face of intensive Soviet counterinsurgency operations, exploiting their knowledge of the mountainous terrain, but were unsuccessful when they attempted to overrun urban areas. They obtained weapons chiefly from the US, Saudi Arabia, Iran, and China, funneled into Afghanistan via Islamic parties in Pakistan, which claimed leadership of the insurrection. Arab Islamic fundamentalists, including Saudi businessman Osama bin Laden, also became involved in the conflict. From 1985 the mujahideen were supplied with American Stinger and British Blowpipe anti-aircraft missiles, which reduced the effectiveness of Soviet helicopters. The Soviets never controlled much of Afghanistan outside the towns and pulled out their troops in 1988–89, having suffered 64,000 casualties.

RPG-7
This Russian-made rocket launcher was regularly used against Soviet forces in Afghanistan.

Asymmetric warfare
Afghan mujahideen stand on the remains of a Russian helicopter brought down by an American-supplied Stinger surface-to-air missile.

SANDINISTA REBELS

The Frente Sandinista de Liberación Nacional (FSLN—Sandinista National Liberation Front) was named after Augusto César Sandino, who launched an anti-American guerrilla campaign in Nicaragua in the 1920s. Sandino was assassinated in 1934 by the Somoza family, which established a US-backed dictatorship. The FSLN was founded in 1962 as a small Marxist guerrilla band in a remote area of Nicaragua. In the 1970s the unpopularity of the Somoza dictatorship allowed the Sandinistas to win the active support of the population. Despite a large-scale counterinsurgency campaign waged by the Somozan National Guard, by September 1978 most of Nicaragua was in Sandinista hands. In July 1979 the dictatorship collapsed after the United States withdrew its support. Ironically, in the 1980s the Sandinista regime was in its turn undermined by a ruthless guerrilla campaign, this time mounted by the US-armed and -financed Contras.

British L1A1
Many of these British army service rifles came to the Sandinistas from Belize, a one-time British colony.

Popular support
Sandinista rebels in a village under Sandinista control near the Honduras border, July 1983.

CUBAN REBEL ARMY

On December 2 1956, Fidel Castro and 81 followers landed on the coast of Cuba intent upon overthrowing the dictatorship of Fulgencio Batista. An encounter with government forces, however, soon reduced their numbers to 22, and from May 1957 they carried out small-scale guerrilla raids to which the Cuban government could not respond. A government offensive in the mountains in spring 1958 was a disaster, with Batista's troops repeatedly defeated by the far inferior guerrilla forces. Meanwhile, the American government withdrew military support from the dictatorship. Then numbering several thousands, the guerrillas went on the offensive against the regime in August 1958. Forces led by an Argentinian doctor, Ernesto "Che" Guevara, marched into Havana on January 1 1959.

> "A REVOLUTION IS A STRUGGLE TO THE DEATH BETWEEN THE FUTURE AND THE PAST."
>
> **FIDEL CASTRO**, SPEAKING IN HAVANA, JANUARY 1, 1961

Castro and his commanders
Fidel Castro and members of his staff planning a raid in 1957. Che Guevara is seated second from the right.

FARC

The FARC (Fuerzas Armadas Revolucionarias de Colombia—Revolutionary Armed Forces of Colombia) was set up in the mid-1960s by Marxists claiming to be fighting on behalf of the Colombian people. From the 1980s, under the influence of Jacobo Arenas, it developed into a self-styled "army of the people" with a plan for mounting a military campaign to seize power in the country. Colombia's remote jungle and mountain regions provided safe havens that the guerrillas could control, while the country's coca crop offered a potential source of revenue to buy sophisticated arms. Although the FARC carried out a number of notable military operations in the 1990s, it has exhibited a tendency to degenerate into a simple criminal organization. It battles with Colombia's powerful right-wing paramilitary groups for control of the drug trade and raises further finance by kidnapping, extortion, and protection rackets. However, in spite of the risks involved, joining the FARC might well seem a sensible career choice amid the poverty and insecurity of rural Colombia, since a member of the group is probably paid far higher than a person working in legitimate employment.

1941 – PRESENT

SAS SOLDIER

PART OF LEARNING TO FIGHT TERRORISTS WAS KNOWING HOW TO BE ONE, AND THE BLOKES

AN ELITE INFANTRY FORMATION first established during World War II, the Special Air Service (SAS) has developed into the core of the British Army's special forces. Originally designed to carry out operations behind enemy lines in the context of a conventional war, it has also engaged in counterinsurgency campaigns against guerrilla forces and in counterterrorist operations, such as the highly publicized storming of the Iranian Embassy in London in 1980. The supreme professionalism of the SAS soldier is recognized worldwide.

The SAS took time to establish its permanent place in the British armed forces. Originally formed in North Africa in July 1941 to carry out raids behind Axis lines in the Desert War, it was disbanded at the end of World War II. The need for special forces to track and destroy guerrillas in the Malayan jungle saw that it was resurrected as part of the regular army in the 1950s. Further successful operations followed against rebels in the Arabian peninsula and Borneo. By the 1970s, the SAS had a firmly established reputation in military circles as a tough, efficient regiment that was likely to see a lot of active service. It was also known for having the hardest selection and training routine in the British Army.

SAS insignia
A winged Sword of Damocles is shown with the SAS motto: "Who Dares Wins."

RECRUITMENT AND TRAINING

SAS recruits are drawn from the regular army or from the regiment's own territorials. All candidates have thus already received at least basic military training before they present themselves for an SAS selection course. Volunteers, whether officers, NCOs, or other ranks, require a recommendation from their commanding officer. Men are attracted by the challenge of testing themselves to their mental and physical limits, as well as by the prestige of belonging to an elite formation. About 1 in 10 applicants fails at the first hurdle, which consists of a thorough medical check and a standard fitness test. The rest embark on a three-week initial selection course that is famous for its demands on physical and mental stamina.

Held in the Brecon Beacons, Wales, the course is conducted in a gentlemanly and civilized manner. Already serving soldiers thoroughly imbued with the basics of discipline, the men are set a series of tests of mounting difficulty in which they pit themselves against the elements and against their own limitations. Making long hikes alone across trackless terrain, burdened with a heavy pack and rifle, may seem a crude test of a man's worth, but those who have taken part testify to the extreme mental resolution required to cope with the effects of exhaustion, exposure, and isolation. Injuries are common, and on several occasions SAS trainees have died on the hills. By the end of the initial selection course, roughly 4 out of 5 candidates will have been rejected and returned to their units.

Counter-revolutionary warfare
An SAS hostage rescue team *(above)* storms a country house armed with MP5 submachine guns fitted with maglites and wearing S10 respirators. The MP5, often used by the SAS, has several variants, including one equipped with a grenade launcher *(right)*.

H&K MP5K SUBMACHINE GUN

Ongoing training
All personnel share skills, including counterterrorist skills in which soldiers learn how to move swiftly in confined spaces *(far right)*. Specialist training depends on the troop a soldier belongs to: Air Troop (airborne insertion), Boat Troop (waterborne insertion), Mobility Troop (land vehicle insertion), or Mountain Troop (climbing and skiing techniques).

> "LIKE THE SAS ITSELF, SAS SELECTION IS SIMPLE, DIRECT AND DEADLY EFFECTIVE."

MICHAEL ASHER, SAS TERRITORIAL VOLUNTEER, WRITING IN *SHOOT TO KILL*

If a candidate survives all this, he is officially a member of the regiment. But he will still undergo a great deal more special training, which could range from learning foreign languages to rock climbing, free-fall parachuting, or field surgery.

The soldier who emerges from this selection and training process is expected to be well-balanced, self-reliant, and both mentally and physically in peak condition. He must be able to operate in a small unit for long periods under trying conditions without falling out with his colleagues. When necessary he must carry on alone and without orders. The SAS are trained to kill in cold blood when deemed essential, but men considered to have too much of a taste for killing are weeded out. Aggression must be strictly controlled and directed. Keeping a cool head under pressure is a defining characteristic of SAS men. They are neither brawlers nor braggarts. Drill and military "bullshit" (as it is known) are kept to a minimum, with distinction of rank less important than skills and performance.

COUNTER-REVOLUTIONARY WARFARE TACTICS

SAS tradition stresses secrecy and anonymity—bragging in public about the regiment's activities is totally discouraged. It was the Iranian Embassy siege that transformed the regiment's public profile. In the late 1960s and 1970s, a spate of hostage-taking and airliner hijackings had announced the arrival of international terrorism on the world scene. The SAS responded by setting up a Counter Revolutionary Warfare (CRW) training school at Hereford, where they developed and practiced techniques for dealing with hostage situations. There was a "killing house" for exercise in storming buildings where hostages were being held and a mock airliner for practice in dealing with hijackings. CRW instant-readiness teams were formed to respond to a terrorist incident at any time. On May 5, 1980, the years of training were put into effect when an SAS team assaulted the Iranian Embassy building in Prince's Gate, London, where a

Model of Iranian Embassy
This wooden model of the Iranian Embassy building was made by the SAS to familiarize soldiers with the rooms they would be entering. Each story was detachable to reveal the layout of the floor beneath.

ENTRY TACTICS

In the 1970s, the SAS played a prominent role in the development of tactics for entering buildings occupied by hostile armed groups holding hostages. The first problem was to gain entry, which might involve blowing in windows or doors with controlled charges. The next step was to disorientate the hostage-takers by throwing in stun grenades or CS gas grenades. Small armed units would follow a thoroughly rehearsed procedure to sweep the whole space rapidly with their automatic weapons, identifying any hostile presence. They were strictly trained to avoid risks of shooting one another or innocent hostages. Each man would be positioned so that no other member of the team came within his line of fire at any time. It was SAS policy to shoot all hostage-takers dead, thus preventing the activation of concealed explosive devices.

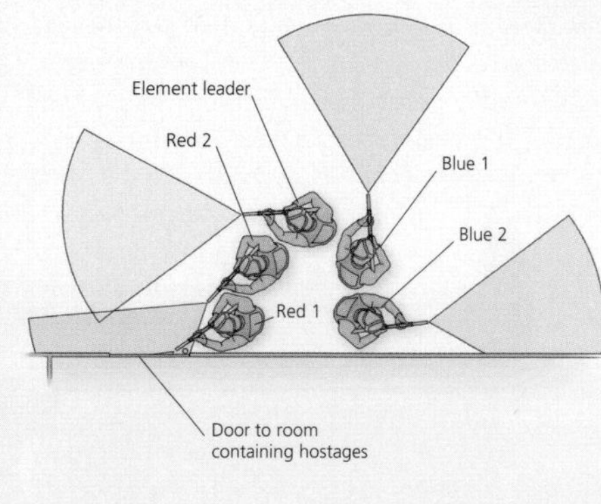

Stacking up
A typical entry team consists of five men; Red 1 and Red 2, who head the team, the element leader, who holds the middle, and Blue 1 and Blue 2 at the rear. To clear a room, the teams starts by "stacking up" at the side of the door where the handle is located.

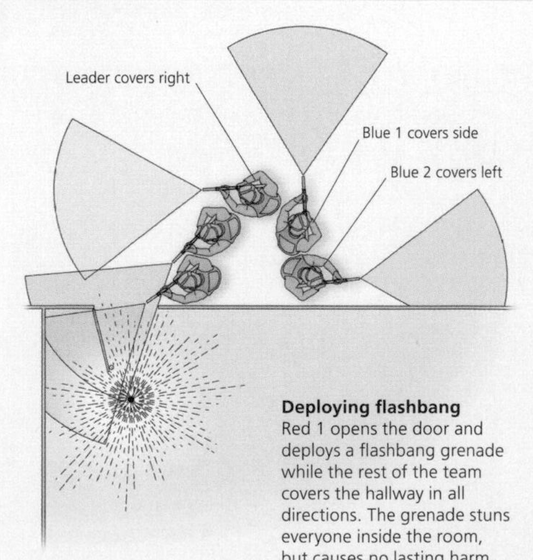

Deploying flashbang
Red 1 opens the door and deploys a flashbang grenade while the rest of the team covers the hallway in all directions. The grenade stuns everyone inside the room, but causes no lasting harm.

group of six Arab terrorists were holding 26 people hostage. Meticulously prepared and executed, the assault took 11 minutes to achieve its objective. Five of the terrorists were shot dead and the other was arrested. Two hostages had also died at the hands of the terrorists. Shown live on television, this operation made the SAS famous throughout the world.

Part of the new SAS image created by the Iranian Embassy siege was of cold-blooded killers, for at least some of the terrorists had been shot dead after ceasing resistance. Criticism of the SAS's allegedly excessive ruthlessness surfaced during the long struggle against IRA terrorism in the 1980s. SAS units were deployed in an undercover role in Northern Ireland with great success, until accusations of a shoot-to-kill policy led to their withdrawal from the province. In a highly publicized operation, in Gibraltar in March 1988, the SAS shot three IRA bombers dead under controversial circumstances. The ruthlessness of the SAS men was praised in some quarters and criticized in others, but no one suggested they had gone beyond their orders.

SPECIALIZED INFANTRY

Despite the publicity attracted by Counter Revolutionary Warfare, the primary role of the SAS has remained as specialist light infantry. How their special skills could be used in a conventional war was demonstrated when Britain went to war with Argentina over possession of the Falkland Islands in 1982.

Iranian Embassy siege
An SAS soldier becomes entangled in his rope during the Iranian Embassy siege in 1980. The team rappelled from the roof to a first floor balcony.

As a British Task Force headed for the islands, which had been occupied by Argentinian troops, four-man SAS patrols were inserted into the islands by helicopter to establish covert observation posts. Surviving for weeks in hiding amid harsh terrain and appalling weather conditions, they transmitted details of the deployment of Argentine forces. After one patrol identified an airstrip as a target for a raid, more than 50 SAS men were flown in by helicopter, destroying 11 Argentinian aircraft on the ground and escaping with only minor casualties. Save for the use of helicopters, this was just the sort of operation that the SAS had carried out against Rommel's forces in the Western Desert during World War II. SAS units were involved in similar behind-the-lines operations in the 1991 Gulf War. Dropped into Iraq by helicopter or driving across the desert border in Land Rovers or on motorbikes, they hunted down and destroyed Scud missile launchers and disrupted enemy communications.

MOVING ON

NCOs and troopers generally only leave the SAS when it is time to return to civilian life. A certain percentage find occupations that employ the skills which they have learned, such as carrying out industrial espionage, being bodyguards, or even mercenaries. Officers only join the SAS on detached duty from their parent regiments and often return to more conventional duties after a time. Some have risen to very senior positions in the British Army, reflecting the high esteem in which the SAS is held.

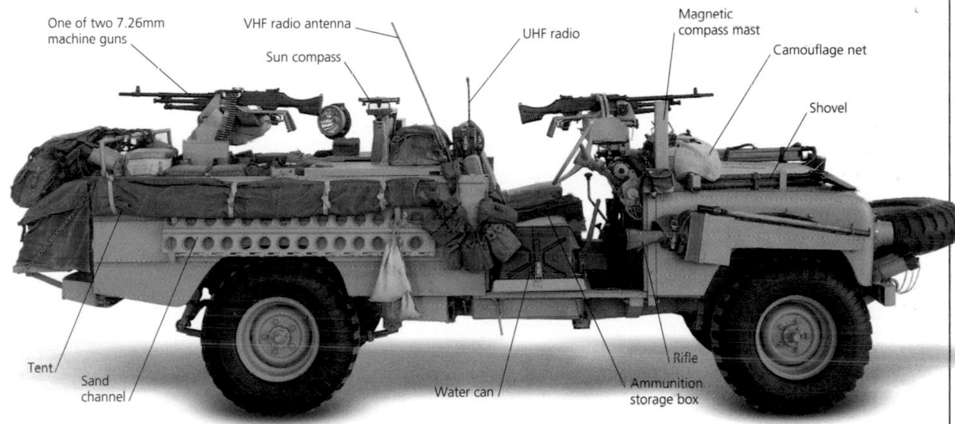

SAS "Pink Panther"
Named after its desert camouflage, this modified Land Rover, in use from the 1960s to the 1980s, had fuel tanks that gave it a range of 1,500 miles (2,400 km).

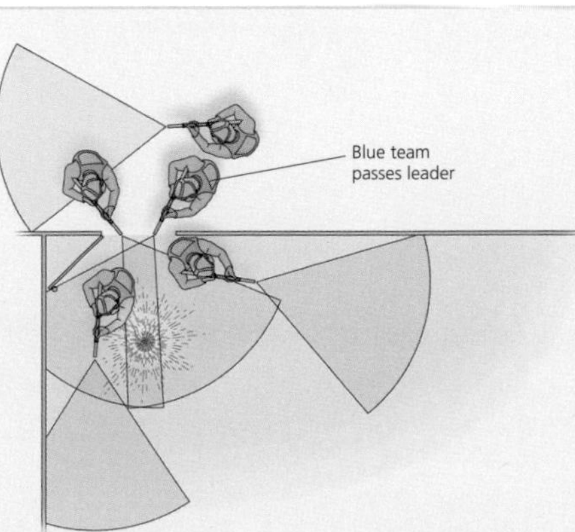

The fatal funnel
Red 1 enters first and covers the right half of the room, then Red 2 follows, covering the left. Blue 1 and Blue 2 prepare to enter while the leader covers the hallway.

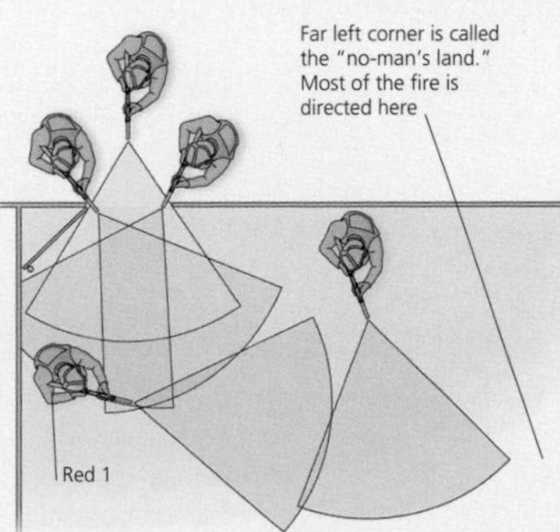

Clearing the room
As Red 1 moves to the far right corner, pointing his weapon at the opposite corner, Red 2 moves to the near left corner, pointing his weapon at the opposite wall.

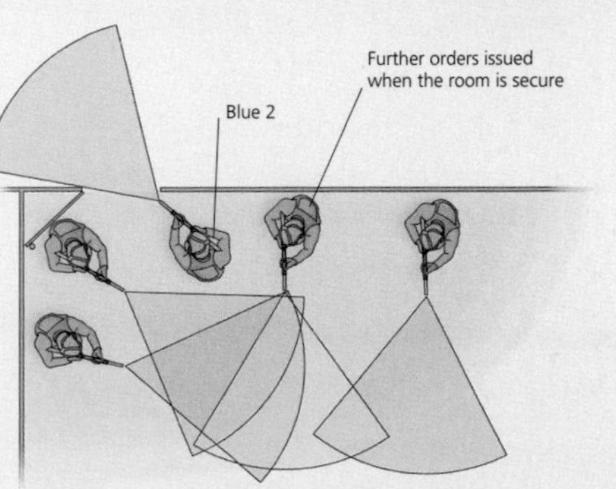

Securing the room
Red 2 clears the near left corner while Red 1 covers the far left. Blue 1 enters and holds the near right corner, followed by Blue 2 who covers the door. Finally the leader enters.

SAS SOLDIER'S GEAR

When they developed their Counter Revolutionary Warfare capacity in the 1970s, the SAS adopted a range of clothing and weaponry suited to assaults on buildings or aircraft in which hostages were being held. In their assault on the Iranian Embassy in Prince's Gate, London, 1981, SAS soldiers used stun grenades and CS gas to disorient the hostage-takers. Their respirators enabled them to operate in the gas-filled environment. Most of the terrorists were killed by fire from the Heckler & Koch MP5s.

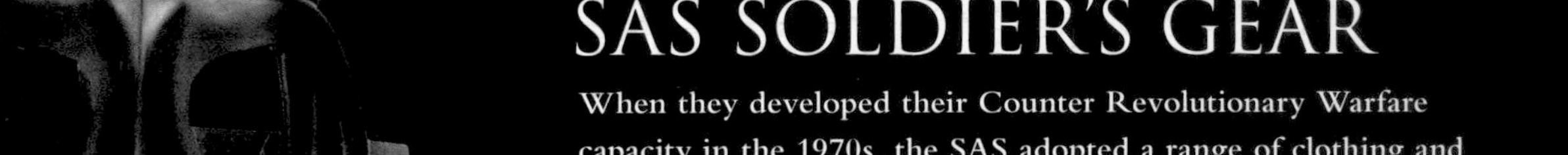

BALACLAVA

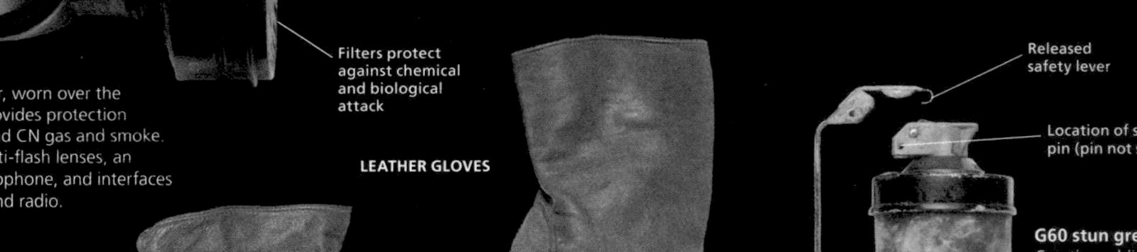

RESPIRATOR

Filters protect against chemical and biological attack

Headgear
The respirator, worn over the balaclava, provides protection against CS and CN gas and smoke. It also has anti-flash lenses, an internal microphone, and interfaces for oxygen and radio.

Black suede combat vest

Knife in sheath

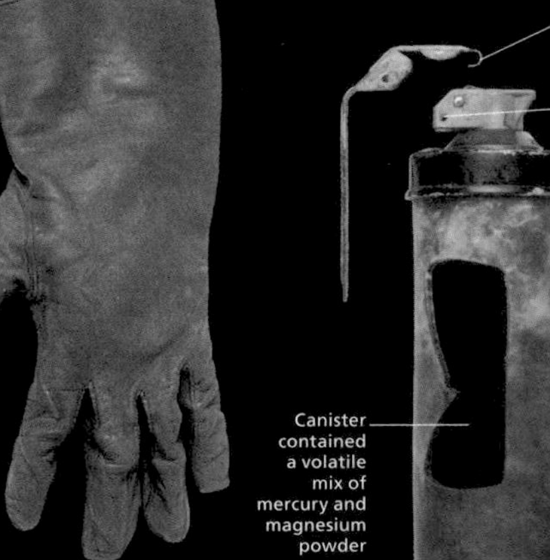

LEATHER GLOVES

Released safety lever

Location of safety pin (pin not shown)

Canister contained a volatile mix of mercury and magnesium powder

G60 stun grenade
Creating a blinding flash and 160 decibels of sound, the stun grenade, or "flash-bang," disorientates anyone within range. The one shown here was used during the Iranian embassy siege of 1980. Current versions also contain CS or CN tear gas.

Bulletproof vest
Incorporating steel plates and padding, the bulletproof vest, or waistcoat, is designed to stop bullets and absorb their kinetic energy.

Assault suit
This one-piece suit, allows for maximum ease of movement. The flame-retardant fabric is black to provide optimum cover at night.

Browning HP pistol
The Browning High Power 9mm pistol has a magazine capacity of 13 rounds.

MP5A5 submachine gun
The MP5 fires at a rate of 800 rpm. This version is also fitted with an ISTEC 40 x 46M grenade launcher.

OTHER SPECIAL FORCES

Since World War II armies have recognized the usefulness of elite troops, capable of operating in small units deep behind enemy lines in conventional warfare or as counterinsurgency forces against guerrillas. All special forces operate rigorous selection procedures and grueling training programs, with an emphasis upon individual initiative, mental strength, controlled aggression, and survival under difficult conditions. In reaction to the mass combat of the World Wars, special forces represent a reassertion of professionalism and of quality over quantity of troops. Since the 1970s, counter-terrorist warfare has been a central concern of special forces, and techniques for dealing with hostage-taking situations have been shared between states.

ISRAELI SPECIAL FORCES

In the guerrilla warfare that led to the creation of the state of Israel in 1948, the Israelis developed a tradition of ruthless covert operations involving raids inside hostile territory, sabotage, and assassination. This was carried forward into their conflict with Arab states and with paramilitary organizations around Israel's borders after independence. Israel's first special forces group, Unit 101, led by Ariel Sharon, was disbanded in 1953 after a notorious raid into the West Bank in which 69 Palestinian civilians were massacred. It was succeeded by other special forces units, however, including Sayeret Golani, Sayeret T'zanhanim, and the most famous, Sayeret Matkal (popularly known as "The Unit").

Founded in 1958, Sayeret Matkal was originally a top-secret unit recruited through personal and family contacts, somewhat like Britain's wartime SOE. This partially explains its close links with Israel's governing elite. Sayeret Matkal is now staffed by volunteers who have survived a ferociously demanding selection course. It has established a formidable reputation for intelligence-gathering and sabotage raids deep into Arab territory. Many of its operations have remained shrouded in secrecy; they are believed often to involve the assassination of suspected enemies of Israel. Sayeret Matkal also specializes in dealing with hostage-taking situations. Its most highly publicized success was the freeing of hostages held by terrorists at Entebbe airport in Uganda in July, 1976.

Rear sight
Fore sight
Muzzle compensator
Tubular butt stock folds left
Cocking handle
Gas regulator
Bipod mounting point
Molded plastic pistol grip
Magazine catch
35-round detachable box magazine

Galil assault rifle
Designed by Israel Galil in 1974, this light, gas-operated assault rifle is the Israeli answer to the Russian AK47. It is based on the Finnish Valmet M62 and chambered for the Amercian 5.56 x 45 round.

GSG-9

Germany's lack of an adequate counter-terrorist force was revealed by a bungled response to hostage-taking by Palestinian terrorists at the 1972 Munich Olympics. GSG-9 (Grenzschutz-gruppe-9, or "Border Guards, Group 9") went operational on April 17, 1973. Its name suggested that it was part of Federal Germany's border guards, although in practice it was a totally new organization within the country's police force. Under the strong leadership of Ulrich Wegener, GSG-9 quickly developed into an elite counter-terrorist organization. In the 1970s, Federal Germany faced a home-grown terrorist movement, known as the Red Army Faction. In October 1977 a group of terrorists led by Zohair Akache, a Palestinian, hijacked a Lufthansa airliner with 86 passengers on board. They demanded the release of Red Army Faction prisoners in Germany in return for the passengers' safe release. After the captain of the aircraft had been murdered by the terrorists, GSG-9 operatives supported by two SAS men stormed the hijacked airliner at Mogadishu airport, Somalia. Three of the four terrorists were killed in an exchange of fire, while only one hostage was injured. The Mogadishu operation made GSG-9's reputation—one which has been confirmed by subsequent operations.

GSG-9 INSIGNIA

Troop carrier
Bell Huey troop carriers are among the helicopters used by GSG-9 to fly officers anywhere in Germany.

US SPECIAL OPERATIONS FORCES

Over the half century since the US Army Special Forces, popularly known as the Green Berets, were tentatively founded in 1952, units devoted to unconventional warfare, counterinsurgency, and counter-terrorism have proliferated in the US armed forces. Since 1987 all have been grouped together under US Special Operations Command in Tampa, Florida. By the early 21st century there were estimated to be around 50,000 men in the US military devoted to special operations.

The Green Berets, primarily based at Fort Bragg, North Carolina, became a high-profile formation after winning the patronage of President John F. Kennedy in his drive to develop a counterinsurgency capacity in the early 1960s. The Berets' reputation was confirmed by their determined efforts to organize mountain tribesmen as anti-communist forces during the Vietnam War. Vietnam also saw the re-formation of the US Army Rangers as a long-range patrol force. Another product of that period's interest in countering guerrilla warfare was the US Navy SEAL (Sea-Air-Land) teams, founded in 1962 and first sent into combat in Vietnam in 1966, specializing in riverine operations. The 1970s brought a different emphasis, with the rise of international terrorism. The US Army's Combat Applications Group, popularly known as Delta Force, was set up by Colonel Charles Beckwith in 1977 primarily as a counter-terrorist warfare unit. It has remained one of the most secretive of unconventional warfare organizations, perhaps partly because the highly publicized failure of its attempt to free American hostages held in Iran in 1980 was such an embarrassment.

US special operations forces have played a prominent role in recent conflicts, notably the invasions of Iraq and Afghanistan, and the prolonged counterinsurgency campaigns in both those countries. The US Defense Department envisages they will have a crucial future role in countering the threat of global terrorism networks.

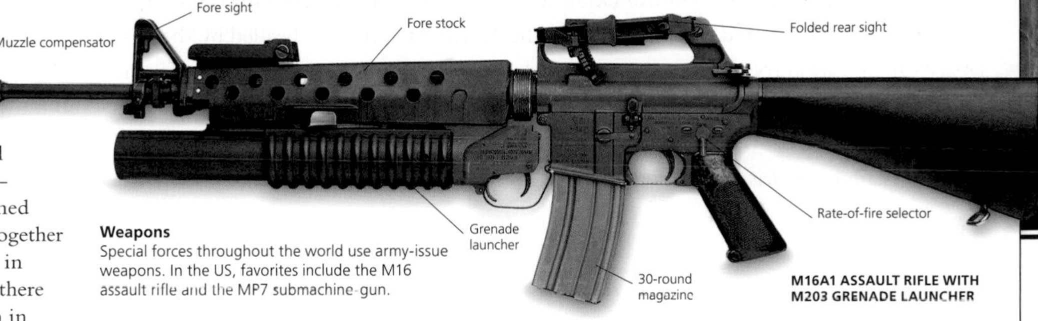

Weapons
Special forces throughout the world use army-issue weapons. In the US, favorites include the M16 assault rifle and the MP7 submachine-gun.

> TRAIN FOR WAR, FIGHT TO WIN, DEFEAT OUR NATION'S ENEMIES.

US NAVY SEAL CODE OF HONOR EXCERPT

Small Boat Unit
US Navy SEALs on a special operation with an SBU (Small Boat Unit) in Panama, 1994. In the foreground a camouflaged soldier bears an M16A3 rifle fitted with an M209 grenade launcher.

MODERN WESTERN INFANTRY

The ending of the Cold War confrontation with the Soviet Union in the late 1980s suggested that the forces of the North Atlantic Treaty Organization (NATO) states might find themselves without an enemy to fight. Instead, the Iraqi invasion of Kuwait in 1990 provoked the US and its allies to fight the Gulf War against Iraq in 1991. Islamic terrorism and Iraqi intransigence further led to the invasions of Afghanistan in 2001 and Iraq in 2003, both headed by the US with Britain in support, and both followed by a troubled occupation. The all-volunteer infantry who fought in these conflicts were well trained and enjoyed a superb level of equipment. But their experience showed that the lot of the soldier on the ground remained as demanding as it had ever been.

US INFANTRYMAN

Since 1973, when the US withdrew from Vietnam, the US Army has been an all-volunteer force committed to equal opportunities. The presence of large numbers of women in the army (up from 2 percent of personnel in 1973 to almost 15 percent by 2006) marked a sharp break with the long tradition of warfare as a male preserve. Volunteers, male or female, primarily came from sections of US society in which other employment prospects were poor, giving the army the problem of training individuals often short on education and potentially resistant to discipline. This was partially alleviated by the imposition of higher admission standards. Recruits are given Basic Combat Training followed by Advanced Individual Training—the latter a specialized course in recognition of the technical demands imposed by modern warfare.

The Gulf War of 1991 and the invasion of Iraq in 2003 demonstrated the overwhelming effectiveness of the US Army in conventional warfare against a less well-equipped, less well-trained foe. With land, sea, and air forces coordinated under a single command, combat proceeded with relentless speed and violence, and its success provided a much-needed boost to US credibility—its competence, at least on the battlefield, had been in question since the Vietnam War. But the subsequent military occupation of Iraq and Afghanistan showed that the US could not suppress an elusive enemy armed with light but sophisticated equipment and a ruthless determination to use it. In spite of regular setbacks, the great majority of US soldiers continued to show a strong commitment to the army and to find in military service a chance to learn valuable skills and to earn a respect often denied them in civilian society.

US infantryman on patrol
A US infantryman, carrying an M16 assault rifle with grenade launcher, patrols in an armored personnel vehicle in Iraq, 2005.

BRITISH INFANTRYMAN

Britain has a long history of employing a small professional army to fight varieties of limited war overseas, a tradition that was only temporarily interrupted in the 20th century by the drafting of a mass of conscripts in two world wars. The return to an all-volunteer regular army since the start of the 1960s has thus been in line with British tradition. In other ways, battle has been joined against the army's traditions, with successive reforms of a regimental system widely regarded as outdated, yet stubbornly defended by its adherents.

Up to the 1990s, the post-World War II British Army was chiefly deployed as part of NATO to fight a defensive war against a Soviet invasion of West Germany that never happened, and in a counter-insurgency role in various British-ruled territories, latterly in Northern Ireland. The end of the Cold War, followed by the cessation of the IRA insurgency, naturally led cost-conscious politicians to cut back on infantry numbers in the 1990s. There was also a shift towards higher investment in advanced technology and training for a war of rapid deployment and maneuver, in line with American military doctrine.

The British Army contributed the second-largest contingent to the UN forces that drove the Iraqis out of Kuwait in the Gulf War of 1991—the largest, of course, was supplied by the US. In the early 21st century, the British again supported the US in the invasions of Afghanistan (2001) and Iraq (2003), and the subsequent counter-insurgency campaigns conducted by the occupying forces. The demands of prolonged warfare on this scale severely tested morale and revealed deficiencies in the army's equipment and logistics.

In 2007, the British Army consisted of over 100,000 full-time soldiers, backed up by around 40,000 part-time Territorials. Partly as a result of low unemployment in Britain, there were shortfalls in domestic recruitment, so that an increasing percentage of soldiers came from abroad, mostly from the British Commonwealth. Whether on patrol in Iraq or fighting the Taliban in Afghanistan's Helmand Province, the British infantryman showed himself time and again to be a thorough professional.

Desert combat uniform
This British Army combat uniform is a light cotton and polyester mix designed for use in the desert. It was worn by troops in Iraq and Afghanistan in the early 2000s.

MK 6 KEVLAR INFANTRY HELMET

"Disruptive pattern" material

CAMOUFLAGE SHIRT

HYDRATION SACK

Drinking tube

Screw-top for 5.3 pint (3 l) water bag

SA80 BAYONET

30-round magazine behind trigger

Plastic pistol grip

SA80 assault rifle
The SA80 is one of only three "bullpup" rifles adopted worldwide; the others are the French FAMAS, and the Austrian AUG. To make the rifle shorter, the action is placed in the butt, with the magazine behind the trigger. This model is the L85A1.

DESERT BOOTS

CAMOUFLAGE TROUSERS

US Marines in Iraq
A squad of US Marines rides a 7-ton truck during operations against insurgents near Fallujah, Iraq, in April 2004. Most are wearing hydration sacks over their flak jackets, and are carrying M16 assault rifles equipped with M203 grenade launchers.

INDEX

Page numbers in **bold** indicate main references

A

B

C

D

E

F

G

H

I

J

K

L

M

ACKNOWLEDGMENTS

The publisher would like to thank the following for their kind permission to reproduce their photographs.

ABBREVIATIONS KEY:
Key: a = above, b = below, c = center, l=-left, r=-right, t=-top, f=-far, s =-sidebar

2-3 Getty Images: AFP. **4 DK Images:** Board of Trustees of the Armouries (tl). **4-5 DK Images:** By kind permission of the Trustees of the Wallace Collection (bc). **5 DK Images:** American Museum of Natural History (bl); Imperial War Museum (cb); Pitt Rivers Museum, University of Oxford (br), Royal Green Jackets Museum, Winchester (bc). **7 DK Images:** State Historical Museum, Moscow (tl). **9 DK Images:** Board of Trustees of the Armouries (tr) (bl). **14 DK Images:** British Museum (c). **14-43 Werner Forman Archive:** British Museum (t/sidebar). **15 DK/**Sharon Spencer: Ermine Street Guard (tr) (bc) (bl). **16-17 akg-images:** Erich Lessing. **17 DK Images:** British Museum (cr). **18 The Art Archive:** Museo di Villa Giulia, Rome / Dagli Orti (t). **Hellenic Navy:** (bl). **19 Alamy Images:** Walter Bibikow (b). **DK Images:** British Museum (cra). **20 The Art Archive:** Archaeological Museum, Naples / Dagli Orti (b). **21 Alamy Images:** The Print Collector (tl). **DK/**Sharon Spencer: Hoplite Society (tr). **22 DK/**Sharon Spencer: Hoplite Society (tr/shield). **24-25 Luisa Ricciarini Photoagency, Milan. 26-27 Corbis:** Araldo de Luca (t). **27 DK Images:** British Museum (crb) (br) (cr). **28-29 DK/** Sharon Spencer: Ermine Street Guard (b). **30 Corbis:** Roger Wood (b). **Lunt Roman Fort:** (tl/fort). **31 Corbis:** Nathan Benn (tr). **32 akg-images:** (tr). **34 DK/**Sharon Spencer: Ermine Street Guard (tr/ cheek guards). **35 DK Images:** Ermine Street Guard (tr). **DK/**Sharon Spencer: Ermine Street Guard (tl/ purse). **36 DK Images:** British Museum (tc). **38 akg-images:** (bl). **Tyne and Wear Museums/**Sharon Spencer: (bc) (br). **The Viking Ship Museum, Roskilde, Denmark:** (tr). **39 Tyne and Wear Museums/** Sharon Spencer. **40 DK Images:** British Museum (fcl) (cla). **Tyne and Wear Museums/**Sharon Spencer: (bl) (ca). **40-41 Tyne and Wear Museums/**Sharon Spencer: (b). **41 DK Images:** British Museum (bc). **Tyne and Wear Museums/**Sharon Spencer:(tl) (br) (tr). **42 Corbis:** Gianni Dagli Orti (b) (cr). **43 Corbis:** Araldo de Luca (cl). **DK Images:** British Museum (bl). **Werner Forman Archive:** British Museum (br). **46 DK Images:** Warwick Castle, Warwick (bl). **DK/**Sharon Spencer: (cb). **46-105 DK Images:** By kind permission of the Trustees of the Wallace Collection (t/sidebar). **47 The Board of Trustees of the Armouries:** (bl) (bc). **The Art Archive:** Laurie Platt Winfrey (t). **DK Images:** Board of Trustees of the Armouries (br). **48-49 Corbis:** The Art Archive / Alfredo Dagli Orti (t). **49 DK Images:** Statens Historiska Museum, Stockholm (cr). **50 Sky High Entertainment, Quebec:** (b). **51 DK Images:** Statens Historiska Museum, Stockholm (cla); Universitets Oldsaksamling, Oslo (br). **52 Corbis:** Werner Forman (tr). **Andrew Horeckyj:** (tc). **53 Corbis:** Ted Spiegel (b). **54 Geoff Buxton:** (tc). **Andrew Horeckyj:** (ftr) (tr). **55 Andrew Horeckyj:** (tl). **58 Mick Baker:** (cl). **The Viking Ship Museum, Roskilde, Denmark:** Erwan Crouan (bl) (bc), Werner Karrasch (br). **59 The Viking Ship Museum, Roskilde, Denmark:** (tl) (l); Erwan Crouan (cra) (crb); Werner Karrasch (tr) (br). **60 The Art Archive:** Musée de la Tapisserie, Bayeux / Dagli Orti (b). **61 akg-images:** Amelot (br). **62 Ancient Art & Architecture Collection:** R. Sheridan (ca). **DK Images:** By kind permission of the Trustees of the Wallace Collection (br). **63 DK Images:** Nigel Hicks (tc). **66-67 akg-images:** British Library. **68 The Board of Trustees of the Armouries:** (bc). **Corbis:** Gianni Dagli Orti (tl). **DK Images:** By kind permission of the Trustees of the Wallace Collection (cr) (br). **69 The Board of Trustees of the Armouries:** (cla). **The Bridgeman Art Library:** British Library, London © British Library Board (br). **70 Corbis:** Bettmann (b). **Getty Images:** Kean Collection / Hulton Archive (t). **71 DK Images:** Board of Trustees of the Armouries (fbl) (bl) (br); By kind permission of the Trustees of the Wallace Collection (r) (bc). **72 DK Images:** By kind permission of the Trustees of the Wallace Collection (bc). **72-73 DK Images:** By kind permission of the Trustees of the Wallace Collection (ca); Warwick Castle, Warwick (b) (bc). **73 DK Images:** Board of Trustees of the Armouries (t/sword) (br/cuisses); Warwick Castle, Warwick (cra/leg protection) (cr) (fbr). **74-75 The Art Archive:** Biblioteca Nazionale Marciana, Venice / Dagli Orti. **76 Corbis:** Darama / zefa (cl); Angelo Hornak (bl). **DK Images:** Order of the Black Prince (cr). **77 National Trust Photographic Library:** Alasdair Ogilvie (bc) (ftl). **Richard White:** (tl) (br) (fbr) (ftr) (tr). **78 DK Images:** Warwick Castle, Warwick (cl). **79 The Bridgeman Art Library:** Bibliothèque Nationale, Paris (br). **80-81 Getty Images:** Bridgeman Art Library (t). **81 DK Images:** Board of Trustees of the Armouries (br). **82 The Art Archive:** British Library (b) (tc). **83 DK Images:** Board of Trustees of the Armouries (b); Robin Wigington, Arbour Antiques Ltd, Stratford-upon-Avon (crb/arrows). **Getty Images:** Stringer / Hulton Archive (c). **86 The Art Archive:** (bl). **The Bridgeman Art Library:** Collection of the Earl of Leicester, Holkham Hall, Norfolk (c). **87 The Board of Trustees of the Armouries:** (bl). **DK Images:** Board of Trustees of the Armouries (crb/bolts); By kind permission of the Trustees of the Wallace Collection (cr). **88-89 akg-images:** (t). **90 Corbis:** Barry Lewis (b). **DK Images:** University Museum of Archaeology and Anthropology, Cambridge (cl). **91 The Bridgeman Art Library:** Private Collection (b). **92 The Board of Trustees of the Armouries:** (bl). **92-93 The Board of Trustees of the Armouries:** (br) (t). **93 The Board of Trustees of the Armouries:** (cl) (tc). **94-95 The Kobal Collection:** Warner Bros. / David James (t). **95 DK Images:** By kind permission of the Trustees of the Wallace Collection (b). **96 Alamy Images:** Photo Japan (tc). **DK Images:** Judith Miller / Barry Davies Oriental Art Ltd (c); Pitt Rivers Museum, University of Oxford (b). **97 Corbis:** Burstein Collection (b). **DK Images:** Judith Miller / Sloan's (tl). **98 DK Images:** Board of Trustees of the Armouries (bl) (cla) (cr). **98-99 DK Images:** Board of Trustees of the Armouries (cr) (c) (t). **99 DK Images:** Board of Trustees of the Armouries (cra). **100 DK Images:** Board of Trustees of the Armouries (cla) (ca/sword & scabbard). **100-101 DK Images:** Board of Trustees of the Armouries (c); Pitt Rivers Museum, University of Oxford (t) (b) (br/top kogai). **101 DK Images:** Board of Trustees of the Armouries (br/top kozuka). **102-103 Alamy Images:** Jamie Marshall / Tribaleye Images. **104 The Art Archive:** University Museum Cuzco / Mireille Vautier (l). **Justin Kerr:** (br). **105 The Art Archive:** Eileen Tweedy (b). **DK Images:** CONACULTA-INAH-MEX / Michel Zabe (tl) (c). **106 TopFoto. co.uk:** Roger-Viollet (b). **108 DK Images:** By kind permission of the Trustees of the Wallace Collection (bl). **108-141 DK Images:** Board of Trustees of the Armouries (t/sidebar). **109 The Board of Trustees of the Armouries:** (bc). **Corbis:** Brooklyn Museum (tr). **DK Images:** Pitt Rivers Museum, University of Oxford (br). **110-111 The Art Archive:** Château de Blois / Dagli Orti (t). **111 DK Images:** By kind permission of the Trustees of the Wallace Collection (br). **112 akg-images:** (b). **Getty Images:** Handout / Hulton Archive (t). **114-115 DK Images:** Board of Trustees of the Armouries (b) (ca) (t); By kind permission of the Trustees of the Wallace Collection (b/armour) (c). **116 akg-images:** (bl). **117 DK Images:** Board of Trustees of the Armouries (clb) (cr). **118-119 The Bridgeman Art Library:** Topkapi Palace Museum, Istanbul, Turkey (t). **120 Alamy Images:** Images&Stories (tr). **The Bridgeman Art Library:** Topkapi Palace Museum, Istanbul, Turkey (tc). **DK Images:** Board of Trustees of the Armouries (br). **121 The Art Archive:** Topkapi Museum Istanbul / Dagli Orti (bl). **124-125 Corbis:** Stapleton Collection (t). **126 The Bridgeman Art Library:** Egyptian National Library, Cairo, Egypt / Giraudon (bl). **DK Images:** National Museum, New Delhi (br). **127 The Board of Trustees of the Armouries:** (ca). **128-129 The Board of Trustees of the Armouries:** (t) (b) (ca). **DK Images:** Board of Trustees of the Armouries (ca/mace). **129 The Board of Trustees of the Armouries:** (br) (crb). **DK Images:** Pitt Rivers Museum, University of Oxford (tl). **130-131 Paul Self:** English Civil War Society (tl). **132 Corbis:** Bettmann (t). **136-137 akg-images:** Rabatti - Domingie. **139 Corbis:** Underwood & Underwood (b). **140-141 akg-images:** (b). **141 DK Images:** Imperial War Museum (r). **144-223 DK Images:** Musée de l'Empéri, Salon-de-Provence (t). **145 The Board of Trustees of the Armouries:** (bl). **DK Images:** Pitt Rivers Museum, University of Oxford (bc). **National Archives and Records Administration, USA:** (tr). **146-147 Military & Historical Image Bank:** (tl). **148 Army Art Collection, U.S. Army Center of Military History:** H. Charles McBarron (tl). **149 Corbis:** William A. Bake (b). **Peter Newark's Military Pictures:** F. C.Yohn (tl). **153 The Art Archive:** (ca). **Art Resource, NY:** (tr). **Getty Images:** Brendan Smialowski / Stringer (bl). **154 The Bridgeman Art Library:** Courtesy of the Council, National Army Museum, London (b). **DK/** Sharon Spencer: **156-157 The Bridgeman Art Library:** Art Gallery of New South Wales (tl). **158 The Art Archive:** Musée de L'Armée, Paris / Dagli Orti (t). **159 The Bridgeman Art Library:** Musée du Louvre, Paris (tl). **DK Images:** David Edge (tl) (br) (cr). **160-161 The Bridgeman Art Library:** Musée Condé, Chantilly, France / Giraudon (b). **166 DK Images:** David Edge (bl) (bc) (cra). **166-167 The Art Archive:** Musée du Château de Versailles / Dagli Orti (bc). **167 The Bridgeman Art Library:** Musée de l'Armée, Brussels / Patrick Lorette (br). **168-169 The Bridgeman Art Library:** National Gallery of Victoria, Melbourne, Australia. **170-171 DK/**Sharon Spencer: (tl). **172 Getty Images:** Time & Life Pictures (tr). **173 Mary Evans Picture Library:** (b). **174 akg-images:** (b). **DK Images:** Royal Green Jackets Museum, Winchester (cr). **180-181 National Maritime Museum, London:** Denis Dioghton (tl). **182 The Bridgeman Art Library:** Stapleton Collection, UK (tl). **182-183 National Maritime Museum, London:** Greenwich Hospital Collection (bc). **186 Alamy Images:** Gary Curtis (br); Richard Naude (cl); Trafalgar 2005 (bc). **Royal Naval Museum, Portsmouth:** (crb). **187 Alamy Images:** Nigel Reed (br). **188 Royal Naval Museum, Portsmouth:** (cl). **189 Royal Naval Museum, Portsmouth:** (cla). **190-191 Getty Images:** Stringer / Hulton Archive (tl). **192 Library Of Congress, Washington, D.C.:** (b) (tr). **194 DK Images:** Confederate Memorial Hall, New Orleans (bl/ except friction matches). **National Archives and Records Administration, USA:** (tl). **Robert Szabo. 195 Library Of Congress, Washington, D.C.:** (b). **Robert Szabo:** (tl). **199 DK Images:** Gettysburg National Military Park, PA (cra/Ketchum hand grenade). **200 The Bridgeman Art Library:** Private Collection (b). **202-203 National Archives and Records Administration, USA. 204-205 Corbis:** Anders Ryman. **205 DK Images:** Pitt Rivers Museum, University of Oxford (b). **206 DK Images:** Pitt Rivers Museum, University of Oxford (ca). **PhotoNewZealand:** Geoff Mason (tr). **207 DK Images:** Pitt Rivers Museum, University of Oxford (bl). **PhotoNewZealand:** (r). **208-209 The Bridgeman Art Library:** Michael Graham-Stewart (b). **210-211 The Kobal Collection. 211 The Board of Trustees of the Armouries:** (br). **DK Images:** Powell-Cotton Museum, Kent (br/ shield). **212 The Board of Trustees of the Armouries:** (bl). **Corbis:** Underwood & Underwood (t). **213 Alamy Images:** The Print Collector (b). **The Bridgeman Art Library:** Stapleton Collection, UK (tr). **214 The Bridgeman Art Library:** Private Collection / Heini Schneebeli (tl). **DK Images:** Powell-Cotton Museum, Kent (tr) (cr/club). **214-215 The Board of Trustees of the Armouries:** (cr). **DK Images:** Powell-Cotton Museum, Kent (br). **215 The Bridgeman Art Library:** Heini Schneebeli. **DK Images:** Powell-Cotton Museum, Kent (tl). **216-217 Corbis:** Brian A. Vikander. **217 DK Images:** Pitt Rivers Museum, University of Oxford (br). **218 Alamy Images:** Visual Arts Library (London) (bl). **DK Images:** American Museum of Natural History (t). **219 Corbis:** (b). **DK Images:** American Museum of Natural History (cr). **220-221 DK Images:** American Museum of Natural History (br) (crb). **221 DK Images:** American Museum of Natural History (cl); British Museum / Museum of Mankind (ca); Pitt Rivers Museum, University of Oxford (knives and sheaths). **222 DK Images:** Board of Trustees of the Armouries (cl). **Getty Images:** MPI / Stringer / Hulton Archive (b). **223 The Bridgeman Art Library:**

Private Collection, Peter Newark's American Pictures (br). **DK Images:** American Museum of Natural History (tl) (tr); British Museum / Museum of Mankind (bl). **225 DK Images:** Collection of Jean-Pierre Verney (cl/canteen). **226 DK/**Sharon Spencer: (c). **227 Corbis:** Bettmann (tr). **228-229 Alamy Images:** Popperfoto. **230 Corbis:** Hulton-Deutsch Collection (tl). **232 Alamy Images:** Popperfoto (b). **234 DK Images:** Board of Trustees of the Armouries (clb). **234-235 DK Images:** Imperial War Museum (bl) (cr/boots). **235 DK Images:** Collection of Jean-Pierre Verney (bc). **236 DK Images:** Board of Trustees of the Armouries (b/bayonet); Collection of Jean-Pierre Verney (cra/no.1 grenade); Imperial War Museum (ca/mills bomb). **237 DK Images:** Collection of Jean-Pierre Verney (t) (c) (ca). **238-239 Corbis:** Bettmann. **239 DK Images:** Board of Trustees of the Armouries (b). **240 Corbis:** Hulton-Deutsch Collection (b). **DK Images:** Collection of Jean-Pierre Verney (tc). **241 Corbis:** Bettmann (br). **244 Corbis:** Bettmann (cl). **DK Images:** Collection of Jean-Pierre Verney (crb). **Peter Gombeir:** Bayernwald Trench (bl) (br). **245 Peter Gombeir:** Bayernwald Trench (tl) (bc) (bl) (br) (c) (tc) (tr). **246 Corbis:** Hulton-Deutsch Collection (bl). **DK Images:** Collection of Jean-Pierre Verney (cb) (cr). **247 Corbis:** Bettmann (cra). **DK Images:** Collection of Jean-Pierre Verney (tr) (bc) (cl); Ministry of Defence Pattern Room, Nottingham (bl). **248 Corbis:** Bettmann (bl). **DK Images:** Collection of Jean-Pierre Verney (tr) (br) (cl) (crb); Firepower, The Royal Artillery Museum, Royal Artillery Historical Trust (cla). **249 Corbis:** Hulton-Deutsch Collection (cra) (fbr/bayonet). **DK Images:** Collection of Jean-Pierre Verney (cla) (clb) (crb); Firepower, The Royal Artillery Museum, Royal Artillery Historical Trust (br/carbine). **250-251 Getty Images:** Stringer / Hulton Archive. **252 Corbis:** EFE (b). **253 The Bridgeman Art Library:** Bibliothèque Nationale, Paris / Archives Charmet (clb). **Robert Hunt Library:** (tc). **254-255 Getty Images:** Arthur Tanner / Stringer / Hulton Archive. **256 Getty Images:** Fox Photos / Stringer (t); Hans Wild / Stringer (bl). **257 Getty Images:** Fox Photos / Stringer (b). **258 Getty Images:** Harry Shepherd / Stringer / Hulton Archive (b). **259 Corbis:** Hulton-Deutsch Collection (tl). **264 Corbis:** Bettmann (b). **265 Alamy Images:** Popperfoto (bl). **266-267 DK/**Sharon Spencer. **268 Getty Images:** Hulton Archive (bl). **269 Corbis:** The Dmitri Baltermants Collection (b). **272 DK/**Sharon Spencer: (fbl) (br). **273 DK/**Sharon Spencer: (bc). **274 DK Images:** Imperial War Museum (bl). **Getty Images:** Horace Abrahams / Stringer / Hulton Archive (cr). **275 DK Images:** Michael Butler Collection (c) (clb) (r). **276-277 Corbis:** Hulton-Deutsch Collection. **278 Getty Images:** Frank Scherschel / Stringer / Time & Life Pictures (bl). **Wikipedia, The Free Encyclopedia:** (tl). **279 Getty Images:** Frank Scherschel / Stringer / Time & Life Pictures (tl). **282 Alamy Images:** Nic Hamilton (fbl). **Getty Images:** Margaret Bourke-White / Stringer / Time & Life Pictures (cl). **283 Alamy Images:** Nic Hamilton (tl). **Getty Images:** Keystone / Stringer / Hulton Archive (c). **284 EAA:** (bl) (bc) (cl). **Brian Lockett (www.air-and-space.com) :** (tr). **285 DK Images:** Board of Trustees of the Armouries (cla). **EAA:** (cr) (br). **286-287 Getty Images:** PNA Rota / Stringer / Hulton Archive. **288 Wikipedia, The Free Encyclopedia:** National Archives and Records Administration (cb); USAF (cr) (bl). **289 Corbis:** Hulton-Deutsch Collection (br). **290-291 The Ronald Grant Archive. 291 DK Images:** Board of Trustees of the Armouries (br). **292 Cody Images:** (cl). **DK Images:** Imperial War Museum (cra). **Imperial War Museum:** (bl). **293 DK Images:** Imperial War Museum (fbl) (bl); Ministry of Defence Pattern Room, Nottingham (b); Royal Green Jackets Museum, Winchester (tr). **The Kobal Collection:** Central Office Of Information (tc). **294 DK Images:** Imperial War Museum (c). **294-295 DK Images:** Imperial War Museum (b). **295 DK Images:** The late Charles Fraser-Smith (tc/lights) (tr); H. Keith Melton Collection (cra) (cr/belt pistol). **296 DK Images:** H. Keith Melton Collection (cl/pipe pistol); Imperial War Museum (c) (br) (fbr). **Imperial War Museum:** (cl/pencil knife). **296-297 DK Images:** RAF Museum, Hendon (c). **297 DK Images:** Imperial War Museum (r). **298 Corbis:** Bettmann. **300 Getty Images:** Time & Life Pictures / Stringer (b). **301 Getty Images:** Time & Life Pictures / Stringer (tc); US Army Air Force / Stringer / Time & Life Pictures (br). **304-305 DK Images:** Board of Trustees of the Armouries (b). **310 DK Images:** Board of Trustees of the Armouries (br). **Getty Images:** Frederic J. Brown / AFP (c). **311 U.S. Army:** PFC Brandon R. Aird (tc). **312-313 Corbis:** Alain Nogues. **313 DK Images:** Board of Trustees of the Armouries (br); Denis Lassus, Paris (c). **314 Corbis:** Robbie Cooper (tc); Pierre Vauthey (tr). **DK Images:** Lieutenant Commander W.M. Thornton MBE RD RNR (c). **315 akg-images:** ullstein bild (b). **DK Images:** Lieutenant Commander W.M. Thornton MBE RD RNR (tl). **318-319 Getty Images:** Three Lions / Stringer / Hulton Archive. **319 DK Images:** Board of Trustees of the Armouries (b); Royal Marines Museum, Portsmouth (c). **320 DK Images:** Board of Trustees of the Armouries (b). **Getty Images:** Paul Schutzer / Stringer / Time & Life Pictures (t). **321 Corbis:** Bettmann (b). **322 Corbis:** Bettmann (bl). **323 Corbis:** Bettmann (r). **DK Images:** Andrew L. Chernack (bl). **328-329 Getty Images:** Paul Schutzer / Stringer / Time & Life Pictures. **330-331 Getty Images:** AFP. **332 Getty Images:** Three Lions / Stringer / Hulton Archive (b). **338 Corbis:** Alain DeJean / Sygma (b). **DK Images:** Board of Trustees of the Armouries (cr). **339 Corbis:** Jean-Louis Atlan / Sygma (ca); Bettmann (bc). **DK Images:** Board of Trustees of the Armouries (tr). **340-341 Military Picture Library. 341 DK Images:** Board of Trustees of the Armouries (br); Royal Signals Museum, Blandford Camp, Dorset (c) (ca). **342 DK Images:** Imperial War Museum (c). **Military Picture Library:** Peter Russell (tl) (tr). **343 Cody Images:** (tl). **DK Images:** Vehicle supplied by Steve Wright, Chatham, Kent (cr). **344-345 DK Images:** Imperial War Museum (clothing). **345 DK Images:** Board of Trustees of the Armouries (tr/submachine-gun, ammunitions and grenade). **346 Cody Images:** (bl). **347 Corbis:** Leif Skoogfors (b). **348 Corbis:** Tim Tadder. **350-351 Corbis:** Lynsey Addario

All other images © Dorling Kindersley
For further information see:
www.dkimages.com

Dorling Kindersley would like to thank the following events, reenactment organizations, and individuals for the modeling and supply of gear, as well as their advice and information:

Events:

Kelmarsh Festival of History event, Kelmarsh Hall, English Heritage

Military Odyssey history event, Detling, Kent Gary Howard

Battle of Hastings event, English Heritage
(Norman and Saxon reenactment)

Organizations and private collectors:

Greek Hoplite Society
(Ancient Greek reenactment),
George Georgiou

www.4hoplites.com
(Ancient Greek gear),
Elaine and Andy Cropper

Ermine Street Guard
(Roman reenactment, gear),
Chris Haines

Tyne & Wear Museums, Discovery Museum Newcastle upon Tyne
(Roman Fort), Alex Croom

Vikings! (of Middle England)
Viking gear supplied by:
Dagmaer Raemundsson
Halfdan Badgerbeard
Hrothgar Sigurdsson
Rafen, The Merkismathir
Bölverkr inn fróthr

Viking Ship Museum, Denmark
(Viking longship tour),
Rikki Tørnsø Johansen

Battle of Hastings event
(Norman and Saxon reenactment),
Thanks to all the groups featured in this book including:
Alan Larsen of **The Troop**
Hag Dik Arnaud Lefèbre
Franko-Flamischoa-Kontingent
Triglav Domsborgelag
Igor Gorewicz

English longbowman model,
Royal Armouries:
Andrew Balmforth

Shogun Fight School
(Samurai reenactment),
Dean Wayland, Mary Gentle,
and Robert Johnson

English Civil War Society
(English musketeer gear),
George Bowyer, Christian Towers

Queen's Rangers
(US War of Independence - Queen's Rangers gear, American rifleman gear), Michael Butterfield, Chris Smith

47th Regiment of Foot
(Redcoats of American Revolutionary War reenactment),
Paul Pattinson, Nigel Hardacre

1er Chasseurs à Cheval de la Ligne, 2e Compagnie
Affiliated to the Napoleonic Association of Great Britain
(Napoleonic cavalryman gear),
John Norris

The Polish Light Horse Display Team Napoleonic cavalry reenactment), George Lubomski

Polish Vistula Legion
(Napoleonic armies reenactment)

33rd Re-enactment
(Redcoats of Napoleonic era reenactment), Kate MacFarlane

68th Durham Light Infantry
(Redcoat of Napoleonic era reenactment, gear), Kevin Walsh

RN Sailor model,
Royal Armouries: Stuart Greig

HMS *Victory*
(Ship of the line tour)
Peter Goodwin, Keeper and Curator

Southern Skirmish Association
(American Civil War reenactment—Union gear, Confederate gear), Roy Daines, Andrew Rose and Steve Boulton

South Staffordshire Regiment Museum, Whittington Barracks, Lichfield, Staffs
(WWI and WWII objects),
Erik Blakely and Willy Turner

Birmingham Pals
(WWI British Infantryman gear),
Richard Sheard, Edwin Field,
Sean Featherstone, and
Malcom Cook

5te. Kompagnie, Infanterie Regiment nr. 28 'von Goeben'
(WWI German Stormtrooper gear),
John Pearce

WWII RAF fighter pilot gear
Private collector, Richard Simms

2nd Guards Rifle Division
(WWII Soviet tank crewman gear),
Adrian Stevenson

Soviet T-34 tank
Private collector: Neil Culham

WWII B-17 bomber crew gear
Private collectors: Tim Parker,
Richard Simms

First Allied Airborne Associaton
(WWII US Paratrooper gear),
Lee Bowden and Neil Galloway
Private collector: Tim Parker

Flame Torbay Costumiers
Lionel Digby (Prussian soldier gear,
German U-boat crew gear,
French Foreign Legionnaire gear)

US Marine gear
Private collector: Tim Parker

Vietnam Rolling Thunder
(Viet Cong guerrilla gear),
Stuart Beeney

Thanks also for assistance from the following groups and individuals not featured due to the limited confines of the book:

The Garrison Keith Brigstock
Ranger Reenactment David Pratt
95th Regiment (Royal Green Jackets) Neil Collins, Andrew Rayfield, Ian Wilkinson, and Rob Gray
Anglesey Hussars Ian Walker

Thanks also to the following for their contributions to this book:

The Royal Armouries in Leeds and Phillip Abbott for his help and advice; Richard Holmes for advice about trenches; John Freeman for the presentation photo shoot; Dennis Bacon for assistance on location photo shoots; Steve Setford Phillip Parker, and Tom Broder for editorial work; Ted Kinsey and Terry Jeavons for design work; Shaz Madani and Sarah Oiestad for design support; Phil Gamble for tactics illustrations; Rob Strachan for DTP support; Sarah Smithies for picture research; Myriam Megharbi for picture research support.

Every effort has been made to correctly credit the contents of this book. Any errors or ommissions will be corrected in future editions on written notification to the publishers.